ENJOY LEARNING JAPANESE KANJI

Discover their Hidden Meanings

Authors Kun Ho Park & Kyung Yong Kong
Translation Young Youp Hwang & Jennifer Jean Lim
Design Jongwoo Lee & Jae Kyoung Shim
Illustration Jae Young Lee
Editor Kyung Yong Kong

Published by KONG & PARK USA, Inc.
475 North Martingale Road, Suite 710, Schaumburg, IL 60173 USA
Tel +1 (847) 241 4845, Fax +1 (312) 757 5553
usaoffice@kongnpark.com
www.kongnpark.com

ISBN 978-1-63519-000-7

Library of Congress Control Number: 2016952764

DISTRIBUTORS
United States: KONG & PARK USA, Inc.
475 North Martingale Road, Suite 710, Schaumburg, IL 60173
Tel +1 (847) 241 4845, Fax +1 (312) 757 5553
usaoffice@kongnpark.com

Canada: Fitzhenry & Whiteside Ltd.
195 Allstate Parkway, Markham, Ontario L3R 4T8
Tel +1 (800) 387 9776, Fax +1 (800) 260 9777
bookinfo@fitzhenry.ca

United Kingdom and Ireland: Kodansha Europe Ltd.
40 Stockwell Street, Greenwich, London SE10 8EY
Tel +44 (0)20-8293-0111, Fax +44 (0)20-8293-5533
info@kodansha.eu

Other countries: KONG & PARK, Inc.
85, Gwangnaru-ro 56-gil, Prime center 1518, Gwangjin-gu, Seoul, 05116 Korea
Tel +82 (0)2 565 1537, Fax +82 (0)2 3445 1080
info@kongnpark.com

Printed in Korea

ENJOY LEARNING JAPANESE KANJI

Discover their Hidden Meanings

Kun Ho Park
Kyung Yong Kong

KONG & PARK

Contents

Introduction 06
User Guide 08

People 12

Human body 14
Head 亠1, 京2, 高3, 頁4, 彡5
Face 自6, 目7, 直8, 見9, 艮10, 良11, 口12, 可13, 奇14, 古15, 囗16, 言17, 音18, 欠19, 舌20, 齒21, 耳22
Body 身23, 骨24, 歹25, 心26, 忄27
Hand 手28, 爪29, 又30, 史31, 彐32, 聿33, 𠂇34, 寸35, 付36, 寺37, 廾38, 其39, 勹40, 勿41, 支42, 攵43
Foot 止44, 正45, 夂46, 舛47, 彳48, 辶49, 廴50

Person 110
"人" 人51, 亻52, 入53, 亼54, 僉55, 𠂊56, 免57, 儿58, 兄59
"大" 大60, 夭61, 夬62, 尢63, 立64
Shape of a person 疒65, 己66, 乙67, 也68, 卩/㔾69, 印70, 令71, 匕72, 北73, 尸74

Title 156
Inherited 巳75, 厶76, 子77, 女78, 母79, 氏80, 耂81, 者82
Social 辛83, 士84, 臣85, 王86

Life 180

War 182
Weapons 弓87, 弋88, 矢89, 至90, 戈91, 戊92, 殳93, 斤94, 刀95, 干96
Transportation 車97, 舟98
Ceremonies 示99, 卜100

Necessities of life 210
Clothes 衣101, 哀102a, 巾103, 糸104, 文105, 白106, 青107, 黄108
Food 食109, 米110, 禾111, 豆112
Shelter 宀113, 广114, 門115, 阝116, 厂117, 冂118, 里119

Agriculture 248

Land	土120, 圭121, 田122, 苗123, 火124
Tools	力125, 方126, 㫃127
Containers	斗128, 用129, 甫129c, 冖131, 覀132, 酉133

Nature 276

Animals 278

Land animals	羊134, 犬135, 豕136, 牛137, 馬138
Other animals	鳥139, 隹140, 羽141, 采142, 虫143, 魚144, 貝145, 网146, 鼎147, 辰148
Animal by-products	皮149, 角150, 肉151, 自152

Natural scenery 314

山153, 金154, 工155, 水156, 氵157, 气158, 雨159, 冫160, 艹161, 生162, 丰163, 木164, 本165, 林166, 東167, 几168, 竹169

Heavenly bodies 348

日170, 昔171, 月172

Miscellaneous 354

一173, 且174, 丁175, 二176, 八177, 十178, 亅179, 乍180, 丶181, 小182

A concluding remark 372
On-Kun pronunciation index 375
Meaning index 388
Radical index 397
Pattern index 406

Introduction

Because kanji are commonly known as pictograms, most Japanese learners wonder if they can possibly learn thousands of characters. For this reason, most people think that it would be more effective to memorize words to expand their vocabulary than to memorize thousands of complicated drawings, and that's why they prefer books with furigana. However, considering that most ancient Chinese who created and used the language, as well as the Chinese and Japanese who use it now are not geniuses, there must be an easier way to learn kanji. This book was written to share that secret with you!

Countries that still use Chinese characters in their vocabulary are China (including Taiwan, Hong Kong and Singapore), Korea and Japan. China, for obvious reasons, uses it most often. The simplified characters are used in China and Singapore, whereas Taiwan and Hong Kong use the original complicated characters. Japan uses a mix of both. Korea has her own alphabet hangeul, but up to 60% of the vocabulary has borrowed meaning from Chinese characters. Therefore, if you don't know them, it is very hard for you to understand their true meanings. For these reasons, many researches on Chinese characters have been carried out mostly in China, Korea and Japan. We consulted opinions from scholars from the above three countries and compiled a list of 3,500 commonly used Chinese characters. This book describes 971 basic characters that appear in JLPT 5-level vocabulary.

Chinese characters are based on inscriptions found on bones and tortoise carapaces used in 12th and 14th century B.C. In the 6th and 7th centuries, they were said to have been passed on to nations in the Korean peninsula at that time, and then passed on to Japan. All languages change with time and Chinese was no exception. The usage of Chinese characters in Korea and Japan retain the original form and meaning from when they were passed on, so it was very helpful to have the input of scholars from the three countries.

This book is an attempt to compile the opinions of scholars from these three countries, and the authors' personal interpretations of the inscriptions on bronze, bones and tortoise carapaces to explain the origin of the characters.
The authors' aim is to help our readers understand the characters, not to become scholars in their own right. But that does not mean this book is a pet project. It is intended to help readers further understand the meanings of all kanji.

User Guide

To learn kanji much more easily, one must understand how they came to be. This book will introduce you to the characters about people, life and nature.

Characters about people

Human body: Though different in color and size, we share the same physical characteristics. Most characters are based on human physical attributes.

Person: Many basic characters depict the form of certain human postures, such as 'standing man,' 'crouching man,' and 'kneeling man.'

Title: From an unborn baby to an elderly man, and from a slave to a king.

Characters about life

War: The history of man might as well be the history of war. Many kanji are related to war, which influenced life greatly.

Necessities of life: Characters related to the necessities of life.

Agriculture: Farming is an occupation that produces food, the most essential element for human existence. It has a long association with the survival of mankind.

Characters about nature

Animals: They can be categorized into 'land animals,' 'other animals' and 'animal by-products.'

Natural scenery: Characters about mountains, minerals, water, greenery and trees are the most-used kanji.

Heavenly bodies: The characters about the sun, moon and stars are combined with other characters, contributing to produce another meaning.

Miscellaneous: Numbers and signs.

By finding out how these kanji were initially developed, and later by and repeatedly using the same basic characters in more complicated ones, you will be able to dissect the complicated ones and appreciate the story each of them tell. If you practice reading and writing these characters repeatedly, your kanji ability will improve surprisingly fast. Furthermore, if you come across new characters not listed in this book, you can guess what their pronunciation would be and what they mean.

Structure of the content

To gain the most from this book, you will need to understand the structure of the content of this book and the intention of the editors. The contents of this book can be divided into two parts, the diagram and the explanation.

The diagram

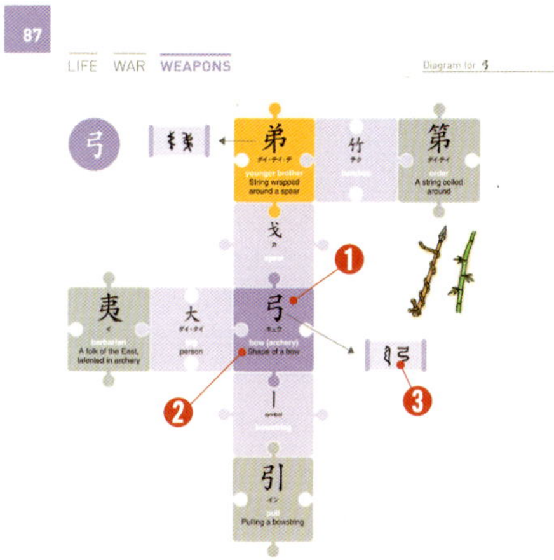

1. The main character
2. Condensed explanation
3. Ancient characters

1. The main character: These may not be part of the 214 radicals that the scholars have identified. But remember that a character doesn't have to be a radical to have an important meaning within another, more complicated, character. In essence, radicals are only used to categorize characters and are seldomly used other than when one is looking up a character up in a dictionary. So, because they are of little importance, this book does not list radicals. By the time you are done reading, you will be able to dissect each kanji into the basic components, and with this information you can look them up in a kanji dictionary. The on-yomi shown on the diagram is written with hiragana. Generally, on-yomi should be written with katakana, but we have written it in hiragana for our readers who have difficulty reading katakana. Of course, the on-yomi is written in katakana in the main body, so if possible, being comfortable reading in katakana would be beneficial.

2. Condensed explanation: Read the short explanation, and you will be able to understand how a certain kanji was originally developed. In the latter part of the book, you will find some kanji appearing in a diagram without much

explanation about them. That is because these characters would have already been explained and therefore a short introduction should be enough to have you guess the origin and meaning of it. When you go back to reread about a certain character, the short introduction and diagram will be enough to jog your memory.

3. Ancient characters: In order to help the readers to better understand the characters in current use, the ancient characters such as the inscriptions on bones and tortoise carapaces, bronze inscriptions and seal characters have been listed in this book. These ancient characters will help the readers to clearly understand the hidden meanings of the kanji by simple storytelling of each character.

The main body

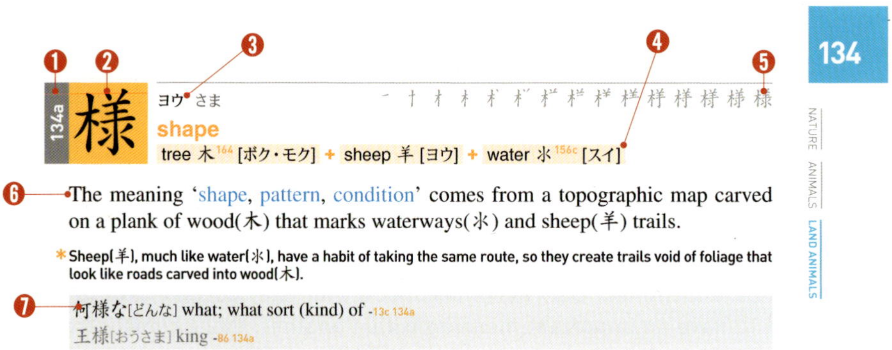

1. Quick reference number
2. Character explained
3. On-yomi and Kun-yomi
4. Dissection
5. Stroke order
6. Vocabulary
7. Explanations and footnotes

1. Quick reference number: Each character in this book has its own quick reference number. This is to aid you in searching for a specific character you do not know or cannot remember. Use them to go back to a certain word or character that appears on another page.

2. Character explained: If the kanji appears on a yellow background, it means it is used in a word from JLPT N5. Even if the background color is not yellow, the character is still important because its radical could connect it to a kanji with greater application.

3. On-yomi and kun-yomi: On-yomi means to read a kanji in its Chinese or Korean pronunciation. In Japan, this would be considered a foreign language, so it's printed in katakana. Of course, Chinese characters had been introduced a long time ago into Japan and had spread gradually over many years, so the current pronunciation does not correspond to that of Mandarin pinyin or Korean hanja. Some kanji originated in Japan and those characters do not have an *On*. Also, some characters are not used as radicals, so these don't have an *On*. In that case, we have used its closest possible pronunciation of kanji.
   Kun-yomi is to read a kanji in Japanese to portray its own meaning. This is a Japanese pronunciation and is printed in hiragana. But, if a kanji was created based on an item or notion that did not exist in Japanese language, its corresponding *Kun* may not exist. One kanji can be used to portray multiple meanings, and can also have different *Kun* based on the period when it was introduced to Japan. Depending on characters, there exist many dozens of *Kun*. In this book, we have only printed those *Kun* characters applicable to those characters used in vocabulary from JLPT N5~N1.

4. Dissection: This explains which basic characters are brought together to make the complicated one. It is also helpful to check how the pronunciation of one affects that of the other. As the epilogue states, most characters not mentioned in this book take the pronunciation of a character it is composed of. Also, there is nothing to worry if the shape of a character changes when it becomes part of another. That change was made over centuries, according to what the people thought would look better.

5. Stroke order: There's a rule to the stroke order when writing a kanji. Left to right, top to bottom. When two strokes meet, write the horizontal stroke first, then the vertical. Follow the stroke order in this book and your kanji will look balanced. It should help if you try to recall the smaller components of each character when writing.

6. Explanations and footnotes: This is the most important part of this book. These explain how a character is made. In some cases, the ancient version of the same character is provided to aid understanding.

7. Vocabulary: Words printed in black have been listed here only when those characters explained are used and applied as kun-yomi. Words printed in grey show a linguistic process where a kanji explained is added to another kanji to develop a new meaning. These words should help you understand how that a specific kanji explained can be used in its applications.

Human body

PEOPLE

Person

Title

Human body

When the ancient Chinese first came up with the shapes that later became the basis of the present kanji, it would have been much easier for them to use something associated with their bodies. Everything from the top of the head to the tip of the toes is depicted in a character.

1. The head can also symbolize a leader.
2. A face has ears, eyes, a nose and a mouth.
3. Which part of the body would be used to describe emotions like happiness, anger, sadness and joy? It's "心 [シン]," the character meaning 'heart.'
4. Which body part is used the most? It's our hands, which is what differentiates us from animals. Of all the body parts,the character for 'hand' is used the most as part of a more complicated character.
5. The second most used body part is 'foot,' which is also part of many other characters.

Person

Many characters in this category describe people, not just body parts. Whereas some mean 'a person,' others now entail a different meaning.

1. Explanations on how the meaning of "人," 'a person,' influences a character.
2. Some characters look like "大," a man with arms and legs splayed out.
3. 'Standing man, crouching man, kneeling man,' and how they change a character's meaning.

Title

Any dictionary will tell you that humans are a social species. In this section, we will find out how titles and classes are inflected in various characters.

1. Some characters describe the class one is born into.
2. There is also the social class that separates kings from commoners. There are more subjects than kings, hence more characters about subjects.

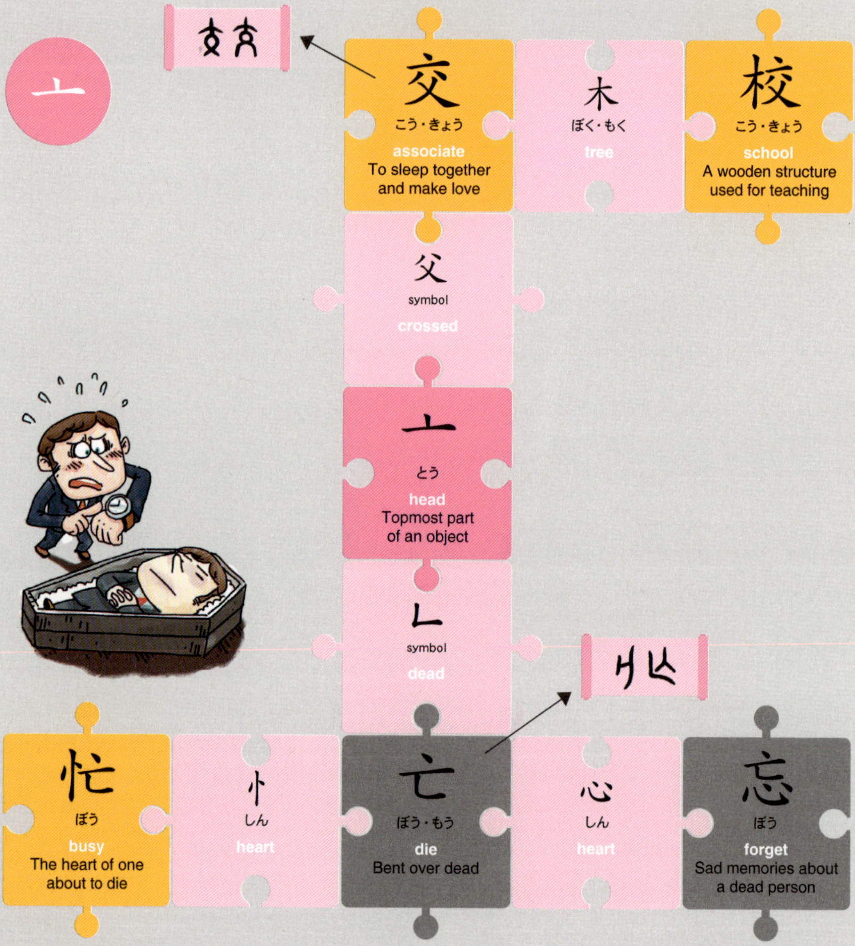

1 亠

トウ

head

The 'head' of a person, an animal, or the 'roof' of a building; the 'upper part' of an object.

1a 交

コウ・キョウ　かわす・まじえる・まじわる

associate with

head 亠 [トウ] + crossed legs 父 [symbol]

When you see an image of two people(亠) with legs crossed/mixed(乂) to make love, this character means 'associate with.' For a man and a woman to be in this posture, it also indicates that they are in love with each other and reciprocate each other's feelings.

* The character that looks like "father 父[30a]" is a pictorial image of crossed legs and has nothing to do with the word. Remember, just because they have the same shape doesn't mean they have the same meaning.

交(わ)す[かわす] exchange; cross
交える[まじえる] mix; exchange; cross
交わる[まじわる] associate with; cross; intersect
交番[こうばん] police box; alternation - 1a 142a

1b 校

コウ・キョウ

一 十 才 木 木' 木' 木' 村 杉 校

school

tree 木[164][ボク・モク] + associate with 交 [コウ・キョウ]

A school is a structure made with wood(木), where teachers and students get together to exchange(交) knowledge.

* An example of an old wooden Chinese structure would be the Forbidden City.

学校[がっこう] school - 77b 1b
校庭[こうてい] schoolyard; campus - 1b 50b
高校[こうこう] high school - 3 1b

1c 亡

ボウ・モウ

丶 亠 亡

die

A person(亠) who usually stands up straight(丨) is considered hunched over and dead(L) due to old age or sickness.

* "亠[トウ]" signifies the top of the body, the head.

死亡[しぼう] death - 25a 1c

1d 忘

ボウ　わすれる

丶 亠 亡 亡 忘 忘 忘

forget

die 亡 [ボウ・モウ] + heart 心[26][シン]

Memories of a dead(亡) loved one breaks the heart(心), so it's best to forget.

忘れる[わすれる] forget

1e 忙

ボウ　いそがしい

丶 丶 忄 忄 忙 忙

busy

heart 忄=心[26] [シン] + die 亡 [ボウ・モウ]

A person about to die(亡) has a 'busy heart(忄)' because there is little time and so much to do.

* The "亡" in "忘" is at the top, which signals it's a memory that has to be forgotten. "忙" has "亡" in front of "忄" which describes the mental state of someone about to die.

忙しい[いそがしい] busy; be busy

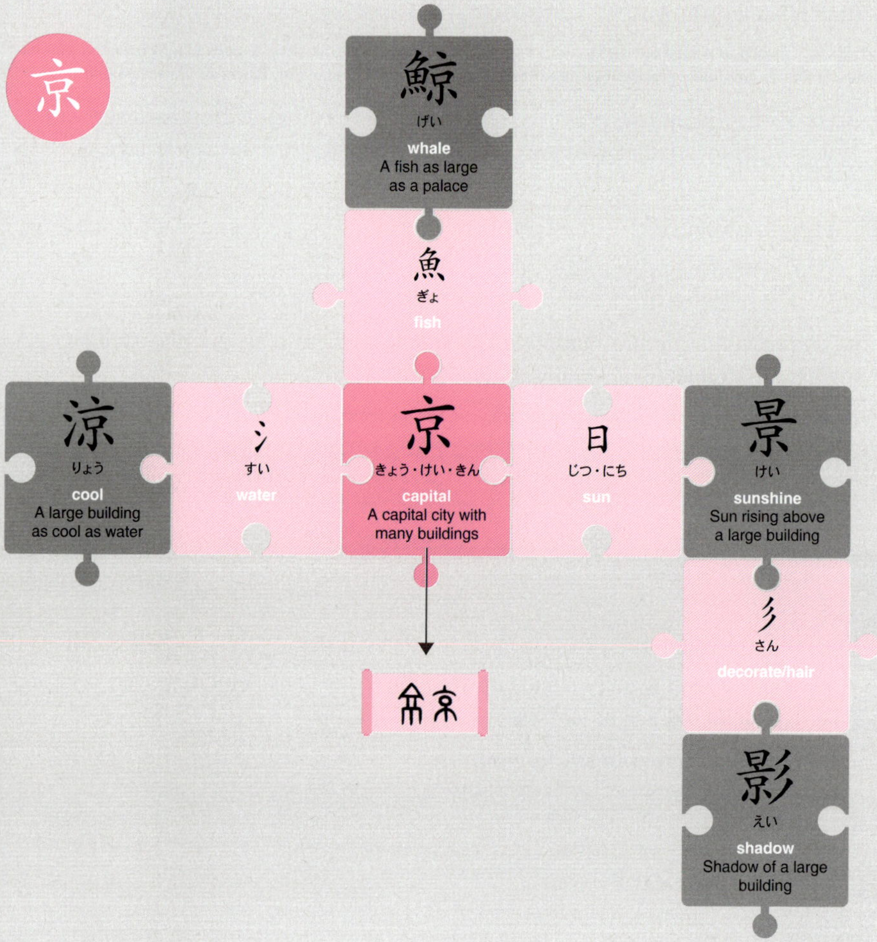

2 京 キョウ・ケイ・キン

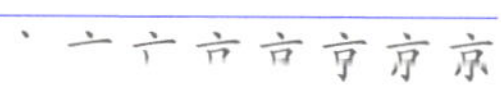

capital

head 亠[トウ] + structure of a building 京 [symbol]

Symbolizing the shape of a high-rise building(京) with a roof(亠), it means something high or large. It also means a large city, like the capital of a nation.

* This character is associated with a building, so "亠[1]" is the roof and the rest is the actual structure. It has nothing to do with "mouth 口[12]" or "small 小[182]."

2a 鯨

ゲイ くじら

ノ ク ク 各 吊 角 角 角 魚 魚 魚 魚` 魚´ 魚亠 魚亡 魚古 魚亭 魚京 鯨

whale

fish 魚 144 [ギョ] + big/capital 京 [キョウ・ケイ・キン]

A whale is described as a fish(魚) as large as a palace(京).

捕鯨[ほげい] whaling; whale fishing -130 2a

2b 景

ケイ

丶 口 日 日 旦 早 早 昙 昙 景 景 景

sunshine

sun 日 170 [ジツ・ニチ] + big/capital 京 [キョウ・ケイ・キン]

The sun(日) shines over a large building(京).

景色[けしき] scenery; landscape; view -2b 75d

風景[ふうけい] landscape; scenery -143c 2b

2c 影

エイ かげ

丶 口 日 日 旦 早 早 昙 昙 景 景 景 景' 影 影

shadow

sunshine 景 [ケイ] + decorate/hair 彡 5 [サン]

When the sun shines(景), buildings cast shadows(彡). Shadows are also used in photographs and movies.

* "Hair 彡" describes the shadow.

撮影[さつえい] photographing; filming -22e 2c

2d 涼

リョウ すずしい・すずむ

丶 冫 氵 氵 氵 氵 汸 汸 泞 涼 涼

cool

water 氵 157 [スイ] + big/capital 京 [キョウ・ケイ・キン]

A large building(京) with a high ceiling and thick walls is cool like water(氵), even in the summer.

涼しい[すずしい] cool; refreshing

涼む[すずむ] cool oneself; enjoy the cool air

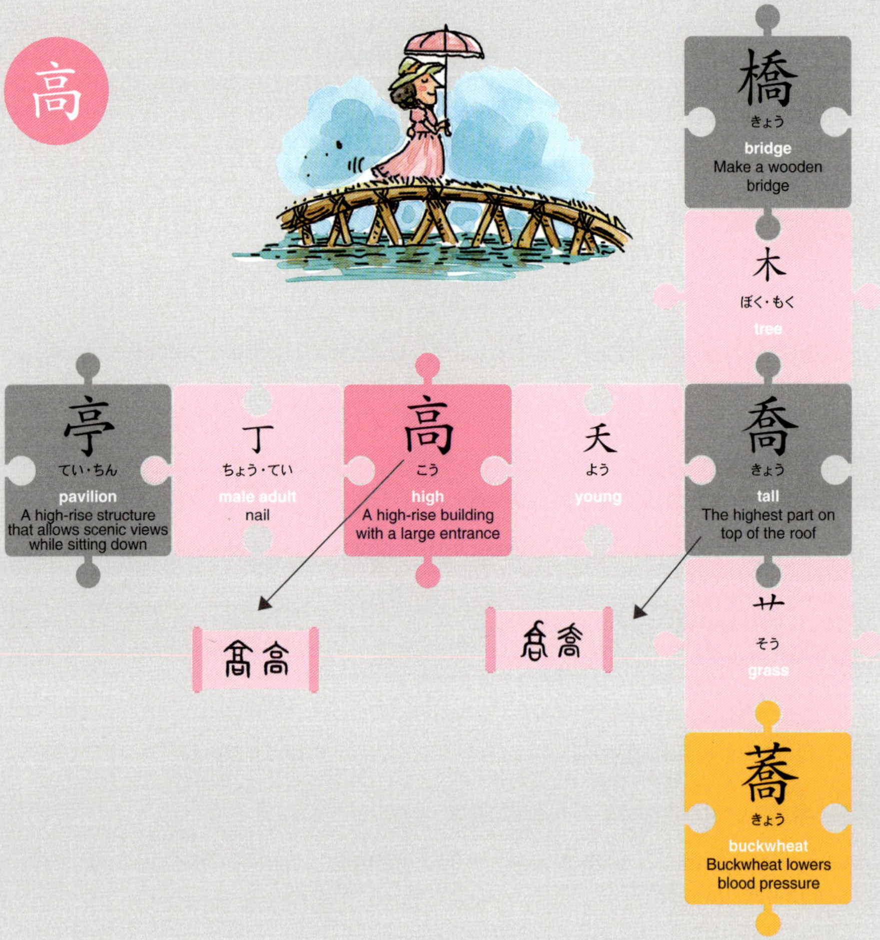

3 高

コウ たかい・たかまる・たかめる

high

丶 亠 亠 亠 亠 亠 亠 高 高 高

The shape of a large palace with a high and large entrance(ロ) for people to enter and exit. Means 'high.'

* As this character is about a building, "亠[tóu]" is the roof.

高い[たかい] high; tall; be tall	高まる[たかまる] get higher; uprise
高める[たかめる] makes it high (higher); enhance	高校[こうこう] high school -3.1b

3a 喬

キョウ

一 二 チ 夭 夭 夭 夭 夭 喬 喬 喬 喬

tall

young 夭[61][ヨウ] + high 高 [コウ]

The character "夭" describes a decoration(夭) on the highest part of the roof, which is the topmost part of a building(高).

* The upper part of the character "高" is omitted to keep the artistic balance in composition.

3b 橋

キョウ はし

一 十 オ 木 木 木 杯 杯 杯 桥 桥 桥 橋 橋 橋 橋

bridge

tree 木[164][ボク・モク] + tall 喬 [キョウ]

To construct a wooden(木) bridge higher(乔) than the water level so that people can cross.

鉄橋[てっきょう] railroad bridge; railway bridge -154d 3b

3c 蕎

キョウ そば

一 十 艹 艹 芒 芦 芺 芺 茶 茶 茶 蕎 蕎 蕎 蕎

buckwheat

grass 艹[161][ソウ] + tall 喬 [キョウ]

In Oriental medicine, buckwheat(艹) is known to lower high(喬) fevers and blood pressure. Rutin is a well-known component of buckwheat and is used as a hypotensive agent.

蕎麦[そば] buckwheat; Soba (an abbreviation for 'そばきり') -3c 163b

3d 亭

テイ・チン

丶 亠 亠 市 古 古 高 亭 亭

pavilion

high 高 [コウ] + nail/male adult 丁[175][チョウ・テイ]

Signifies a gazebo, that is built to rise high(高) on a scenic area, that allows one to sit down(丁) and enjoy.

* "丁" contains the meaning, to nail down something, and 'stabilize,' which came to mean to sit down firmly on a place.

亭主[ていしゅ] house owner; husband -3d 181a

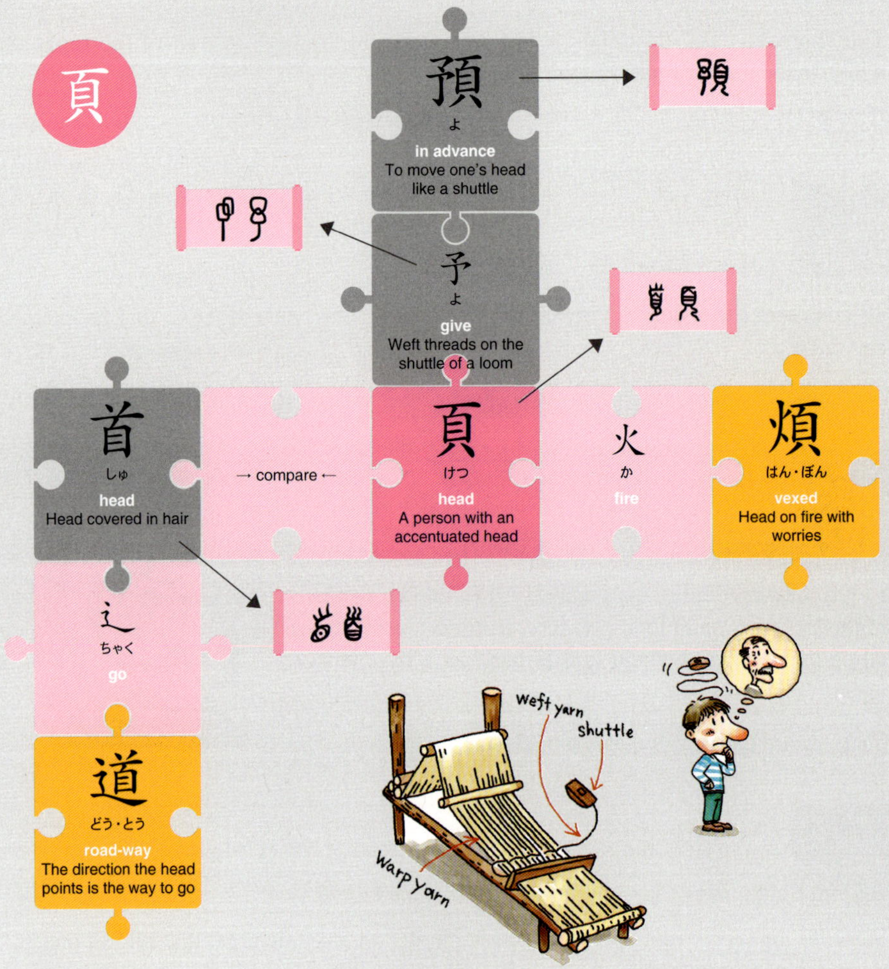

4	頁

ケツ

head

一 丆 丆 丙 丙 百 百 頁 頁

A head(一) above a person's(儿) legs and face(冂) put together to mean 'head.'

4a	予

ヨ あらかじめ・かねて

give / beforehand(豫)

フ マ 孑 予

Symbolizes two hooks that are interconnected together, or the shape of a flying shuttle in traditional looms. As the shuttle moves back and forth to release string, the meaning of 'to give' is derived.

* "豫," a traditional character which was a combination of "予" and "象,"meaning an elephant, became "予," a simplified version that is solely used today. "予" means that an elephant(象) knows beforehand when it will be destined to die, and therefore, find its own gravesite.

予め[あらかじめ] beforehand	予て[かねて] previously
予約[よやく] reservation; booking -4a 104a	予習[よしゅう] preparation(s) -4a 141a
予定[よてい] schedule -4a 45b	天気予報[てんきよほう] weather (fore)cast -60b 158a 4a 30b

4b 預

ヨ あずかる・あずける

フ マ ヌ 予 予 予 予 預 預 預 預 預 預

in advance / deposit

shuttle/give 予 [ヨ] + head 頁 [ケツ]

When weaving with a loom, the weft yarn that goes horizontally is woven through the vertical warp yarn with a flying shuttle(予). This character means that a man's head(頁) or thoughts are moving to and fro, as fast as a shuttle, to think of many options in advance so that he can plan ahead. From saving up for the future came the meaning 'to assign or entrust.'

* When instinctively forecasting the future, we can use the kanji "豫" that includes the elephant(象 136b). When planning or preparing for the future, use "預" with the head(頁).

預(か)る[あずかる] take care of; look after	預ける[あずける] deposit; entrust
預金[よきん] deposit; savings -4b 154	

4c 煩

ハン・ボン

丶 丷 火 火 火 灯 灯 炘 烦 煩 煩 煩 煩

vexed

fire 火 124 [カ] + head 頁 [ケツ]

Anyone with a head(頁) on fire(火) would be in much trouble.

煩い[うるさい] noisy; distressed

4d 首

シュ くび

丶 丷 䒑 䒑 产 肖 首 首 首

head

A person's face(自) with hair(䒑) on top to mean a head.

* In this character, "self 自 6 [zi]" is the nose, which is the boldest feature on one's face.

首都[しゅと] capital city -4d 82d

4e 道

ドウ・トウ みち

丶 丷 䒑 䒑 产 肖 首 首 首 首 道 道

road-way; moral

head 首 [シュ] + go 辶 49 [チャク]

The direction the head(首), or the leader goes(辶), is the way his men must follow. This character also means morals, because it's the way one must go, the right way.

歩道[ほどう] sidewalk; pavement -44a 4e	横道[よこみち] byway; side road; digression -108a 4e

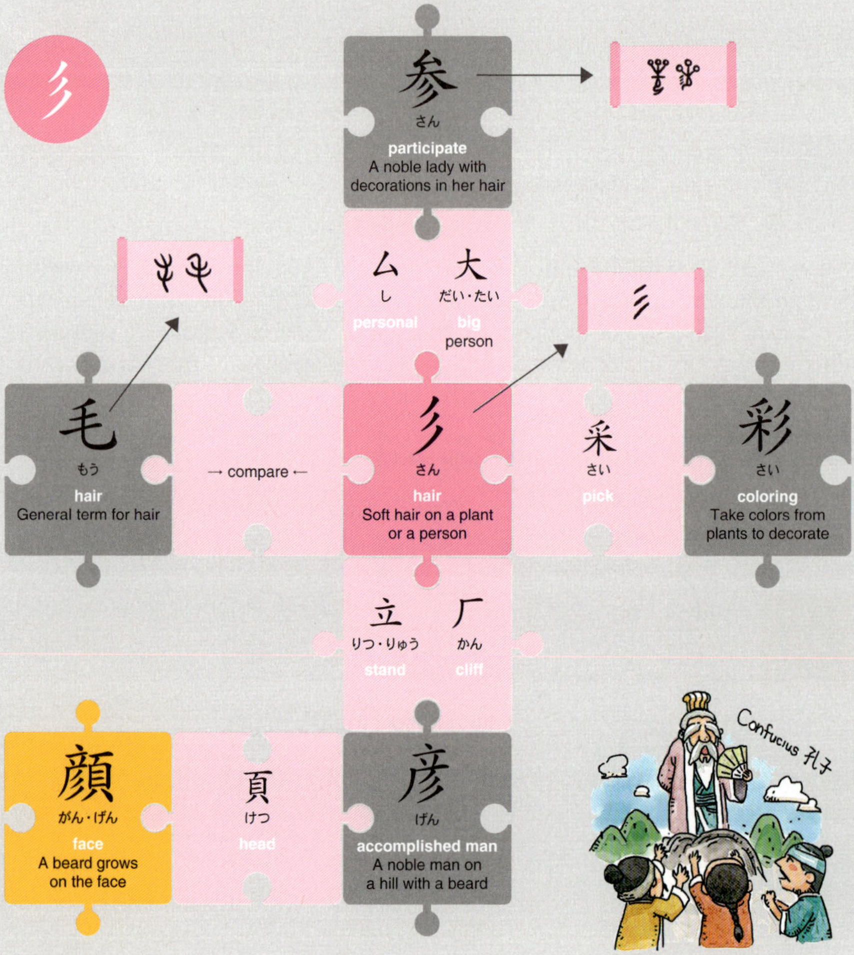

5

彡

リン

hair

ノ 彡 彡

The soft hair on a plant or a person. Hair on the head keeps one warm, but hair elsewhere is more decorative than functional. Characters that include this character have something to do with decorations or the act of decorating.

5a 参

サン まいる

participate

personal ム[76] [シ] + person/big 大[60] [ダイ・タイ] + decorate/hair 彡 [サン]

When taking part in a party, a noble lady(大) decorates(彡) her hair with an accessory(ム).

* The traditional character(參) takes the shape of decorations(厽) in the hair(dark and bushy 㐱 [シン]) to attend a party or a function.

参る[まいる] (honorific) go, come, visit
参加[さんか] participation -5a 125b
持参[じさん] bringing; bearing -37b 5a
参考[さんこう] reference -5a 81c

5b 彩

サイ

coloring

pick 采[29c] [サイ] + decorate/hair 彡 [サン]

To take the leaves(采) of a tree or plant and create different colors to dye material or clothes for decoration(彡) purposes.

色彩[しきさい] color -75d 5b

5c 彦

ゲン

accomplished man

stand 立[64] [リツ・リュウ] + cliff 厂[117] [カン] + hair 彡 [サン]

A learned nobleman with a long beard(彡) standing(立) on top of a hill(厂).

5d 顔

ガン・ゲン かお

face

accomplished man 彦 [ゲン] + head 頁[4] [ケツ]

Virtuous men who were respected(彦) grew long beards(彡). The part of one's head(頁) with long strands of hair is one's face.

笑顔[えがお] a smiling (beaming) face -61a 5d

5e 毛

モウ け

hair

Refers to any type of hair, be it human, animal, plant, or even fruit.

毛皮[けがわ] fur; pelt -5e 149
毛布[もうふ] blanket -5e 103c

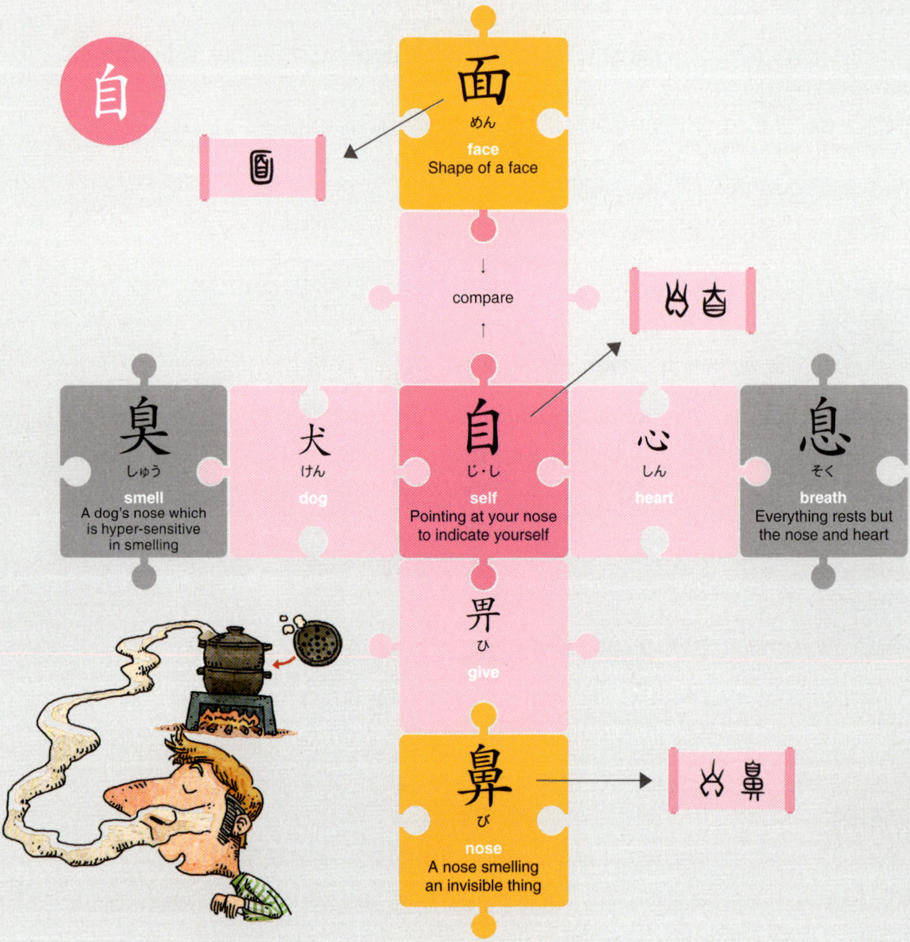

6 自

ジ・シ　みずから・おのずから

self

The nose is the most prominent feature of a face. When someone points to indicate himself or herself, they usually point at his own nose.

* A nose appears in a lot of sayings or proverbs about pride or arrogance. This is more proof on how a nose can mean oneself.

自ら[みずから] oneself; personally; in person
自ら[おのずから] naturally; spontaneously; of its own accord
自分[じぶん] (one)self; I; myself -6 95a
自由[じゆう] freedom; liberty -6 123e
自動車[じどうしゃ] car; vehicle; automobile -6 119b 97

6a 面

メン おも

face; flour

The shape of a face with an eye(目[7]), a nose(自[6]), and a mouth(口[12]). Regardless of the meaning, the pronunciation is identical to that of a powdered grain, especially flour, and came to mean 'flour or noodles.'

面白い[おもしろい] interesting; amusing -6a 106
洗面[せんめん] wash up, wash one's face -58e 6a
側面[そくめん] side; flank -147b 6a
面接[めんせつ] interview -6a 83b

6b 息

ソク いき

breath; rest

nose/self 自 [ジ・シ] + heart 心[26][シン]

The nose(自) and the heart(心) are organs that help breathing, and they work until one breathes his last breath. Only when the nose and the heart are working, it means one is resting.

消息[しょうそく] news -182d 6b

6c 鼻

ビ はな

nose

The character, "self 自 [ジ]," is a character borrowed from the image of the nose. Its meaning is derived from its original meaning by adding a phonetic element, "畀 [ヒ]."

* The character, "give 畀 [ヒ]," shows an image where a steamer(田) is placed on a stand(丌) with a hole through which steam comes up from its bottom. This suggests emphasis on the function of the nose that can smell something invisible like steam. Refer to "真[8d]."

6d 臭

シュウ くさい

smell

nose/self 自 [ジ・シ] + dog 大→犬[135][ケン]

The dog(犬) has been long known to have a well-developed nose(自) and having a sense of smell. Humans use that incredible sense of smell to locate harmful chemicals or to save people who need rescuing.

臭い[くさい] stinking; suspicious

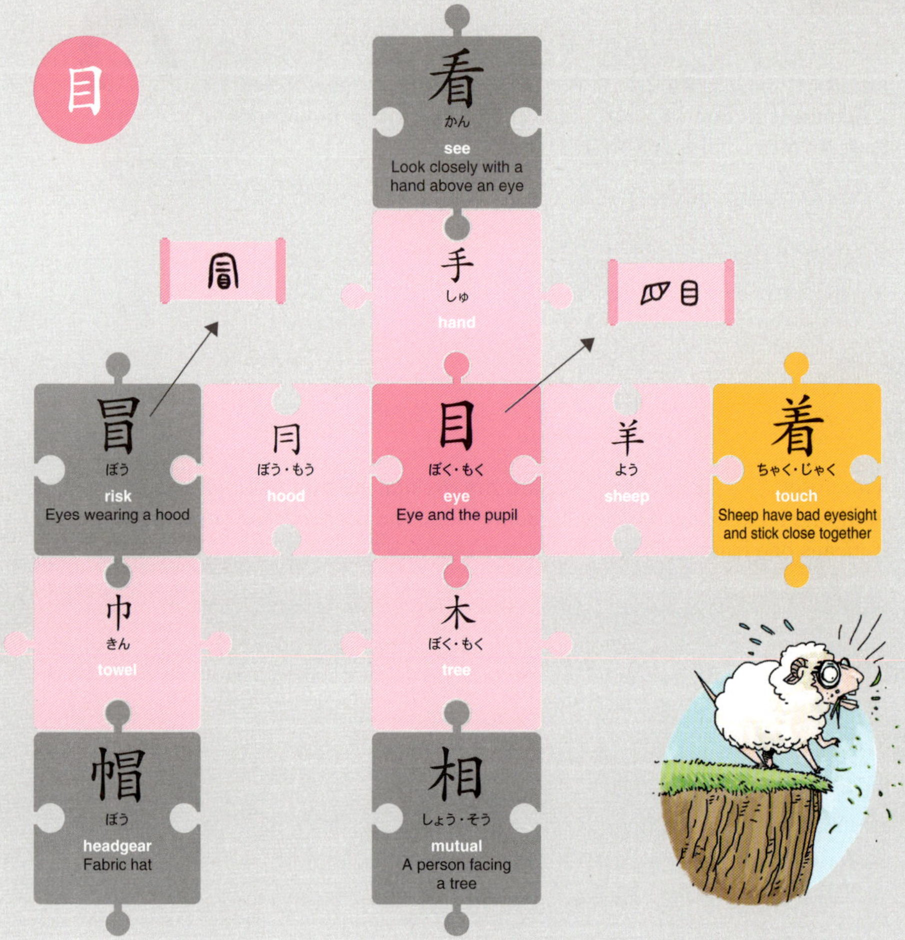

7	目	ボク・モク め	丨 冂 月 月 目

eye

The shape of an eye with a pupil.

7a	看	カン	一 二 三 手 手 看 看 看 看

see

hand 手[28] [シュ] + eye 目 [ボク・モク]

To put a hand(手) above an eye(目) to look at something closely.

看板[かんばん] billboard; sign(board) -7a 117c 看病[かんびょう] nursing -7a 65a

7b 着

チャク・ジャク つく・きる

丶 丷 䒑 䒑 ⺷ 羊 𦍌 羊 着 着 着 着

touch; stick

sheep ⺷→𦍌[134] [ヨウ] + eye 目 [ボク・モク]

Sheep(羊), known to have terrible eyesight(目), stick close enough to touch each other so as to not get lost.

* Sheep are actually so nearsighted, that they can't tell a cliff from a forest.

着く[つく] stick (to); touch; arrive (at, in) 着る[きる] put on; wear
上着[うわぎ] coat; outerwear -173a 7b 下着[したぎ] underwear; underclothes -173b 7b

7c 相

ショウ・ソウ あい

一 十 才 木 木 相 相 相 相

mutual

tree 木[164] [ボク・モク] + eye 目 [ボク・モク]

A man is standing in front of a tree(木) and looking(目) at it to see if it is good to cut down for timber. The character shows a man and a tree facing each other.

* Trees provide us with food and wood, and we, in turn, plant and care for them. We have taken care of each other since the beginning of time.

相手[あいて] opponent; counterpart -7c 28 相当[そうとう] considerable; equality -7c 118e
相談[そうだん] counseling; consultation -7c 17c

7d 冒

ボウ

丨 冂 冃 冃 冐 冐 冒 冒 冒

risk

hood 日→冃 [ボウ・モウ] + eye 目 [ボク・モク]

To wear a hood(冃) deep enough to cover the eyes(目). It came to mean 'to take a risk' because people wearing a hood would do things they wouldn't usually consider to attempt in normal situations.

* "冃" is the hood worn on one's head.

冒険[ぼうけん] venture; adventure -7d 116c

7d 帽

ボウ

丨 冂 巾 巾 帄 帄 帽 帽 帽 帽 帽 帽

headgear

towel 巾[103] [キン] + risk 冒 [ボウ]

When a hood worn above one's eyes(冒) came to mean 'risk,' the kanji added "巾," meaning 'fabric,' to make a character meaning 'hat.'

帽子[ぼうし] hat; cap -7e 77

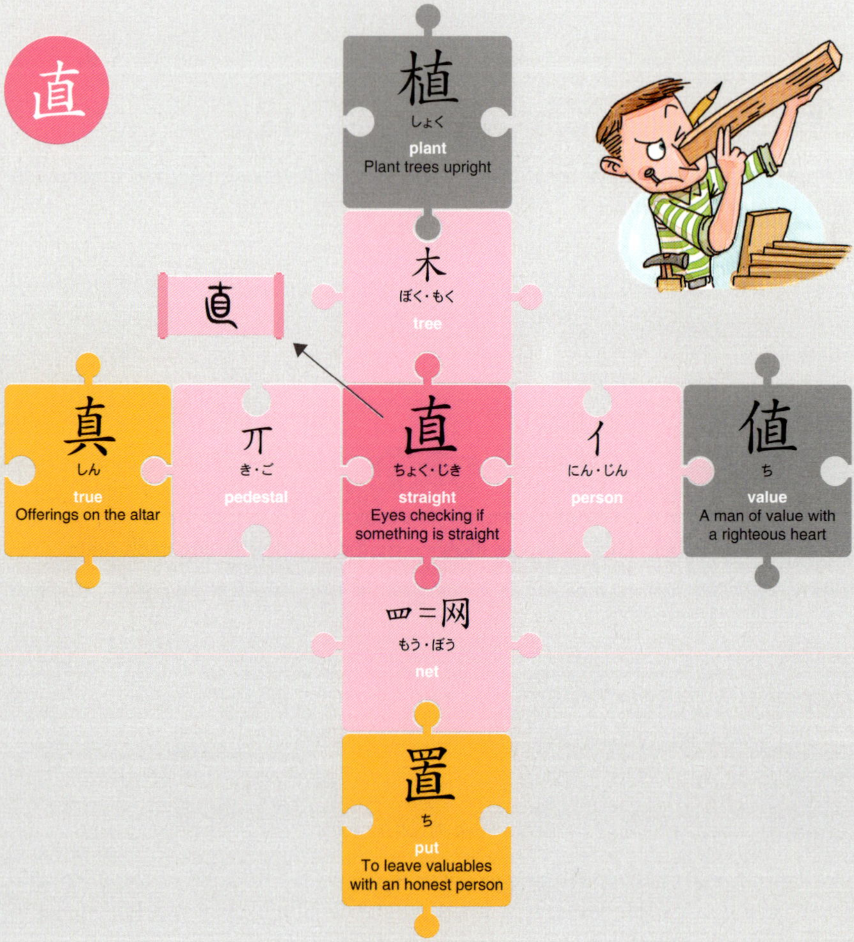

8 **直**

チョク・ジキ なおす・なおる・ただちに

一 十 𠂇 冇 冇 有 直 直

straight

verticality・horizontal 十 [symbol] + eye 目 [ボク・モク] + materials 乚 [symbol]

A carpenter or artisan takes a piece of wood(乚) and uses his eyes(目) to see if it is horizontally and vertically(十) straight.

直す[なおす] correct; reform; improve
直る[なおる] be corrected; be reformed; recover
直ちに[ただちに] at once; immediately; instantly
真っ直ぐ[まっすぐ] straight; upright; straightforward; honest -8d 8
正直[しょうじき] honesty; uprightness -45 8

8a **植** シヨク うえる

一 十 オ 木 木 木 杧 杧 杭 植 植 植

plant

tree 木 164 [ボク・モク] + straight 直 [チョク・ジキ]

Planting trees(木) upright(直) so they grow well.

植える[うえる] plant; raise; grow; sow (barley)
植物[しょくぶつ] plant (vegetable); vegetation -8a 41a
植木[うえき] garden shrubs; potted plant -8a 164

8b **値** チ ね・あたい

ノ イ 亻 仁 什 佶 佶 侑 値 値

value

person 亻 52 [ニン・ジン] + straight 直 [チョク・ジキ]

Being rich or learned doesn't necessarily mean that you are a valued friend. A truly valuable person(亻) is one with a straight, honest(直) heart.

値段[ねだん] price; cost -8b 93a

8c **置** チ おく

丶 冖 冖 罒 罒 罒 罒 罕 罟 罟 署 置 置

put; set

net 罒=网 146 [モウ・ボウ] + straight 直 [チョク・ジキ]

To leave/put(罒) one's life or valuables in the hands of an honest or upright(直) person.

* Baggage or crops were kept in a net or basket(罒), where the meaning 'to put' came from.

置く[おく] put; place
物置[ものおき] storage room; storeroom -41a 8c
位置[いち] position; situation -64a 8c

8d **真** シン ま

一 十 十 冇 冇 百 直 直 真 真

true

straight 直→直 [チョク・ジキ] + pedestal 丌→丌 39 [キ・ゴ]

Flawless(直) offerings are placed on an altar(丌) to the gods, and with their blessings, the humans hope to learn the truth.

* The ancient character depicts the gods using cutlery(匕 72) to eat the food offered up in a bronze pot or a cooker with legs(鼎 147), and then sharing their wisdom and truth with the humans in return.

真っ直[まっすぐ] straight; upright; straightforward; honest -8d 8
写真[しゃしん] photograph; photo -131a 8d

見

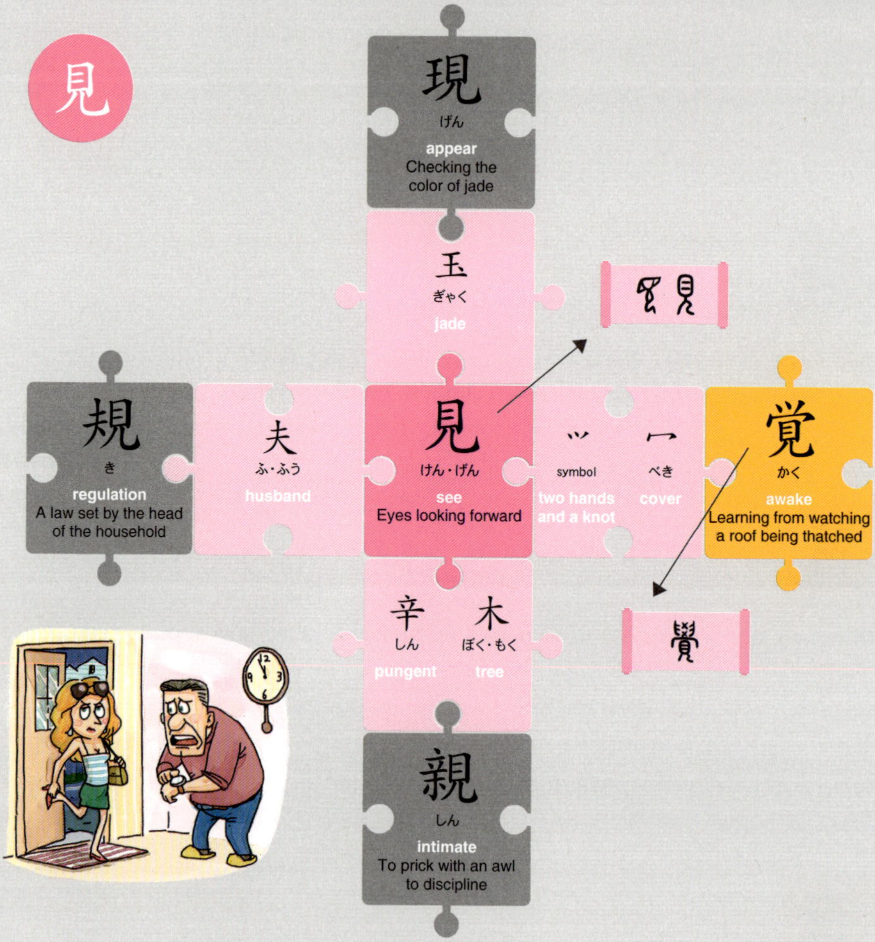

9 見

ケン・ゲン みる・みせる・みえる

see

A man(儿[58]) with open eyes(目[7]) looking straight ahead means that he is staring forward.

見る[みる] see; look (at); look over	見せる[みせる] show; display
見える[みえる] be seen; look	意見[いけん] opinion; idea; view -18b 9

9a 現

ゲン あらわれる・あらわす

一 二 千 王 王 玑 玑 玥 珇 現 現

appear

jade 王→玉[86b] [ギャク] + see 見 [ケン・ゲン]

When holding a jade(玉) object under the sun to see(見) the purity and check the value, the sun's reflection causes many colors to appear on the jade.

* When it becomes part of a more complicated character, "玉" often loses the dot(丶[181]) to look like "king 王[86] [オウ]."

現(わ)れる[あらわれる] come out; appear; come in sight
現(わ)す[あらわす] show, reveal, expose
現代[げんだい] today; present day -9a 86d
表現[ひょうげん] expression -101a 9a

9b 覚

カク おぼえる・さます・さめる

丶 ⺍ ⺍ ⺍ 𰀁 ⺍ 学 常 常 常 覚 覚

awake

two hands and a knot ⺍ [symbol] + cover 冖[131] [ベキ] + see 見 [ケン・ゲン]

A young boy watches(見) the adults tie straw together(⺍) to cover a roof (冖), and 'becomes aware of (realizes) the wisdom of daily life from the adults.'

* The traditional character(覺) shows that a boy learns from watching(見) men cover a roof(冖) with bundles(乂) of hay using their hands(臼[29]).

覚える[おぼえる] remember, learn, feel
覚ます[さます] awaken; realize; grasp
覚める[さめる] wake; become conscious

9c 親

シン おや・したしい

丶 亠 亠 立 立 立 辛 辛 亲 亲 新 新 親 親 親 親

intimate; parent

awl/pungent 立→辛[83] [シン] + tree 木[164] [ボク・モク] + see 見 [ケン・ゲン]

This character shows a parent looking out(見) for the child and using an awl(辛) to discipline so the child grows(木) well.

親しい[したしい] close; intimate; be on good (friendly) terms
父親[ちちおや] father -30a 9c
母親[ははおや] mother -79 9c

9d 規

キ

一 二 于 夫 夫 犯 玑 邦 担 規 規

regulation

husband 夫[60a] [フ・フウ] + see 見 [ケン・ゲン]

In a patriarchal society, what the father(夫) looked(見) at and what he decided was 'right or correct,' and therefore it finally became the law or rule.

規律[きりつ] rule, regulation, discipline, order -9d 33a
規則[きそく] rule; regulations -9d 147a
規準[きじゅん] standard; criterion; canon -9d 140c

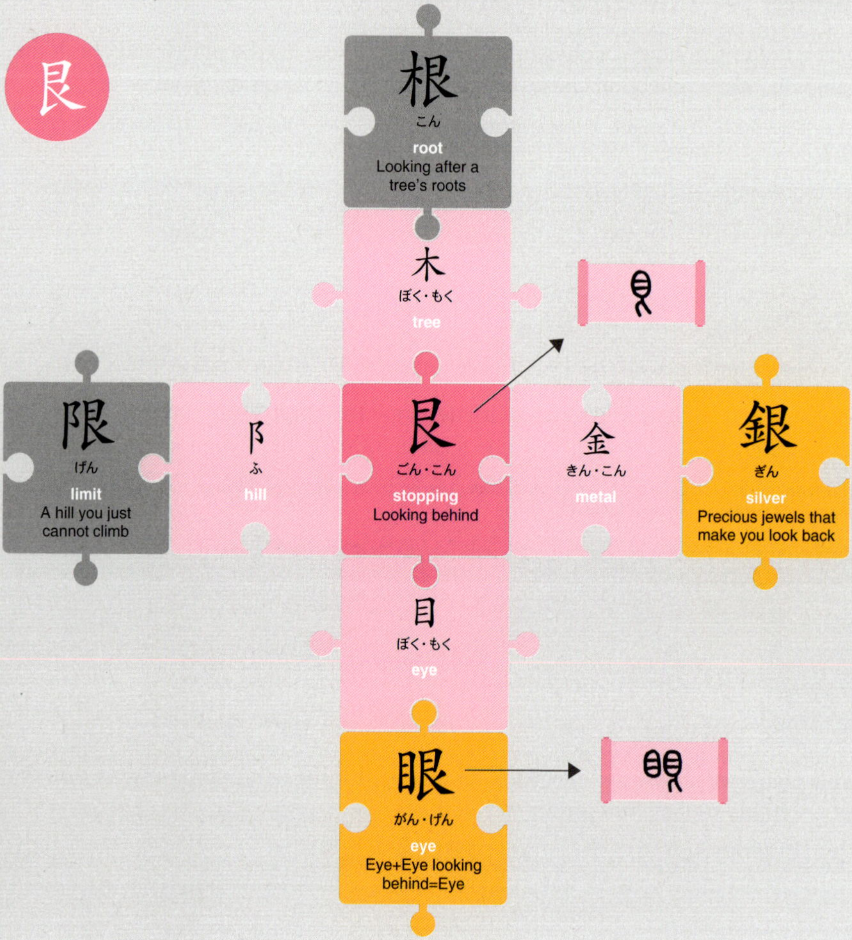

10 艮

ゴン・コン

stopping

ㄱ ㅋ ヨ 巳 艮 艮

The opposite of "見," which means 'to look straight at.' "艮" is the shape of someone turning to look behind and means 'stopping or look back.'

10a **根**

コン　ね

root

tree 木[164] [ボク・モク] + look back/stopping 艮 [ゴン・コン]

A tree(木) needs to be looked after(艮) until its root firmly attaches into the soil.

根性[こんじょう] nature; spirit; grit -10a 27a

10b **銀**

ギン　しろがね

silver

metal 金[154] [キン・コン] + look back/stopping 艮 [ゴン・コン]

Silver used to be prized more than gold because it was harder to find in the natural state and was very hard to purify. To find a metal(金) as precious as silver means that one has to keep looking everywhere, including behind(艮) himself.

銀行[ぎんこう] bank -10b 48a

10c **眼**

ガン・ゲン　め

eye

eye 目[7] [ボク・モク] + look back/stopping 艮 [ゴン・コン]

"目" meaning 'eye' and "艮" meaning 'backwards' were put together to mean 'eye' but with a different pronunciation.

眼鏡[めがね] glasses; spectacles -10c 18e

10d **限**

ゲン　かぎる

limit

hill 阝[116] [フ] + look back/stopping 艮 [ゴン・コン]

However hard you look at it(艮), in order to overcome your limit or boundary, you are facing a hill(阝) that you cannot scale over or go around.

限る[かぎる] limit; set bounds (limits); restrict　　限界[げんかい] limit; bounds -10d 51b
限度[げんど] limit; bounds -10d 114b

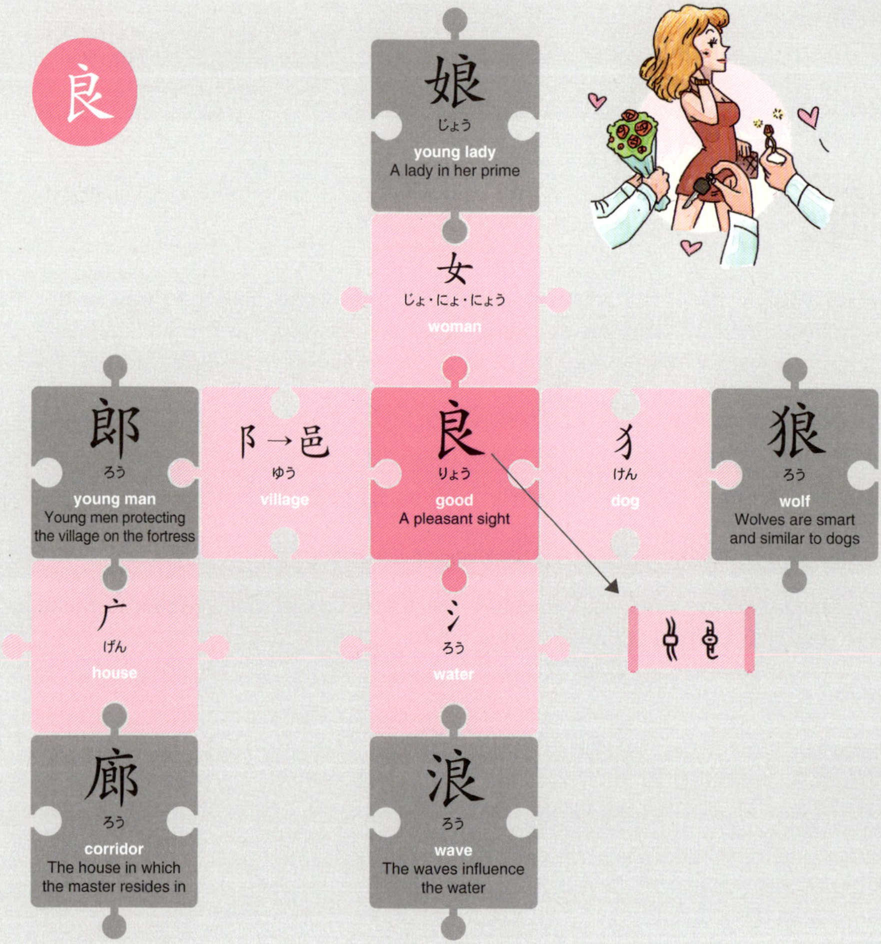

11 良

リョウ よい

good

The long corridor of a palace or a well-maintained castle wall is always good to see.

* Has no correlation with "stopping 艮10 [ゴン・コン]."

良い/善い[よい] good; fine; excellent -11.134b
良い/善い[いい] (spoken language) good, fine, excellent -11.134b

11a 娘

ジョウ むすめ

く 女 女 女' 女ᄀ 女ᄏ 女ᄏ 娘 娘 娘

young lady

woman 女[78] [ジョ・ニョ・ニョウ] + good 良 [リョウ]

The best(良) time in a woman's(女) life is when she is a young lady.

娘さん[むすめさん] (honorific) daughter, young lady

11b 狼

ロウ おおかみ

ノ 犭 犭 犭' 犭ᄀ 犭ᄏ 犭ᄏ 狼 狼 狼

wolf

dog 犭[135b] [ケン] + good 良 [リョウ]

Wolves(犭) are smart and possess a keen(良) sense of what to do. Native Americans used to revere wolves for their loyalty and cunningness.

* "犭" means the animal looks like or is similar in size to a dog.

11c 浪

ロウ なみ

丶 氵 氵 氵' 氵ᄀ 氵ᄏ 氵ᄏ 浪 浪 浪

wave

water 氵[157] [スイ] + good 良 [リョウ]

Waves or ripples have a good(良) effect on water(氵). A popular Korean proverb goes "stagnant water will rot." Waves or ripples are nature's way of showing that water is alive and moving. Plankton is said to rely on the currents and waves to move around.

11d 郎

ロウ

丶 ㇇ ㇇ ㇇ 自 自 良 良' 良ʒ 郎

young man

good 良 [リョウ] + village 阝→邑[75c] [ユウ]

Young men or soldiers protecting the village(邑) that is surrounded by a fortress(良).

* "Hill 阝[116] [フ]" on the right of a character means "邑."

11e 廊

ロウ

丶 亠 广 广 庐 庐 庐 庐 庐 廊' 廊ʒ 廊

corridor

house 广[114] [ゲン] + young man 郎→郎 [ロウ]

This character depicts a large house(广) with a detached house where the master(郎) resides in and entertains guests. Because the detached house is connected to the main building with a corridor, it also means 'hallway or corridor.'

廊下[ろうか] corridor; hall(way); passage(way) -11e 173b

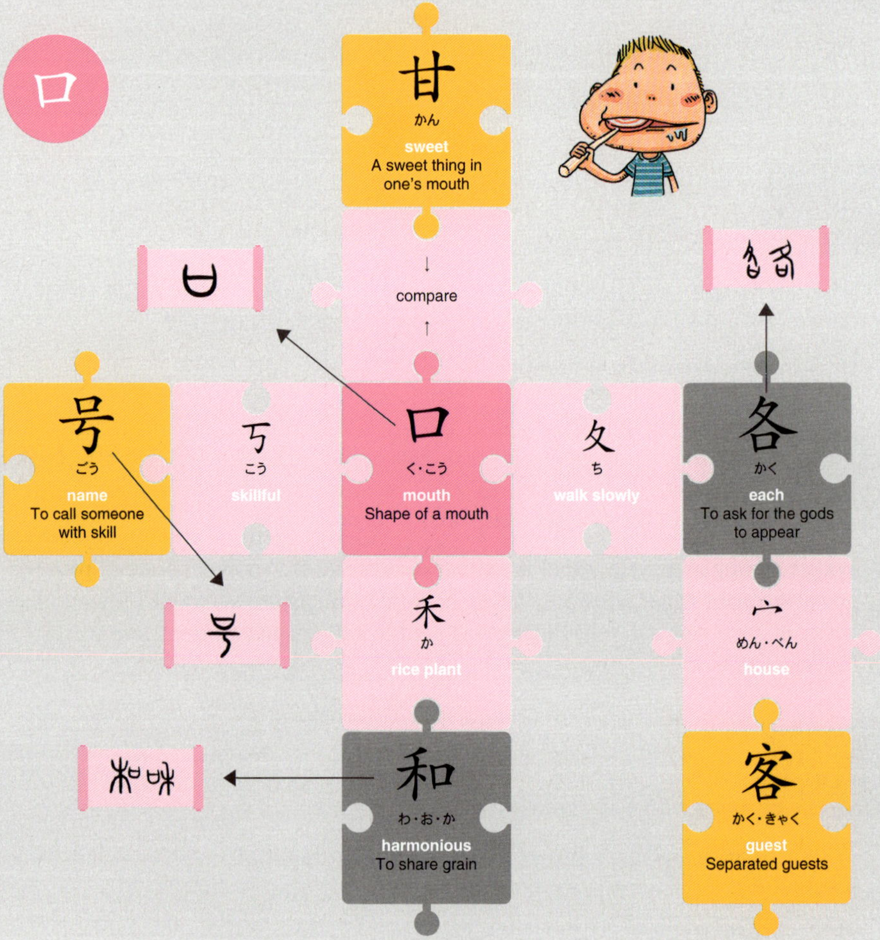

12 口

ク・コウ くち

mouth

丨 冂 口

The shape of a mouth. When used as part of another character, it describes an action done with a mouth, like 'eat, speak and cry.' But there are characters out there that look like "ロ," but have nothing to do with it.

* Kanji have changed over the centuries. Therefore, there exist numerous characters which look similar but originate from different sources of characters. Just because the two characters look the same doesn't necessarily mean that they have the same meaning.

入(り)口[いりぐち] entrance; doorway; root; beginning -53 12　出口[でぐち] exit; way out -131c 12

12a 甘

カン　あまい・あまえる・あまやかす　　一 十 廿 廿 甘

sweet

This character depicts the image of holding a sweet thing(-) in one's mouth(廿 → ロ) without swallowing it.

甘い[あまい] sweet; sugary　甘える[あまえる] play on affection; behave like a spoiled child
甘やかす[あまやかす] pamper; spoil

12b 各

カク　おのおの　　ノ ク 夂 夂 各 各

each; every

foot/walk slowly 夂[46] [チ] + mouth ロ [ク・コウ]

"夂" is a foot facing downwards. So "各" is a mouth(ロ) begging the gods for help and feet(夂) facing the mouth. Everyone wishes(ロ) that the gods would come(夂) and help them.

12c 客

カク・キャク　　丶 丶 宀 宀 岁 安 客 客 客

guest

house 宀[113] [メン・ベン] + each 各 [カク]

Men together in one house(宀) but separated(各) is 'a guest.'

お客さん[おきゃくさん] (honorific) guest　乗客[じょうきゃく] passenger - 165d 12c

12d 和

ワ・オ・カ　やわらげる・なごやか　　一 二 千 千 禾 和 和 和

harmonious; Japan

rice aplant 禾[111] [カ] + mouth ロ [ク・コウ]

People living in harmony are willing to share food(ロ) made with their harvest(禾). Japan is an island nation and the belief that they might perish if they didn't live in harmony became a philosophy and culture in the form of "和."

* The ancient character describes someone blowing(ロ) a pipe or a flute(龠→禾) and meant that music had to be harmonious.

和らげる[やわらげる] soften; relieve　和やか[なごやか] mild; calm; gentle
和食[わしょく] Japanese food; Japanese-style meal - 12d 109

12e 号

ゴウ　さけぶ　　丨 口 口 旦 号

name; number

mouth ロ [ク・コウ] + skillful 丂 [コウ]

It takes much skill(丂) to remember one's name so that you can call out(ロ) to him from within a crowd. But, when there are too many people to call everyone's name, it's easier to use numbers.

* "丂" is a carving knife used for delicate work.

番号[ばんごう] number - 142a 12e　記号[きごう] sign; symbol; mark - 66b 12e
符号[ふごう] mark; sign; symbol - 36b 12e

Diagram for 可

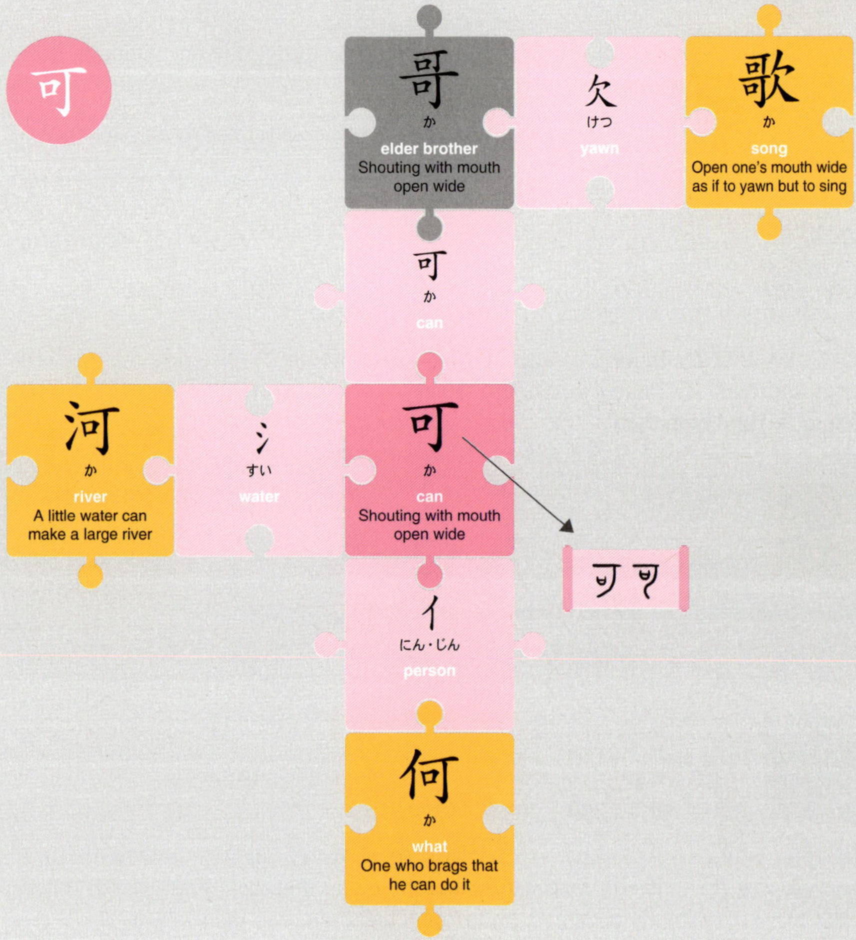

13 **可**

カ

can

mouth 口 12 [ク・コウ] + mouth open wide 丁 [symbol]

Shouting with one's mouth(口) wide open(丁) means that one is not shy and can do something or ask for the approval of something.

可愛い[かわいい] lovely; charming; sweet -13 29e
許可[きょか] permission; approval; license -96d 13

13a 哥

カ

一 丆 丙 可 可 哥 哥 哥 哥 哥

elder brother

can 可 [カ] + can 可 [カ]

Not one but two mouths(ロ) wide open(丁) to shout(可＋可) originally meant 'to sing.' Nowadays, it means that the elder brother is the one who gets to pull a prank and shout in the house.

13b 歌

カ うた・うたう

一 丆 丙 可 可 哥 哥 哥 哥 哥 哥 歌 歌 歌

song

song/elder brother 哥 [カ] + yawn 欠[19] [ケツ]

When singing(哥), one must open his/her mouth wide, as if to yawn(欠). After the meaning of "哥" went from 'to sing' to 'older brother,' the kanji added "欠" to the character to make one to mean 'to sing.'

歌う[うたう] sing (a song)

13c 何

カ なに・なん

ノ イ 仁 仃 佰 何 何

what

person 亻[52] [ニン・ジン] + can 可 [カ]

A person(亻) boastfully saying he can(可) do whatever it takes.

何時も[いつも] always; all the time -13c 37a
何時[いつ] when; (at) what time -13c 37a
何の[どの] which; what
何れ[どれ] which; which one; either; any
何故[なぜ] why; for what reason -13c 15a
如何[どう] how -78d 13c
如何して[どうして] why; how -78d 13c
如何致しまして[どういたしまして] You are welcome -78d 13c 90d
何卒[どうぞ] please; kindly; by all means; in any case -13c 181d
何処/何所[どこ] where; what place -13c 46d 13c 115e
何方[どなた] (honorific) who -13c 126
何方[どちら] which -13c 126
何様な[どんな] what; what sort (kind) of -13c 134a

13d 河

カ かわ

丶 丶 氵 氵 汀 沪 河 河

river

water 氵[157] [スイ] + can 可 [カ]

A little water(氵) gathers to make a stream, and a few streams can(可) make a river.

河/川[かわ] river; stream -13d 156e

Diagram for 奇

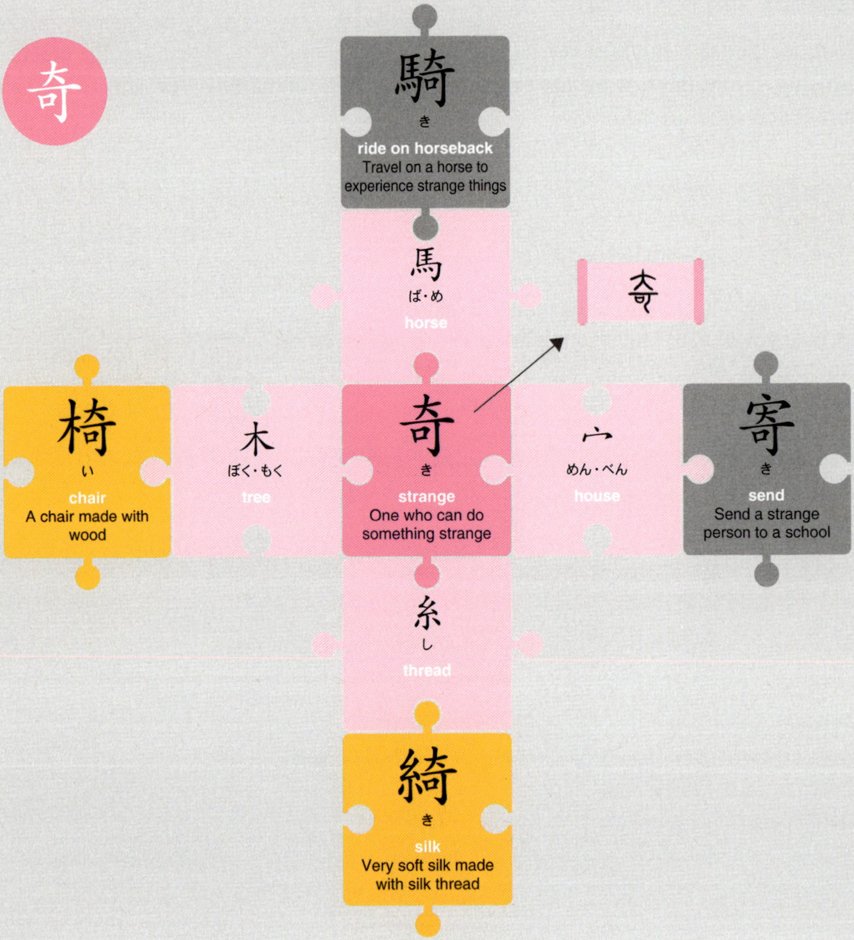

14 **奇**

キ

strange

person/big 大[60] [ダイ・タイ] + can 可 [カ]

一 ナ 大 大 太 奇 奇 奇

A person(大) who can(可) carry out strange activities which others cannot.

奇麗[きれい] beautiful; pretty; lovely -14 150c

14a 騎

キ

丨 𠃌 𠃌 𠃌 𠃌 馬 馬 馬 馬 馬 馬 馬 馬 馬 騎 騎 騎 騎

ride on horseback

horse 馬 [138] [バ・メ] + strange 奇 [キ]

Depicts a man who rides a horse(馬) to travel and see strange(奇) things he cannot see in his hometown.

14b 寄

キ よる・よせる

丶 丶 宀 宀 宀 宀 宀 宀 宀 寄 寄

send

house 宀 [113] [メン・ベン] + strange 奇 [キ]

A person who can do strange(奇) things that others cannot are sent to a school (宀) to develop their skills.

寄る[よる] visit; drop in; approach	寄せる[よせる] come near; bring near

14c 綺

キ

𠃋 幺 幺 糸 糸 糸 糸 糸 糸 綺 綺 綺 綺 綺

silk; beautiful

thread 糸 [104] [シ] strange 奇 [キ]

Silk is made with silk thread(糸) that comes from a silk worm, an insect, but it is wonderfully and amazingly(奇) soft.

綺麗[きれい] beautiful; pretty; lovely - 14c 150c

14d 椅

イ こしかけ

一 十 才 木 木 木 木 木 椅 椅 椅 椅

chair

tree 木 [164] [ボク・モク] + strange 奇 [キ]

Strangely(奇), unlike other animals, only humans live on their two feet. Wooden(木) chairs became a very useful tool which changed their lives forever.

椅子[いす] chair - 14d 77

Diagram for 古

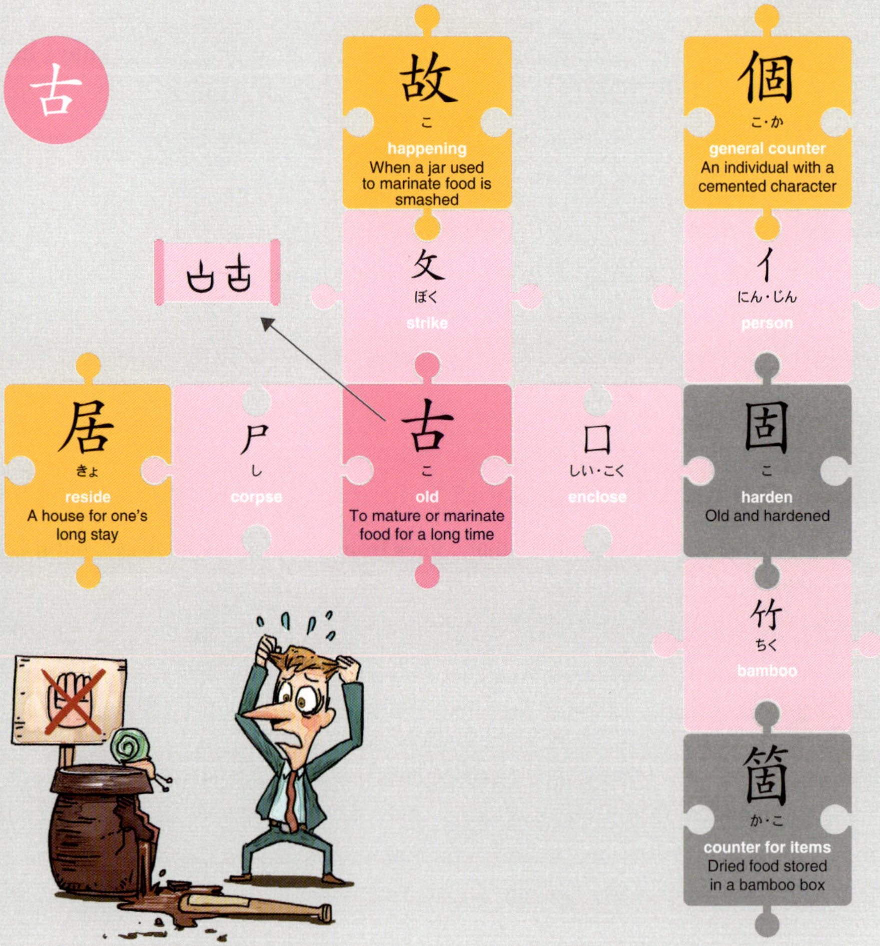

15	古	コ ふるい **old**	一 十 十 古 古

To put food in a jar(ロ) and tighten the lid with a heavy stone(十) on top of it in order to marinate or ripen the food for a long time.

* In this character, "ロ" has nothing to do with 'mouth.' Here, it's the shape of a container.

古い[ふるい] old; worn (out)　　中古[ちゅうこ] used article; secondhand article - 179d 15

15a 故

コ ゆえ

一 十 ナ 古 古 古 古 故 故

happening; reason

old 古 [コ] + strike 攵 [43] [ボク]

In the olden days, when there were no refrigerators, if someone smashed(攵) a pot that was used to store food for a long period of time(古), it was considered a terrible happening because there were only a few ways to preserve food.

何故[なぜ] why; for what reason - 13c 15a　　事故[じこ] accident - 32c 15a

15b 固

コ かたまる・かためる

丨 冂 冂 冂 冂 冃 固 固

harden

enclose 口 [16] [イ・コク] + old 古 [コ]

This character depicts a jar or urn used to ferment food for a long time(古) that is covered up(口), and it came to mean something that has hardened after time.

固まる[かたまる] harden; become hard　　固める[かためる] harden; solidify; strengthen
固定[こてい] fix; settle - 15b 45b

15c 個

コ・カ

ノ イ 亻 们 们 們 們 個 個 個

individual; general counter

person 亻 [52] [ニン・ジン] + harden 固 [コ]

As every person(亻) has their own character or habit that has hardened(固) and become difficult to change, this character means 'each or individual.' It's also used as a general counter when counting objects or persons.

一個・一箇[いっこ] one (object); a piece - 173 15c 173 15d　　個人[こじん] individual - 15c 51

15d 箇

カ・コ

ノ ト ケ ケ' ケケ 竹 竹 竹 笛 笛 筒 筒 箇 箇

counter for items

bamboo 竹 [169] [チク] + harden 固 [コ]

This character came to mean 'each or one' because it depicts dried, hard(固) foods stored separately in an airy bamboo(竹) box.

* "個" is used for people and "箇" is used for items.

15e 居

キョ いる・おる

コ コ 尸 尸 尸 尸 居 居

reside

house/corpse 尸 [74] [シ] + old 古 [コ]

This character symbolizes a house(尸) where one can live for the longest period(古) of time, right from the time of his or her birth.

居る[いる] to be; exist; stay
居る[おる] to be, exist, (after the 'て' form of a verb) verb indicating continuing action or state
居間[いま] living room - 15e 115b　　住居[じゅうきょ] dwelling; residence; living - 181b 15e

Diagram for 口

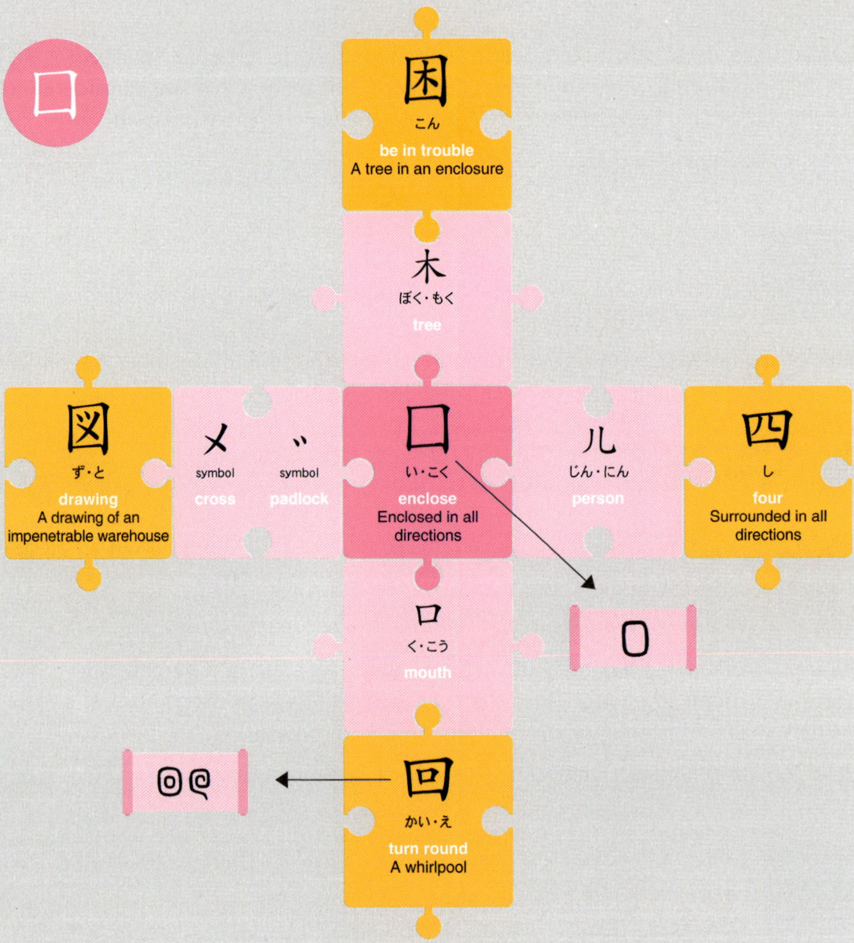

16 口

イ・コク

enclose

丨 冂 口

To be enclosed in all directions by something like a castle wall.

* This character has the same shape as "mouth ロ [12] [ク・コウ]," but is much larger and encircles other characters.

16a 困

コン こまる

be in trouble

enclose 囗 [イ・コク] + tree 木[164][ボク・モク]

To enclose a tree(木) or a person within a frame(囗) means to imprison or shut in.

困る[こまる] difficult; tough; embarrassing 困難[こんなん] difficult; tough -16a 108d

16b 四

シ よん・よっつ

four; 4

enclose 囗 [イ・コク] + person 儿[58][ジン・ニン]

A person(儿) surrounded(囗) from all four directions.

四つ[よっつ] four; 4 四季[しき] four seasons -16b 72d

16c 回

カイ・エ まわる・まわす

turn round; times

A body of water whirling in circles in the same place. This character came to mean 'number of times an action takes place.'

* This character has nothing to do with "enclose 囗 [コク]" or "mouth ロ[12][ク・コウ]."

回る[まわる] turn; rotate 回す[まわす] turn; spin
一回[いっかい] once; one time -173 16c 何回[なんかい] how many times -13c 16c

16d 図

ズ・ト はかる

drawing; plan

enclose 囗 [イ・コク] + cross㐅 [symbol] + padlock丷 [symbol]

The drawing or layout(囗) of a grain warehouse so well-built with a padlock (丷) that can't be penetrated(㐅) gave this character's meaning for 'drawing, layout or figure.'

* The traditional character(圖) shows a plan(囗) of a storing facility for grain(啚) with something heavy(ロ) put on top of the grain hold(亩) so that no one can get into what is inside.

図る[はかる] plot; plan; attempt 図書館[としょかん] library -16d 33e 152d
地図[ちず] map -68b 16d

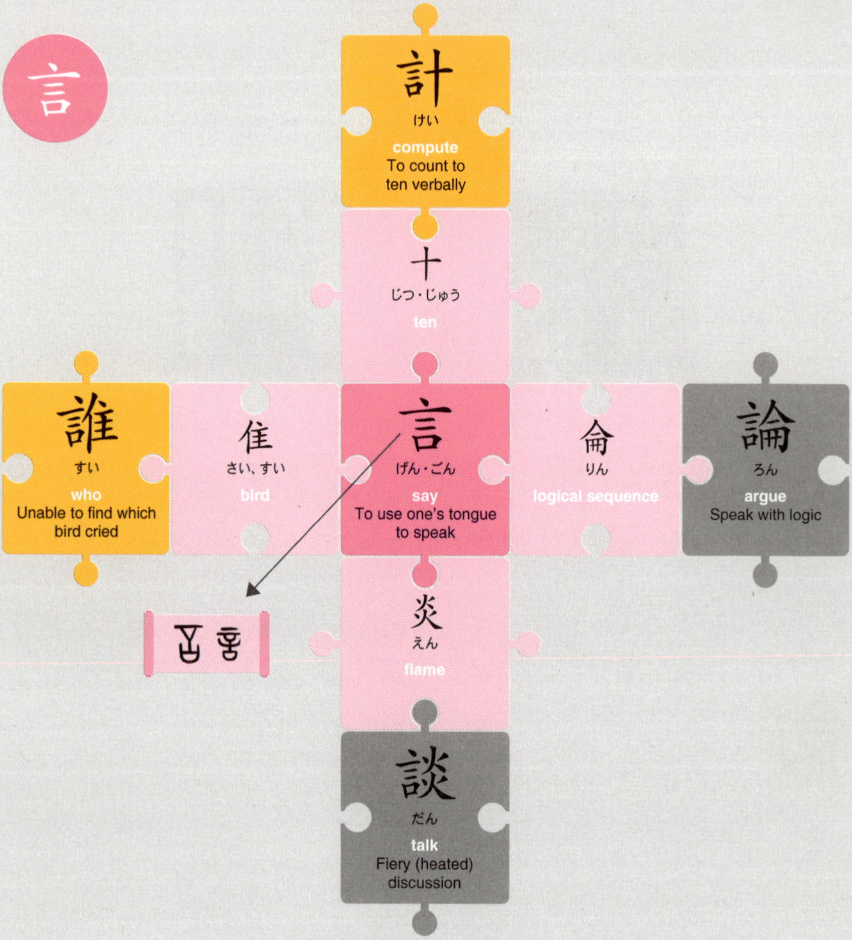

17 **言** ゲン・ゴン いう・こと

say

To speak a word in earnestness by sticking one's tongue out of one's mouth(口 12).

言う[いう] say; speak; talk; tell
言葉[ことば] speech; language; word; phrase -17 162d
助言[じょげん] advice -174c 17

17a 計

ケイ はかる

丶 亠 亠 亖 亖 言 言 訁 計

compute

say 言 [ゲン・ゴン] + ten 十[178][ジツ・ジュウ]

To count up to ten(十) verbally, with words(言).

はかる[計る] measure; weigh; survey
時計[とけい] watch; clock -37a 17a
計画[けいかく] plan (for); program; scheme; design -17a 122d
計算[けいさん] calculation; reckoning -17a 38e

17b 論

ロン

丶 亠 亠 亖 亖 言 言 訁 訃 訃 訡 訡 論 論 論

argue

say 言 [ゲン・ゴン] + logical sequence 侖 [リン]

To use logic(侖) when speaking(言) means 'to argue or discuss.'

* "侖" means a lot of books(冊[169c]) are gathered together(亼[54]).

結論[けつろん] conclusion -84b 17b
勿論[もちろん] of course -41 17b

17c 談

ダン

丶 亠 亠 亖 亖 言 言 言 訁 訁 訁 訁 談 談 談

talk

say 言 [ゲン・ゴン] + flame 炎 [エン]

A heated discussion or conversation is initiated as words(言) come together in fiery or scorching fashion(炎).

* "炎" stacked two fires(火[124]) on top of each other to signify intense burning.

相談[そうだん] counseling; consultation -7c 17c

17d 誰

スイ だれ

丶 亠 亠 亖 亖 言 言 訁 訁 訁 訁 訁 誰 誰 誰

who

say 言 [ゲン・ゴン] + bird 隹[140] [サイ、スイ]

It is hard to find who cried(言) out when a group of small birds(隹) sit together.

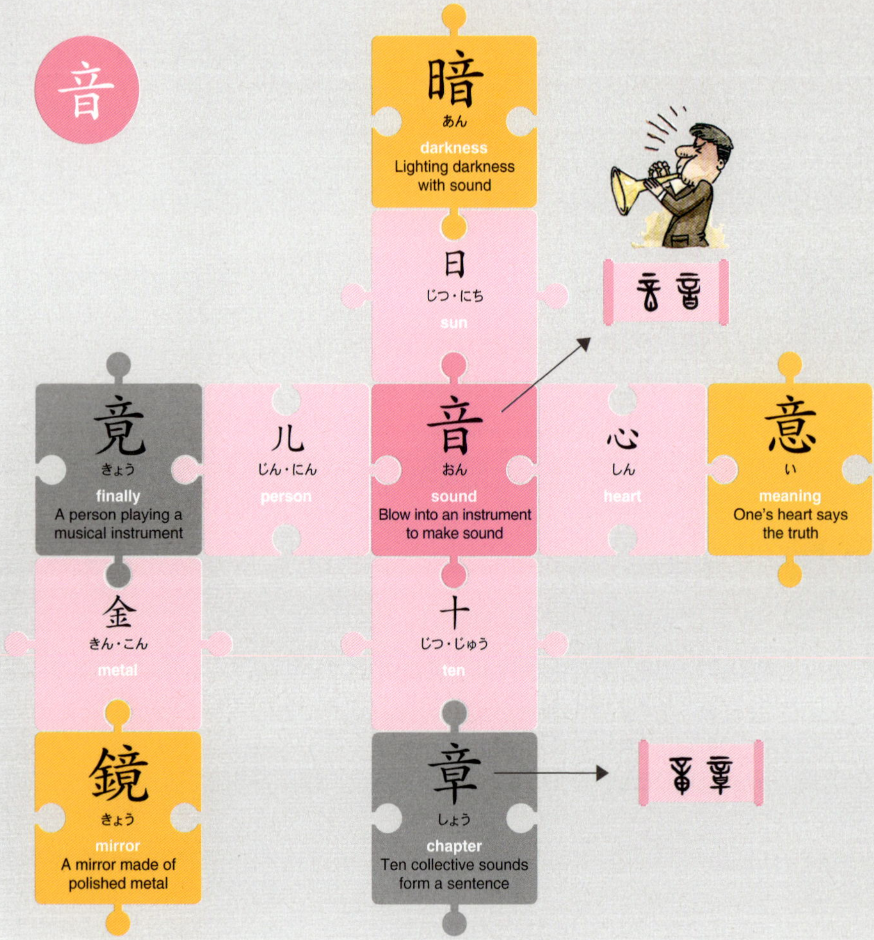

18 **音** オン おと・ね

sound

Ancient kanji text shows that "言[17]" and "音" have something to do with blowing into an instrument. At first they were used interchangeably until "音" came to stress sound and "言" was used to stress context.

* The upper part of "音" looks like "stand 立[64] [リツ・リュウ]" but is unrelated.

音楽[おんがく] music -18 161c　　騒音[そうおん] noise -138a 18
雑音[ざつおん] noise -140b 18

18a 暗

アン くらい

darkness

sun 日[170][ジツ・ニチ] + sound 音 [オン]

When the sun(日) goes down and it becomes dark, you need sound(音) to distinguish things.

暗い[くらい] dark; gloomy

18b 意

イ

meaning

sound 音 [オン] + heart 心[26][シン]

What the heart(心) says(音) is what one really means to say.

意味[いみ] meaning; sense; intention - 18b 164c　　意志[いし] will; intention - 18b 26d

18c 章

ショウ

chapter

sound 音 [オン] + ten 十[178][ジツ・ジュウ]

Many(十) sounds(音) make a sentence, and many sentences make phrases and paragraphs.

* Ancient characters show that a sharp tool like an awl or a gimlet(辛[83]) was used to draw tattoos, which is how this character came to mean 'writing.' A lot(十) of writing makes a sentence or a chapter.

文章[ぶんしょう] sentence; writing - 105 18c

18d 竟

キョウ

finally

instrument/sound 音 [オン] + person 儿[58][ジン・ニン]

This character describes a person(儿) who is playing a musical instrument (音), such as a trumpet. Even if someone knows how to make a sound from the instrument, we cannot conclude that he is very good at playing musical instruments. In that context, this letter means 'eventually or finish,' because the ability of a player of a musical instrument should eventually reach a certain level of competence if the player is considered to be good at it.

18e 鏡

キョウ かがみ

mirror; lens

metal 金[154][キン・コン] + finally 竟 [キョウ]

In ancient times, mirrors were made of silver or copper(金). To make a mirror, the surface of the metal(金) was polished such that a face could eventually(竟) be looked at. During the 12th–13th centuries, the mirror was made of glass, and the meaning of lens was derived from this character.

眼鏡[めがね] glasses; spectacles - 10c 18e

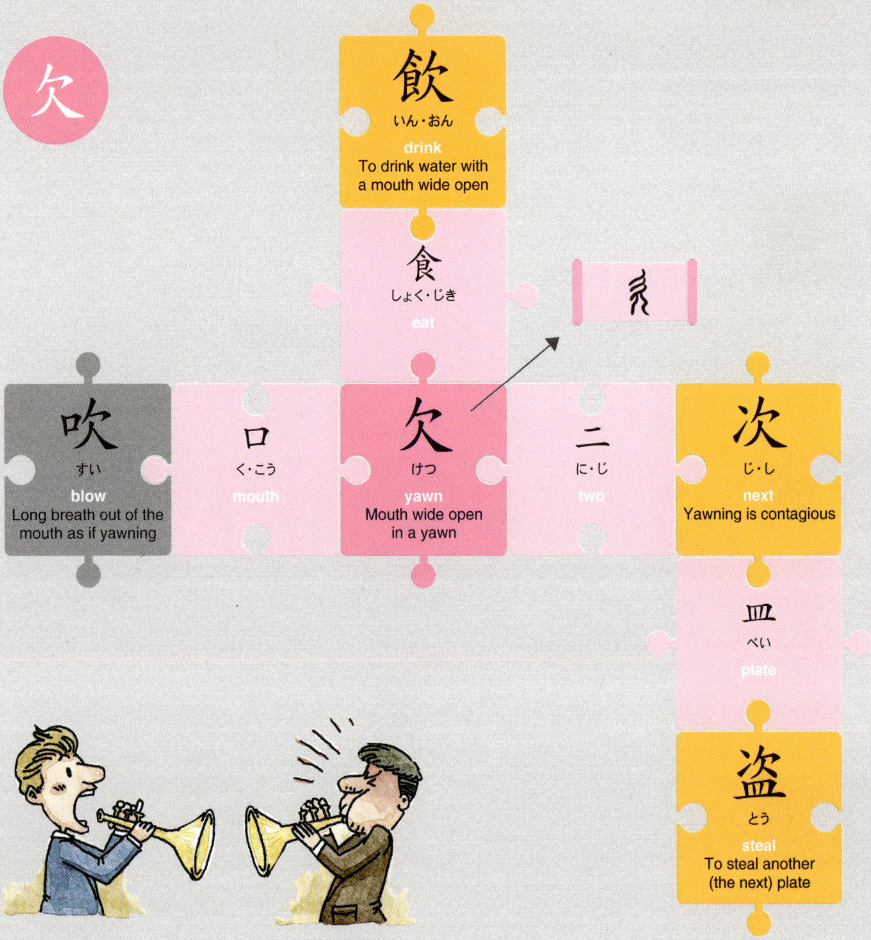

19 **欠** ケツ かける・かく

yawn

A person(人[51]) opening his mouth wide to yawn.

欠[あくび] yawning; yawn	欠ける[かける] wane; be lacking; be insufficient; be chipped
欠く[かく] lack; chip; be missing	

19a 飲

イン・オン のむ

ノ 𠆢 𠆢 今 今 今 今 食 食 飣 飲 飲

drink

eat 飠=食[109][ショク・ジキ] + yawn 欠 [ケツ]

When you are thirsty, you open your mouth as if you yawn(欠) to drink(食) water.

飲む[のむ] drink
飲(み)物[のみもの] a drink; a beverage -19a 41a
飲酒[いんしゅ] drinking -19a 133a

19b 次

ジ・シ つぎ・つぐ

丶 冫 冫 冫 次 次

next

two 二[176] [ニ・ジ] + yawn 欠 [ケツ]

Many animals yawn, but contagious yawning is only found in human beings and a few species of primates. This character means that after one person yawns (欠), it moves on to the next, the second(二) person. It is also used to count numbers of actions.

次次[つぎつぎ] one after another; one by one; in succession
次ぐ[つぐ] rank next (to); come after

19c 盗

トウ ぬすむ

丶 冫 冫 冫 次 次 次 盗 盗 盗 盗

steal

next 次 [ジ・シ] + plate 皿[132d][ベイ]

You own the best plate(皿), yet you want the next(次) one as well, so you steal it.

盗む[ぬすむ] steal; rob (a person of a thing); plagiarize

19d 吹

スイ ふく

丨 口 口 口 吅 吹 吹

blow

mouth 口[12] [ク・コウ] + yawn 欠 [ケツ]

To breathe in as if yawning(欠), then exhaling through the mouth(口) to blow on an instrument.

吹く[ふく] blow, play (wind instrument)
吹雪[ふぶき] snowstorm; blizzard -19d 159a

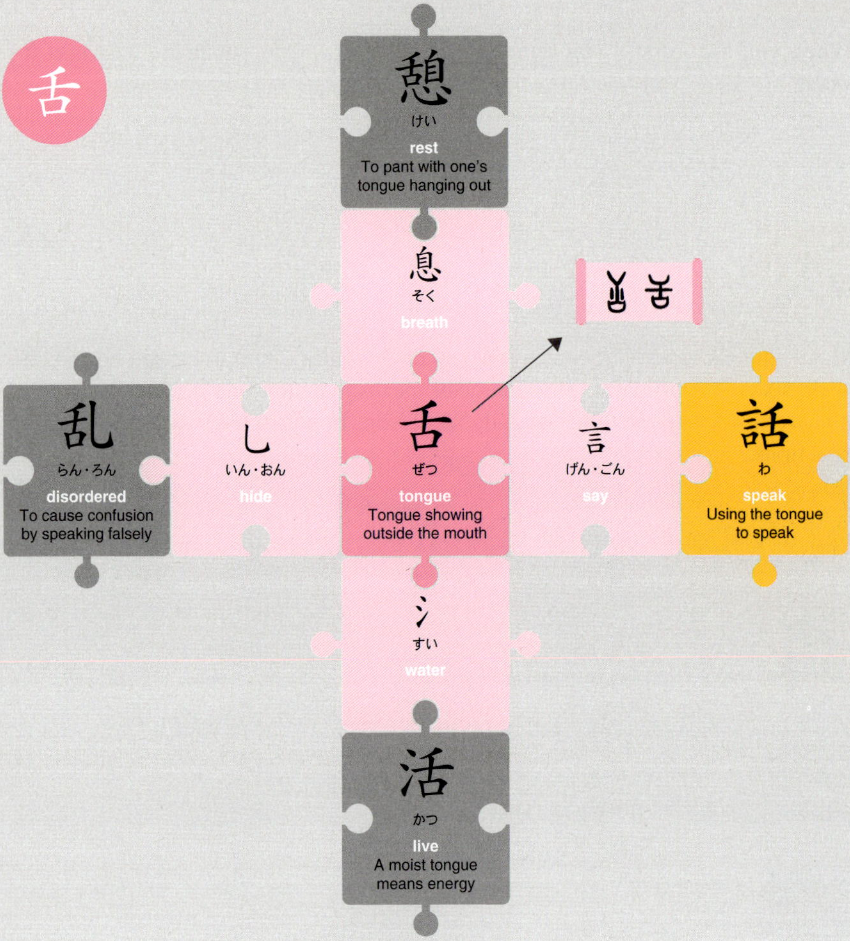

20 舌

ゼツ した

tongue

This character came to mean tongue because it's the shape of a tongue(千) sticking out of a mouth(ロ [ク・コウ]).

20a 憩

ケイ

丿 二 千 千 舌 舌 舌' 乱 乱 甜 甜 甜 甜 憩 憩 憩

rest; relax

tongue 舌 [ゼツ] + breath 息[6b] [ソク]

A description of someone at rest, panting and out of breath(息), with the tongue(舌) hanging out after hard work or exercise.

休憩[きゅうけい] rest; recess; interval -165a 20a

20b 話

ワ はなし・はなす

丶 亠 亠 亖 言 言 言 訁 訂 訐 話 話 話

speak

say 言[17] [ゲン・ゴン] + tongue 舌 [ゼツ]

To speak or to say something(言), one needs to use his tongue(舌).

話す[はなす] say; tell; speak; talk
話し[はなし] story; talk; conversation
電話[でんわ] telephone -159c 20b

20c 活

カツ

丶 丶 氵 氵 汗 汗 汗 活 活

live

water 氵[157] [スイ] + tongue 舌 [ゼツ]

When a person's tongue(舌) is moist with water(氵), it means one is healthy and alive.

* The small bumps on the tongue(舌) are able to excrete fluid(氵), so the tongue of a healthy and energetic person is always moist.

活動[かつどう] activity; action -20c 119b
生活[せいかつ] life; existence; livelihood; living -162 20c

20d 乱

ラン・ロン みだれる・みだす

丿 二 千 千 舌 舌 乱

disordered

tongue 舌 [ゼツ] + hunched stance/hide 乚[67c] [イン・オン]

To have a crooked(乚) tongue(舌) means you said something wrong and caused confusion.

* "乚" doesn't mean much, and can be translated in many ways.

乱れる[みだれる] be disordered; be disarranged
乱す[みだす] throw out of order; disarrange

Diagram for 齒

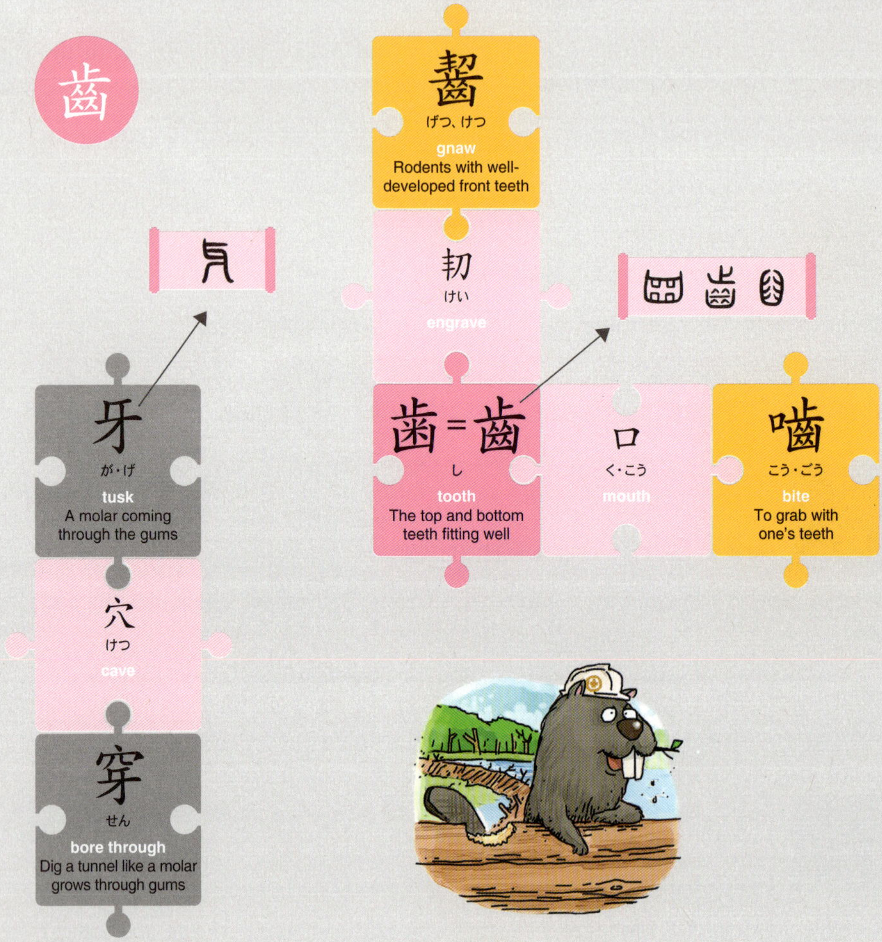

21 歯

シ は

tooth

丨 ⺊ 𠂇 止 止 歩 歩 歯 歯 歯 歯 歯

The depiction of a mouth(口[12]) with the top and bottom row of teeth(㸚) in a perfect fit(止[44]). The pronunciation comes from "止[シ]" and shows that chewing requires two rows of healthy teeth.

* The lower part of the character(㐫) has been simplified, but when combined with another character, the traditional form(齒) is used.

歯医者[はいしゃ] dentist -21 89a 82
歯磨(き)[はみがき] brushing one's teeth; tooth powder; toothpaste -21 165c
虫歯[むしば] dental caries; cavity -143 21

21a 齧

ゲツ、ケツ かじる

gnaw; nibble

engrave 契 [ケイ] + tooth 歯 [シ]

Rodents, such as squirrels, have well-developed front teeth(歯) so they can gnaw(契) on nuts. They also use their teeth(歯) to bite(契).

* '契' means to use a blade(刀[95]) to carve(丰) a mark or a letter in wood, to mark a contract or show quantity.

齧る[かぶる] snap at; bite into	齧る[かじる] nibble; gnaw; chew

21b 噛

コウ・ゴウ かむ

bite; gnaw

mouth ロ[12] [ク・コウ] + tooth 歯 [シ]

To grab or bite with one's teeth(歯) to eat(ロ) food.

噛る[かぶる] snap at, bite into	噛む[かむ] bite; chew; gnaw

21c 牙

ガ・ゲ

tusk

A molar is a tooth that grows in the innermost corners of the mouth.

象牙[ぞうげ] ivory - 136b 21c

21d 穿

セン はく

bore through; wear

cave 穴[113a] [ケツ] + tusk 牙 [ガ・ゲ]

One digs a tunnel or a cave(穴), like a molar(牙) penetrates the gums. Squirming around in clothes, while trying to figure out where your arms and legs go has a similar imagery, so this character came to mean 'to wear (clothes or socks).'

穿く[はく] put on; wear

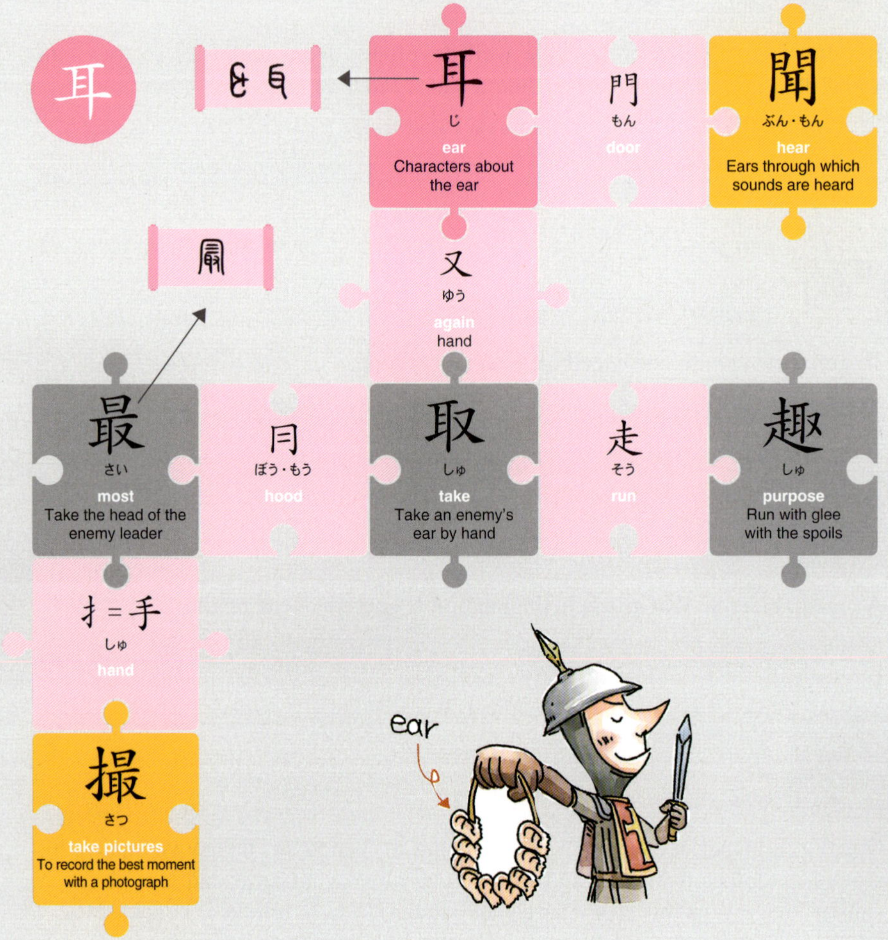

22 耳

じ みみ

ear

Shaped like a human's ear.

22a 聞

ブン・モン く・きこえる

hear

door 門[115] [モン] + ear 耳 [ジ]

As people go through doors(門), sounds are heard through the ears(耳).

聞く[きく] hear; listen (to) 聞(こ)える[きこえる] hear; be considered; be interpreted
新聞[しんぶん] newspaper -94b 22a

22b 取

シュ とる

一 丅 F F 耳 耳 耶 取

take

ear 耳 [ジ] + hand/again 又 30 [ユウ]

Victorious soldiers took the ears(耳) of their fallen enemies and carried them in their hands(又).

* This depicts the old custom where the ears of the fallen enemies were taken(取) back as prizes.

取る[とる] take; pick up; catch

22c 趣

シュ おもむき

一 十 土 丰 丰 走 走 走 走 赶 趄 趄 趄 趣 趣

purpose

take 取 [シュ] + run 走 44c [ソウ]

The victorious soldiers have taken(取) the spoils, and are running(走) home with a cheerful heart because their main interests are the spoils.

趣旨[しゅし] meaning; poin; purposet -22c 73b

22d 最

サイ もっとも

丨 口 日 日 旦 早 早 早 早 星 最 最

most

hood 日→冃 [ボウ・モウ] + take 取 [シュ]

In a war, the most important prize and honor is to take(取) the enemy leader's head(冃).

* "冃" is the hood worn on one's head. Refer to "冒 7d."

最も[もっとも] most; extremely
最近[さいきん] most recent; lately; nowadays -22d 94a
最初[さいしょ] first; earliest; beginning -22d 102
最低[さいてい] least; lowest; worst -22d 80b

22e 撮

サツ とる

一 扌 扌 扌 扌 扌 扌 扌 扌 捍 捍 揖 揖 撮 撮

take pictures

hand 扌=手 28 [シュ] + most 最 [さい]

To gather the spoils of war by hand(扌) to decide which soldier accomplished the greatest(最) feat. It also means 'to take a photograph or movie' to record the moment you wish to remember the most(最) by hand(扌).

撮る[とる] take (a photo); record (video, audio, etc.)
撮影[さつえい] photographing; filming 22e 2c

Diagram for 身

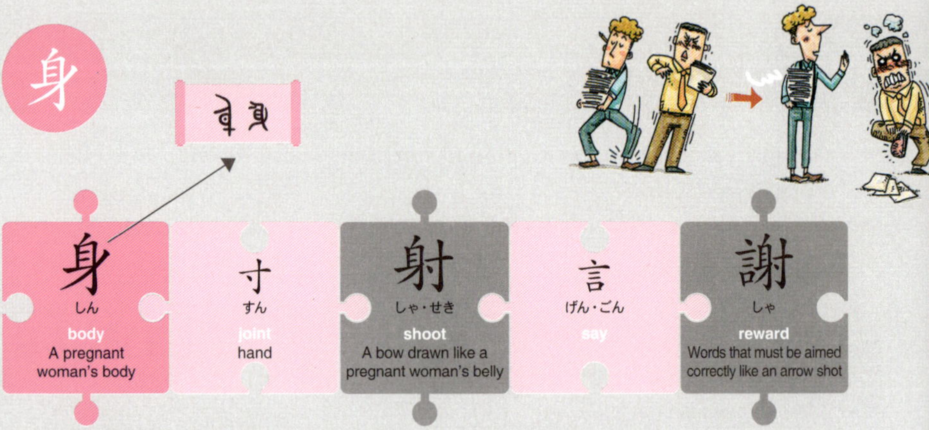

23 身

シン み

body

A side profile of a pregnant woman's body.

23a 射

シャ・セキ いる

shoot

pregnant woman/body 身 [シン] + hand/joint 寸[35] [スン]

To shoot an arrow, one must draw the bow back with one's hand(寸). When done, the bow is curved, like a pregnant woman's side profile(身).

射る[いる] shoot

23b 謝

シャ あやまる

reward; apologize

say 言[17] [ゲン・ゴン] + shoot 射 [シャ・セキ]

A word(言) of thanks has to be aimed well, like an arrow shot(射) at a target. It is of no use when said at the wrong time or without sincerity.

謝る[あやまる] apologize; refuse

Diagram for 骨

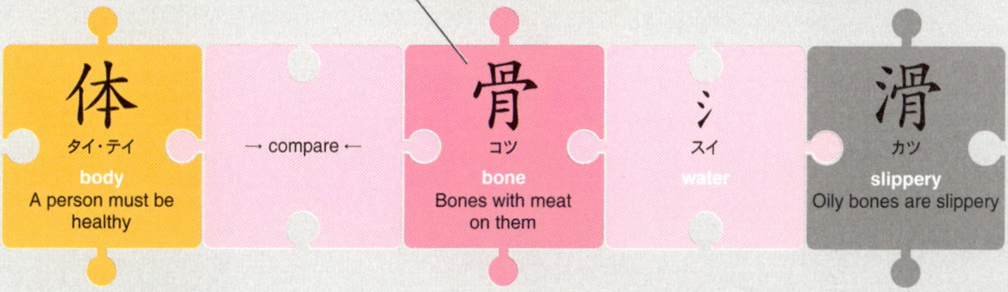

24 骨

コツ　ほね

bone

Bones(⾻) with meat(月) are still bones. "⾻ [カ]" means bones without the surrounding meat.

* "Moon 月 [172]" as part of another character usually means "meat 肉 [151] [ニク]."

骨折[こっせつ] fracture -24 94c

24a 滑

カツ　すべる・なめらか

slippery

water 氵 [157] [スイ] + bone 骨 [コツ]

When there is water(氵) on the bone(骨), it means the meat is oily. Oily bones are slippery.

滑る[すべる] slip; slide; glide　　滑らか[なめらか] smooth; glassy; slippery

24b 体

タイ・テイ　からだ

body

person 亻 [52] [ニン・ジン] + root 本 [165] [ホン]

"To lose a fortune is to lose a lot. To lose one's health is to lose all." The root (本) of a person(亻) is his healthy body.

* The traditional character(體) portrayed a body with bones(骨) and plentiful(豊 [148e]) flesh.

全体[ぜんたい] whole; entirety -53a 24b　　体重[たいじゅう] weight -24b 119a

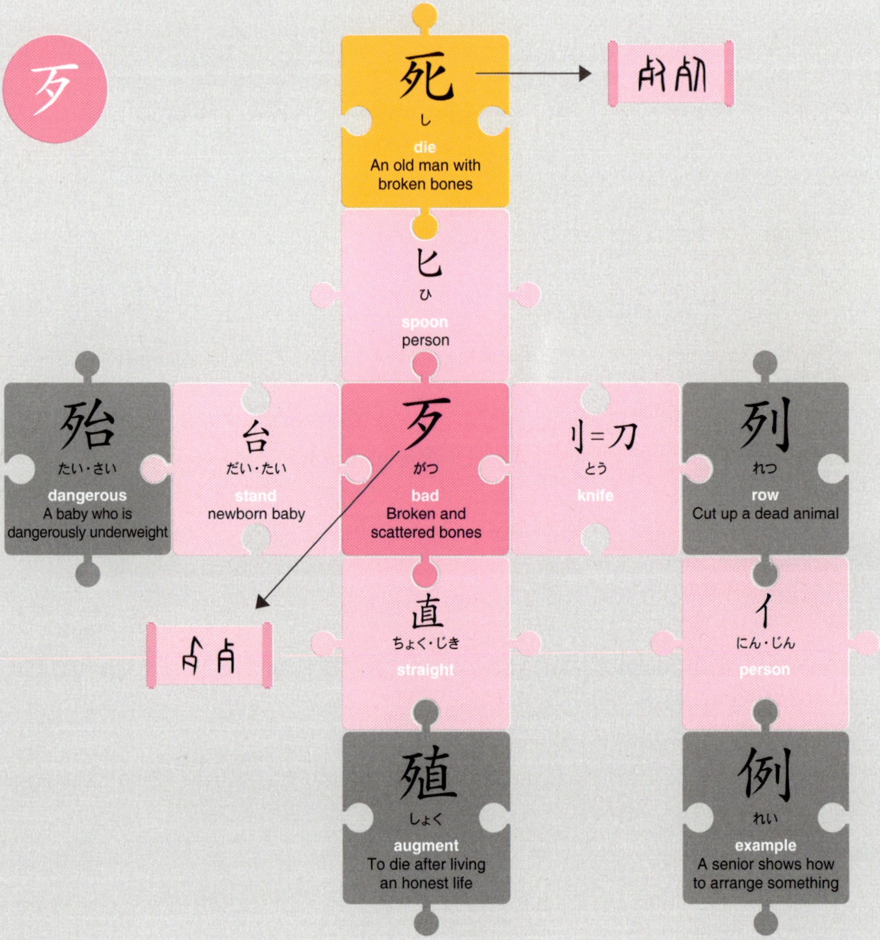

25 歹

ガツ

bad

一 ア 歹 歹

Broken bones with no flesh on them. When used on its own, this character means 'bad,' and used alongside another character, it means 'death and disaster.'

25a 死

シ しぬ

一 ア 歹 歹 歹 死

die

broken bone/bad 歹 [ガツ] + person/spoon 匕[72][ヒ]

Broken bones(歹) and an old man(匕) can only mean 'death.'

* "匕" is another character meaning person(人), but the crooked angle means 'old person.'

死ぬ[しぬ] die; pass away　　死亡[しぼう] death -25a 1c

25b 列

レツ

一 ア 歹 歹 列 列

row; line

dead/bad 歹 [ガツ] + knife 刂=刀[95][トウ]

Using a knife(刂) to cut up a dead(歹) animal and arrange the pieces.

列車[れっしゃ] train -25b 97

25c 例

レイ たとえる

ノ イ 仁 仁 伢 伢 例 例

example

person 亻[52][ニン・ジン] + row 列 [レツ]

There are rules as to how one must cut up and arrange(列) pieces of a carcass. This character shows a senior(亻) giving a demonstration.

例える[たとえる] exemplify; give an example; compare　　例外[れいがい] exception -25c 172b

25d 殖

ショク ふえる・ふやす

一 ア 歹 歹 歹 歹 歹 殖 殖 殖 殖 殖

augment; increase

dead/bad 歹 [ガツ] + straight 直[8][チョク・ジキ]

As the ancient believed one must live an upright(直) and honest life and then die(歹) for the descendants to prosper, this character came to mean 'to increase, extend or to propagate.'

殖える[ふえる] increase; multiply　　殖す[ふやす] increase; augment

25e 殆

タイ・サイ ほとんど

一 ア 歹 歹 歹 殆 殆 殆 殆

almost; dangerous

broken bone/bad 歹 [ガツ] + newborn baby/stand 台[76b] [ダイ・タイ]

Describes a dangerous situation where an already vulnerable baby(台) is left with just bones(歹). Since having just bones or having broken bones can represent a dying situation, this character came to mean 'almost, approximately or dangerous.'

* "台" is the shape of a baby(ム[76]) speaking(口[12]) in baby talk.

殆ど[ほとんど] mostly; nearly; practically　　危殆[きたい] danger; jeopardy -69b 25e

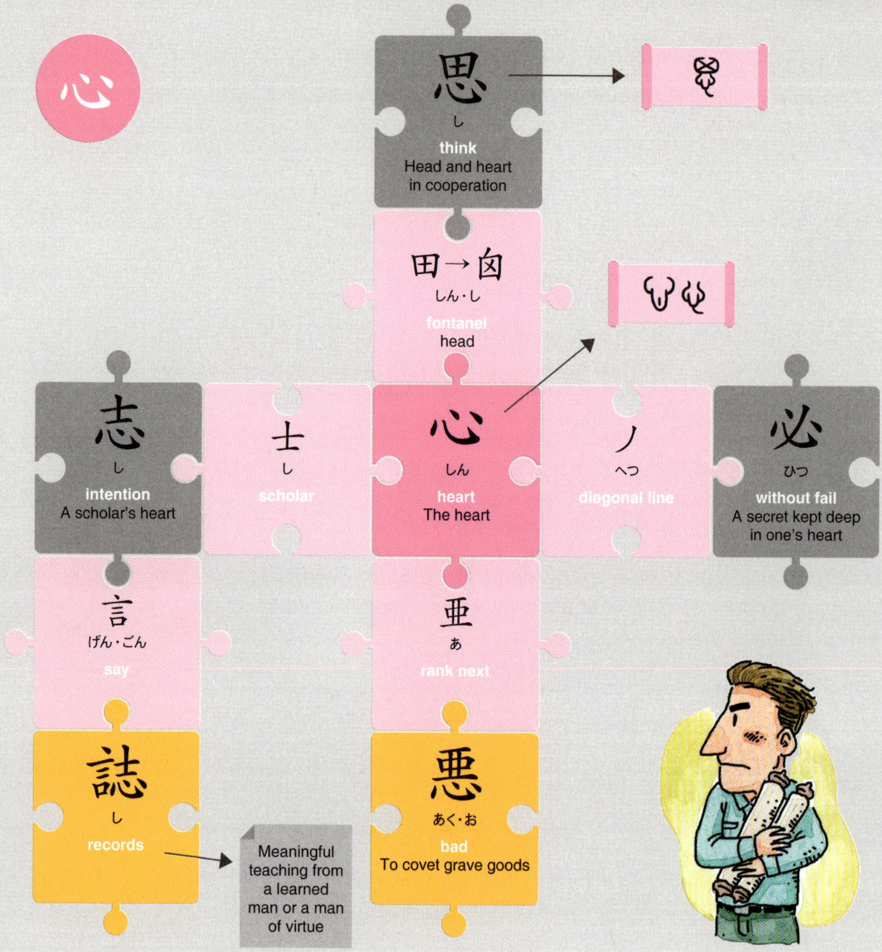

26 **心**

シン こころ

heart

This is what a heart is said to look like. It means 'heart,' but in other characters it symbolizes emotion or characteristics.

心配[しんぱい] worry; anxiety; concern -26 66d　　安心[あんしん] peace of mind; relief -78a 26

26a 思

シ おもう

丶 口 口 田 田 田 思 思 思

think

head/fontanel 田→囟 [シン・シ] + heart 心 [シン]

A thought is something you have when your head(囟) works alongside your heart(心). The ancient kanji thought it was about reason(囟) and emotion(心).

* Ancient characters are proof that "田" is a simplified version of "囟." The dot on the top is the hole in the top of a baby skull, before the bones fuse. Refer to "細[104c]."

思う[おもう] think; consider; regard　思い出す[おもいだす] recall; remember -26a 131c

26b 必

ヒツ かならず

丶 心 心 必 必

without fail

heart 心 [シン] + diagonal line ノ[179e][ヘツ]

A secret buried(ノ) deep within one's heart(心) must be kept.

* "ノ" has no specific meaning and can be interpreted differently.

必ず[かならず] always; surely; without fail　必要[ひつよう] need; necessity -26b 132b

26c 悪

アク・オ わるい

一 丆 丙 亜 亜 亜 亜 悪 悪 悪 悪

bad; evil

rank next 亜 [ア] + heart 心 [シン]

In ancient times, powerful people were buried with grave goods in a large chamber in preparation for the next(亜) life or afterlife. It is evil to covet or want(心) someone's grave goods(亜).

* "亜" is the shape of a grave of a king or a powerful person when looked at from above.

悪い[わるい] bad; evil; sinful　悪化[あっか] deterioration -26c 52a

26d 志

シ こころざし・こころざす

一 十 士 志 志 志 志

intention

scholar 士[84][シ] + heart 心 [シン]

The heart(心) of a scholar(士) that does not care for riches or titles but only for the realization of truth through continuous studies has a 'great goal' in mind.

志す[こころざす] intend; plan　意志[いし] will; intention -18b 26d

26e 誌

シ

丶 亠 亠 亠 言 言 言 言 計 計 計 誌 誌 誌

records

say 言[17][ゲン・ゴン] + intention 志 [シ]

To leave records so words(言) with deep meaning(志) can be left for future generations.

雑誌[ざっし] journal; magazine -140b 26e

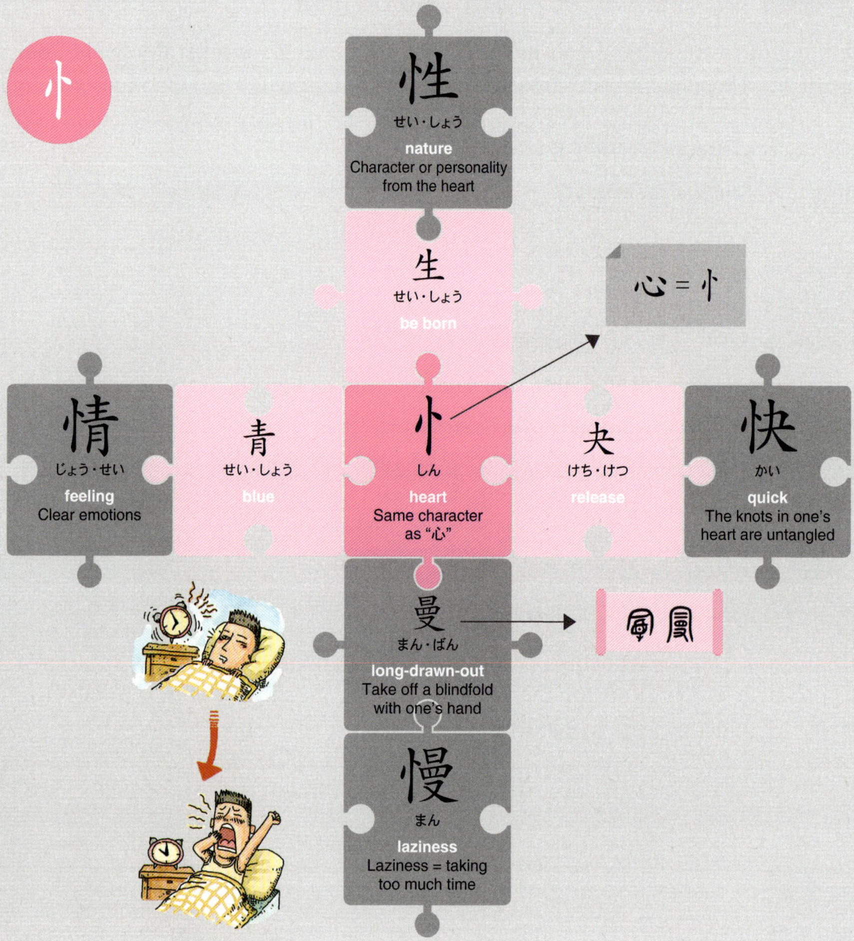

27	忄

シン

heart

"忄" is the same character as "heart 心[26]," but takes this shape when used as a radical and placed on the left of a character.

27a	性

セイ・ショウ　さが

nature; sex

heart 忄＝心 [シン] ＋ be born 生[162] [セイ・ショウ]

Something that comes out of(生) one's heart(忄) is that person's nature.

根性[こんじょう] nature; spirit; grit -10a 27a　　女性[じょせい] woman; female; lady -78 27a
男性[だんせい] man; male -125a 27a

27b 快

カイ　こころよい

quick

heart 忄=心 [シン] + release 夬[62][ケチ・ケツ]

When a problem is solved, one's heart(忄) feels free(夬) and troubles disappear instantaneously.

* "夬" shows a hand(ヨ[32]) on the notch of an arrow(矢[89]). This means that one feels a cool relief, as when an arrow(矢) is released(ヨ) from the bow very quickly.

快い[こころよい] refreshing; pleasant

27c 曼

マン・バン

long-drawn-out

hood 日→冃[7d] [ボウ・モウ] + eye 罒→目[7] [ボク・モク] + hand/again 又[30][ユウ]

Picture a hand(又) taking off a hood(冃) that was used to cover someone's eyes(目). It takes a while for that person to grow accustomed to the light, which is how this character came to mean 'take time.'

* There's a protein called rhodopsin in the retina. When hit with light, rhodopsin has a chemical reaction and releases energy which makes us see. When one steps suddenly into a bright light, rhodopsin dissolves to release energy in a short burst, which is why we are blinded temporarily. But after a while, the rhodopsin dissolves and we recover.

27d 慢

マン

laziness; arrogant

heart 忄=心 [シン] + long-drawn-out 曼 [マン・バン]

A lazy(忄) person who is slow all the time takes a while(曼) to wake up.

* "心" is all about emotion or characteristics and means lazy.

驕慢[きょうまん] arrogance -138b 27d

27e 情

ジョウ・セイ　なさけ

feeling

heart 忄=心 [シン] + blue 青[107][セイ・ショウ]

Blue water symbolizes clarity, and a blue(青) heart(忄) means one's emotions are not complicated. When one is not confused, one's 'feelings or emotions' are strong.

情け[なさけ] affection; pity; sympathy　　愛情[あいじょう] love; affection -29e 27e

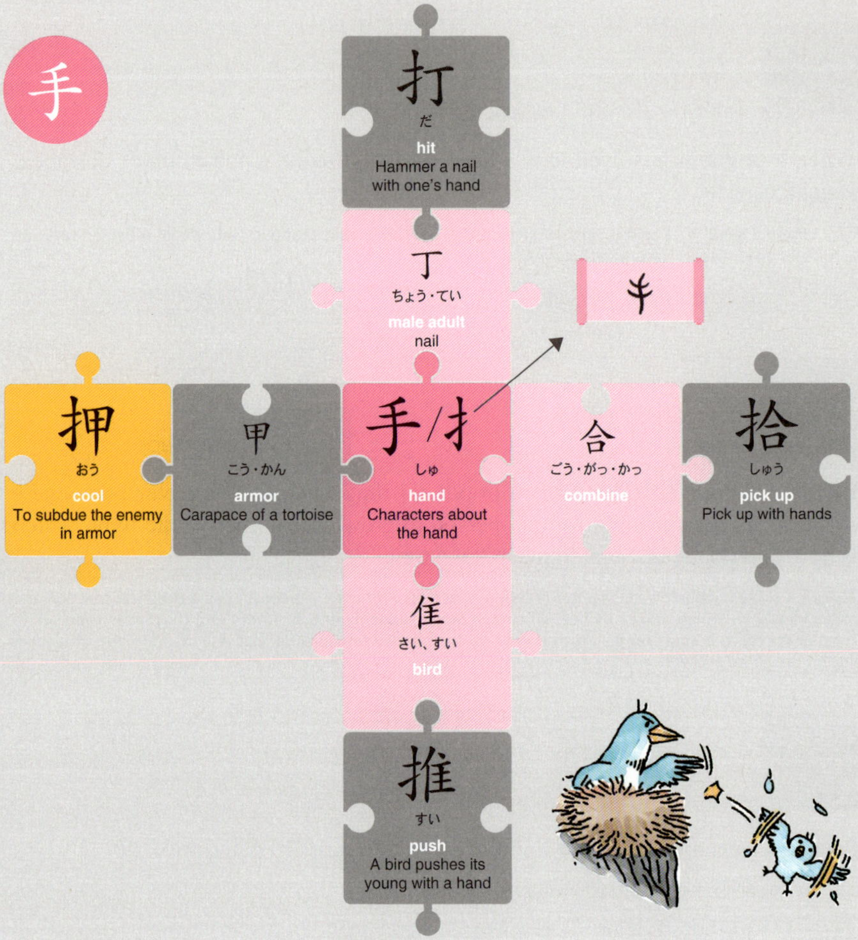

28 手

シュ て

hand

A hand has five outstretched fingers. Whereas "手" is an independent character or used in the center of a more complicated character, "扌" is a radical that comes on the left.

切手[きって] stamp -95b 28	上手[じょうず] excellent skill, skillful; expert -173a 28
手紙[てがみ] letter -28 80a	下手[へた] unskillful; poor (at); clumsy -173b 28

28a 打

ダ　うつ　　一 扌 扌 扌 打

hit; strike

hand 扌=手 [シュ] + nail/male adult 丁[175] [チョウ・テイ]

Using one's hand(扌) to hold a hammer and hit a nail(丁).

打つ[うつ] hit; strike; knock

28b 拾

シュウ　ひろう　　一 扌 扌 扌 扌 扌 扌 拾 拾

pick up

hand 扌=手 [シュ] + combine 合[54a] [ゴウ・ガッ・カッ]

This character is the image of someone using his hand(扌) to pick up or to collect something(合) from the ground.

拾う[ひろう] pick up; gather; find

28c 推

スイ　　一 扌 扌 扌 扌 扌 扌 扌 推 推 推

push; support

hand 扌=手 [シュ] + bird 隹[140] [サイ、スイ]

A mother bird lightly pushes her young(隹) one with a wing(扌) to see if it is ready to leave the nest.

28d 甲

コウ・カン　きのえ　　丨 冂 日 日 甲

armor; carapace

A tortoise's carapace or the hard outer layer of a seed, when spread out evenly, looks like a suit of armor. This character is the first of ten calendar signs and also means the first in the order.

28e 押

オウ　おす・おさえる　　一 扌 扌 扌 扣 扣 押 押

push; press

hand 扌 =手 [シュ] + armor 甲 [コウ・カン]

The depiction of soldiers in armor(甲) oppressing the enemy or prisoners with their hands(扌) came to mean 'to press, to push down on, suppress.'

押す[おす] push; press　　押(さ)える[おさえる] restrain; seize; suppress

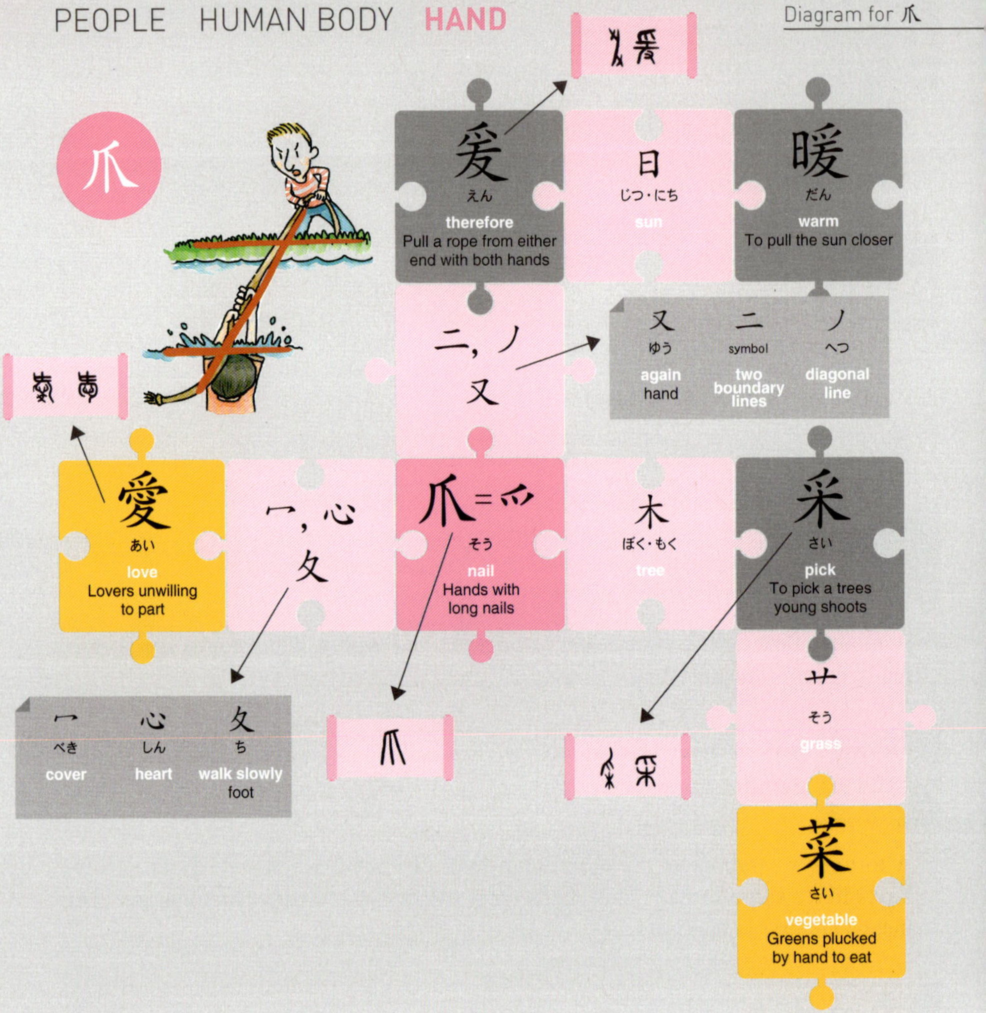

29	爪

ソウ つめ

nail

This character depicts a hand with long fingernails trying to grasp something. When used as part of another character, it means 'hand' and sometimes changes into "爫."

* Two symmetrical hands(爪) with fingers pointing downward means "both hands 臼 [コク]."

29a 爰

エン

therefore

diagonal line ノ [179e][ヘツ] + hand/again 又 [30][ユウ] + hand/nail ⺥=爪 [ソウ] + two boundary lines 二 [symbol] +

The hand(⺥) of someone by the water(一) and the hand(又) of someone in the water(一) are tied together with a rope(ノ). It's the image of someone trying to pull a drowning person to shore. The meaning gradually changed to 'therefore.'

* "ノ" doesn't mean anything specific and can be translated differently depending on the character.

29b 暖

ダン　あたたかい・あたたまる・あたためる

warm

sun 日 [170][ジツ・ニチ] + pull/therefore 爰 [エン]

If you pull(爰) the sun(日) closer to you, how warm would that be now!

暖かい[あたたかい] warm; mild; genial　　暖まる[あたたまる] warm up; get warm
暖める[あたためる] warm; heat

29c 采

サイ　とる

pick

hand/nail ⺥=爪 [ソウ] + tree 木 [164][ボク・モク]

To pick a tree's(木) young shoots, tea leaves, or fruit by hand(⺥).

採る[とる] pick; take; adopt (proposal)

29d 菜

サイ

vegetable

grass 艹 [161][ソウ] + pick 采 [サイ]

Vegetables are plants(艹) that are picked by hand(采), which is true because most edible vegetation can be picked by hand.

野菜[やさい] vegetable - 119e 29d

29e 愛

アイ

love

foot/stop ⺥→止 [44][シ] + cover 冖 [131][ベキ] + heart 心 [26][シン] + foot/walk slowly 夂 [46][チ]

"止" and "夂" are feet facing opposite directions and between them is a heart(心) that is covered up(冖). Love is the hidden(冖) feelings of the heart(心) of lovers who don't wish to part(止・夂).

* The old pictogram shows that the character which looks like a hand(⺥) is a modified form developed from "foot(止)."

可愛い[かわいい] cute; adorable; lovely - 13 29e　　愛情[あいじょう] love; affection - 29e 27e

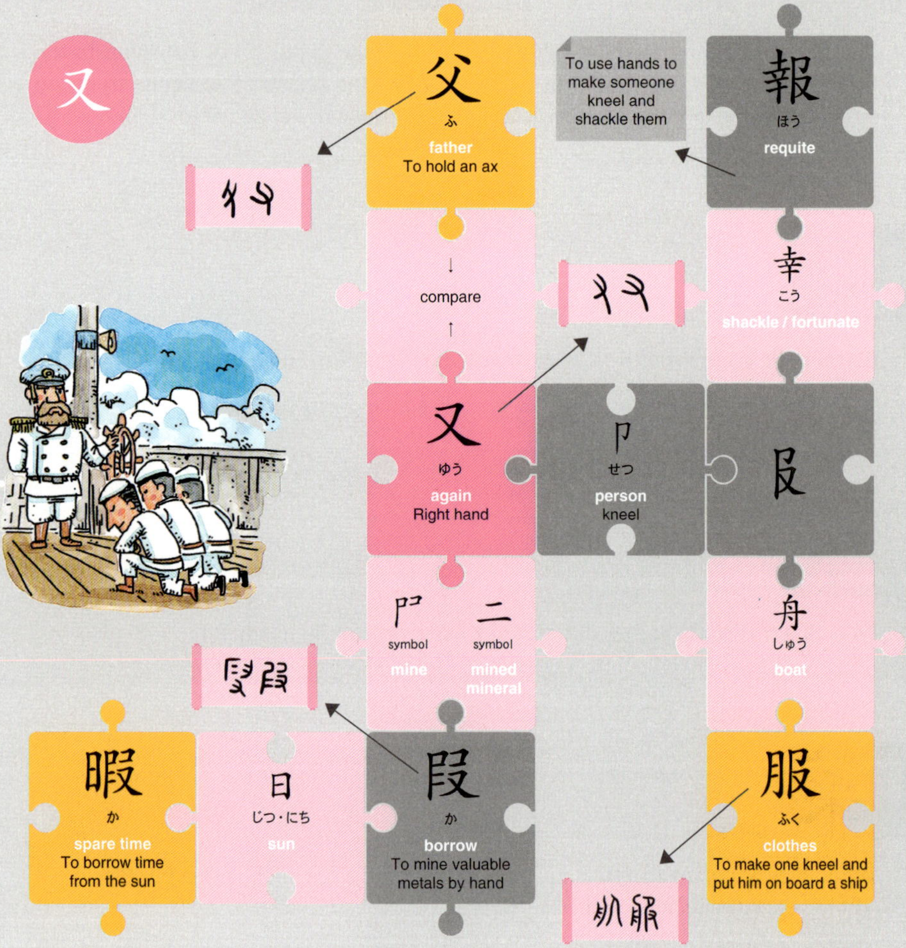

30 又

ユウ　また

again

フ 又

When the character was first created, it meant 'right hand,' but because most people are right-handed and use it for most chores, it came to mean 'again.' When used as part of a more complicated character, it's better to think it means 'hand.'

又は[または] or; otherwise

30a **父**

フ ちち

ノ ハ ケ 父

father

A father holding a hammer or a stick in his hand(又) to hunt for the family.

お父さん[おとうさん] (honorific) father
お祖父さん[おじいさん] (honorific or a friendly) grandfather - 174d 30a
小父さん[おじさん] (honorific) uncle, old man, mister - 182 30a
祖父[そふ] grandfather - 174d 30a
父親[ちちおや] father 30a 9c

30b **報**

ホウ

一 十 土 圥 去 坴 坴 幸 幸 𡙸 報 報

requite; inform

shackle/fortunate 幸 83e [コウ] + kneel/person 卩 69 [セツ] + hand/again 又 [ユウ]

To use one's hands(又) to make a prisoner kneel(卩) in defeat and shackle(幸) them. It came to mean 'to inform' because one would wish to spread the good news that they made their enemies pay.

* Shackles: Ancient shackles were made of wood and used to secure both wrists and ankles.

天気予報[てんきよほう] weather (fore)cast - 60b 158a 4a 30b
電報[でんぽう] telegram - 159c 30b

30c **服**

フク

丿 刀 月 月 月 肌 服 服

clothes; obey

boat 月→舟 98 [シュウ] + kneel/person 卩 69 [セツ] + hand/again 又 [ユウ]

You force(又) a man to kneel(卩) and keep him in your ship(舟). To take someone on board meant you made him serve you, and to differentiate such people from your original crew, you made them wear special clothes.

* In the ancient version of the character, the "月 172" in "服" is actually "舟."

洋服[ようふく] suit (Western clothes) - 134d 30c
衣服[いふく] clothes; dress - 101 30c
和服[わふく] Japanese clothes - 12d 30c

30d **叚**

カ

ㄱ ㄱ 戸 戸 戸 戸 戸 叚 叚

borrow

mine [symbol] + mined mineral 二 [symbol] + hand/again 又 [ユウ]

This character seems to describe a man's hand(又) mining valuable metals(二) in a mine(戸). There's a philosophical interpretation to this character that says the metals are only borrowed from nature.

* Because kanji have changed over the centuries, sometimes it's hard to decipher the exact meaning.

30e **暇**

カ ひま

丨 冂 日 日 日 日 𣅃 𣅃 𣅃 𣅃 𣅃 暇 暇

spare time

sun 日 170 [ジツ・ニチ] + borrow 叚 [カ]

To borrow(叚) from the sun(日) to make 'spare time' to rest.

休暇[きゅうか] holiday - 165a 30e

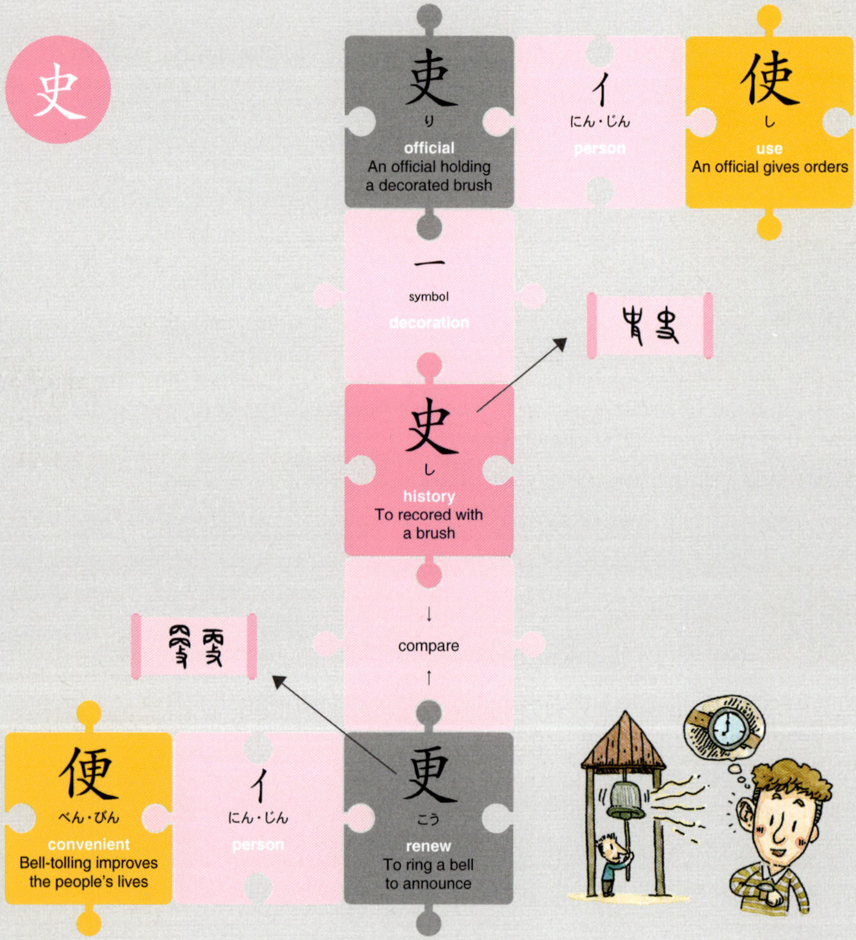

31 史 シ
history

丶 口 口 中 史

Writing by holding a brush in hand(乂→"又[30] [ユウ]") is how a government official writes when recording facts. These facts become history.

31a 吏

リ

一 ㄷ 亓 戸 声 吏

official

decoration 一 [symbol] + brush in hand/history 史 [シ]

"史" is a hand holding a brush with a decoration(一). "史" is an official taking records, but "吏" is a man holding a special brush and therefore a highranking official.

31b 使

シ つかう

ノ イ 亻 仁 佢 佢 使 使

use; envoy

person 亻[52][ニン・ジン] + official 吏 [リ]

A government official(吏) can 'use' his subordinate(亻) and make him do as he bids.

使う[つかう] use; employ; handle　　大使館[たいしかん] embassy -60 31b 152d

31c 更

コウ ふける

一 ㄷ 戸 百 亘 更 更

renew

strike 攴→攵 [ボク] + say 曰[33e][エツ]

At the start of every hour, the governmental office rang a bell(攴→攵) to announce(曰) the time. Each time the bell was rung, a prayer was chanted to wish for more blessings for a better life.

* The "曰" shape in the ancient character is a bell(曰→丙) that has been hung up.

更ける[ふける] get late　　更新[こうしん] renewal -31c 94b

31d 便

ベン・ビン たより

ノ イ 亻 亻 仁 佢 佰 便 便

convenient

person 亻[52][ニン・ジン] + sound of the bell/renew 更 [コウ]

The bell(更) helped people(亻) tell the time and follow a schedule, which made things more convenient.

便り[たより] news; letter; correspondence　　便利[べんり] convenient; handy; useful -31d 111d
船便[ふなびん] by ship (sea, water); surface mail -98a 31d
不便[ふべん] inconvenience; inexpediency -173c 31d

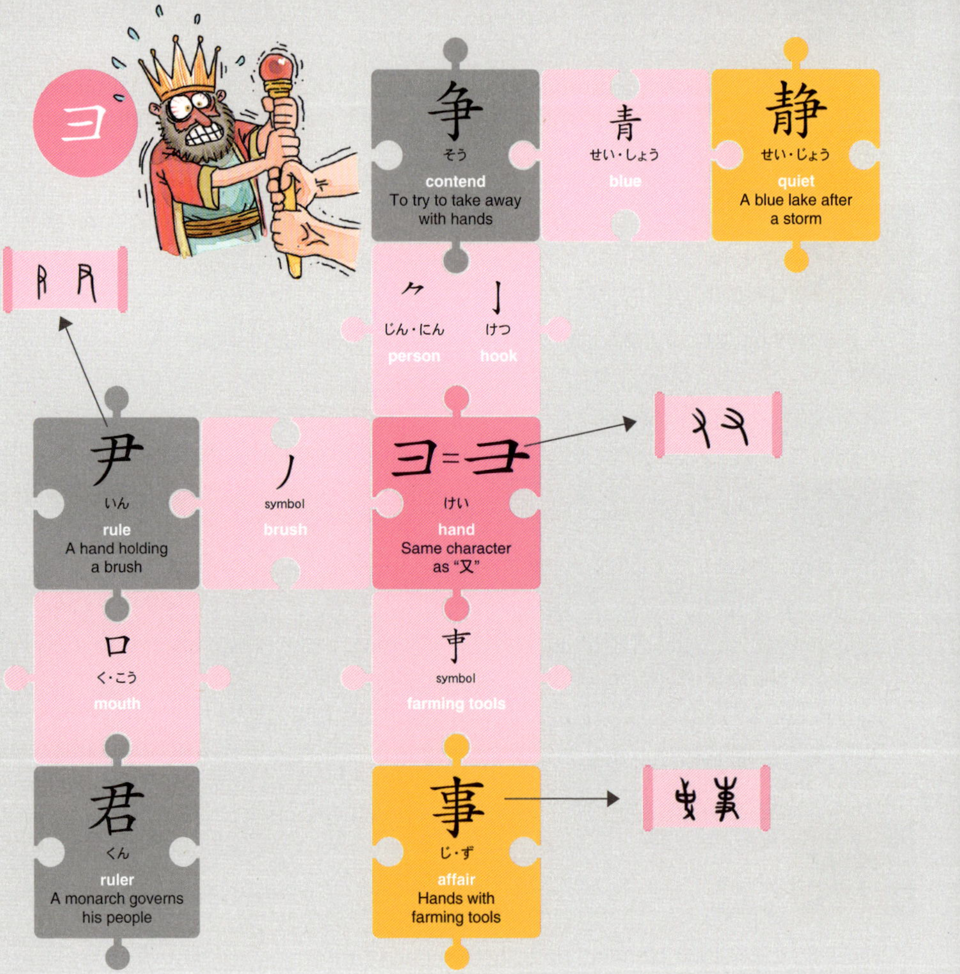

32 ヨ

ケイ

hand

Ancient records show this is the same character as "hand 又[30] [ユウ]" that also means 'hand.'

* This character is never used on its own and is not a radical, but it is useful to remember. It doesn't have its own phonetic value either.

32a 争

ソウ あらそう

ノ ク ク 刍 刍 争

contend

person ⺈[56] [ジン・ニン] + hand ヨ [ケイ] + hook 亅[179] [ケツ]

A person(⺈) is holding something(亅) which another person is contending and trying to take away by hand(ヨ).

* The traditional character(爭) shows two hands(爫[29], ヨ) trying to take something(亅). "亅" is called a hook because it looks like one, but can be interpreted in many ways.

争う[あらそう] contend; fight; compete

32b 静

セイ・ジョウ しずか・しずまる

一 二 キ 丰 丰 青 青 青 青 青' 青' 静 静 静

quiet

blue 青[107] [セイ・ショウ] + contend 争 [ソウ]

After a storm(争) passes, the sky becomes blue(青) and calm as a lake.

* The blue color of the water is a reflection of the sunlight. The clearer the sky and calmer the water, the bluer the water is.

静か[しずか] quiet; peaceful　静まる[しずまる] quieten down; calm down

32c 事

ジ・ズ こと

一 一 亓 亓 亖 亖 亖 事

affair

farming tools 亊 [symbol] + hand ヨ [ケイ]

In an agricultural society, working with farming tools(亊) like rakes and spades in their hands(ヨ) was a common affair.

仕事[しごと] work; business; job -84e 32c　火事[かじ] fire; blaze -124 32c
事故[じこ] accident -32c 15a　領事[りょうじ] consul -71d 32c

32d 尹

イン

フ ヨ ヨ 尹

rule

This character gives us the image of a hand(ヨ) that holds a brush(丿). In ancient times, the ruling class used the letters, therefore, they came to mean 'to control or to govern.'

32e 君

クン きみ

フ ヨ ヨ 尹 尹 君 君

ruler

rule 尹 [イン] + mouth 口[12] [ク・コウ]

Among the ruling class, a 'monarch' is a person who controls(尹) his people with his words(口). It's affixed at the end of the name of a friend or someone of lower social standing to show respect.

君主[くんしゅ] ruler; monarch; sovereign -32e 181a

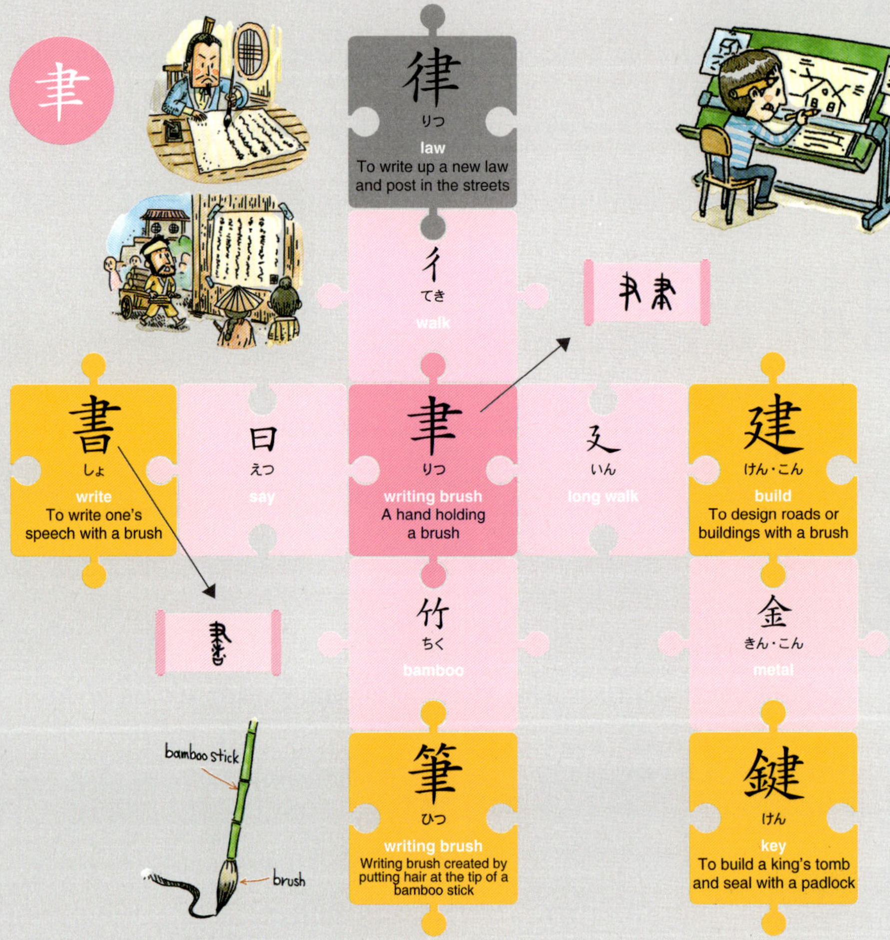

33 **聿**

リツ

writing brush

A hand(ヨ[32][イン]) holding a brush(⺘), which corresponds to a fountain pen in the present day.

33a 律

リツ

law

walk 彳[48][テキ] + writing brush 聿 [リツ]

To write out a new law with a brush(聿) so that people walking(彳) in the streets could read them.

規律[きりつ] rule; regulation; discipline; order -9d 33a	法律[ほうりつ] law -63d 33a

33b 建

ケン・コン　たてる・たつ

build

writing brush 聿 [リツ] + long walk 廴[50][イン]

"廴" means a narrow and winding road while "聿" is a brush. To build roads(廴) or buildings, they needed a brush(聿) to design them first.

建てる[たてる] build; construct	建つ[たつ] be built
建物[たてもの] building -33b 41a	

33c 鍵

ケン　かぎ

key

metal 金[154][キン・コン] + build 建 [ケン・コン]

A well-built(建) tomb in the form of a maze that is secured with a metal(金) padlock.

33d 筆

ヒツ　ふで

writing brush

bamboo 竹[169][チク] + writing brush 聿 [リツ]

Symbolizes a brush for writing(聿), created by attaching animal hair at the tip of a bamboo(竹) straw. Now used to refer to any stylus or writing tools, including pen and pencil.

鉛筆[えんぴつ] pencil -154a 33d	筆記[ひっき] note-taking; record -33d 66b
筆者[ひっしゃ] writer; author -33d 82	万年筆[まんねんひつ] fountain pen -161e 96e 33d

33e 書

ショ　かく

write; writing

writing brush 聿 [リツ] + say 曰 [エツ]

It means 'writing or to write' because you use a brush(聿) to record someone's words(曰).

* "曰" is the one speaking, with his tongue(一) coming out of his mouth(口[12]).

葉書[はがき] postcard -152d 33e	図書館[としょかん] library -16d 33e 152d
辞書[じしょ] dictionary; lexicon -83d 33e	読書[どくしょ] reading -146c 33e

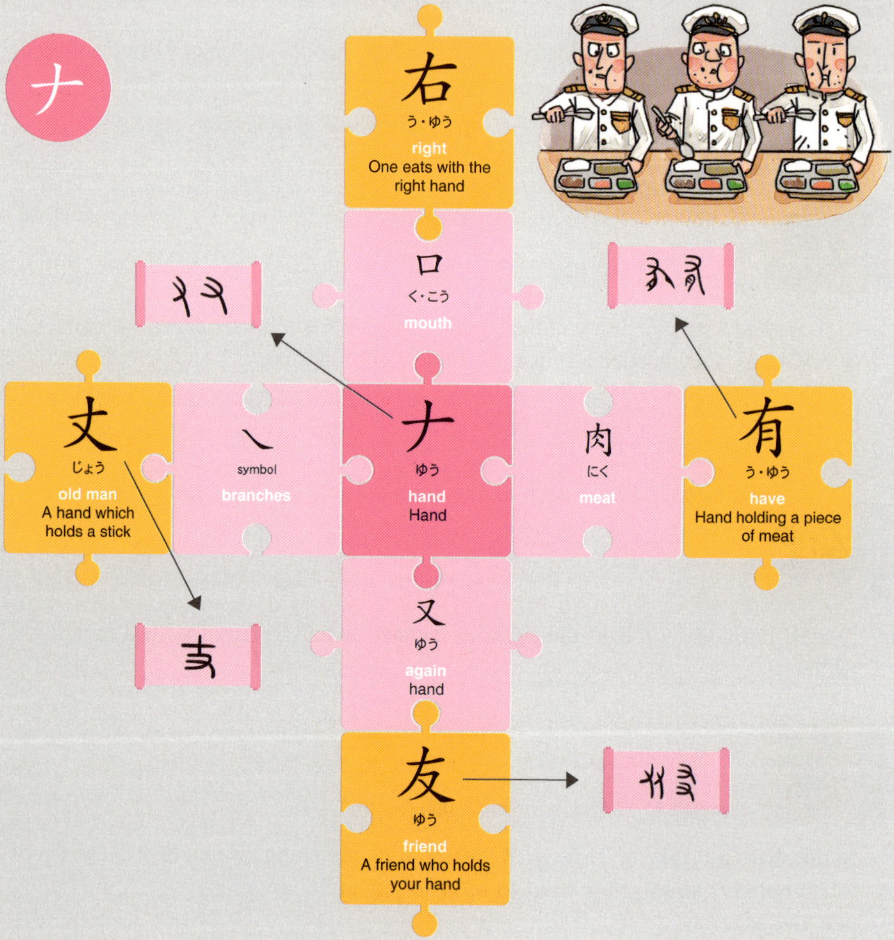

34 **ナ** ユウ

hand

一 ナ

"ナ," "又[30] [ユウ]" and "ヨ[32] [ケイ]" are all different shapes, but ancient texts say they all mean 'hand.'

* This character is never used alone and has no phonetic value by itself. This character is used only for convenience.

34a 右

ウ・ユウ　みぎ　　一ナオ右右

right

hand ナ [ユウ] + mouth ロ [12] [ク・コウ]

The hand(ナ) that helps the mouth(ロ). In other words, it's the 'right' hand used to eat. Although some people are left-handed, most people in China use chopsticks with their right hand.

左右[さゆう] left and right -155c 34a

34b 有

ウ・ユウ　ある　　一ナオ有有有

have; exist

hand ナ [ユウ] + meat 月→肉 [151] [ニク]

A hand(ナ) holding meat(肉), which is a sacrifice. It came to mean 'have or exist.'

* "Moon 月 [172] [ゲツ・ガツ]" as part of another character means "肉."

有る[ある] exist; have
有名[ゆうめい] famous; well-known -34b 172d
有(り)難い[ありがたい] thankful; grateful -34b 108d
有難う[ありがとう] Thank you; Thanks -34b 108d

34c 友

ユウ　とも　　一ナ方友

friend

hand ナ [ユウ] + hand/again 又 [30] [ユウ]

Two overlapping hands(ナ, 又) means 'cooperation.' A friend is someone who offers a hand when one is in need.

友達[ともだち] friend; companion -34c 49d
友人[ゆうじん] friend -34c 51
友情[ゆうじょう] friendship -34c 27e

34d 丈

ジョウ　たけ　　一ナ丈

old man

hand ナ [ユウ] + branches ㇏ [symbol]

This character depicts the image of an old man who is holding a stick(㇏) in his hand(ナ).

丈夫[じょうぶ] healthy; strong; robust -34d 60a
大丈夫[だいじょうぶ] safe; all right; okay -60 34d 60a

寸

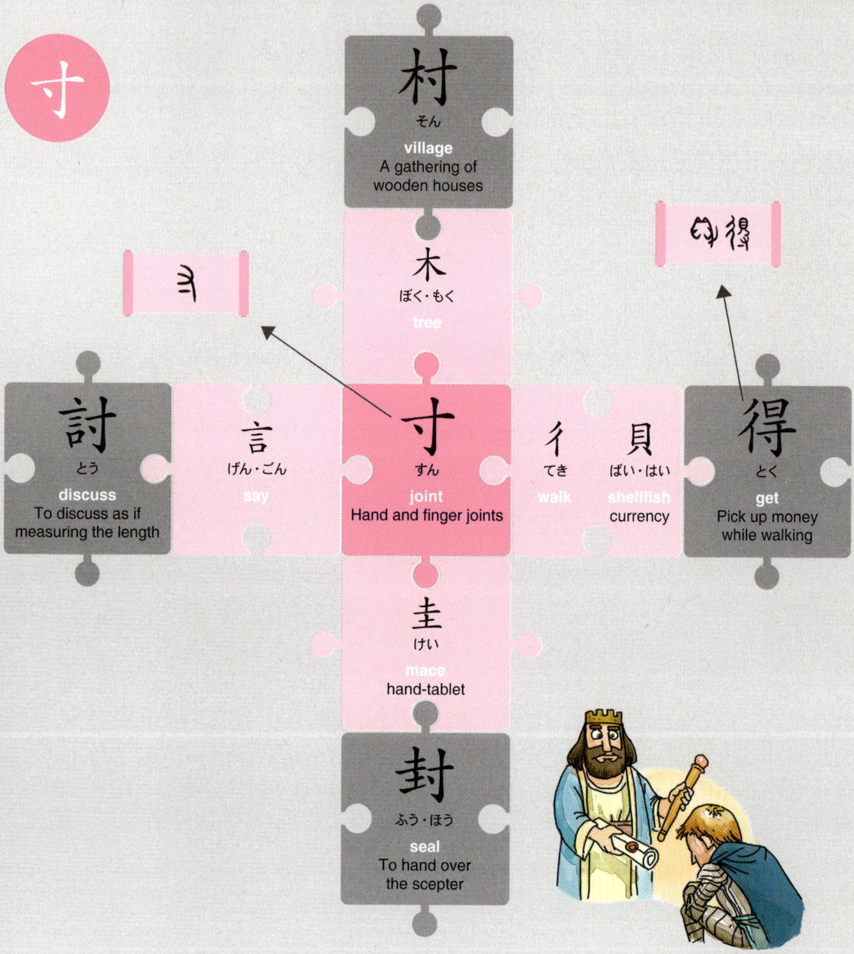

35	寸	スン **joint**	一 十 寸

One presents gifts and offerings with one's 'hand.' The dot in the character means joint but is also used as a measurement of length.

* Most ancient cultures, regardless of location, used body parts to measure length.

一寸[ちょっと] some; a little; a few -173 35
寸法[すんぽう] measurement; size; extent; dimension -35 63d

35a 村

ソン むら　一 十 才 木 木一 村 村

village; town

tree 木 164 [ボク・モク] + hand/joint 寸 [スン]

This character depicts a village with many houses built by hand(寸) with wood(木).

* The Forbidden City is China's most famous wooden construction.

漁村[ぎょそん] fishing village - 144b 35a
農村[のうそん] farm village; agricultural community - 148d 35a

35b 得

トク うる・える　ノ ノ 彳 彳 彳口 彳日 彳旦 彳旦 得 得 得

get; gain

walk 彳 48 [テキ] + currency/shellfish 旦→貝 145 [バイ・ハイ] + hand/joint 寸 [スン]

To pick up by hand(寸) and therefore obtain seashells(旦→貝), used as money, while walking(彳).

* The ancient character shows that "旦 170a" was originally a seashell(貝).

得る[うる] [literary] get; obtain; be able to~: can　得る[える] get; obtain; be able to~: can

35c 封

フウ・ホウ　一 + 土 圭 圭 圭 圭一 封 封

seal; closing

hand-tablet/mace 圭 121 [ケイ] + hand/joint 寸 [スン]

A king is handing(寸) his servant a sealed letter of appointment and a scepter(圭) to award a title.

* "圭" is a decoration of sorts that the king's subjects held whenever in his presence.

開封[かいふう] unsealed letter; breaking the seal - 38d 35c

35d 討

トウ うつ　` 亠 亠 亠 言 言 言 言一 討 討

discuss; attack

say 言 17 [ゲン・ゴン] + joint 寸 [スン]

During a discussion, you do not speak whatever is on your mind. You speak(言) carefully, after considerations, and carefully measuring(寸) what to say. This character also means 'to attack' with words.

討つ[うつ] attack; defeat; destroy　検討[けんとう] examination; review - 55a 35d

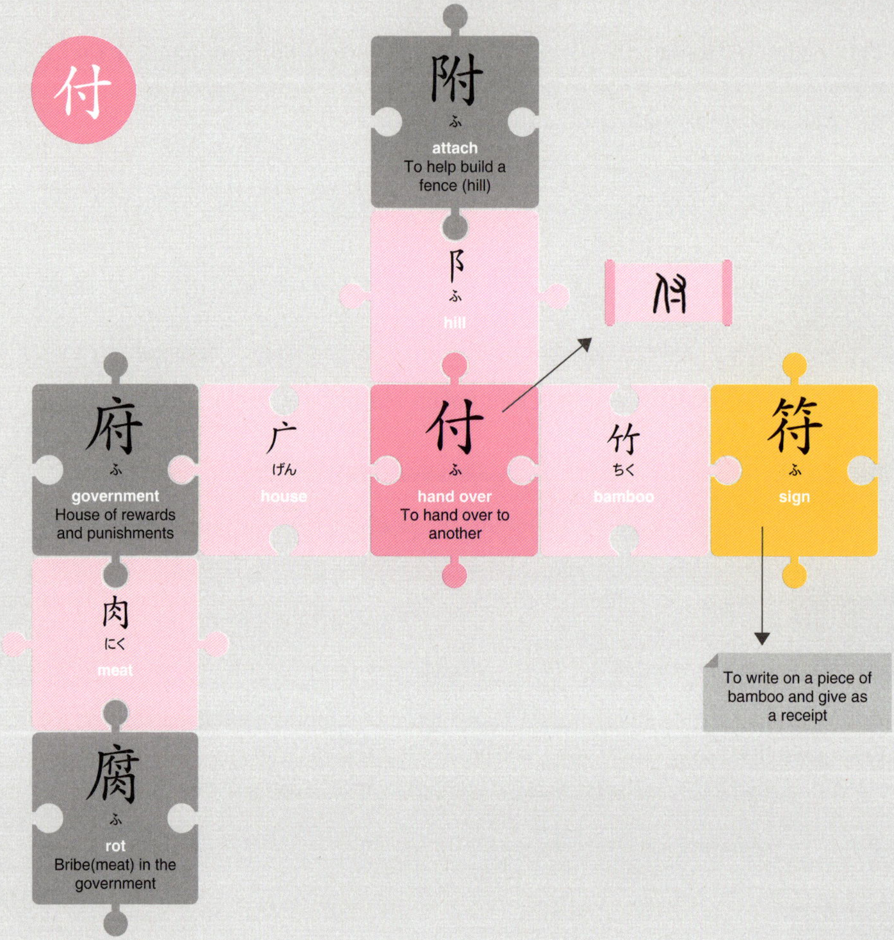

36 **付**

フ つく・つける　　ノ イ 仁 付 付

hand over; attach

person イ [52][ニン・ジン] + hand/joint 寸 [スン]

To hand over something to another person(イ) by hand(寸). As time passed, it gained the meaning 'to give → to request → to attach.'

付く[つく] stick (to); adhere (to); be attached　　付ける[つける] stick; attach; affix

36a 附

フ つく・つける

ʾ 阝 阝' 阝' 阝' 阝什 附

attach

hill 阝[116] [フ] + hand over 付 [フ]

To build a hill(阝) or a fence for protection, the less powerful needed to offer or add(付) their services to the rich and powerful. They had to approach the corrupt officials just so they could survive.

付く/附く[つく] stick (to); adhere (to); be attached -36 36a
付ける/附ける[つける] stick; attach; affix -36 36a

36b 符

フ

ノ ト ト ト' ト' ト' 竹 符 符 符 符

sign; mark

bamboo 竹[169] [チク] + hand over 付 [フ]

In China, before paper was invented, an important deal was written on a strip of bamboo(竹). They then broke it in half and gave(付) it to the other party so that each party had a mark (sign).

切符[きっぷ] ticket -95b 36b　　符号[ふごう] mark; sign; symbol -36b 12e

36c 府

フ

丶 亠 广 广 庁 庁 府 府

government

house 广[114] [ゲン] + hand over 付 [フ]

A government house(广) hands out rewards(付) as well as punishments(付).

* "广" is the shape of a house with one wall torn down, because that open space was where the official sat.

政府[せいふ] government; administration -45c 36c

36d 腐

フ くさる

丶 亠 广 广 广 广 府 府 府 腐 腐 腐 腐 腐

rot

government 府 [フ] + meat 肉[151] [ニク]

The government(府) is the center of power, and when meat(肉) is offered as a bribe, it is a sign of corruption.

腐る[くさる] rot; decay; spoil　　腐敗[ふはい] corruption; decomposition -36d 147c

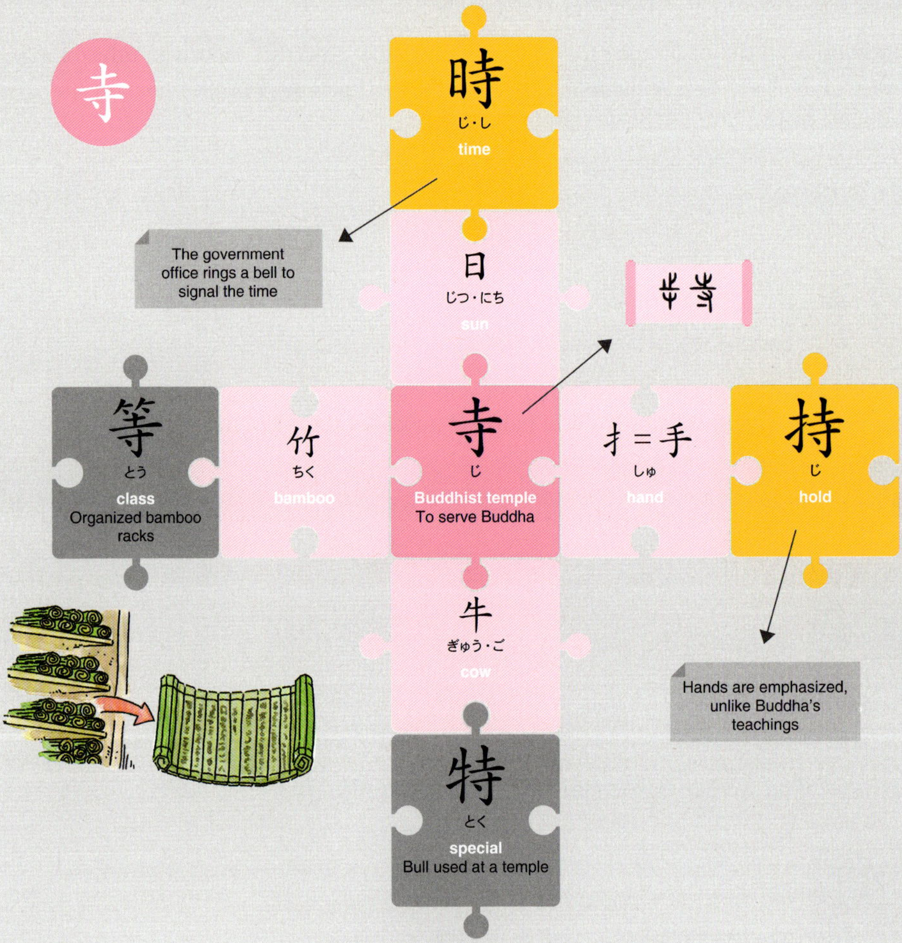

37	寺	ジ てら **Buddhist temple** foot/stop 土→止[44][シ] + hand/joint 寸 [スン]	一 十 土 圭 寺 寺

To serve as one's feet(止) and hands(寸). At first, it was used to describe an office of the king, but it became 'temple' after Buddhism was brought into China.

* "土[120]" is a variation of "止," the shape of a foot.

寺院[じいん] temple -37 56c

37a 時

ジ・シ とき

丨 ∏ 月 日 日一 日+ 日土 日圭 時 時

time

sun 日 170 [ジツ・ニチ] + Buddhist temple 寺 [ジ]

The local office(寺) checked the sun(日) dial and rang a bell to inform the people of the time.

何時[いつ] when; (at) what time -13c 37a
一時[いちじ] moment; a time; a while -173 37a
時計[とけい] watch; clock -37a 17a
何時[なんじ] when; (at) what time -13c 37a
何時も[いつも] always; all the time -13c 37a
時間[じかん] time; hours -37a 115b
時時[ときどき] sometimes; at times

37b 持

ジ もつ

一 十 扌 扌一 扌+ 扌土 扌圭 持 持

hold; have

hand 扌=手 28 [シュ] + Buddhist temple 寺 [ジ]

A famous Buddhist teaching goes, "You come with nothing, you leave with nothing." One must never covet material possessions. But unlike those teachings taught at a temple(寺), some hands(扌) crave riches, so this character came to mean 'to keep or hold.'

持つ[もつ] have; hold; possess
持参[じさん] bringing; taking; carrying -37b 5a

37c 特

トク

丿 ⺧ 牛 牜 牜一 牜+ 牜土 牜圭 特 特

special

cow 牛 137 [ギュウ・ゴ] + Buddhist temple 寺 [ジ]

Buddhists do not kill animals or eat meat. When a bull(牛) is offered to a Buddhist temple(寺), it is considered as a special offering.

* The people offered a bull of best quality as a sacrifice.

特急[とっきゅう] limited express (train) -37c 56d
特売[とくばい] special (bargain) sale -37c 146b

37d 等

トウ など・ひとしい

丿 ⺈ ⺮ 竹 竹 竺 笁 笙 等 等

class; equal

bamboo 竹 169 [チク] + Buddhist temple 寺 [ジ]

In temples(寺), Buddhist teachings were written on slices of bamboo(竹) and organized according to importance or level of difficulty.

* The Chinese used bamboo(竹) to make books before paper was invented.

等しい[ひとしい] equal; similar; like
平等[びょうどう] equality -96a 37d

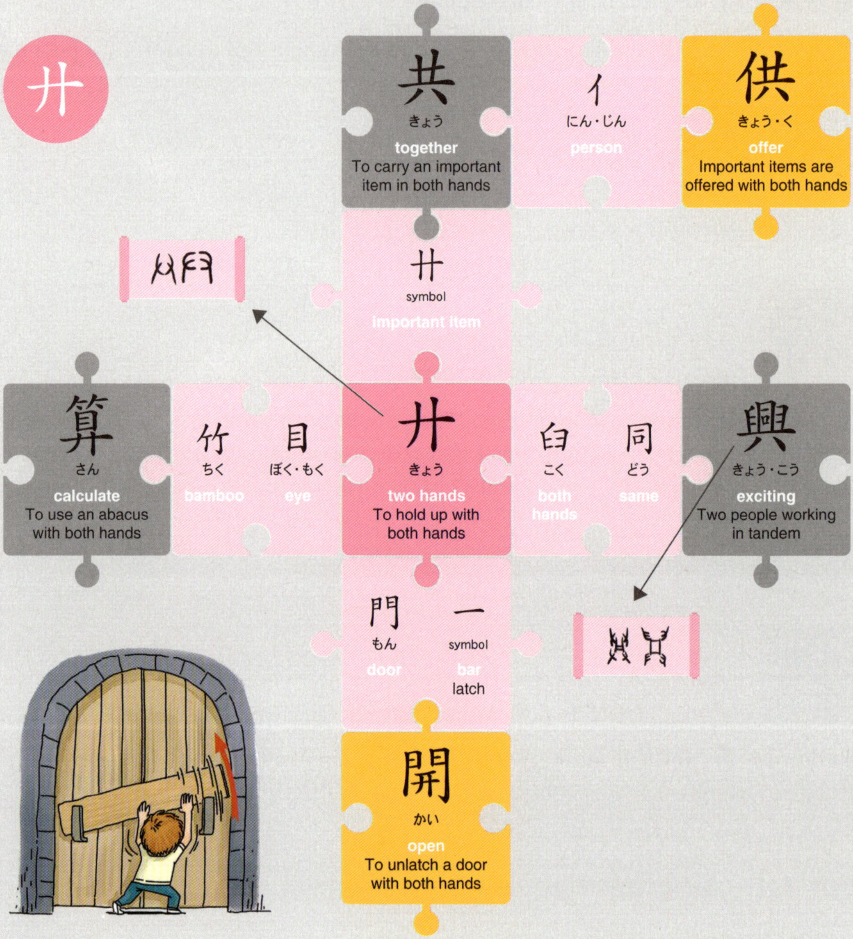

38 廾

キョウ

two hands

一 ナ 廾

The shape of two hands holding something upwards. The character changes shape when used as part of another character.

38a 共

キョウ　とも

together

important item 廾 [symbol] + two hands 六→廾 [キョウ]

To bring two hands(廾) together to carry something important(廾).

＊"廾" is shaped like a "一" above an "八[177]," for aesthetic reasons.

共に[ともに] together	公共[こうきょう] public; whole society -76e 38a
共通[きょうつう] commonness; be common -38a 129b	

38b 供

キョウ・ク　とも

offer; serve

person 亻[52][ニン・ジン] + together 共 [キョウ]

Two hands(共) offering an item of importance to the master(亻) came to mean 'to offer, provide or supply.'

子供[こども] child; children -77 38b

38c 興

キョウ・コウ

exciting

both hands 臼[29][コク] + same 同[118a][ドウ] + two hands 六→廾 [キョウ]

To hold the same(同) thing together, with two hands(臼) above and two hands(廾) below. It describes two people cheerfully working together.

興味[きょうみ] interest (in) -38c 164c

38d 開

カイ　など・あく・あける・ひらく

open

door 門[115][モン] + latch/bar 一 [symbol] + two hands 廾 [キョウ]

Using two hands(廾) to push up a latch(一) and open the gate(門).

開く[あく] open; begin; start	開ける[あける] open; throw open
開く[ひらく] open; spread out	開封[かいふう] unsealed letter; breaking the seal -38d 35c

38e 算

サン

calculate

bamboo 竹[169][チク] + eye 目[7][ボク・モク] + two hands 廾 [キョウ]

Using both hands(廾) to flick the bamboo(竹) abacus beads(目) to calculate.

＊The abacus came into Asia from Europe around 500 B.C. and the Chinese used bamboo to make them.

計算[けいさん] calculation; reckoning 17a 38e	算数[さんすう] arithmetic -38e 110b

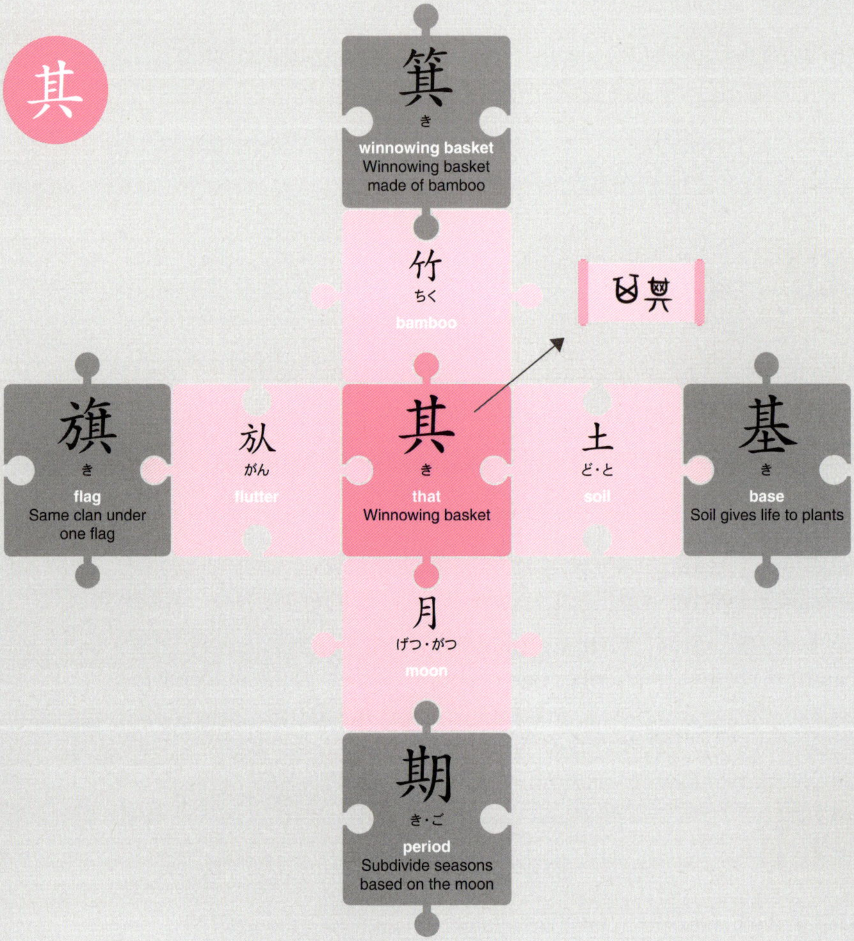

39 **其** キ その それ

that

一 十 卄 廾 甘 甘 其 其

The shape of a winnowing basket(甘) used to sort grain is leaning against a stand(丌). The character took the meaning of 'that' because that's how people referred to the grain.

* The "丌[キ・ゴ]" part is the pedestal on which items can be placed. Refer to "典 169d."

其処/其所[そこ] there (place); that place; that time (moment) -39 46d / 39 115e
其方[そちら] that way (direction); there -39 126
其の[その] that; the
其れ[それ] that; it; then; there

39a **箕** キ み ノ ⺈ ⺮ ⺮ ⺮ ⺮ 竺 竿 笄 笄 笄 筫 箕 箕

winnowing basket

bamboo 竹[169][チク] + winnowing basket/that 其 [キ]

When the character that originally referred to a winnowing basket(其) became a pronoun, the character for bamboo(竹) was added to create a character for the basket.

39b **基** キ もと 一 十 廾 廾 甘 甘 甘 其 其 其 基

base

winnowing basket/that 其 [キ] + soil 土[120][ド・ト]

Grain that is winnowed(其) is grown from the soil(土).

基準[きじゅん] standard; basis; criterion -39b 140c　基本[きほん] foundation; basis -39b 165

39c **期** キ・ゴ 一 十 廾 廾 甘 甘 甘 其 其 期 期 期

period

winnowing basket/that 其 [キ] + moon 月[172][ゲツ・ガツ]

Before taking grains to winnow(其), farmers checked the moon(月) to ascertain the seasonal period. In Asia where the lunar calendar is still often used, the moon(月) is an important factor when judging the right time or period to sow and harvest.

延期[えんき] delay; postponement -50d 39c　期間[きかん] period; term -39c 115b
期待[きたい] expectation; anticipation -39c 48d　短期[たんき] short term -89c 39c

39d **旗** キ はた 丶 亠 亍 方 方 方 扩 扩 旂 旂 旃 旗 旗 旗

flag

flutter 㫃[127][ガン] + winnowing basket/that 其 [キ]

People who share winnowed(其) grains lived under the same flag,which is shown by a fluttering(㫃) flag.

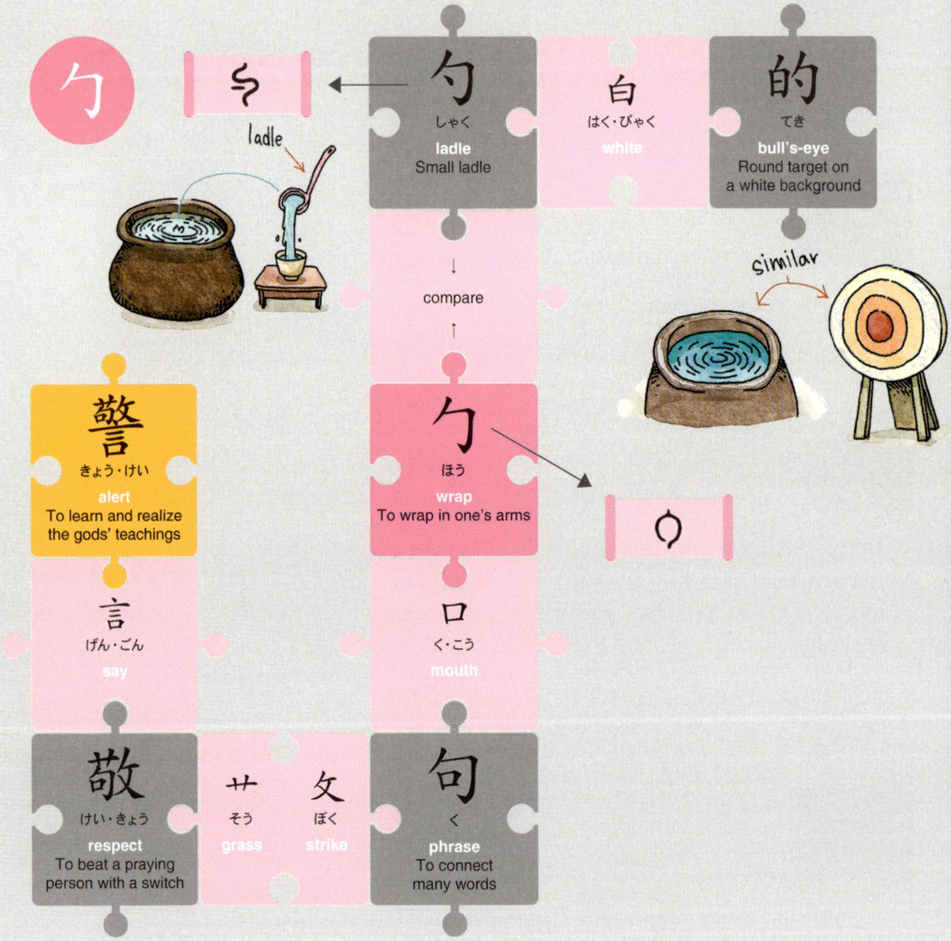

40 勹

ホウ

wrap

丿 勹

The shape of a pregnant woman or a woman holding a child wrapped in her arms.

40a 勺
シャク　　丿 勹 勺
ladle

A small ladle used to serve wine from a jar.

* The ancient character shows that it has nothing to do with the "wrap 勹 [ホウ]" character.

40b 的
テキ　まと　　′ 亻 ⺊ 白 白 的 的 的
bull's-eye
white 白 [106] [ハク・ビャク] + ladle 勺 [シャク]

Round ripples shaped like a shooting target form when a ladle(勺) is used to serve wine. Most targets are drawn on white(白) backgrounds so that they are visible from a distance.

40c 句
ク　　丿 勹 勹 句 句
phrase
wrap 勹 [ホウ] + mouth 口 [12] [ク・コウ]

To wrap(勹) the mouth(口) with both arms is an analogical way of saying a sentence is many words(口) brought together(勹).

文句[もんく] phrase; complaint - 105 40c

40d 敬
ケイ・キョウ　うやまう　　一 十 廾 艹 芍 芍 苟 苟 苟 苟 敬 敬
respect
grass 艹 [161] [ソウ] + phrase 句 [く] + strike 攵 [43] [ボク]

Hitting someone on the back with a switch(攵) when he is making a wish(句) to the gods wearing a decoration(艹) on their head. This means one must respect the gods.

* Records show that "艹" means a decoration on the head.

敬う[うやまう] respect; honor; worship　　敬語[けいご] honorific; honorific language - 40d 176c

40e 警
ケイ　　一 十 廾 艹 芍 芍 苟 苟 苟 苟 敬 敬 敬 敬 警 警 警 警 警
alert
respect 敬 [ケイ・キョウ] + say 言 [17] [ゲン・ゴン]

One must revere(敬) the gods to be alerted to their teachings(言).

警官[けいかん] policeman - 40e 152c　　警察[けいさつ] police - 40e 99b

Diagram for 勿

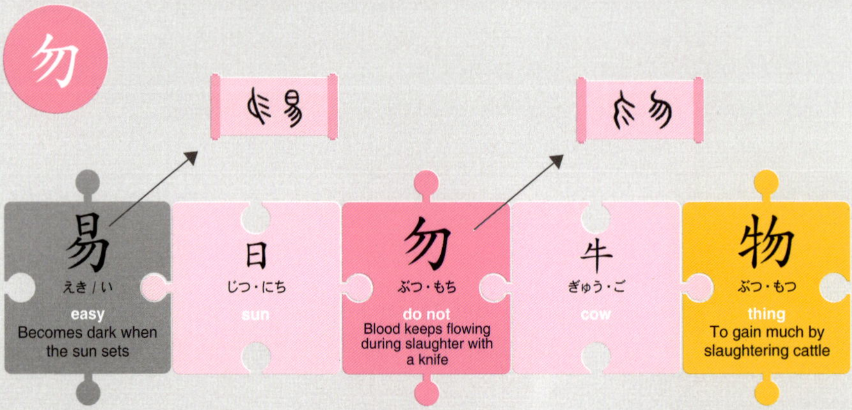

41 **勿**

ブツ・モチ　　ノ 勹 勺 勿

do not

knife 刀[95] [トウ] + flowing blood ノ[179e] [symbol]

Ancient texts suggest it is a description of a slaughtering knife(刀) and flowing blood(ノ). Using a knife(刀) to draw blood(ノ) is never ideal, so it came to mean 'do not.'

＊When "勿" is used to describe inanimate objects, "ノ" is the shape of a flying banner or a haze.

勿論[もちろん] of course -41 17b

41a **物**

ブツ・モツ　もの　　ノ ⺈ 牛 牛 牜 牞 物 物

thing

cow 牛[137] [ギュウ・ゴ] + kill with a knife/do not 勿 [ブツ・モチ]

In the ancient agricultural society, cattle(牛) was a valuable possession. When one was slaughtered(勿), the family could gain meat and leather, and purchase other things they needed.

買(い)物[かいもの] shopping; purchase 144a 41a
建物[たてもの] building 03b 41a
食べ物[たべもの] food; provisions -109 41a
飲(み)物[のみもの] a drink; a beverage -19a 41a
動物[どうぶつ] animal -119b 41a

41b **易**

エキ・イ　やさしい　　丨 冂 日 日 旦 昜 昜 易

easy / exchange

sun 日[170] [ジツ・ニチ] + haze/do not 勿 [ブツ・モチ]

When the sun(日) sets, a haze(勿) appears on the horizon. Day changes to night in a second. Because the sun(日) disappears beyond the horizon fast, this character came to mean 'easy.'

易しい[やさしい] easy
安易[あんい] easy; easy-going -78a 41b

Diagram for 支

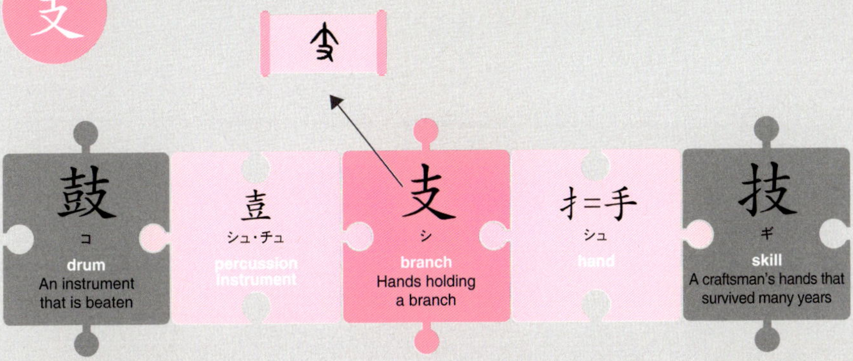

42 支

シ　ささえる

一 十 支 支

branch; support

This character means 'branch' and the ancient texts show a hand(又[30][ユウ]) holding a split branch(十). It also means 'support,' because it is the shape of a hand(又) propping up a branch(十).

支える[ささえる] support; sustain　　支社[ししゃ] branch office -42 99e

42a 技

ギ　わざ

一 † 扌 扌 扌 扌 技

skill

hand 扌=手[28] [シュ] + support 支 [シ]

When you see a building that has withstood(支) centuries, you can feel the craftsman's touch(扌) and 'skill and talent.'

42b 鼓

コ

一 十 士 士 吉 吉 吉 吉 壴 壴 壴 鼓 鼓

drum

percussion instrument 壴[112a][シュ・チュ] + branch/support 支 [シ]

This character depicts someone who is hitting the top of a a drum(壴) that has decorated legs with a drumstick(支).

* Another character with "士" that means to be decorated on the top is "声[112b]."

鼓舞[こぶ] inspiration; encouragement -42b 47b

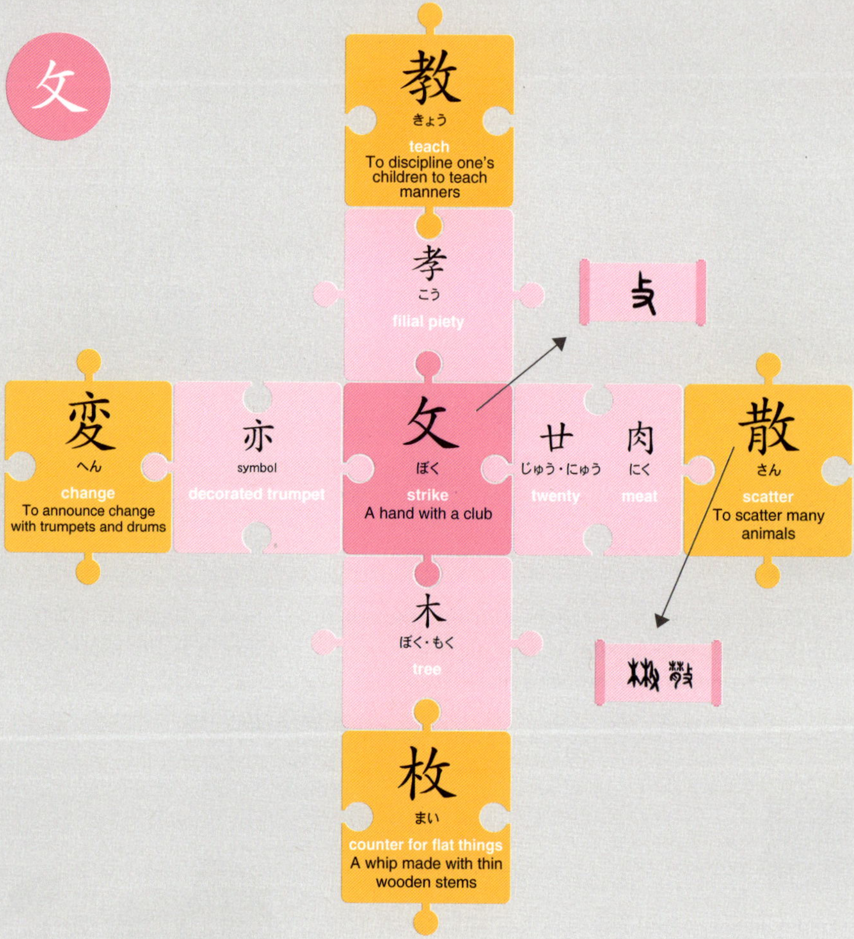

43 攵

ボク

strike

ノ ト ケ 攵

This character means 'strike,' because it is a hand(又[30]) holding a club(丨).

* It is always a hand that beats or whips.

43a 教

キョウ おしえる・おそわる

一 十 土 耂 耂 考 孝 孝 教 教 教

teach

filial piety 孝[81b][コウ] + strike 攵 [ボク]

If one teaches his/her child with an appropriate amount of discipline(攵), the child will be filial(孝).

* "攵" means discipline because it's the shape of a hand holding a stick.

教える[おしえる] teach; instruct　教わる[おそわる] be taught; get a lesson; learn
教室[きょうしつ] classroom -43a 90a　教育[きょういく] education; training -43a 151c

43b 散

サン ちらす・ちらかす・ちる・ちらかる

一 十 卄 廾 廾 昔 昔 昔 背 背 散 散

scatter

twenty 廿→龷 [ジュウ・ニュウ] + meat 月→肉[151][ニク] + strike 攵 [ボク]

To hit(攵) and scatter twenty(廿) animals(肉) with a stick because they are ruining the crops.

* "廿" is two "ten, 十[178]" characters written to overlap. In ancient texts, "forest(林[166])" describes hitting(攵) with a stick. When one hits a fruit tree with a stick, the fruits fall and scatter.

散らかす[ちらかす] scatter, litter up　散らかる[ちらかる] be scattered; be dispersed
散らす[ちらす] scatter; disperse; diffuse
散る[ちる] fall (e.g. blossoms, leaves), scatter; be dispersed
散歩[さんぽ] walk; stroll -43b 44a

43c 枚

マイ

一 十 才 木 木' 杧 杪 枚

counter for flat things

tree 木[164][ボク・モク] + strike 攵 [ボク]

Someone beating down(攵) with a whip made with thin stems of a tree(木). This character is the counter for flat things such as paper, boards, or farmland.

一枚[いちまい] one sheet (flat things) -173 43c　何枚[なんまい] how many flat objects -13c 43c

43d 変

ヘン かえる・かわる

丶 亠 亣 亣 亦 亦 亦 变 変

change; unusual

decorated trumpet 亦 [symbol] + strike 夂→攵[43][ボク]

When there was a huge change, like the coronation of a new king, the men blew trumpets(亦) with tassels and beat(攵) drums.

* The traditional character(變) is the shape of someone blowing into a wind instrument(言[17]) with tassels(糸[104]) and beating a drum(攵).

変える[かえる] change; alter; switch　変(わ)る[かわる] change; be transformed
大変[たいへん] very; greatly; awfully -60 43d

Diagram for 止

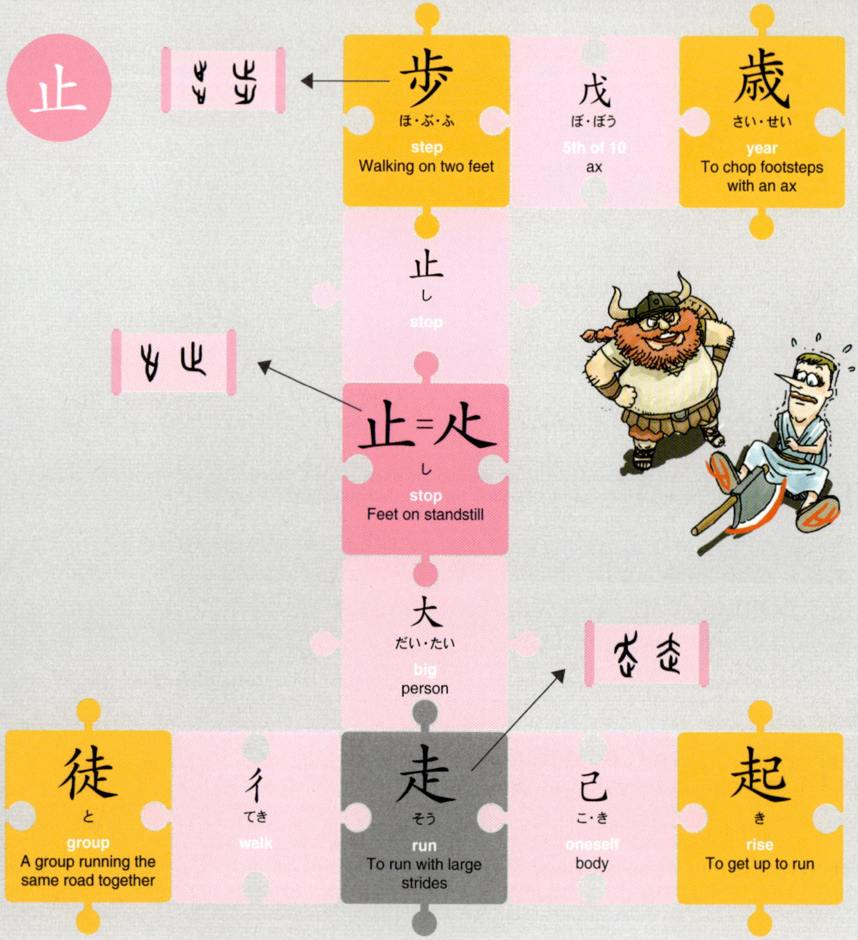

44 止

シ　とどまる・とどめる・とまる・とめる・やむ・やめる

stop

This character is the shape of a foot that is waiting to move, but because it is not moving at the moment, it means 'stop.'

止まる[とどまる] remain; abide; stay	止める[とどめる] stop; stay; remain
止(ま)る[とまる] stop; halt; cease; die	止める[とめる] stop; turn off
止む[やむ] stop, cease, be over	止める[やめる] stop; cease; cancel

44a 歩

ホ・ブ・フ　あるく・あゆむ

step; walk

foot/stop 止 [シ] + foot/stop 少→止 [シ]

Two feet(止, 止), the left(止) and the right(止) on the move, walking.

歩く[あるく] walk
歩く[あるく] walk (informal term)
散歩[さんぽ] walk; stroll 43b 44a
歩道[ほどう] sidewalk; pavement -44a 4e

44b 歳

サイ・セイ　とし

year; age

step 歨→歩 [ホ・ブ・フ] + ax/5th of 10 戊[92][ボ・ボウ]

Time and tide wait for no man, and as the years go by, a person gets weaker, which is depicted by footsteps(歩) being chopped up with an ax(戊).

二十歳[はたち] 20 years old; twenty -176 178 44b

44c 走

ソウ　はしる

run

person/big 土→大[60][ダイ・タイ] + foot/stop 止 [シ]

This character describes a person(大) running with two feet(止) and two arms.

* The ancient character shows that "土[120]" means 'person(大).'

走る[はしる] run; dash; run away
走狗[そうく] hunting dog; tool of another person -44c 135c

44d 起

キ　おきる・おこす・おこる

rise

run 走 [ソウ] + body/oneself 己[66][コ・キ]

An athlete raising his body(己) to run(走) as soon as the signal is given.

起きる[おきる] get up; rise; wake up
起(こ)す[おこす] raise; wake (up)
起(こ)る[おこる] occur; happen
起床[きしょう] getting out of bed; rising -44d 114a

44e 徒

ト

group

walk 彳[48][テキ] + run 走 [ソウ]

People running(走) along the same road(彳) together is 'a group.'

* "彳" means 'road' because it's the left part of "行," which is a crossroad.

生徒[せいと] pupil; student -162 44e

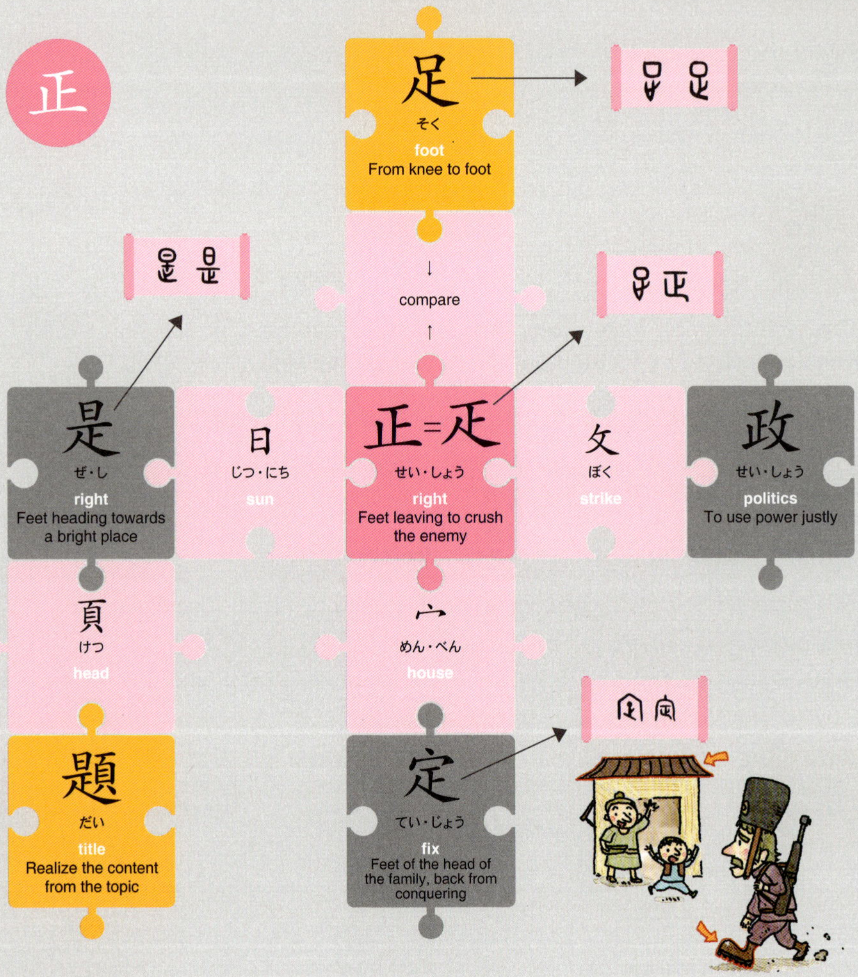

45 正

セイ・ショウ ただしい

right

enemy camp 一 [symbol] + foot/stop 止[44] [シ]

一 丅 下 亡 正

This character describes that the feet(止) of the soldiers are off to attack the enemy(一) and means 'to conquer.' To do so is the 'right' thing.

* The ancient character shows 'feet(止) facing a castle(口[16]).'

正しい[ただしい] right; correct; righteous	正月[しょうがつ] New Year('s Day); January -45 172
正直[しょうじき] honesty; uprightness -45 8	正式[せいしき] official; formality -45 88a

45a 足
ソク　あし・たす・たりる
丨 口 口 ⻊ 早 足 足

foot

This character means 'foot,' but it refers to the shin, calf, ankle, and foot.

足す[たす] add　　足りる[たりる] be enough, be sufficient

45b 政
セイ・ショウ
一 丅 下 正 正 正' 正' 政 政

politics

right 正 [セイ・ショウ] + strike 攵[43] [ボク]

Politics is the power(攵) that should be used justly(正) to improve the nation and its people.

* "攵" is a hand(又) holding a stick(丨), which symbolizes power that gives the right to punish others.

政治[せいじ] politics 45c 76d　　政府[せいふ] government; administration -45c 36c

45c 定
テイ・ジョウ　さだまる・さだめる
丶 丶 宀 宀 宀 宀 宁 定

fix

house 宀[113] [メン・ベン] + conquer/right 正 [セイ・ショウ]

Feet that went out to conquer(正) are now heading home(宀). When the head of the family comes home, stability returns.

* The lower part is the same shape as "foot 疋[166c] [ソ・ショ]," but the stroke at the top(一) makes it different from "正."

定まる[さだまる] be set; be fixed; be decided　　定める[さだめる] decide; determine; establish
固定[こてい] fix; settle -15b 45b　　予定[よてい] schedule -4a 45b

45d 是
ゼ・シ
丨 口 日 日 旦 早 早 早 是

right

sun 日[170] [ジツ・ニチ] + conquer/right 正 [セイ・ショウ]

Feet heading out to conquer(正) are facing the sun(日). To head towards the light means it is the right thing to do.

* When the two characters were put together, the lower part of "正" was changed for aesthetic reasons.

是非[ぜひ] right and wrong -45d 141d

45e 題
ダイ
丨 口 日 日 旦 早 早 是 是 是 是 是 題 題 題 題 題 題

title; subject

right 是 [ゼ・シ] + head 頁[4] [ケツ]

To accurately(是) recognize the contents of a book, the subject is written at the head(頁), or the front of it.

宿題[しゅくだい] homework -106b 45e　　問題[もんだい] question; problem -115a 45e
課題[かだい] task; assignment; mission -123d 45e

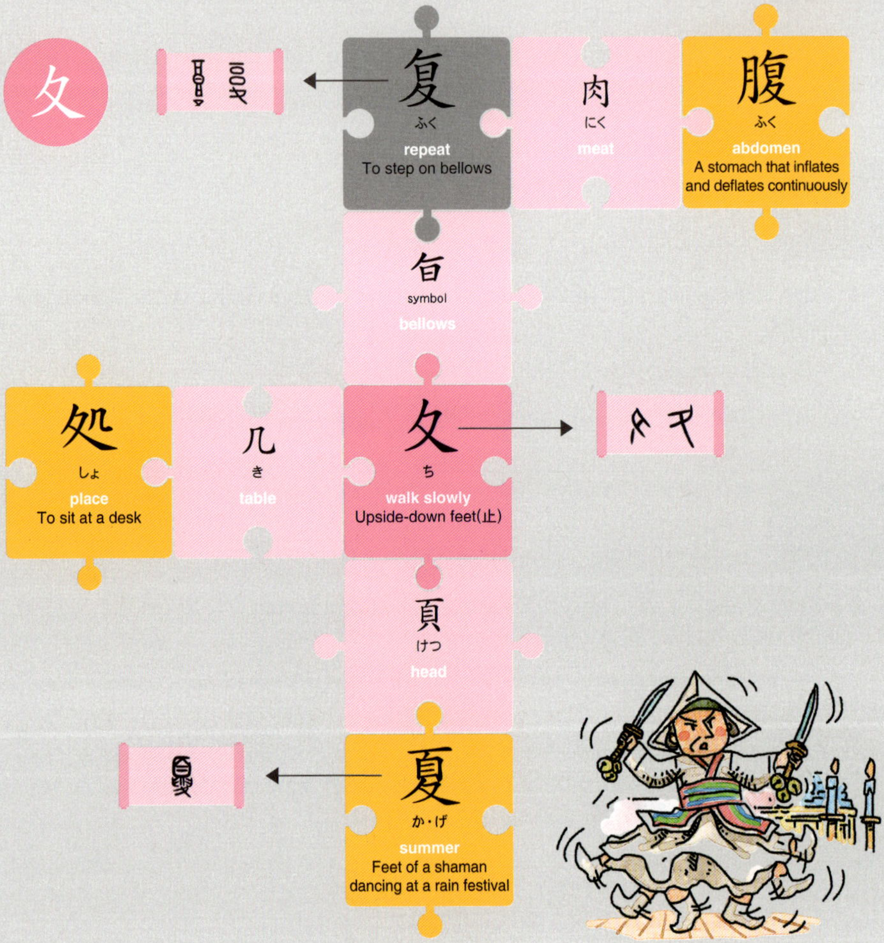

46 夊

チ

walk slowly

ノ ク 夊

Upside-down feet(止[44]) because someone pulled a man down from behind. When one is being stopped from walking at normal speed, one has to 'walk slowly or fall behind others.'

46a 复

フク ノ ㇒ 𠂉 𠂉 𠂉 𠂉 𠂉 复 复 复

repeat

bellows 𠂉 [symbol] + foot/walk slowly 夂 [チ]

Ancient texts show that this character originally took the shape of a foot(夂) stepping on bellows(𠂉). Bellows inflate and deflate repeatedly.

46b 腹

フク

abdomen

meat 月→肉[151][ニク] + repeat 复 [フク]

The abdomen is a part of the body(月) that repeatedly(复) 'inflates and deflates' each time one breathes.

御腹[おなか] abdomen; belly; stomach -69c 46b

46c 夏

カ・ゲ なつ 一 丁 丆 丙 丙 百 百 頁 夏 夏

summer

head 百→頁[4] [ケツ] + foot/walk slowly 夂 [チ]

Some say this character describes a shaman(頁) with wildly dancing feet(夂). Of all the rites, the most important was to pray for rain, so in the Eastern Zhou (東周, 770~256 BC) Dynasty, this character came to mean 'summer.'

* "頁" the top part of "夏," is the shaman dancing in a long-sleeved outfit and shows both hands. When a shaman is dancing in a trance, the feet look like they are upside down, which is why "夂" was used.

夏休み[なつやすみ] summer vacation; summer holiday -46c 165a

46d 処

ショ ところ ノ ク 夂 処 処

place; stay

foot/walk slowly 夂 [チ] + table 几[168][キ]

To find a good location, put a desk(几) there and sit in place(夂). "夂" is an inverted foot meaning the person is staying.

* The ancient Chinese believed tigers(虎) were holy animals that chased away evil. The traditional character(處) indicates one staying(夂) in an auspicious location a tiger(虎) is protecting.

彼処[あそこ] there; that place -149a 46d

此処[ここ] here; this place -72a 46d

其処[そこ] there (place); that place; that time (moment) -39 46d

何処[どこ] where; what place -13c 46d

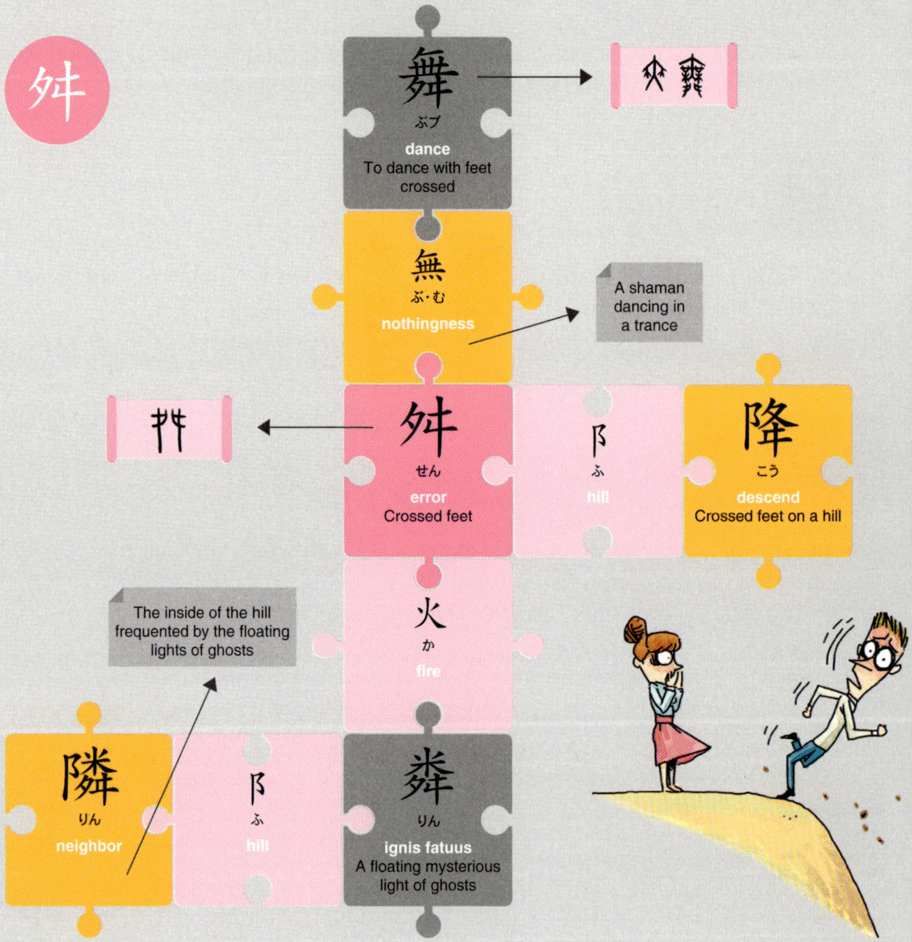

47 **舛** セン

error

The character on the left, "夕," is a variation of the downward turned "夂[46]." The character on the right is a shape of a foot(午→止[44]), and when used together it means 'error' because feet should face the same direction, not be crossed.

47a 無

ブ・ム ない

nothingness

a shaman danced 無 [symbol] + four dots 灬 [symbol]

This character is the shape of a shaman(無) holding a sacred object like feathers and dancing in a trance so fast that the feet are only visible as four dots(灬). Because the feet are almost invisible, the character also means 'none.'

* Even now in China, shamans dance with swords decorated with feathers or tassels.

無い[ない] nonexistent; not being (there); nonoccurrence

47b 舞

ブ まい, まう

dance

nothingness 無 [ぶ・む] + crossed feet/error 舛 [セン]

"無" originally indicated someone dancing, but when people used it to mean 'none,' crossed feet(舛) replaced the four dots to depict someone dancing.

舞い[まい] dance; dancing
舞う[まう] dance; wander; flutter
鼓舞[こぶ] inspiration; encouragement -42b 47b
仕舞う[しまう] finish; stop; end -84e 47b

47c 降

コウ おりる・おろす・ふる

descend

hill 阝[116][フ] + crossed feet/error 夅→舛 [セン]

Feet crossed(舛) on top of a hill(阝). When this happens, you will fall down.

降りる[おりる] descend; come down; go down
降る[ふる] fall; come down; drop
降ろす[おろす] take down; drop off

47d 粦

リン

ignis fatuus

fire 米→火[124][カ] + crossed feet/error 舛 [セン]

An unexplainable ignis fatuus or will-o'-the-wisp(火) floating around(舛) or blinking continually(舛).

* A variant of this character(粦) shows the top half isn't rice(米[110]) but fire(火).

47e 隣

リン となり

neighbor

hill 阝[116][フ] + ignis fatuus 粦 [リン]

A neighbor isn't someone who lives over the hill(阝) where strange lights(粦) appear, but someone close enough whom you can visit even at night.

隣接[りんせつ] adjacency; abuttal -47e 83b

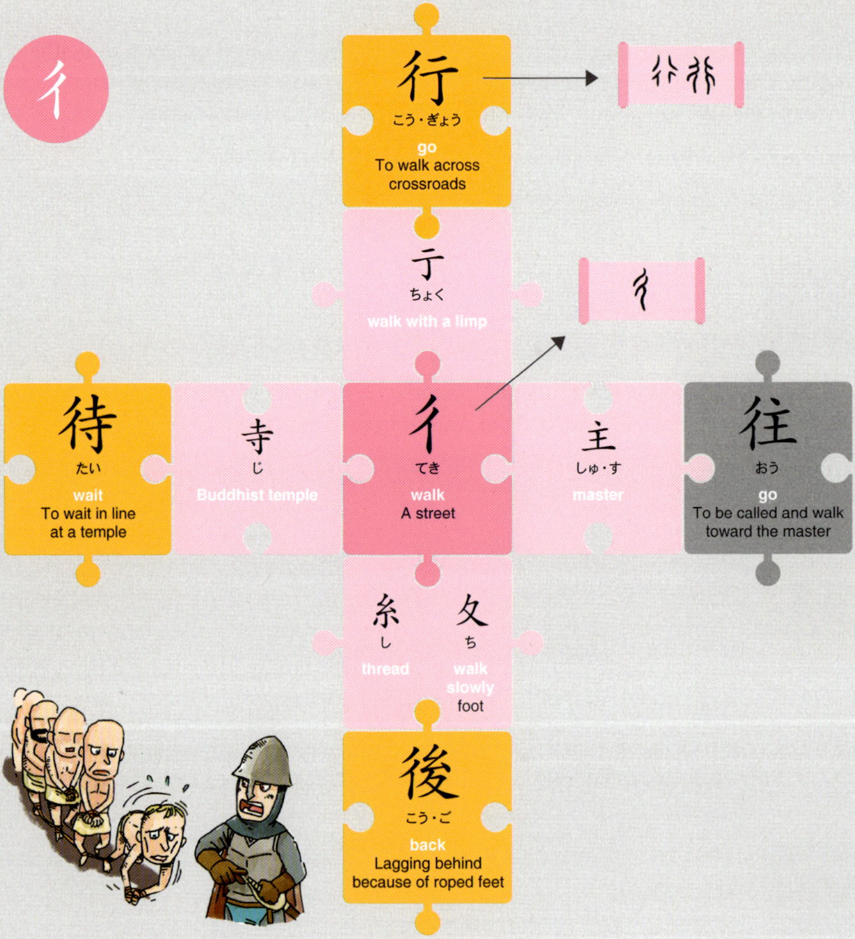

48 彳

テキ

walk

The left side of "go 行[48a][コウ・ギョウ]," which is a crossroad. It means 'road or walk.'

* We can tell this character is associated with feet by the meanings 'road' and 'walk.'

48a 行

コウ・ギョウ いく・おこなう・ゆく

ノ ク 彳 彳 行 行

go

walk 彳 [テキ] + walk with a limp 亍 [チョク]

Taking the shape of a crossroad, this character means 'to go or walk.'

* "彳" is the left of the crossroad, "亍" is the right. Neither character(彳, 亍) is used on its own.

行く[いく] go; proceed
行く[ゆく] go; proceed
飛行機[ひこうき] airplane; aircraft -128d 48a 91e
行(な)う[おこなう] do; perform
銀行[ぎんこう] bank -10b 48a

48b 往

オウ

ノ ク 彳 彳 彳 往 往 往

go

walk 彳 [テキ] + master 主 181a [シュ・ス]

To be summoned and walk(彳) toward one's master(主). The pronunciation comes from the traditional character of "主," which is "king 王 86 [オウ]."

往来[おうらい] coming and going -48b 110e

48c 後

コウ・ゴ あと・うしろ・のち

ノ ク 彳 彳 彳 後 後 後 後

back; after

walk 彳 [テキ] + thread 幺→糸 104 [シ] + foot/walk slowly 夂 46 [チ]

Prisoners walking(彳) in single file with their feet(夂) tied up with a long rope(糸). Because people with feet tied up(糸) can only walk(彳) slowly(夂), this character came to mean 'behind, next, later or in the back.'

後ろ[うしろ] back; rear; behind
午後[ごご] afternoon; p.m. -96c 48c
明後日[あさって] day after tomorrow -170d 48c 170
後悔[こうかい] repentance; regret -48c 79d

48d 待

タイ まつ

ノ ク 彳 彳 彳 往 待 待 待

wait

walk 彳 [テキ] + Buddhist temple 寺 37 [ジ]

When you go(彳) to a busy government office or a temple(寺), you must wait in line until it's your turn.

待つ[まつ] wait
期待[きたい] expectation; anticipation -39c 48d

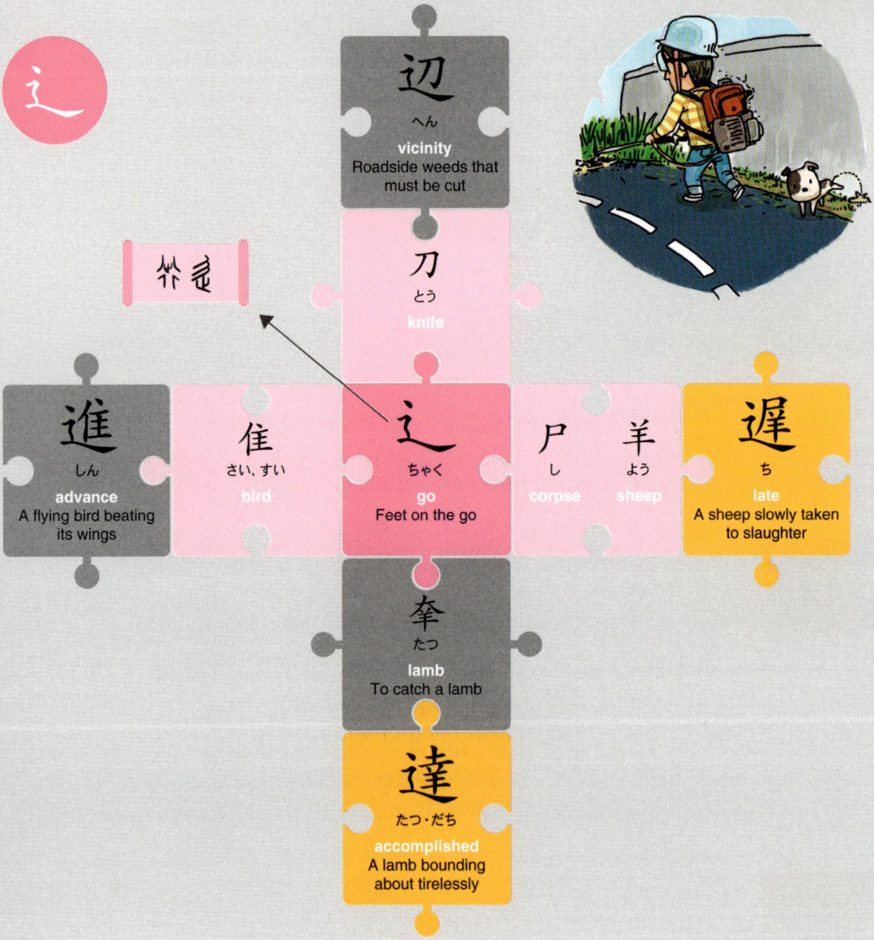

49 辶 チャク

go

The ancient character shows a combination of "行[48a] (crossroad)" and "止[44] (foot)," which means 'a road describing distance,' or 'to go.'

49a 辺

ヘン あたり・べ・ほとり

フ 刀 刀 刃 辺

vicinity

knife 刀 [95][トウ] + go ⻌ [チャク]

Weeds that grow by or around the road(⻌) must be cut with a blade(刀).

* If you come across the traditional character(邊), imagine a dog passing by(⻌) and sticking its nose(自 [6]) into a corner(方 [126]), or a hold(穴 [113a]) on the road.

辺り[あたり] by the side of; neighborhood; vicinity
海辺[うみべ] beach; seaside; seashore - 79c 49a
周辺[しゅうへん] surroundings; circumference - 122a 49a

49b 遅

チ おくれる・おそい

フ コ 尸 尸 尸 尸 尸 尸 犀 犀 遅 遅

late; slow

corpse 尸 [74] [シ] + sheep 羊 [134][ヨウ] + go ⻌ [チャク]

A sheep(羊) used to be used as a sacrifice(尸). Think of a ceremonial sheep(羊) walking(⻌) slowly toward the slaughterhouse(尸).

* The traditional character(遲) shows a large horned bull(犀) walking(⻌) slowly.

遅い[おそい] late; slow
遅れる[おくれる] be late; be delayed

49c 幸

タツ

一 ナ 大 太 夳 夳 夳 查 幸

lamb

person/big 大 [60][ダイ・タイ] + sheep 羊 [134] [ヨウ]

A person(大) catching a lamb as it's being born from a sheep(羊), an important ceremonial animal.

49d 達

タツ・ダチ たち

一 十 土 キ 去 去 圭 幸 幸 幸 達 達

accomplished; reach

lamb 幸→ 幸 [タツ] + go ⻌ [チャク]

An accomplished person who is able to work tirelessly, like a lamb(幸) that never stops running(⻌) amongst the flock is a well-trained expert.

友達[ともだち] friend; companion 34c 49d
配達[はいたつ] delivery - 66d 49d
速達[そくたつ] express mail; special delivery - 167b 49d

49e 進

シン すすむ・すすめる

ノ イ イ 亻 亻 亻 隹 隹 隹 進 進

advance

bird 隹 [140][サイ、スイ] + go ⻌ [チャク]

A bird(隹) about to take flight runs(⻌) forward as it beats its wings.

進む[すすむ] advance; go forward
進める[すすめる] propel; move forward
進歩[しんぽ] progress; advance 49e 44a
進行[しんこう] progress; head (toward) 49e 48a

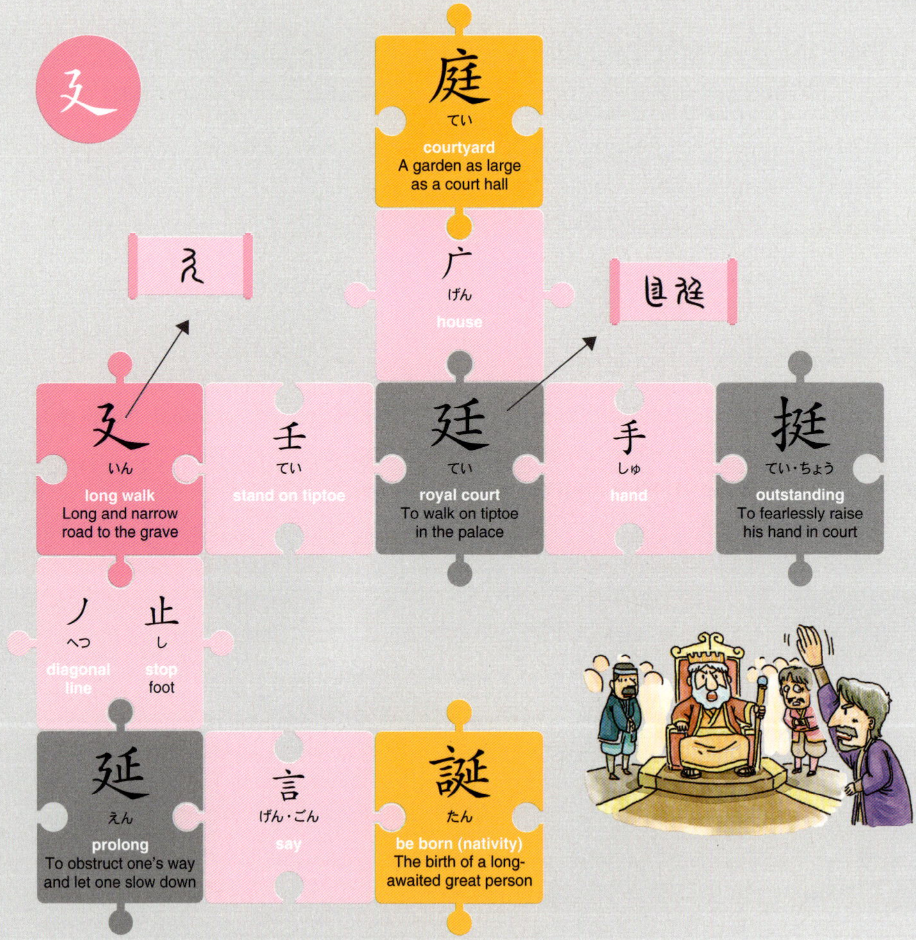

50 廴 イン

long walk

This character describes a long and narrow road to the king's tomb, to mean 'a long walk or a narrow road.'

* A king's tomb contain many treasures and artifacts, so they were designed to be reached only by a long and narrow road. Think of a man walking carefully.

50a 廷

テイ

royal court

stand on tiptoe 𡈼 [テイ] + long walk 廴 [イン]

Subjects walking(廴) carefully on tiptoe(𡈼) in court. "𡈼" is the shape of a foot(止) with the heel lifted above the ground, which also gives the character its pronunciation.

* "𡈼" is the same shape as "9th of 10 壬 [ジン]," but a completely different character.

50b 庭

テイ　にわ

courtyard; garden

house 广[114][ゲン] + royal court 廷 [テイ]

In the old days, most large Asian houses had a yard without walls within the house. The meaning 'yard or hall' originated from it being a large space like a court(廷) within a house(广).

* "广" is the shape of a house with one wall taken down.

家庭[かてい] home; family -136a 50b　　校庭[こうてい] schoolyard; campus -1b 50b

50c 挺

テイ・チョウ

outstanding

hand 扌=手[28][シュ] + royal court 廷 [テイ]

A distinguished subject raising his hand(扌) in court(廷) to speak his mind.

50d 延

エン　のばす・のびる

prolong; stretching

diagonal line ノ[179e][ヘツ] + foot/stop 止[44][シ] + long walk 廴 [イン]

This character means 'to prolong or extend' because it depicts someone blocking(ノ) the front of someone else's feet(止) to make them go(廴) slowly.

* "ノ" has no distinct meaning and can be interpreted in various ways.

延ばす[のばす] prolong; delay; postpone　　延びる[のびる] extend; stretch; be prolonged
延期[えんき] delay; postponement -50d 39c　　延長[えんちょう] extension -50d 81d

50e 誕

タン

be born (nativity)

say 言[17][ゲン・ゴン] + prolong 延 [エン]

To inform(言) the people of the birth of a prince or someone great that everyone had been waiting for a long time(延).

誕生日[たんじょうび] birthday -50e 162 170　　誕生[たんじょう] birth; creation -50e 162

Diagram for 人

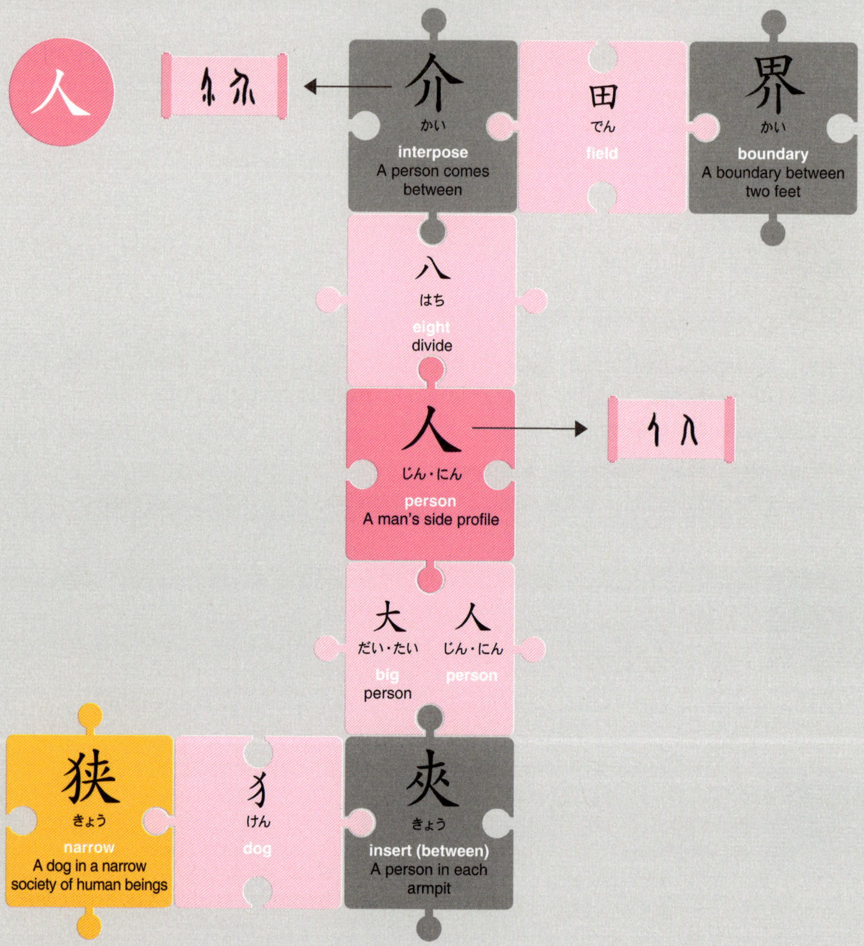

51 人

ジン・ニン ひと

ノ 人

person

The side profile of a person which means 'man.'

男の人[おとこのひと] man; male -125a 51	大人[おとな] adult -60 51
女の人[おんなのひと] woman; female -78 51	外国人[がいこくじん] foreigner; alien -172b 86a 51
何人[なんにん] how many (people) -13c 51	一人[ひとり] one person -173 51
個人[こじん] individual -15c 51	友人[ゆうじん] friend -34c 51

51a 介

カイ

ノ 人 介 介

interpose

person 人 [ジン・ニン] + divide/eight 八[177] [ハチ]

A person(人) interjects into something that is divided in two(八) to solve a problem or to introduce others.

紹介[しょうかい] introduction -95d 51a　厄介[やっかい] trouble; nuisance; bother; burden -69a 51a

51b 界

カイ　さかい

丶 口 田 田 田 甲 甲 界 界

boundary

field 田[122] [デン] + interpose 介 [カイ]

"田" is a ditch dividing two rice paddies and means 'rice paddy or farming land.' This character is the boundary between(介) two fields(田).

世界[せかい] the world -162c 51b　限界[げんかい] limit; bounds -10d 51b

51c 夾

キョウ

一 ア ス ズ 双 夾 夾

insert (between)

person/big 大[60] [ダイ・タイ] + person 人 [ジン・ニン] + person 人 [ジン・ニン]

A man(大) with one person(人) lodged in each armpit.

51d 狭

キョウ

ノ 犭 犭 犭 犷 犷 狂 狭 狭

narrow

dog 犭[135b] [ケン] + insert 夾→夹 [キョウ]

The dog(犭) was mankind's first domesticated pet and got stuck(夹) in the narrow human society.

狭い[せまい] narrow; small

52 亻

ニン・ジン

ノ 亻

person

It looks different, but it is the same character as "person 人[51]." This shape is only used when it's on the left of a more complicated character.

52a 化

カ・ケ ばける

ノ 亻 亻' 化

change

person 亻 [ニン・ジン] + person/spoon ヒ → ヒ[72] [ヒ]

A man standing(亻) and a man upside down(ヒ). A person(亻) is born as baby but dies an old man(ヒ), which means that everything changes.

化ける[ばける] turn oneself into; disguise oneself as	悪化[あっか] deterioration -26c 52a
化石[かせき] fossil; petrifaction -52a 153a	消化[しょうか] digestion -182d 52a

52b 花

カ・ケ はな

一 十 艹 艹 艿 芲 花

flower

grass 艹[161] [ソウ] + change 化 [カ・ケ]

As a person goes from a baby to an elderly person, plants(艹) change(化) into beautiful flowers with time.

花瓶[かびん] (flower) vase -52b 64f	花見[はなみ] flower viewing; cherry-blossom viewing -52b 9

PEOPLE PERSON "入"

Diagram for 入

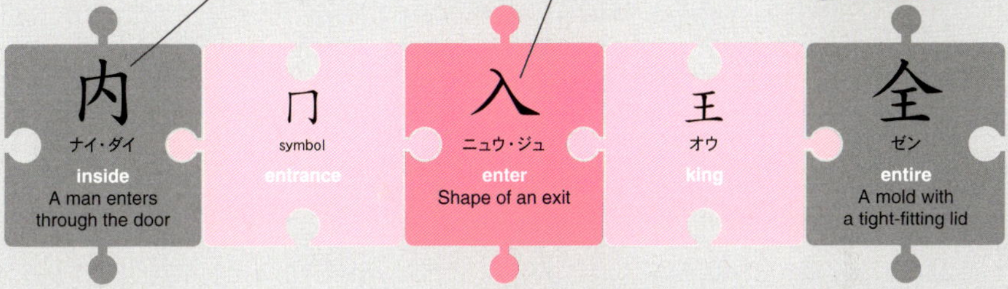

53 **入** ニュウ・ジュ　いれる・はいる　ノ 入

enter

The entrance to a cave or a mud hut. It means 'to enter.'

* It is a radical but no one is sure of the origin. Not to be confused with "person 人[51] [ジン・ニン]."

入れる[いれる] put in; take in; insert	入る[はいる] enter, go (come, get) in
入(り)口[いりぐち] entrance; doorway; root; beginning -53 12	
入浴[にゅうよく] bathing; enter a bath -53 153e	

53a **全** ゼン　まったく　ノ 入 𠆢 仝 仝 全

entire

enter 入 [ニュウ・ジュ] + king 王[86] [オウ]

A mold with a body(王) and a lid(入) that fits the mold completely.

* Regardless of the shape, "王" is the container and "入" is the lid. The ancient character(仝) describes a mold used to make farming tools(工[155]) and its lid(入).

全く[まったく] quite; entirely; completely; wholly	安全[あんぜん] safety; security -78a 53a
全部[ぜんぶ] all; entire; whole -53a 116d	全体[ぜんたい] whole; entirety -53a 24b

53b **内** ナイ・ダイ　うち　丨 冂 内 内

inside

enter 入 [ニュウ・ジュ] + entrance 冂 [symbol]

A man goes(入) inside through the entrance(冂).

家内[かない] (my) wife; one's family -136a 53b	内部[ないぶ] interior; inside -53b 116d

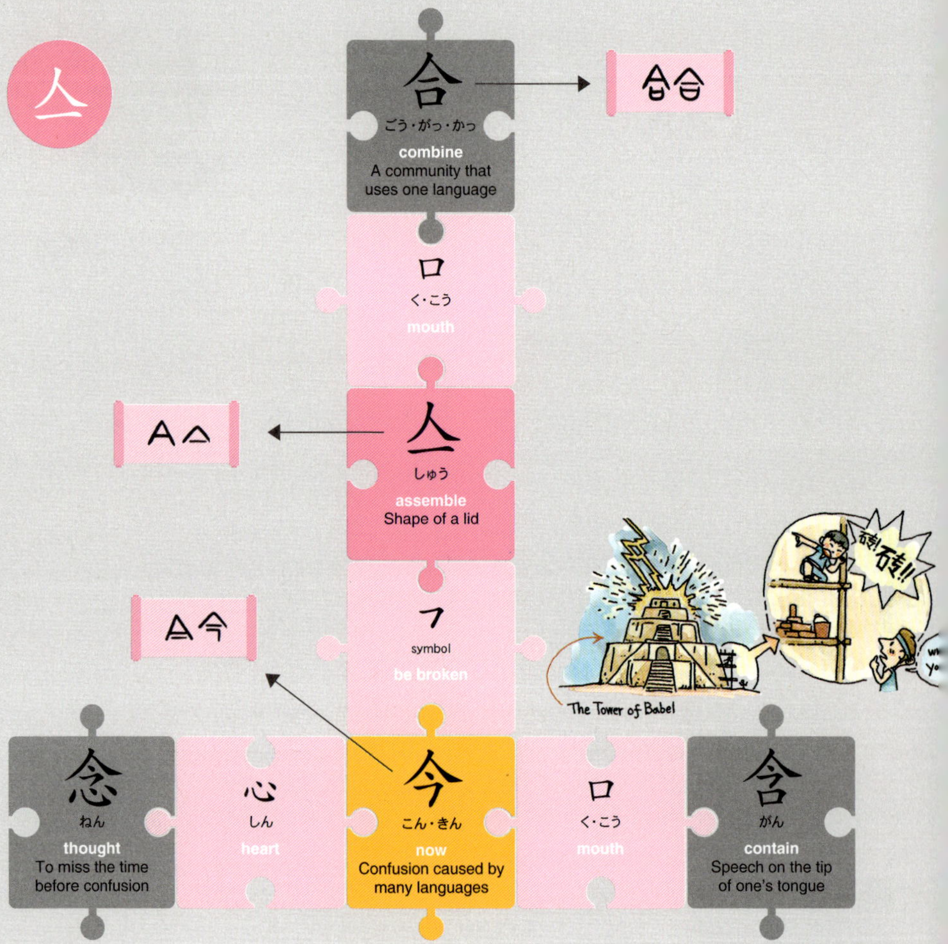

54 **亼**

シュウ

assemble

ノ 人 亼

A container(一) and its lid(人) must be assembled or kept together.

* This character is listed here because of the "人[51]" component, not the meaning.

54a 合

ゴウ・ガッ・カッ あう・あわせる・あわす

ノ 人 亼 亼 合 合

combine

assemble 亼 [シュウ] + mouth 口[12] [ク・コウ]

This character describes the time when man spoke one language(口) in one community(亼) before the Tower of Babel had been built.

* The ancient character shows a rice bowl(口) and its lid(亼) fitting perfectly.

合う[あう] come together; merge; unite; meet
合わす[あわす] match; join together; make a pair of
合(わ)せる[あわせる] match; join together; unite
試合[しあい] game; contest -88b 54a

54b 今

コン・キン いま

ノ 人 亼 今

now

assemble 亼 [シュウ] + be broken ㇇ [symbol]

Before they built the Tower of Babel, man used one language(口) which made the human beings unite as a single community(亼). But when the tower was built, God became angry with them, and broke(㇇) the languages so they couldn't communicate. Such an important incident changed history, so this character means 'now.'

* "㇇" is the shape of a broken "口[12] (mouth)" and symbolizes that one language was broken into many.

今朝[けさ] this morning -54b 98e
今日は[こんにちは] good afternoon -54b 170
今晩は[こんばんは] good evening -54b 57b
今年[ことし] this year -54b 96e
今月[こんげつ] this month -54b 172
今晩[こんばん] tonight; this evening -54b 57b
今週[こんしゅう] this week -54b 122b
今日[きょう] today; this day -54b 170

54c 含

ガン ふくむ・ふくめる

ノ 人 亼 今 今 含 含

contain

confused language/now 今 [コン・キン] + mouth 口[12] [ク・コウ]

When God caused confusion(今) with the languages, people spoke(口) but could not understand each other. This looks like speech(口) on the tip of one's tongue, '(keep) in the mouth,' not knowing what to say.

含む[ふくむ] contain; include; hold in the mouth
含める[ふくめる] include; instruct; put in (someone's) mouth

54d 念

ネン

ノ 人 亼 今 今 念 念 念

thought

confused language/now 今 [コン・キン] + heart 心[26] [シン]

With the language in confusion(今), people scattered, but in their hearts(心) they missed the time they were one community.

記念[きねん] commemoration -66b 54d

Diagram for 佥

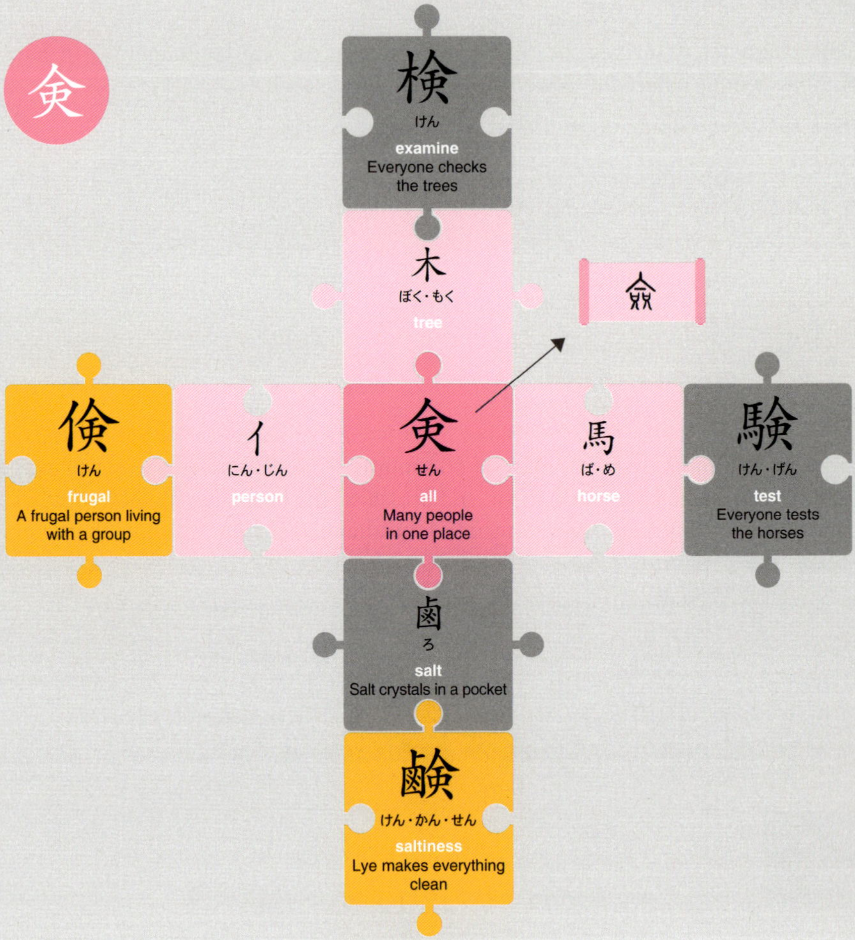

55 佥

セン

all

assemble 亼 [シュウ] + mouth ロ [12] [ク・コウ] + person 人 [51] [ジン・ニン]

Many people(人) gather(亼) all in one place to speak(ロ) their opinions.

* The traditional character(僉) shows many people(人人) gathered(亼) all in one place and speaking(ロロ).

55a **検**

ケン

一 十 才 木 木' 木^ 朩^ 朩^ 朩^ 枠 梌 検

examine

tree 木[164] [ボク・モク] + all 㑒 [セン]

All(㑒) the people are checking the trees(木) to see if they are good building material.

検査[けんさ] inspection; examination -55a 174a 　 検討[けんとう] examination; review -55a 35d

55b **験**

ケン・ゲン

丨 𠂉 𠃊 ⺕ 馬 馬 馬 馬 馬 馬 馬' 馬^ 馬^ 馬^ 騐 騐 験 験

test

horse 馬[138] [バ・メ] + all 㑒 [セン]

All(㑒) the people are testing the horses(馬) by making them run and jump.

* Part of the character "検" is a tree(木) that is a plant which tests can be run on. But a horse(馬) is an animal whose build and movement cannot be tested(験) in a lab. Remember the difference.

試験[しけん] test -88b 55b

55c **鹵**

ロ

丶 ⺊ 𠂉 卢 卤 卤 卤 卤 卤 卤 鹵

salt

The shape of a salt crystal in a pocket.

55d **鹸**

ケン・カン・セン

丶 ⺊ 𠂉 卢 卤 卤 卤 卤 卤 卤 鹵 鹵' 鹵^ 鹵^ 鹵^ 鹸 鹸 鹸 鹸

saltiness

salt 鹵 [ロ] + all 㑒 [セン]

This character refers to lye that was used before soap was created. Lye is an alkaline(鹵) solution that worked like soap to make everything(㑒) clean.

石鹸[せっけん] soap -153a 55d

55e **倹**

ケン

丿 亻 亻' 亻^ 亻^ 亻^ 佮 佮 倹 倹

frugal

person 亻[52] [ニン・ジン] + all 㑒 [セン]

When everyone(㑒) lives in a group, one must be frugal since there are other people(亻) watching.

節倹[せっけん] economy; frugality; thrift -109e 55e
倹約[けんやく] thrift; frugality; economy -55e 104a

Diagram for 𠂊

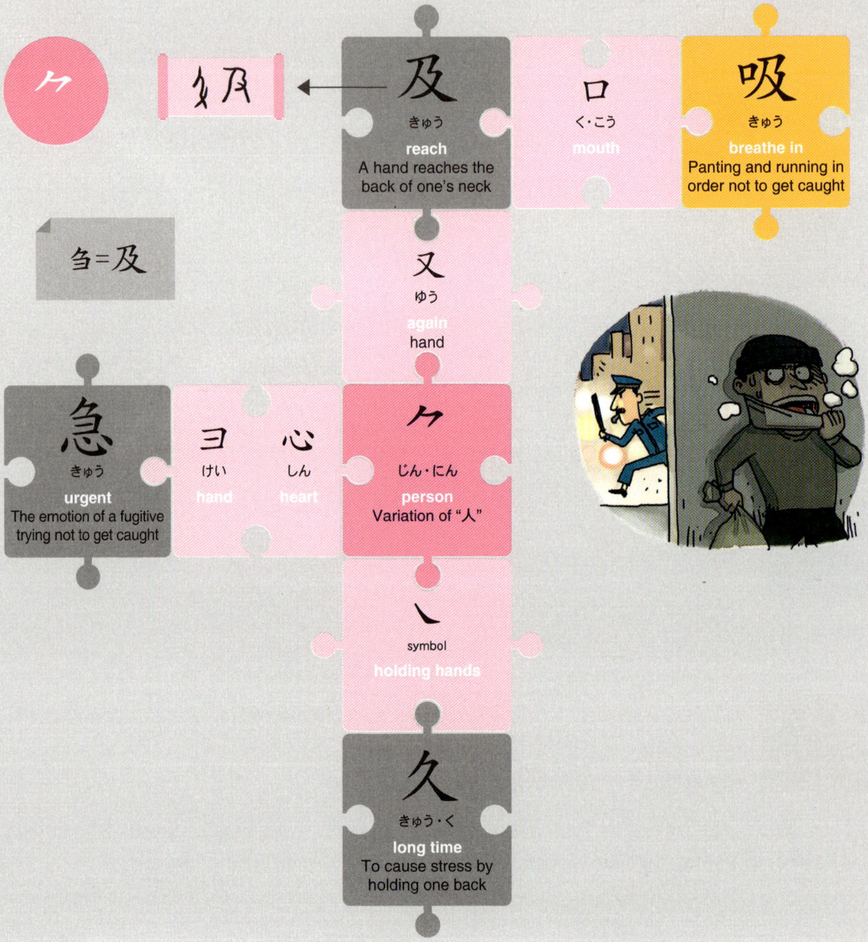

56 𠂊

ジン・ニン

person

ノ 𠂊

This character has a different shape but means the same as a “person 人[51].” It is sometimes used to give a different meaning to a character. The same shape doesn't necessarily mean that it always has the same meaning.

* This character isn't used alone and isn't a radical, but we mention it here because it has many uses. For the sake of convenience, we will call it ‘person.’

56a 及

キュウ　および・およぶ・およぼす　　ノ 乃 及

reach

person 𠂊 [ジン・ニン] + hand/again 又[30][ユウ]

Someone's hand(又) is about to reach the back of a man(𠂊) who is running away.

及び[および] and; as well as	及ぶ[およぶ] reach; extend
及ぼす[およぼす] reach out	普及[ふきゅう] diffusion; dissemination -64c 56a

56b 吸

キュウ　すう　　丨 口 口 口 吖 吸 吸

breathe in

mouth 口[12][ク・コウ] + reach 及 [キュウ]

A person running as fast as they can so that they don't get caught(及) will be out of breath(口).

吸う[すう] breathe in; inhale; suck	呼吸[こきゅう] breathing; breath -179b 56b

56c 久

キュウ・ク　ひさしい　　ノ ク 久

long time

person 𠂊 [ジン・ニン] + holding hands ㇏ [symbol]

The shape of a person(𠂊) pulling someone else back(㇏). When one is being stopped from walking at normal speed, it takes 'a long time.'

久しい[ひさしい] long-time; old	永久[えいきゅう] permanent; foreverness -156a 56c

56d 急

キュウ　いそぐ　　ノ ク 午 刍 刍 刍 急 急 急

urgent

person 𠂊 [ジン・ニン] + hand ヨ[32][ケイ] + heart 心[26][シン]

This character describes the impatience(心) of a man(𠂊) running as fast as he can to avoid getting caught(ヨ). 𠂊 + ヨ = 及

急ぐ[いそぐ] hurry; hasten; rush	特急[とっきゅう] limited express (train) -37c 56d
急行[きゅうこう] express train; express -56d 48a	至急[しきゅう] urgent; pressing -90 56d

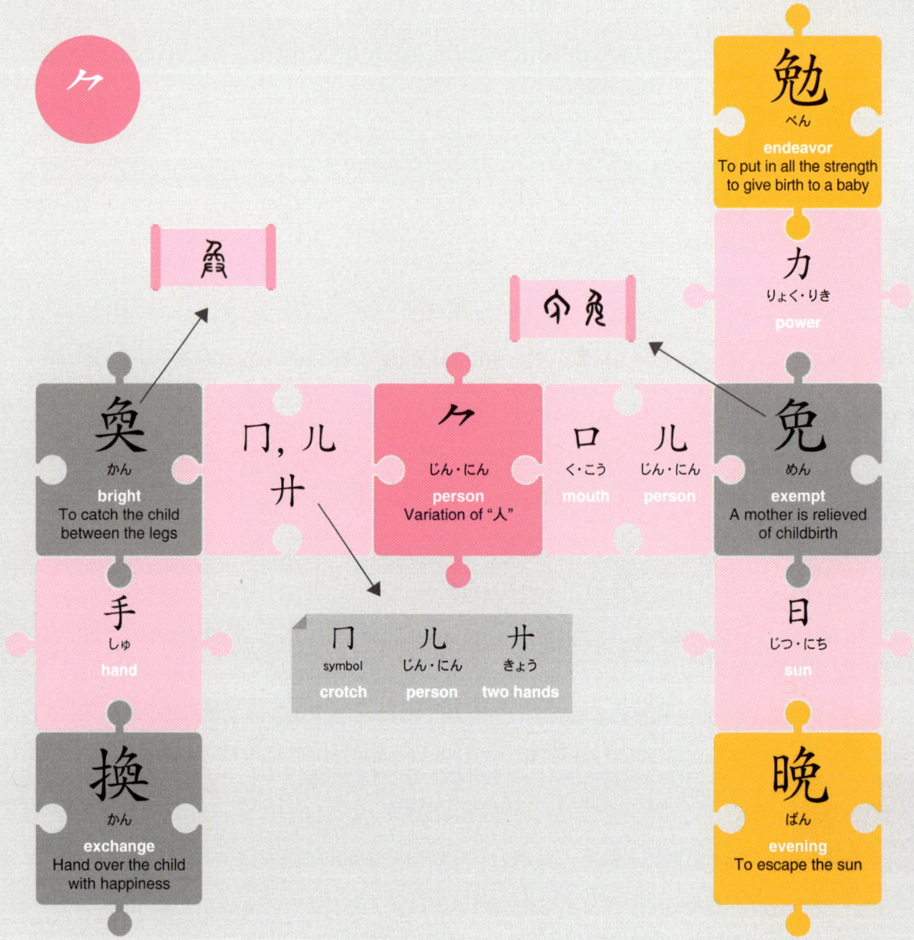

57 免

メン まぬかれる

ノ ⺈ ⺈ 㐫 ... 免

exempt

person ⺈ [ジン・ニン] + mouth 口[12][ク・コウ] + person 儿[58][ジン・ニン]

A mother(⺈) gives birth to a child(儿) from her womb(口). It signifies that she has 'escaped' from the pain, or from the guilt of not being able to bear children.

* In the past, not being able to have children was reason for divorce in China.

免れる[まぬかれる] escape; avoid; evade　　免許[めんきょ] license -57 96d

57a 勉

ベン

endeavor

exempt 免 [メン] + power 力[125] [リョク・リキ]

When a woman gives birth(免), she puts in all the strength(力) she has with great endeavor.

勉強[べんきょう] study; diligence -57a 143a

57b 晩

バン

evening; late

sun 日[170] [ジツ・ニチ] + exempt 免 [メン]

To escape(免) the sun(日) means it is evening. As the day ends, it also means late.

今晩[こんばん] tonight; this evening -54b 57b
今晩は[こんばんは] good evening -54b 57b
晩御飯[ばんごはん] dinner -57b 69c 117b
毎晩[まいばん] every evening; every night -79a 57b

57c 奐

カン

bright

person ⺈ [ジン・ニン] + crotch 冂 [symbol] + person 儿[58] [ジン・ニン] + two hands 大→廾[38] [キョウ]

A midwife catches the child(儿) with both hands(廾) from between the mother's(⺈) legs(冂). For a woman, childbirth is the most amazing miracle, a 'shining' accomplishment.

57d 換

カン かえる

exchange

hand 扌=手[28] [シュ] + bright 奐 [カン]

With her hands(扌), the midwife hands over the child to the mother who is shining(奐) with happiness. As she is now a mother, this character signifies change.

換える[かえる] exchange; interchange
交換[こうかん] exchange; interchange -1a 57d
乗(り)換え[のりかえ] transfer (trains, buses, etc.); connection -165d 57d

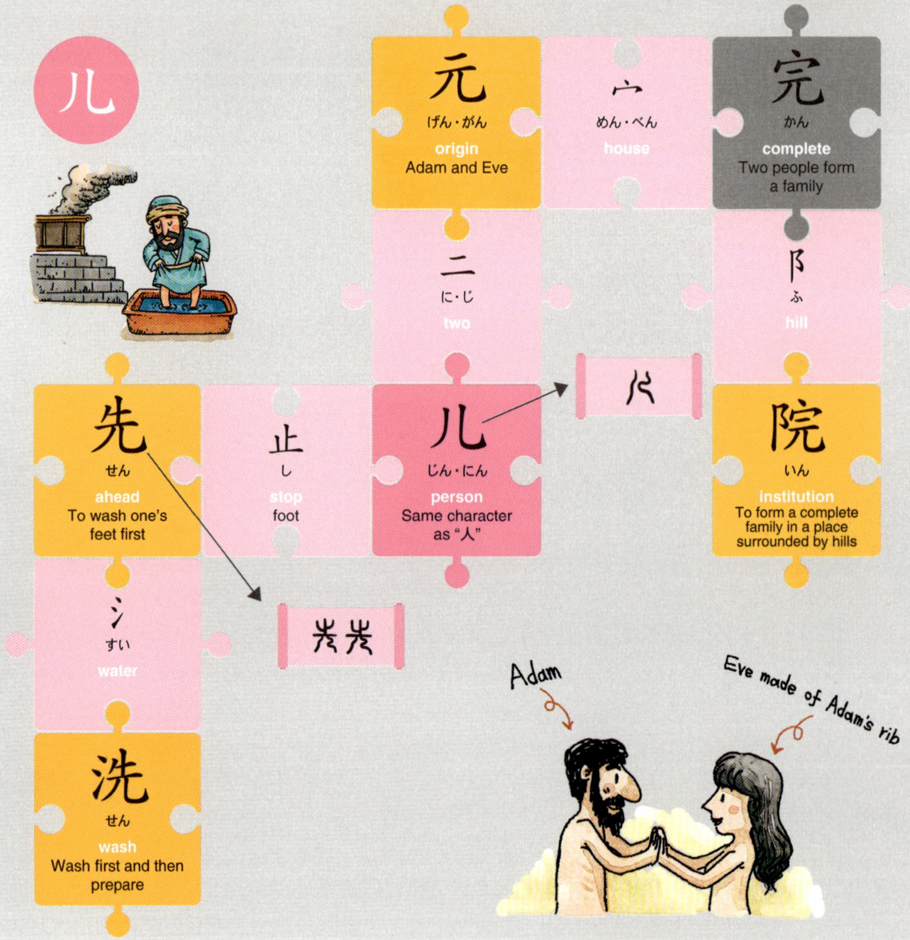

58 **儿**

ジン・ニン

丿 儿

person

The ancient character shows that it is the same character as “人,[51]” and it means the same thing, ‘person.’

58a 元

ゲン・ガン もと

一 二 テ 元

origin

two 二[176][ニ・ジ] + person 儿 [ジン・ニン]

The Bible says that two(二) people(儿), Adam and Eve, were the origin of all people.

元気[げんき] energy; vitality; vigor -58a 158a　　元年[がんねん] first year -58a 96e

58b 完

カン

丶 丷 宀 宀 宇 宇 完

complete

house 宀[113][メン・ベン] + origin 元 [ゲン・ガン]

God created people(元) by forming Eve out of Adam's rib and told them to form a family(宀). The last living form God created to complete creation was Eve.

完成[かんせい] completion -58b 92a

58c 院

イン

⁷ 阝 阝' 阝'' 阝宀 阝宀 阝宀 陉 院

institution

hill 阝[116][フ] + complete 完 [カン]

God prepared a place called Eden, surrounded by hills(阝), for Adam and Eve's perfect(完) family. This character means 'a home surrounded by a wall with a countyard in the middle.' It is used to name public institutions like hospitals or courthouses.

病院[びょういん] hospital -65a 58c　　寺院[じいん] temple -37 58c

58d 先

セン さき

ノ 𠂉 十 生 牛 先

ahead

foot/stop 㐅→止[44][シ] + person 儿 [ジン・ニン]

Before entering a sacred place, a person(儿) must first wash his feet(止).

* "止" is the shape of a foot and means 'foot.'

先月[せんげつ] last month -58d 172　　先週[せんしゅう] last week -58d 122b
先生[せんせい] teacher; doctor; (honorific) sir -58d 162
先頭[せんとう] head; vanguard; first -58d 112c

58e 洗

セン あらう

丶 丶 氵 氵 汁 汁 洪 洪 洗

wash

water 氵[15][スイ] + ahead 先 [セン]

To enter into where the altar is, one must first(先) wash with water(氵) and prepare for the service.

洗う[あらう] wash, launder　　洗面[せんめん] wash up, wash one's face -58e 6a

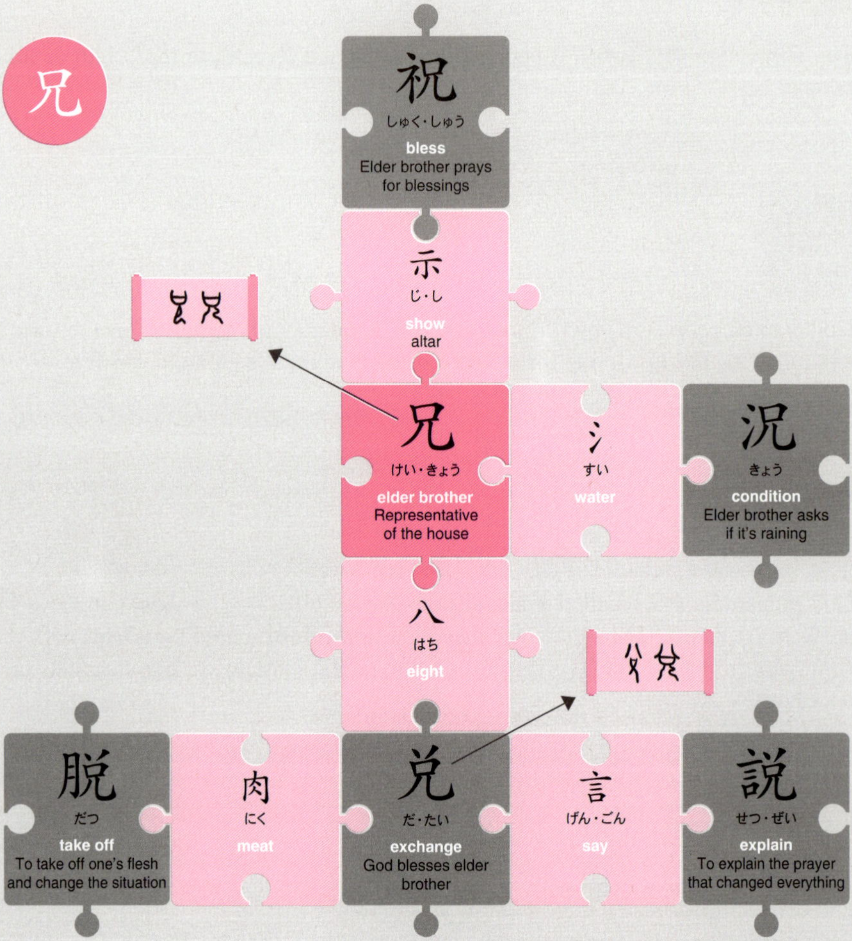

59 **兄** ケイ・キョウ あに

elder brother

mouth 口[12] [ク・コウ] + person 儿[58] [ジン・ニン]

A person(儿) with a large mouth(口). This is the person(儿) who speaks up(口) when discussing family matters and means 'elder brother.'

お兄さん[おにいさん] elder (older) brother	兄弟[きょうだい] brother; sibling -59 87a

59a 祝

` ラ ネ ネ ネ' ネ'' ネ口 ネ므 祝

シュク・シュウ いわう

bless; celebrate

altar/show ネ=示[99][ジ・シ] + elder brother 兄 [ケイ・キョウ]

As representative of the family, the elder brother(兄) goes to the altar(示) to pray for his wish to come true.

* "ネ" is the shape of the altar or pedestal.

祝う[いわう] congratulate; celebrate 祝日[しゅくじつ] national holiday -59a 170

59b 況

` ` 氵 氵' 氵'' 氵口 氵므 況

キョウ

condition

water 氵[157][スイ] + elder brother 兄 [ケイ・キョウ]

The elder brother(兄) who was praying for rain(氵) during the drought is enquiring with someone about the situation.

好況[こうきょう] booming economy -78c 59b

59c 兑

` ` ` ` ` ` 兑

ダ・タイ

exchange

eight ソ→八[177][ハチ] + elder brother 兄 [ケイ・キョウ]

God is touched by the brother's(兄) prayer and sends down(八) blessings in the form of rain, which changes the situation.

* The "八" in this character describes 'blessings coming down from the heavens.'

59d 説

` 二 二 三 言 言 言 言 言' 言'' 言口 言므 説 説

セツ・ゼイ とく

explain

say 言[17][ゲン・ゴン] + exchange 兑 [ダ・タイ]

The elder brother who changed the situation(兑) explains in words(言) how he prayed.

説く[とく] explain; preach; persuade
解説[かいせつ] explanation; commentary; exposition -150a 59d

59e 脱

丿 刀 月 月 月' 月'' 月口 月므 脱 脱 脱

ダツ ぬぐ

take off

meat 月→肉[151][ニク] + exchange 兑 [ダ・タイ]

Thanks to the gods' blessings, he has escaped the pain of the flesh(肉) and changed(兑) his life.

* When "月[172]" is used as part of another character it means "肉."

脱ぐ[ぬぐ] take off; undress; strip (off) 脱出[だっしゅつ] escape; break-out -59e 131c

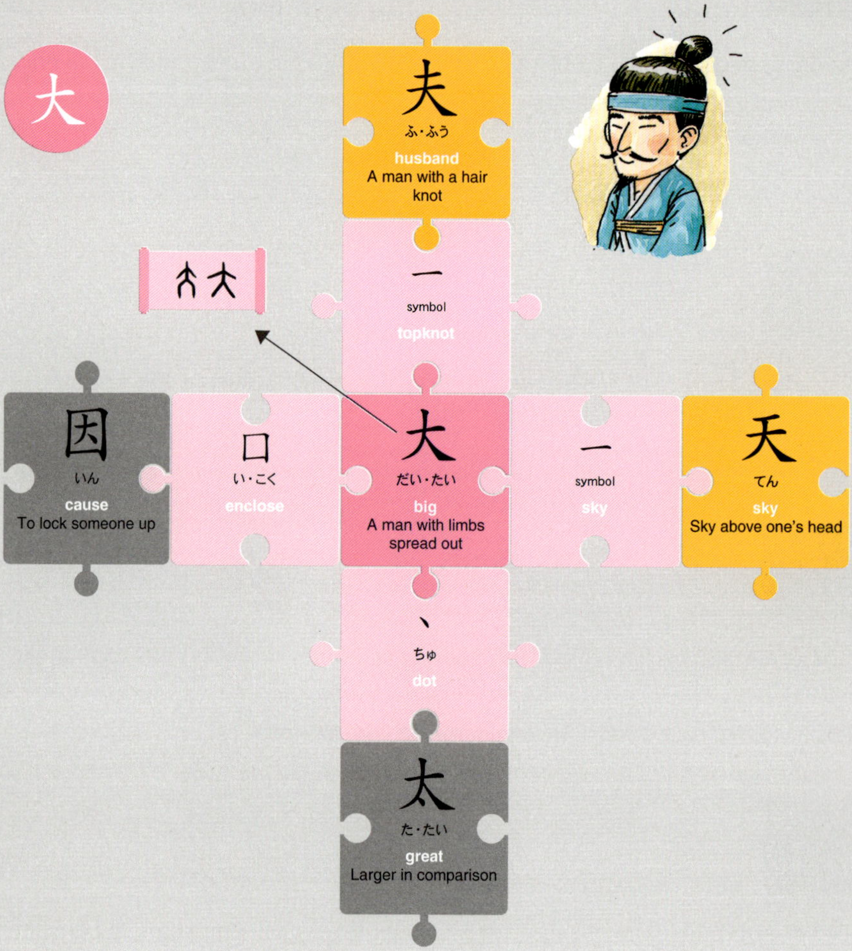

60 **大** ダイ・タイ おお・おおいに・おおきい

一 ナ 大

big

A person(人[51]) with four limbs spread out(一). This character is just another form of a 'person.'

大きい[おおきい] big; large; great
大きな[おおきな] big; large; great
大ぜい[おおぜい] large (great) number of people; many
大人[おとな] adult -60 51
大いに[おおいに] very; much; greatly
大変[たいへん] very; greatly; awfully -60 43d
大学[だいがく] university -60 77b
大好(き)[だいすき] loveable; very likeable -60 78c
大丈夫[だいじょうぶ] safe; all right; okay -60 34d 60a
大使館[たいしかん] embassy -60 31b 152d

60a 夫

一 二 夫 夫

フ・フウ おっと

husband

top knot 一 [symbol] + person/big 大 [ダイ・タイ]

In ancient China, a married man tied his hair up on the top of his head. A man(大) with a hair knot(一) therefore means 'husband.'

＊"一" symbolizes the hair knot and has no extra meaning.

丈夫[じょうぶ] healthy; strong; robust -34d 60a　大丈夫[だいじょうぶ] safe; all right; okay -60 34d 60a
夫妻[ふさい] man and wife; married couple -60a 78e

60b 天

一 二 チ 天

テン

sky

sky 一 [symbol] + person/big 大 [ダイ・タイ]

The sky is high above our heads and is described with "一" above a person(大).

＊"一" symbolizes the sky and has no extra meaning.

天気[てんき] weather -60b 158a　天気予報[てんきよほう] weather (fore)cast -60b 158a 4a 30b

60c 太

一 ナ 大 太

タ・タイ ふとい・ふとる

great

big 大 [ダイ・タイ] + dot 丶 [チュ]

"大" with a dot(丶) stresses the size and means 'great, grand or thick.'

太い[ふとい] fat; thick　太る[ふとる] grow fat; gain weight

60d 因

丨 冂 冃 冄 因 因

イン よる

cause

enclose 囗[16] [イ・コク] + person/big 大 [ダイ・タイ]

A person(大) is arrested and taken to prison(囗) because there is a reason for him to be locked up.

因る[よる] be caused by; result from; be due to　原因[げんいん] cause -106d 60d

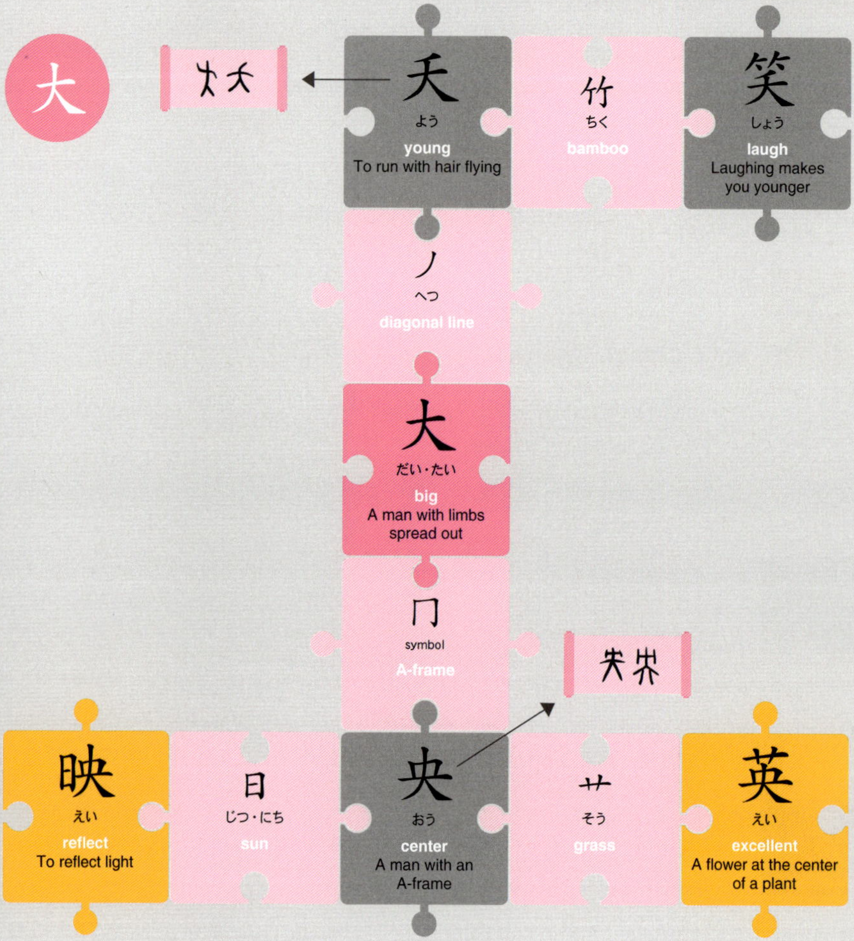

61 夭

ヨウ

young

person/big 大 [ダイ・タイ] + diagonal line ノ [179e][ヘツ]

ノ 二 チ 夭

A man(大) running energetically with hair flying(ノ) is a young man.

* “ノ” has no set meaning and can be interpreted in many ways.

61a 笑

ノ ト ⺮ 𥫗 ⺮ 竺 笑 (stroke order)

ショウ　わらう

laugh

bamboo 竹[169][チク] + young 夭 [ヨウ]

A popular Chinese saying goes, "One laugh makes you younger, one frown makes you older." When you laugh, you appear younger(夭) and will live longer(竹) too.

* Bamboo(竹) lives for many years, stays green all year round, and has the same pronunciation as "bless 祝[59a] [シュク・シュウ]." It is a symbol of longevity and is often used to pray with.

笑う[わらう] laugh; smile; bloom　　笑顔[えがお] a smiling (beaming) face -61a 5d

61b 央

丶 冂 口 央 央

オウ

center

person/big 大 [ダイ・タイ] + A-frame 冂 [symbol]

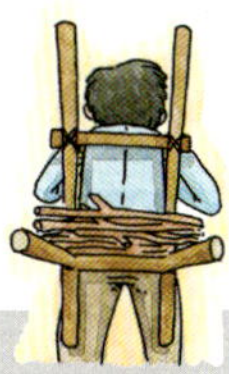

A man(大) carrying an A-frame(冂) in the center of his back to carry heavy things.

中央[ちゅうおう] center; middle -179d 61b

61c 英

一 十 艹 艹 芇 苎 英 英

エイ

excellent

grass 艹[161][ソウ] + center 央 [オウ]

The center(央) of any plant(艹) is the flower, because it's beautiful and is used to multiply. The meaning of 'flower or excel' comes from that. This character is used in the kanji name for Great Britain, the land 'where the sun never set.'

英語[えいご] English -61c 176c　　英国[えいこく] Great Britain -61c 86a

61d 映

丨 冂 月 日 日' 日冖 日口 映 映

エイ　うつす・うつる

reflect; project

sun 日[170] [ジツ・ニチ] + center 央 [オウ]

To reflect the sun(日) with a mirror and make it shine in the center(央).

映す[うつす] reflect; project　　映る[うつる] be reflected; be projected
映画館[えいがかん] movie theater; cinema -61d 122d 152d
映画[えいが] movie; film -61d 122d

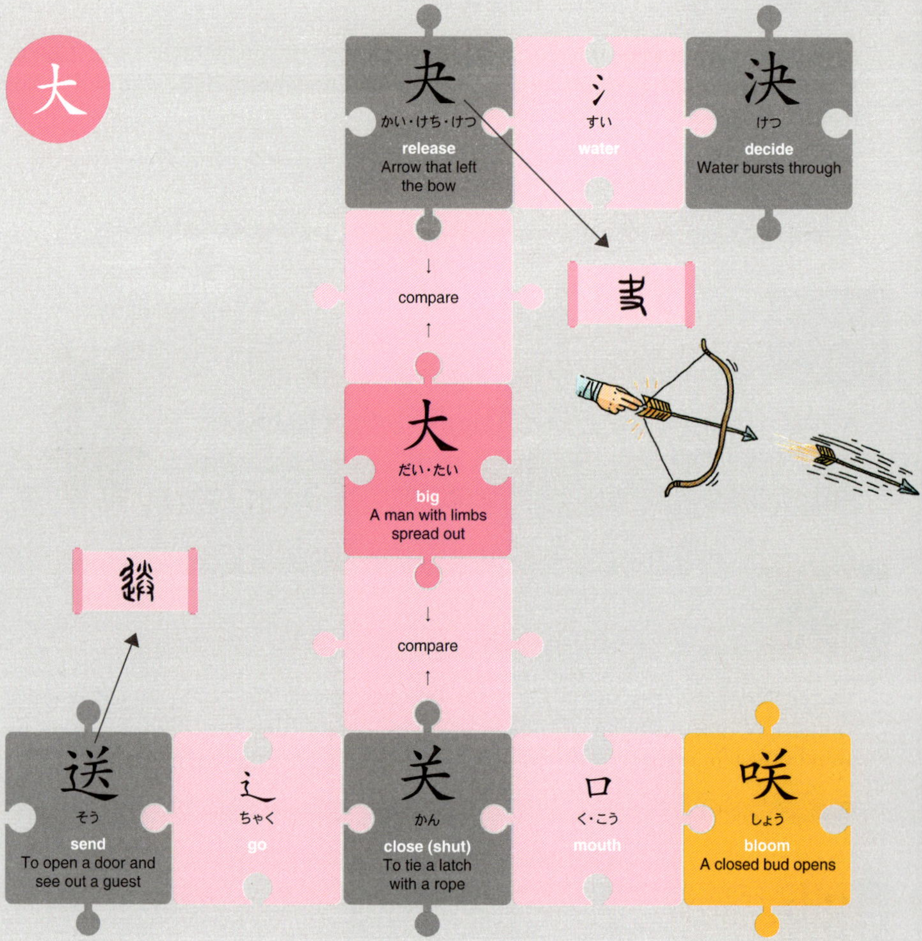

62 **夬**

カイ・ケチ・ケツ

release; open

arrow 矢[89] [シ] + hand ヨ[32] [ケイ]

A hand(ヨ) fitting the notch of the arrow(矢) into the bowstring. An arrow flies, which is where this character got its meaning of 'open or release.'

* Notch of arrow: The part at the end of the arrow that fits into the bowstring.

62a 決

ケツ きまる・きめる

丶 丷 氵 氵 江 決 決

decide

water 氵[157] [スイ] + release 夬 [ケチ・ケツ]

When a timely decision provides a permanent solution to a persistent problem, it can be said that 'everything works out like water(氵) bursting through(夬).'

決(ま)る[きまる] be decided; be settled
決める[きめる] decide; settle
解決[かいけつ] settlement; solution -150a 62a

62b 关

カン

丶 丷 丷 兰 并 关

close (shut)

thread 丷→糸[104] [シ] + latch/bar 一 [symbol] + two hands 大→廾[38] [キョウ]

To close a door means to tie down the door latch(一) with a rope(糸) so it can't be undone, even with both hands(廾).

* The traditional character(關) shows the rope(丝→絲) tied around the latch(丱) on the door(門[115]). Compare with "開[38d]".

62c 咲

ショウ さく

丨 ㄇ 口 口' 口丷 口䒑 口兰 咩 咲

bloom

mouth 口[12] [ク・コウ] + close 关 [カン]

When a closed(关) flower bud opens its mouth(口), a flower blooms.

咲く[さく] bloom

62d 送

ソウ おくる

丶 丷 丷 兰 并 关 关 关 送

send

close 关 [カン] + go 辶[49] [チャク]

To let a guest leave, one must open the closed(关) door so the guest can go out(辶).

* The ancient character shows a person holding up a light or fire(火[124]) with both hands(廾[38]), sending off the guest who is leaving(辶).

送る[おくる] send; dispatch
送金[そうきん] remittance -62d 154
放送[ほうそう] broadcasting -126d 62d
輸送[ゆそう] transport; transportation -98d 62d

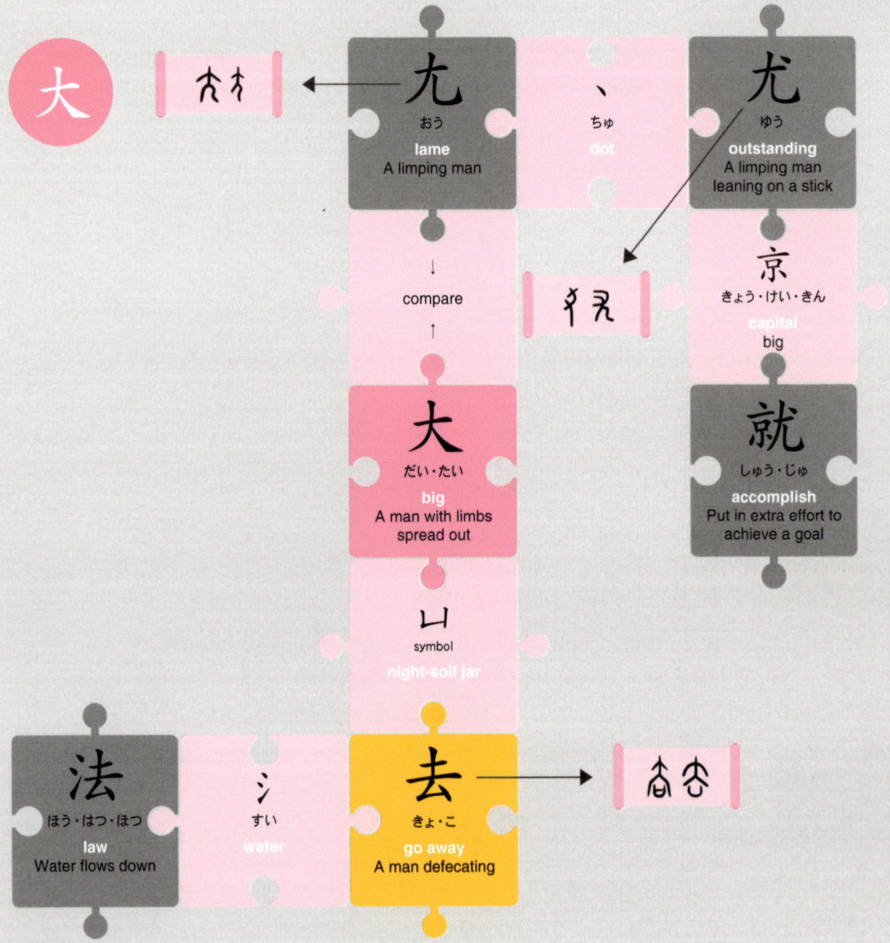

63 尢

オウ

lame

一 ナ 尢

"大[60]" is the shape of an adult standing with arms spread out. One leg of the character is hook-shaped(し[67c]), showing that he's lame.

63a 尤

ユウ もっとも — 一 ナ 尢 尤

outstanding

lame 尢 [オウ] + dot 丶 181 [チュ]

A limping man(尢) with a cane(丶) will stand out.

尤も[もっとも] (quite) right; plausible; natural
尤物[ゆうぶつ] something superior; beautiful woman - 63a 41a

63b 就

シュウ・ジュ つく・つける — 丶 亠 亠 六 亩 亨 亨 京 京 就 就 就

accomplish

big/capital 京 2 [キョウ・ケイ・キン] + outstanding 尤 [ユウ]

This character shows a physically challenged person(尤) who puts in extra effort to get closer to achieving a large goal(京).

* "京" is the shape of a large building, so it includes the meaning 'large.'

就く[つく] enter; ascend; take (seat, position, etc.)
就ける[つける] install (a person in a position); appoint (to a post)

63c 去

キョ・コ さる — 一 十 土 去 去

go away

person/big 土→大 60 [ダイ・タイ] + night-soil jar ム→凵 [symbol]

A man(大) sitting above a toilet(凵) to defecate(夻). Because feces exit the body, this character came to mean 'to go.'

* The "ム 76 [シ]" in "去" does not mean 'personal' or 'fetus.' Same shape doesn't always translate to same meaning.

去る[さる] leave, go away, pass
去年[きょねん] last year - 63c 96e

63d 法

ホウ・ハツ・ホツ — 丶 丶 氵 氵 汁 注 法 法

law

water 氵 157 [スイ] + go away 去 [キョ・コ]

It is a natural phenomenon for water(氵) to flow(去) from high to low altitudes. For people to live in harmony, there are laws that must be adhered to.

* For water(氵) to go(去), it has to flow.

文法[ぶんぽう] grammar - 105 63d
法則[ほうそく] law; rule - 63d 147a
法律[ほうりつ] law - 63d 33a

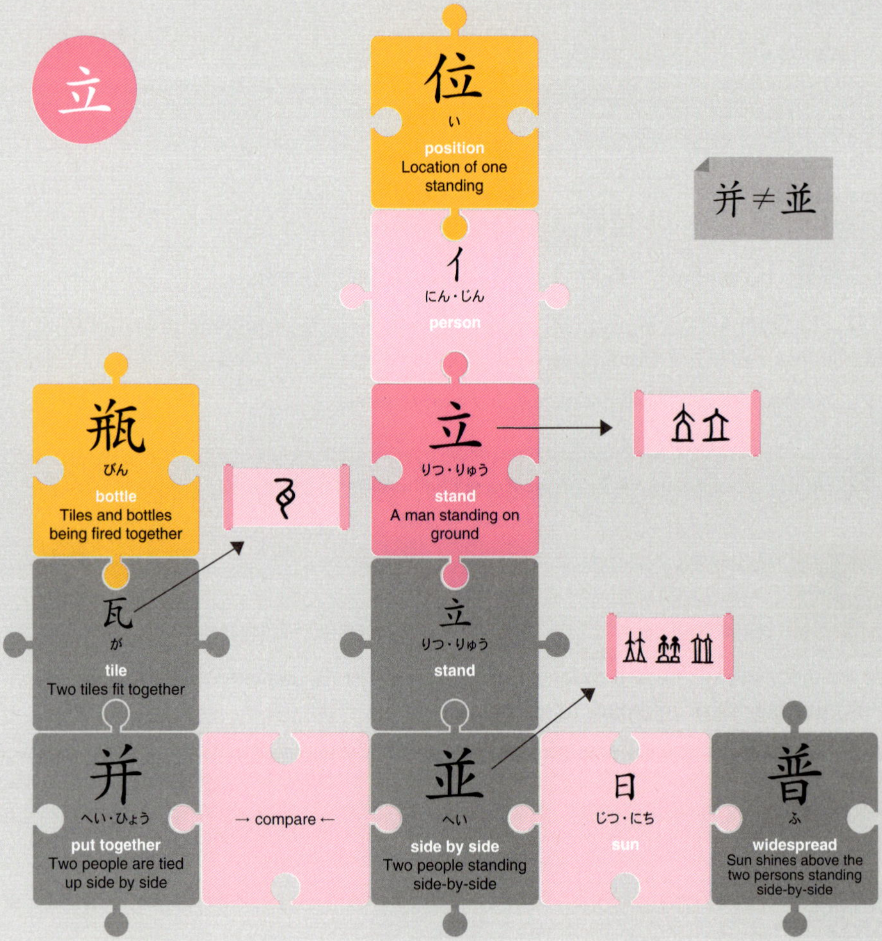

64 **立** リツ・リュウ たつ・たてる ` 亠 亣 立 立

stand

A man(大[60]) standing with two feet firmly on the ground(一).

立つ[たつ] stand; rise	立てる[たてる] stand up; put up; erect
立派[りっぱ] splendid; fine; handsome; elegant -64 157b	

64a **位** イ くらい ノ 亻 亻' 亻亠 亻亣 亻立 位

position

person 亻[52][ニン・ジン] + stand 立 [リツ・リュウ]

The location or position of where a person(亻) is standing(立) shows his title.

位地[いち] status; position; rank -64a 68b　　位置[いち] position; situation -64a 8c

64b 並

ヘイ　ならびに・ならべる・ならぶ・なみ

丶 丷 䒑 䒑 並 並 並 並

side by side

stand 立 [リツ・リュウ] + stand 立 [リツ・リュウ]

Two people(竝) standing(立) beside each other.

並びに[ならびに] and; as well as　　並べる[ならべる] line up; set up
並ぶ[ならぶ] stand in a queue (row); stand in line
並(み)[なみ] average; common; ordinary

64c 普

フ

丶 丷 䒑 䒑 並 並 並 並 普 普 普 普

widespread

side by side 並 [ヘイ] + sun 日 170 [ジツ・ニチ]

This character portrays the image of the sun(日) shining above two persons standing side-by-side(並). The Sun(日) shines and disseminates its light to everybody(並), and, therefore, the meaning of 'general' is derived out of it.

普通[ふつう] usual; ordinary; general -64c 129b

64d 并

ヘイ・ヒョウ

丶 丷 䒑 丷 并 并

put together

Two people(从) are tied up(二) side by side so they do not part.

64e 瓦

が　かわら

一 厂 F 瓦 瓦

tile

Tiles shaped to lock together as in a pair of male and female parts.

煉瓦[れんが] brick -167d 64e

64f 瓶

ビン

丶 丷 䒑 丷 并 并 并 瓶 瓶 瓶 瓶

bottle

put together 并 [ヘイ・ヒョウ] + tile 瓦 [ガ]

To put bottles (ceramic ware) and tiles(瓦) together(并) into a kiln and fire them up.

* China was the first East-Asian country to use ceramics as everyday items.

花瓶[かびん] (flower) vase -52b 64f

Diagram for 疒

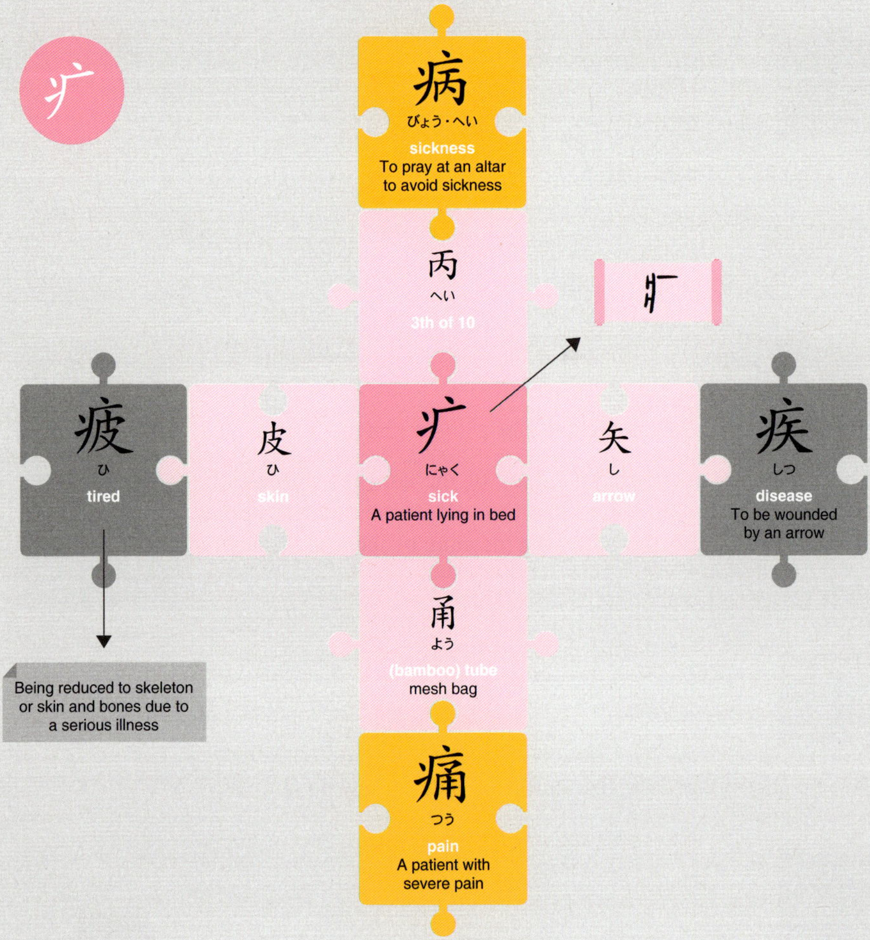

65 疒 ニャク

丶 亠 广 疒 疒

sick

A patient(亠[1]) is sick and is lying in bed(丬[168b]).

65a 病 ビョウ・ヘイ　やむ

丶 亠 广 广 疒 疒 疔 病 病 病

sickness

sick 疒 [ニャク] + 3rd of 10 丙 [ヘイ]

To pray to the ancestors on the high tables(丙) so that no one will be sick(疒).

＊"丙" depicts a table with very long legs where tablets of one's ancestors are kept.

病む[やむ] fall ill; be ill	病院[びょういん] hospital -65a 58c
病気[びょうき] disease; illness; sickness -65a 158a	看病[かんびょう] nursing -7a 65a

65b 疾

シツ

丶 亠 广 疒 疒 疒 疒 疒 疾 疾

disease

sick 疒 [ニャク] + arrow 矢[89] [シ]

A soldier wounded by an arrow(矢) and lying in bed(疒) is a good example of a sick person.

疾病[しっぺい] disease; illness -65a 65b

65c 痛

ツウ　いたい・いたむ・いためる

丶 亠 广 疒 疒 疒 疒 疒 疖 痌 痛 痛

pain

sick 疒 [ニャク] + mesh bag/(bamboo) tube 甬[129a] [ヨウ]

A sick(疒) man suffering from pain that feels like wind seeping through a net(甬).

痛い[いたい] painful; sore	痛む[いたむ] hurt; suffer
痛める[いためる] hurt; injure; cause pain	頭痛[ずつう] headache -112c 65c

65d 疲

ヒ　つかれる

丶 亠 广 疒 疒 疒 疒 疒 疲 疲

tired

sick 疒 [ニャク] + skin 皮[149] [ヒ]

A tired, exhausted person is someone who is sick(疒) and is so thin that there's nothing left but skin(皮) on bones.

疲れる[つかれる] tired; exhausted

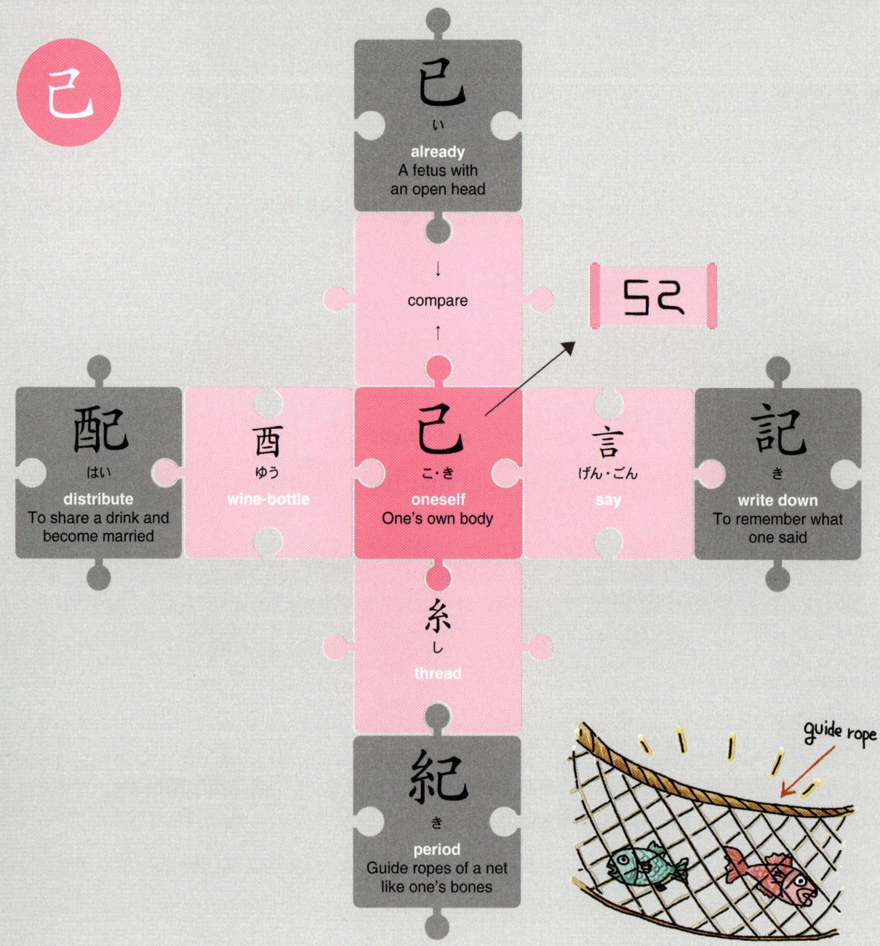

66 己

コ・キ

oneself; body

㇆ コ 己

We cannot tell what "己" originally meant by its ancient character. But nowadays, it means 'body or self.'

* It looks similar to "已" and "巳," but the three are completely different.

自己[じこ] self; ego -6 66

66a 已

イ すでに

ㄱ コ 已

already; cease

A depiction of a fetus in the mother's womb. We can't be sure of the root of this character, but let's assume the opening in the head means the fetus' life is already over.

* The ancient character looks similar to "巳."

已に[すでに] already

66b 記

キ しるす

﹅ 亠 亠 亖 言 言 言 訁 訂 記

write down; remember

say 言 17 [ゲン・ゴン] + oneself 己 [コ・キ]

One must remember what words(言) you(己) spoke.

記す[しるす] write (put) down; note	記者[きしゃ] journalist; reporter - 66b 82
日記[にっき] diary; journal - 170 66b	筆記[ひっき] note-taking; record - 33d 66b

66c 紀

キ

𠃋 幺 幺 糸 糸 糸 紀 紀 紀

period; discipline

thread 糸 104 [シ] + body/oneself 己 [コ・キ]

A skeleton is a frame and helps maintain the shape of one's body(己). A fishing net has something similar called a guide rope, a thick rope(糸) that goes around the net to retain its shape. That is why this character means a period, because such frames need to be in regular intervals to be effective. Also, society needs rules to stay in working form.

世紀[せいき] century; era - 162c 66c

66d 配

ハイ くばる

一 丆 万 丙 两 西 酉 酉 酉 配

distribute

wine-bottle 酉 133 [ユウ] + body/oneself 己 [コ・キ]

A man and a woman must share a drink(酉) at the wedding to become a married couple, with one body(己).

* The wine that the bride and groom share in a traditional Chinese ceremony is a ritual to wish fertility.

配る[くばる] distribute; deal out; apportion	心配[しんぱい] worry; anxiety; concern - 26 66d
配達[はいたつ] delivery - 66d 49d	

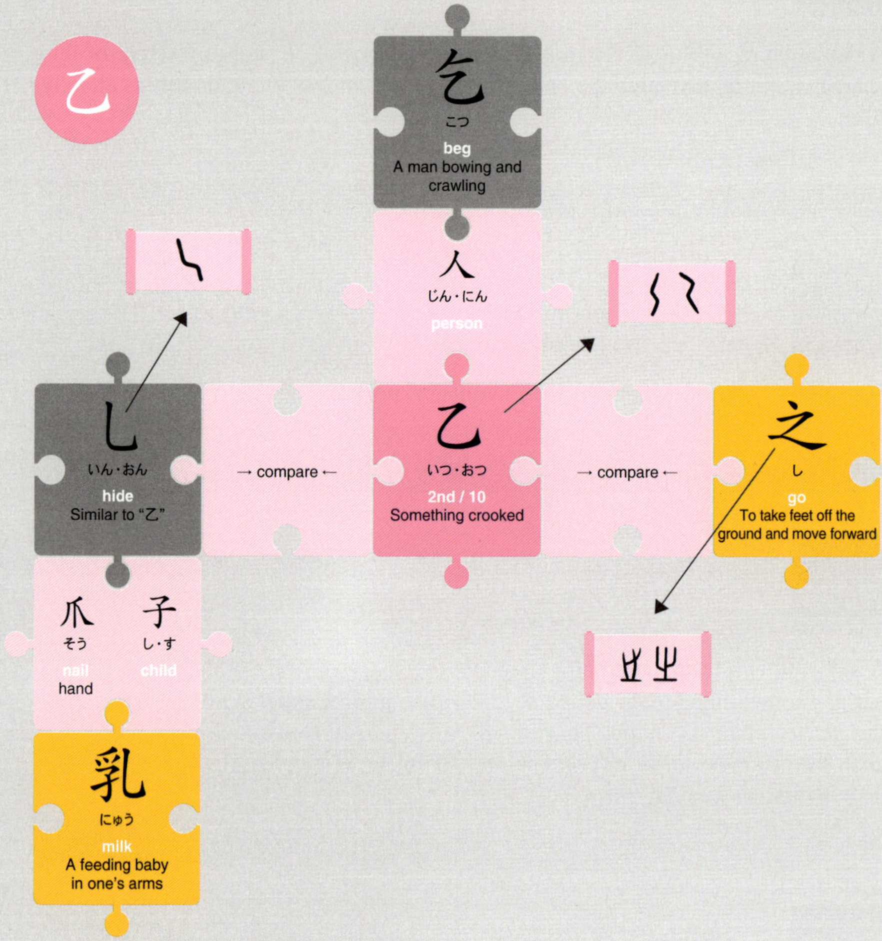

67 乙

イツ・オツ

2nd/10

In the spring, new buds and sprouts emerge, crooked and curved at first. This character is also the shape of someone cowering and begging. It's also the second out of the ten calendar signs.

67a 乞

ノ 𠂉 乞

コツ

beg

person 𠂉→人[51][ジン・ニン] + hunched stance/2nd of 10 乙 [イツ・オツ]

A man(人) is hunched over(乙) in a cowardly posture to beg.

67b 之

丶 ㇇ 之

シ これ

go

Although it looks similar to "乙," this character depicts a foot(止[44]) stepping on ground(一) to go somewhere.

之/此れ[これ] this; this person; now -67b / 72a

67c 乚

乚

イン・オン

hide

It is never used as a separate character and it means 'to hide.' But when used as part of another character, instead of adding any meaning, it just represents 'something crooked.'

* It's considered a radical like "乙."

67d 乳

乳

ニュウ ちち

milk

hand/nail 爫 = 爪[29][ソウ] + child 子[77] [シ・ス] + hide 乚 [イン・オン]

A child(子) held in its mother's hands(爫) drinking milk from the breast(乚).

牛乳[ぎゅうにゅう] (cow's) milk -137 67d

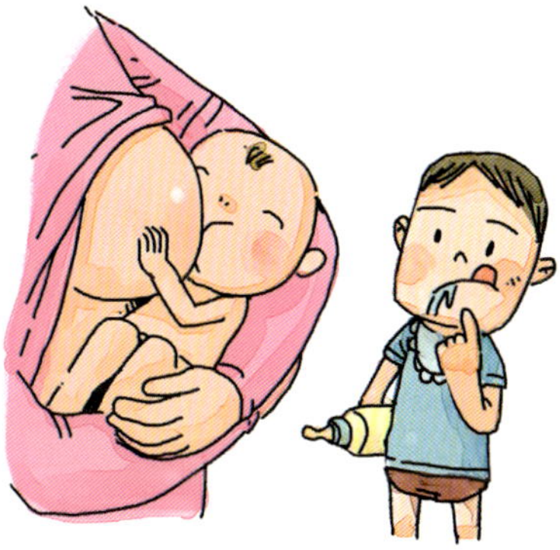

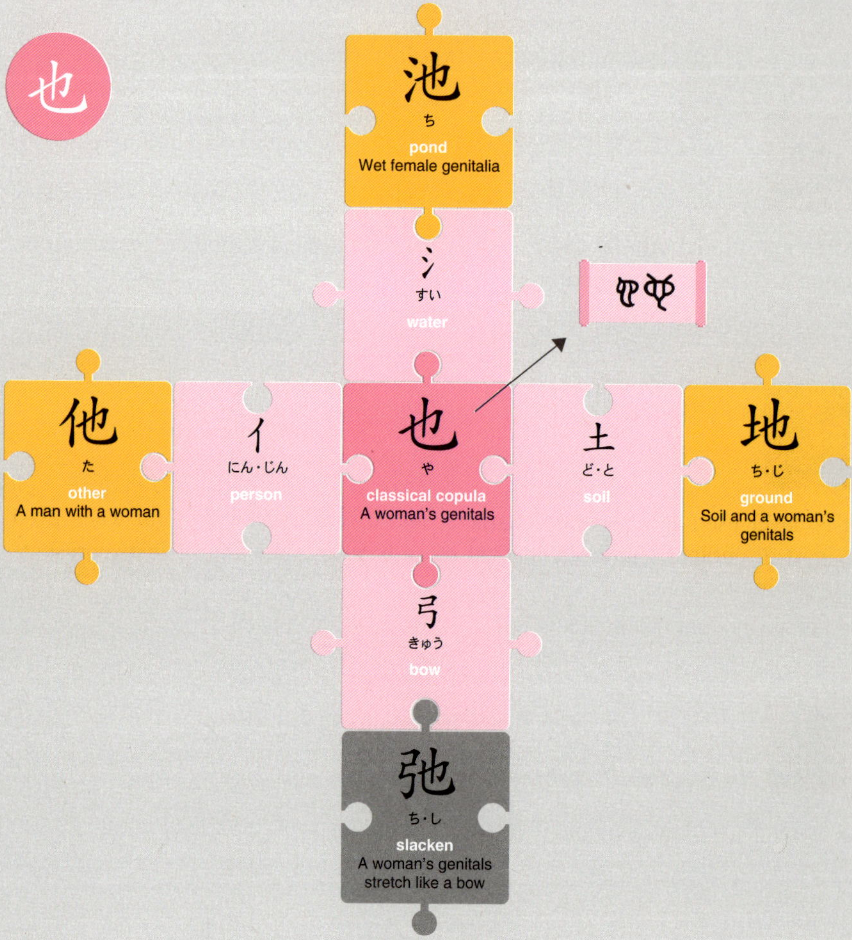

68 也

ヤ

classical copula

It's said to be the shape of a woman's genitals. It's also a postpositional particle that comes at the end of a sentence.

* This character is listed here because the radical of "也" is "乙[67]."

68a 池

チ いけ

、 丶 氵 汁 汋 池

pond

water 氵[157] [スイ] + female genitals/copula 也 [ヤ]

A woman's genitals(也) are usually damp(氵) like a pond full of water(氵).

電池[でんち] battery -159c 68a

68b 地

チ・ジ

一 十 土 圠 坾 地

ground

soil 土[120] [ド・ト] + female genitals/copula 也 [ヤ]

Soil or the land is where the food chain begins and is the basis of all life forms. This character is formed with soil(土), which most ground is made of, and a woman's genitals(也).

地下鉄[ちかてつ] subway -68b 173b 154d

地図[ちず] map -68b 16d

位地[いち] status; position; rank -64a 68b

地理[ちり] geography -68b 86e

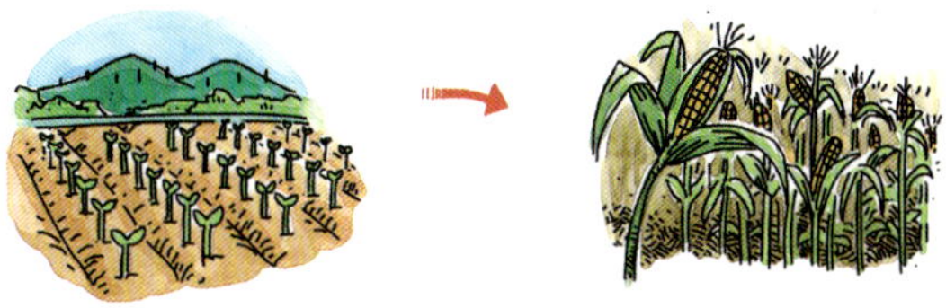

68c 弛

チ・シ ゆるむ

乛 コ 弓 弜 弛 弛

slacken

bow 弓[87] [キュウ] + female genitals/copula 也 [ヤ]

A woman's genitals(也) stretch like a bow(弓) when she gives birth, so this character came to mean 'relax.'

弛む[ゆるむ] loosen; slacken; relax

68d 他

タ ほか

ノ イ 仂 他 他

other

person 亻[52] [ニン・ジン] + female genitals/copula 也 [ヤ]

A person(亻) beside a woman's genitals(也) means 'other things or other people.' It also means that a man(亻) and a woman(也) have different characters.

他界[たかい] pass away; die; another world -68d 51b

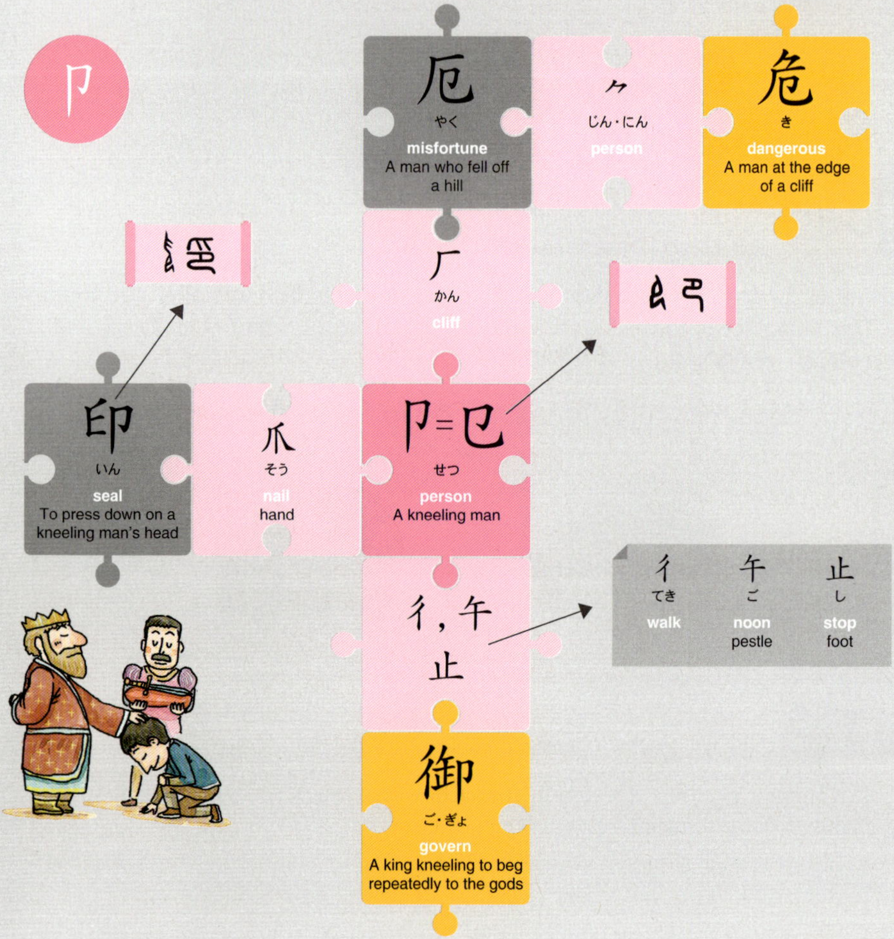

69	卩	ヒツ **person**	㇇ 卩

A person crouching in a deep bow or a person who is kneeling.

69a 厄

ヤク

一 厂 厅 厄

misfortune

cliff 厂[117][カン] + kneel/person 㔾=卩 [セツ]

A person(㔾) who met a disaster by falling off a cliff(厂).

厄介[やっかい] trouble; nuisance; bother; burden -69a 51a

69b 危

キ あぶない・あやうい

ノ ク 仒 产 户 危

dangerous

person ⺈[56][ジン・ニン] + misfortune 厄 [ヤク]

A man(⺈) standing dangerously at the edge of a cliff, where 'falling' means a certain disaster(厄).

危ない[あぶない] dangerous; risky; anxious　危うい[あやうい] dangerous; risky
危険[きけん] danger; risk; hazard -69b 116c

69c 御

ゴ・ギョ お

ノ 彡 彳 彳 𠂉 彳 ... 御

govern

walk 彳[48][テキ] + pestle/noon 午[96c][ゴ] + foot/stop 止[44][シ] + kneel/person 卩 [セツ]

A king who rules or reigns went to the gods(彳, 止) and knelt(卩) repeatedly(午) to ask for guidance. This character is also affixed to nouns to show respect and humility.

* Someone using a pestle makes a repetitive movement, like a king asking repeatedly.

御中/御腹[おなか] abdomen; belly; stomach -69c 179d / 69c 46b
御飯[ごはん] expression of politeness for '食事(meal)' -69c 117b
昼御飯[ひるごはん] lunch; midday meal -170b 69c 117b　晩御飯[ばんごはん] dinner -57b 69c 117b

69d 印

イン しるし

´ 𠂆 F E E7 印

seal; print

hand/nail E→爪[29] [ソウ] + kneel/person 卩 [セツ]

As an act of acceptance, the Chinese gently placed a hand(爪) on the head of a kneeling man(卩). This character means 'seal or print.'

印象[いんしょう] impression -69d 136b　矢印[やじるし] arrow (mark or symbol) -89 69d

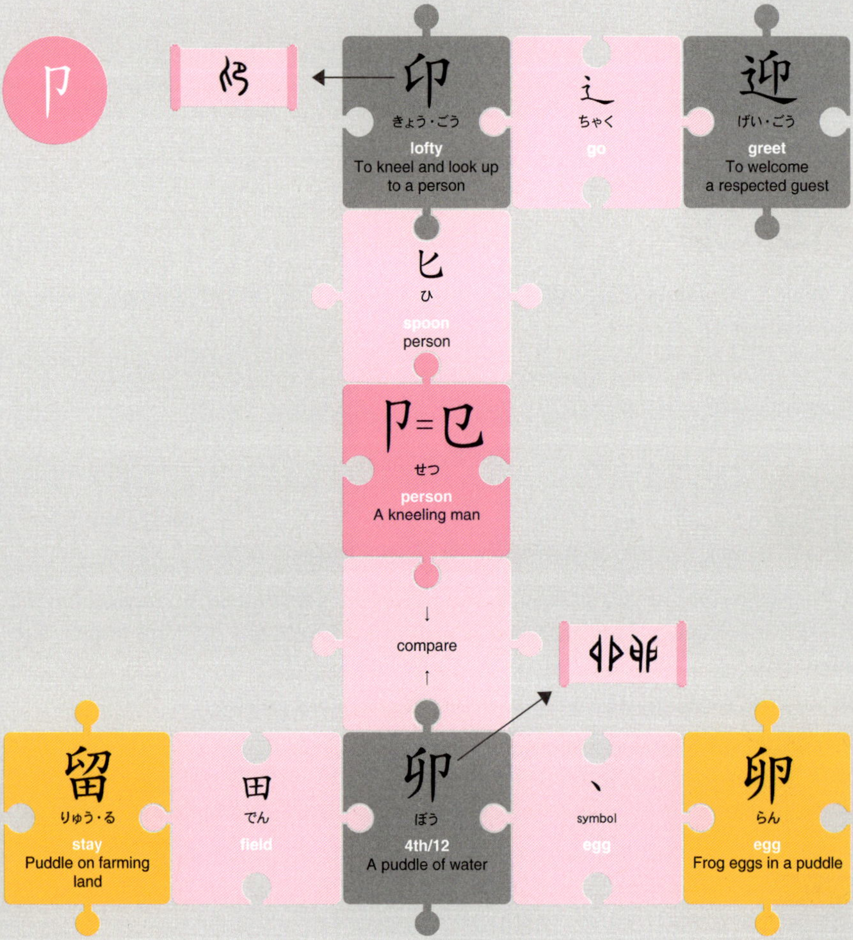

70 印

キョウ・ゴウ

lofty

person/spoon ⺊→匕[72] [ヒ] + kneel/person 卩[69] [セツ]

A kneeling(卩) person looking up to a person standing up(匕).

70a 迎

ゲイ・ゴウ むかえる

Stroke order: ノ ㇄ 卬 卬 卬 迎 迎

greet

look up to/lofty 卬 [キョウ・ゴウ] + go 辶[49] [チャク]

A man going out(辶) to welcome a guest who is much respected(卬).

迎える[むかえる] meet; receive; accept
迎え[むかえ] meeting; greeting; welcome

70b 卯

ボウ

Stroke order: ノ ㇄ 卯 卯 卯

4th/12

This character depicts a long puddle by the side of a field or a rice paddy, and is the fourth sign of the Chinese zodiac.

* Ancient characters show that despite looking like "卩[69]," the two characters have no connections.

70c 卵

ラン たまご

Stroke order: ノ ㇄ ㇄ 卯 卯 卵 卵

egg

puddle/4th of 12 卯 [ボウ] + egg 丶 [symbol]

In the spring, one can often find a puddle(卯) with toad or frog eggs(丶).

70d 留

リュウ・ル とめる, とまる

Stroke order: ノ ㇄ ㇄ 𠂎 丣 丣 留 留 留 留

stay; study abroad

puddle/4th of 12 丣→卯 [ボウ] + field 田[122] [デン]

To water one's farming land(田), the puddle(卯) always has to have excess water. This character also means 'to study abroad.'

* Ancient characters show that the top of this character is a variation of "卯."

留める[とめる] stop (keep); fix
留(ま)る[とまる] stay; languish; be fixed
留学生[りゅうがくせい] international student; student studying abroad -70d 77b 162

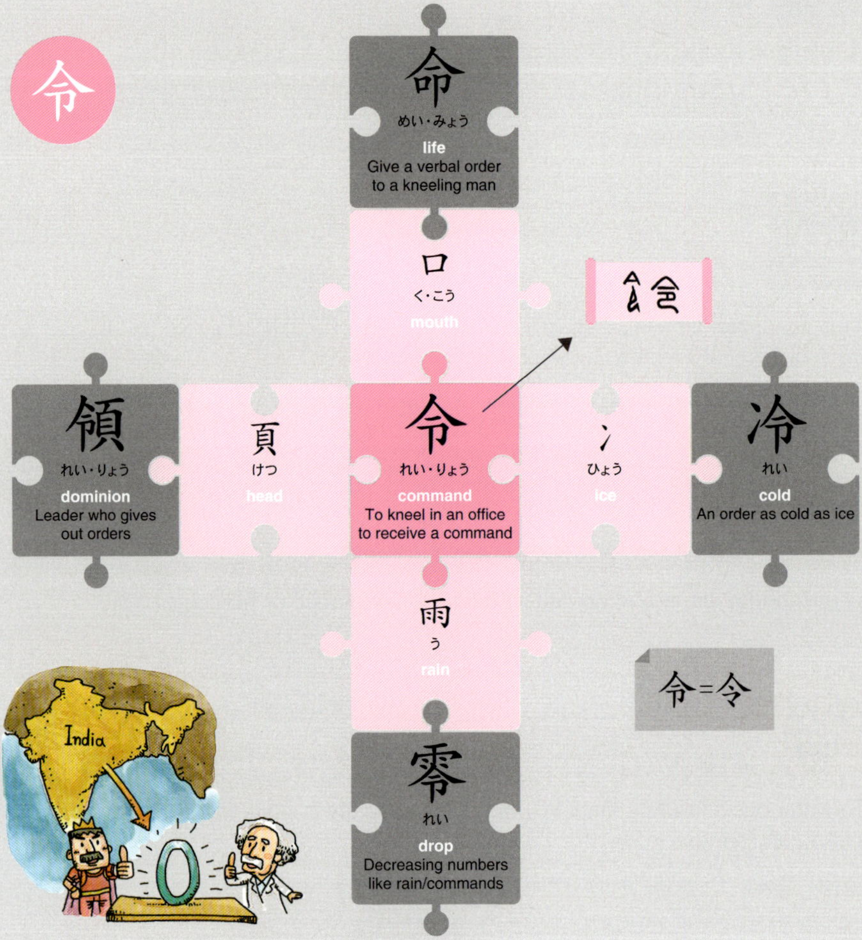

71 令

レイ・リョウ

command

assemble 亼[54] [シュウ] + kneel/person ㄗ→ 卩[69] [セツ]

A man kneeling(卩) in an office, the seat of power(亼), to receive a command.

命令[めいれい] orders; command; decree -71a 71

71a 命

メイ・ミョウ　いのち

ノ 人 人 人 合 合 合 命

life; order

command 令 [レイ] + mouth 口 12 [ク・コウ]

To give a command(令) verbally(口) in an office to a kneeling man. To disobey the order of a powerful man certainly meant death, so this character also means 'life.'

革命[かくめい] revolution - 149c 71a
命令[めいれい] orders; command; decree - 71a 71
生命[せいめい] life - 162 71a

71b 冷

レイ　さます・さめる・つめたい・ひえる・ひやかす・ひやす

` 冫 冫 冫 冫 冷 冷

cold

ice 冫 160 [ヒョウ] + command 令 [レイ]

However softly put, a command(令), or an order is always cold as ice(冫).

冷ます[さます] cool (down/off)
冷める[さめる] become cool; come down (fever)
冷たい[つめたい] chilly; icy; cold
冷える[ひえる] cool (down/off); grow cold; get chilly
冷やす[ひやす] cool; cool (down/off)
冷(や)かす[ひやかす] tease; banter; ridicule

71c 零

レイ　こぼれる

一 广 戸 雨 雨 雨 雨 雫 雫 雫 雫 零 零

drop; zero

rain 雨 159 [ウ] + command 令 [レイ]

Commands(令) come from the top down, just like rain(雨) from the sky. When you count down from a large number, you are bound to reach zero.

* The ordinary people in the ancient world did not use "zero." However, "zero," first used in India was the best invention for scientists and rulers because they needed to express numbers as large as possible. Thus, just like rain(雨) falling down from the sky, it may be assumed that the number "zero," originating in this country run by the Gods, was passed down to rulers who commanded(令) that it be used.

零れる[こぼれる] overflow; spill; flow out
零点[れいてん] zero (points) - 71c 100c

71d 領

レイ・リョウ

ノ 卜 ト 牟 牟 令 令 令 領 領 領 領 領 領

dominion

command 令 [レイ] + head 頁 4 [ケツ]

The head(頁) of a team who leads and gives orders(令).

領事[りょうじ] consul - 71d 32c
占領[せんりょう] occupation - 100a 71d

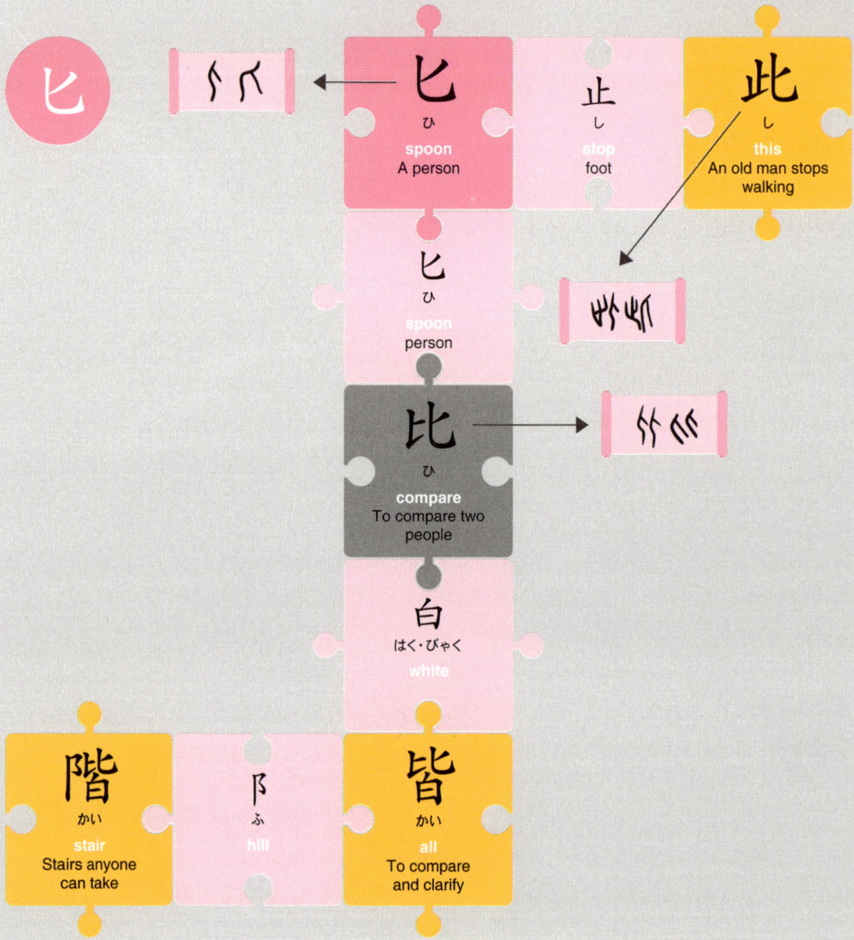

72 **匕**

し

spoon

ノ 匕

It means 'spoon,' but is more often used to mean 'person.' Ancient texts explain that because it looks like a mirrored "person 人[ニン・ジン]," it also means 'the elderly,' a frail person.

72a 此

シ　この・これ

this

foot/stop 止[44] [シ] + old-person/spoon 匕 [ヒ]

A weak old man(匕) stops walking(止) and instead uses only what he can reach. This character means 'this,' item that is close by.

此の[この] this; these
此れ[これ] this
此処/此所[ここ] here; this place -72a 46d / 72a 115e
此方[こちら] this way (direction); here -72a 126

72b 比

ヒ　くらべる

compare

person/spoon 匕 [ヒ] + person/spoon 匕 [ヒ]

To compare the height or the build of two people(匕) facing the same direction.

比べる[くらべる] compare
比較[ひかく] comparison -72b 97a

72c 皆

カイ　みな

all

compare 比 [ヒ] + white 白[106] [ハク・ビャク]

To compare(比) two people and reveal everything clearly(白).

皆さん[みなさん] all; everyone (conversational tone of '皆様 -134a[みなさま]')
皆[みんな(spoken)←みな] all; everyone; everything

72d 階

カイ

stair; story

hill 阝[116] [フ] + all 皆 [カイ]

The reason any(皆) person can climb a hill(阝) is because there are stairs. This character is also used to indicate the floor or story of a building.

階段[かいだん] stairs; staircase -72d 93a
一階[いっかい] one floor; first floor -173 72d
何階[なんがい] what floor -13c 72d

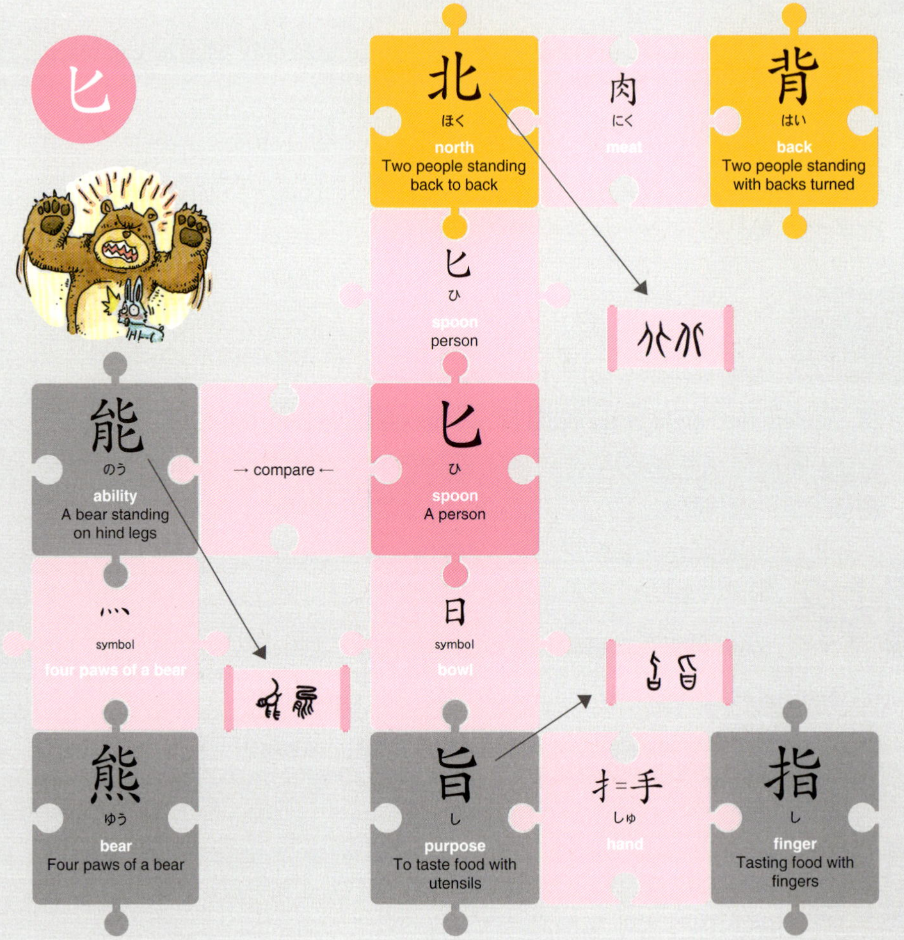

73 **北**

ホク きた

丨 ⺊ 丬 丬 北

north

person/spoon 丬→ヒ[72] [ヒ] + person/spoon ヒ [ヒ]

Two people(ヒ) standing facing away from each other means 'to turn one's back.' People prefer to face the light and build houses facing south, so this character came to mean 'north,' the direction one faces when their back is turned to the south.

北米[ほくべい] North America - 73 110 南北[なんぼく] south and north - 178a 73

73a 背

ハイ せ・せい・そむく・そむける

back; betray

north 北 [ホク] + meat 月→肉[151] [ニク]

When people started using "北," which previously meant 'back' to mean 'north,' they added a character to indicate the human body(肉) to create a character meaning back. To turn one's back means 'to betray' or to measure one's height(せい).

背く[そむく] turn one's back on; betray
背ける[そむける] turn against; turn one's face away

73b 旨

シ うまい

purpose; tasty

spoon 匕 [ヒ] + bowl 日 [symbol]

To taste food in a bowl(日) with cutlery(匕). Some people use fingers to taste food, so this character came to mean 'finger.' Fingers are also used to point out a direction or a goal, so this character also means 'purpose.'

* The ancient text explains "旨" is a spoon(匕) hovering over a bowl(日).

旨い[うまい] delicious; tasty; appetizing
趣旨[しゅし] meaning; point; purpose -22c 73b

73c 指

シ さす・ゆび

finger; point to

hand 扌=手[28] [シュ] + finger/purpose 旨 [シ]

After "旨" came to mean 'purpose,' the kanji added a hand(扌) to stress the meaning of 'finger.' This character also means 'to point.'

指す[さす] point; indicate
指示[しじ] directions; instructions -73c 99

73d 能

ノウ

ability

bear 𦫳 [symbol] + bear's foot 匕 [symbol]

A bear(𦫳) standing on its hind legs with its front paws(匕+匕) held high. A bear is very strong, and for it to pose as if to attack means that one can do anything.

* The ancient character describes a bear(𦫳) posing to attack prey with its front paws(匕+匕).

知能[ちのう] intellect; intelligence -89b 73d
能力[のうりょく] ability; capacity -73d 125

73e 熊

ユウ

bear

ability 能 [ノウ] + four paws of a bear 灬 [symbol]

The pictogram of the character was created to mean bear "能," and four paws(灬) were added to reinforce its original meaning 'bear.'

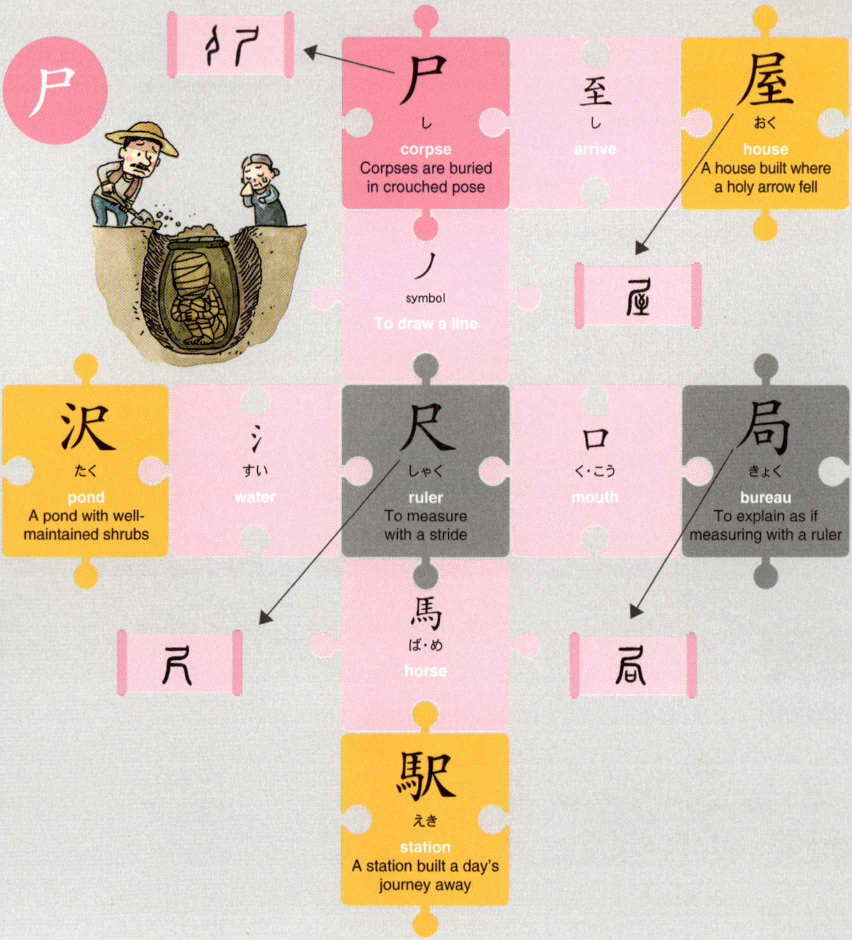

74	尸	シ **corpse**	㇇ ㇋ 尸

This character describes a person crouching in a sitting position but with only the feet on the ground. Because people were buried in that posture, this character means 'corpse.' The ancient Chinese believed in afterlife, so the biers used to transport corpses were made to look like houses, and people were buried with some of their possessions. This is why this character sometimes means house.

* Qin Shi Huang's(秦始皇, 259-210 BC) tomb is a good example of how the Chinese prepared a house within a tomb to prepare for the afterlife.

74a 屋

オク や

フ コ 尸 尸 尸 层 层 屋 屋

house

house/corpse 尸 [シ] + arrive 至 90 [シ]

In ancient China, when building a house(尸), they shot a specially decorated arrow and built the house in the spot where the arrow landed(至).

* "至" is the actual shape of a decorated sacred arrow(矢 89) stuck upside down in the ground (一).

八百屋[やおや] vegetable shop; greengrocer - 177 106a 74a
部屋[へや] room - 116d 74a
屋上[おくじょう] rooftop - 74a 173a
屋外[おくがい] outdoor; open air - 74a 172b

74b 尺

シャク

フ コ 尸 尺

ruler; Shaku

To draw a line(丿 179e) between a person's(尸) legs to measure the distance. It was a common way to measure distance, so this character means 'ruler or a unit of length.'

* "尸" is a crouching man, so in essence it means 'person.'

74c 局

キョク

フ コ 尸 月 局 局 局

bureau; situation

ruler 尺 [シャク] + mouth 口 12 [ク・コウ]

An official verbally(口) describes the situation as if measuring(尺) the facts. This character also means office, because that is where official business takes place.

薬局[やっきょく] pharmacy - 161d 74c

74d 駅

エキ

丨 厂 F F 甲 馬 馬 馬 馬 馬 馬 馬 駅 駅

station

horse 馬 138 [バ・メ] + ruler 尺 [シャク]

Stations were erected at regular intervals, with the distance(尺) between them being a day's ride on a horse(馬), so both the horse and messenger could rest.

* The traditional character(驛) shows a station where the horse(馬) rests and a prisoner(幸 83e) is kept locked up and guarded(罒→目 7).

74e 沢

タク さわ

丶 丶 氵 氵 氵 沢 沢

pond

water 氵 157 [スイ] + ruler 尺 [シャク]

A well-maintained house, with a pond(氵) surrounded by plants kept at an appropriate length(尺), is owned by someone 'well-off.'

* The traditional character(澤)shos that guarded(罒→目 7)prisoners(幸 83e) shed tears(氵 157) that gathered to make a 'pond.'

沢山[たくさん] many; much; a lot; plenty of - 74e 153

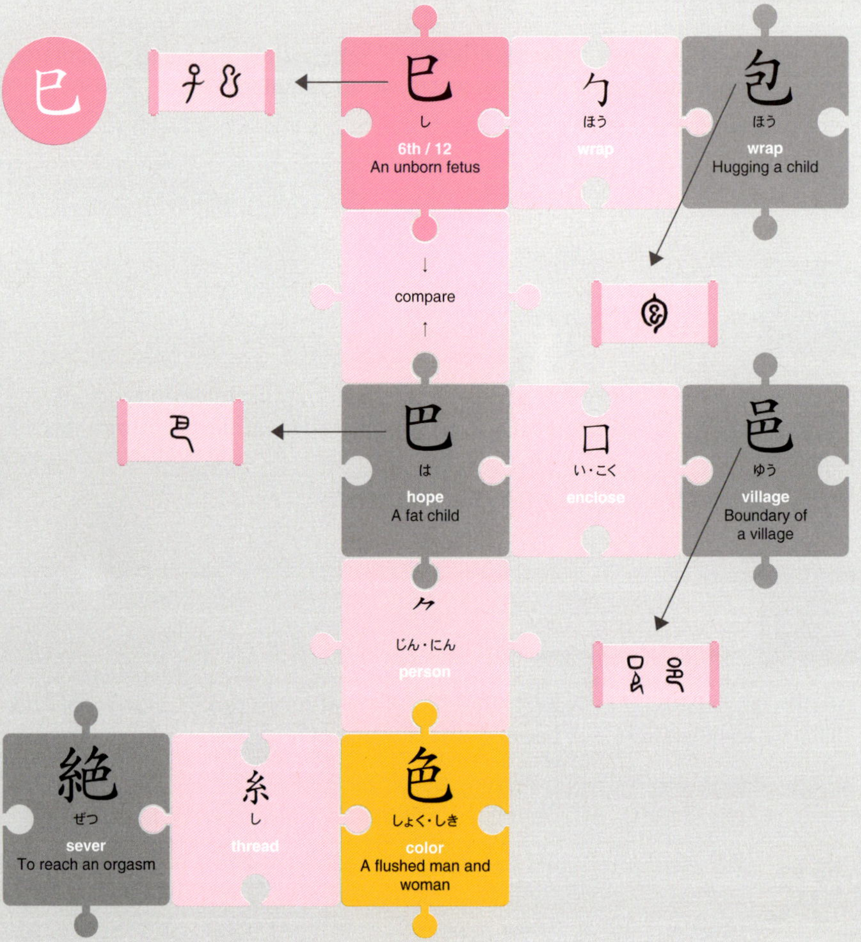

75 巳 シ

6th/12

A fetus still in the mother's womb, or a newborn baby. It's the sixth out of the twelve Chinese zodiac signs.

75a 包

ホウ　つつむ

丿 勹 勹 匀 包

wrap

wrap 勹[40] [ホウ] + unborn child/6th of 12 巳→巳 [シ]

The shape of a pregnant woman hugging(勹) her unborn child(巳) in her belly, or wrapping(勹) the child(巳) in her two arms.

包む[つつむ] wrap; pack; cover　　小包[こづつみ] package; parcel -182 75a

75b 巴

ハ

ㄱ ㄲ 卫 巴

hope

If "巳" is a fetus or a newborn baby, "巴" is a baby with more weight that can be considered a person. It signifies the wish that one wishes their children to be healthy.

75c 邑

ユウ

丶 ㄇ 口 吕 吕 另 邑

village

person/hope 巴 [ハ] + enclose 口[16] [イ・コク]

The boundary(口) surrounding a town where people(巴) live. When it is on the right of a more complicated character, it takes the shape of "阝."

* When "阝[116]" is on the left it means 'hill,' when it's on the right it means 'town(邑).'

75d 色

ショク・シキ　いろ

丿 ク ㇇ 今 刍 色

color

person ⺈[56] [ジン・ニン] + person/hope 巴 [ハ]

One person(⺈) on top of another(巴) making love. As they will both be flushed, this character means 'color.'

色色/種種[いろいろ] various; various colors (kinds) -75d 75d/119d 119d
黄色い[きいろい] yellow -108 75d
好色[こうしょく] lust; sensuality -78c 75d
色彩[しきさい] color; colour -75d 5b

75e 絶

ゼツ　たえる

ㄥ 幺 幺 糸 糸 糸 糸' 糸ク 糸ク 絈 絶 絶

sever; extremely

thread 糸[104] [シ] + color 色 [ショク・シキ]

When a person(⺈) is on top of another person(巴) having intercourse(色), and the ecstasy reaches a climax, the 'severity or extremity' could be likened to the second before a length of thread(糸) snaps.

絶える[たえる] be cut off; cease to exist
絶頂[ぜっちょう] summit; peak; climax -75e 175b

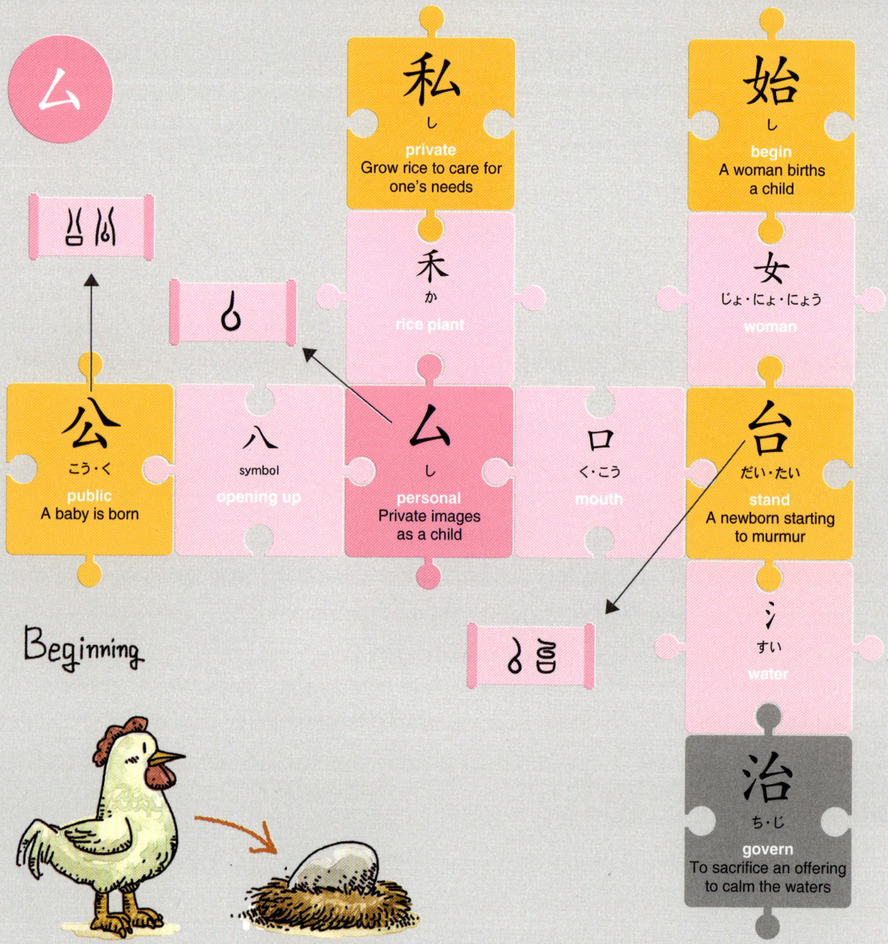

76 ム シ

ム ム

personal

We can't be sure what this ancient character meant, but if we consider the meanings of all the characters that include "ム," it seems to mean 'a newborn baby.' Such images are for private viewing.

76a 私

シ　わたくし・わたし

丿 二 千 禾 禾 私 私

private

rice plant 禾[111] [カ] + newborn baby/personal ム [シ]

In the old days, one grew rice(禾) not to sell, but for their own(ム) personal consumption. That is how this character came to mean 'private or me.'

私鉄[してつ] private railroad (railway) -76a 154d　私立[しりつ] private (establishment) -76a 64

76b 台

ダイ・タイ

ㄥ ム 厶 台 台

stand; pedestal

newborn baby/personal ム [シ] + mouth ロ[12] [ク・コウ]

To hold a murmuring(ロ) newborn(ム) in glee. It also means 'pedestal' as one would put the baby on an altar to show gratitude.

台所[だいどころ] kitchen -76b 115e　寝台[しんだい] bed; berth -168d 76b
舞台[ぶたい] stage -47b 76b

76c 始

シ　はじまる・はじめる

く 女 女 女 女 女 始 始

begin

woman 女[78] [ジョ・ニョ・ニョウ] + newborn baby/stand 台 [ダイ・タイ]

This character proves that the chicken comes before the egg. It shows a woman (女) giving birth to a child(台), which signaled the beginning of a life.

始(ま)る[はじまる] begin; start
始めまして[はじめまして] I am glad to meet you (greetings on a first meeting)

76d 治

チ・ジ　おさまる・おさめる

丶 丶 氵 氵 氵 氵 治 治

govern

water 氵[157] [スイ] + stand 台 [ダイ・タイ]

Whenever there was a drought or a flood, the people offered sacrifices on the altar(台) to calm or rule the waters(氵). The Chinese believed the gods had power over natural phenomena.

治(ま)る[おさまる] be at peace; calm down　治める[おさめる] rule; govern; heal
政治[せいじ] politics -45c 76d

76e 公

コウ・ク　おおやけ

丿 八 公 公

public

opening up 八 [symbol] + newborn baby/personal ム [シ]

The womb opens(八) and a fetus(ム) is born. It means that a baby is now a member of the public, and no longer under the sole protection of its mother.

* The "八" part of "公" is the shape of something opening up.

公園[うえん] park -76e 102d　公共[こうきょう] public; whole society -76e 38a
公害[こうがい] pollution; public nuisance -76e 163e

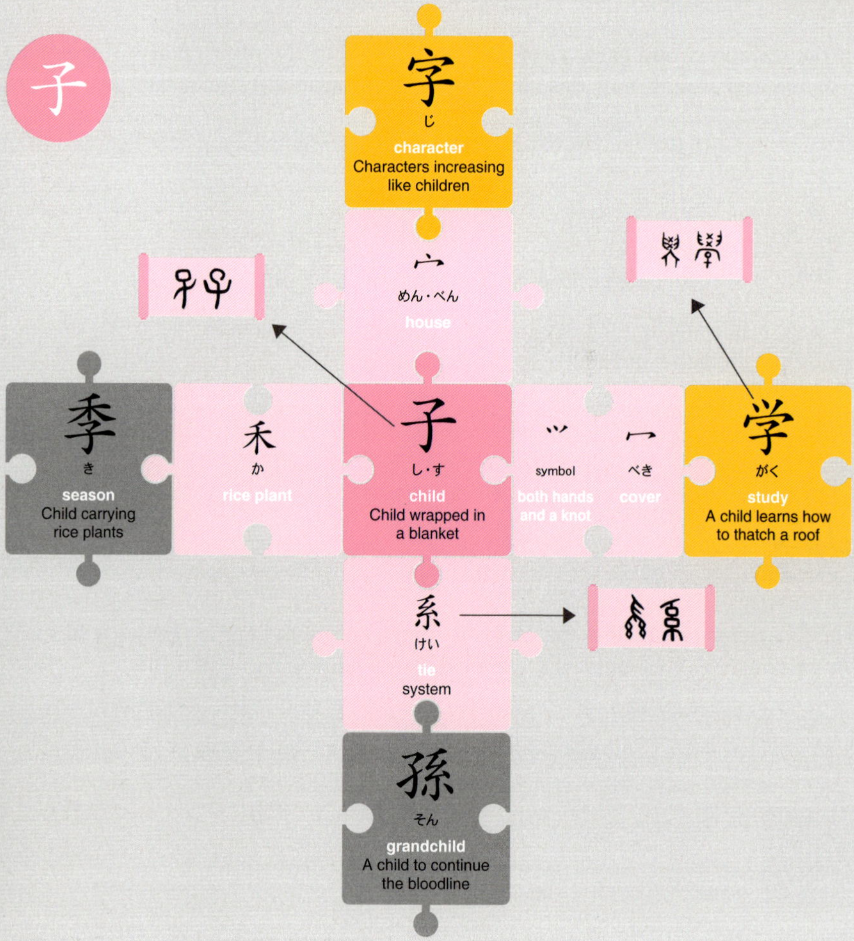

77 **子** シ・ス　こ

child; suffix

㇇ 了 子

A child wrapped in a blanket means 'sons and daughters,' but more often 'son' than 'daughter' because Confucianism caused parents to prefer sons. This character is also used as a meaningless suffix.

椅子[いす] chair -14d 77	男の子[おとこのこ] boy -125a 77
女の子[おんなのこ] girl -78 77	子供[こども] child; children -77 38b

77a 字

ジ

character; letter

house 宀[113] [メン・ベン] + child 子 [シ・ス]

Just like the number of children(子)in a household(宀) increases, new characters are made. Kanji is mostly pictograms, and one character usually means only one thing, so new characters have to be made to reflect the changing times. In comparison, the alphabet has changed much less.

漢字[かんじ] Chinese characters; kanji -108c 77a
文字[もじ] letter (of alphabet); character -105 77a

77b 学

ガク まなぶ

study

both hands and a knot ⺍ [symbol] + cover 冖[131] [ベキ] + child 子 [シ・ス]

A boy(子) watching and learning from the adults who were thatching a roof (冖) with their hands(⺍).

* The traditional character(學) shows that the boy(子) learns from watching men cover a roof(冖) with bundles(メ) of hay using their hands(臼[29]).

学生[がくせい] student -77b 162
学校[がっこう] school -77b 1b
大学[だいがく] university -60 77b
留学生[りゅうがくせい] international student; student studying abroad -70d 77b 162

77c 孫

ソン まご

grandchild

child 子 [シ・ス] + system/tie 系 [ケイ]

A child(子) that continues(系) the bloodline is 'a grandson or a descendant.'

* "系" is a thread(糸[104]) connected to another with a knot at one end(ノ [179e]).

子孫[しそん] descendant; offspring -77 77c

77d 季

キ

season

rice plant 禾[111] [カ] + child 子 [シ・ス]

In autumn, the harvest season of the year, a child(子) is picking up ears of rice(禾) and carrying a sheaf of rice(禾).

季節[きせつ] seasons; solar term -77d 109e
四季[しき] four seasons -16b 77d

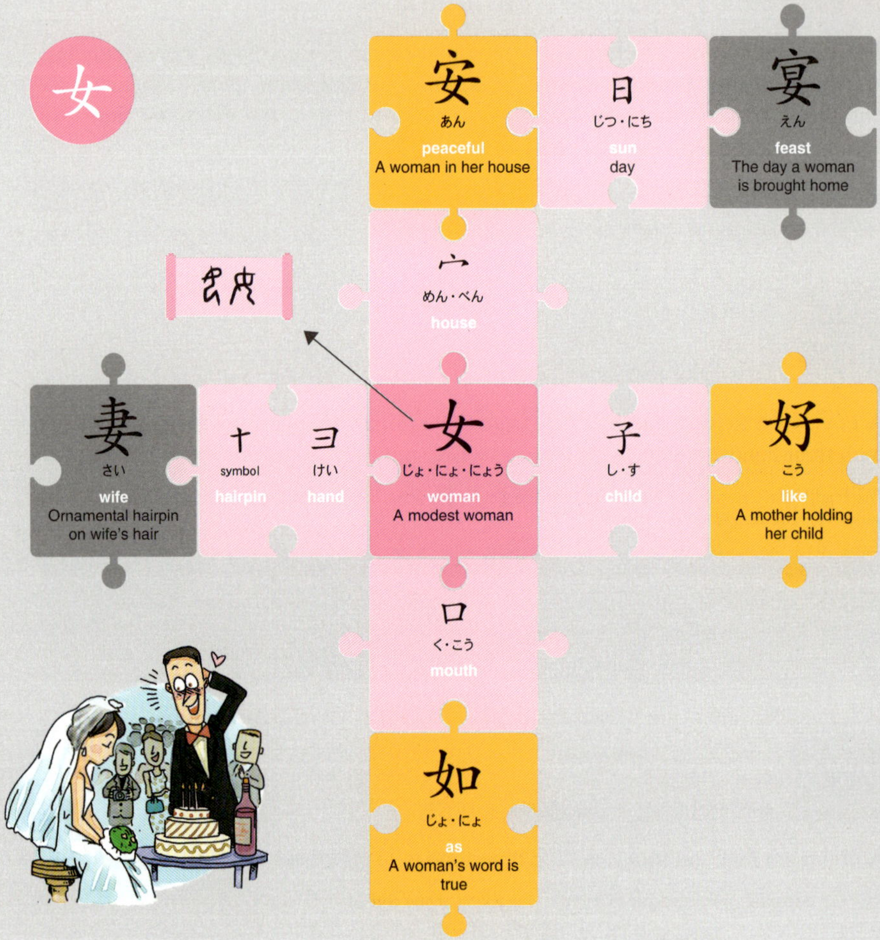

78 **女**

ジョ・ニョ・ニョウ　おんな

woman

A woman sitting with her hands on her knees.

女の子[おんなのこ] girl -78 77
少女[しょうじょ] girl; young lady -182a 78
女性[じょせい] woman; female; lady -78 27a

78a 安

アン やすい

丶 丷 宀 宄 安 安

peaceful

house 宀 [113] [メン・ベン] + woman 女 [ジョ・ニョ・ニョウ]

A woman(女) is relatively weaker than a man, so she feels peaceful and safe when at home(宀).

安い[やすい] cheap; inexpensive; comfortable; tranquil
安易[あんい] easy; easy-going -78a 41b
安心[あんしん] peace of mind; relief -78a 26
安全[あんぜん] safety; security -78a 53a

78b 宴

エン

丶 丷 宀 宀 宁 宣 宣 宴 宴 宴

feast

house 宀 [113] [メン・ベン] + day/sun 日 [170] [ジツ・ニチ] + woman 女 [ジョ・ニョ・ニョウ]

To hold a feast to celebrate bringing a woman(女) home(宀) on the man's wedding day(日).

宴会[えんかい] party; banquet -78b 158d

78c 好

コウ このむ・すく

く 女 女 女 好 好

like

woman 女 [ジョ・ニョ・ニョウ] + child 子 [77] [シ・ス]

It's always a 'good' thing for a mother(女) to hold her child(子).

好き[すき] liking, fondness, love
大好き[だいすき] loveable; very likeable -60 78c
好況[こうきょう] booming economy -78c 59b

78d 如

ジョ・ニョ

く 女 女 如 如 如

as; like

woman 女 [ジョ・ニョ・ニョウ] + mouth ロ [12] [ク・コウ]

This character got the 'just like~' meaning because what a woman(女) says (ロ) is closer to the truth.

如何[どう] how -78d 13c
如何致しまして[どういたしまして] You are welcome -78d 13c 90d
如何して[どうして] why; how -78d 13c

78e 妻

サイ つま

一 ヨ ヨ ヨ clustering 妻 妻 妻

wife

hairpin 十 [symbol] + hand ヨ [32] [ケイ] + woman 女 [ジョ・ニョ・ニョウ]

This character symbolizes a married woman(女) who has her ornamental hairpin(十) on her hair or keep it up(ヨ) in a chignon.

* In ancient China, only married women tied up their hair with an ornamental hairpin.

夫妻[ふさい] man and wife; married couple -60a 78e

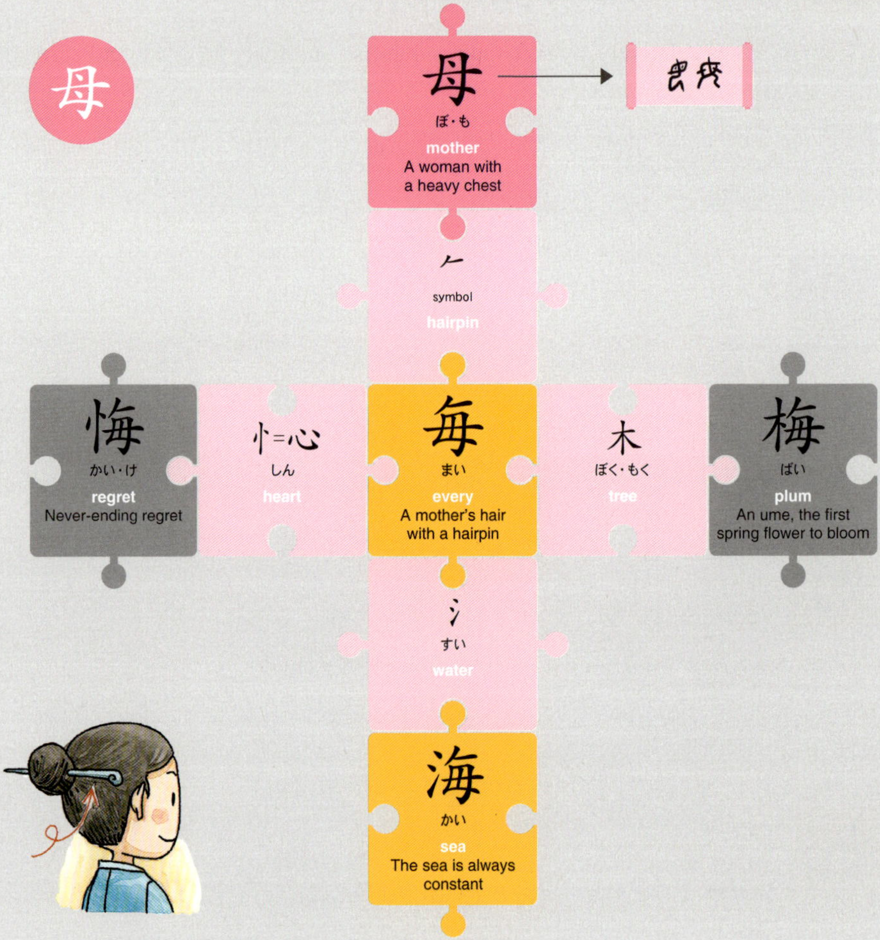

79 母 ボ・モ はは

mother

Skew the "女" character to the side, add two dots(、) to accentuate breastfeeding, and the character means 'mother.'

お母さん[おかあさん] mother; honorific of mother
お祖母さん[おばあさん] (honorific or a friendly) grandmother -174d 79
小母さん[おばさん] (honorific) old lady, madam
祖母[そぼ] grandmother -174d 79 母親[ははおや] mother -79 9c

79a 毎

マイ

ノ ㇒ 𠂉 𠂉 毎 毎

every

hairpin 𠂉 [symbol] + mother 毋→母 [ボ・モ]

A mother(母) usually pulls her hair up with a hairpin(𠂉), which is why this character means 'every or each.'

* "𠂉" is not a person, but a traditional Asian hairpin that is placed through a woman's hair. In ancient China, only married women tied up their hair with one.

毎朝[まいあさ] every morning -79a 98e	毎月[まいげつ] every month -79a 172
毎週[まいしゅう] every week -79a 122b	毎日[まいにち] everyday; daily -79a 170
毎年[まいねん] every year -79a 96e	毎晩[まいばん] every evening; every night -79a 57b

79b 梅

バイ うめ

一 十 才 木 木' 木𠂉 杧 梅 梅 梅

plum

tree 木[164] [ボク・モク] + every 毎 [マイ]

In spring, the ume, or the Japanese plum tree(木), is always(毎) the first to bloom. Asians thought highly of this tree(木) because it bloomed in the cold as if it braved adversity with its upright(毎) character. It also means heavy rains that people wished for around the time the flower blooms.

梅雨[つゆ] rainy season; (summer) monsoon -79b 159

79c 海

カイ うみ

丶 冫 氵 氵' 氵𠂉 汇 海 海 海

sea

water 氵[157] [スイ] + every 毎 [マイ]

The sea never overflows or dries up, and it always(毎) maintains the same water (氵) level.

海辺[うみべ] beach; seaside; seashore -79c 49a

海外[かいがい] overseas; foreign; abroad -79c 172b

79d 悔

カイ・ケ くやしい・くやむ

丨 忄 忄 忄' 忄𠂉 忙 悔 悔 悔

regret; repent

heart 忄=心[26] [シン] + every 毎 [マイ]

Regret is an emotion that always(毎) remains in the heart(忄).

悔しい[くやしい] vexing; regrettable

悔(や)む[くやむ] repent; regret; mourn

後悔[こうかい] repentance; regret -48c 79d

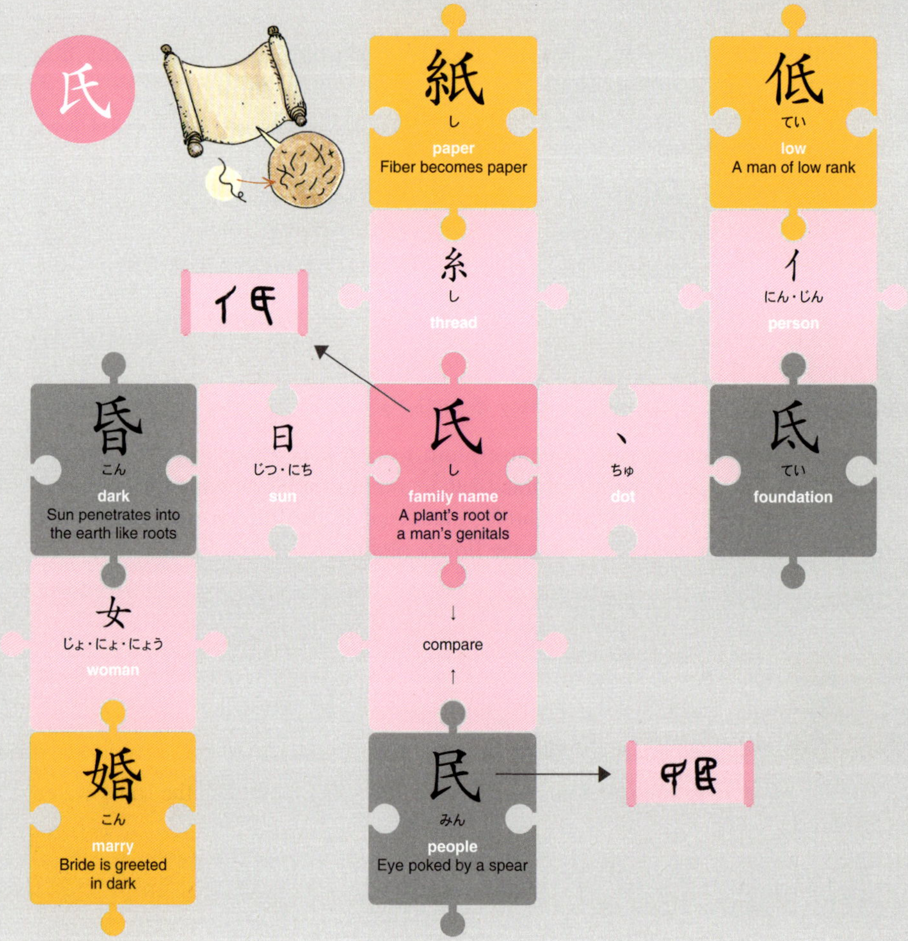

80 **氏** シ

family name

One cannot be sure, but the ancient text suggests the meaning 'surname' came from the fact that this character looks like a root, or a man's genitals.

氏名[しめい] full name; identity -80 172d

80a **紙**

シ かみ

幺 幺 幺 糸 糸 糸 糸 紅 紅 紙

paper

thread 糸 104 [シ] + root/family name 氏 [シ]

The root(氏), which is the main material paper is made of, is thread(糸). Paper was made with(氏) fiber which is a thready(糸) substance.

* China's Cai Lun(蔡伦, 50 AD~121) was the first man to make paper, and he used flax fiber.

手紙[てがみ] letter - 28 80a　用紙[ようし] paper; blank form - 129 80a

80b **低**

テイ ひくい

ノ イ イ 化 仾 低 低

low

person イ 52 [ニン・ジン] + foundation 氐 [テイ]

'Base(氐)' implies 'below, the floor,' and a man(イ) whose social rank is below(氐) others is a 'low' person.

* When "氏" became 'surname' instead of 'genitals,' the kanji added a dot(丶) at the bottom of its character to mean "foundation 氐."

低い[ひくい] low; short　最低[さいてい] least; lowest; worst - 22a 80b

80c **民**

ミン

フ コ 尸 尸 民

people

War prisoners were made slaves by blinding them in one eye(目 7) with a spear(矛). The meaning later changed to 'people.'

* The ancient character shows it's a spear(矛) poking an eye(目). "矛[ム・ボウ]" is a long spear with a tip as sharp as an awl.

国民[こくみん] nation; people - 86a 80c　市民[しみん] citizen - 103a 80c
農民[のうみん] farmers; peasants - 148d 80c

80d **昏**

コン

一 ㇀ 乊 氏 氏 昏 昏 昏

dark

root/family name 氏 [シ] + sun 日 170 [ジツ・ニチ]

This character depicts the image of sunlight(日) penetrating deep into the earth like the roots(氏) of trees, and it means 'dark.'

80e **婚**

コン

く 女 女 女 妒 妒 娇 娇 婚 婚 婚

marry

woman 女 78 [ジョ・ニョ・ニョウ] + dark 昏 [コン]

As the sun sets and it gets dark(昏), a bride(女) is greeted. This character illustrates the traditional wedding custom of old China.

結婚[けっこん] marriage - 84b 80e

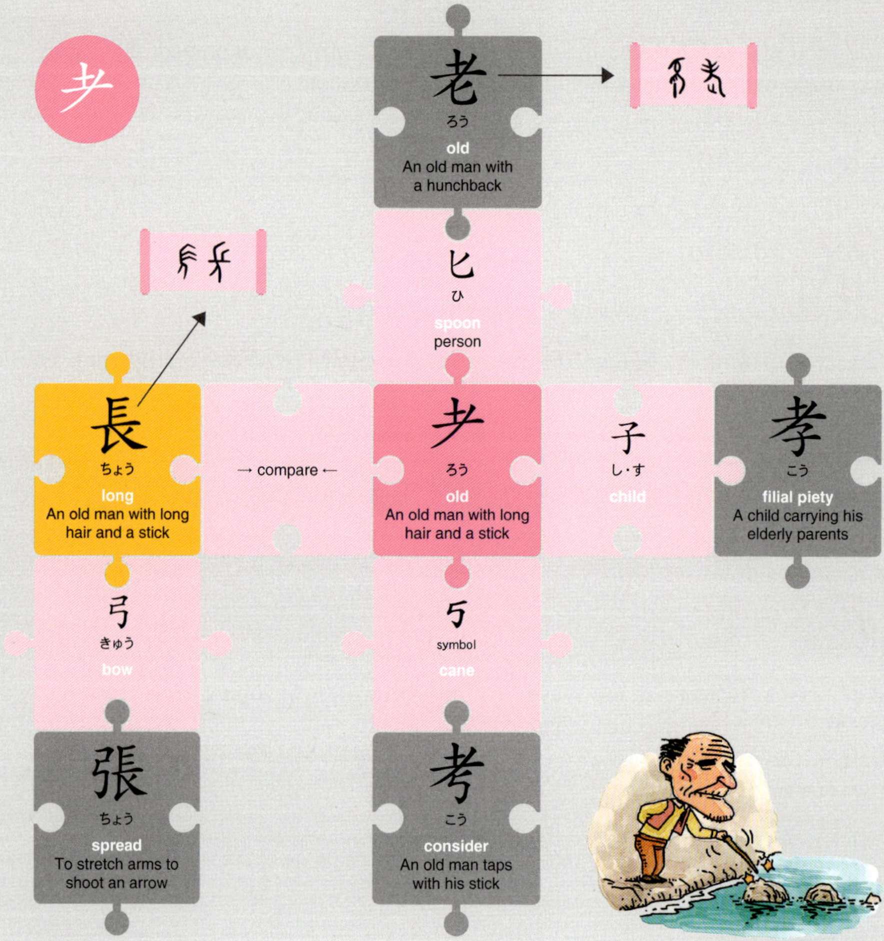

81 **耂**

ロウ

old

一 十 土 耂

An old man with a hunched back and long flying hair(丿) is using a stick to help him tread the ground(土).

81a 老

ロウ おいる・ふける

一 十 土 耂 耂 老

old

old 耂 [ロウ] + person/spoon 匕 72 [ヒ]

As "耂" cannot be used on its own, the kanji added the character for "old 匕" to stress the meaning.

* "匕" is a mirror reflection of a person(人 51) and is used to describe the elderly.

老いる[おいる] age; grow old; decrepit
老ける[ふける] age; grow old; be old
老人[ろうじん] the aged; old person -81a 51

81b 孝

コウ

一 十 土 耂 耂 考 孝

filial piety

old 耂 [ロウ] + child 子 77 [シ・ス]

A filial son(子) is one who cares for his old(耂) parents.

孝行[こうこう] filial duty (piety) -81b 43a

81c 考

コウ かんがえる

一 十 土 耂 耂 考

consider

old 耂 [ロウ] + cane 丂 [symbol]

A wary old(耂) man who uses his stick(丂) to tap and inspect where he is treading.

* Ancient text shows that the lower half is the crooked stick.

考える[かんがえる] think; consider
参考[さんこう] reference -5a 81c

81d 長

チョウ ながい

丨 ┌ F F 巨 𠀐 長 長

long; chief

Like "老," this character is also an old man with long hair and a stick. But whereas "老" came to mean 'old,' "長" came to mean 'long.' "長" describes long hair, but it also means 'a chief or to grow.'

長い[ながい] long; lengthy; prolonged
延長[えんちょう] extension -50d 81d
社長[しゃちょう] president; CEO (Chief Executive Officer) -99e 81d
課長[かちょう] section chief (head) -123d 81d

81e 張

チョウ はる

フ コ 弓 弓 弓 弓 弓 弓 張 張 張

spread

bow 弓 87 [キュウ] + long 長 [チョウ]

To shoot an arrow, one must hold a bow(弓) and stretch out(長) the arms very tightly.

張る[はる] stretch; spread; strain
出張[しゅっちょう] business trip; official tour -131c 81e

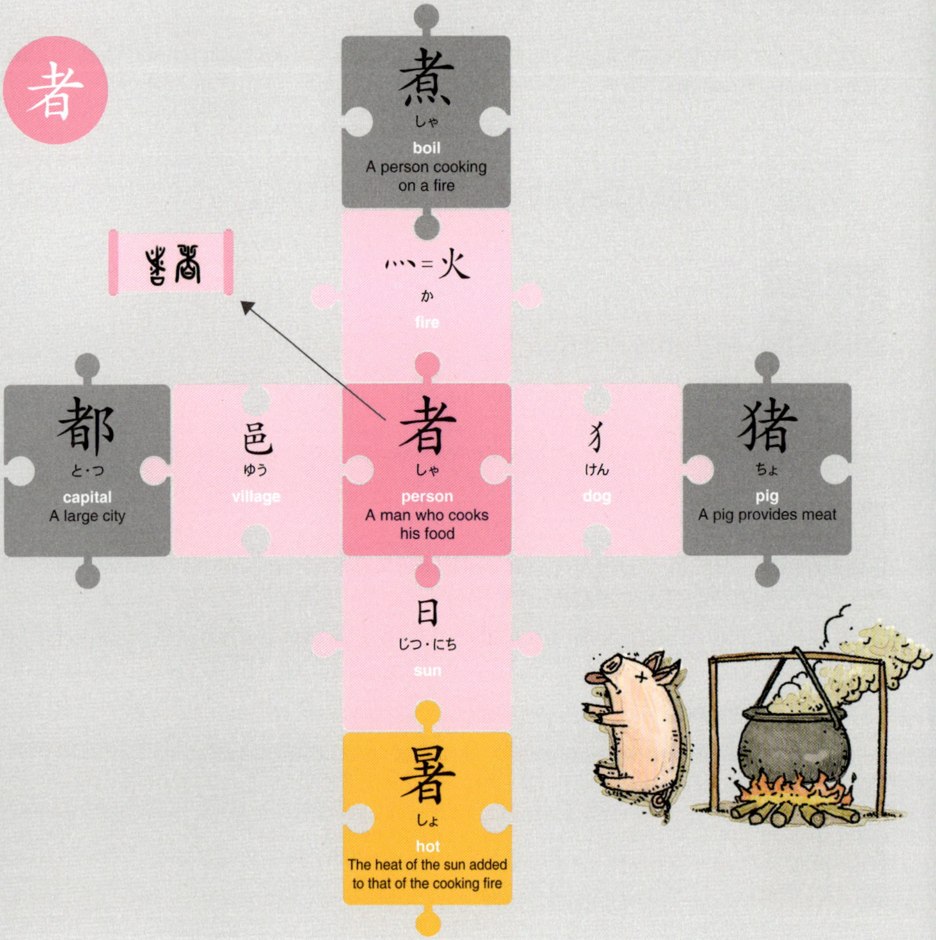

82 者

シャ もの

一 十 土 耂 耂 者 者 者

person; -ist, -er (person)

This character describes someone cooking with a pot and has nothing to do with "耂." Only people are known to do that. Now, this character is used after a verb or an adjective to describe a person or an object with certain qualities.

医者[いしゃ] doctor -89a 82	記者[きしゃ] journalist; reporter -66b 82
歯医者[はいしゃ] dentist -21 89a 82	筆者[ひっしゃ] writer; author -33d 82

82a 煮

シャ にえる・にる

一 十 土 耂 耂 者 者 者 者 煮 煮 煮

boil

cooking/person 者 [シャ] + fire 灬=火 124 [カ]

When 'to boil' gained the meaning 'person,' "灬" was added to include the meaning of fire to create a character for 'boil.'

煮える[にえる] boil; cook; be cooked
煮る[にる] boil; simmer; stew

82b 猪

チョ

丿 犭 犭 犭 犭 犭 犭 犭 猪 猪 猪

pig

dog 犭 135b [ケン] + cooking/person 者 [シャ]

A pig is an animal(犭) that provides meat to a person who cooks(者). This shows that pigs have provided us with food for many centuries.

* "犭" symbolizes an animal, the size of a large dog.

82c 暑

ショ あつい

丨 冂 日 日 旦 早 昊 昊 昊 暑 暑 暑

hot; summer heat

sun 日 170 [ジツ・ニチ] + cooking/person 者 [シャ]

The heat of cooking(者) plus the heat of the sun(日) can be very hot.

暑い[あつい] hot
暑さ[あつさ] heat; hotness

82d 都

ト・ツ みやこ

一 十 土 耂 耂 者 者 者 都 都

capital

cooking/person 者 [シャ] + village 阝→邑 75c [ユウ]

A large village(邑) with many people who cook(者). To distinguish this word from a mere village(邑), kanji added "者" to say 'capital.'

* "Hill 阝 116 [フ]" on the right of a character means "邑."

首都[しゅと] capital city -4d 82d
都市[とし] city; town -82d 103a

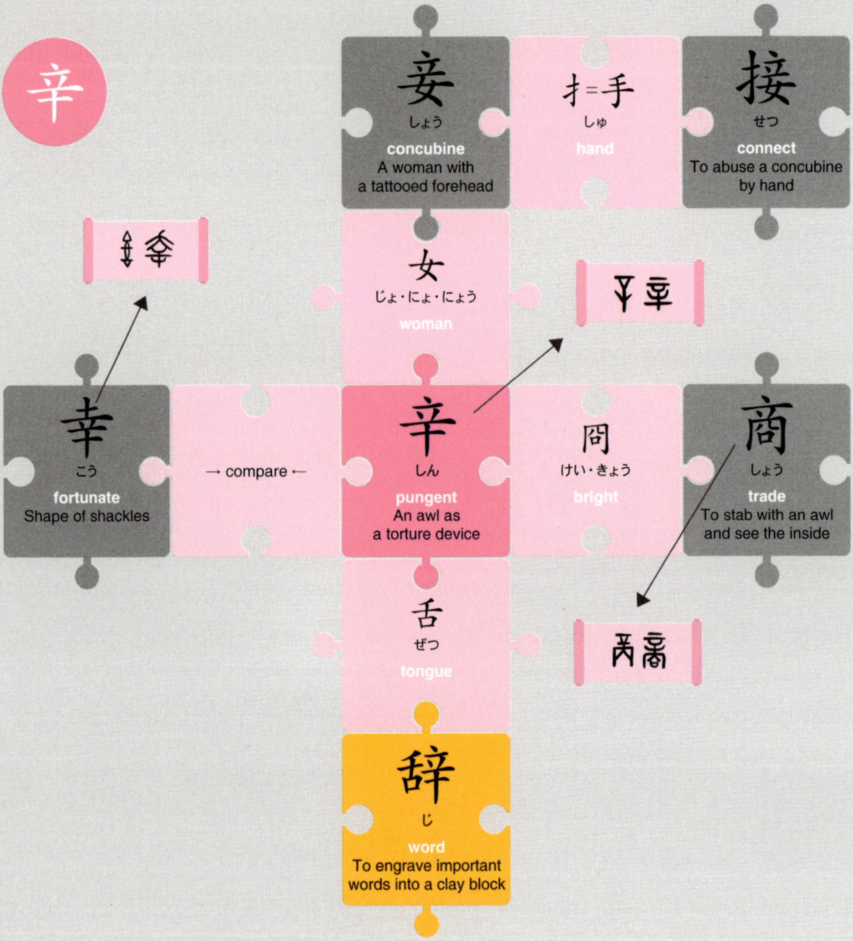

83 辛

シン からい・つらい

pungent; pain

The shape of 'an awl, something long and sharp, a torture device' signifies pain. It also means 'spicy,' a taste that can be described as painful.

* The spicy taste is not felt by tastebuds on the tongue but by nerve endings that sense pain.

辛い[からい] spicy; hot; painful
辛い[つらい] painful; distressed; bitter

83a 妾

ショウ

concubine

awl/pungent 立→辛 [シン] + woman 女[78] [ジョ・ニョ・ニョウ]

To use an awl(辛) to tattoo a woman's(女) forehead and make her a man's slave or a concubine. In ancient China, female(女) prisoners or the wives and daughters of dead criminals were tattooed on the forehead with an awl(辛), and then taken as slaves or concubines.

* The upper part of "妾," the ancient character, has nothing to do with "stand 立[64] [リツ・リュウ]."

83b 接

セツ つぐ

connect; contact

hand 扌=手[28] [シュ] + concubine 妾 [ショウ]

To tease a concubine(妾) with one's hand(扌) means to have an heir to succeed the family name, or to 'receive' her servitude.

接ぐ[つぐ] join; connect; piece together
面接[めんせつ] interview -6a 83b
隣接[りんせつ] adjacency; abuttal -47e 83b

83c 商

ショウ

trade

awl/pungent 立→辛 [シン] + bright 冏 [ケイ・キョウ]

To secure the best products, a merchant must stab with an awl(辛) and reveal(冏) the inside to check the quality.

* The character "冏" has a hole(口[12]) through(内[53b]) which light shines.

83d 辞

ジ ことば・やめる

word; resign

tongue 舌[20] [ゼツ] + awl/pungent 立→辛 [シン]

To use an awl(辛) to engrave important words(舌) into a clay block. When someone 'refuses or resigns,' they tend to finish with elaborate words(辞).

* The traditional character(辭) shows two hands(爪[29]+又[30]) holding yarn and needles(辛) to knit. It indicates that a speech must flow logically as if one were untangling a mess of yarn.

辞める[やめる] resign; retire; quit
辞書[じしょ] dictionary; lexicon -83d 33e

83e 幸

コウ さいわい・しあわせ

fortunate

The shape of wooden shackles to restrain one's hands and feet. This character means 'to be lucky' that one is not in shackles.

* This character was made because in the ancient times, rulers threatened the people with imprisonment.

幸い[さいわい] luck; fortune; luckily; fortunately
幸せ[しあわせ] fortune; luck; happiness

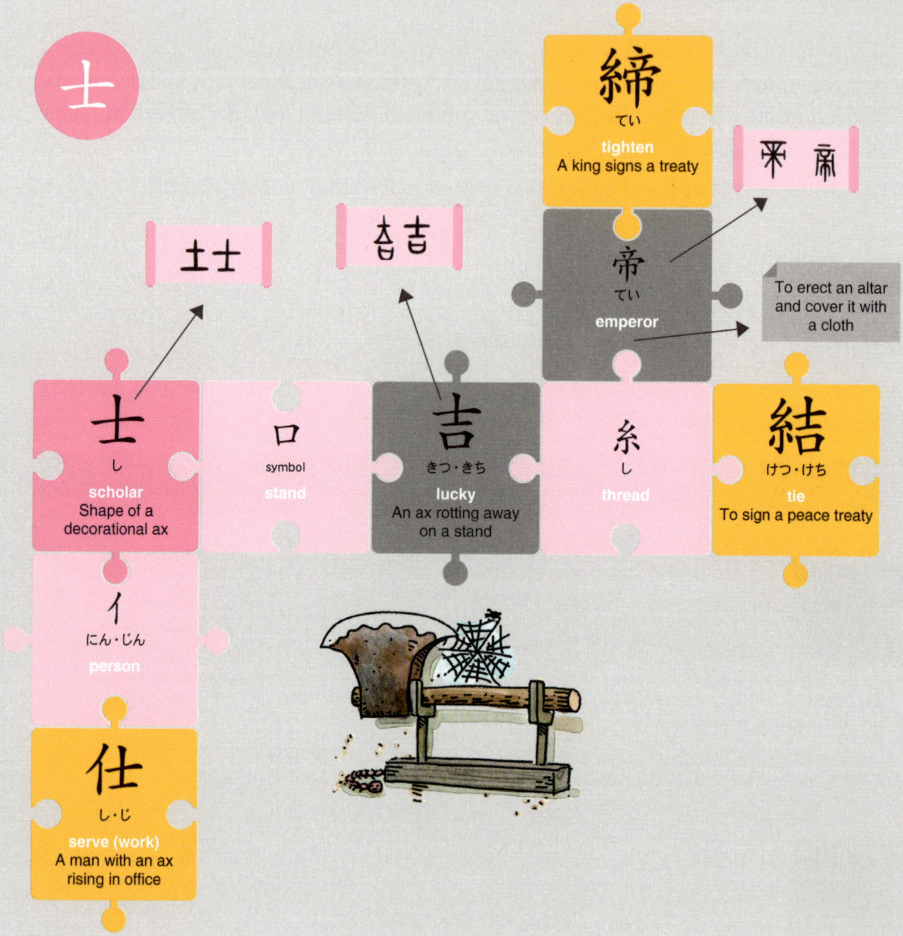

84 **士** シ

一 十 士

scholar; profession suffix

A decorational ax(士) shows authority. Only a scholar has enough knowledge to gain authority that comes with a title.

武士[ぶし] samurai; warrior -88c 84

84a

吉

キツ・キチ

一 十 士 吉 吉 吉

lucky

ax/scholar 士 [シ] + stand ロ [symbol]

An ax(士), a symbol of authority and also used as a weapon, is lying neglected on a stand(ロ). For the handle of an ax to rot away, it means that there has been peace for many years, which is considered 'lucky.'

不吉[ふきつ] bad luck; ominous -173c 84a

84b

結

ケツ・ケチ むすぶ

纟 纟 幺 糸 糸 糸 糸 紅 紅 結 結 結

tie; bear (fruit)

thread 糸 104 [シ] + peaceful/lucky 吉 [キツ・キチ]

To sign or agree to(糸) a peace(吉) treaty means to 'tie' two or more villages together.

* "糸" is used to tie or connect the parties.

結ぶ[むすぶ] tie; bind; bear (fruit)
結婚[けっこん] marriage -84b 80e
結果[けっか] result; consequence -84b 123c
結論[けつろん] conclusion -84b 17b

84c

帝

テイ

丶 亠 亠 立 产 产 产 帝 帝

emperor

An altar is erected and covered with a cloth(巾 103) prior to a ceremony held by the emperor.

* Ancient characters carved on shell and bone show altars made with pieces of erected wood shaped like an 'X,' which had nothing to do with "巾."

84d

締

テイ しめる

纟 纟 幺 糸 糸 糸 糸 紵 紵 紵 紵 綷 綷 締 締

tighten; tie

thread 糸 104 [シ] + emperor 帝 [テイ]

A king(帝) making/tie(糸) a peaceful deal with a neighboring nation to end the fight.

* Signing treaties and making peace was a task only for the most powerful, such as a king(帝).

締める[しめる] tie; fasten; tighten
締結[ていけつ] conclusion -84d 84b

84e

仕

シ・ジ つかえる

ノ 亻 亻 什 仕

serve (work)

person 亻 52 [ニン・ジン] + ax/scholar 士 [シ]

A man(亻) with a ceremonial ax(士) who accepts office 'to serve and work.'

仕える[つかえる] attend; serve
仕事[しごと] work; business; job -84e 32c

Diagram for 臣

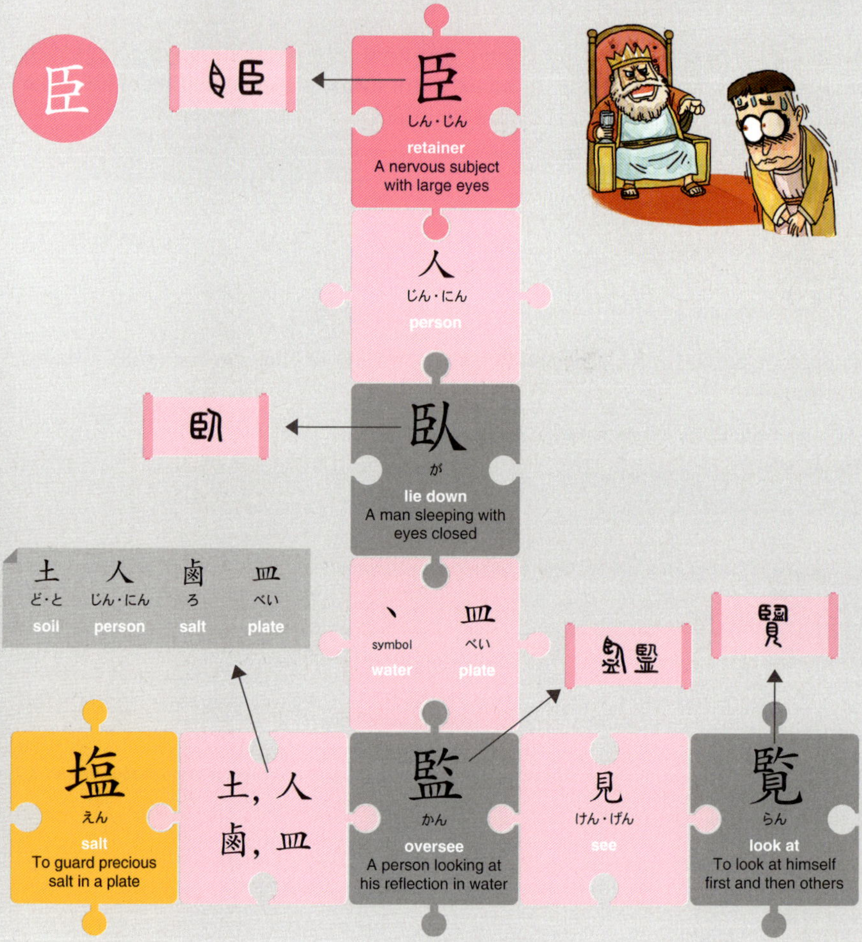

85 **臣**

シン・ジン

retainer

一 丅 丂 丂 予 臣

This character is the side profile of a nervous person with eyes wide open. Subjects were not allowed to face the king directly, so they looked at him sideways, either with a lowered head or from a right angle. A nervous subject could not dare to relax and close his eyes in the king's presence.

大臣[だいじん] cabinet minister -60 85

85a 臥

ガ

一 丁 𫝀 𫝀 𫝀 臣 臥 臥

lie down

retainer 臣 [シン・ジン] + person 人[51] [ジン・ニン]

A person(人) lying down to sleep is accentuated with "臣," an eye.

85b 監

カン

一 丁 𫝀 𫝀 𫝀 臣 臣' 臣' 臣' 臣' 監 監 監 監 監

oversee

eye/retainer 臣 [シン・ジン] + person 人[51] [ジン・ニン] + water 丶 [symbol] + plate 皿[132d] [ベイ]

Before mirrors were invented, people(人) looked at(臣) their reflections in a bowl(皿) of water(丶), which came to mean 'supervise or inspect.'

* "臣" is the shape of eyes wide open.

監察[かんさつ] inspection; inspector - 85b 99b

85c 覧

ラン

一 丁 𫝀 𫝀 𫝀 臣 臣' 臣' 臣' 臣' 覧 覧 覧 覧 覧 覧 覧

look at

oversee 監 [カン] + see 見[9] [ケン・ゲン]

The depiction of someone looking at(監) himself in the water first before looking(見) at others.

* The traditional character(覽) is a combination of "監" and "見."

回覧[かいらん] reading in turn - 16c 85c
遊覧[ゆうらん] sightseeing - 127d 85c

85d 塩

エン しお

一 十 土 𡈽 圹 圹 圹 垆 垆 塩 塩 塩 塩

salt

soil 土[120] [ド・ト] + person 人[51] [ジン・ニン] + salt ロ→鹵[55c] [ロ] + plate 皿[132d] [ベイ]

A person(人) takes valuable rock salt(鹵) extracted from soil(土) to put into a plate(皿) and guard it.

* The traditional character(鹽) shows that in ancient times, salt(鹵) was guarded(監) well because it was as precious as money.

食塩[しょくえん] table salt - 109 85d

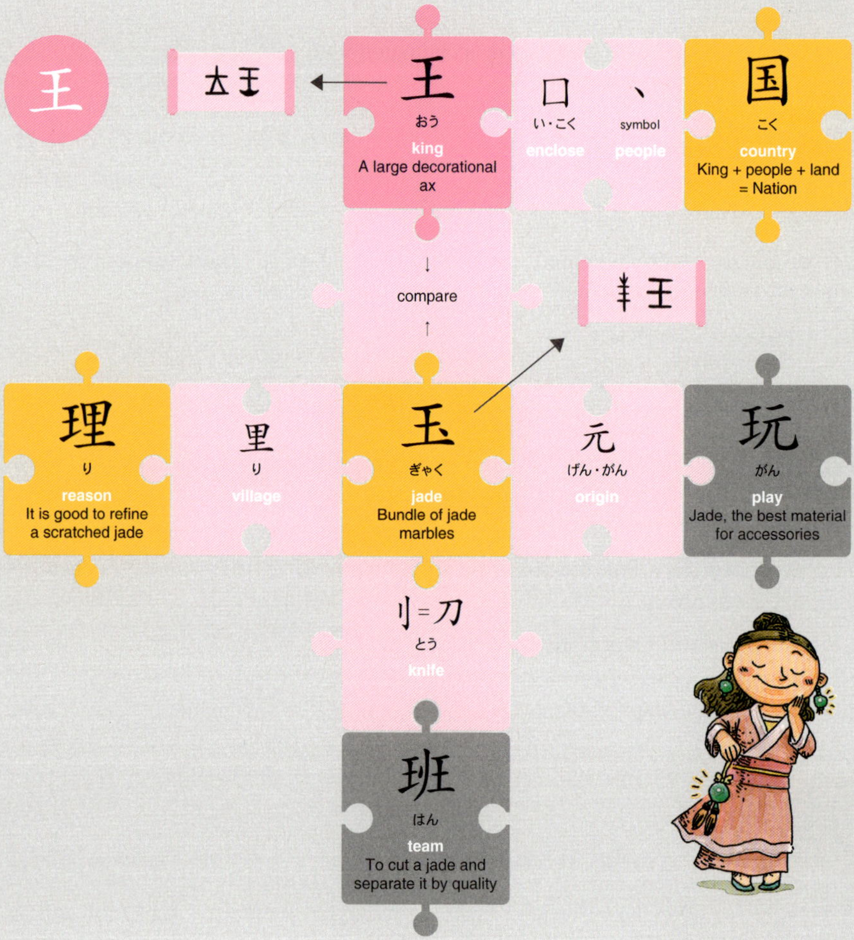

86 **王** オウ **king** 一 二 干 王

If a small ax symbolizing authority became "士[84]," then a larger ax can mean something substantial as in 'king.'

* The radical of "王" is "jade 玉[86b] [ギャク]," and when "玉" is used as part of another character, it changes into "王."

王様[おうさま] king -86 134a
国王[こくおう] king; sovereign -86a 86

86a 国

コク くに

country

enclose 口[16] [イ・コク] + king 王 [オウ] + people 丶 [symbol]

A king(王), people(丶), and a boundary(口) makes a nation. These are the three basic components of a country.

* The traditional character(國) is a combination of people(ロ[12]), land(一), a spear(戈[91]) and a boundary(口[16]).

外国人[がいこくじん] foreigner; alien -172b 86a 51	英国[えいこく] Great Britain -61c 86a
国王[こくおう] king; sovereign -86a 86	国民[こくみん] nation; people -86a 80c

86b 玉

ギャク たま

jade

A few jade marbles are made into a bundle by passing threads(丶) into the center hole.

* Usually changes its shape to "王" when combined with other characters.

86c 玩

ガン

play

jade 王→玉 [ギャク] + origin 元[58a] [ゲン・ガン]

Symbolizes the fact that jade(玉) was the best(元) material to create women's favorite playing accessories.

* Chinese people started to make jade since the early stone ages. Jade has been used accessories since 500 B.C.

愛玩[あいがん] being fond of; prizing; treasuring -29e 86c

86d 班

ハン

team; squad

jade 玉 [ギャク] + knife 刂=刀[95] [トウ]

This character describes someone dividing a jade(玉) with a knife(刂) and grouping the pieces according to quality. It means 'class or group.'

86e 理

リ

reason

jade 王→玉 [ギャク] + village 里[119] [リ]

It is only reasonable to refine a defective jade(玉) into a jewel instead of discarding it. "里" is where the character gets its pronunciation.

* Regardless of however much jade(玉) a village(里) can produce, it's still reasonable to refine them all and put them to use.

料理[りょうり]cooking; cookery -128b 86e	地理[ちり] geography -68b 86e
理由[りゆう] reason; excuse; pretext -86e 123e	

War

LIFE

Necessities of life

Agriculture

War

Which events shaped the ancient societies? War probably affected people more than any other event because it was a matter of life and death. Many kanji are about war.

1. No war is fought without a weapon. Characters for 'arrow,' 'spear,' 'ax,' 'sword' and 'shield' are all part of more complicated characters.
2. Any nation going to war needs a secure supply line. Means of transportation, such as carts and ships are important characters.
3. Before going to war, the ancient Chinese prayed to the gods. Characters for 'altar' and 'fortunetelling' appear frequently.

Necessities of life

Regardless of which country you live in, the three necessities that we all need are food, housing, and clothing.

1. Clothes are made with fabrics, and fabrics are made with threads. These connections are reflected in the Chinese characters. Fabrics were dyed to give their color, so there are many color-related characters as well.
2. From characters about cooked and uncooked rice to beans, to "食," its the shape of a bowl of rice covered with a lid. There are many characters regarding food.
3. Some characters describe the shape of a house, and some others describe the markings on a door. As many people lived in caves or mud huts, there are also many characters associated with hills.

Agriculture

Agriculture has been the very basis of human civilization since its beginning, since it produces most basic foods for people.

1. This section will deal with characters related to land, such as crop fields and earth, as well as fire, as people created fields by setting land on fire in the early days.
2. As agriculture developed, requirement of tools became evident. You will see that 'plow' is used as a basic element of the character for many different symbols and meanings.
3. Harvested crops need vessels and plates to hold them. Many basic characters related to items such as wine bottles, measuring cups, mesh bags, and covers will be covered in this section.

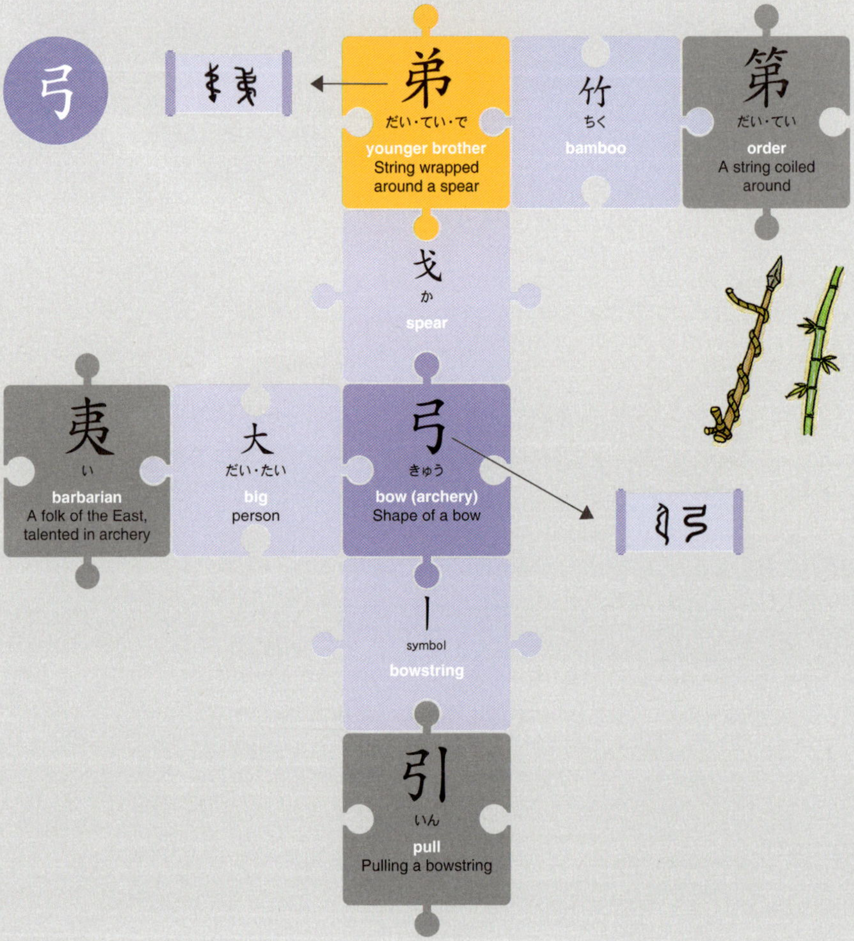

87 弓

キュウ ゆみ

bow (archery)

The most efficient weapon was the bow. This character takes the shape of a drawn bow.

87a **弟**

ダイ・テイ・デ　おとうと　　丶 丷 丷 当 弚 弟 弟

younger brother

spear 丫→戈[91] [カ] + coiled around/bow 弓 [キュウ]

Means 'order' because it describes a string coiled around(弓) a spear(戈). This character also means 'younger brother' because there's a top and bottom to a coil.

* Ancient characters show that this "弟" character originally describes a string wrapped around(弓) a spear(戈), not a bow.

兄弟[きょうだい] brother; sibling -59 87a

87b **第**

ダイ・テイ　　ノ ト ⺮ ⺮ ⺮ ⺮ 笃 笃 笃 第 第

order

bamboo 竹[169] [チク] + younger brother 弟 [ダイ・テイ・デ]

When "弟," the shape of a bow's drawstring coiled around something came to mean 'younger brother,' the Chinese combined it with the character for bamboo(竹), giving this character the meaning 'order.' It's also used as a prefix when counting.

87c **引**

イン　ひく　　フ コ 弓 引

pull

bow 弓 [キュウ] + bowstring 丨 [symbol]

To pull the string(丨) of a bow(弓).

引く[ひく] pull; draw; tug
字引[じびき] dictionary -77a 87c

87d **夷**

イ　　一 ㇇ 弓 弓 夷 夷

barbarian

person/big 大[60] [ダイ・タイ] + bow 弓 [キュウ]

This character signifies the alien people who used to live in the Eastern part of old China. They were very good at archery(弓). It is interesting to note that the people of Goguryeo were horse-riding people(大) who were also talented in archery(弓). Goguryeo was a kingdom which was established in the eastern part of old China in about 1st century B.C.

* The letter of Ju Mong, the founder's name of Goguryeo, means a person(大) who is very good at archery(弓).

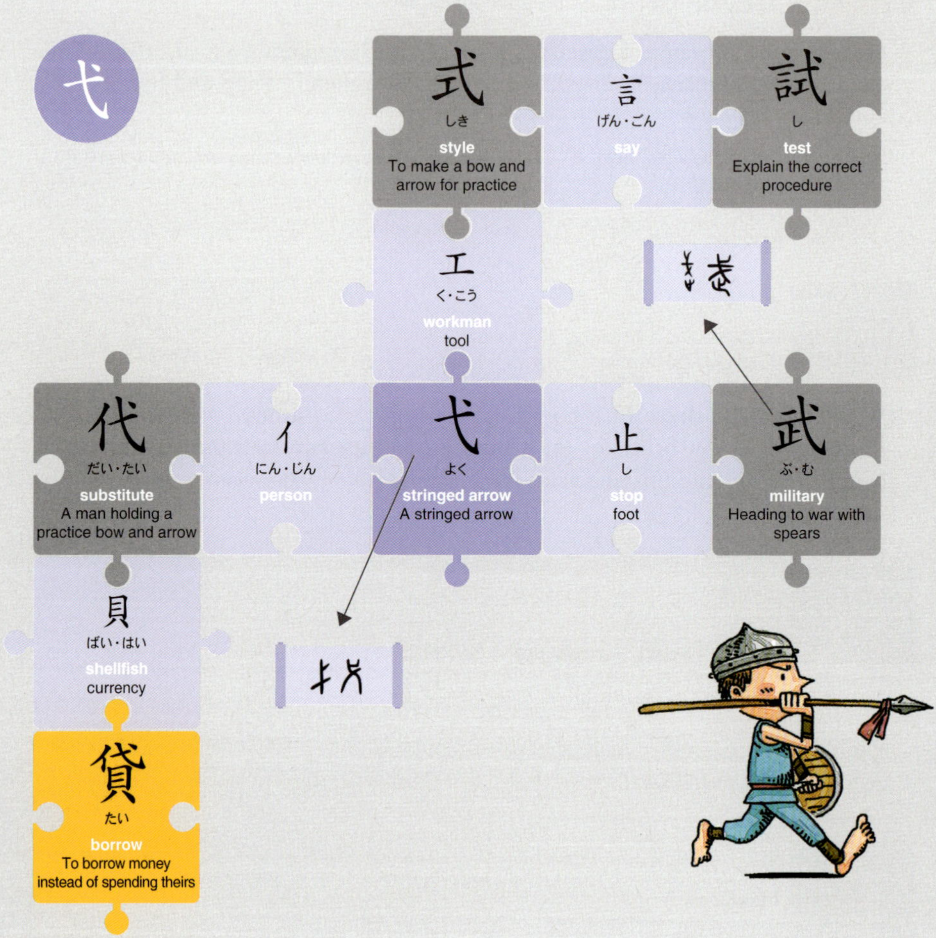

88 弋

ヨク

stringed arrow

This character takes the shape of an arrow connected to the bow with a string used for shooting practice.

88a **式**

シキ 一 二 亍 王 式 式

style; ceremony

stringed arrow 弋 [ヨク] + tool/workman 工 155 [ク・コウ]

A bow and arrow used for practice(弋) is made with tools(工). Even though they are only used for practice, they have to be made according to certain procedures.

公式[こうしき] formula; formality -76e 88a
正式[せいしき] official; formality -45 88a

88b **試**

シ こころみる・ためす

test

say 言 17 [ゲン・ゴン] + style 式 [シキ]

A test is to check whether one can explain(言) or follow the correct procedures (式).

試みる[こころみる] exam; test	試す[ためす] try; exam; test
試合[しあい] game; contest -88b 54a	試験[しけん] test -88b 55b

88c **武**

ブ・ム

military

spear 戈 91 [カ] + foot/stop 止 44 [シ]

The feet(止) of men heading to war carrying spears (戈) is how the Chinese portrayed an army.

* This character shows that instead of a "stringed arrow 弋 [yi]," it's a spear with an extra stroke(戈) with a set of feet(止).

武士[ぶし] samurai; warrior -88c 84

88d **代**

ダイ・タイ かわる・かえる ノ イ 仁 代 代

substitute; period

person 亻 52 [ニン・ジン] + stringed arrow 弋 [ヨク]

A person(亻) using a practice bow and arrow(弋) instead of the one used in the war. Because the following era in history takes the place of the previous one, this character came to mean 'historical periods.'

代(わ)る[かわる] replace; substitute (for)	代える[かえる] replace; substitute
時代[じだい] period; era -37a 88d	現代[げんだい] today; present day -9a 88d

88e **貸**

タイ かす

borrow

substitute 代 [ダイ・タイ] + currency/shellfish 貝 145 [バイ・ハイ]

To borrow someone else's money(貝) instead(代) to satisfy their needs.

貸す[かす] lend; loan; lent out	貸家[かしや] rented house -88e 136a

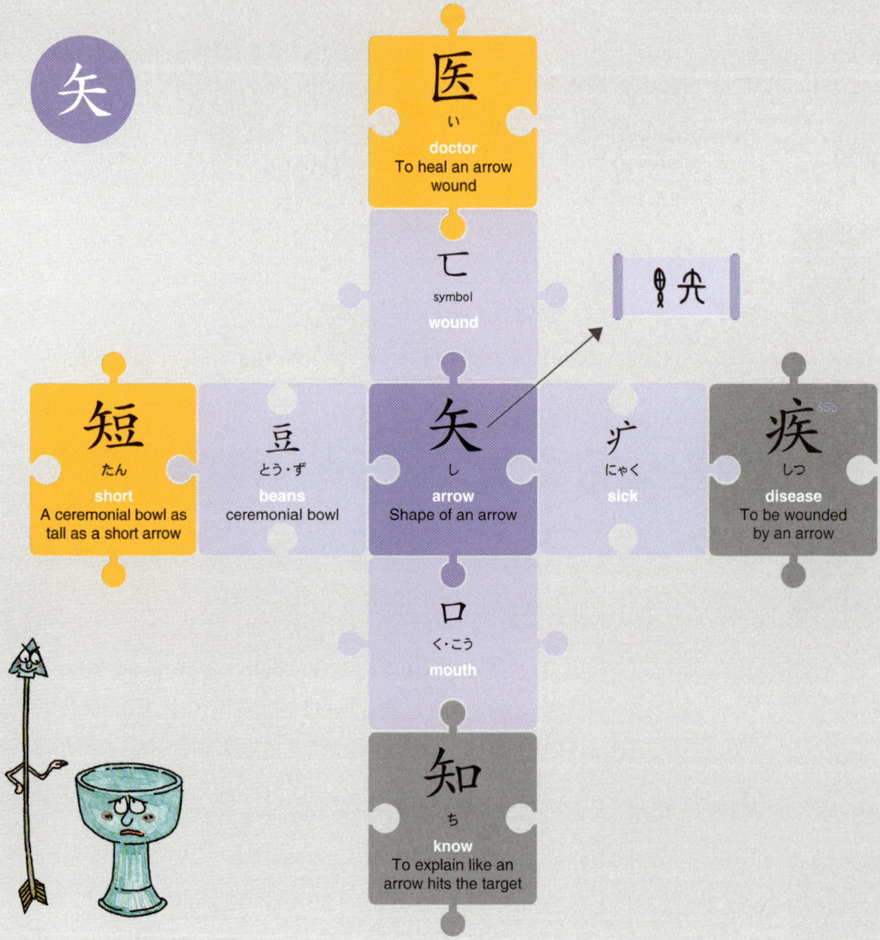

89 **矢** シ や
arrow

The shape of an arrow including the head, body, and notch.

矢印[やじるし] arrow (mark or symbol) -89 69d

89a 医

一 丆 丆 匸 至 医 医

イ

doctor

wound 匸 [symbol] + arrow 矢 [シ]

A doctor is someone who pours alcohol on wounds(匸) caused by arrows(矢) to help them heal.

* The traditional character(醫) shows liquor(酉[133]) used to disinfect an open wound(匸) caused by an arrow(矢), then a splint(殳[93]) used to secure the body part.

医者[いしゃ] doctor -89a 82
医師[いし] doctor; physician -89a 152b
歯医者[はいしゃ] dentist -21 89a 82

89b 知

ノ 𠂉 ⺧ 午 矢 矢 知 知

チ しる

know

arrow 矢 [シ] + mouth ロ[12] [ク・コウ]

'To know' about something means you can verbally(ロ) explain, like how an arrow(矢) hits the bulls-eye.

知る[しる] know; recognize
知能[ちのう] intellect; intelligence -89b 73d

89c 短

ノ 𠂉 ⺧ 午 矢 矢 矢 知 知 短 短 短

タン みじかい

short

arrow 矢 [シ] + ceremonial bowl/beans 豆[112] [トウ・ズ]

It can be said that the stem of a ceremonial bowl(豆) that's as long as the stem of a wine glass cannot even come close to the length of an arrow(矢). This came to mean 'short.'

* "豆" is the shape of a ceremonial bowl that has a stem or legs.

短い[みじかい] short; brief
短期[たんき] short term -89c 39c

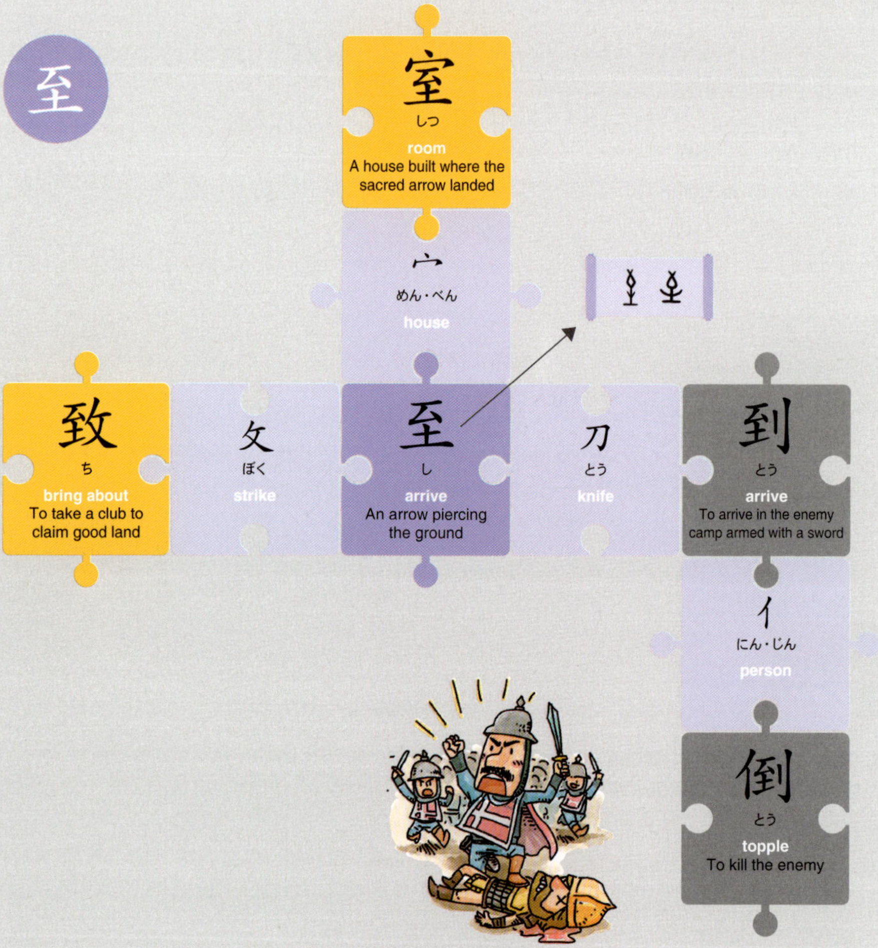

90 **至**

シ いたる

arrive

一 工 云 亖 至 至

An arrow(矢) that has been shot into the ground(土 120) has reached its target.

* In the ancient days, a sacred arrow(矢) was shot, and where it landed(一) was where they built important buildings or temples.

至る[いたる] arrive (at/in); reach; get (to)

至急[しきゅう] urgent; pressing -90.56d

90a 室

丶 丷 宀 宀 宀 宏 宏 室 室

シツ

room

house 宀[113] [メン・ベン] + arrive 至 [シ]

Tradition dictated that sacred arrows were shot, and houses(宀) with rooms were built where the arrow landed(至). This character also came to mean 'wife,' who's someone who shares a man's room.

* The Chinese believed in building and living in sacred locations.

教室[きょうしつ] classroom - 43a 90a
室内[しつない] indoor - 90a 53b

90b 到

一 ㇐ ㇐ 云 至 至 到 到

トウ　いたる

arrive; reach

arrive 至 [シ] + knife 刂=刀[95] [トウ]

An arrow that hits its mark(至), and a sword(刂) symbolizes war. To arrive(至) at the enemy camp armed with a sword(刀) gave the meaning 'to arrive or to go~.'

到る[いたる] arrive (at/in); reach; get (to)
到着[とうちゃく] arrival - 90b 7b

90c 倒

丿 亻 亻 任 任 侄 侄 侄 倒 倒

トウ　たおす・たおれる

topple

person 亻[52] [ニン・ジン] + arrive 到 [トウ]

Soldiers(亻) who have reached(到) the enemy camp are throwing down the enemies backwards.

倒す[たおす] throw down; blow down
倒れる[たおれる] fall (down); collapse
倒産[とうさん] bankruptcy; insolvency - 90c 117e

90d 致

一 ㇐ ㇐ 云 至 至 到 致 致 致

チ　いたす

bring about

arrive 至 [シ] + strike 攵[43] [ボク]

Taking a club or a stick(攵) to reach and claim the land the sacred arrow landed on(至) means to 'bring about.'

致す[いたす] bring; cause; lead to
如何致しまして[どういたしまして] You are welcome - 78d 13c 90d

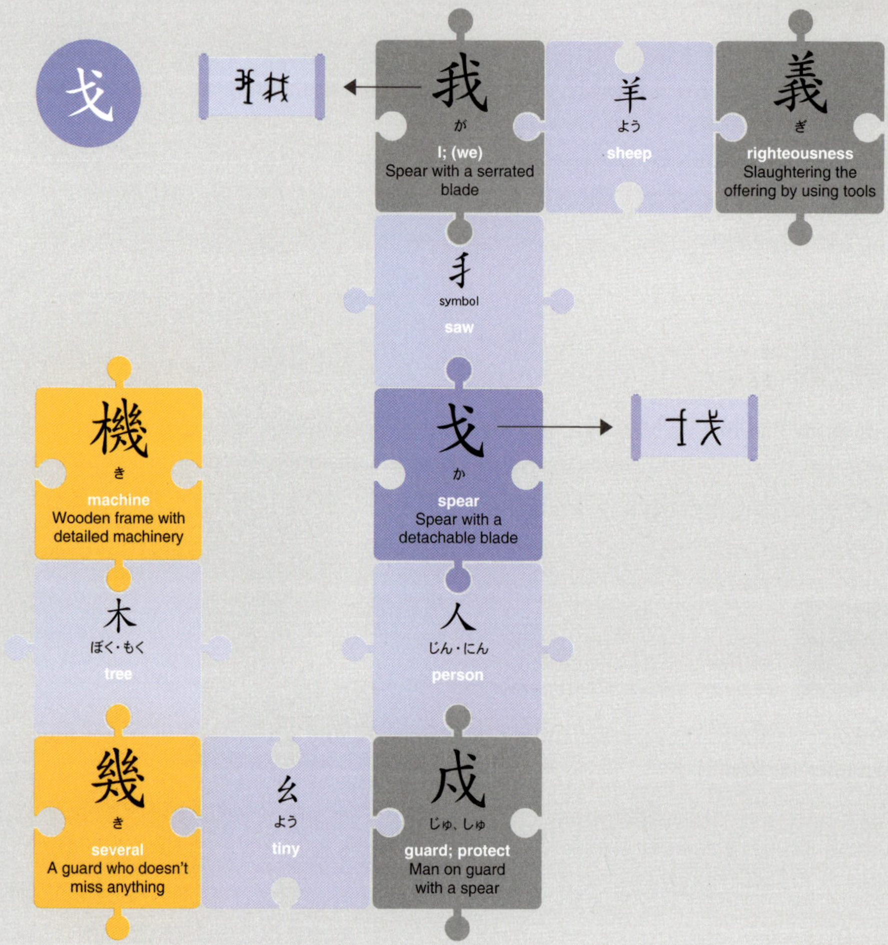

91 戈 カ

spear

一 弋 戈 戈

The shape of a spear with a curved detachable blade.

91a 我

ガ わ·われ　㇒ 二 于 手 我 我 我

I; we

saw 扌[symbol] + spear 戈 [カ]

This character originally meant 'saw' because of the serrated(扌) blade on the spear(戈), but later it meant 'me or us' because of the similar pronunciation.

* It's interesting to note that Chinese geese have serrated edges on the base of their bills. That explains why the character "goose 鵝 [ガ]" is a combination of a saw(我) and a bird(鳥[139]).

我がまま[わがまま] self-indulgence; selfishness
怪我[けが] injury; hurt -120c 91a

91b 義

ギ　丶 丷 䒑 䒑 ⺷ 羊 羊 差 羊 羊 義 義 義

righteousness

sheep 羊[134] [ヨウ] + spear with a serrated edge / I (me) 我 [ガ]

To slaughter(我) a sheep(羊) to serve it as an offering. To offer a sacrifice to the gods is 'right.'

意義[いぎ] meaning; significance -18b 91b
主義[しゅぎ] principle; belief -181a 91b

91c 戍

ジュ·シュ　一 厂 厂 戊 戍 戍

guard; protect

spear 戈 [カ] + person ⺊→人[51] [ジン·ニン]

A person(人) standing guard with a spear(戈) is there 'to protect.'

91d 幾

キ いく　𠃋 幺 幺 幺 幺幺 幺幺 丝 幾 幾 幾 幾 幾

several

tiny 幺 [ヨウ] + guard 戍 [ジュ、シュ]

Soldiers who guard(戍) the borders must pay attention to detail and small(幺) changes, and that means 'several or how many.'

* "幺" is one strand of thin thread(糸[104]) and means 'small.'

幾つ[いくつ] how many; how old
幾ら[いくら] how much; how many

91e 機

キ　一 十 才 木 木 朩 朩 朩 朩 朩 朩 朩 朩 機 機 機

machine

tree 木[164] [ボク·モク] + several 幾 [キ]

A detailed(幾) machine made of wood(木) such as a loom.

飛行機[ひこうき] airplane; aircraft -128d 48a 91e

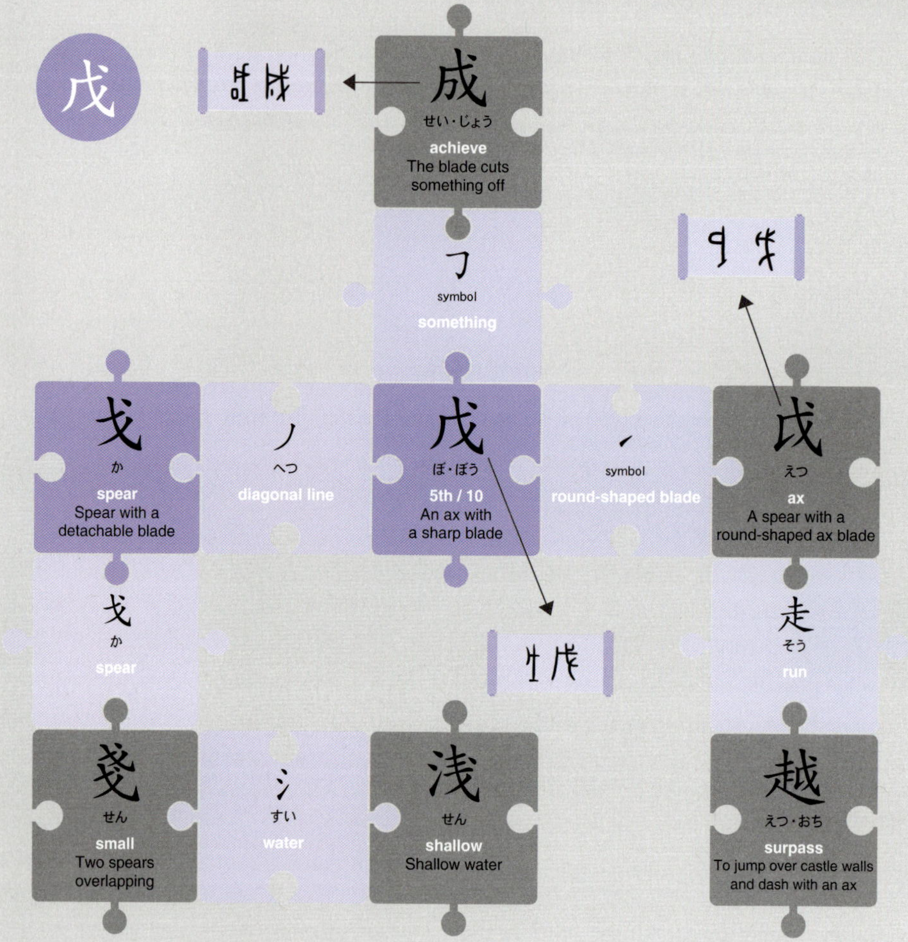

92 戊

ボ・ボウ

5th/10

diagonal line 丿 [179e] [ヘツ] + spear 戈 [91] [カ]

This character is a combination of two characters. They are the spear(戈), of which the main purpose is to stab, and the axe(丿), which is used to cut or chop down. It is also the fifth of the ten calendar signs.

* "丿" has no meaning and can be interpreted in many ways.

92a 成

セイ・ジョウ　なる　　一 厂 万 成 成 成

achieve

ax/5th of 10 戊 [ボ・ボウ] + something 𠃌 [symbol]

Something(𠃌) has been cut off by the blade(丿) of an ax(戊). To accomplish at war means to cut off the opposing commander's head(𠃌) with one's ax(戊).

成る[なる] be; become; come true
完成[かんせい] completion -58b 92a

92b 戉

エツ　　一 厂 弋 戊 戉

ax

spear 戈[91] [カ] + round-shaped blade ⺃ [symbol]

"戉" is a character which is formed by the combination of a spear(戈) and a blade(丿). The character of "戉" shows that the function of its spear has been improved as a more offensive weapon due to the rounded blade of an ax.

* Its ancient character clearly shows that there is an ax blade on the left side of the spear.

92c 越

エツ・オチ　こえる・こす　　一 + 土 キ 丰 未 走 走 走 赵 越 越

surpass

run 走[44c] [ソウ] + ax 戉 [エツ]

This character symbolizes a soldier who jumps over castle walls and makes a dash(走) at the enemy with an ax(戉), as a weapon that has been much improved for offense.

越える[こえる] cross over; cross; pass
越す[こす] cross over; go over

92d 戔

セン　　一 𠂇 戈 戈 戈 戔 戔 戔

small

spear 戈[91] [カ] + spear 戈[91] [カ]

A spear(戈) is used to hurt or kill, so the two written together means 'to injure.' It also means 'little or few' because spears pile up easily without taking up much space.

92e 浅

セン　あさい　　丶 丶 氵 氵 氵 浐 浅 浅 浅

shallow

water 氵[157] [スイ] + small 戋 → 戔 [セン]

Little(戔) water(氵) means that it's shallow.

浅い[あさい] shallow; non-deep

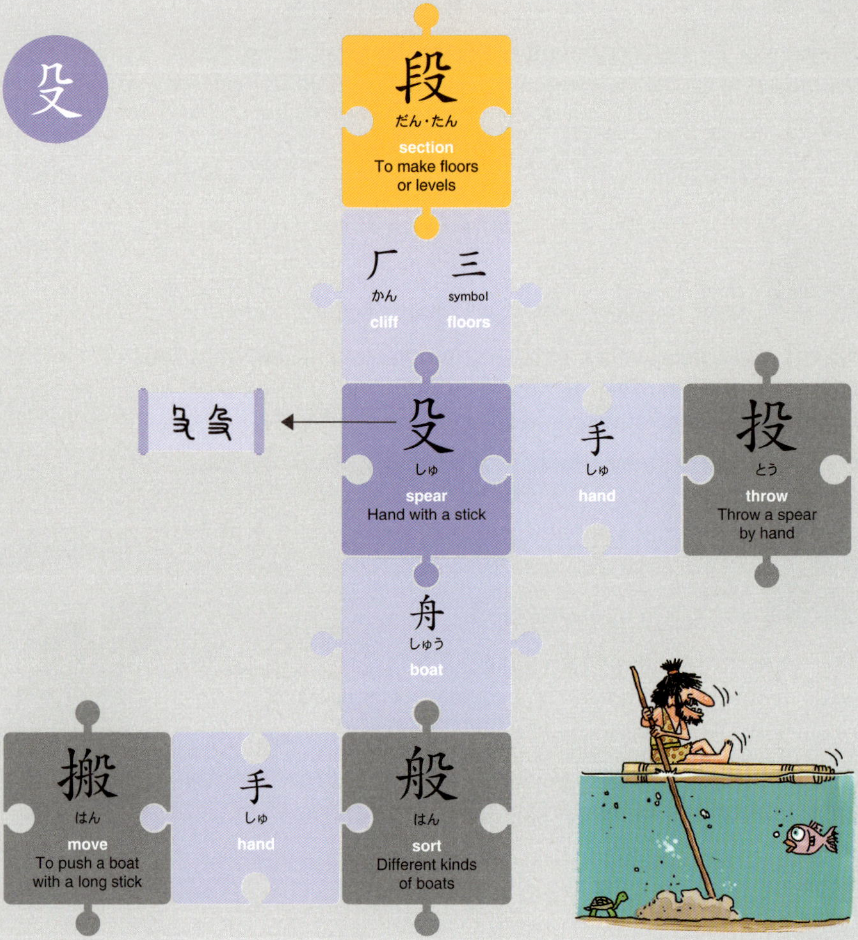

93 **殳** シュ

spear

This character is a hand(又[30]) holding a stick, much like the body of a spear. It means 'stick or strike.'

93a 段

ダン・タン

´ 丨 𠂆 𠂇 𦣝 𣪠 𣪨 段 段

section; step

cliff 厂[117] [カン] + floors 三 [symbol] + strike/spear 殳 [シュ]

To divide a hill(厂) into sections, then use tools to beat(殳) the ground into levels(三).

階段[かいだん] stairs; staircase -72d 93a
段段[だんだん] gradually; by degrees -93a 93a
値段[ねだん] price; cost -8b 93a

93b 投

トウ なげる

一 十 扌 扌 扌 抃 投

throw

hand 扌=手[28] [シュ] + spear 殳 [シュ]

To throw a spear(殳) very far by hand(扌).

投げる[なげる] throw; cast away; shine
投手[とうしゅ] pitcher -93b 28

93c 般

ハン

´ 丿 力 月 舟 舟 舟 舟 般 般

sort

boat 舟[98] [シュウ] + stick/spear 殳 [シュ]

The type of boat(舟) differs depending on the shape of the sail or the oar(殳) used.

* Older boats were pushed along with a long stick(殳) instead of being rowed.

一般[いっぱん] general; ordinary -173 93c

93d 搬

ハン

一 十 扌 扌 扌 扚 扚 扚 扚 搬 搬 搬 搬

move

hand 扌=手[28] [シュ] + sort 般 [ハン]

To transport items in the kind(般) of boat that is pushed by a hand(扌) holding a long stick.

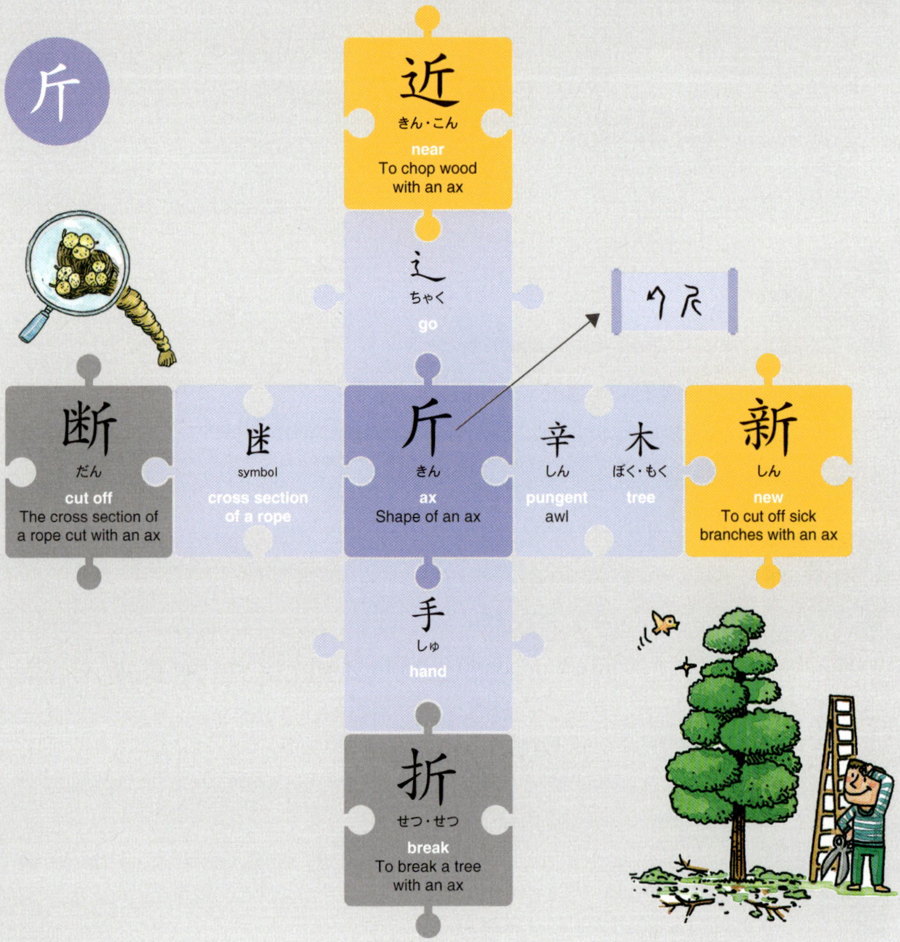

94 斤 キン

ax

An ax is used as a tool to chop up wood or a weapon to kill. The Chinese adopted this character to measure weight.

* One "斤" is 600 grams.

94a 近

キン・コン ちかい

丿 厂 斤 斤 䜣 䜣 近

near

ax 斤 [キン] + go ⻍[49] [チャク]

One stays near his house or work site when taking an ax(斤) to go(⻍) and chop firewood.

近い[ちかい] close (to); near
近く[ちかく] near; neighborhood; vicinity
最近[さいきん] most recent; lately; nowadays -22d 94a
近所[きんじょ] neighborhood; vicinity -94a 115e

94b 新

シン あたらしい・あらた

丶 亠 亠 立 立 立 辛 辛 亲 亲 新 新 新

new

awl/pungent 立→辛[83] [シン] + tree 木[164] [ボク・モク] + ax 斤 [キン]

If disciplining with an awl(辛) fails to help a child become something worthy(木), then one must take an ax(斤) to cut off the sick branches and help grow new ones.

新しい[あたらしい] new; fresh
新聞[しんぶん] newspaper -94b 22a
新た[あらた] new; fresh; newly; freshly
更新[こうしん] renewal -31c 94b

94c 折

セツ おり・おる・おれる

一 十 扌 扌 扩 扩 折

break; snap

hand 扌=手[28] [シュ] + ax 斤 [キン]

To break a tree by hitting it with an ax(斤) in your hand(扌).

折(り)[おり] time; moment; opportunity; chance
折る[おる] fold; bend; break
折れる[おれる] fold, be folded, break, be broken
骨折[こっせつ] fracture -24 94c

94d 断

ダン たつ・ことわる

丶 丷 丷 半 米 米 迷 迷 断 断 断

cut off

cross section of a rope 㡭 [symbol] + ax 斤 [キン]

A depiction of the cross section(㡭) of a thick rope made with many thinner strands of thread cut by an ax(斤).

* The traditional character(斷) shows that the cut(斤) rope was made with many strands of thread(糸[104]).

断つ[たつ] sever; cut off
断(わ)る[ことわる] refuse; decline
不断[ふだん] constancy; ceaselessness; continuity -173c 94d
断水[だんすい] water outage -94d 156

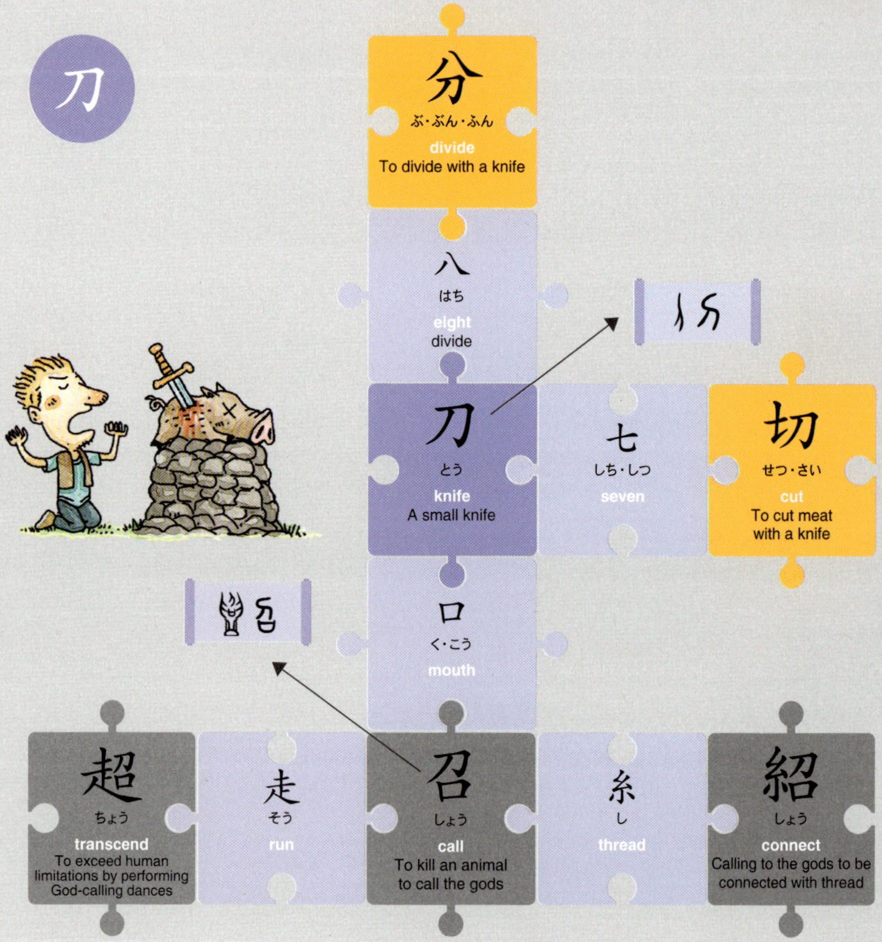

95 刀

トウ かたな

knife

フ 刀

The shape of a knife with a handle.

95a **分** ブ・ブン・フン　わかる・わかれる・わける　丿 八 分 分

divide

divide/eight 八 177 [ハチ] + knife 刀 [トウ]

To divide in half(八) with a knife(刀). A 'minute' is a division of time.

*"八" means 'to be divided' because of the identical left and right shapes.

一分[いっぷん] a minute, one minute - 173 95a
何分[なんぷん] what minute - 13c 95a
分(か)る[わかる] know; understand; be proved
分(か)れる[わかれる] crack; split; divide
分ける[わける] divide; split; separate
自分[じぶん] (one)self; I; myself - 6 95a

95b **切** セツ・サイ　きる・きれる　一 七 切 切

cut

seven 七 178b [シチ・シツ] + knife 刀 [トウ]

The shape of meat(七) cut up with a knife(刀).

*"七" is the shape of the cutting action, left-right, top-bottom.

切る[きる] cut; sever; amputate
切れる[きれる] snap, cut, break
切手[きって] stamp - 95b 28
切符[きっぷ] ticket - 95b 36b

95c **召** ショウ　めす　フ 刀 刀 召 召

call

knife 刀 [トウ] + mouth 口 12 [ク・コウ]

To kill an animal with a knife(刀) and call out(口) to the gods.

*The ancient character shows a man holding up his sacrifice to call the gods, but the modern character only shows the knife(刀) and a mouth(口) calling out to the gods.

召す[めす] honorific of 'call, eat, drink'

95d **紹** ショウ　𠃋 幺 幺 糸 糸 糸 紹 紹 紹 紹 紹

connect

thread 糸 104 [シ] + call 召 [ショウ]

A depiction of a man and gods becoming connected with thread(糸) after calling out(召).

*The meaning of the thread(糸), which is to tie and connect, helped define the meaning.

紹介[しょうかい] introduction - 95d 51a

95e **超** チョウ　一 十 土 キ キ 走 走 起 起 超 超 超

transcend; super

run 走 44c [ソウ] + call 召 [ショウ]

This character depicts a shaman who is dancing, frequenting(走) the two different worlds of body and soul beyond the limitations of human faculties in order to call up(召) to God.

超える[こえる] pass (by); exceed
超す[こす] cross over; go over; surpass; exceed

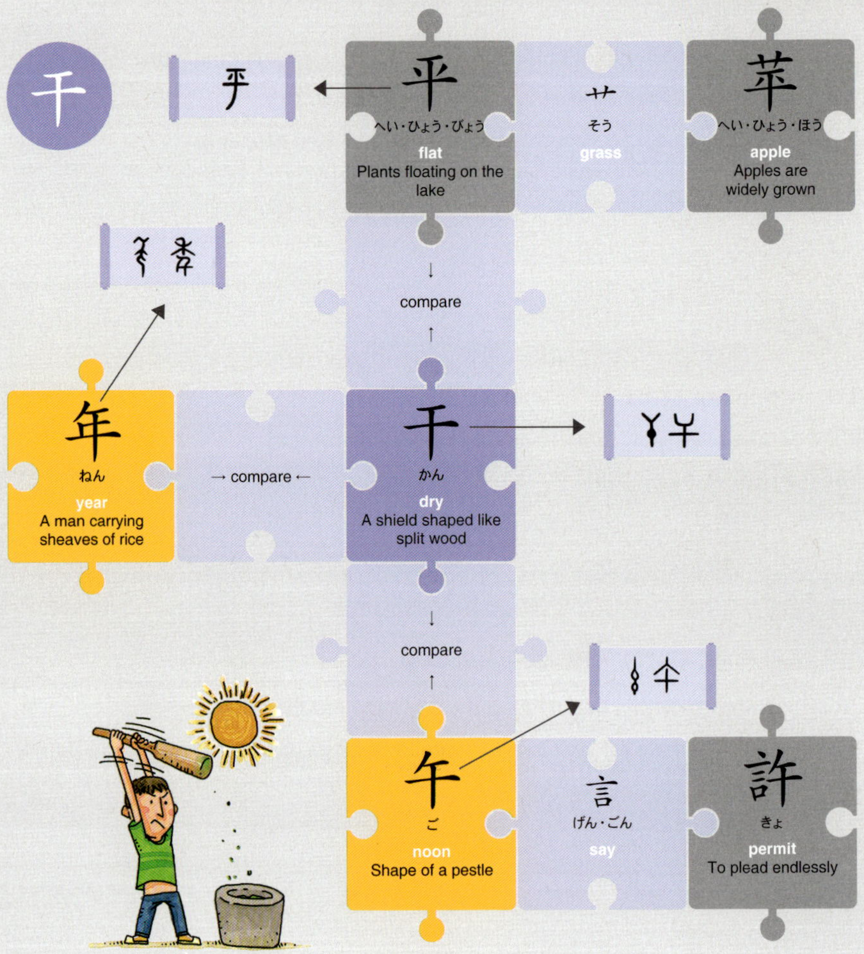

96	干	カン ほす **dry**	一 二 干

The shape of a shield split at the top to defend and attack. This character is rarely used to mean a shield. Instead, it means 'dry,' which has the same pronunciation.

干す[ほす] dry; desiccate

96a	平	ヘイ・ヒョウ・ビョウ たいら **flat; calm**	一 ㄷ ㄷ 立 平

A description of plants covering a lake's flat surface.

* Shirakawa Shizuka(白川静, 1910~2006), a Japanese scholar, says this character is the shape of woodchips flying as a man uses a plane(干) to shave a flat surface on a piece of wood(丷).

平ら[たいら] flatness; level; even	平等[びょうどう] equality -96a 37d

96b 苹

ヘイ・ヒョウ・ホウ

一 十 艹 艹 芒 芏 苙 苹

apple

grass 艹[161] [ソウ] + flat 平 [ヘイ・ヒョウ・ビョウ]

An apple is a fruit(艹) grown evenly(平) all around the world, so the Chinese decided to use this characteristic to describe it. This character is only used as part of the word "apple 苹果."

* The apple is the most evenly(平) grown fruit(艹) in the world, meaning production is not limited to one area.

苹果[りんご] apple -96b 123c

96c 午

ゴ

ノ 𠂉 𠂈 午

noon

This character depicts a pestle standing upright in a mortar which is used to grind grains into powder. When the sun shines directly above the center of the mortar, it is noon time.

* The ancient character shows that this is the shape of a mill with a mortar and a pestle under the roof of a building.

午後[ごご] afternoon; p.m. -96c 48c	午前[ごぜん] morning; a.m. -96c 98b

96d 許

キョ　ゆるす

丶 亠 亠 亠 言 言 言 訁 訂 訐 許

permit

say 言[17] [ゲン・ゴン] + pestle/noon 午 [ゴ]

'Strike enough times and any tree will fall' is a popular adage. Like one pounding a pestle(午) endlessly, if one asks(言) for permission enough times, one will get it.

許す[ゆるす] permit; allow	許可[きょか] permission; approval; license -96d 13
免許[めんきょ] license -57 96d	

96e 年

ネン　とし

ノ 𠂉 𠂈 仁 仨 年

year

person 𠂉→人[51] [ジン・ニン] + rice plant 丰→禾[111] [カ]

A man(人) carrying sheaves of rice(禾) reminds us of harvests. The Chinese harvest once a year, so this character means 'year.'

* Ancient texts show that this character's a combination of rice(禾) and a person(人).

一階[いちねん] one year; first year -173 96e	一昨年[おととし] year before last -173 180b 96e
今年[ことし] this year -54b 96e	去年[きょねん] last year -63c 96e
何年[なんねん] what year; how many years -13c 96e	毎年[まいねん] every year -79a 96e
来年[らいねん] next year -110e 96e	少年[しょうねん] boy; youth -182a 96e

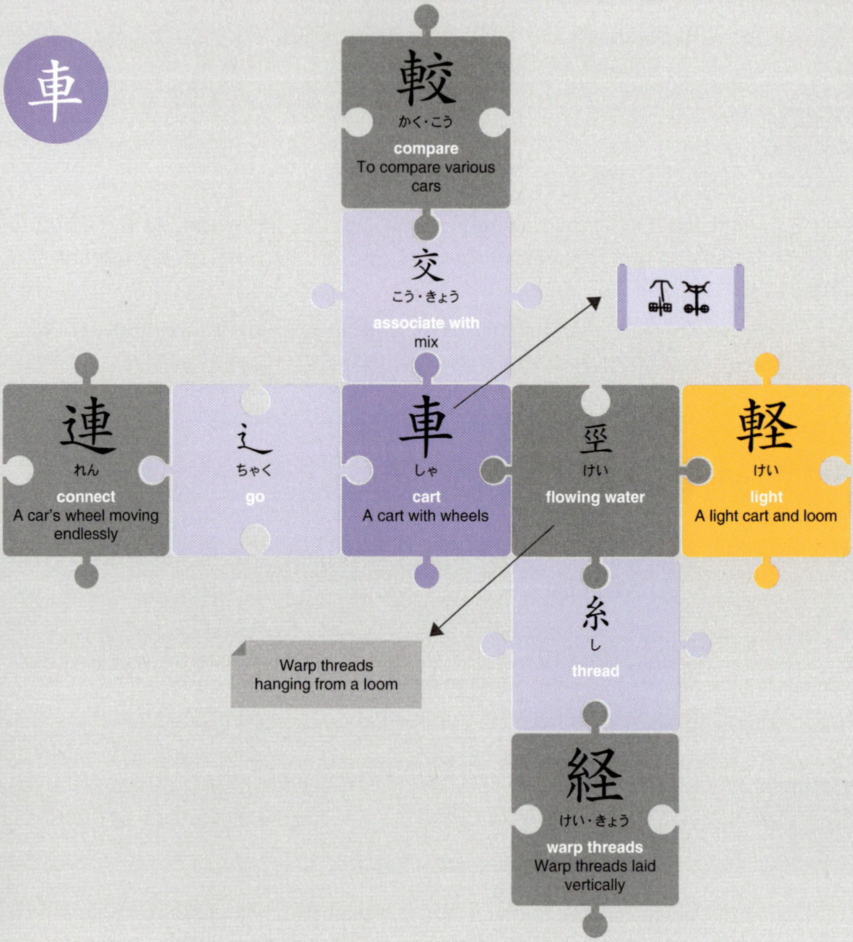

97 **車** しゃ くるま

cart; car

The shape of a cart with wheels, drawn by horse or cattle. Now it means 'car.'

汽車[きしゃ] train; steam train (original meaning) -158b 97
自動車[じどうしゃ] car; vehicle; automobile -6 119b 97
列車[れっしゃ] train -25b 97

97a **較**

カク・コウ くらべる

一 ㄏ 币 百 亘 車 車 軟 軟 較 較

compare

cart 車 [シャ] + mix/associate with 交 1a [コウ・キョウ]

Out of an assortment of(交) cars(車), they are comparing which one is better.

*Even in ancient China, they compared cars or carts to judge who was better off.

較べる[くらべる] compare　　比較[ひかく] comparison - 72b 97a

97b **巠**

ケイ

一 ㄏ 巛 巠 巠 巠 巠

flowing water

A loom from which warp threads(巛) are being held down with weights(工). This character means 'streams of water or underground streams,' because that's what hanging threads look like.

97c **軽**

ケイ かるい

一 ㄏ 币 百 亘 車 車 軒 軽 軽 軽 軽

light

cart 車 [シャ] + loom/flowing water 圣→巠 [ケイ]

The light movement of a cart's(車) wheels and the swift movement of a loom (巠).

*The right side of the traditional character(輕) is a variation of "巠," which is the original shape of a 'loom.'

軽い[かるい] light (i.e. not heavy)　　手軽[てがる] simple; convenient; easy - 28 97c

97d **経**

ケイ・キョウ たつ・へる

ㄥ 幺 幺 糸 糸 糸 紀 経 経 経 経

warp threads

thread 糸 104 [シ] + loom/flowing water 圣→巠 [ケイ]

Threads(糸) laid vertically on a loom(巠) are called 'warp threads.' It also means 'to pass through,' because the shuttle on the loom carries the weft thread that is laid horizontally through these wrap threads.

*The right-hand side of The traditional character(經) is a variation of "巠."

経つ[たつ] pass; go by　　経る[へる] pass (by); pass (through)

97e **連**

レン つれる・つらねる・つらなる

一 ㄏ 币 百 亘 車 車 連 連 連

connect

cart 車 [シャ] + go 辶 49 [チャク]

A car(車) turns its wheels endlessly to go forward(辶). Something that never ends is 'connected or continuous.'

連れる[つれる] bring along; take along; accompany
連ねる/列ねる[つらねる] line up; put in a row - 97e/25b
連なる/列なる[つらなる] be in a line, stand in a row - 97e/25b
連休[れんきゅう] consecutive holidays - 97e 165a

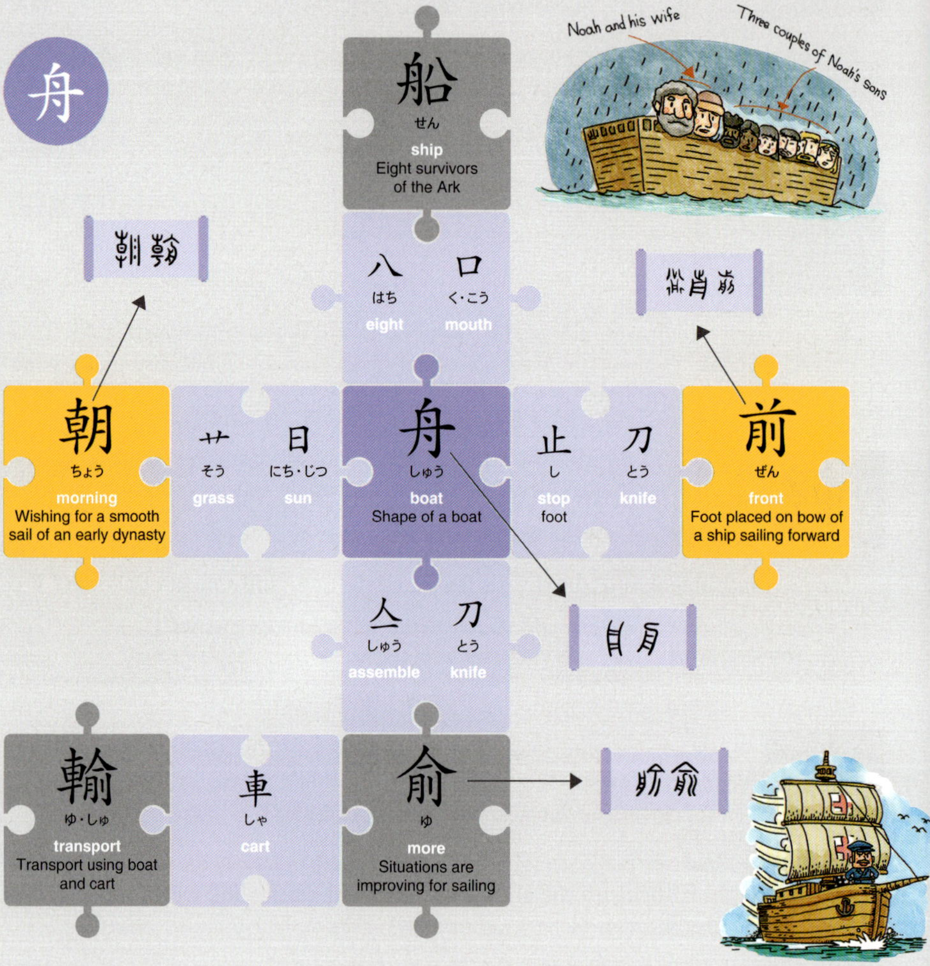

98 舟

シュウ ふね

boat

A small boat made by carving out a whole piece of wood.

98a 船

センふね

丿 亅 介 舟 舟 舟 舟 舟 舟 船 船

ship

boat 舟 [シュウ] + eight 八[177] [ハチ] + mouth ロ[12] [ク・コウ]

This character means boats and ships of all sizes. The bible states that eight(八) people(ロ) survived in Noah's Ark(舟), and this character seems to explain that.

＊A mouth(ロ) is used to eat and speak and it also describes people.

漁船[ぎょせん] fishing boat (vessel) -144b 98a
船便[ふなびん] by ship (sea, water); surface mail -98a 31d

98b 前

ゼンまえ

丶 丷 䒑 䒑 前 前 前 前 前

front; before

foot/stop 䒑→止[44] [シ] + boat 月→舟 [シュウ] + knife 刂=刀[95] [トウ]

Symbolizes the feet(止) of a man standing on the bow or the front of a ship (舟), sailing forward(刂) on water.

＊Sword(刂) is used here to symbolize water being spilt into sides when a ship sails forward. The ancient character shows a feet(止) of a person standing on a bow of a ship(舟) moving(行[48a]) forward.

午前[ごぜん] morning; a.m. -96c 98b
名前[なまえ] name -172d 98b

98c 俞

ユ

丿 人 亼 亼 俞 俞 俞 俞 俞

more

assemble 亼[54] [シュウ] + boat 月→舟 [シュウ] + knife 刂=刀[95] [トウ]

The collective(亼) circumstances are getting better for a ship(舟) to sail forward(刂).

98d 輸

ユ・シュ

一 丆 戸 百 百 亘 車 車 軡 軡 軡 輪 輸 輸 輸 輸

transport

cart 車[97] [シャ] + more 俞 [ユ]

Signifies transportation of goods using boats and carts(車) as winds and conditions get better(俞).

輸送[ゆそう] transport; transportation -98d 62d

98e 朝

チョウあさ

一 十 𠂇 古 古 吉 直 卓 朝 朝 朝 朝

morning; dynasty

grass 艹[161] [ソウ] + sun 日[170] [ニチ・ジツ] + boat 月→舟 [シュウ]

Originally meant as a morning sun(日) rising above the grass(艹) field. In the bronze inscription, however, ship(舟) was added to imply a smooth voyage – symbolizing a wish for the smooth(舟) sailing of a newly established dynasty.

＊The ancient character shows that "moon 月[172] [ゲツ・ガツ]" used in "朝" actually looks like "舟."

今朝[けさ] this morning -54b 98e
毎朝[まいあさ] every morning -79a 98e
朝ご飯[あさごはん] breakfast -98e 117b

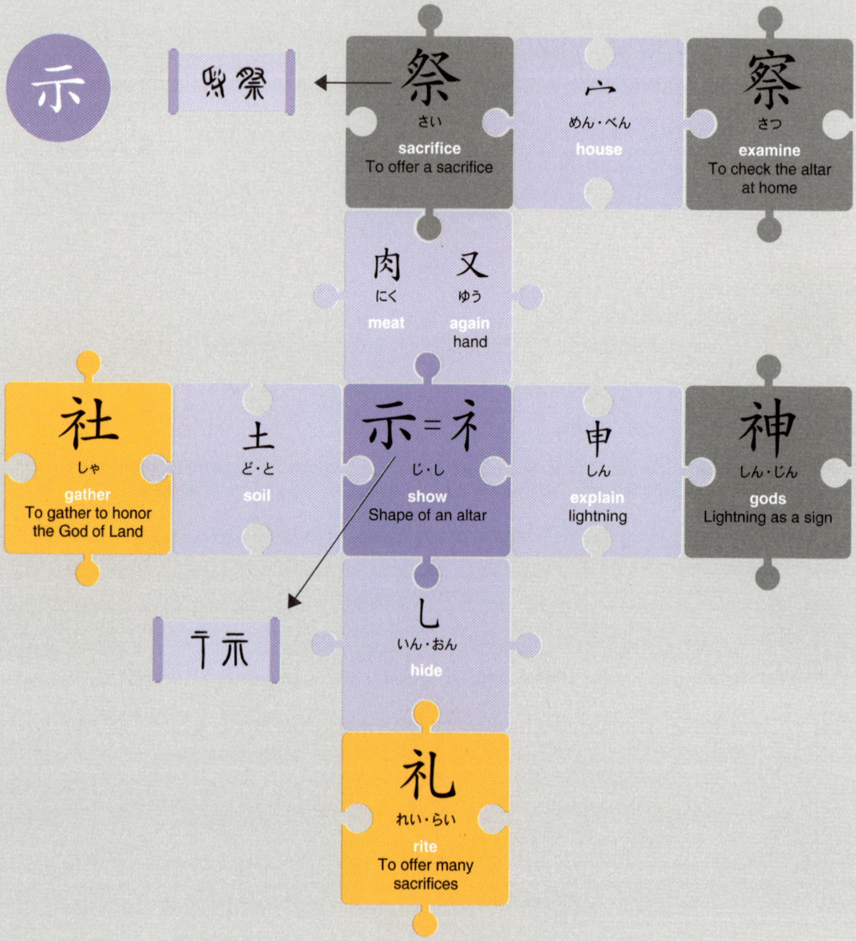

99 **示**

ジ・シ しめす

一 二 亍 亓 示

show

The shape of an altar used to offer sacrifices to the gods. In return, the gods show the people something. When combined to become part of another character, it sometimes changes into "ネ."

示す[しめす] point; indicate; denote	指示[しじ] directions; instructions -73c 99

99a **祭**

サイ まつり・まつる

ノ ク タ タ タ' 夕又 夕又 夕又 夕又 祭 祭

sacrifice

meat タ→月→肉[151] [ニク] + hand/again ヌ→又[30] [ユウ] + altar/show 示 [ジ・シ]

To sacrifice, in which meat(肉) is offered(又) on an altar(示).

* "又" is a variation of 'hand' used here because less strokes balance the character out.

祭(り)[まつり] ancestral rites; festival; feast
祭る[まつる] perform ancestral rites; worship one's spirit
祭日[さいじつ] sacrificial day; festival day -99a 170

99b 察

サツ

` ' 宀 宀 ⺈ ⺈ ⺈ ⺈ 宊 宊 宊 察 察 察

examine

house 宀[113] [メン・ベン] + sacrifice 祭 [サイ]

To check carefully if the offerings(祭) set up at home(宀) for the ancestors are appropriate.

* All East-Asian countries have set rules on which food is offered and where they are set on the table.

監察[かんさつ] inspection; inspector -85b 99b 警察[けいさつ] police -40e 99b

99c 神

シン・ジン かみ

` ⺀ ネ ネ ネ ネ口 ネ口 祀 神

gods

show ネ=示 [ジ・シ] + lightning/explain 申[159b] [シン]

This character means 'god or supernatural' because lightning(申) was considered a sign from the gods(ネ) and was feared. It also means 'spirit' because gods are invisible as are souls.

* "申" is the shape of lightning that spreads.

精神[せいしん] mind; spirit -107b 99c 神社[じんじゃ] (Shinto) shrine -99c 99e

99d 礼

レイ・ライ

` ⺀ ネ ネ 礼

rite; ceremony

altar/show ネ=示 [ジ・シ] + hide し[67c] [イン・オン]

To have a ceremonial rite with many(し) offerings on the altar(ネ).

* The traditional character(禮) is a better description of an altar(示) overflowing(豊[148e]) with offerings. "し" has no set meaning and can be interpreted depending on the character. Here, it gives the character its pronunciation.

失礼します[しつれいします] (an idiom) pardon me; excuse me -154c 99d
失礼[しつれい] discourtesy; impoliteness -154c 99d

99e 社

シャ

` ⺀ ネ ネ ネ一 ネ十 社

gather

altar/show ネ=示 [ジ・シ] + soil 土[120] [ド・ト]

In agricultural society, soil(土) was considered sacred that made everything grow. This character describes people gathered in front of an altar(ネ) to worship the God of Land(土). As this character describes a group of people gathered for a specific purpose, it came to mean 'society.'

会社[かいしゃ] company -158d 99e 支社[ししゃ] branch office -42 99e
社会[しゃかい] society; community -99e 158d 社長[しゃちょう] president; CEO -99e 81d

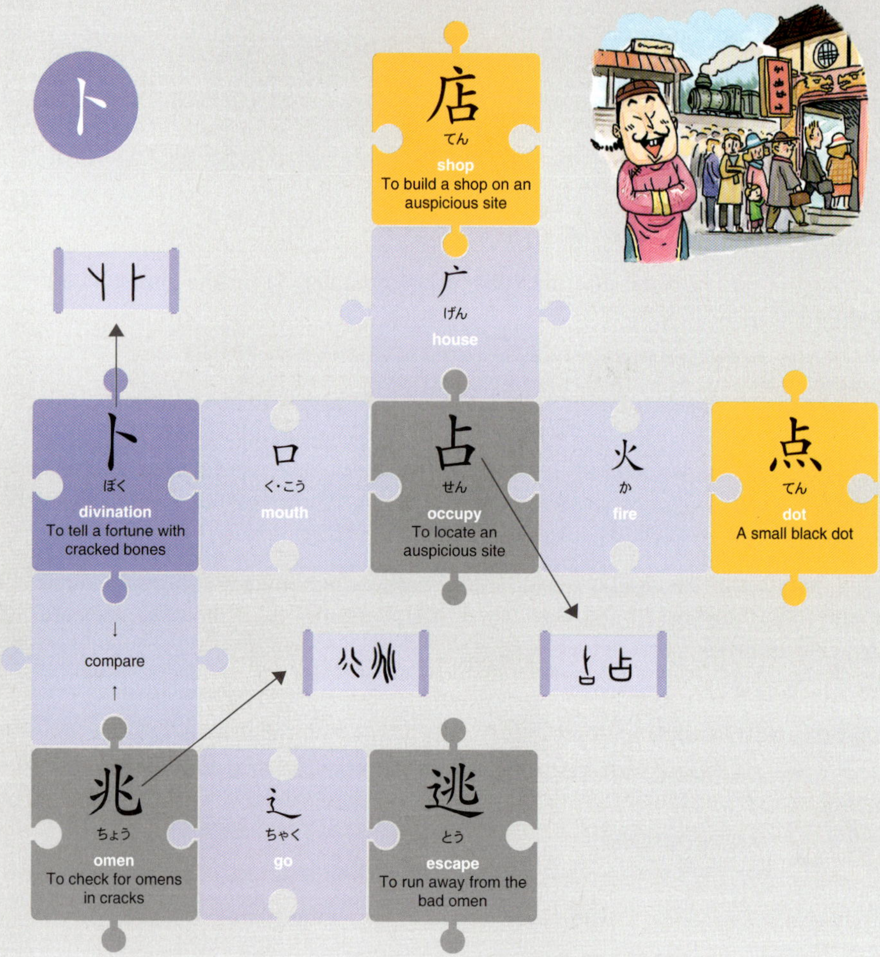

100 卜

ボク うらなう

divination

丨 卜

When you drill a hole in a cow bone or a tortoise shell, then put it in a fire, it cracks. The Chinese told fortunes based on them back in the day.

トう[うらなう] divine; tell a fortune

100a 占

セン うらなう・しめる

丨 ⺊ ⺊ 占 占

occupy

divination 卜 [ボク] + mouth 口 12 [ク・コウ]

A description of someone being told(口) of an auspicious site through fortunetelling(卜) and occupying the site.

占う[うらなう] divine; tell a fortune
占める[しめる] occupy; capture
占領[せんりょう] occupation -100a 71d
独占[どくせん] monopoly; exclusive -143d 100a

100b 店

テン みせ

丶 亠 广 广 广 庐 店 店

shop; store

house 广 114 [ゲン] + occupy 占 [セン]

To occupy an auspicious site(占), construct a building(广), and open a 'shop.'

* "广" is a house with one wall taken down, so think of a shop with a front window to display products.

喫茶店[きっさてん] teahouse, tea room -163d 161b 100b
店員[てんいん] (sales) clerk; shop assistant -100b 147d

100c 点

テン つける

丨 ⺊ ⺊ 占 占 占 点 点 点

dot; point

occupy 占 [セン] + fire 灬=火 124 [カ]

To make a character meaning 'dot,' the Chinese used the character for "fire 灬" that makes ash, and combined it with "occupy 占" to borrow the pronunciation.

* The traditional character(點) can also imply that the fire(灬) is "black 黑 124c." Burning the bones black to tell a fortune(占) also influenced the meaning.

点ける[つける] light (fire); switch on (light)
百点[ひゃくてん] full marks; perfect score -106a 100c
交差点[こうさてん] crossing; intersection 1a 1-55d 100c

100d 兆

チョウ きざし

丿 丿 扌 扌 兆 兆

omen

When you drill a hole in a cow bone or tortoise shell then put it in a fire, it cracks. This character means 'omen' and got its meaning in the similar way to "divination 卜." Because there are so many different ways something may crack, it came to mean 'a trillion.'

兆し[きざし] sign; symptom; omen

100e 逃

トウ にがす・にげる・のがす・のがれる

丶 冫 扌 兆 兆 兆 兆 逃

escape

omen 兆 [チョウ] + go 辶 49 [チャク]

The description of a man running away(辶) at the news of a negative omen(兆).

逃(が)す[にがす] release; let escape; set free
逃げる[にげる] escape; run away
逃す[のがす] release; let escape; set free
逃れる[のがれる] escape; run away

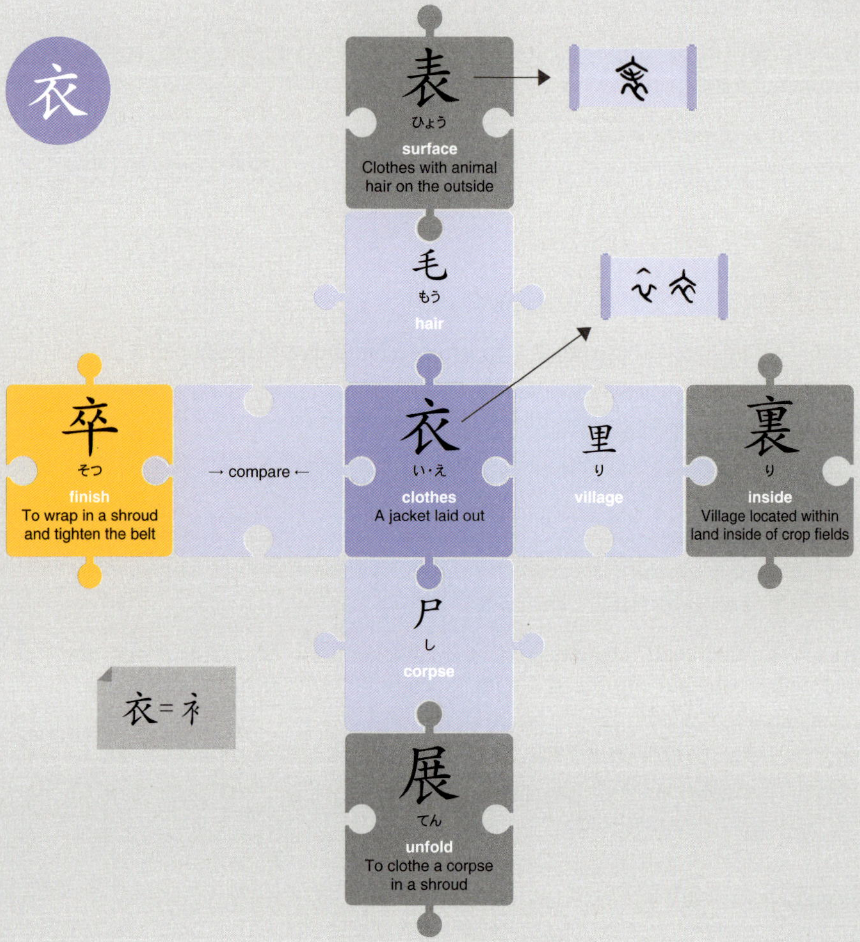

101 **衣**

イ・エ

clothes

A jacket, an item of clothing, spread out on the floor. When combined to become part of another character, it sometimes changes into "衤."

衣服[いふく] clothes; dress -101 30c

101a 表

ヒョウ おもて・あらわす

一 = 丰 主 丰 耒 表 表

surface

hair 毛[5e] [モウ] + clothes 衣 [イ・エ]

To make and wear clothes(衣) with animal hair(毛) on the outside.

表(わ)す[あらわす] show, reveal, expose
表現[ひょうげん] expression -101a 9a

101b 裏

リ うら

inside; back (rear)

clothes 衣 [イ・エ] + village 里[119] [リ]

Just as clothes(衣) were a means of protection, people formed villages(里) inside forests or places surrounded by mountains to hide from invaders.

裏口[うらぐち] back door, rear door -101b 12

101c 展

テン

unfold; display

corpse 尸[74] [シ] + shroud(衣) 𧘇 [symbol]

A shroud(𧘇) has been spread out to clothe the corpse(尸).

展示[てんじ] exhibit; display -101c 99

101d 卒

ソツ

finish; end

clothes 衣 [イ・エ] + a tightened waist 一 [symbol]

When a body is wrapped in a shroud(衣), rolled up in a cloth and tied up(一), funeral preparations are 'finished.' This character also looks like a soldier with a tight belt, so it means 'pawn, soldier or servant.'

何卒[どうぞ] please; kindly; by all means; in any case -13c 101d

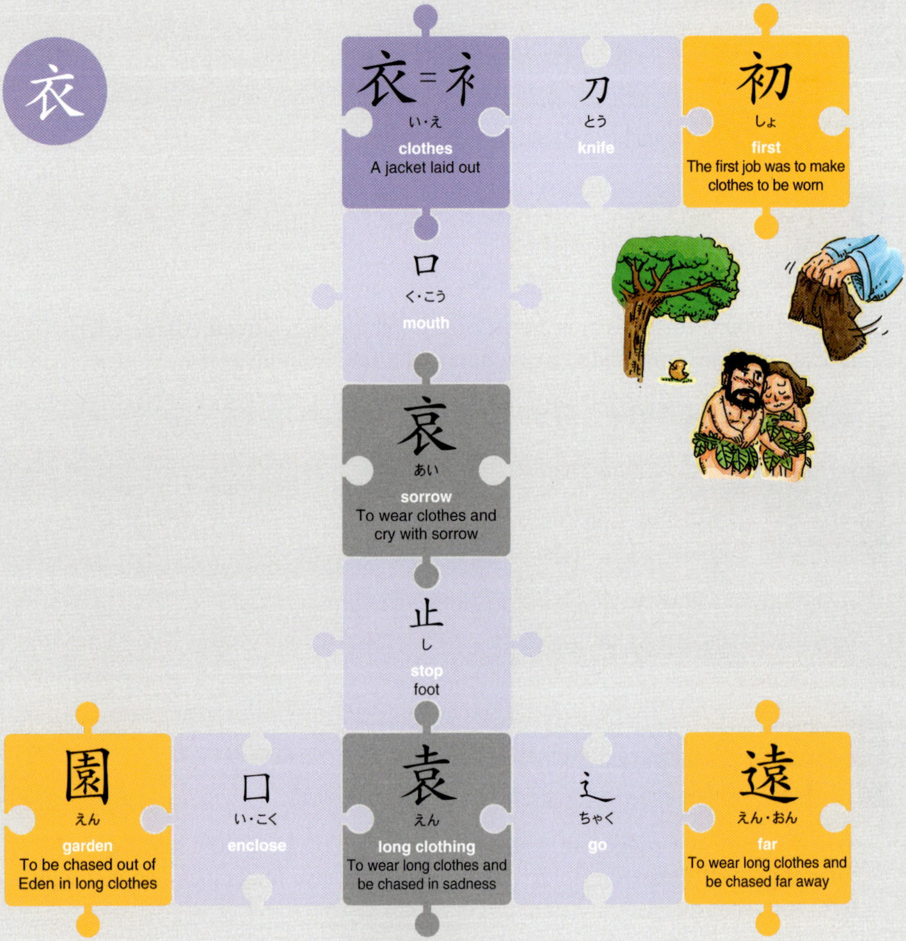

102 初

ショ　はつ・はじめ・はじめて

` ラ ネ ネ ネ 初 初

first

clothes ネ=衣 [イ・エ] + knife 刀[95] [トウ]

The first thing that God did after Adam and Eve ate the forbidden fruit of good and evil was to make(刀) them clothes(衣).

* The first thing one does when making clothes(ネ) is to cut the fabric with a knife(刀).

初め[はじめ] beginning; first　　初めて[はじめて] primally; for the first time
初めまして[はじめまして] I am glad to meet you (greetings on a first meeting)
最初[さいしょ] first; earliest; beginning -22d 102

102a 哀

アイ あわれ

sorrow; pity

clothes 衤=衣 [イ・エ] + mouth 口[12] [ク・コウ]

After Adam and Eve sinned, they wore clothes(衣) God created and cried(口)in sadness.

哀れ[あわれ] pitiful; pathetic; pitiable

102b 袁

エン

long clothing

foot/stop 土→止[44] [シ] + sorrow 哀 [アイ]

Adam and Eve wore long leather clothes when they were chased(止) out of the Garden of Eden in sadness(哀).

* Genesis 3:21 mentions God creating long leather clothes for Adam and Eve to wear after they ate the forbidden fruit.

102c 遠

エン・オン とおい

far; distant

long clothing 袁 [エン] + go 辶[49] [チャク]

Once they had been chased out of the Garden of Eden in their long leather clothes(袁), Adam and Eve were unable to return(辶). The Garden of Eden became a place that was too 'far' away for them.

遠い[とおい] far; distant　永遠[えいえん] eternity -156a 102c

102d 園

エン その

garden; park

enclose 囗[16] [イ・コク] + long clothing 袁 [エン]

The place Adam and Eve were chased out of in their long leather clothes(袁) was a lovely garden surrounded(囗) by a fence.

公園[こうえん] park -76e 102d

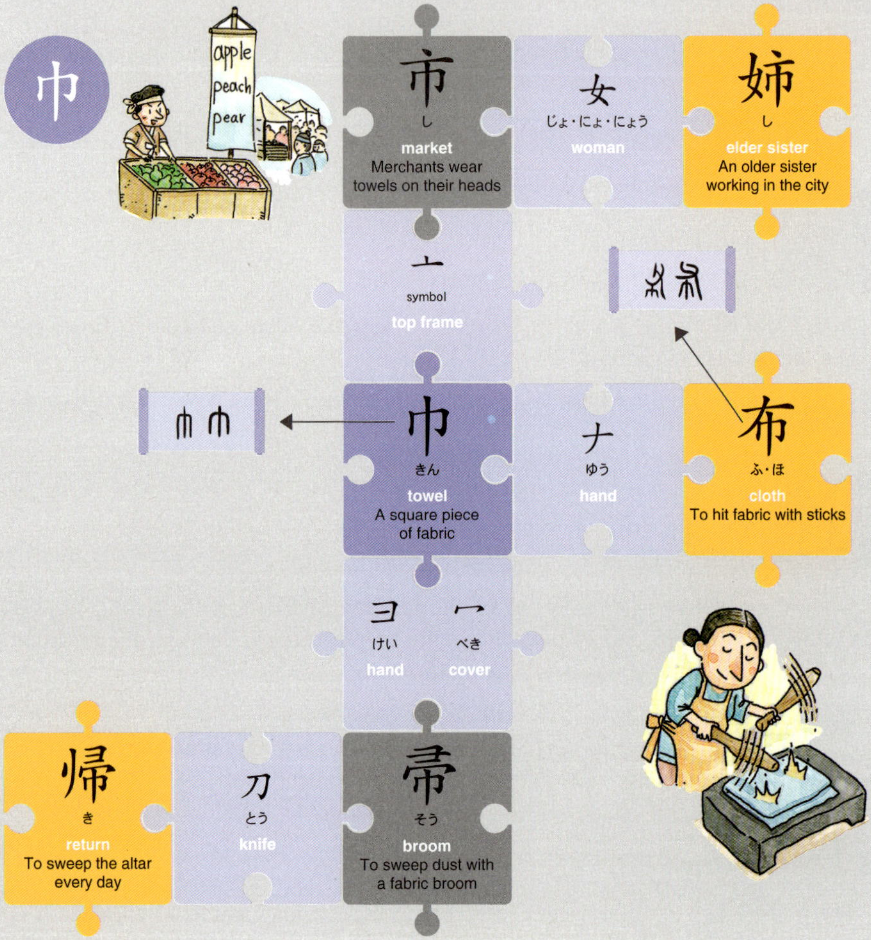

103 **巾**

キン

towel

丨 冂 巾

A towel is a square piece of fabric used to wipe hands.

103a 市

シ いち

丶 亠 亠 亠 市

market; city

top frame 亠[1] [symbol] + towel 巾 [キン]

Back in the day, shop signs were pieces of fabric(巾) hanging from a horizontal pole with a top frame(亠), and markets were full of them. A place with many markets is a 'city.'

市民[しみん] citizen -103a 80c　　都市[とし] city; town -82d 103a

103b 姉

シ あね

く 女 女 女' 女' 女' 妬 姉

elder sister

woman 女[78] [ジョ・ニョ・ニョウ] + market 市 [シ]

An 'older sister' is a female(女) sibling who works in the market or the city(市) for her younger siblings.

お姉さん[おねえさん] honorific of "姉[あね]"　　姉妹[しまい] sisters -103b 164d

103c 布

フ・ホ ぬの

一 ナ 才 右 布

cloth; spread

towel 巾 [キン] + hand ナ[34] [ユウ]

To spread cloth(巾) under a flat stone and beat it with handheld(ナ) sticks. Fabric treated that way became flat, like it was ironed, so this character also means 'to spread.'

* The ancient character shows that "ナ" is the shape of a hand holding a stick. China and Korea also used sticks to beat and flatten fabric.

財布[さいふ] wallet -145a 103c　　毛布[もうふ] blanket -5e 103c

103d 帚

ソウ ほうき

㇇ ⺕ ⺕ 彐 帚 帚 帚 帚

broom

hand ヨ[32] [ケイ] + cover 冖[131] [ベキ] + towel 巾 [キン]

To hold a broom made with fabric(巾) in one's hand(ヨ) to clear away the dust covering(冖) the floor.

* A hand(扌[28]) holding a broom(帚) became "sweep 掃 [ソウ]."

103e 帰

キ かえる

丨 刂 刂 刂 归 归 帰 帰 帰 帰

return

knife 刂=刀[95] [トウ] + broom 帚 [ソウ]

The altar where the sacrifice is slaughtered(刂) is a holy place. One must 'return' to clean such a place with a broom(帚) every day.

* The traditional character(歸) shows a person with a broom(帚) going(止[44]) to the altar where the sacrifice(𠂤) is made.

帰る[かえる] return; come (go) back　　帰国[きこく] homecoming; return to one's country -103e 86a

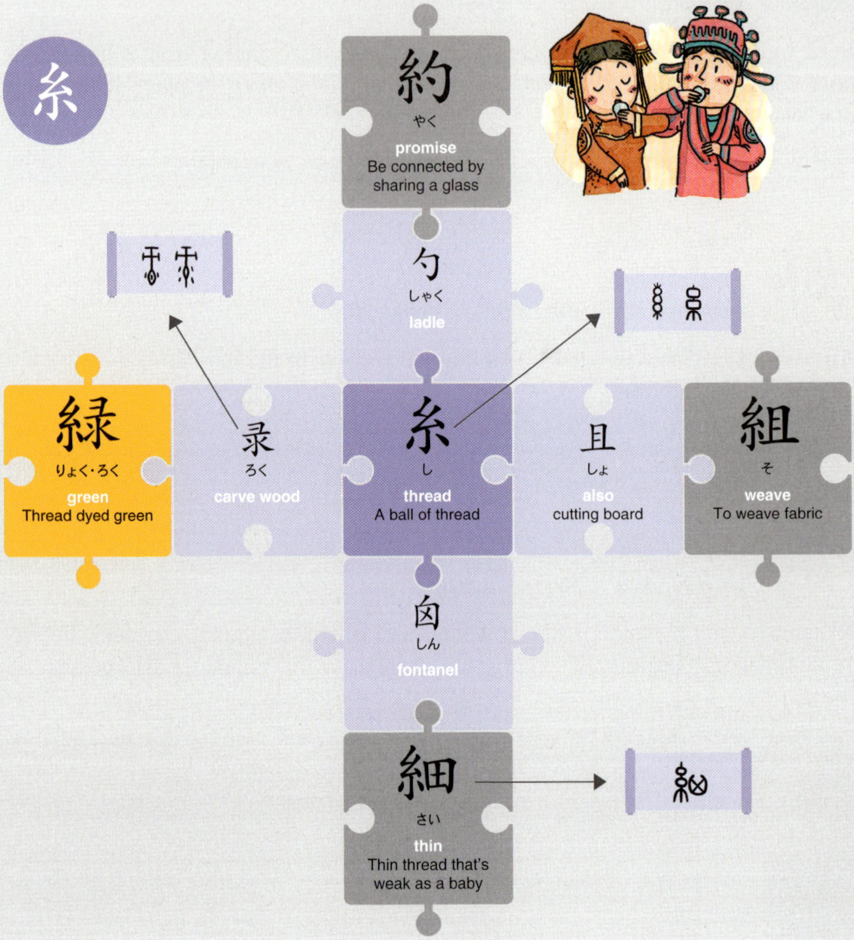

104 糸

シ いと

thread

A ball of rolled-up thread(糸). When used as part of a character, it adds the meaning of thread that 'ties, or connects.'

104a 約

ヤク

ㄥ ㄠ 幺 糸 糸 糸 糸 約 約

promise

thread 糸 [シ] + ladle 勺 [40a] [シャク]

Symbolizes a ceremony of sharing a glass of wine(勺) with a promise to be together for the rest of life, thereby connecting(糸) the bride and the groom in a covenant.

* Sharing of wine in the Chinese traditional weddings signifies a promise, an act originating from a blessing for many children.

契約[けいやく] contract; agreement - 163c 104a
約束[やくそく] promise; appointment; convention; rule - 104a 167a
予約[よやく] reservation; booking - 4a 104a

104b 組

ソ くみ・くむ

ㄥ ㄠ 幺 糸 糸 糸 糸 糹 絅 絈 組

weave

thread 糸 [シ] + cutting board/also 且 [174] [ショ]

"且"is a description of a cutting board with slices of meat piled on it and means 'layers of.' Weaving is the result of thread(糸) being layered together(且). This character also means 'to organize.'

組み[くみ] set (of); group; team　　組む[くむ] cross (legs or arms); weave; make a set

104c 細

サイ こまかい・ほそい

ㄥ ㄠ 幺 糸 糸 糸 糸 紅 細 細 細

thin; slender

thread 糸 [シ] + fontanel 田→囟 [シン]

New thread(糸) is thin and delicate, like a baby whose hole in the skull(囟) still has not fused.

* The ancient characters shows that "田" is a variation of "囟," which is the hole in a newborn baby's skull that disappears when the skullbones fuse. Refer to "思 [26a]."

細かい[こまかい] small; fine; detailed　　細い[ほそい] thin; slender; narrow

104d 緑

リョク・ロク みどり

ㄥ ㄠ 幺 糸 糸 糸 糸 糸 紀 綠 綠 綠 緑 緑

green

thread 糸 [シ] + carve wood 彔 [ロク]

The Chinese dyed fabric or threads(糸), and this character meaning 'green' gets its pronunciation from "彔."

* "彔" describes the action of poking a hole in a tree/green. Refer to "録 [156d]."

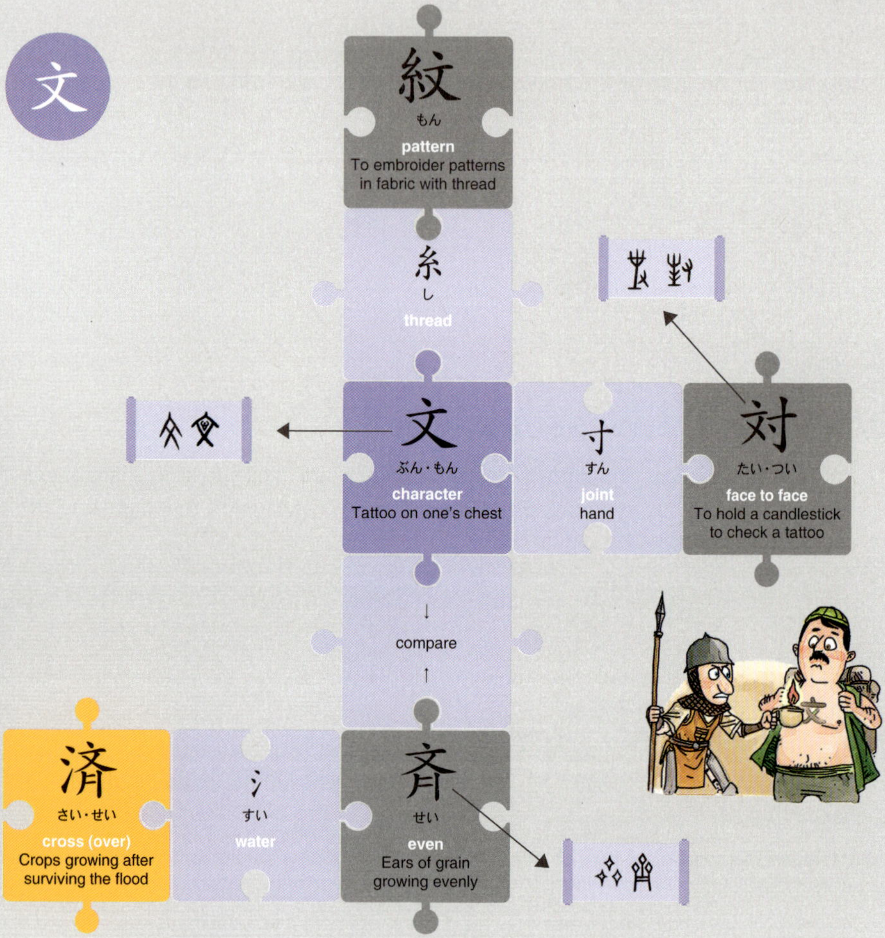

105 文

ブン・モン

character; script

丶 亠 ナ 文

A man with a tattoo on his chest(乂), which is below the head(亠[1]). Chinese characters began as rough tattoo-like drawings, so this character means 'character or writing.'

作文[さくぶん] writing; composition -180a 105	文章[ぶんしょう] sentence; writing -105 18c
文法[ぶんぽう] grammar -105 63d	文字[もじ] letter (of alphabet); character -105 77a

105a 紋

モン　　　 ㇐ 幺 幺 糸 糸 糸 糹 紋 紋 紋

pattern; crest

thread 糸[104] [シ] + tattoo/character 文 [ブン・モン]

To embroider a pattern in fabric with thread(糸) just like a tattoo(文).

家紋[かもん] family crest - 136a 105a
指紋[しもん] fingerprint - 73c 105a

105b 対

タイ・ツイ　　　 ㇔ 亠 ナ 文 文 対 対

face to face; opposite

tattoo/character 文 [ブン・モン] + hand/joint 寸[35] [スン]

Before talking to someone, you would raise the hand(寸) holding the candlestick to check the tattoo(文) to see if the person is your friend or foe. This is where the meaning 'face to face or answer' came from.

* The left-hand side of the traditional character(對) is the candlestick.

反対[はんたい] opposite; contrary; reverse - 117a 105b
対立[たいりつ] opposition; confrontation - 105b 64

105c 斉

セイ　　　 ㇔ 亠 ナ 文 产 斉 斉 斉

even; equal

Ears of grain are growing in neat and even lines.

* This character has nothing to do with "文" and is used as a radical.

一斉[いっせい] all at once; simultaneous - 173 105c

105d 済

サイ・セイ　すます・すむ　　　 ㇔ ㇔ 氵 氵 氵 氵 済 済 済 済 済

cross (over); finish

water 氵[157] [スイ] + even 斉 [セイ]

This character describes a neat row of crops(斉) growing well after surviving a drought or a flood(氵). To survive a hardship means that one has 'crossed over or finished.'

済ます[すます] finish; complete
済む[すむ] end, finish, be completed
済みません[すみません] sorry; excuse me; thank you

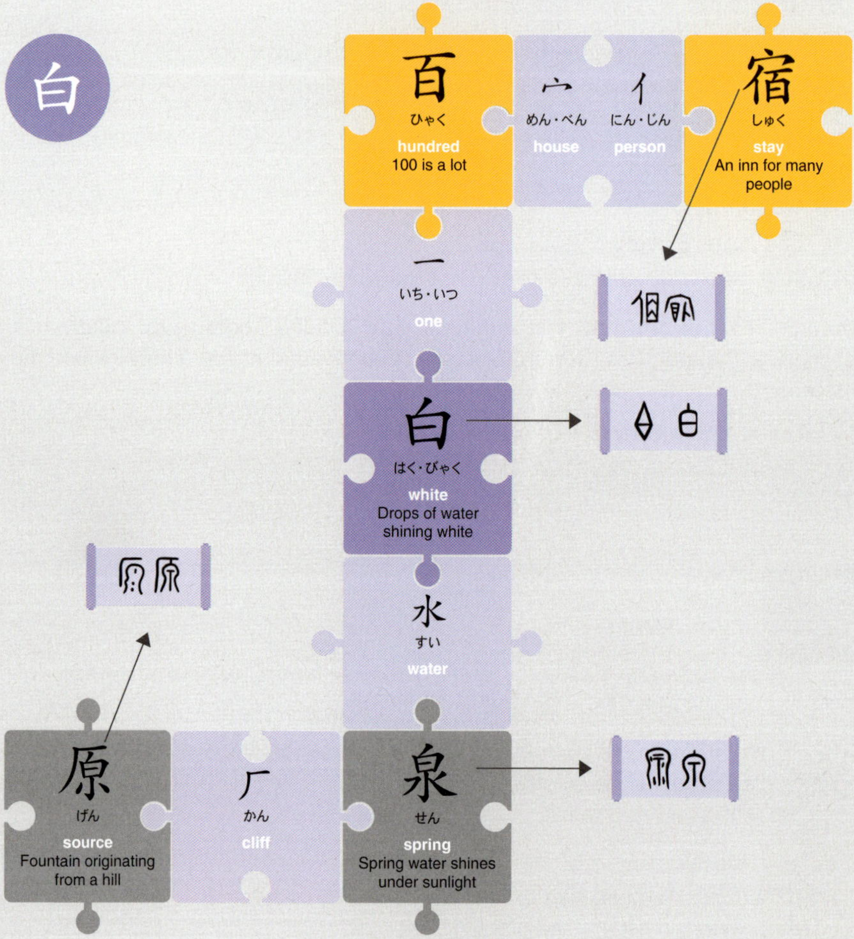

106 **白** ハク・ビャク しろ・しろい

white

A drop of water reflecting the sun(日 [170]) and shining(丶) white. In ancient times, the Chinese revered the color white, so it also means 'best.'

白い[しろい] white
面白い[おもしろい] interesting; amusing -6a 106

106a 百

ヒャク

一 丆 丆 百 百 百

hundred; 100

one 一[173] [イチ・イツ] + best/white 白 [ハク・ビャク]

The number one(一) combined with the best(白) means 'hundred.'

百点[ひゃくてん] full marks; perfect score - 106a 100c
八百屋[やおや] vegetable shop; greengrocer - 177 106a 74a

106b 宿

シュク やど

宿 宿 宿 宿 宿 宿 宿 宿 宿 宿 宿

stay; lodging

house 宀[113] [メン・ベン] + person 亻[52] [ニン・ジン] + hundred 百 [ヒャク]

An inn or a hotel is a house(宀) where many(百) people(亻) can stay the night.

* The ancient characters explain that "百" is the shape of a mat used for sleeping on, and that this character is the shape of a house(宀) with sleeping mats(百) for people(亻).

宿題[しゅくだい] homework - 106b 45e

106c 泉

セン

泉 泉 泉 泉 泉 泉 泉 泉 泉

spring; fountain

white 白 [ハク・ビャク] + water 水[156] [スイ]

Water(水) springing in the fountain between the stones is shining(白) under sunlight.

温泉[おんせん] spa; hot spring; thermal spring - 132e 106c

106d 原

ゲン はら・もと

原 原 原 原 原 原 原 原 原 原

source; original

cliff 厂[117] [カン] + spring 泉 [セン]

All rivers originate from a small source fountain(泉) in between boulders located in high grounds(厂).

* Note that the water(水) below "泉" is simplified into "小[182]."

原[はら] field; plain
原因[げんいん] cause - 106d 60d

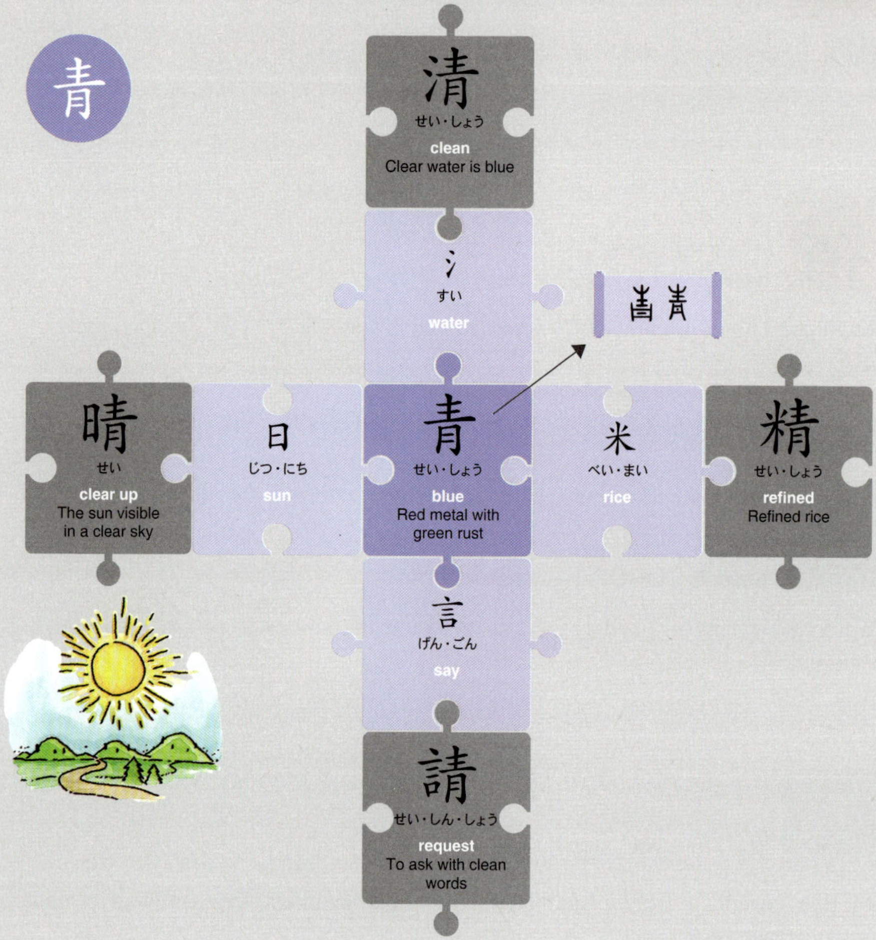

107 青

セイ・ショウ あお・あおい

blue; green

一 = ‡ 丰 丰 青 青 青

Green rust appearing(生) on a red(円→丹) metal-like copper.

* The ancient characters show that this is a combination of "be born 生[162] [セイ・ショウ]" and "red 丹 [タン]." "丹" describes a well(井[176d]) dug within a structure to stop it from caving in from which red minerals (丶[181]) like copper were extracted.

青い[あおい] blue; pale
青年[せいねん] young man -107 96e

107a 清

セイ・ショウ きよい

丶 ⺀ 氵 氵 氵 氵 氵 浐 清 清 清

clean; pure

water 氵[157] [スイ] + blue 青 [セイ・ショウ]

When sunlight hits clear water, the infrared rays and red lights are absorbed, and only the blue lights are reflected. So the clearer the water, (氵) the bluer (青) it is.

清い[きよい] clear; pure; noble

107b 精

セイ・ショウ

refined

rice 米[110] [ベイ・マイ] + blue 青 [セイ・ショウ]

Blue water symbolizes clarity, and blue(青) rice(米) means it is clean to eat. This character also means 'refined.'

精神[せいしん] mind; spirit -107b 99c

107c 請

セイ・シン・ショウ

request

say 言[17] [ゲン・ゴン] + blue 青 [セイ・ショウ]

Blue water symbolizes clarity, and blue(青) words(言) mean 'clear' speech. When making a request, one must be polite.

107d 晴

セイ はれる

clear up

sun 日[170] [ジツ・ニチ] + blue 青 [セイ・ショウ]

The sun(日) shines in a cloudless blue(青) sky when the weather is clear.

晴れる[はれる] clear up; become clear

晴天[せいてん] clear sky; fine weather -107d 60b

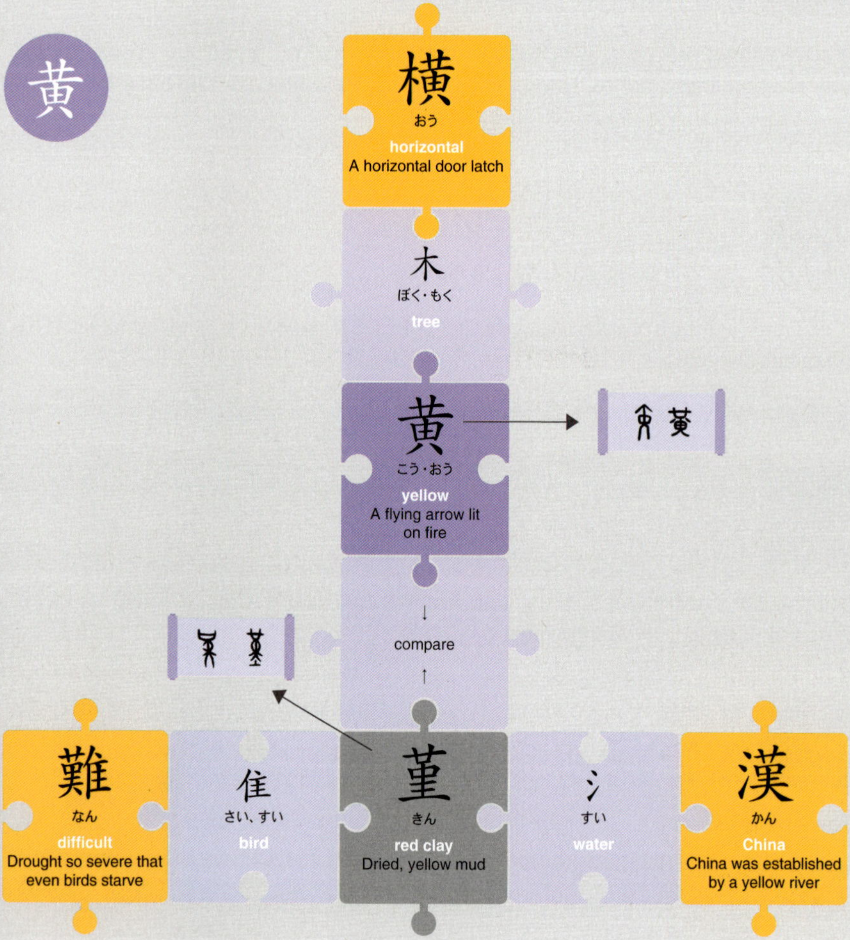

108 **黄** コウ・オウ き

yellow

Some scholars say that "矢[89]" and "黄" all symbolize an arrow. We are not sure with the modern character, but an arrow lit on fire, then shot across the night sky looks "yellow 黄".

黄色い[きいろい] yellow -108 75d
黄金[おうごん] gold -108 154

108a 横

オウ よこ

一 十 オ 木 朩 栌 栌 栟 栟 栟 椯 椯 横 横 横

horizontal; sideways

tree 木[164] [ボク・モク] + yellow 黄 [コウ・オウ]

As an arrow on fire(黄) flies across the sky, the wooden(木) latch was used across the door to lock it. From this description, the character got the meaning of 'sideways or on the side.'

横断[おうだん] crossing; traversing -108a 94d
横道[よこみち] byway; side road; digression -108a 4e

108b 堇

キン

一 十 廾 廾 廾 芇 芇 苎 苎 革 堇

red clay

yellow 黄 [コウ・オウ] + soil 土[120] [ド・ト]

Dry ground(土) of cracked yellow(黄) clay without a single blade of grass.

* The version carved on the turtle shells and animal bones show the character for a shaman who prayed for rain with an exaggerated mouth.

108c 漢

カン

` ゛ 氵 汁 汁 汁 汁 浐 浐 溄 溄 漢 漢

Sino-; China

water 氵[157] [スイ] + red clay 堇 [キン]

This character refers to the Han River(漢江), which is a tributary of the Yangtze River(長江). The Han Dynasty was named after this river as it was established nearby its yellow(黄) clay waters(氵). It created the culture of China that the Chinese currently think of as tradition.

漢字[かんじ] Chinese characters; kanji -108c 77a

108d 難

ナン むずかしい

一 十 廾 廾 芇 芇 苎 苎 革 莫 莫 歎 歎 歎 歎 歎 難 難

difficult

red clay 堇 [キン] + bird 隹[140] [サイ、スイ]

A drought so difficult to survive in that the only thing in the air is dust from the yellow mud(堇). Also, the flying birds(隹) have nothing to eat.

難しい[むずかしい] difficult; hard
困難[こんなん] difficult; tough -16a 108d
非難[ひなん] criticism -141d 108d

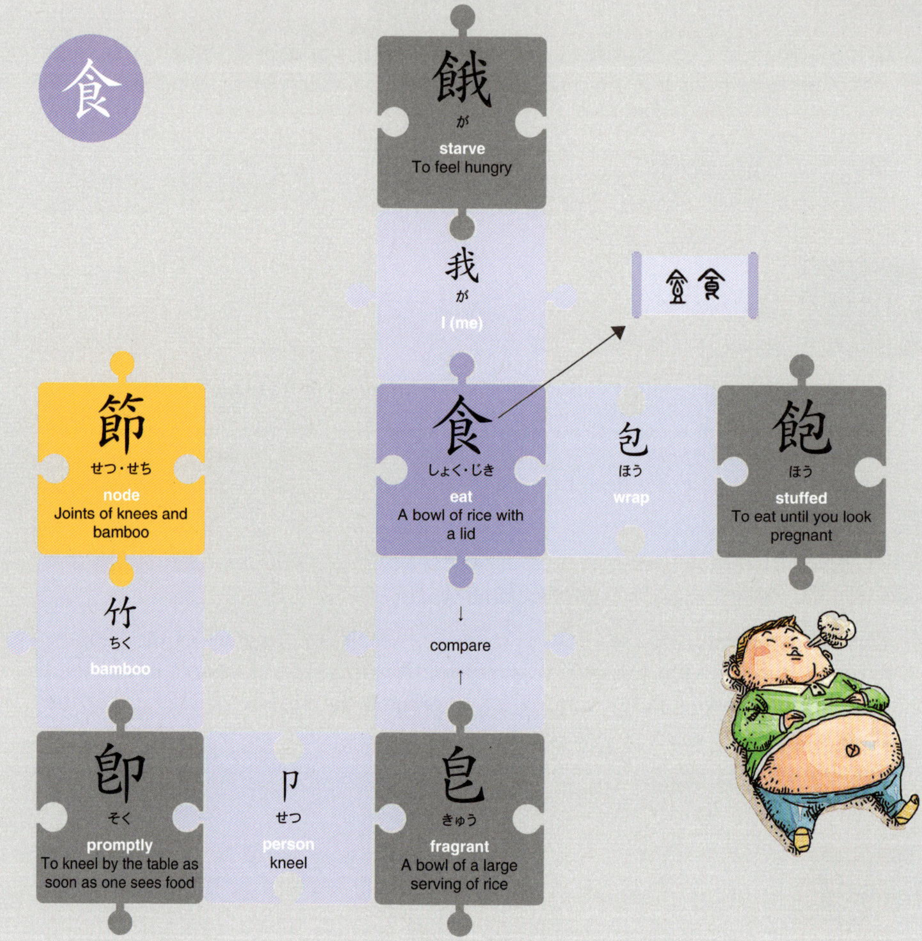

109 食

ショク・ジキ　く(う)・た(べる)

eat; food

A bowl of food(皀) and a lid(亼[54]) to keep it warm means ‘food or to eat’ when used as part of a character.

* The ancient characters show that “皀” in the “食” character has nothing to do with “look back 艮[ゴン・コン].”

食う[くう] eat	食べる[たべる] eat
食べ物[たべもの] food; provisions -109 41a	食堂[しょくどう] restaurant -109 118d
食塩[しょくえん] table salt -109 85d	
和食[わしょく] Japanese food; Japanese-style meal -12d 109	

109a 餓

ガ　うえる

starve; hungry

eat 食 [ショク・ジキ] + I (me) 我[91a] [ガ]

You cannot tell if someone else is hungry unless you ask. You(我) feel hungry when it's time to eat(食).

餓える[うえる] starve; be hungry

109b 飽

ホウ　あきる

stuffed; sated

eat 食 [ショク・ジキ] + wrap 包[75a] [ホウ]

To be 'full' means you eat(食) so much that you look like a woman who has a child inside(包) her.

飽きる[あきる] get tired of; be fed up

109c 皀

キュウ

fragrant; grain

A bowl(匕) with legs like the stems of a wine glass containing a large serving of tasty rice(白).

* The character is made up of what looks like dagger/spoon(匕[72]) and white(白[106]), but they are not connected.

109d 卽

ソク　すなわち

promptly

grain/fragrant 皀 [キュウ] + kneel/person 卩[69] [セツ]

A hungry person who sees food(皀) will immediately kneel(卩) by the table.

即ち[すなわち] that is; namely; i.e.

109e 節

セツ・セチ　ふし

node; joint

bamboo 竹[169] [チク] + promptly 即→卽 [ソク]

The combination of the joints of a man kneeling(卩) by a table of food(皀) and the nodes of a bamboo(竹) mean 'joints.' It also means 'seasons,' which are an important part of rice(皀) farming and come by regularly, like the nodes(卩) on bamboo(竹).

節倹[せっけん] economy; frugality; thrift -109e 55e
季節[きせつ] seasons; solar term -77d 109e

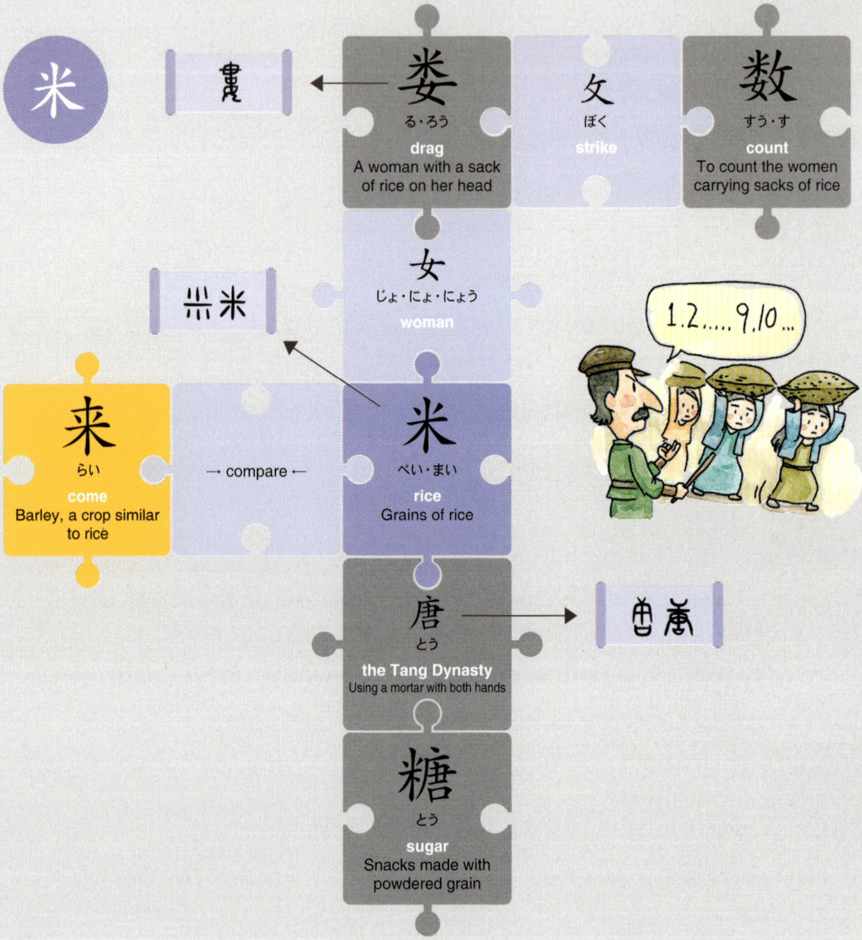

110 米

ベイ・マイ こめ

rice

The shape of rice grains that were milled. Because of the similar pronunciation, it means 'meter.'

* In Japan, America is written as '亜米利加' and '米' is often used as an abbreviation to mean America.

北米[ほくべい] North America -73 110
南米[なんべい] South America -175a 110

110a 娄

ル・ロウ

丶 丷 ⺌ 䒑 半 米 娄 娄 娄

drag; pull

rice 米 [ベイ・マイ] + woman 女[78] [ジョ・ニョ・ニョウ]

A woman(女) carrying a sack of rice(米) on her head would be so tired and would have to drag her feet.

＊The traditional character(婁) describes a woman carrying a lot of things on her head.

110b 数

スウ・ス かず・かぞえる

count; number

rice 米 [ベイ・マイ] + woman 女[78] [ジョ・ニョ・ニョウ] + strike 攵[43] [ボク]

An official with a baton in his hand(攵) is counting the number of rice(米) sacks the women(女) are carrying on their heads.

＊"攵" is the shape of a hand(又[30]) holding a stick(|).

数える[かぞえる] count; enumerate
算数[さんすう] arithmetic - 38e 110b

110c 唐

トウ

the Tang Dynasty (618-907)

To hold the pestle(午[96c]) in hand(ヨ[32]) and grind whatever is in the mortar(ロ). It later meant the 'Tang Dynasty.'

＊The ancient character shows both hands holding the pestle. That is why "ロ" is not actually a person's mouth but a mortar.

110d 糖

トウ

sugar

rice 米 [ベイ・マイ] + pounding/Tang Dynasty 唐 [トウ]

One can make snacks or sweets with grains(米) powdered in a mortar(唐).

110e 来

ライ くる・きたす・きたる

come; next

tree 木[164] [ボク・モク] + rice 米 [ベイ・マイ]

Symbolizes barley, which is a crop(木) similar to rice(米). Barley bears its grain in spring after a long winter, signifying that long-sought spring is coming with barley.

＊Imagine how the ancient people waited for spring to come during harsh winters when they had no food.

来る[くる] come; approach
来す[きたす] cause; induce; bring about
来週[らいしゅう] next week - 110e 122b
来る[きたる] come; arrive; coming
来月[らいげつ] the next month - 110e 172
来年[らいねん] next year - 110e 96e

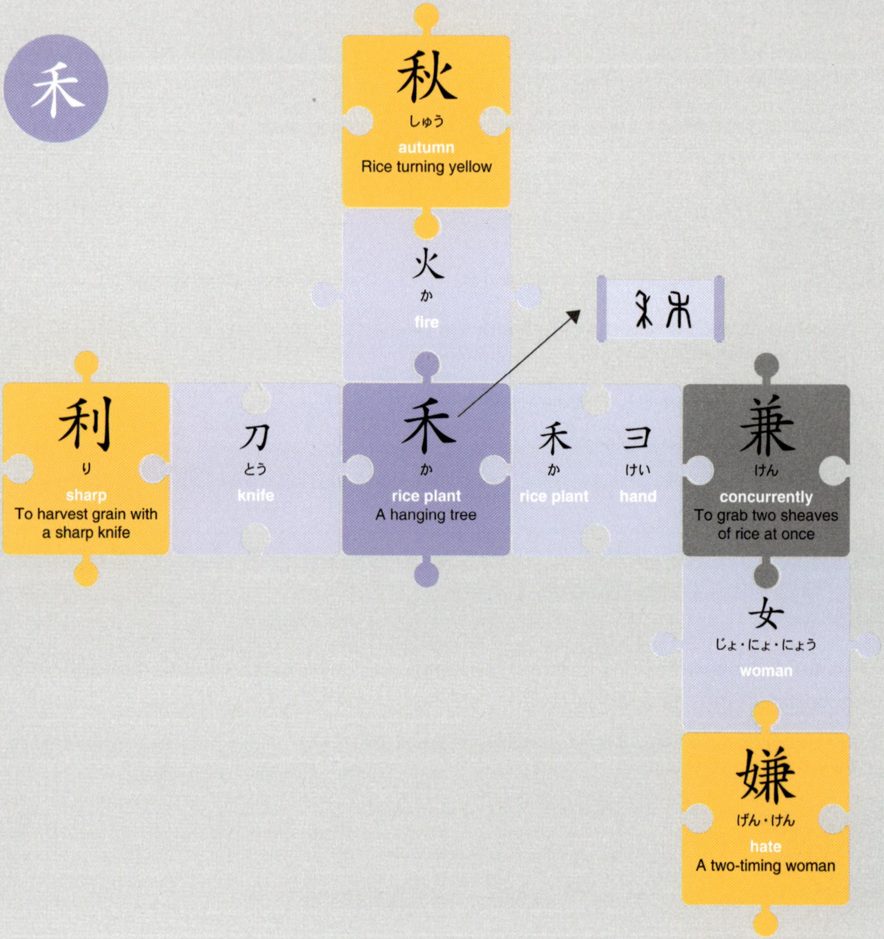

111 禾

カ

rice plant

丿 二 千 才 禾

A rice stalk is a kind of a tree(木[164]) that hangs its head(丿[179e]) as it ripens.

* An Asian saying goes, "The riper the rice, the lower it bows." It means the more one knows, the humbler he is. This shows how Asians thought rice stalks bowed.

111a 秋

シュウ　あき

ノ 二 千 千 禾 禾 禾' 秒 秋

autumn; fall

rice plant 禾 [カ] + fire 火[124] [カ]

Rice(禾) fields that are turning yellow as if they are catching fire(火) is another way of saying the rice is ripe and almost ready to harvest. This also means it is autumn.

* Asians liken the autumn rice(禾) paddies to a field that caught fire(火).

111b 兼

ケン　かねる

丶 丷 䒑 当 当 当 争 争 兼 兼

concurrently

rice plant 禾 [カ] + rice plant 禾 [カ] + hand ヨ[32] [ケイ]

To grab two sheaves(秝) of rice(禾) by hand(ヨ) at once to harvest.

兼ねる[かねる] combine; together

111c 嫌

ゲン・ケン　いや・きらう

く 女 女 女' 女'' 女'' 女弓 女弓 女弓 女弟 女弟 嫌 嫌

hate; dislike

woman 女[78] [ジョ・ニョ・ニョウ] + concurrently 兼 [ケン]

A woman(女) holding on to the crotches of two men at the same time(兼) is 'dislikable or disgusting.'

嫌う[きらう] hate; dislike
嫌い[きらい] hate, dislike, (negative) tendency

111d 利

リ

ノ 二 千 千 禾 和 利

sharp; advantage

rice plant 禾 [カ] + knife 刂=刀[95] [トウ]

Before using a knife(刂) to harvest rice(禾), the farmer has to make sure that it is indeed sharp. Harvest is considered advantageous for everyone.

便利[べんり] convenient; handy; useful -31d 111d
利用[りよう] use -111d 129

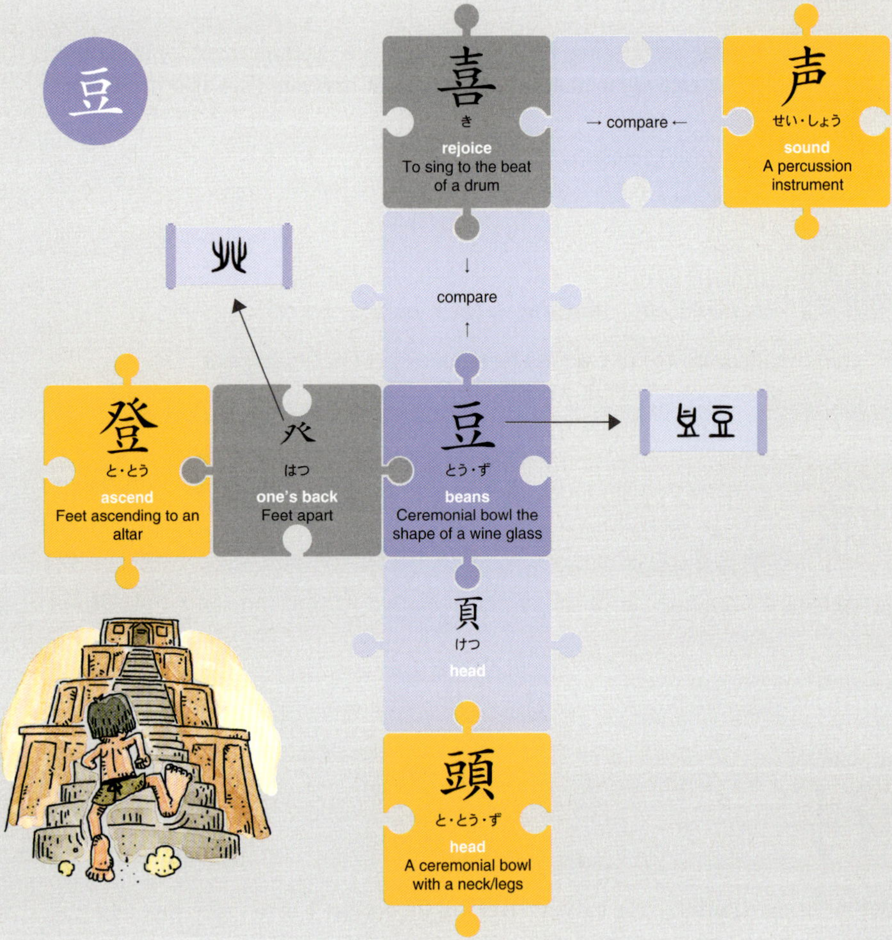

112 **豆**

トウ・ズ まめ

beans

A ceremonial bowl or an altar has a stem or legs like a wine glass. The shape is like that of a bean.

豆腐[とうふ] tofu; bean-curd -112 36d

112a 喜

キ よろこぶ

一 十 士 吉 吉 吉 吉 吉 壴 喜 喜 喜

rejoice

percussion instrument 壴[42b] [シュ・チュ] + mouth 口[12] [ク・コウ]

"壴" is a drum(豆) raised on legs with a decoration(士) on top, and a person singing with their mouth(口) to that drumbeat(壴) would be 'happy.'

* "豆" and "壴" are both mentioned here because they look similar, but they have no connection.

喜ぶ [よろこぶ] be glad; be delighted; take pleasure in

112b 声

セイ・ショウ こえ

一 十 士 韦 韦 声 声

sound; voice

frame 士 [symbol] + stone plate 尸 [symbol]

To make a sound by hitting a stone plate(尸) hanging on a frame(士).

* The traditional character(聲) shows an ear(耳[22]) listening to the sound of a musical instrument made with a thin stone(石[153a]) plate(尸) that's played with a stick(殳[93]). The kanji just shows a stone plate(尸) and a hanging frame(士).

声明[せいめい] statement; announcement - 112b 170d

112c 頭

ト・トウ・ズ あたま

一 丆 亓 戸 戸 豆 豆 豆 豇 豇 頭 頭 頭 頭 頭 頭

head

ceremonial bowl/beans 豆 [トウ・ズ] + head 頁[4] [ケツ]

A ceremonial bowl(豆) where the main part is on raised legs like a head(頁).

先頭[せんとう] head; vanguard; first - 58d 112c

頭痛[ずつう] headache - 112c 65c

112d 癶

ハツ

フ ヲ ヺ ヺ 癶

one's back; splay

Two feet splayed apart or upward means 'to part.' When this character is included, think of feet.

112e 登

ト・トウ のぼる

フ ヲ ヺ ヺ 癶 癶 癶 癶 登 登 登 登

ascend; climb up

two feet/one's back 癶 [ハツ] + altar/beans 豆 [トウ・ズ]

Two feet(癶) ascending to a high altar(豆) to offer a sacrifice to the gods.

登る[のぼる] ascend; climb up; go up

登山[とざん] climbing - 112e 153

Diagram for 宀

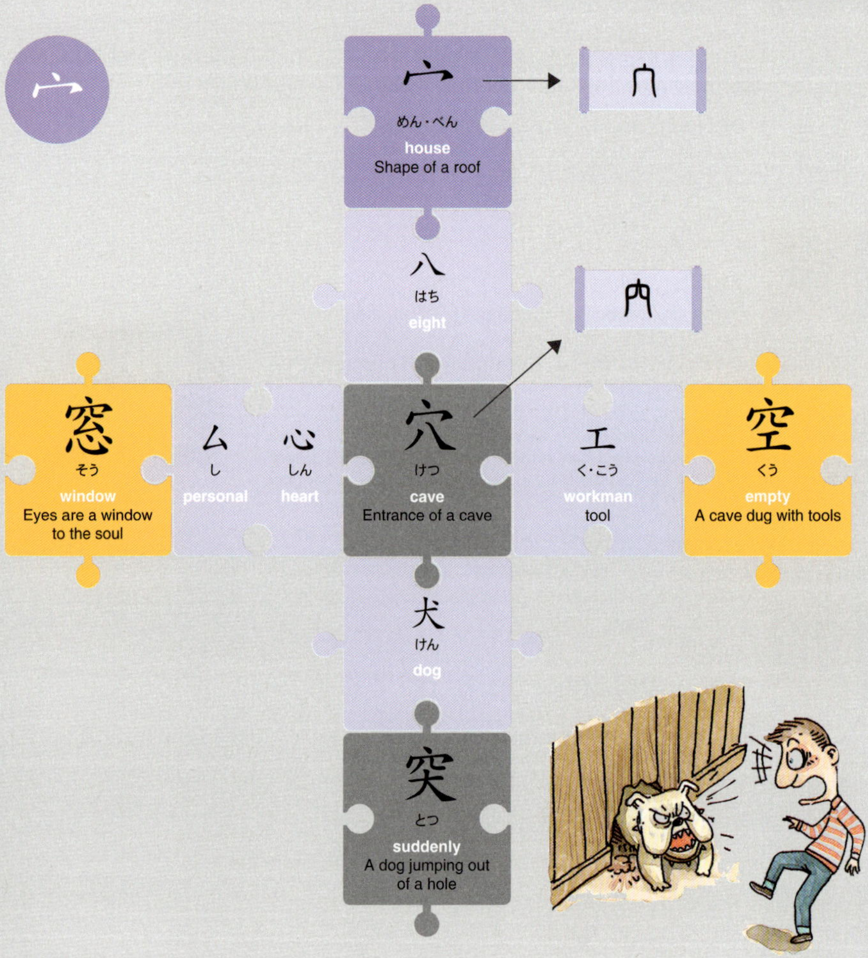

113 宀

メン・ベン

house

A house represented by its roof. When part of another character, it gives the meaning of a house where people live.

113a 穴

ケツ　あな　　、 丶 宀 穴 穴

cave; hole

house 宀 [メン・ベン] + eight 八[177] [ハチ]

Back in the day, many people used caves as houses(宀). This character depicts the entrance(八) to the cave.

*"八" is an open entrance.

113b 空

クウ　そら・から・あく・あける・すく　　、 丶 宀 穴 穴 空 空 空

empty; sky; air

cave 穴 [ケツ] + tool/workman 工[155] [ク・コウ]

An empty cave(穴) dug out with tools(工). An empty space is only filled with air.

空く[あく] be empty; be vacant; unoccupied
空ける[あける] empty (out); clear out
空く[すく] get empty (crack, time, space, etc.); be hungry
空気[くうき] air; atmosphere - 113b 158a

113c 突

トツ　つく・つつく　　、 丶 宀 穴 穴 空 突 突

suddenly

cave 穴 [ケツ] + dog 大→犬[135] [ケン]

A dog(犬) suddenly jumping out of a cave-like(穴) hole and surprising a person. A dog(犬) suddenly jumping out of a hole(穴) came to mean 'dash or protrude.'

突く[つく] prick; stab; strike
突く[つつく] poke; peke at; pick at
突然[とつぜん] suddenly; unexpectedly - 113c 124d

113d 窓

ソウ　まど　　、 丶 宀 穴 穴 空 空 窓 窓 窓 窓

window

cave 穴 [ケツ] + personal ム[76] [シ] + heart 心[26] [シン]

A person's eyes/holes(穴) are windows that show what's hidden(ム) within the heart(心).

窓口[まどぐち] ticket window; point of contact - 113d 12

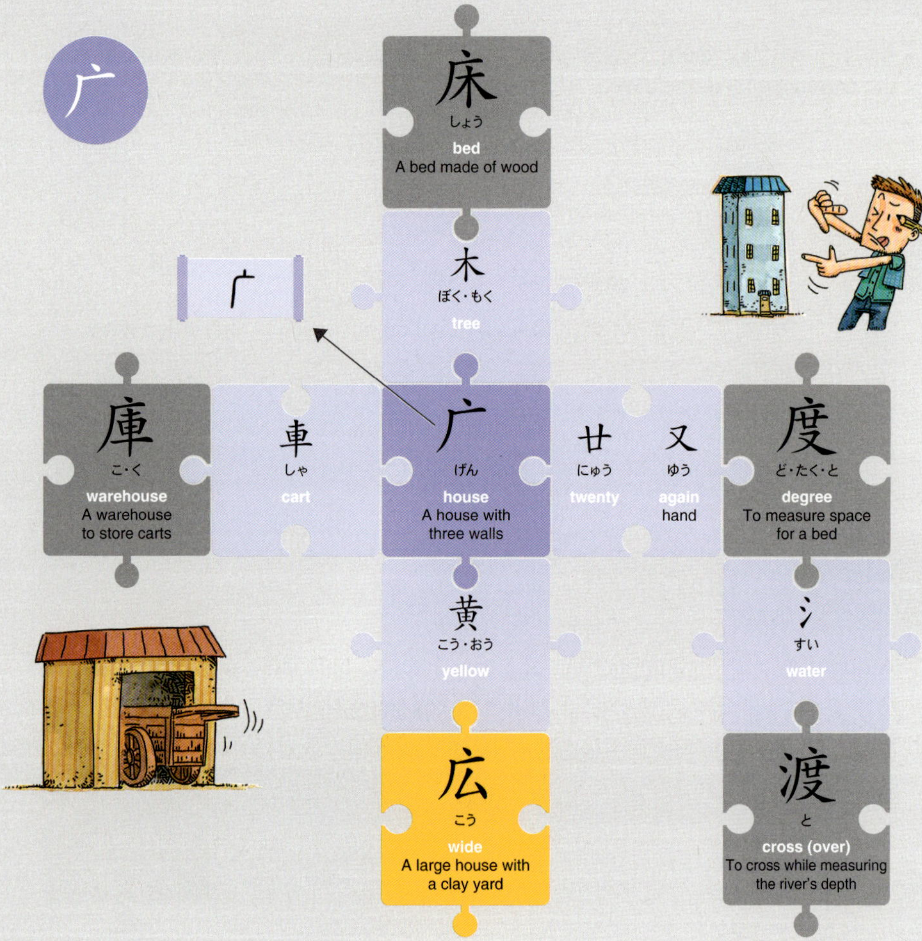

114 广

ゲン

house

丶 亠 广

Offices in old palaces and buildings had one wall torn down where the king or officials would sit. This character describes a house with three walls.

114a 床

ショウ ゆか

丶 亠 广 庁 庁 床 床

bed; floor

house 广 [ゲン] + tree 木[164] [ボク・モク]

A 'bed or floor' is the flat space in a house(广) made of wood(木).

起床[きしょう] getting out of bed; rising -44d 114a

114b 度

ゲン

丶 亠 广 广 庐 庐 庐 度 度

degree

house 广 [ゲン] + twenty 廿 [ニュウ] + hand/again 又[30] [ユウ]

To use a hand(又) to measure many sides(廿) of a large house(广) to judge how much space there is. It's also a suffix that indicates things like temperature, humidity, angle, altitude, longitude, etc.

* "廿" is two "ten 十[178] [ジツ・ジュウ]" overlapping.

度[たび] time; moment; number (of times)	高度[こうど] altitude; height -3 114b
今度[こんど] now; this time; next time 5-4b 114b	限度[げんど] limit; bounds -10d 114b

114c 渡

ト わたす・わたる

丶 丶 氵 氵 氵 汁 沪 沪 浐 浐 渡 渡

cross (over)

water 氵[157] [スイ] + degree 度 [ド・タク・ト]

To cross a river(氵) safely while measuring(度) the depth.

渡す[わたす] ferry across; carry across; hand over
渡る[わたる] cross over; go across

114d 広

コウ ひろい・ひろがる・ひろげる・ひろめる

丶 亠 广 広 広

wide; broad

house 广 [ゲン] + yellow ム→黄[108] [コウ・オウ]

A palace(广) with a wide clay(黄) garden that's open to one side so that the servants could gather.

* The traditional character(廣) shows that '黄' was simplified.

広い[ひろい] wide; broad; spacious	広がる[ひろがる] widen, broaden, spread
広げる[ひろげる] widen, broaden, extend	広める[ひろめる] widen, broaden; propagate

114e 庫

コ・ク くら

丶 亠 广 广 庐 庐 庐 庐 庐 庫

warehouse

house 广 [ゲン] + cart 車[97] [シャ]

A warehouse means a house(广) or a place where carts(車) are stored.

車庫[しゃこ] garage -97 114e

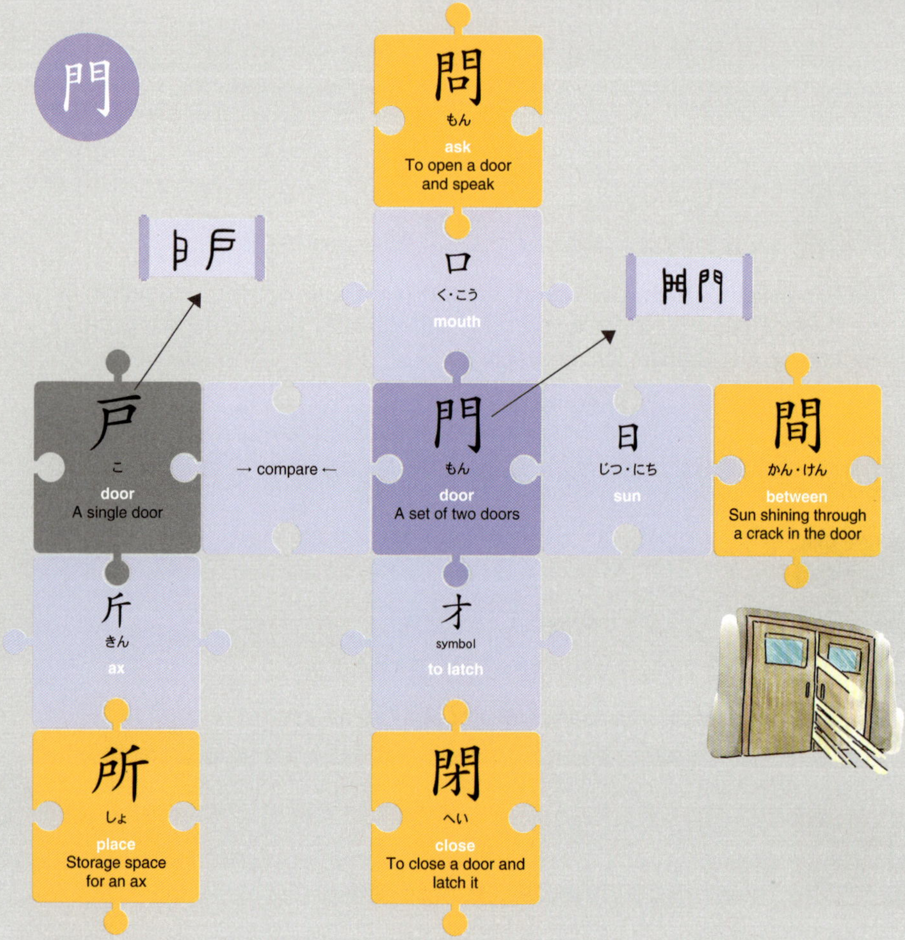

115 **門**

モン

door; gate

Palaces and large houses had doors that came in a set of two.

正門[せいもん] front gate; main gate -45 115

115a 問

モン　とい・とう

ask; question

door 門 [モン] + mouth ロ 12 [ク・コウ]

To open a door(門) and ask(ロ) if he is at the right house.

問(い)[とい] question; query
問う[とう] ask, inquire
問題[もんだい] question; problem -115a 45e
訪問[ほうもん] visit -126a 115a

115b 間

カン・ケン　あいだ・ま

between; interval

door 門 [モン] + sun 日 170 [ジツ・ニチ]

This describes the sun(日) shining through a space in the door(門). It came to mean 'room,' the space between two walls, and is also a quantifier used to count the number of rooms.

時間[じかん] time; hour -37a 115b
居間[いま] living room -15e 115b
期間[きかん] period; term -39c 115b

115c 閉

ヘイ　しめる・とじる

close; shut

door 門 [モン] + to latch オ [symbol]

A door(門) that is closed with a latch(オ) put across it.

閉める[しめる] close; shut
閉(ま)る[しまる] be closed; close; be shut
閉じる[とじる] close; shut

115d 戸

コ　と

door

Small huts or storage rooms had a single door, smaller than the larger double doors(門).

雨戸[あまど] rain shutter door; shutters -159 115d

115e 所

ショ　ところ

place

door 戸 [コ] + ax 斤 94 [キン]

A storage room is a place with a single door(戸) where farming tools such as an ax(斤) are kept.

彼所[あそこ] there; that place -149a 115e
此所[ここ] here; this place -72a 115e
其所[そこ] there (place); that place; that time (moment) -39 115e
台所[だいどころ] kitchen -76b 115e
何所[どこ] where; what place -13c 115e

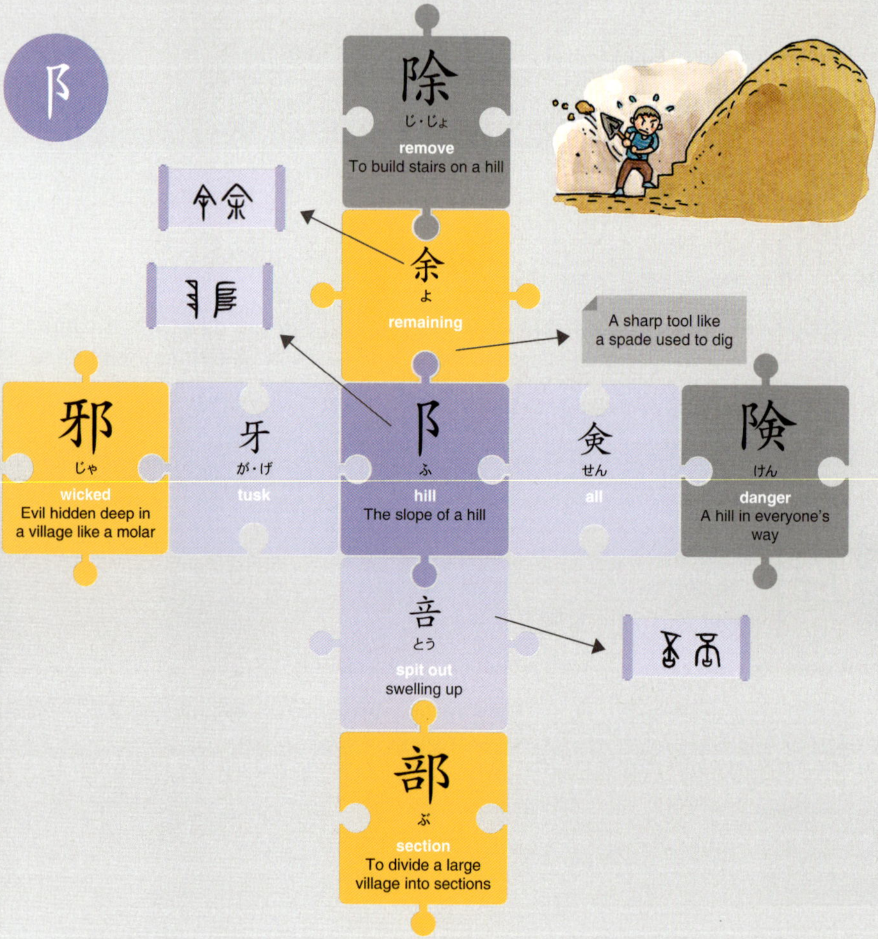

116 ⻖

ソ

hill

This character describes the slope of a hill. When used on the left of a character, it means 'hill,' but when used on the right, it means "town 邑[75c] [ユウ]."

116a 余

ヨ あまる

ノ 𠆢 今 全 仐 余 余

remaining

Characters carved on bones or shells show a shape of a tool with a sharp edge used to dig. This character is also the abbreviation of "餘" meaning 'to have leftovers,' because there is enough food(食[109]) to be scooped with a spade(余), not a spoon.

余る[あまる] remain; be in excess
余り[あまり] remainder; surplus; too much

116b 除

ジ・ジョ のぞく

⻖ 阝 阝 阶 阾 除 除 除 除

remove

hill 阝 [フ] + digging tool/remaining 余 [ヨ]

To use tools(余) to carve stairs in a hill(阝) to make it easier to climb. This character came to mean 'to eliminate' because stairs in a steep hill eliminate much of the hard work.

除く[のぞく] remove; eliminate; exclude

116c 険

ケン けわしい

⻖ 阝 阝 阶 阾 険 険 険 険 険 険

danger

hill 阝 [フ] + all 㑒[55] [セン]

A hill(阝) that is in everybody's(㑒) way is a large mountain or obstacle, which is where the meaning 'danger' comes from.

険しい[けわしい] rough; rugged; dangerous
危険[きけん] danger; risk; hazard -69b 116c
冒険[ぼうけん] venture; adventure -7d 116c

116d 部

ブ べ

丶 亠 亠 立 立 产 咅 咅 咅⻏ 部

section

swelling up/spit out 咅 [トウ] + village 阝→邑[75c] [ユウ]

A village(邑) that has swelled(咅) or grown has to be divided into parts for better maintenance.

* "咅" is a bumpy(口) or swollen ground because new shoots are sprouting up(立). Refer to "倍[173e]."

部屋[へや] room -116d 74a
全部[ぜんぶ] all; entire; whole -53a 116d
内部[ないぶ] interior; inside -53b 116d
部分[ぶぶん] part; section; portion -116d 95a

116e 邪

ジャ

一 𠂉 匚 牙 牙 牙⻏ 邪 邪

wicked

tusk 牙[21c] [ガ・ゲ] + village 阝→邑[75c] [ユウ]

The depiction of a shady person who does evil and hides deep in the village(邑), like a molar or tusk(牙).

風邪[かぜ] cold (illness); influenza -143c 116e

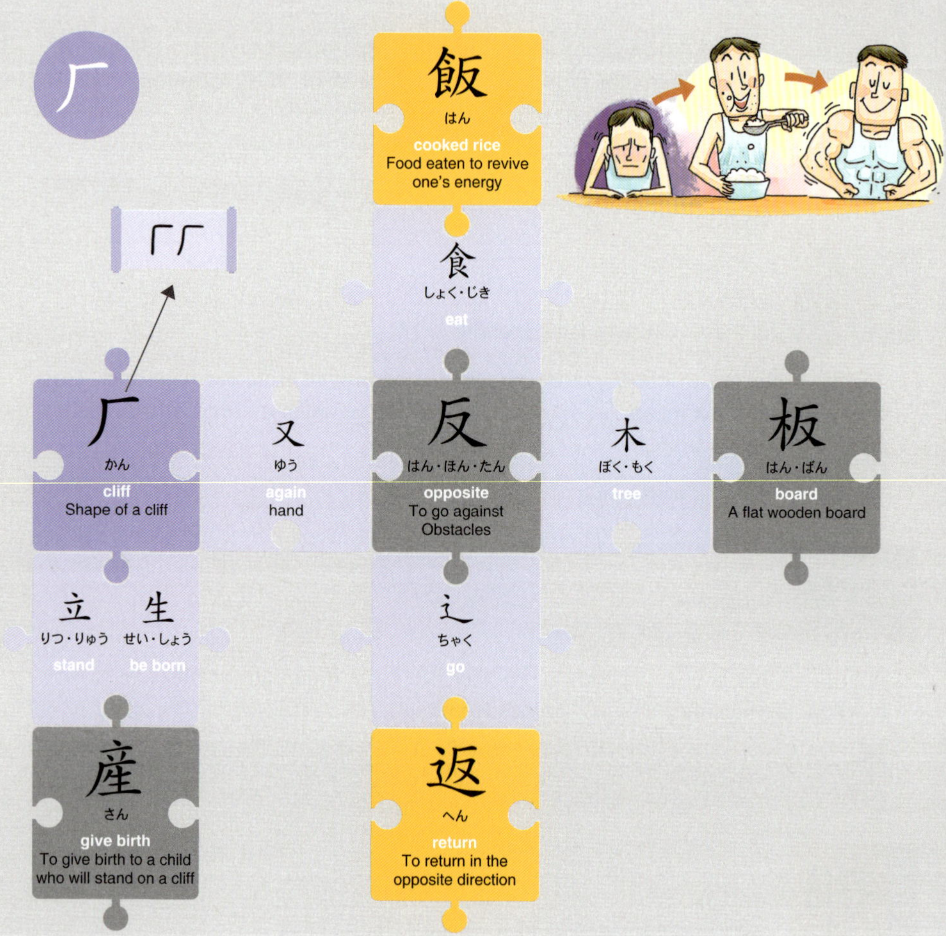

117 **厂**

カン

cliff

一厂

A cliff with stones jutting out at the edge.

117a 反

ハン・ホン・タン　そらす・そる

一 厂 万 反

opposite

cliff 厂 [カン] + hand/again 又[30] [ユウ]

To put one's hand(又) against the cliff(厂) to overcome it and oppose the effect.

反らす[そらす] bend; warp; curve　　反る[そる] be bent; be warped; be curved
反省[はんせい] self-reflection, self-examination -117a 182b
反対[はんたい] opposite; contrary; reverse -117a 105b

117b 飯

ハン　めし

ノ 𠆢 𠆢 今 今 今 食 食 飠 飣 飯 飯

cooked rice; meal

eat 食[109] [ショク・ジキ] + opposite 反 [ハン]

One eats(飠) three meals a day to recover(反) one's energy.

＊ In Asia, this character usually refers to cooked rice.

朝ご飯[あさごはん] breakfast -98e 117b
御飯[ごはん] expression of politeness for '食事(meal)' -69c 117b
昼御飯[ひるごはん] lunch; midday meal -170b 69c 117b
晩御飯[ばんごはん] dinner -57b 69c 117b　　夕飯[ゆうはん] evening meal -172a 117b

117c 板

ハン・バン　いた

一 十 才 木 木 朾 板 板

board

tree 木[164] [ボク・モク] + opposite 反 [ハン]

If you take a piece of wood(木) and flatten it on both sides, then you have a board that can be used even when flipped over(反).

看板[かんばん] billboard; sign(board) -7a 117c　　黒板[こくばん] blackboard -124c 117c

117d 返

ヘン　かえす・かえる

丶 ⻌ 返 辶 𨑕 返 返

return

opposite 反 [ハン] + go ⻌[49] [チャク]

To go along a road(⻌) and then return in the opposite(反) direction.

返す[かえす] return; turn over; pay back　　返る[かえる] return; come back; turn over
返事・返辞[へんじ] reply; answer; response -117d 32c 117d 83d

117e 産

サン

丶 亠 亠 立 立 产 产 产 産 産 産

give birth; produce

stand 立[64] [リツ・リュウ] + cliff 厂 [カン] + be born 生[162] [セイ・ショウ]

A person standing(立) tall on a cliff(厂) indicates a hero who will lead the people against adversity. A mother giving birth(生) to a child wishes for him to become someone great.

生産[せいさん] production; manufacture -162 117e　　倒産[とうさん] bankruptcy; insolvency -90c 117e

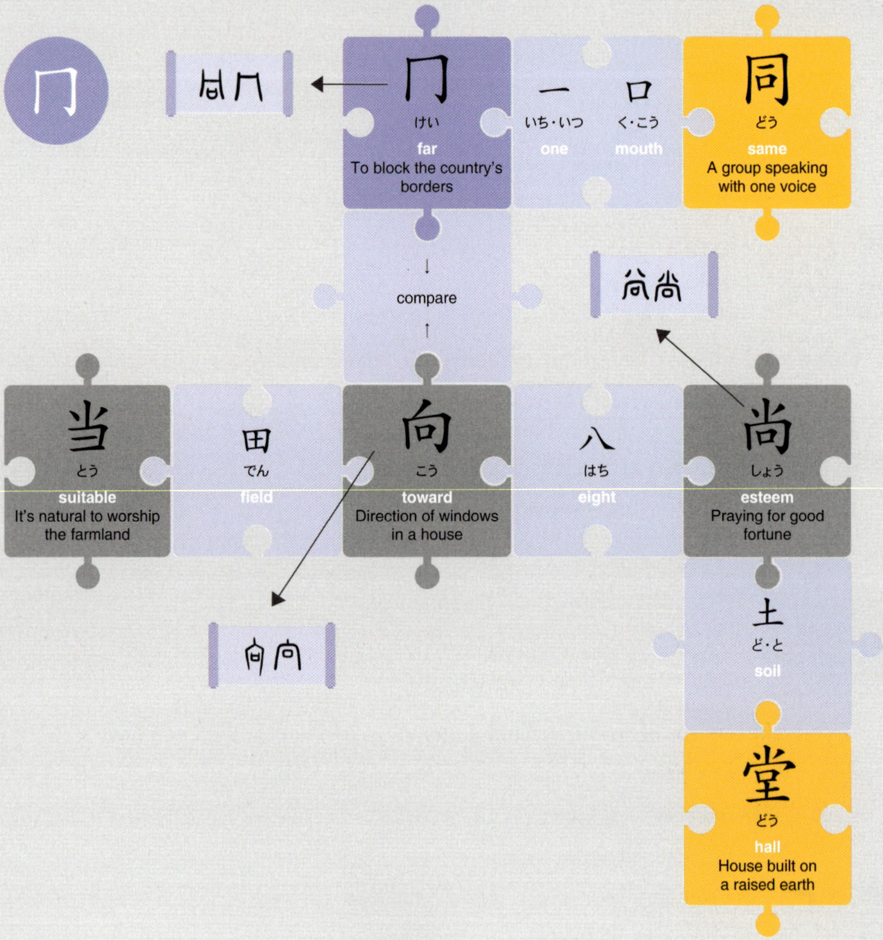

118 冂

ケイ

far

丨 冂

When a border crossing is closed, it becomes a boundary that is just too far away and impossible to cross.

＊When used as part of another character, it's usually for the shape, not the meaning.

118a **同** ドウ おなじ
丨 冂 冂 同 同 同
same
one 一[173] [イチ・イツ] + mouth ロ[12] [ク・コウ] + boundary/far 冂 [ケイ]

To speak in one(一) voice(ロ) means it is the same group(冂).

* "冂" is a boundary, so think of this as a group within the same boundaries.

同じ[おなじ] same; identical; equal
合同[ごうどう] combination; union; joint -54a 118a

118b **向** コウ むかう・むく・むける・むこう
′ 丫 白 向 向 向
toward; face
house 宀[113] [メン・ベン] + windows ロ [symbol]

Signifies looking/facing towards the windows(ロ) inside a house(宀).

* "mouth ロ[12] [ク・コウ]" symbolizes a 'window' in this case.

向かう[むかう] face; confront; go toward
向く[むく] face; turn toward
向ける[むける] turn toward; point at
向こう[むこう] other side; opposite direction

118c **尚** ショウ
丨 丨 丷 𭕄 尚 尚 尚 尚
esteem
eight ソ→八[177] [ハチ] + toward 向 [コウ]

Praying towards(向) the gods asking for blessings to be sent down(八) means 'to esteem, to value or still.'

* "八" symbolizes 'fortunes or blessings descending from heaven.'

118d **堂** ドウ
丨 丨 丷 𭕄 尚 尚 尚 尚 堂 堂 堂
hall
esteem 尚 [ショウ] + soil 土[120] [ド・ト]

Meaning of hall is derived from the ancient practices of building a house or a building on top of the highly raised(尚) earth(土) to prevent water damage from rain.

* When used as part of another character, it's usually for the shape, not the meaning.

食堂[しょくどう] restaurant -109 118d

118e **当** トウ あてる・あたる
丨 丨 丷 当 当 当
suitable; right; hit
esteem ⺌→尚 [ショウ] + field ヨ→田[122] [デン]

Farmland(田) on which crops were grown was rightly revered(尚), so the meaning of this character came from 'rightly → right → to hit.'

* Traditional character(當) combines "田" and "尚," which is simplified into the current version.

当(た)る[あたる] be hit; fit; hit the mark (target)
当てる[あてる] hit; hit the mark (target); guess (an answer)
相当[そうとう] considerable; equality -7c 118e
当然[とうぜん] natural; a matter of course -118e 124d

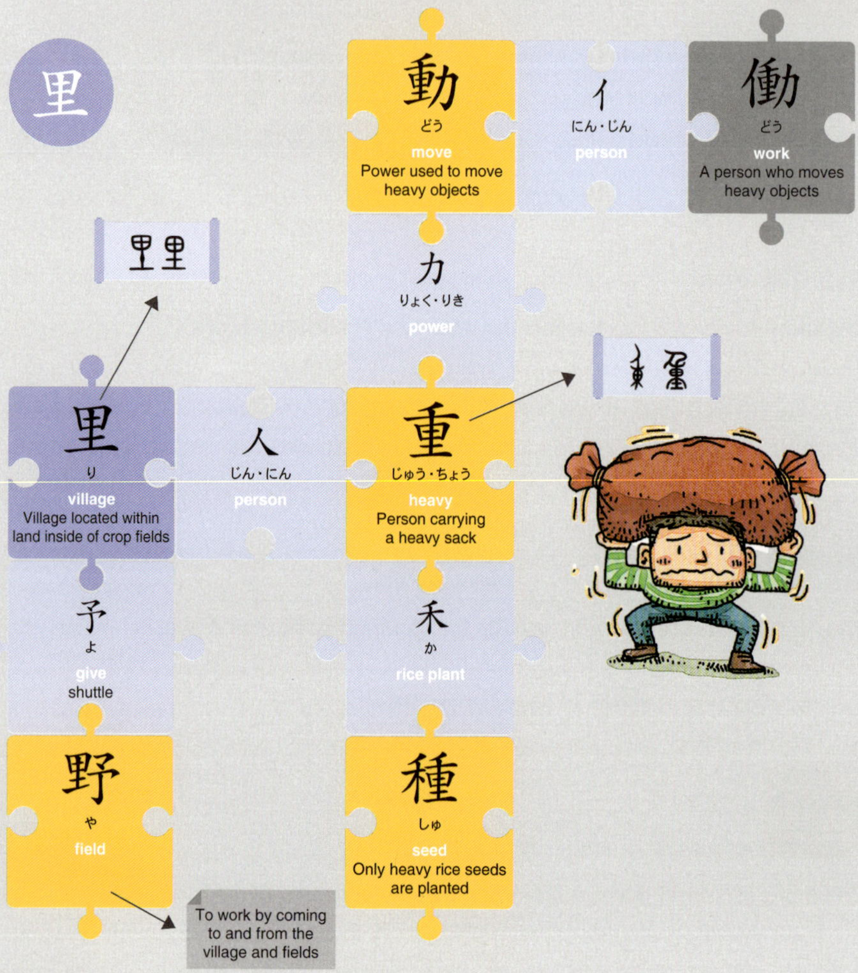

119 **里**

リ さと

village

丨 冂 冃 日 甲 甲 里

A village is located on land(土 [120]) close to the crop fields(田 [122]).

古里/故里 [ふるさと] home town; birthplace - 15 119 / 15a 119

119a **重**

ジュウ・チョウ　おもい・え・おもんずる・かさなる・かさねる

heavy; -fold

person 千→人[51] [ジン・ニン] + sack/east 里→東[167] [トウ]

Signifies a person(人) carrying a heavy sack(東) on his back.

* "東" signifies a sack with both ends tied up; the ancient character clearly shows a sack(東) together with a man(人).

重い[おもい] heavy; weighty
重んずる[おもんずる] lay (put) stress on; respect
重なる[かさなる] be piled up; overlap; repeat
重ねる[かさねる] pile up; heap up; repeat
体重[たいじゅう] weight -24b 119a

119b **動**

ドウ　うごかす・うごく

move

heavy 重 [ジュウ・チョウ] + power 力[125] [リョク・リキ]

Power or strength(力) is needed to move something heavy(重).

動かす[うごかす] move
動く[うごく] move; operate
動物[どうぶつ] animal -119b 41a
活動[かつどう] activity; action -20c 119b
自動車[じどうしゃ] car; vehicle; automobile -6 119b 97

119c **働**

ドウ　はたらく

work

person イ[52] [ニン・ジン] + move 動 [ドウ]

A person(イ) moving(動) heavy objects indicates work or labor.

働く[はたらく] work; do; be active

119d **種**

シュ　たね

seed

rice plant 禾[111] [カ] + heavy 重 [ジュウ・チョウ]

Light kernels that float in water are discarded and only the heavy(重) rice seeds(禾) are kept to be planted as seeds.

種種/色色[いろいろ] various; various colors (kinds) -119d 119d / 75d 75d
人種[じんしゅ] race; ethnicity -51 119d
播種[はしゅ] sowing; seeding -142b 119d

119e **野**

ヤ

field

village 里 [リ] + shuttle/give 予[4a] [ヨ]

Like the shuttle(予) on a loom weaving between the warp threads, people go between the village(里) and the fields to work.

野菜[やさい] vegetable -119e 29d
野生[やせい] wild -119e 162

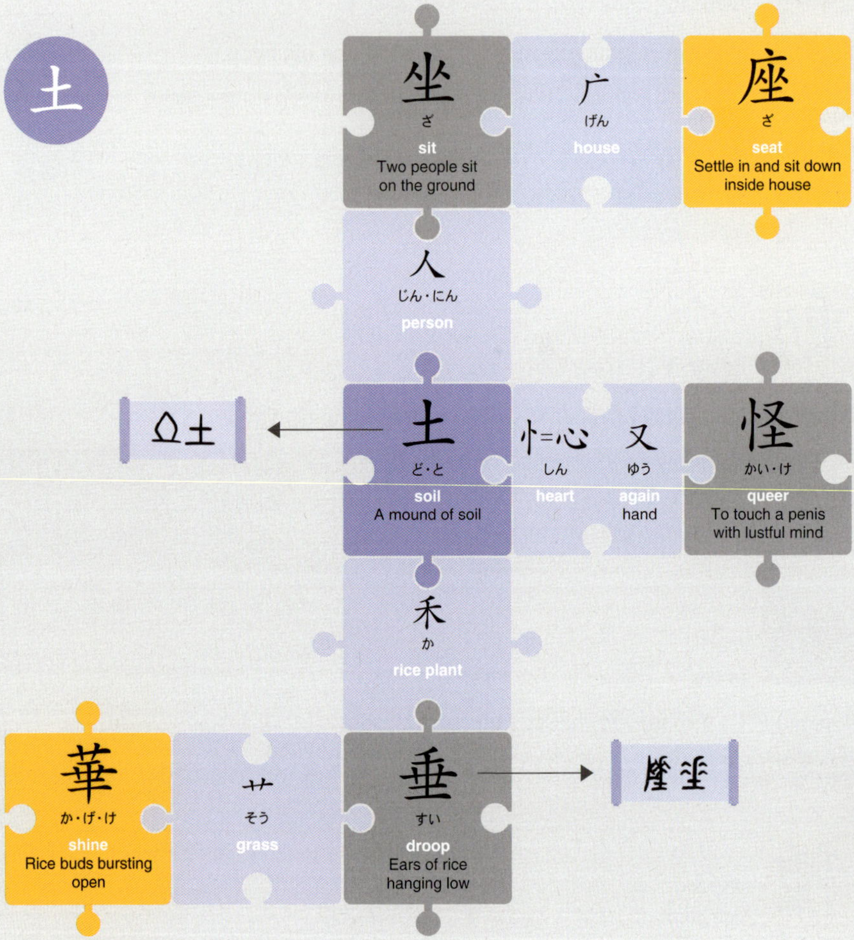

120	土	ド・ト つち **soil**	一 十 土

Signifies a mound of earth or soil. Also came from the model of male penis made from earth.

土曜日[どようび] Saturday -120 141c 170
土地[とち] land; ground -120 68b

120a 坐

ザ

ノ 人 从 从 丛 坐 坐

sit

person 人[51] [ジン・ニン] + soil 土 [ド・ト]

Signifies two people(人) sitting down on the ground(土) to have a chat.

120b 座

ザ すわる

丶 亠 广 广 広 応 応 应 座 座

seat; place

house 广[114] [ゲン] + sit 坐 [ザ]

Signifies a person who is comfortably seated(坐) inside a house(广).

＊"广" symbolizes a large house with an open wall on the side.

座る[すわる] sit, fill a position

120c 怪

カイ・ケ あやしい

丨 忄 忄 忄 怪 怪 怪 怪

queer

heart 忄=心[26] [シン] + hand/again 又[30] [ユウ] + male penis/soil 土 [ド・ト]

Out of an image of having a lustful mind(忄) and touching a penis(土) with one's hands(又), the meaning of 'queer' is derived.

怪しい[あやしい] suspicious; strange; weird
怪我[けが] injury; hurt -120c 91a

120d 垂

スイ たれる

ノ 二 三 千 丘 岳 垂 垂

droop

Ears of rice(禾[111]) or plant stems drooping enough to reach the earth(土) like weeping willows.

垂れる[たれる] hang; droop
垂直[すいちょく] verticality -120d 8

120e 華

カ・ゲ・ケ はな

一 十 艹 艹 芒 芒 苔 苔 萃 華

shine

grass 艹[161] [ソウ] + droop 垂→垂 [スイ]

The sight of rice(垂) buds(艹) bursting open is grand and shiny to those whose staple is cooked rice.

華/花[はな] flower -120e / 52b
華やか[はなやか] splendor; brilliant

Diagram for 圭

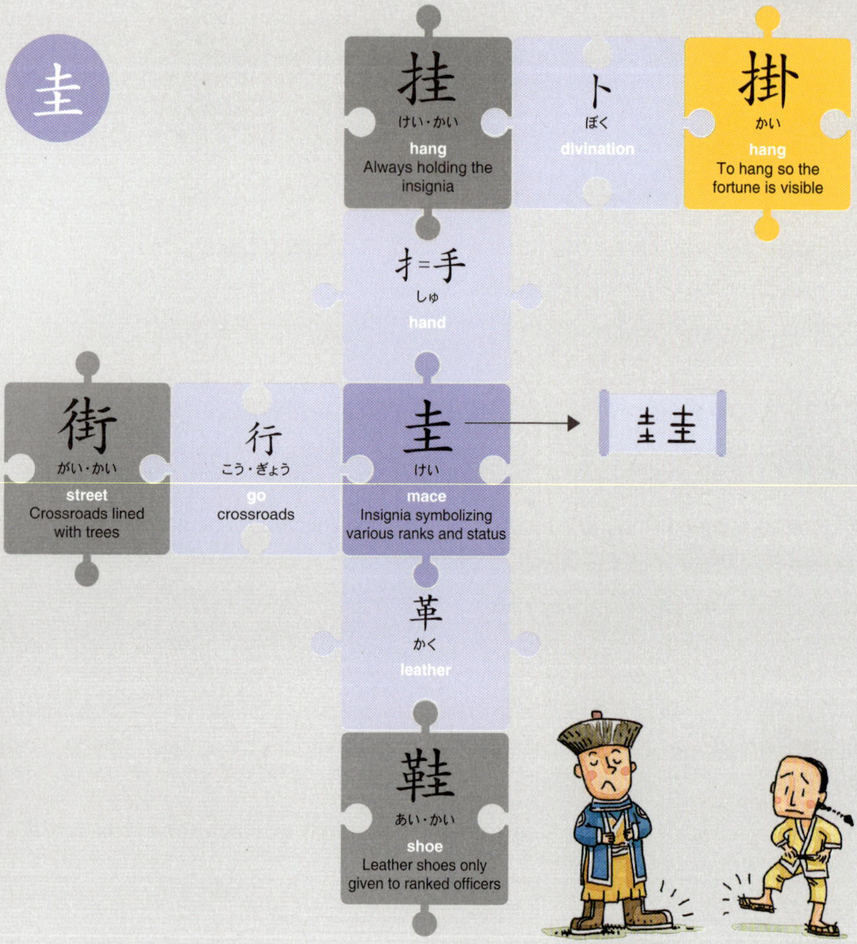

121 **圭**

ケイ

一 十 土 圭 圭 圭

mace; hand-tablet

Symbolizes a small traditional insignia which is rectangular in shape. It is made from jade or wood (therefore a small tablet) that was used as an appointment certificate and also as marks that distinguished various ranks of government officers.

* Although this has no relation to "soil 土[120] [ド・ト]," it's covered here due to its similar shape and the fact that it takes "土" as its radical.

121a 挂

ケイ・カイ

hang

hand 扌=手[28] [シュ] + hand-tablet/mace 圭 [ケイ]

A king's servants and officers always held(扌) onto the insignia tablets(圭) when handling national affairs – almost as if the insignia(圭) is hanging from their hands(扌).

121b 掛

カイ かかる・かける

hang; set

hang 挂 [ケイ・カイ] + divination 卜[100] [ボク]

To hang(挂) the auspicious fortune(卜) where it can be seen clearly.

掛(か)る[かかる] hang; be set over; lean against
掛ける[かける] hang; set; lock; fasten (up)

121c 鞋

アイ・カイ

shoe

leather 革[149c] [カク] + hand-tablet/mace 圭 [ケイ]

Officers and servants who are given the insignia tablet(圭) (therefore a prestigious position in the office) from the king could wear shoes made of leather(革).

* In ancient China, leather shoes were only allowed to be worn by nobles whereas commoners could only afford to wear them during their wedding ceremony.

121d 街

ガイ・カイ まち

street

crossroads/go 行[48a] [コウ・ギョウ] + hand-tablet/mace 圭 [ケイ]

This character means 'street' because a crossroad(行) lined with trees looks just like the king's men standing in rows holding their ceremonial scepters(圭).

街角[まちかど] street corner - 121d 150

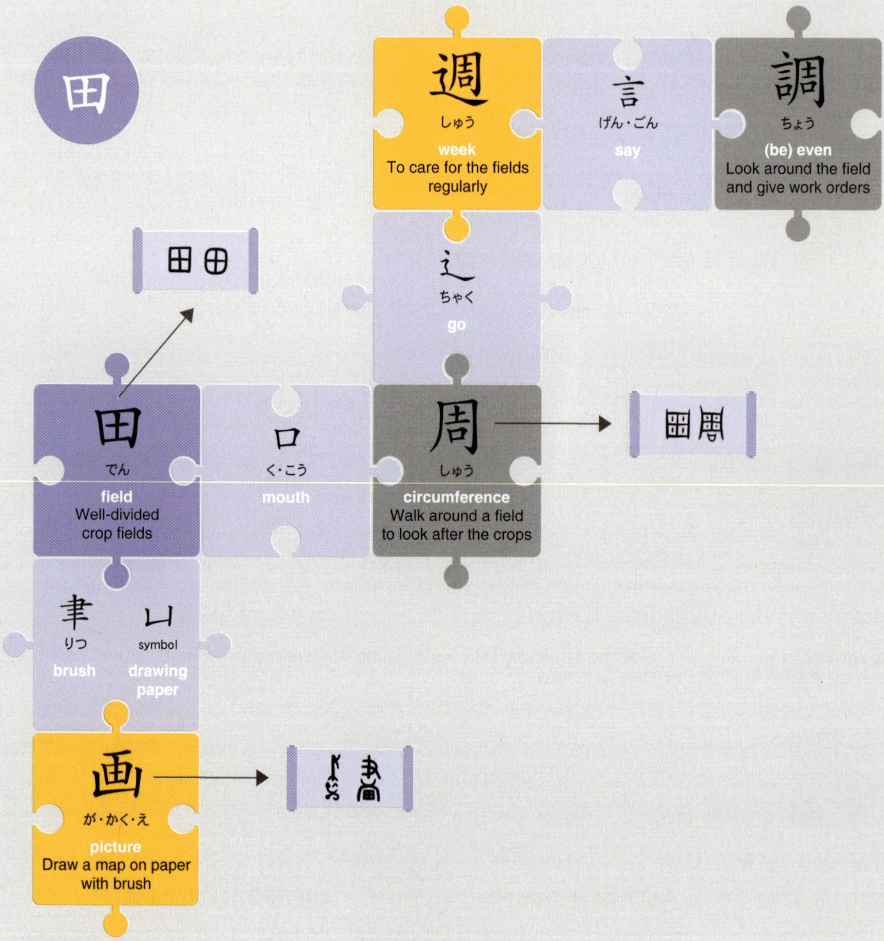

122 田

テン た

field; rice paddy

Signifies crop fields that are clearly divided by drains and mounds (banks).

122a 周

シュウ まわり

丿 冂 冂 円 円 周 周 周

circumference; circuit

field 円→田 [デン] + mouth ロ[12] [ク・コウ]

Signifies the act of regularly circling or going around the circumference (bounds) of the field(田) to take care of crops that will become food for the mouth (ロ).

* Ancient bone-letters show dots(丶) inside a field(田), signifying regularly maintained fields that help crops(丶) to grow well.

周り[まわり] circumference; surroundings
周辺[しゅうへん] surroundings; circumference -122a 49a

122b 週

シュウ

丿 冂 冂 円 円 周 周 周 凋 调 週

week

circumference 周 [シュウ] + go 辶[49] [チャク]

The sight of farmers looking around(辶) their fields regularly(周) came to mean 'week.'

今週[こんしゅう] this week -54b 122b	先週[せんしゅう] last week -58d 122b
毎週[まいしゅう] every week -79a 122b	来週[らいしゅう] next week -110e 122b

122c 調

チョウ しらべる

丶 亠 亠 亠 言 言 言 言 訂 訂 訶 訶 調 調 調

(be) even; investigate; tone

say 言[17] [ゲン・ゴン] + circumference 周 [シュウ]

Signifies circling(周) of fields to see or investigate if crops are growing evenly, and then giving various work orders by words(言).

調べる[しらべる] investigate; inquire into; research
強調[きょうちょう] emphasis; highlight -143a 122c
調査[ちょうさ] investigation; examination -122c 174a

122d 画

ガ・カク・エ えがく

一 丅 丙 丙 両 画 画 画

picture; draw

brush 丅→聿[33] [リツ] + field 田 [デン] + drawing paper 凵 [symbol]

Signifies drawing or painting of a map(田) or a picture on a canvas(凵) with a brush(聿).

* Traditional character(畫) shows painting of a map(田) on a paper(凵) with a brush(聿).

画く[えがく] draw; paint
映画館[えいがかん] movie theater; cinema- 61d 122d 152d
映画[えいが] movie; film -61d 122d
計画[けいかく] plan (for); program; scheme; design -17a 122d

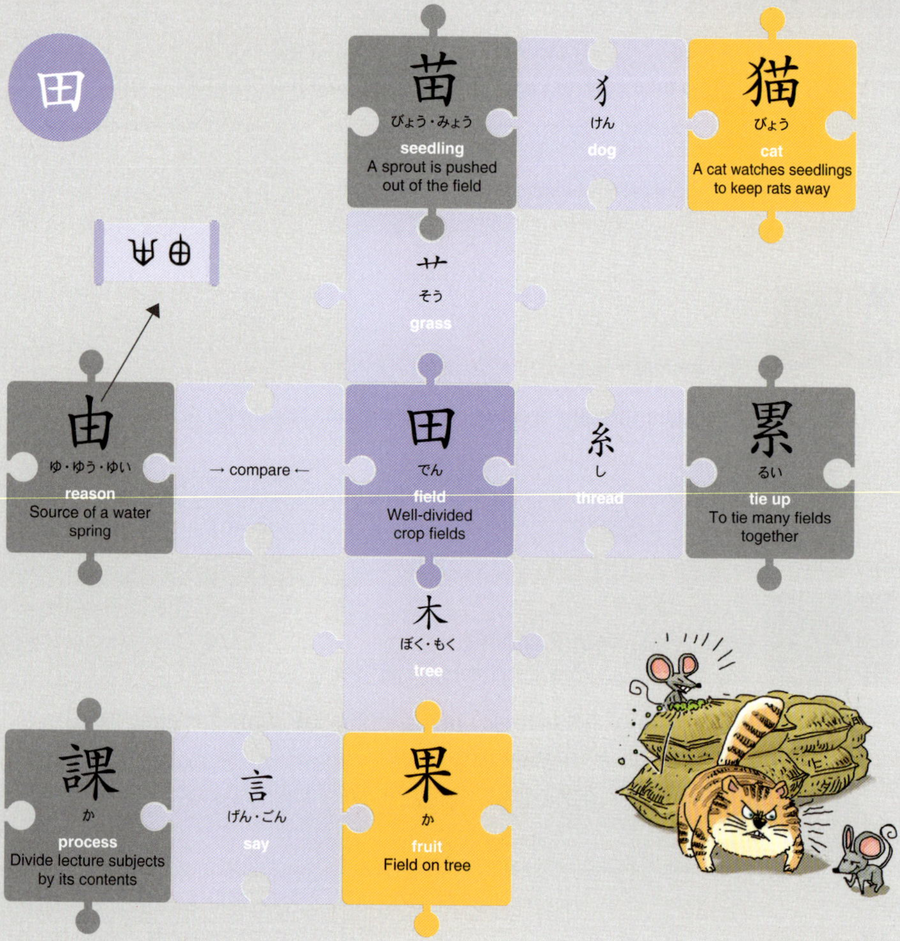

123 苗

ビョウ・ミョウ

一 十 艹 艹 芇 苗 苗 苗

seedling

grass 艹 161 [ソウ] + field 田 122 [デン]

This character has the image of a sprout(艹) which is coming up out of the field(田) in the spring.

123a 猫

ビョウ ねこ

丿 犭 犭 犭 犭 犭 犭 猎 猫 猫 猫

cat

dog 犭 135b [ケン] + seedling 苗 [ビョウ・ミョウ]

This character has the image of a cat(犭) that keeps watching the seedlings(苗) to be sown in the spring time in order to keep the rats away from a granary.

* "犭" is used as a stroke, meaning that an animal is big as a dog.

123b 累

ルイ

丶 ㄇ 冂 冂 田 甲 罗 罗 累 累 累

tie up

field 田 122 [デン] + thread 糸 104 [シ]

A description of many fields(田) tied together with thread(糸).

* The traditional character(纍) shows three rice paddies(田) tied(糸) together.

累算[るいさん] total -123b 38e

123c 果

カ はたす・はて・はてる

丶 ㄇ 日 日 旦 甲 果 果

fruit

field 田 122 [デン] + tree 木 164 [ボク・モク]

A crop field(田) hanging from trees(木) signifies fruits hanging from tree branches.

果(た)す[はたす] carry out; accomplish	果て[はて] end, extremity; limit
果てる[はてる] end; be finished; die	果物[くだもの] fruit -123c 41a
結果[けっか] result; consequence -84b 123c	苹果[りんご] apple -96b 123c

123d 課

カ

丶 亠 亠 亠 言 言 言 言 訂 訂 訂 詚 課 課 課

process; section

say 言 17 [ゲン・ゴン] + fruit 果 [カ]

Symbolizes division of subjects or lessons based on the content(果) of a lecture (言).

* "果" signifies the fruit of learning, with emphasis on its contents in this character.

課長[かちょう] section chief (head) -123d 61d
課題[かだい] task; assignment; mission -123d 45e

123e 由

ユ・ユウ・ユイ

丨 ㄇ 巾 由 由

reason

Symbolizes a deep well with water springs – a source or cause of water for people.

* Has no relation to "field 田 122 [デン]," but is covered here due to the similar shape and because it uses "田" as its radical.

自由[じゆう] freedom; liberty -6 123e	理由[りゆう] reason; excuse; pretext -86e 123e

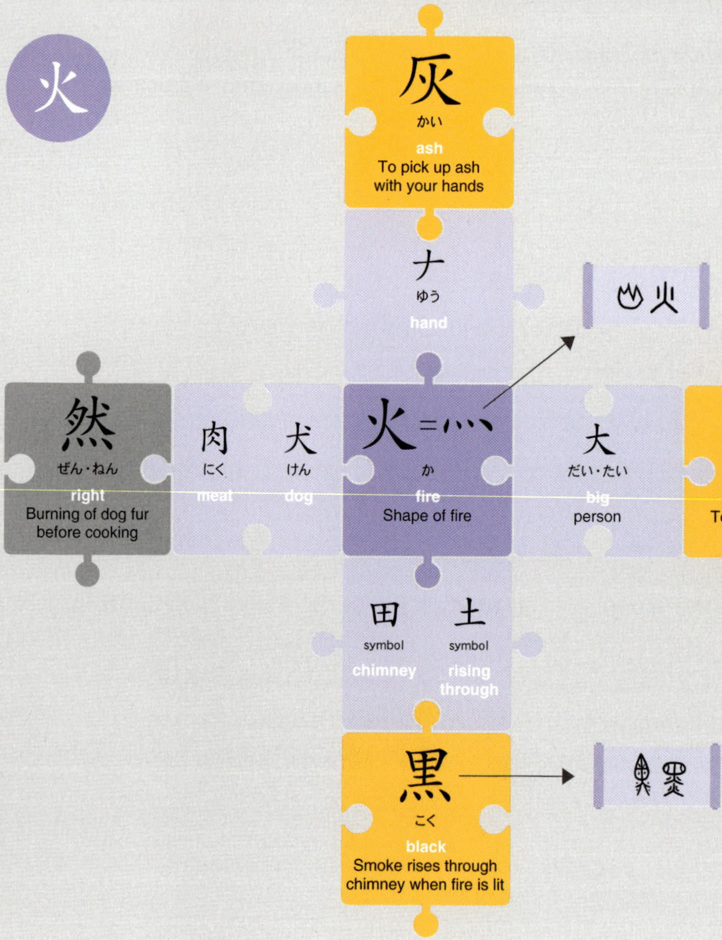

124 火

カ ひ

fire

A simple representation of fire as a shape. When merged and placed under other characters, it takes the shape of "灬."

*"Fire 火" is being covered in this section since in the old days, crop fields were created by burning down mountains and fields.

火曜日[かようび] Tuesday -124 141c 170
火山[かざん] volcano -124 153
火事[かじ] fire; blaze -124 32c

124a 灰

一 厂 厂 尸 灰 灰

カイ　はい

ash

hand 厂→ナ[34] [ユウ] + fire 火 [カ]

Fire(火) you can pick up with your hand(ナ) is ash.

灰皿[はいざら] ashtray -124a 132d
灰色[はいいろ] ash gray; gray -124a 75d

124b 赤

一 十 土 ナ 赤 赤 赤

セキ・シャク　あか・あかい

red

person/big 土→大[60] [ダイ・タイ] + fire 火 [カ]

To burn(火) a prisoner(大) to death came to mean 'red.'

赤い[あかい] red; crimson, ruddy, communist
赤道[せきどう] equator -124b 4e

124c 黒

丶 冂 冂 日 甲 甲 里 里 里 黒 黒

コク　くろ・くろい

black

chimney 田 [symbol] + rising through 土 [symbol] + fire 灬=火 [カ]

Fire(灬) causes black smoke to rise into the chimney(田) and exit(土), turning everything near it into black charcoal.

* In the bronze inscription, the chimney is shown to turn black when fire(灬) is lit from below.

黒い[くろい] black; dark; illicit
黒板[こくばん] blackboard -124c 117c

124d 然

ノ ク タ タ 夕 外 外 外 然 然 然 然

ゼン・ネン　しかし・しかり

right; so

meat タ→月→肉[151] [ニク] + dog 犬[135] [ケン] + fire 灬=火 [カ]

The fur is removed by burning(灬) prior to cooking dog(犬) meat(肉). It was rightly so that such cooked dog meat would appear in ceremonial tables and offerings.

* Dog meat was an exquisite delicacy that always appeared in large ceremonies and offerings in the old dynasties of China. When "moon 月[172] [ゲツ・ガツ]" combines with other characters, it means "肉."

然し[しかし] but; however; though
然り[しかり] yes; right; be so
当然[とうぜん] natural; a matter of course -118e 124d
突然[とつぜん] suddenly; unexpectedly -113c 124d

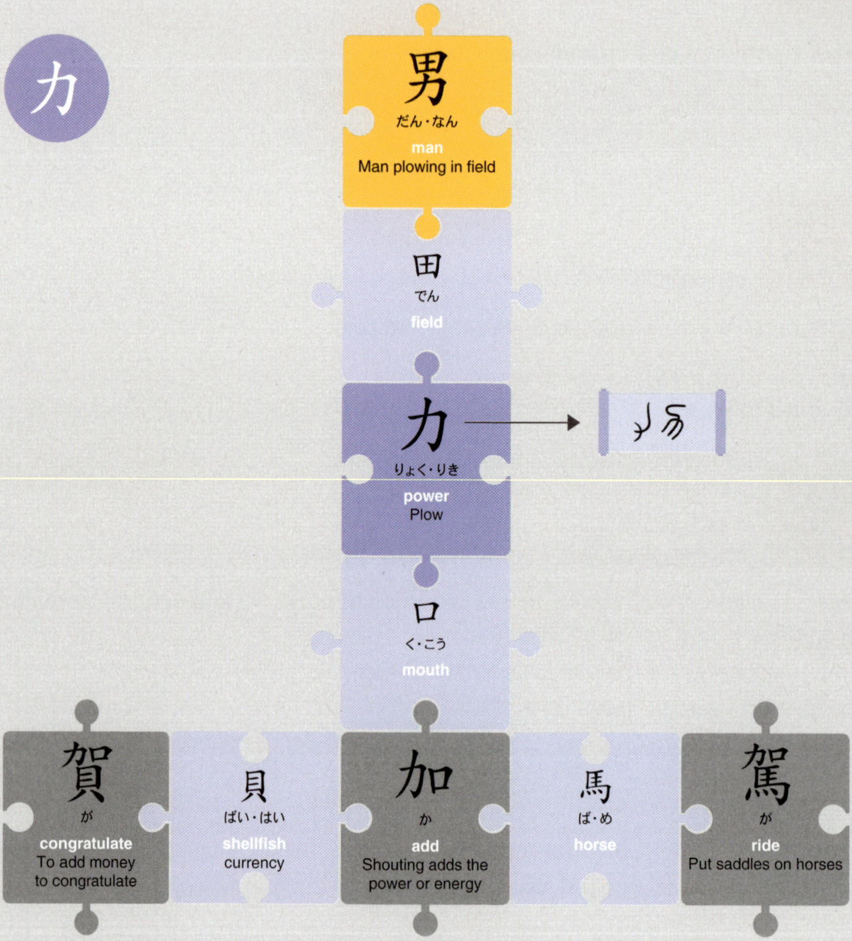

125 **力**

リョク・リキ ちから　　フ 力

power

Symbolizes a plow, a critical tool in agriculture. Power is needed to pull the plow in fields.

力強い[ちからづよい] reassuring; encouraging; powerful; strong -125 143a
電力[でんりょく] electricity; (electric) power -159c 125
能力[のうりょく] ability; capacity -73d 125

125a 男

ダン・ナン おとこ

man

field 田[122] [デン] + plow/power 力 [リョク・リキ]

Signifies a man working in the field(田) using plows(力) at the time of agrarian society.

男の子[おとこのこ] boy -125a 77
男の人[おとこのひと] man; male -125a 51
男性[だんせい] man; male -125a 27a

125b 加

カ くわえる・くわわる

add

plow/power 力 [リョク・リキ] + mouth ロ[12] [ク・コウ]

Farmers using all their physical power into plowing(力) the field. Shouting or singing from their mouth(ロ) adds more power to each stroke or push that they need to give.

加える[くわえる] add; append; increase
加わる[くわわる] be added; be appended, increase
参加[さんか] participation -5a 125b

125c 駕

ガ

ride

add 加 [カ] + horse 馬[138] [バ・メ]

A horse(馬) is ready to be ridden when its saddles are properly put on(加).

125d 賀

ガ

congratulate

add 加 [カ] + currency/shellfish 貝[145] [バイ・ハイ]

When going to congratulate someone, you should bring money(貝) to give or add(加) to them.

祝賀[しゅくが] congratulation; celebration -59a 125d

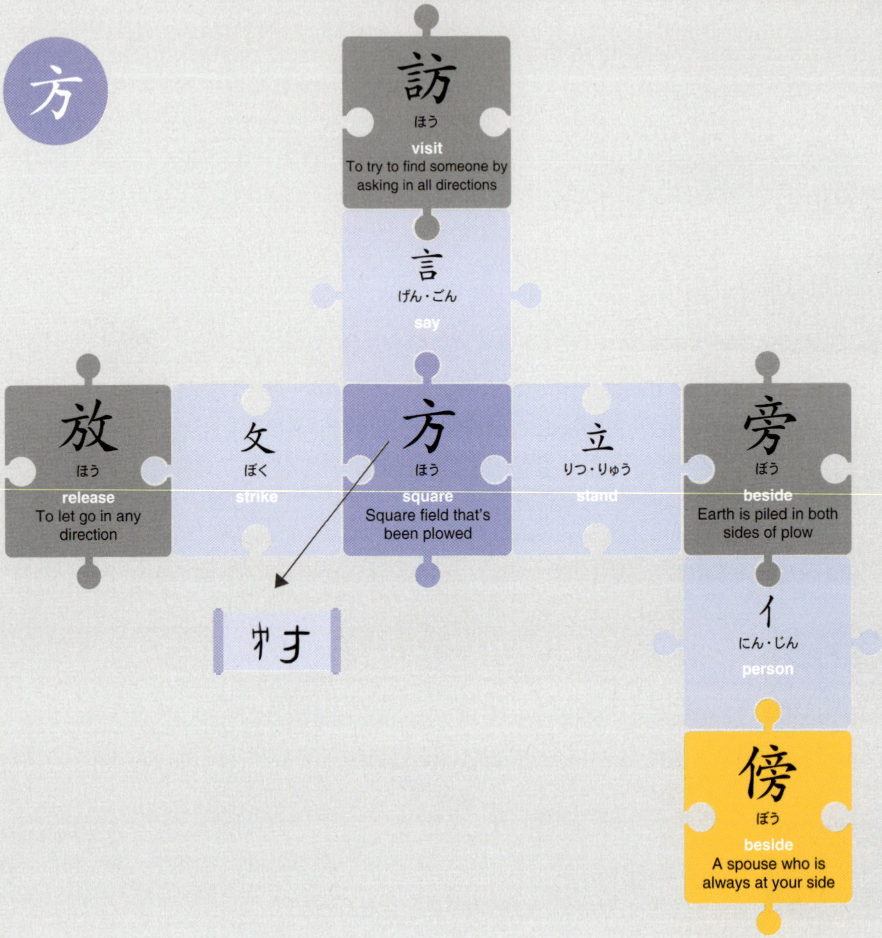

126 **方**

ホウ かた

square; direction

A variation on the shape of a plow(方). A field is square shaped after proper plowing. It also signifies direction since a square has points facing all four directions.

彼方[あちら] that way (direction); there -149a 126

貴方/貴下[あなた] (honorific) you -145c 126 / 145c 173b

此方[こちら] this way (direction); here -72a 126

其方[そちら] that way (direction); there -39 126

何方[どなた] (honorific) who -13c 126

何方[どちら] which -13c 126

夕方[ゆうがた] sunset; dusk; evening (time) -172a 126

126a 訪

ホウ　おとずれる・たずねる

visit

say 言[17] [ゲン・ゴン] + direction/square 方 [ホウ]

Signifies the act of visiting a famous teacher or a doctor by asking(言) around in all directions(方).

訪れる[おとずれる] visit; call on
訪ねる[たずねる] visit, call on
訪問[ほうもん] visit - 126a 115a

126b 旁

ボウ

beside

stand 立[64] [リツ・リュウ] + plow/square 方 [ホウ]

Earth is dug up and piled(立) to each side of a plow(方).

126c 傍

ボウ　そば・かたわら

beside

person 亻[52] [ニン・ジン] + beside 旁 [ボウ]

A spouse(亻) or a partner who is always beside(旁) you or 'at your side.'

傍ら[かたわら] beside; while

126d 放

ホウ　はなす・はなれる・ほうる

release

direction/square 方 [ホウ] + strike 攵[43] [ボク]

To whip(攵) and then release a prisoner so he can go in any direction(方) he chooses.

放す[はなす] release; set free
放れる[はなれる] be released; get free
放る[ほうる] throw; throw away; neglect
放送[ほうそう] broadcasting - 126d 62d

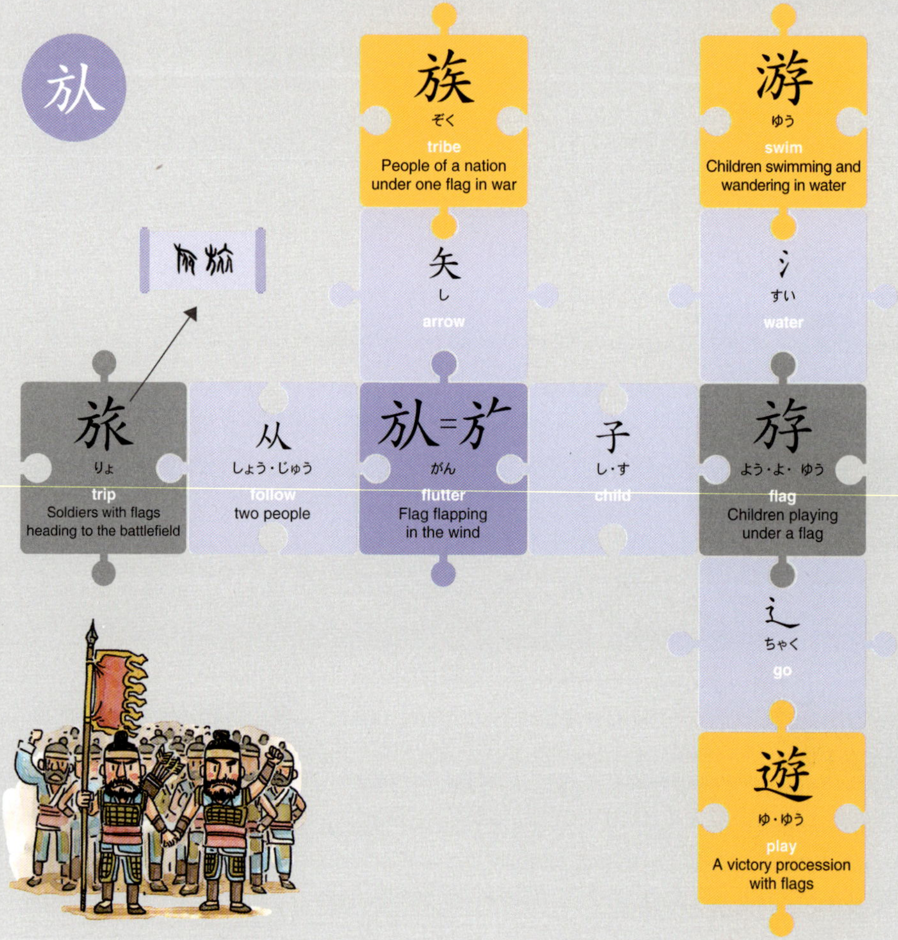

127 㫃

ガン

`丶 亠 方 方 㫃 㫃`

flutter

square 方 [ホウ] + waving flag 人 [symbol]

Signifies a rectangular(方) flag(人) flapping or fluttering in the wind.

* Although the right side looks the same as a person "人[51]," it symbolizes a flapping flag. Its shape can change(𠂉) when combined with other characters.

127a **族**

ゾク ` ㅗ 亠 方 方 方 方 於 於 族 族

tribe; family

flutter 㫃 [ガン] + arrow 矢[89] [シ]

Waving the flag(㫃) and the arrow(矢) signifies war. When people are gathered under one flag(㫃) in a time of war, it means 'the people are from the same tribe or clan of long generations, sharing the same culture and language.'

家族[かぞく] family - 136a 127a
貴族[きぞく] aristocrat; nobility - 145c 127a

127b **斿**

ヨウ・ヨ・ユウ ` ㅗ 亠 方 方 方 方 斿 斿

flag

flutter 㫃 [ガン] + child 子[77] [シ・ス]

The sight of children(子) running and playing under a fluttering(㫃) flag.

127c **游**

ユウ およぐ ` ` 氵 氵 氵 汸 汸 汸 汸 游 游 游

swim; float

water 氵[157] [スイ] + flag 斿 [ヨウ・ヨ・ユウ]

Signifies children(子) swimming or wandering in water(氵), under the protection of the flag(㫃) or adults.

游ぐ/泳ぐ[およぐ] swim - 127c / 156b

127d **遊**

ユ・ユウ あそぶ ` ㅗ 亠 方 方 方 方 斿 斿 斿 游 遊

play

flag 斿 [ヨウ・ヨ・ユウ] + go 辶[49] [チャク]

The sight of children running and playing between soldiers carrying a flag(斿) in a victory procession(辶) came to mean 'play or travel.'

遊ぶ[あそぶ] play; make an excursion
遊覧[ゆうらん] sightseeing - 127d 85c

127e **旅**

リョ たび ` ㅗ 亠 方 方 方 方 於 旅 旅

trip; travel

flutter 㫃 [ガン] + two people/follow 𠂉→从 [ショウ・ジュウ]

'Two men(从) under a fluttering(㫃) flag' describes 'soldiers heading to war.' It came to mean 'travel' because soldiers fight away from home.

* "从" depicts a person(人[51]) following the person(人) in front.

旅館[りょかん] traditional Japanese inn - 127e 152d

斗

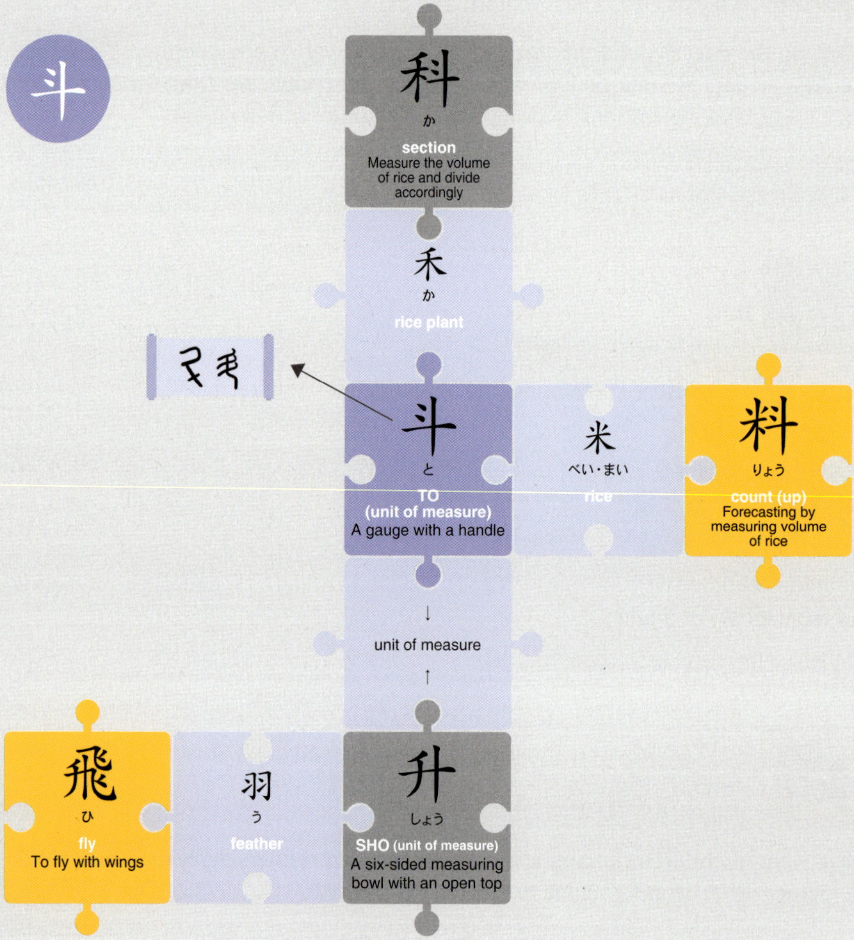

128 斗

ト

TO (unit of measure)

A gauge with a handle that's used to weigh grain. This character came to mean 'unit of measure.'

128a **科**

カ

ノ 二 千 禾 禾 禾 禾 科 科

section

rice plant 禾[111] [カ] + measure/TO 斗 [ト]

Harvested rice(禾) is measured with a measuring scale(斗) and is divided to each purpose, such as tax, rent, and distribution of seeds.

＊For example, science is a systematically divided(科) study of nature for easier understanding(学[77b]).

科学[かがく] science - 128a 77b
内科[ないか] internal medicine - 53b 128a

128b **料**

リョウ

丶 丷 䒑 半 米 米 米 米 料 料

count (up); materials

rice 米[110] [ベイ・マイ] + measure/TO 斗 [ト]

To measure(斗) the amount of rice(米) to calculate the amount to eat. It also means 'ingredients or to cook' with the measured rice.

料理[りょうり] cooking; cookery - 128b 86e
料金[りょうきん] charge; fee - 128b 154

128c **升**

ショウ

ノ 二 チ 升

SHO (unit of measure); ascend

To scoop up grain with a six-sided measuring bowl and pour into a bag means 'SHO or to ascend.'

128d **飛**

ヒ　とぶ・とばす

乁 乁 飞 飞 飞 飞 飛 飛 飛

fly

feather 羽[141] [ウ] + ascend/SHO 升 [ショウ]

A large bird spreading its wings(羽) to fly up(升).

飛ぶ[とぶ] fly
飛ばす[とばす] fly; spatter; skip over
飛行機[ひこうき] airplane; aircraft - 128d 48a 91e
飛行場[ひこうじょう] airfield; airport - 128d 48a 171c

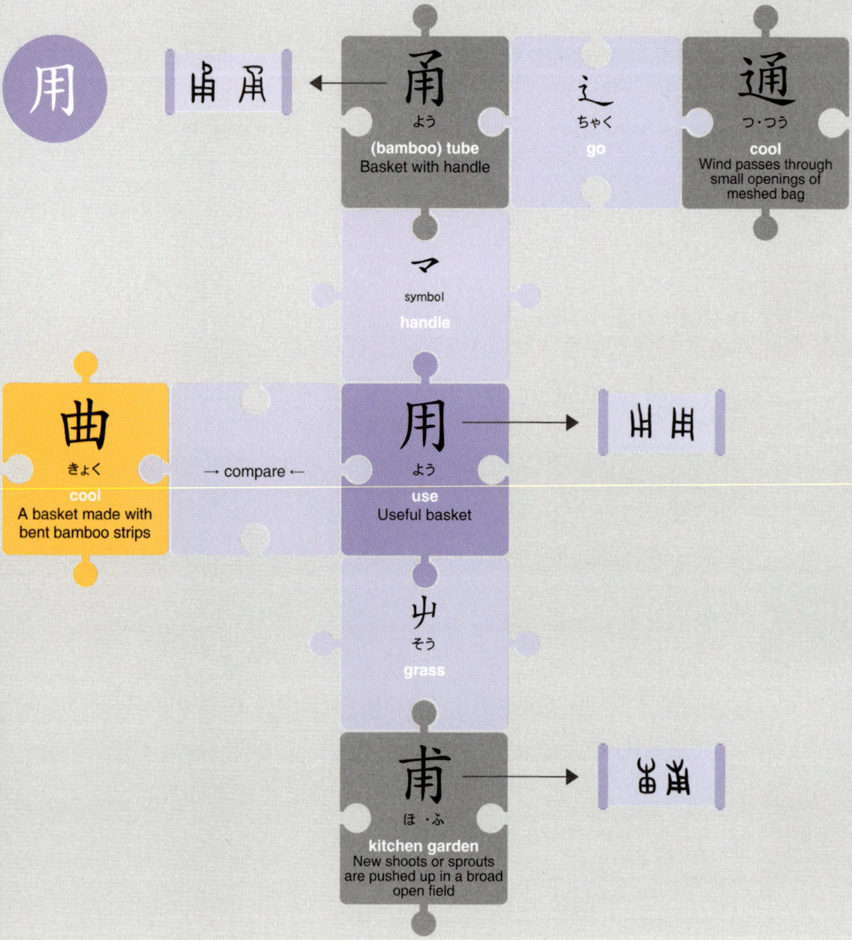

129 **用**

ヨウ もちいる

ノ 冂 月 月 用

use

Symbolizes the shape of a traditional basket which can be conveniently used for containing agricultural crops or other things.

用いる[もちいる] utilize; use
利用[りよう] use -111d 129

129a 甬

ヨウ

(bamboo) tube

handle ⺕ [symbol] + basket/use 用 [ヨウ]

ㇷ ㇷ ㇷ 乃 乃 甬 甬

A mesh bag(用) with a handle(⺕) shaped like a tube.

＊"甬" also means 'crown of a bell' because it looks like a bell with a handle. A ringing bell creates a ripple in the air, and air flows through nets, so consider this character to mean a net.

129b 通

ツウ・ツ かよう・とおす・とおる

pass through

mesh bag/(bamboo) tube 甬 [ヨウ] + go ⻌[49] [チャク]

Wind can pass through(⻌) the holes of a mesh basket(甬).

通う[かよう] go back and forth; commute
通す[とおす] let pass; pass through
通る[とおる] pass; get through
共通[きょうつう] commonness; be common -38a 129b
交通[こうつう] traffic; transport 1a -129b
普通[ふつう] usual; ordinary; general -64c 129b

129c 甫

ホ・フ

kitchen garden; just

一 厂 冂 冃 甬 甫 甫

Vegetables just started to spring their young sprouts(⺘→屮[161]) in a field(用→田[122]).

＊This character belongs to this section because the radical is "用," but it has nothing to do with its meaning.

129d 曲

キョク まげる・まがる

bend; curve

丨 冂 巾 曲 曲 曲

A character shaped like a bag or basket made with bent bamboo strips or dried plant stalks.

曲(が)る[まがる] curve; bend; turn
曲げる[まげる] bend

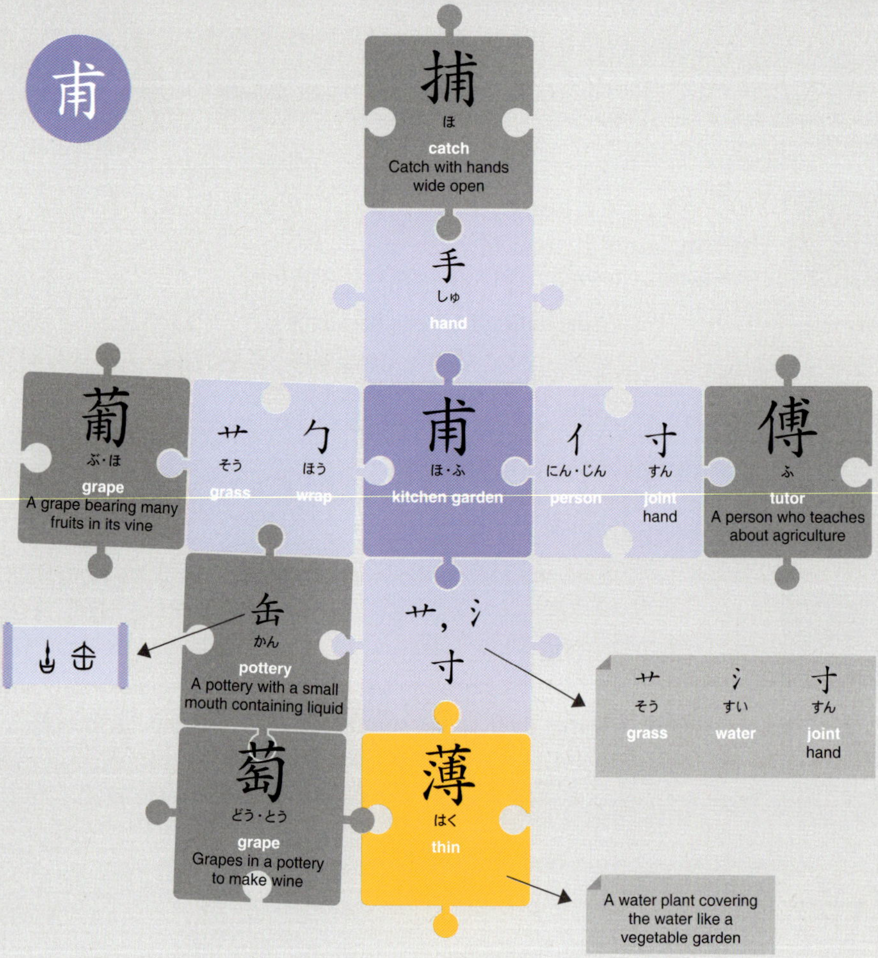

130 捕

ホ

catch

hand 扌=手[28] [シュ] + kitchen garden 甫 [ホ・フ]

一 十 扌 扌 扩 拆 挏 捐 捕 捕

To catch by hand(扌) an animal ruining the vegetable garden(甫).

捕鯨[ほげい] whaling; whale fishing - 130 2a

130a 傅

フ

tutor

person 亻[52] [ニン・ジン] + kitchen garden 甫 [ホ・フ] + hand/joint 寸[35] [スン]

A tutor is a person(亻) who teaches or gives a hand to(寸) you on how to farm in order to yield lots(甫) of harvest. It tells us that 'agriculture' has its long history in human civilization because it brings about the staple food necessary for their survival.

130b 薄

ハク うすい・うすめる

thin

grass 艹[161] [ソウ] + water 氵[157] [スイ] + kitchen garden 甫 [ホ・フ] + hand/joint 寸[35] [スン]

A thin layer of plants(艹) covering the water(氵) like a vegetable garden(甫), well-tended to by hand(寸).

薄い[うすい] thin; dilute; pale
薄める[うすめる] dilute

130c 葡

ブ・ホ

grape

grass 艹[161] [ソウ] + wrap 勹[40] [ホウ] + kitchen garden 甫 [ホ・フ]

This character illustrates the image of a grape vine which is covered by its creeping(勹) vines(艹) with many fruits(甫) hanging on them.

葡萄[ぶどう] grape - 130c 130e

130d 缶

カン

pottery

This character symbolizes a pottery which is used to contain liquid. Its belly is a bit bulged and has a small mouth. The container was used, in ancient times, as a percussion instrument.

130e 萄

ドウ・トウ

grape

grass 艹[161] [ソウ] + wrap 勹[40] [ホウ] + pottery 缶 [カン]

This character portrays the image of making wine in the pottery(缶). The wine is made from clusters of grapes grown in a grapevine covered with its creeping (勹) vines(艹).

葡萄[ぶどう] grape - 130c 130e

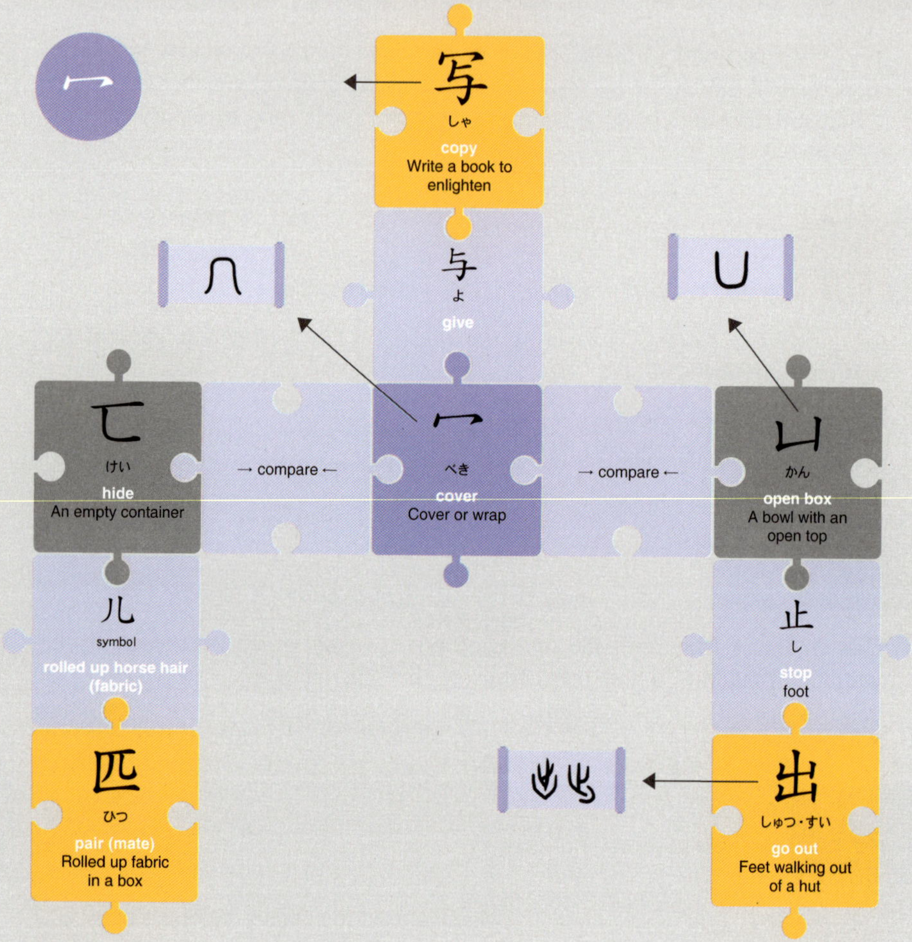

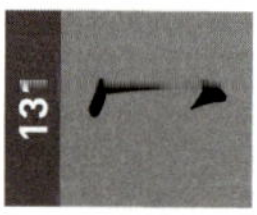

ベキ ノ 冖

cover

Symbolizes a cloth or wrap to cover food or goods.

131a 写

シャ　うつす・うつる

丶 冖 冖 写 写

copy

cover 冖 [ベキ] + give 与 [ヨ]

Writing a book and passing(与) it to someone can enlighten people and help them escape from the 'cover(冖) of ignorance.'

*Traditional character(寫) shows a nest(宀 113) of a magpie bird(舄), which looks the same as if it was transcribed regardless of where it is.

写す[うつす] copy; describe; take a photograph
写る[うつる] be seen through; be photographed
写真[しゃしん] photograph; photo -131a 8d

131b 凵

カン

𠃊 凵

open box

A character with variable interpretations, which can either mean an open-mouthed bowl or an open-top vessel.

131c 出

シュツ・スイ　だす・でる

𠃊 凵 屮 出 出

go out

foot/stop 止 44 [シ] + open box 凵 [カン]

According to the ancient character, it signifies the symbol of feet(止) walking out of a hut(凵).

出す[だす] put out; take out; send
出口[でぐち] exit; way out -131c 12
脱出[だっしゅつ] escape; break-out -59e 131c
出る[でる] go out; come out; go forth
出張[しゅっちょう] business trip; official tour -131c 81e

131d 匸

ケイ

一 匸

hide; empty box

'To hide' something with an empty container or bowl.

131e 匹

ヒツ　ひき

一 丆 兀 匹

pair (mate); counter for animals

empty box/hide 匸 [ケイ] + rolled up horse hair (fabric) 儿 [symbol]

A pair of bundles of horse hair or fabric(儿) in a box(匸) rolled up in the opposite direction to prevent entanglement. This character comes behind a number when used to count horses or animals.

一匹[いっぴき] one animal (or a fish); one roll of cloth -173 131e
何匹[なんびき] how many (animal) -13c 131e

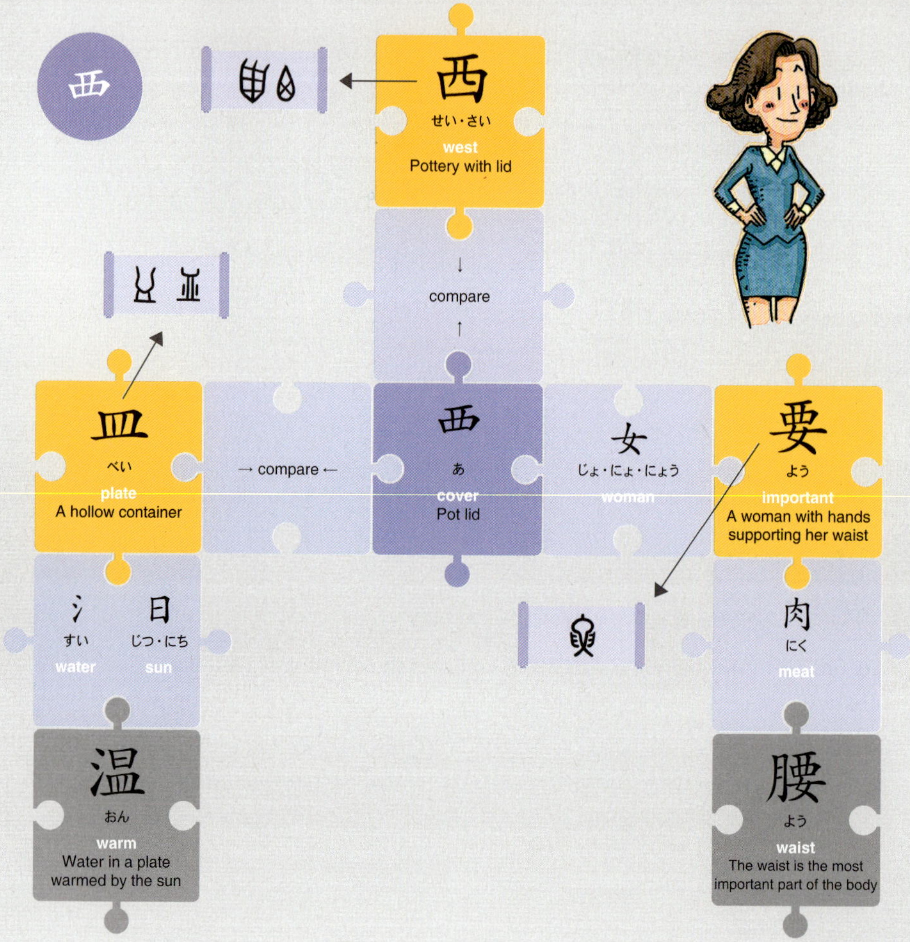

132 襾

ア

cover

Simple form of a cover used to close bottles or pots.

132a **西**

セイ・サイ　にし　　一 丆 冂 丙 襾 西

west

Symbolizes an earthenware(口) that holds water, with a lid(儿) on top. Borrowed to mean the concept of west since the pronunciation is same.

* Ancient version of this character clearly shows a lid being added on top of a pottery.

西洋[せいよう] the West; the Occident -132a 134d

132b **要**

ヨウ　いる　　一 丆 襾 襾 襾 西 要 要 要

important

cover 襾 [ア] + woman 女[78] [ジョ・ニョ・ニョウ]

A woman(女) is standing while supporting her waist with two hands(襾→臼); derived to mean 'essential, must or need' as the waist is the most critical part of a body.

* Ancient version of this character shows "襾" as the shape of two hands, "both hands 臼[29*] [コク]."

要る[いる] need; want
必要[ひつよう] need; necessity -26b 132b

132c **腰**

ヨウ　こし　　丿 刀 月 月 肝 肝 肝 肝 肝 腰 腰 腰 腰

waist

meat 月→肉[151] [ニク] + important 要 [ヨウ]

When the character for waist gained the meaning 'useful, important(要),' they added the character for meat(肉) to create a new character.

132d **皿**

ベイ　さら　　丨 冂 冂 皿 皿

plate; dish

This character shows an image of a vessel which is hollow.

お皿[おさら] dish; plate
灰皿[はいざら] ashtray -124a 132d

132e **温**

オン　ぬるい　　丶 丶 氵 氵 氵 氵 氵 温 温 温 温 温

warm

water 氵[157] [スイ] + sun 日[170] [ジツ・ニチ] + plate 皿 [ベイ]

Water(氵) in a plate(皿) is warmed by the sun(日).

温い[ぬるい] lukewarm; tepid
温泉[おんせん] spa; hot spring; thermal spring -132e 186c

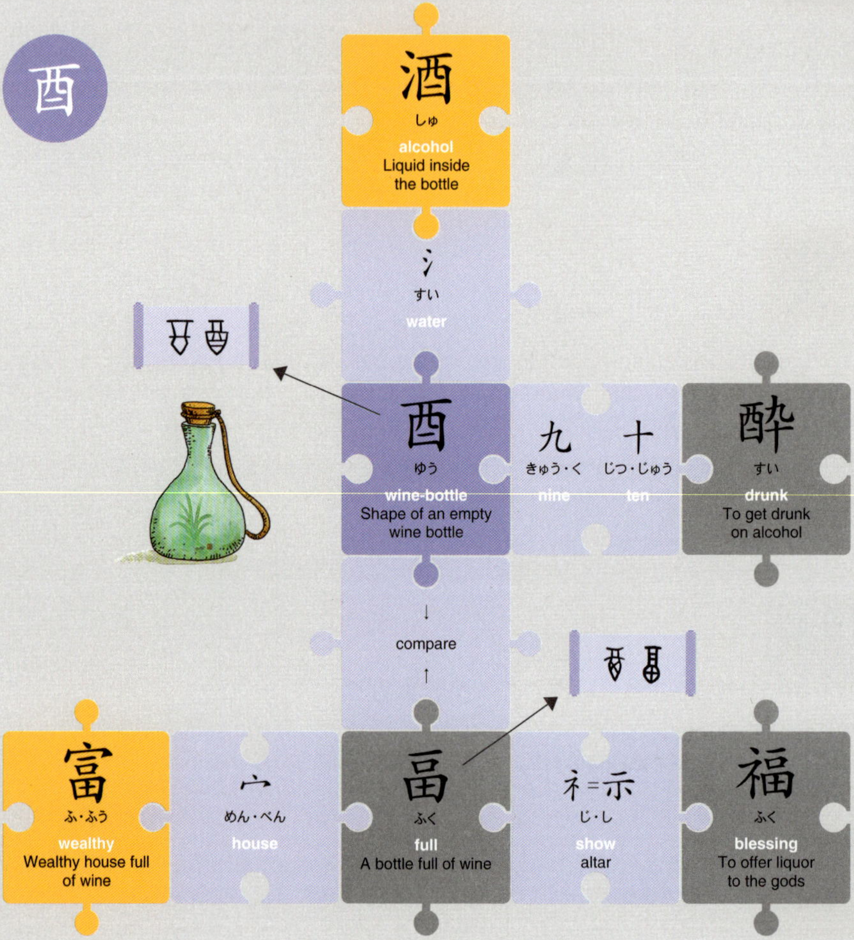

133 西

ユウ

一 丆 丙 丙 两 西 西

wine-bottle

Meaning of an empty wine bottle is derived from the shape of a traditional vessel that held wine.

133a **酒**

シュ さけ

` ﾞ 氵 汀 汀 沔 洒 洒 酒 酒

alcohol; sake

water 氵[157] [スイ] + wine-bottle 酉 [ユウ]

An empty bottle(酉) is filled with wine (or alcohol in general) in the form of a liquid(氵).

お酒[おさけ] alcohol
飲酒[いんしゅ] drinking -19a 133a

133b **酔**

スイ よい・よう

一 丅 万 丙 丙 西 酉 酉丿 酔 酔 酔

drunk

wine-bottle 酉 [ユウ] + nine 九[177b] [キュウ・ク] + ten 十[178] [ジツ・ジュウ]

Add the largest number in the decimal system, nine with ten(九+十), and that becomes the character for a bar(酉), which means one had too much to drink and is drunk.

酔い[よい] drunkenness; intoxication
酔う[よう] get drunk
麻酔[ますい] anesthesia -165b 133b

133c **畐**

フク

一 𠂉 戸 戸 戸 畐 畐 畐 畐

full

Symbolizes a bottle(酉) full of wine.

133d **福**

フク

` 礻 礻 礻 礻 礻 礻 礻 礻 福 福 福 福

blessing

altar/show 礻=示[99] [ジ・シ] + liquor bottle/full 畐 [フク]

In the agricultural society, wine(畐) was a must on any altar(礻). That was because the foam from a fermented wine symbolizes a field rich with grains. To offer alcohol(畐) to the gods(礻) guaranteed a blessing.

幸福[こうふく] happiness; blessedness -83e 133d

133e **富**

フ・フウ とみ・とむ

` 丶 宀 宀 宀 宀 宀 宀 富 富 富 富

wealthy

house 宀[113] [メン・ベン] + full 畐 [フク]

A household(宀) owning a lot(畐) of wine or alcohol could only mean a rich or wealthy family.

富む[とむ] be rich; abound in
豊富[ほうふ] abundance -148e 133e

NATURE

Animals

Natural scenery

Heavenly bodies

Miscellaneous

Animals

Animals play a very important role in the food chain, where humans reside on top.

1. Land animals which are most friendly with humans, such as sheep, dog, pig and cow appear as basic characters.
2. Other animals included are the birds, whose flight fascinated mankind for years, as well as insects and fish. Shellfish also plays an important role as it was used for currency in ancient times.
3. Animal by-products such as fur, skin, horn and meat are also used as basic characters.

Natural scenery

Mountains and natural resources including animals, are the key components of nature. Humans needed tools to manage such resources. Water, grass and trees provide the most basic source of food to the natural food chain. The characters in this section will show how these components play role as basic characters.

Heavenly bodies

All things on earth are affected by the movement of the heavens. Therefore, it is very natural to have the symbol of heavens to become a basic character. This section will explain how the basic characters, from the sun to moon are combined to form new characters and meanings, along with the explanation of their background.

Miscellaneous

The numbers and codes are the last step in the formation of the basic characters. Codes were used to convey meanings that were difficult to express with shapes. You will find additional numbers that were skipped before, and the basic strokes '丨, 丶, 丿' which are just symbols (codes) without specific meaning. Try to understand the background and the process of how these strokes are incorporated into the basic characters.

羊

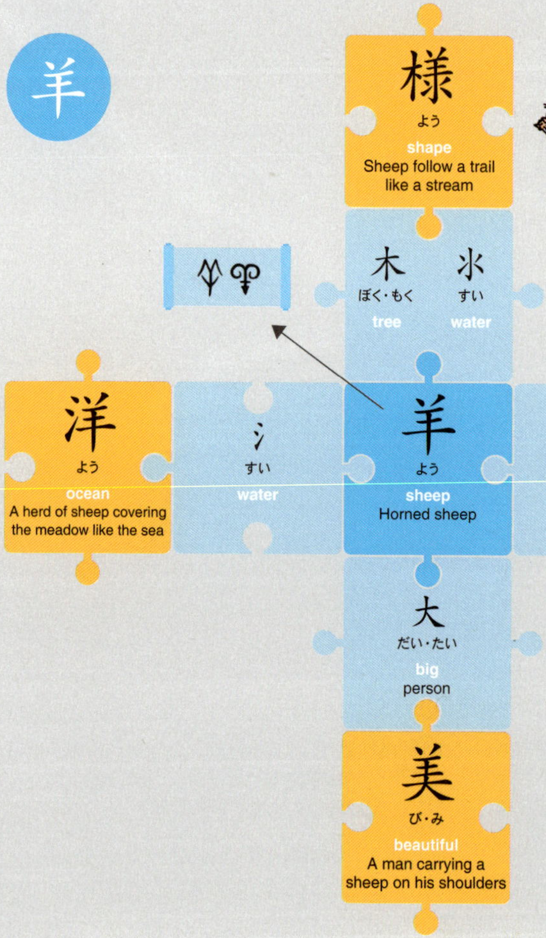

134 羊

コウ

sheep

Symbolizes a sheep with horns when one looks at it from the front.

羊毛[ようもう] wool -134.5e

134a **様**

ヨウ さま

一 十 オ 木 木 木 木 栏 栏 样 样 样 様 様 様

shape

tree 木 164 [ボク・モク] + sheep 羊 [ヨウ] + water 氺 156c [スイ]

The meaning 'shape, pattern or condition' comes from a topographic map carved on a plank of wood(木) that marks waterways(氺) and sheep(羊) trails.

* Just as water(氺) tends to flow downhill naturally, sheep(羊) have the natural tendency to take the same route. Therefore, the trail that the sheep take can be easily distinguished, just like a map carved on wood(木).

何様な[どんな] what; what sort (kind) of - 13c 134a
王様[おうさま] king - 86 134a

134b **善**

ゼン よい

丶 丷 丷 䒑 䒑 羊 羊 羊 盖 盖 善 善

goodness

sheep 羊 [ヨウ] + quarrel 誩 [ケイ・キョウ]

A sheep(羊) is considered a mystical or holy animal, and when two people are in a verbal(言 17) fight(誩), it decides who is good.

善い/良い[よい] good; fine; excellent - 134b / 11
善い/良い[いい] (spoken language) good, fine, excellent - 134b / 11

134c **美**

ビ・ミ うつくしい

丶 丷 丷 䒑 䒑 羊 羊 美 美

beautiful

sheep 羊 [ヨウ] + person/big 大 60 [ダイ・タイ]

A man(大) carrying a sheep(羊) to offer to the gods was considered a 'beautiful or grand' sight.

美しい[うつくしい] beautiful; lovely; pretty
美味しい[おいしい] delicious; tasty - 134c 164c
美人[びじん] beautiful person (woman) - 134c 51

134d **洋**

ヨウ

丶 冫 氵 氵 氵 氵 氵 洋 洋

ocean

water 氵 157 [スイ] + sheep 羊 [ヨウ]

A herd of sheep(羊) covering a field looks like the sea(氵).

洋服[ようふく] suit (Western clothes) - 134d 30c
西洋[せいよう] the West; the Occident - 132a 134d
東洋[とうよう] the East; the Orient - 167 134d

犬

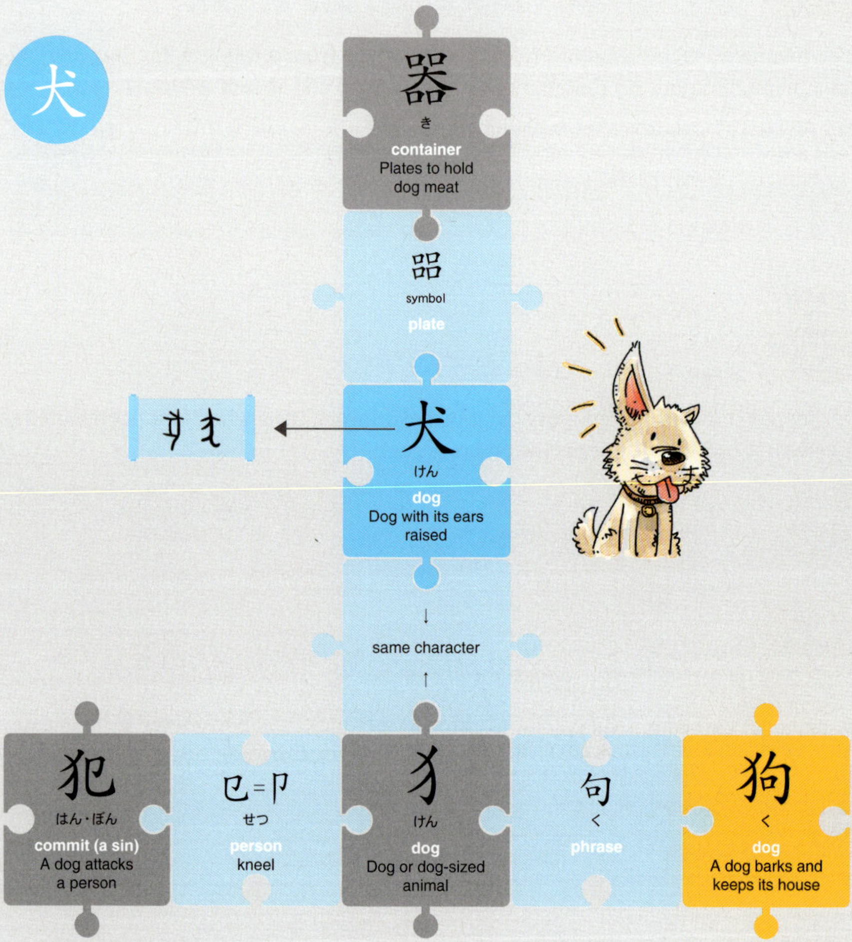

135 **犬** ケン いぬ

dog

一 ナ 大 犬

Symbolizes a dog with its ears(丶) raised.

135a 器

キ うつわ

丶 ㄇ ㅁ 吅 吅 吅 吅 哭 哭 哭 哭 哭 器 器 器

container; utensil

plate 㗊 [symbol] + dog 大→犬 [ケン]

Symbolizes the shape of plates(㗊) that held dog meat(犬) used in ceremonies and sacrifices.

* Dog meat was an essential part of ceremonies and events.

楽器[がっき] musical instrument - 161c 135a
食器[しょっき] the dishes; tableware - 109 135a

135b 犭

ケン

ノ 犭 犭

dog

Used only in combination with other characters to replace dog "犬" or to symbolize a small dog-sized animal.

135c 狗

ク いぬ

ノ 犭 犭 犭 犳 狗 狗 狗

dog

dog 犭 [ケン] + phrase 句 40c [ク]

A faithful dog(犭) keeps barking(句) at a stranger to protect his owner's house.

* It's easy to remember that '句,' from which the pronunciation comes from, describes a dog barking continuously.

走狗[そうく] hunting dog; tool of another person - 44c 135c

135d 犯

ハン・ボン おかす

ノ 犭 犭 犯 犯

commit (a sin)

dog 犭 [ケン] + kneel/person 㔾=卩 69 [セツ]

A dog(犭) which attacks a person(㔾) 'commits' a bad deed.

犯す[おかす] commit (a sin); violate
犯人[はんにん] criminal; offender - 135d 51

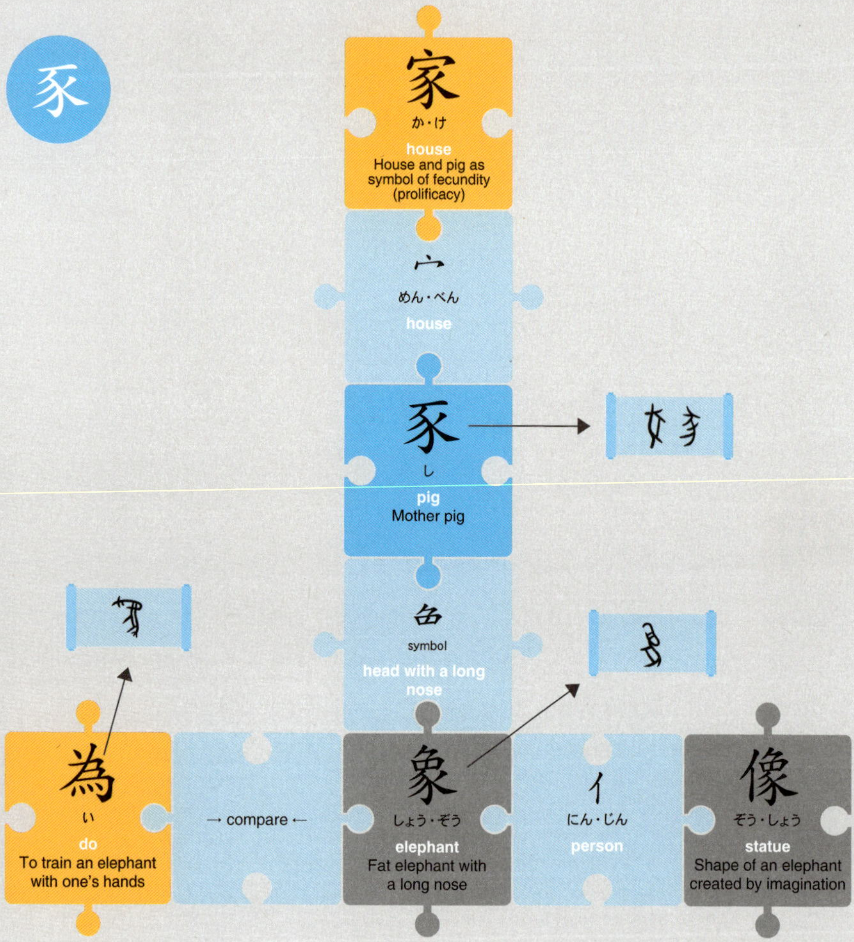

136 豖

し

pig

Symbolizes a well-fed pig lying sideways to give milk to her young one.

136a 家

カ・ケ いえ

丶 宀 宀 宀 宇 宇 家 家 家 家

house

house 宀[113] [メン・ベン] + pig 豕 [シ]

Combination of the house(宀) and the pig(豕), which gives birth to large litters. It came to mean a family. This character shows a type of Chinese humor in favor of prolificacy.

＊A pig produces 8 to 12 babies in a single birth.

家族[かぞく] family -136a 127a
家庭[かてい] home; family -136a 50b
家内[かない] (my) wife; one's family -136a 53b

136b 象

ショウ・ゾウ

elephant

head with a long nose ⺈ [symbol] + pig 豕 [シ]

An elephant has a head with a long nose(⺈) and a fat body like a pig(豕). It also means shape, as an elephant was more of an exotic, imaginary creature to the people of northern China, which is where Chinese characters originated.

印象[いんしょう] impression -69d 136b
象牙[ぞうげ] ivory -136b 21c

136c 像

ゾウ・ショウ

statue; image

person 亻[52] [ニン・ジン] + elephant 象 [ショウ・ゾウ]

Ancient Chinese people(亻) in the northern area could only imagine how a shape of an elephant(象) would look like. The meaning of 'likeness' is derived from the similar unique shape of the "imaginary elephant" and the actual elephant.

映像[えいぞう] reflection; image -61d 136c

136d 為

イ する・ため・なす

do

Ancient character shows the training of elephants(象) by hand(爪[29]) in order for them to do hard tasks.

為る[する] do
為す/作す[なす] do; perform -136d / 180a

Diagram for 牛

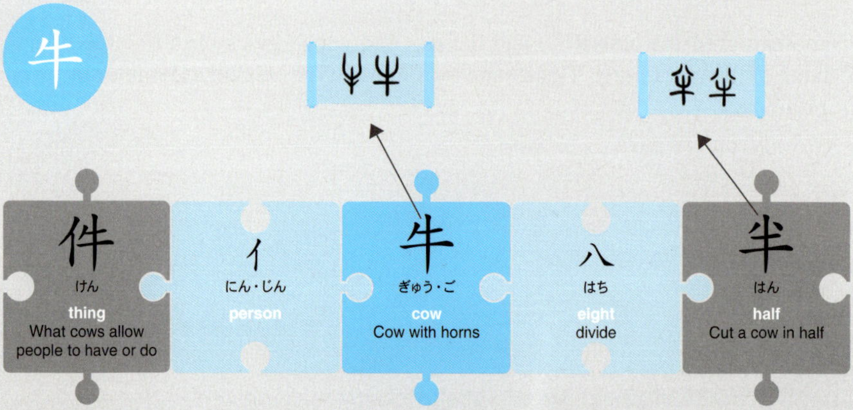

137 **牛**

ギュウ・ゴ うし

ノ ㄏ 㐅 牛

cow

Symbolizes the front view of a cow with horns.

牛肉[ぎゅうにく] beef - 137 151	牛乳[ぎゅうにゅう] (cow's) milk - 137 57d

137a **半**

ハン なかば

丶 丷 䒑 兰 半

half

divide/eight 八[177] [ハチ] + cow 牛 [ギュウ・ゴ]

Signifies a cow(牛) which is being butchered and cut in half(八).

* "八" is a symbol of symmetry in half, signifying to divide.

半ば[なかば] half; middle; semi-	半島[はんとう] peninsula - 137a 139d

137b **件**

ケン

ノ 亻 亻 亻 仁 件

thing; affair

person 亻[52] [ニン・ジン] + cow 牛 [ギュウ・ゴ]

Cows(牛) provided people(亻) with many important things. They helped with plowing, were used as sacrifices, and gave people leather and meat. To emphasize that cows allowed people to do many things, this character came to mean 'things or events.'

事件[じけん] case; affair; event - 32c 137b

Diagram for 馬

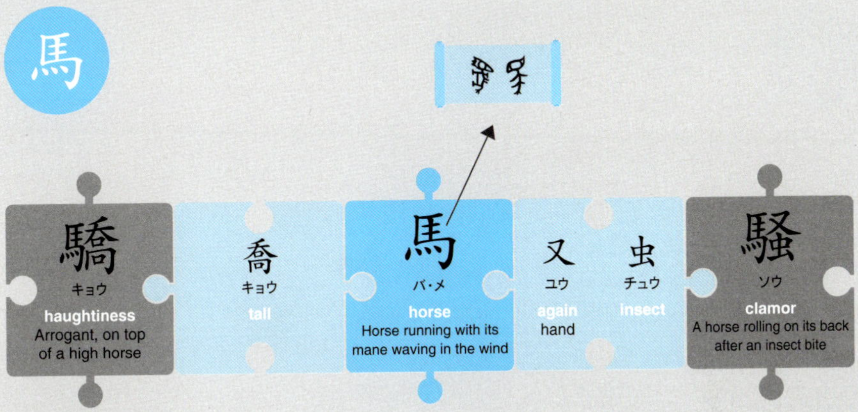

138 馬

バ・メ うま

horse

A symbol of a horse running fast with four feet(灬) and its mane waving in the wind.

* The four legs were simplified into four dots(灬).

馬鹿[ばか] fool; idiot (A fool who can't tell a deer and a horse apart) - 138 150b

138a 騒

ソウ さわぐ

clamor

horse 馬 [バ・メ] + hand/again 又 [30] [ユウ] + insect 虫 [143] [チュウ]

When an insect(虫) such as a flea bites a horse(馬), which has no hands(又) to scratch with, it rolls on the ground which causes a 'clamor or noise.'

騒ぐ[さわぐ] make noise; clamor   騒音[そうおん] noise - 138a 18

138b 驕

キョウ

haughtiness

horse 馬 [バ・メ] + tall 喬 [3a] [キョウ]

A man on a tall horse(馬) looks down on others from up high(喬), and that seems 'arrogant.'

驕慢[きょうまん] arrogance - 138b 27d

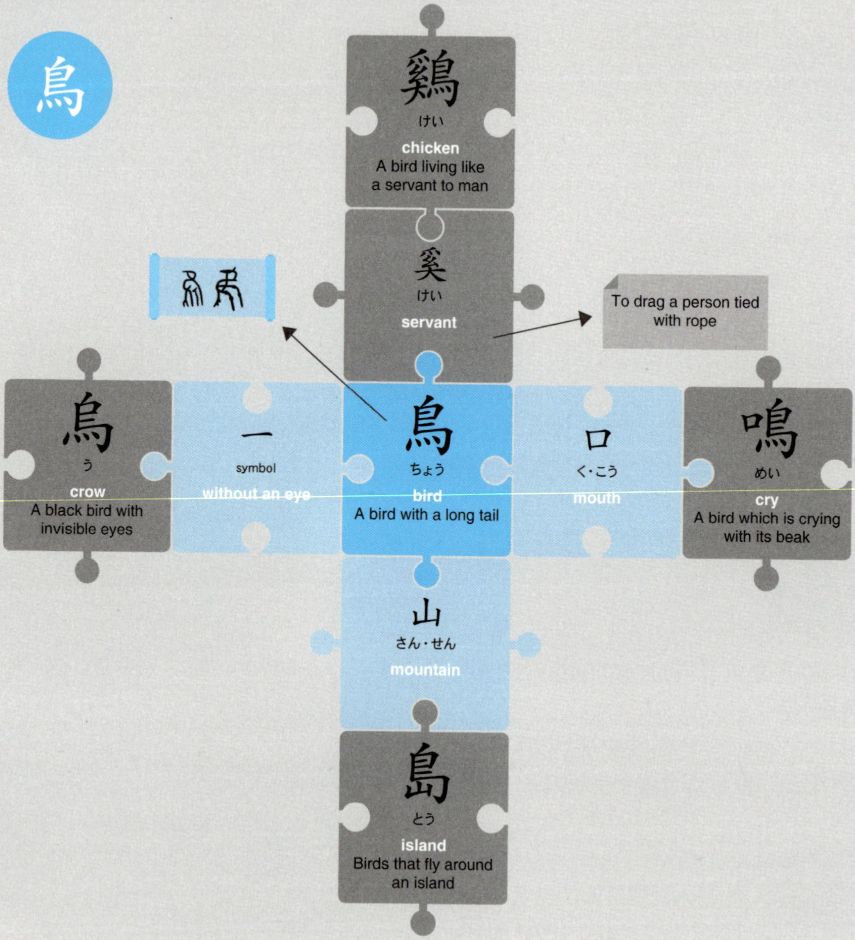

139 **鳥** チョウ とり

bird

Symbolizes a bird with a long tail, beak and legs.

鳥肉[とりにく] chicken meat -139 151

139a 奚

ケイ

servant; what

hand/nail 爫=爪[29] [ソウ] + thread 糸[104] [シ] + person/big 大[60] [ダイ・タイ]

To drag a person(大) tied up with rope(糸) by hand(爪) implicates a 'servant or what.'

139b 鶏

ケイ にわとり

chicken

servant 奚 [ケイ] + bird 鳥 [チョウ]

A chicken is bred and raised by a man, and it lives the life of a bird(鳥) treated like a servant(奚).

鶏肉[けいにく・とりにく] chicken meat -139b 151

139c 鳴

メイ なく・ならす・なる

cry

mouth 口[12] [ク・コウ] + bird 鳥 [チョウ]

Signifies a bird(鳥) crying with its beak(口). This character is used to mean the cry of birds or animals.

鳴く[なく] chirp; cry; weep
鳴らす[ならす] ring; make a sound (noise)
鳴る[なる] sound; ring

139d 島

トウ しま

island

bird 鳥 [チョウ] + mountain 山[153] [サン・セン]

A small island, like that of a small mountain(山) in the middle of the sea, has lots of birds (鳥) flying around freely.

* It can also be thought of as birds(鳥) being able to freely approach the islands(山).

半島[はんとう] peninsula -137a 139d

139e 烏

ウ

crow

bird 鳥 [チョウ] - eye 一 [symbol]

A crow has black eyes that are hard to see, making it a bird(鳥) without an eye(一).

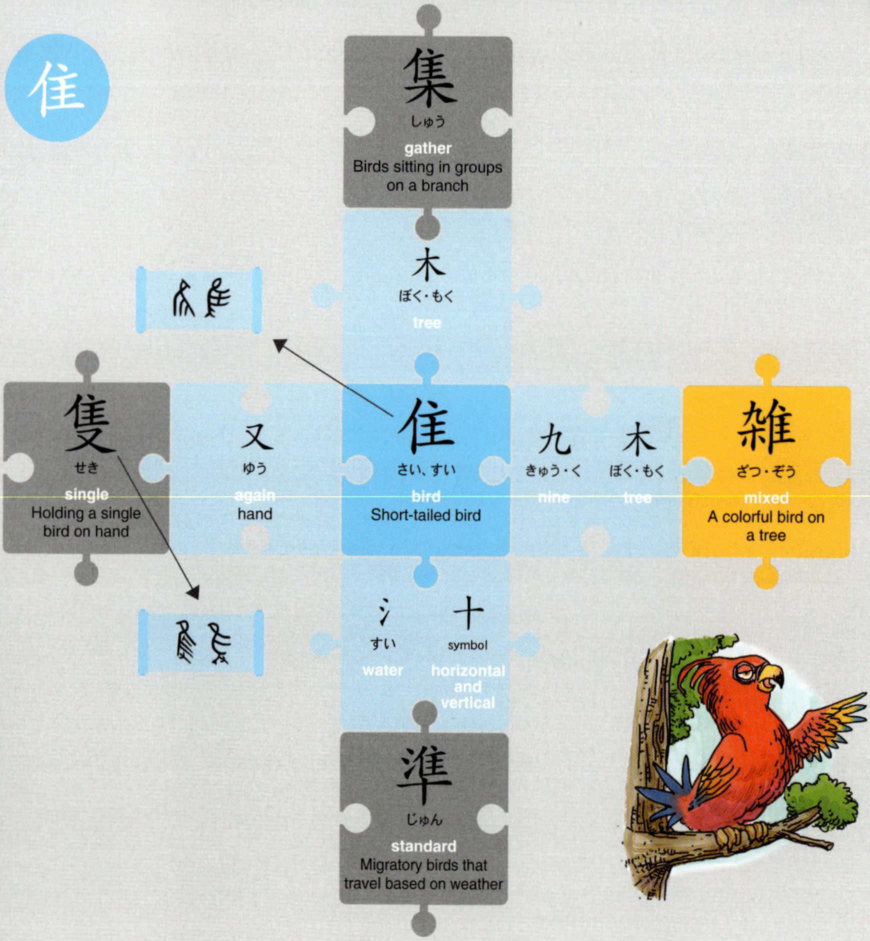

140 **隹** サイ・スイ

bird

丿 亻 亻 亻 亻 亻 隹 隹

Signifies a side view of a small bird. While "鳥[139]" is used to signify the long-tailed and larger birds, this character is a general term to mean 'short-tailed and smaller birds.'

140a 集

シュウ　あつまる・あつめる

ノ イ イ' 代 代 信 隹 隹 隼 隼 集 集

gather

bird 隹 [サイ、スイ] + tree 木 164 [ボク・モク]

Symbolizes the small birds(隹) gathered onto a branch of a tree(木) and chatting or chirping.

集まる[あつまる] gather; assemble
集める[あつめる] collect; gather; assemble
集中[しゅうちゅう] concentration - 140a 179d

140b 雑

ザツ・ゾウ

ノ 九 九 卆 卆 杂 杂 刹 刹 新 新 雑 雑 雑

mixed

nine 九 177b [キュウ・ク] + tree 木 164 [ボク・モク] + bird 隹 [サイ、スイ]

Signifies a bird(隹) with feathers of many(九) mixed colors sitting on a tree(木).

* The traditional character(雜) shows a bird(隹) on a tree(木) in feathers/clothes(衣) of mixed colors.

雑誌[ざっし] journal; magazine - 140b 26e
雑音[ざつおん] noise - 140b 18

140c 準

ジュン

、 ⺀ 氵 氵 氵 汁 汁 汁 汻 淮 淮 準 準

standard

water 氵 157 [スイ] + bird 隹 [サイ、スイ] + horizontal and vertical 十 [symbol]

Water(氵) is always leveled, and migratory birds(隹) leave when the weather reaches a certain standard(十) of temperature, so this character came to mean 'standard.'

基準[きじゅん] standard; basis; criterion - 39b 140c
規準[きじゅん] standard; criterion; canon - 9d 140c

140d 隻

セキ

ノ イ イ' 代 代 仁 件 隹 隻 隻

single

bird 隹 [サイ、スイ] + hand/again 又 30 [ユウ]

Symbolizes only one bird(隹) being held on one hand(又). Used as unit to count a single item in a given pair, or when counting birds, arrows or ships.

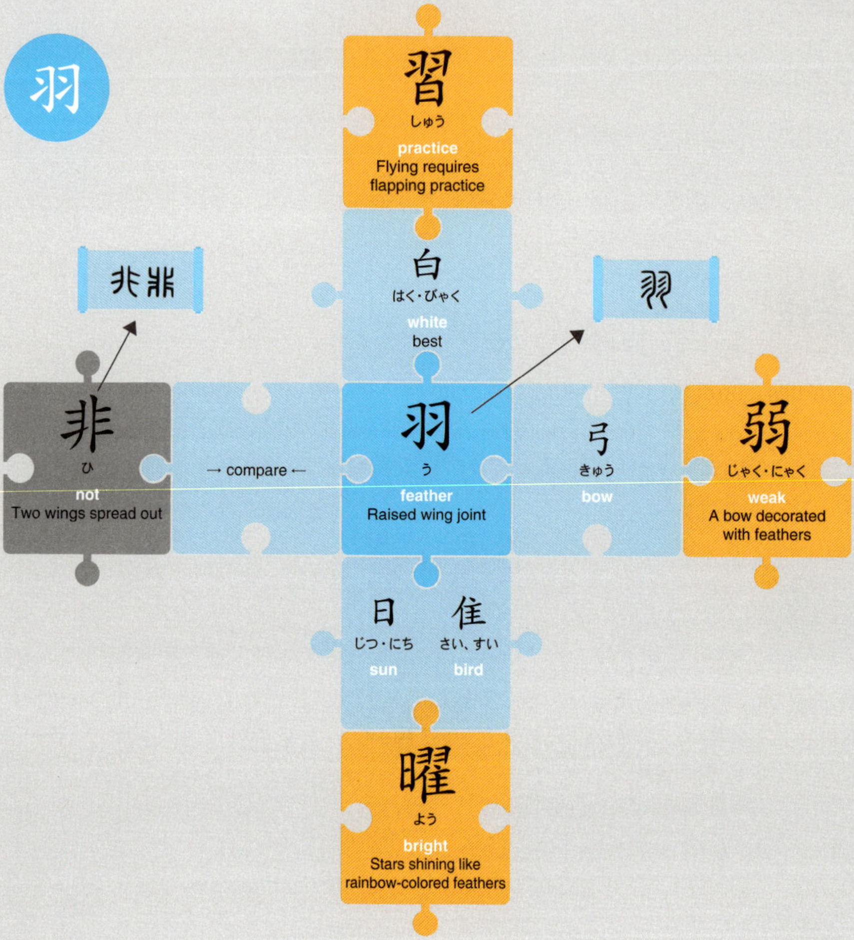

141 **羽**

ウ はね

feather

Symbolizes a bird with its wings raised high to show its feathers.

141a **習**

シュウ ならう

practice

feather 羽 [ウ] + best/white 白 106 [ハク・ビャク]

For a bird to reach a level(白) where it can fly freely, it must 'practice or learn' to flap its wings(羽).

* In ancient times, the Chinese revered the color white "白," so it also means 'best.'

習う[ならう] practice; master; learn
習慣[しゅうかん] custom; habit -141a 145e
予習[よしゅう] preparation(s) -4a 141a
練習[れんしゅう] practice; exercise -167e 141a

141b **弱**

ジャク・ニャク よわい・よわまる・よわめる・よわる

weak

bow 弓 87 [キュウ] + feather 羽 [ウ]

A bow(弓) decorated with feathers(羽) was an ornament not used in battle, so this character means 'weak.'

弱い[よわい] weak; feeble; frail
弱まる[よわまる] weaken; abate; wane
弱める[よわめる] weaken; attenuate
弱る[よわる] weaken; wane; be emaciated

141c **曜**

ヨウ

bright; day of the week

sun 日 170 [ジツ・ニチ] + feather 羽 [ウ] + bird 隹 140 [サイ、スイ]

Like the shiny, multi-colored feathers(羽) of a pheasant(隹), the sun, moon and five planets(日) of the solar system shine, and that's why we have seven 'days of the week.'

* "翟" is a pheasant(隹) with feathers(羽) shining in all colors of the rainbow.

月曜日[げつようび] Monday -172 141c 170
火曜日[かようび] Tuesday -124 141c 170
水曜日[すいようび] Wednesday -156 141c 170
木曜日[もくようび] Thursday -164 141c 170
金曜日[きんようび] Friday -154 141c 170
土曜日[どようび] Saturday -120 141c 170
日曜日[にちようび] Sunday -170 141c 170

141d **非**

ヒ

not; un-

Symbolizes a bird spreading its wings wide; each wing, when spread out, will not meet the other wing. Therefore it is used as negation.

是非[ぜひ] right and wrong -45d 141d
非難[ひなん] criticism -141d 108d

142 **采** ハン・ベン

distinguish

Symbolizes a footprint, which can be used to distinguish what the animal was by looking at it.

* Used only as a combination to add meaning to other characters.

142a 番

バン

一 丷 䒑 亠 平 平 采 采 番 番 番 番

sequence; numberical order

footprints/distinguish 釆 [ハン・ベン] + field 田[122] [デン]

Signifies footprints(釆) of animals printed one after another on a field(田). It also means a sequential 'level, grade or frequency.'

一番[いちばん] number one, first, best -173 142a
交番[こうばん] police box; alternation -1a 142a
何番[なんばん] what number -13c 142a
番号[ばんごう] number -142a 12e

142b 播

ハ・バン まく

一 十 扌 扌 扌 扌 扌 扌 扌 扌 扌 播 播 播 播

sow

hand 扌=手[28] [シュ] + sequence 番 [バン]

Signifies continued(番) seeding(扌) or sowing of crops, one after another, on a field. Also used as the meaning for broadcast, since electro-magnetic waves are seeded onto the air.

* Hands(扌) represent the act of seeding in this case.

播く[まく] sow; seed
播種[はしゅ] sowing; seeding -142b 119d

142c 審

シン

丶 丷 宀 宀 宀 宀 宀 宀 宷 宷 宷 審 審 審 審

examine; judge

house 宀[113] [メン・ベン] + sequence 番 [バン]

To catch a criminal, one must examine the footprints left in the house(宀) in order(番). Also, in court(宀), everything is judged in a sequence(番).

結審[けっしん] conclusion of trial (hearing) -84b 142c28
審査[しんさ] ju\dging; inspection; examination -142c 174a

142d 翻

ホン

一 丷 䒑 亠 平 平 采 采 番 番 番 番 番 翻 翻 翻 翻 翻

turn over

sequence 番 [バン] + feather 羽[141] [ウ]

A bird is continuously(番) flapping its wings(羽), resulting in wings being turned over as it flaps from top to bottom.

翻訳[ほんやく] translation

142e 奥

オウ おく

丿 亻 冂 向 + two hands 大→廾[38] [キョウ]

interior

house 宀[113] [メン・ベン] + footprints/distinguish 米→釆 [ハン・ベン]

To investigate who messed up the inside of the house(宀), one must hold important evidence, such as footprints(釆), with both hands(廾) and look carefully.

奥さん[おくさん] your wife; married lady; madam
奥様[おくさま] honorific of Man's wife; madam -142e 134a

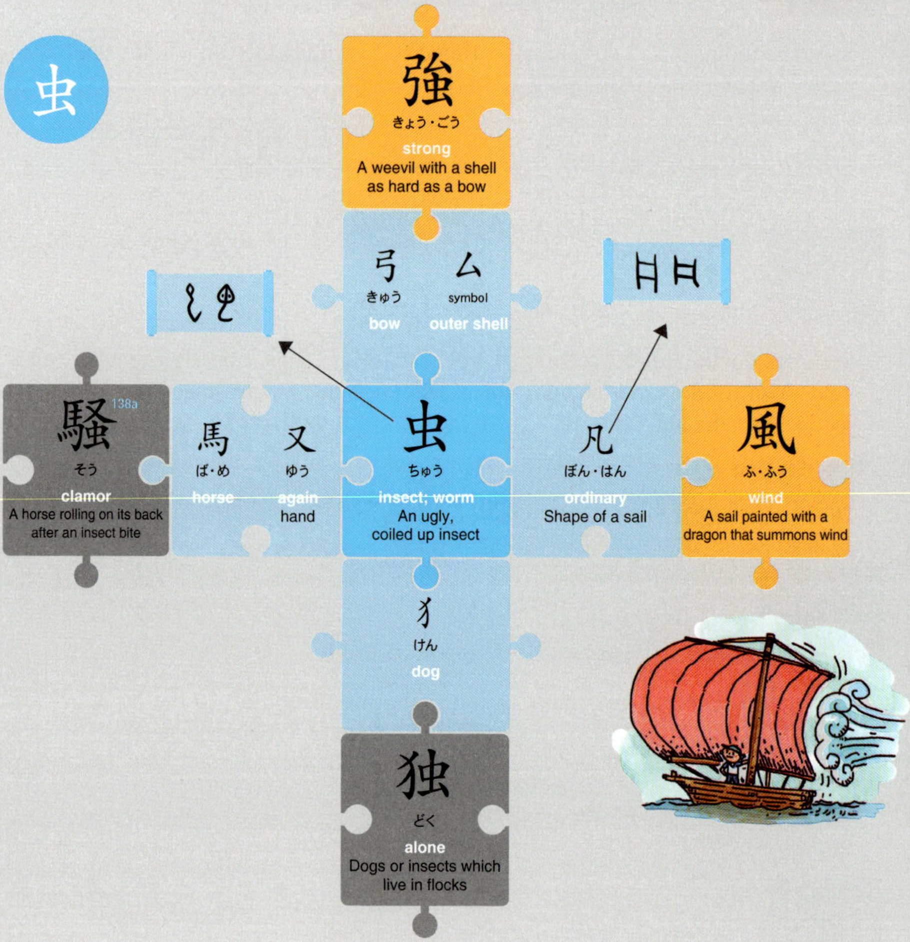

143 虫

チュウ むし

insect; worm

丶 口 口 中 虫 虫

Symbolizes a snake coiled up on the ground. Used to describe any insects, long or short.

虫歯[むしば] dental caries; cavity -143 21

143a 強

キョウ・ゴウ　しいる・つよい・つよまる・つよめる

strong

bow 弓[87] [キュウ] + outer shell ム [symbol] + insect 虫 [チュウ]

A weevil(虫) has a hard shell(ム) and curves like a bow(弓), so it is 'strong or powerful.'

* The ancient version of "強" indicates a weevil, which is an insect(虫) with a shell(ム) as hard as a bow(弓).

強い[つよい] strong; powerful
強いる[しいる] force; compel; press
強まる[つよまる] become strong
強める[つよめる] strengthen; emphasize
強調[きょうちょう] emphasis; highlight - 143a 122c

143b 凡

ボン・ハン　およそ

ordinary

This is the shape of a sail on a boat, which gives the boat power through the wind. Because wind is very common and ordinary among us, this character came to mean 'ordinary or common.'

凡そ[およそ] roughly; generally; approximately
平凡[へいぼん] commonness; ordinary - 96a 143b

143c 風

フ・フウ　かぜ

wind

sail/ordinary 凡 [ボン・ハン] + insect 虫 [チュウ]

A depiction of a sail(凡) that utilizes wind with a drawing of an insect(虫) place of a dragon that summons wind and rain.

* The version of "風" carved in shells or bones showed a bird or a sail(凡), but when the two merged, it was replaced with an insect(虫) that symbolized a dragon.

風邪[かぜ] cold (illness); influenza - 143c 116e
風景[ふうけい] landscape; scenery - 143c 2b
風俗[ふうぞく] manners; customs - 143c 153d

143d 独

ドク　ひとり

alone

dog 犭[135b] [ケン] + insect 虫 [チュウ]

Among dogs(犭) or group of insects(虫) which live in flocks, there is always a leader standing alone in the center.

独り[ひとり] alone; solitary; single
独占[どくせん] monopoly; exclusive - 143d 100a

魚

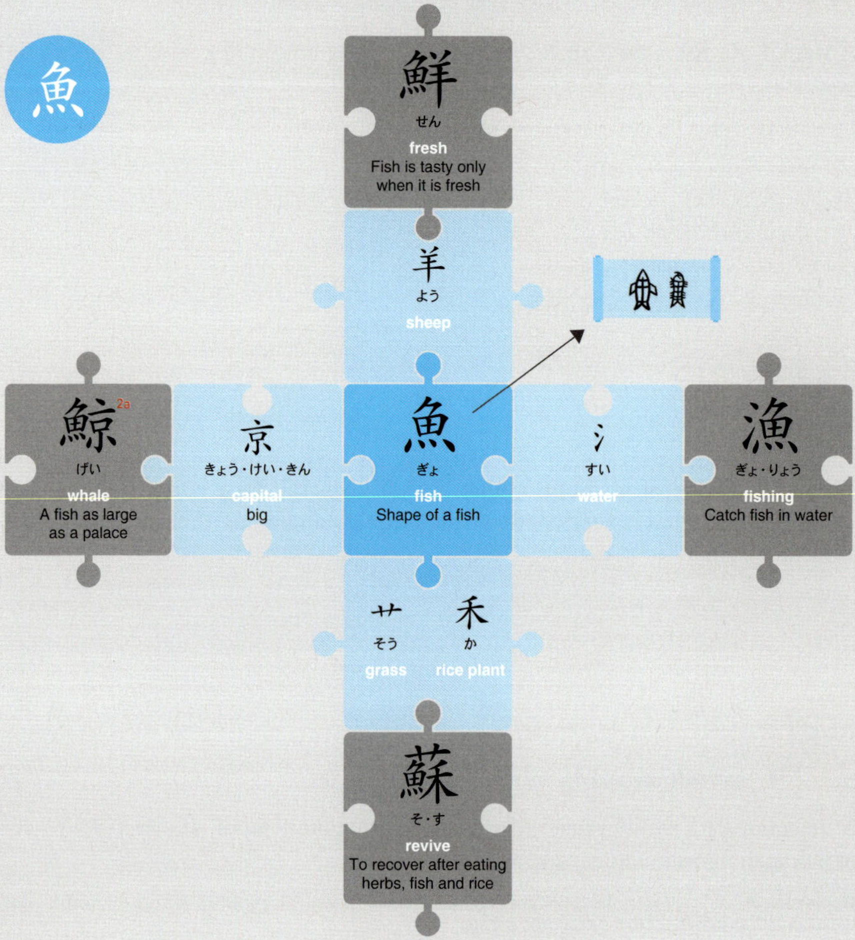

144 **魚**

ギョ うお・さかな

fish

丿 ⺈ ⺈ 𠂊 角 角 甶 魚 魚 魚 魚

Head(⺈), body(田) and tail(灬) are combined together to form a fish.

144a 鮮

セン あざやか

丿 ⺈ ⺈ 各 角 角 角 角 魚 魚 魚 魚 魚 魚 魚 魚 鮮 (stroke order)

fresh

fish 魚 [ギョ] + sheep 羊 134 [ヨウ]

Fish(魚) caught for the purpose of eating can go bad very fast. It can be as delicious as lamb(羊) meat only when it's fresh.

* Lamb(羊) has been known as a delicacy due to the fiber being very thin and soft.

鮮やか[あざやか] vivid; clear; fresh
新鮮[しんせん] fresh -94b 144a

144b 漁

ギョ・リョウ

fishing

water 氵 157 [スイ] + fish 魚 [ギョ]

One can catch fish(魚) in the waters(氵), such as the river or the ocean.

漁船[ぎょせん] fishing boat (vessel) -144b 98a
漁村[ぎょそん] fishing village -144b 35a
漁師[りょうし] fisherman -144b 152b

144c 蘇

ソ・ス よみがえる

revive

grass 艹 161 [ソウ] + fish 魚 [ギョ] + rice plant 禾 111 [カ]

A sick person would 'recover or revive' after eating herbs(艹), fish(魚) and rice(禾).

* Chinese medicine does use animal products like a bear's gall bladder and deer antlers, but most ingredients are herbs(艹).

蘇る[よみがえる] revive; resuscitate
蘇生[そせい] revival; resuscitation -144c 162

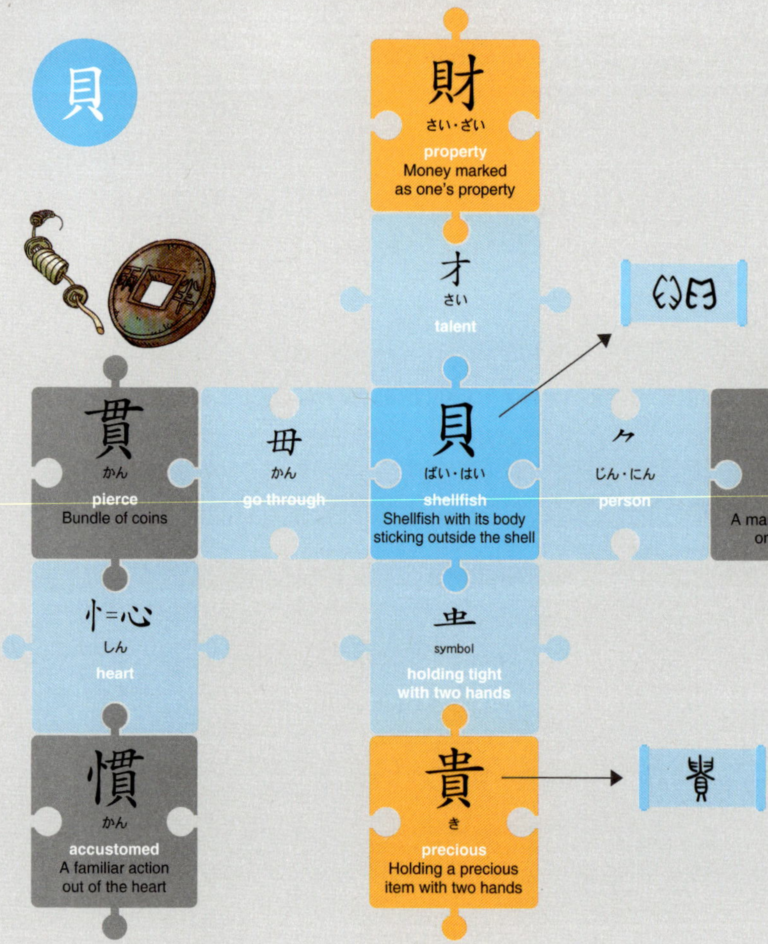

145 **貝**

バイ・ハイ

shellfish; currency

The body(八) of the shellfish is sticking out from its shell(目). Back in the Yin(殷) and Jiu(周) Dynasties, purple-colored shellfish(貝) were used as currency by the inhabitants of the region.

145a 財

サイ・ザイ

丨 冂 冃 月 目 貝 貝 貝一 財 財

property

currency/shellfish 貝 [バイ・ハイ] + talent 才 [サイ]

Money(貝) that's piled up and marked(才) as someone's belongings is 'property.'

* The character "才" is a location where the gods give gifts or talents marked(丿) with a stick(十) in the ground.

財布[さいふ] wallet - 145a 103c　　財産[ざいさん] property; assets; fortune - 145a 117e

145b 負

フ おう・まかす・まける

丿 ⺈ 𠂊 ⺈ 角 角 負 負 負

bear; bear debt

person ⺈ 56 [ジン・ニン] + currency/shellfish 貝 [バイ・ハイ]

Symbolizes a person(⺈) bearing a sack of money(貝) on his back. Money signifies debt.

負う[おう] bear on the back; bear (responsibility)
負かす[まかす] put (a load) on something; defeat　　負ける[まける] lose; be defeated

145c 貴

キ

丶 口 口 中 虫 冉 貴 貴 貴 貴 貴 貴

precious

holding tight with two hands 虫 [symbol] + currency/shellfish 貝 [バイ・ハイ]

Symbolizes grabbing of a precious, high-priced(貝) item with two hands(虫).

貴方/貴下[あなた] (honorific) you - 145c 126 / 145c 173b　　貴族[きぞく] aristocrat; nobility - 145c 127a

145d 貫

カン つらぬく

乚 口 毌 毌 毌 貫 貫 貫 貫 貫 貫

pierce

go through 毌 [カン] + currency/shellfish 貝 [バイ・ハイ]

Signifies a bundle of coins(貝) created by passing through(毌) a piece of thread through the hole in the middle.

* "毌" symbolizes a coin with string passing through the middle. Qin Shi Huang(秦始皇, 259~210 BC) of the Qin dynasty(秦, 221~206 BC) had unified the mainland China for the first time and built the Great Wall. He also created metal coins with hole in the middle. This became the standard form of all Chinese currency.

貫く[つらぬく] pass through; pierce

145e 慣

カン

丨 ⺊ 忄 忄 忄 忄 忄 慣 慣 慣 慣 慣 慣 慣

accustomed

heart 忄=心 26 [シン] + pierce 貫 [カン]

A habit is an action which someone does from the heart(忄), without thinking. The person is used to doing the same action for a long period of time; i.e putting many coins into one bundle by passing through(貫) strings in each one of them.

慣行[かんこう] habitual (usual) practice - 145e 48a　　習慣[しゅうかん] custom; habit - 141a 145e

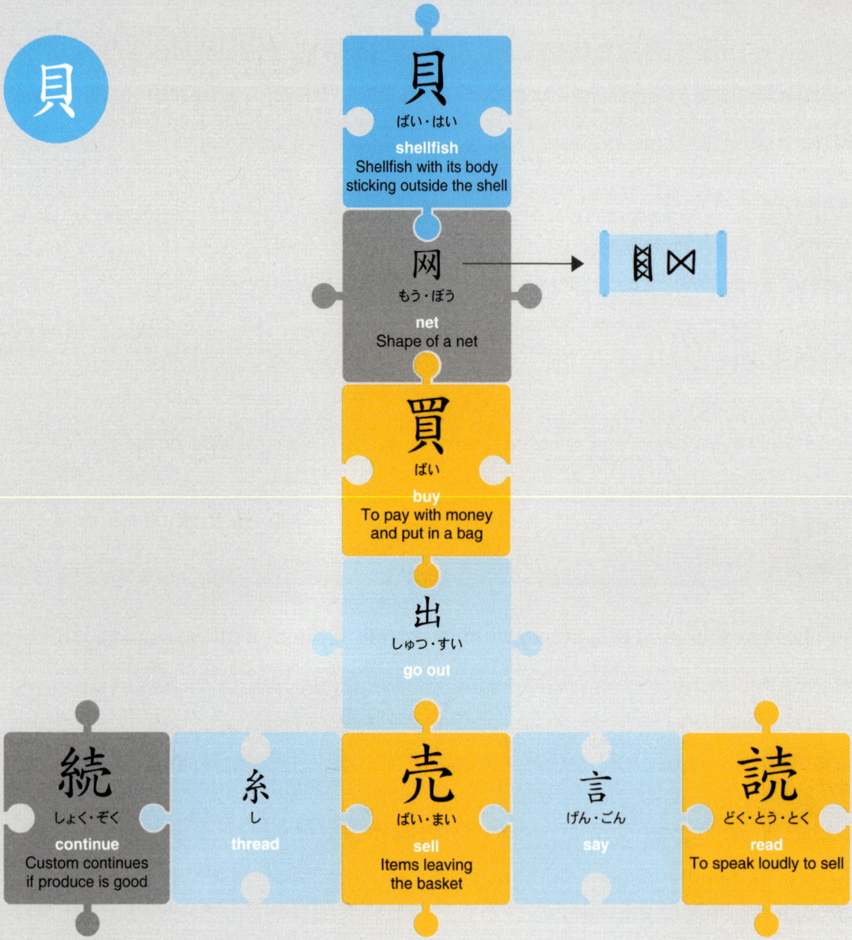

146 网

モウ・ボウ

net

Symbolizes a net to catch birds or fish. Sometimes changes its shape to "罒" for visual appearance when combined with other characters.

146a **買**

バイ　かう

丶 冂 罒 罒 罒 罒 罒 罒 買 買 買 買

buy

net 罒=网 [モウ・ボウ] + currency/shellfish 貝[145] [バイ・ハイ]

Paying with money(貝) to purchase an item and put it in a mesh bag(罒).

買う[かう] buy; purchase
買(い)物[かいもの] shopping; purchase -146a 41a
売買[ばいばい] buying and selling; trade -146b 146a

146b **売**

バイ・マイ　うる・うれる

一 十 士 士 声 売 売

sell

go out 士→出[131c] [シュツ・スイ] + net 冖→罒=网 [モウ・ボウ] + currency/shellfish 儿→貝[145] [バイ・ハイ]

To take out(出) items from the basket(罒) and sell them for more money(貝).

売る[うる] sell; sell (oneself to the public)
売れる[うれる] sell; be well known
特売[とくばい] special (bargain) sale -37c 146b
売買[ばいばい] buying and selling; trade -146b 146a

146c **読**

ドク・トウ・トク　よむ

丶 亠 ∸ 亖 言 言 言 訁 訁 訁 訁 読 読 読

read

say 言[17] [ゲン・ゴン] + sell 売 [バイ]

To use words(言) and read from a list of items to sell(売).

読む[よむ] read; count
読書[どくしょ] reading -146c 33e

146d **続**

ショク・ゾク　つづく・つづける

ㄥ 幺 幺 糸 糸 糸 糸 紆 紆 紆 紆 続 続

continue

thread 糸[104] [シ] + sell 売 [バイ]

One must sell(売) good products for a good price if he desires continuous(糸) commercial transaction.

* Thread(糸) means connections or continuity.

続く[つづく] continue; go on; follow
続ける[つづける] continue; keep up
続続[ぞくぞく] successively; one after another -146d 146d

鼎

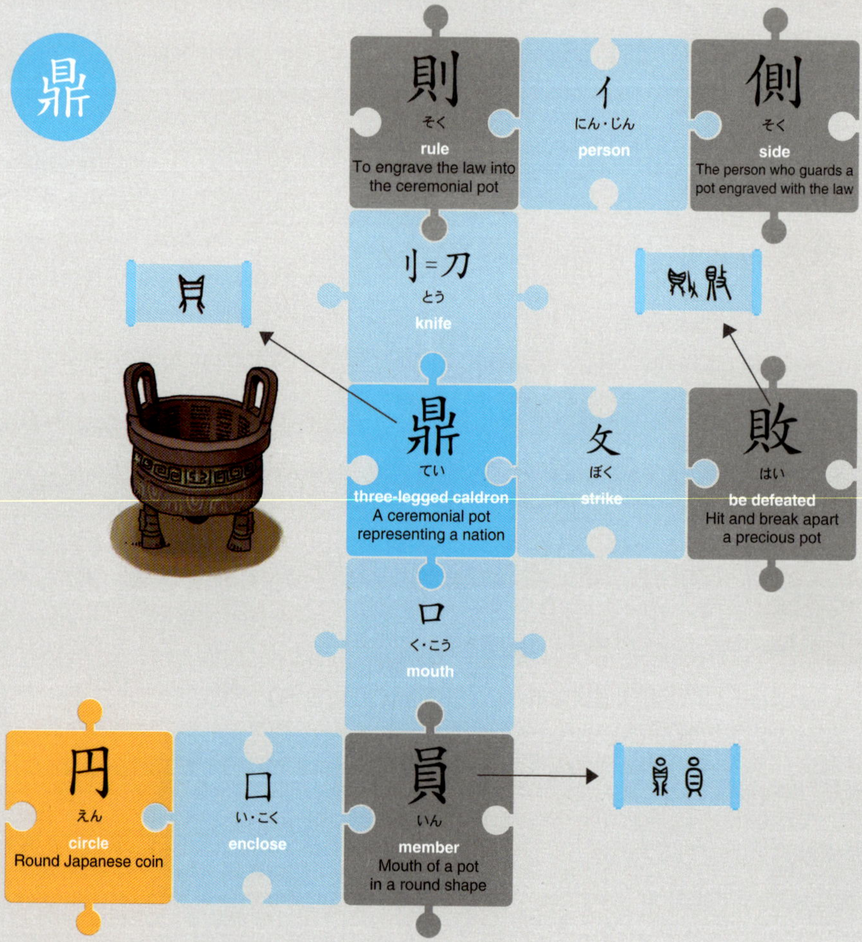

147 **鼎**

テイ

three-legged caldron

A ceremonial pot with three legs and two handles. In ancient times, a large pot or caldron used in ceremonies represented the nation. "鼎" is too complicated to merge with another character, so it was simplified to "貝[145]."

* In the ancient times of China, a variety of Chinese scripts were engraved on bronze-made bells or tripodal cauldrons. They were called 'Bronze inscriptions.'

147a 則

ソク

丨 冂 冃 月 目 貝 貝 貝 則

rule

caldron 貝→鼎 [テイ] + knife 刂=刀 95 [トウ]

To carve the basic law or rules onto the ceremonial pot(鼎) with a blade(刂).

規則[きそく] rule, regulations -9d 147a　法則[ほうそく] law; rule -63d 147a

147b 側

ソク　そば・かわ

丿 亻 亻 仴 仴 侀 但 俱 俱 側 側

side

person 亻 52 [ニン・ジン] + rule 則 [ソク]

The person(亻) who guards the ceremonial pot engraved with the law(則) is close to the king and often stands 'beside' him.

側面[そくめん] side; flank -147b 6a

147c 敗

ハイ　やぶれる

丨 冂 冃 月 目 貝 貝 貝' 貝ᅩ 貶 敗

be defeated

caldron 貝→鼎 [テイ] + strike 攵 43 [ボク]

In ancient China, pots with decorated feet were used as a symbol of royals in many special ceremonies. When defeated in war, enemies would destroy such pots(鼎) with heavy maces(攵).

敗れる[やぶれる] be defeated, lose　失敗[しっぱい] failure -154c 147c

腐敗[ふはい] corruption; decomposition -36d 147c

147d 員

イン

丶 口 口 尸 肙 肙 肙 員 員 員

member

mouth 口 12 [ク・コウ] + caldron 貝→鼎 [テイ]

Used to signify the circle from the shape of the mouth(口) in a pot(鼎). Now it became to mean a member (as in "someone inside the circle 員") or someone who takes part in a group.

定員[ていいん] fixed number of regular personnel; capacity -45b 147d

店員[てんいん] (sales) clerk; shop assistant -100b 147d

147e 円

エン　まるい

丨 冂 円 円

circle; yen

enclose 囗 16 [イ・コク] + member 員 [イン]

When "員," meaning 'round' gained the meaning 'number of people,' "囗" was added to stress the meaning 'round.' Ancient coins were round, so this character indicates currency and is simplified to "円."

円い[まるい] circular; round　一円[いちえん] one yen; whole area (district, region) -173 147e

円周[えんしゅう] circumference -147e 122a

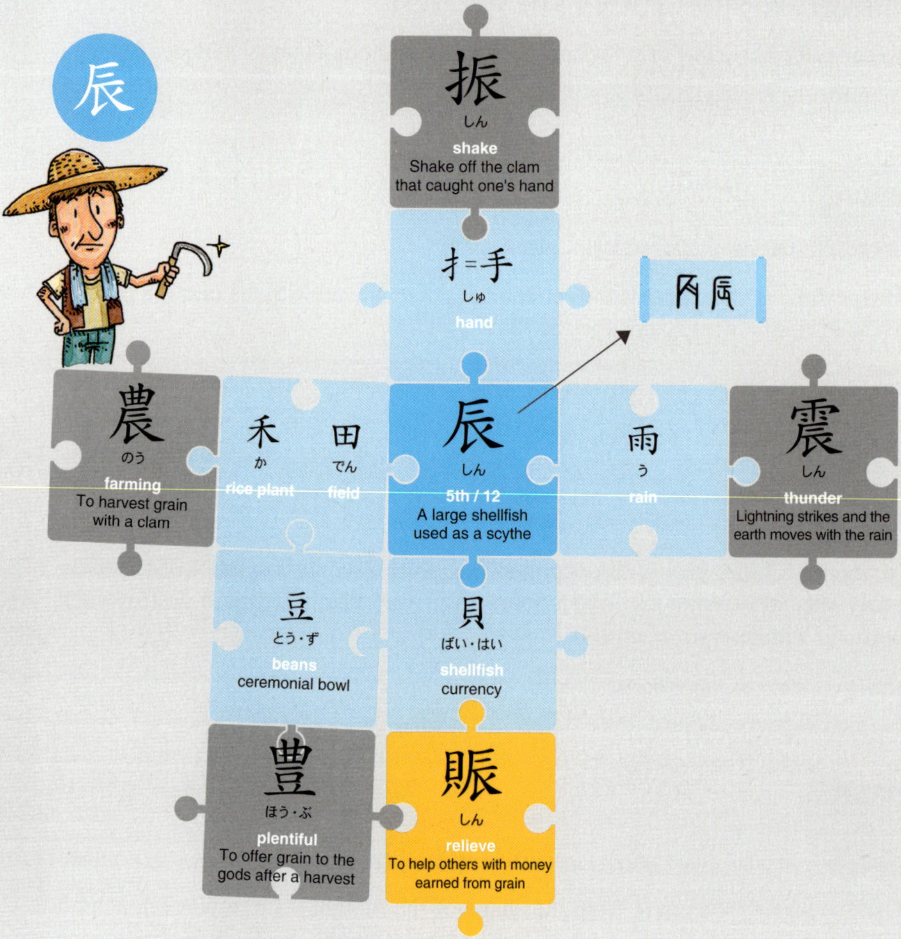

148 **辰**

しん

5th/12

一 厂 F 尸 斤 后 辰

The ancient script shows a large clam with its body sticking out. The clam, with its large and strong shell, was used as a scythe in ancient times when harvesting. It is now defined as the fifth order of the twelve Chinese zodiacs.

* When used with other characters, it can replace "振 148a" to mean 'to shake or move.'

148a 振

シン ふる

一 十 扌 扌 扩 扩 扩 扼 扼 振

shake; swing

hand 扌=手[28] [シュ] + clam/5th of 12 辰 [シン]

Symbolizes a person shaking off the large clam(辰) that caught his hand(扌).

振る[ふる] shake; wave; swing
振動[しんどう] vibration -148b 119b

148b 震

シン ふるえる

一 𠂉 𠆢 币 币 帀 雨 雨 雨 雫 雫 雫 雫 震 震

thunder; quake

rain 雨[159] [ウ] + to shake/5th of 12 辰 [シン]

A depiction of a lightning strike and the sky and earth shaking(辰) when it rains(雨).

震える[ふるえる] shake; quake
地震[じしん] earthquake -68b 148b

148c 賑

シン にぎやか・にぎわう

丨 冂 冂 月 目 目 貝 貝 貝 貯 貯 貯 賑 賑 賑

relieve; flourish

currency/shellfish 貝[145] [バイ・ハイ] + sickle/5th of 12 辰 [シン]

To 'flourish or relieve' means to help others with the excess riches(貝) accumulated from the harvest(辰).

* "辰" is a clam and signifies a sickle with which grain is cut.

賑やか[にぎやか] bustling; crowded
賑わう[にぎわう] prosper; be crowded

148d 農

ノウ

丶 冂 巾 曲 曲 曲 曲 曲 農 農 農 農 農

farming

rice plant 禾[111] [カ] + field 田[122] [デン] + clam/5th of 12 辰 [シン]

This character describes a man using a shell(辰) to harvest grains(田+禾=曲).

農村[のうそん] farm village; agricultural community -148d 35a
農民[のうみん] farmers; peasants -148d 80c

148e 豊

ホウ・ブ ゆたか

丶 冂 巾 曲 曲 曲 曲 曲 曹 曹 曹 曹 豊

plentiful

rice plant 禾[111] [カ] + field 田[122] [デン] + ceremonial bowl/beans 豆[112] [トウ・ズ]

The depiction of a ceremonial bowl(豆) full of offerings(田+禾=曲) after a bountiful harvest.

豊か[ゆたか] plentiful; abundant
豊富[ほうふ] abundance -148e 133e

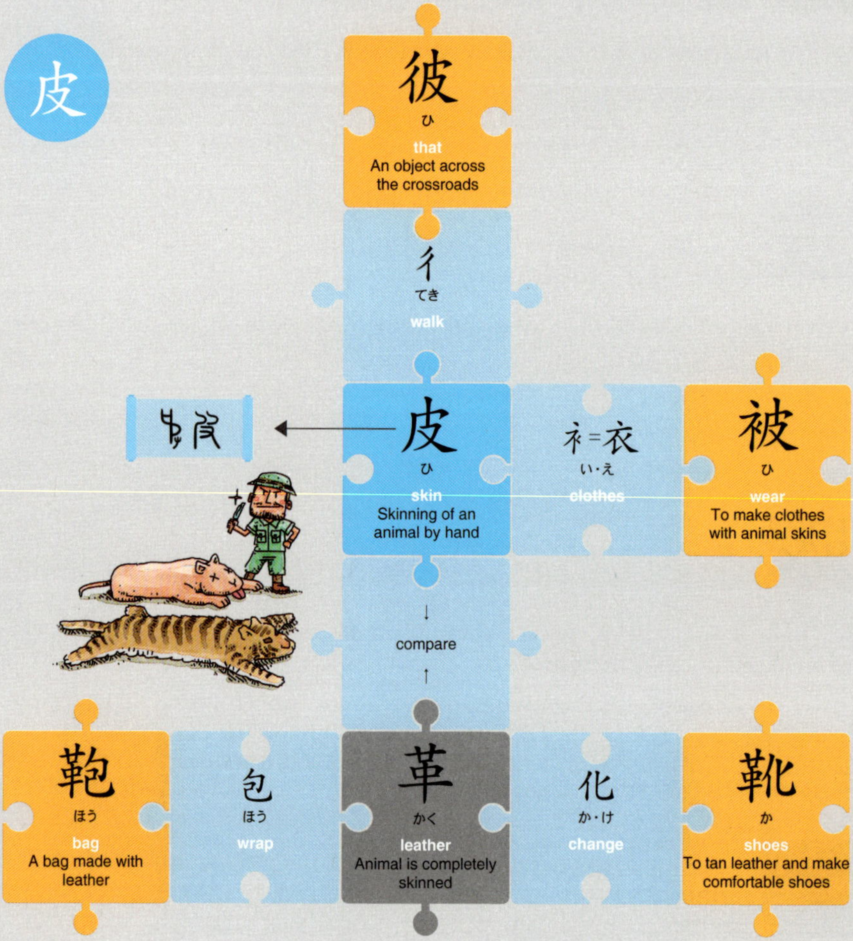

149 **皮**

ヒ かわ

skin

一 厂 广 皮 皮

Symbolizes the skinning of an animal using hand(又 30) tools and means the unprocessed raw skin of an animal.

毛皮[けがわ] fur; pelt -5e 149
皮肉[ひにく] skin and flesh; cynicism; sarcasm -149 151

149a 彼

ヒ かれ・かの

that; the

left side of an intersection/walk 彳[48] [テキ] + skin 皮 [ヒ]

A pronoun(皮) indicating a person or an object across(彳) the crossroads that means 'that, the or there.'

* "皮" is the skin that represents an animal, like a pronoun represents something or someone.

彼処/彼所[あそこ] there; that place -149a 46d / 149a 115e
彼方[あちら] that way (direction); there -149a 126
彼の[あの] that

149b 被

ヒ かぶる

wear

clothes 衤=衣[101] [イ・エ] + skin 皮 [ヒ]

People took the skin(皮) of animals to make clothes(衤) to wear, so the meaning of this character changed from 'wear → put on (cover) → be subjected to.'

被る[かぶる] wear; put on (cover); be covered with
被害[ひがい] damage; harm -149b 163e

149c 革

カク かわ

leather; reform

An animal is cut in the shape of "十" and its skin is removed completely. Whereas "皮" signifies untouched leather, "革" signifies processed leather with furs removed. It also derived to mean reform, as a leather changes its shape after processing.

革新[かくしん] innovation; reform -149c 94b
革命[かくめい] revolution -149c 71a

149d 靴

カ くつ

shoes

reform/leather 革 [カク] + change 化[52a] [カ・ケ]

In the hands of a craftsman, tanned leather(革) becomes(化) shoes.

靴下[くつした] socks -149d 173b

149e 鞄

ホウ かばん

bag

reform/leather 革 [カク] + wrap 包[75a] [ホウ]

A leather(革) bag made to put things in(包) that can be carried or slung on shoulders.

角

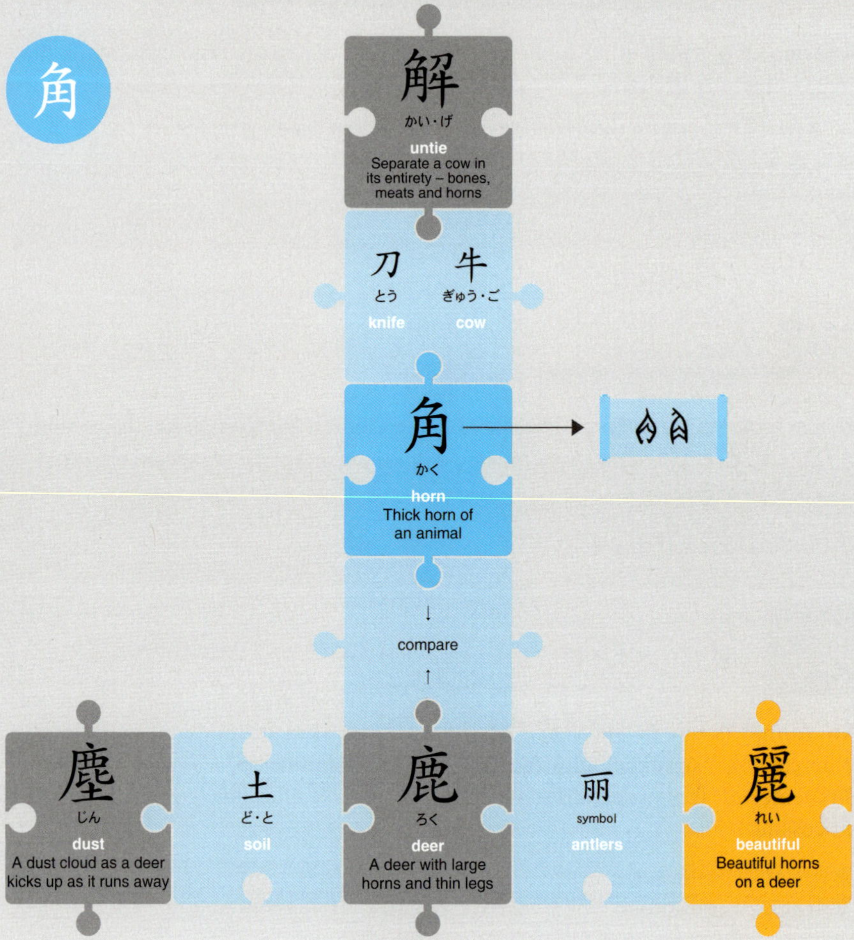

150 **角** カク かど・すみ・つの

horn; angle

ノ ク ⺈ 斤 角 角 角

Symbolizes thick horns present in animals, such as cows and sheep. The angles of such horns are all different.

角度[かくど] angle -150 114b
街角[まちかど] street corner -121d 150

150a 解

カイ・ゲ　とく・とける・ほどく

untie; understanding

horn 角 [カク] + knife 刀[95] [トウ] + cow 牛[137] [ギュウ・ゴ]

This character depicts a scene where a cow(牛) is butchered by a knife(刀) and becomes completely separate parts, such as the meat, bones and even its horns(角). Also came to mean 'understand' by understanding everything in its entirety by dividing them into such smaller parts.

解く[とく] solve; untie
解ける[とける] be solved; come untied
解く[ほどく] unfasten; untie
解説[かいせつ] explanation; commentary; exposition - 150a 59d
解決[かいけつ] settlement; solution - 150a 62a

150b 鹿

ロク　しか

deer

A character showing the large horns(广), nimble body(⾋), and thin legs(比) of a deer.

* "鹿" is the radical, so remember "广" and "比" as one, instead of separating them.

馬鹿[ばか] fool; idiot (A fool who can't tell a deer and a horse apart) - 138 150b

150c 麗

レイ

beautiful

antlers 丽 [symbol] + deer 鹿 [ロク]

A depiction of the beautiful symmetrical horns(丽) on the head of a deer(鹿).

奇麗/綺麗[きれい] beautiful; pretty; lovely - 14 150c / 14c 150c

150d 塵

ジン　ごみ・ちり

dust; trash

deer 鹿 [ロク] + soil 土[120] [ド・ト]

The dust(土) that a herd of deer(鹿) kick up as they run away are made up of tiny 'specks.'

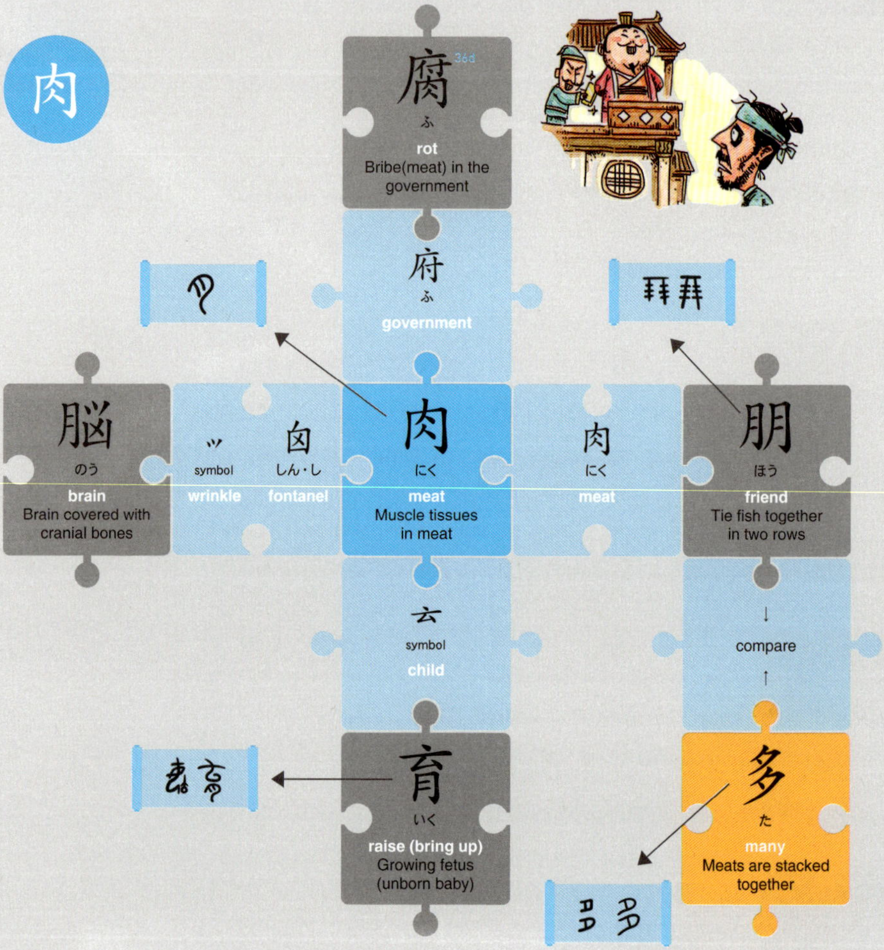

151 肉

一ク

meat

丨 冂 内 内 肉 肉

Represents the shape of the tissues(仌) that appears when a meat is cut(冂).

＊Changes into “月 172” in most cases when combined with other characters.

牛肉[ぎゅうにく] beef - 137 151
鳥肉[とりにく] chicken meat - 139 151
皮肉[ひにく] skin and flesh; cynicism; sarcasm - 149 151

151a 朋

ホウ

丿 月 月 月 月 朋 朋 朋

friend

meat 月→肉 [ニク] + meat 月→肉 [ニク]

Two similar-sized fish(肉) are tied together to form a two-row bundle of fish, representing people who share similar ideas becoming friends.

151b 多

タ おおい

ノ ク タ 多 多 多

many

meat 夕→月→肉 [ニク] + meat 夕→月→肉 [ニク]

Many pieces of meat(肉) are stacked together to describe the meaning of many.

* The ancient character shows that "夕 172a" is in fact meat, instead of a crescent moon.

多い[おおい] many; much
多少[たしょう] more or less; somewhat; a little -151b 182a
多分[たぶん] many; much; perhaps; probably -151b 95a

151c 育

イク そだつ・そだてる

丶 亠 亠 云 产 育 育 育

raise (bring up); grow up

child 𠫓 [symbol] + meat 月→肉 [ニク]

This character comes from 'growing.' A child(𠫓) is nourished when his or her body grows in flesh(肉).

* "𠫓" is an upside-down form of "child 子 77 [シ・ス]," with identical meaning. Refer to "流 157a."

育つ[そだつ] be brought up; grow up
育てる[そだてる] raise; rear; bring up
教育[きょういく] education; training -43a 151c

151d 脳

ノウ

丿 月 月 月 月' 月'' 月''' 脳 脳 脳 脳

brain

meat 月→肉 [ニク] + wrinkle ⺍ [symbol] + fontanel 凶→囟 [シン・シ]

A depiction of a wrinkled(⺍) brain, the most important part of the body(肉), that's enclosed in(囟) a skull.

* We look at its traditional character(腦), "凶" is a changed form of "囟". A fontanel is a crown of a newly-born child's head. It has a very mild membrane that pulses whenever the heart beats.

首脳[しゅのう] head; leader -4d 151d
頭脳[ずのう] head; brains -112c 151d

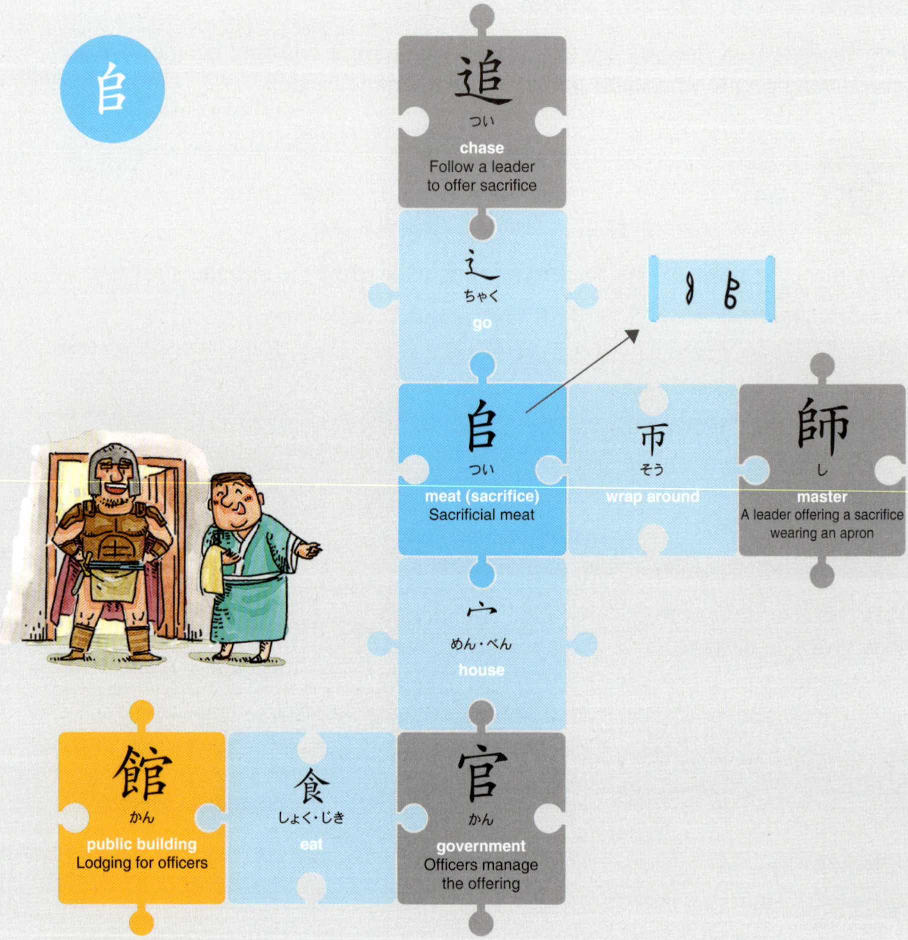

152	𠂤	ツイ **meat (sacrifice)**

Symbolizes a piece of sacrificial meat used for ceremonies.

* The ancient character depicts the shape of a meat, but this character is not used by itself.

152a 追

ツイ おう

chase

sacrifice/meat 𠂤 [ツイ] + go 辶[49] [チャク]

Symbolizes people pursuing(辶) a leader to offer sacrifice(𠂤) to God.

追う[おう] chase; follow
追放[ついほう] exile; banishment; expel - 152a 126d

152b 師

シ

master

wrap around 帀 [ソウ] + sacrifice/meat 𠂤 [ツイ]

A leader wearing(帀) the ceremonial robes conducts a ceremony with the offering(𠂤).

* "帀" describes a large piece of fabric(巾) wrapped around a body.

医師[いし] doctor; physician - 89a 152b
漁師[りょうし] fisherman - 144b 152b

152c 官

カン

government

house 宀[113] [メン・ベン] + sacrifice/meat 𠂤→𠂤 [ツイ]

Sacrificial offering was a major national event in ancient Chinese dynasties; government officials(宀) then managed the offering(𠂤) used in such events.

外交官[がいこうかん] diplomat - 172b 1a 152c

152d 館

カン

public building

eat 食[109] [ショク・ジキ] + government 官 [カン]

Symbolizes a place where the traveling government officials(官) can rest and eat(食), which in turn became to mean a public place used for official purposes. Due to the similar purpose, it also became to mean hotels or lodges in general.

映画館[えいがかん] movie theater; cinema - 61d 122d 152d
図書館[としょかん] library - 16d 33e 152d
大使館[たいしかん] embassy - 60 31b 152d
旅館[りょかん] traditional Japanese inn - 127e 152d

Diagram for 山

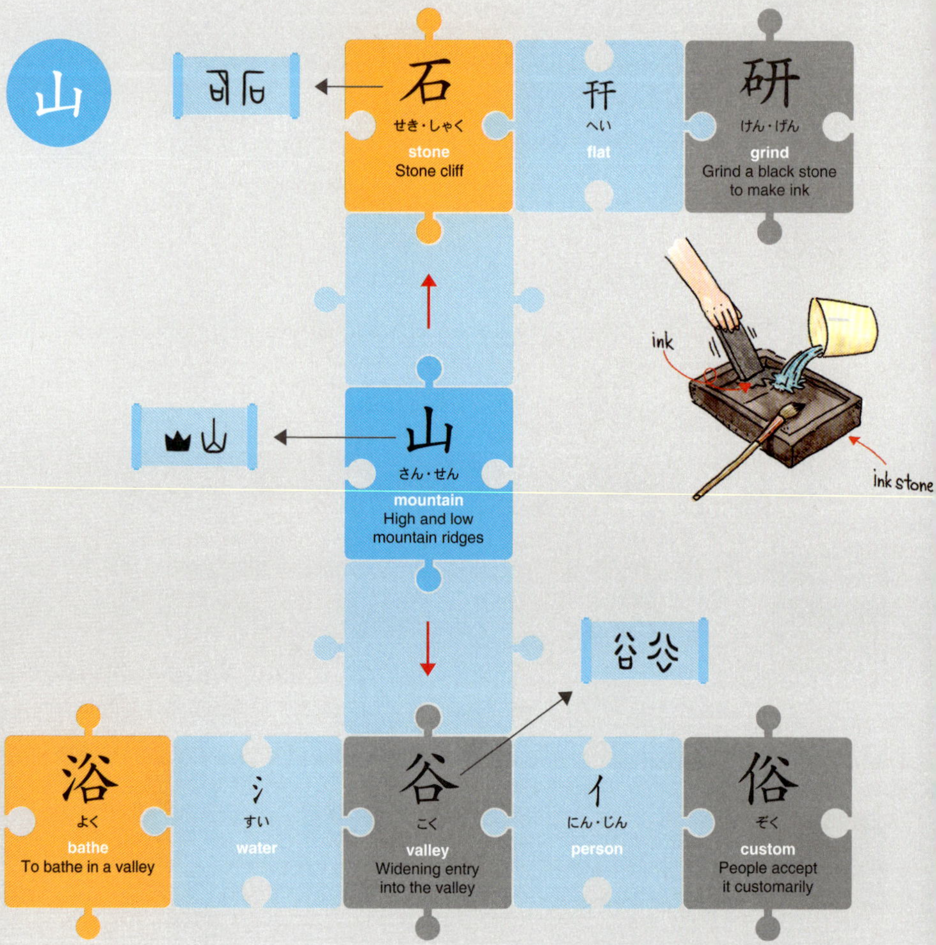

153 **山** リン・セン やま

mountain

Represents a mountain with summit and ridges in different heights.

沢山[たくさん] many; much; a lot; plenty of -74e 153
火山[かざん] volcano -124 153
山林[さんりん]forest; forest woods -153 166
登山[とざん] climbing -112e 153

153a **石** セキ・シャク いし 一ア不石石

stone

Derived to mean stone by symbolizing large boulders(ロ) forming cliffs(ア→厂[117]).

石鹸[せっけん] soap -153a 55d
化石[かせき] fossil; petrifaction -52a 153a

153b **研** ケン・ゲン とぐ 一ア不石石石'石=矸研

grind

stone 石 [セキ・シャク] + flat 幵 → 幵 [ヘイ]

Chinese traditional ink was made by grinding a black stone(石) on top of inkstone(幵) with water. This character is derived to mean research, in the sense that academic research began by writing texts.

* "幵" symbolizes two shields(干[96]) put together in the front to make it flat.

研ぐ[とぐ] grind; sharpen; scour
研究[けんきゅう] study; research -153b 177c

153c **谷** コク たに ノハク⽕⽕谷谷

valley

valley 仌 [symbol] + mouth ロ[12] [ク・コウ]

Symbolizes an entrance(ロ) of a valley(仌) which gets wider as it accepts more water down the way.

153d **俗** ゾク ノイイ'イ\`仫俗俗俗俗

custom

person イ[52] [ニン・ジン] + valley 谷 [コク]

Like a valley(谷) which accepts all waters, customs represent something that's been customarily accepted(谷) and passed down for many generations of people(イ).

風俗[ふうぞく] manners; customs -143c 153d

153e **浴** ヨク あびる 丶丶氵氵'氵\`汃浴浴浴浴

bathe

water 氵[157] [スイ] + valley 谷 [コク]

If you go to a valley(谷) where water(氵) flows, you can 'bathe or get drenched.'

浴びる[あびる] bathe; be bathed (in sunlight); be charged with (a crime)
入浴[にゅうよく] bathing; enter a bath -53 153e

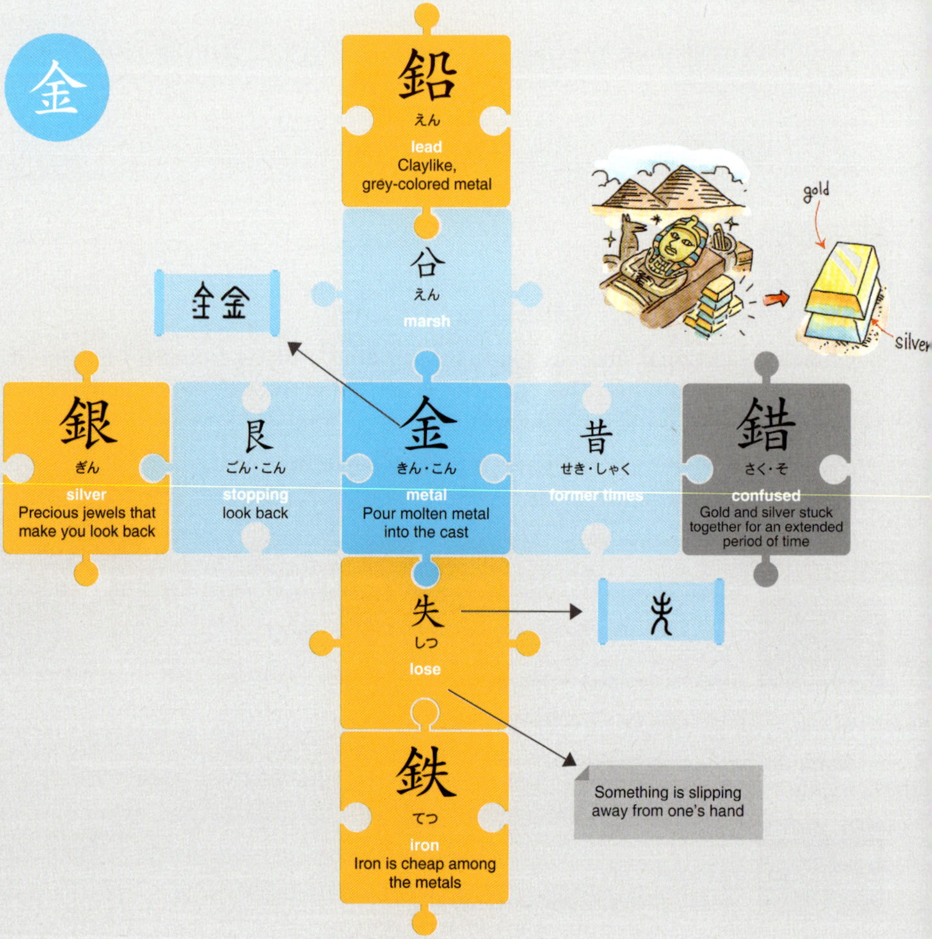

154 **金** キン・コン かね

丿 人 𠆢 今 全 全 金 金

metal; gold

Metals(丶) taken from the earth(土) were melted and poured into the cast (亼). Therefore, it became to represent gold as the first valuable metal – beautiful, easy to manipulate, does not rust – that attracted human attention. Refer to "全[53a]."

* Gold is actually the earliest of metals to be used by humans, it first being used in Mesopotamia around 6.000 B.C.

お金 [おかね] money	金曜日[きんようび] Friday -154 141c 170
黄金[おうごん] gold -108 154	送金[そうきん] remittance -62d 154
預金[よきん] deposit; savings -4b 154	料金[りょうきん] charge; fee -128b 154

154a 鉛

エン なまり

ノ ト ト ト 牟 余 金 金 鈆 鈆 鉛 鉛 鉛

lead

metal 金 [キン・コン] + marsh 㕣 [エン]

Symbolizes lead, a metal(金) with blueish grey color like a swamp(㕣).

* "㕣" represents clays opening up(八) and sucking in everything like a mouth(口) – when something falls into a swamp it becomes very difficult to take it out.

鉛筆[えんぴつ] pencil - 154a 33d

154b 錯

サク・ソ

ノ ト ト ト 牟 余 金 金 金 金 鉡 錯 錯 錯 錯 錯

confused; mix

gold/metal 金 [キン・コン] + former times 昔[171] [セキ・シャク]

If gold(金) and silver are stuck together for an extended period of time(昔), their materials start to flow to each other and mix. Such mixing is considered wrong and inauspicious to happen to pure gold.

* In fact, gold(金) and silver will diffuse into each other when left in contact for too long(昔).

錯雑[さくざつ] complication; intricacy - 154b 140b

154c 失

シツ うしなう

ノ ⺈ 二 生 失

lose

hand 生→手[28] [シュ] + something slipping away ㇏ [symbol]

This character depicts an image of something which is slipping away(㇏) from under one's hand(手), and the meaning of 'to lose' is derived from it.

失う[うしなう] lose
失礼します[しつれいします] (an idiom) pardon me; excuse me - 154c 99d
失礼[しつれい] discourtesy; impoliteness - 154c 99d
失敗[しっぱい] failure - 154c 147c

154d 鉄

テツ

ノ ト ト ト 牟 余 金 金 金 金 金 鉄 鉄

iron

metal 金 [キン・コン] + lose 失 [シツ]

Iron is widely used by human beings. It is cheap(失) and easily available(失) among the metals(金).

* Let us try to think that the character "失" has been changed to indicate the negative meaning.

地下鉄[ちかてつ] subway - 68b 173b 154d
鉄橋[てっきょう] railroad bridge; railway bridge - 154d 3b

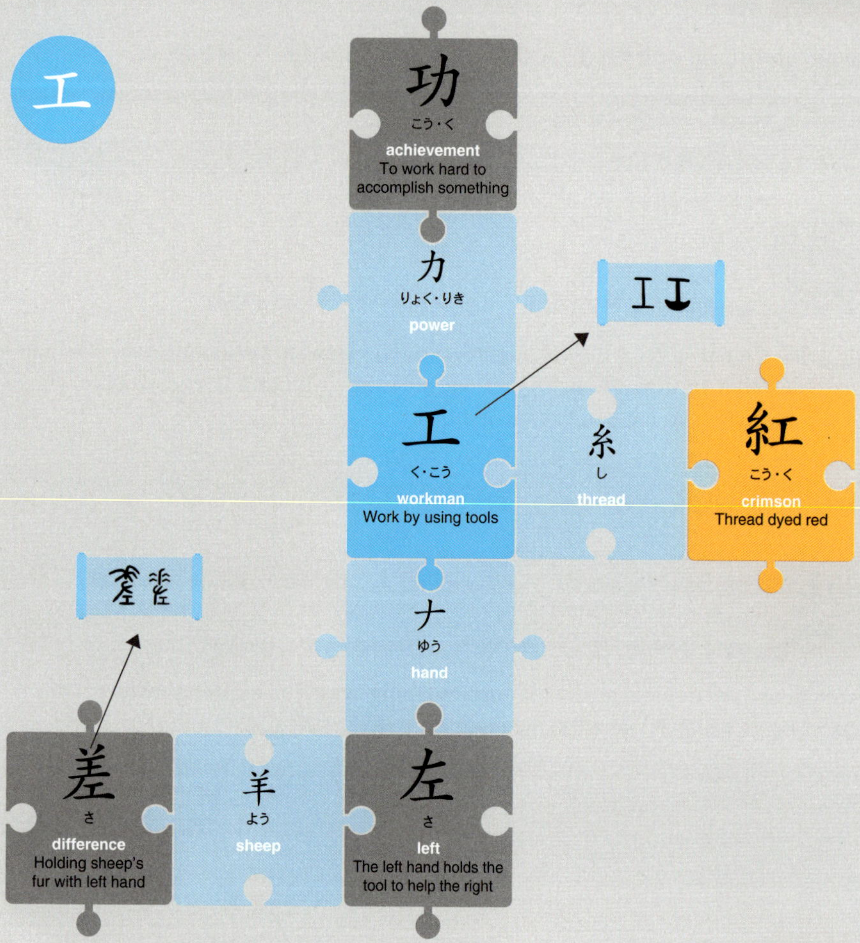

155 工

ク・コウ

一 丅 工

workman

Symbolizes a tool used to make things or used while performing sacrifices. It means work in general.

加工[かこう] manufacturing; processing -125b 155
工事[こうじ] construction work; construction -155 32c
工場[こうじょう・こうば] factory -155 171c

155a 功

コウ・ク

一 丅 工 功 功

achievement; merits

tool/workman 工 [ク・コウ] + power 力 125 [リョク・リキ]

A craftsman good at using tools(工) uses all his strength(力) to make an accomplishment.

155b 紅

コウ・ク

𠃋 幺 幺 糸 糸 糸 糸 紅 紅

crimson

thread 糸 104 [シ] + tool/workman 工 [ク・コウ]

The Chinese dyed fabric or threads(糸), and this character meaning 'red' got its pronunciation from "工."

* "工" is a tool but also a sacrificial artifact. It will be easier to remember 'red' if you think of the blood on a sacrificial tool.

紅茶[こうちゃ] black tea -155b 161b
紅葉[こうよう] autumn colors (leaves) -155b 162d

155c 左

サ ひだり

一 ナ 𠂇 左 左

left

hand ナ 34 [ユウ] + tool/workman 工 [ク・コウ]

A hand(ナ) holding a tool(工). It means 'left' because that's the hand that holds the tool to help the right hand do the work.

左右[さゆう] left and right -155c 34a

155d 差

サ さす

丶 丷 䒑 𦍌 𦍌 羊 差 差 差

difference

sheep 羊 134 [ヨウ] + left 左 [サ]

When holding the sheep(羊) with the left hand(左) to shear the fur, the length of the fur differs from one part of the sheep to another.

* Ancient character shows holding of crops(禾) with the left(左) hand to signify that even crops from the same field are of different lengths.

差す[さす] hold up; (of water) rise; be visible
交差点[こうさてん] crossing; intersection 1a -155d 100c

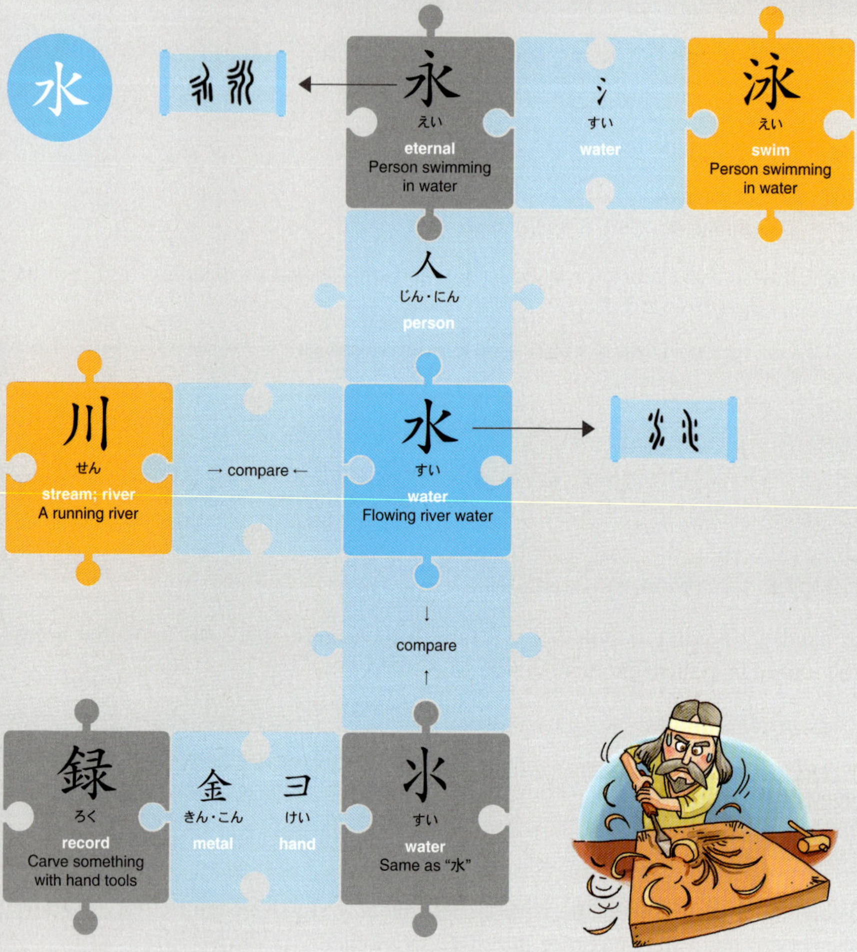

156 水

スイ みず

water

亅 才 水 水

Symbolizes water by representing water flowing in rivers(水).

水曜日[すいようび] Wednesday -156 141c 170
水道[すいどう] water supply (service) -156 4e
断水[だんすい] water outage -94d 156

156a 永

エイ ながい

丶 亅 刁 永 永

eternal

water 水 [スイ] + person 丶→人[51] [ジン・ニン]

The character was initially used to symbolize a person(人) swimming in the river(水), but later derived to mean forever, as in things floating endlessly down the river.

永い[ながい] eternal; everlasting　永久[えいきゅう] permanent; foreverness -156a 56c
永遠[えいえん] eternity -156a 102c

156b 泳

エイ およぐ

丶 丶 氵 氵 氵 汀 汸 泳

swim

water 氵[157] [スイ] + eternal 永 [エイ]

As "永" came to mean forever, water(氵) is added to restore the meaning of swimming.

泳ぐ/游ぐ[およぐ] swim -156b / 127c　水泳[すいえい] swimming -156 156b

156c 氺

スイ

亅 亅 氵 氺 氺

water

A different form of "water 水" which is used only in combination with other characters.

156d 録

ロク

ノ 𠂉 𠂉 𠂉 𠆢 今 金 金 金 釒 釕 釕 鈩 録 録 録

record

metal 金[154] [キン・コン] + hand ヨ→ヨ[32] [ケイ] + water 氺 [スイ]

Ancient inscriptions show a carving(金) or a record of something on wood by hand (ヨ). "氺" does not seem to suggest water, but rather wood particles spraying outward during carving. Refer to "緑[104d]."

記録[きろく] record; write down -66b 156d　登録[とうろく] registration -112e 156d

156e 川

セン かわ

丿 川 川

stream; river

A river flowing around hills.

川/河[かわ] river; stream -156e / 13d

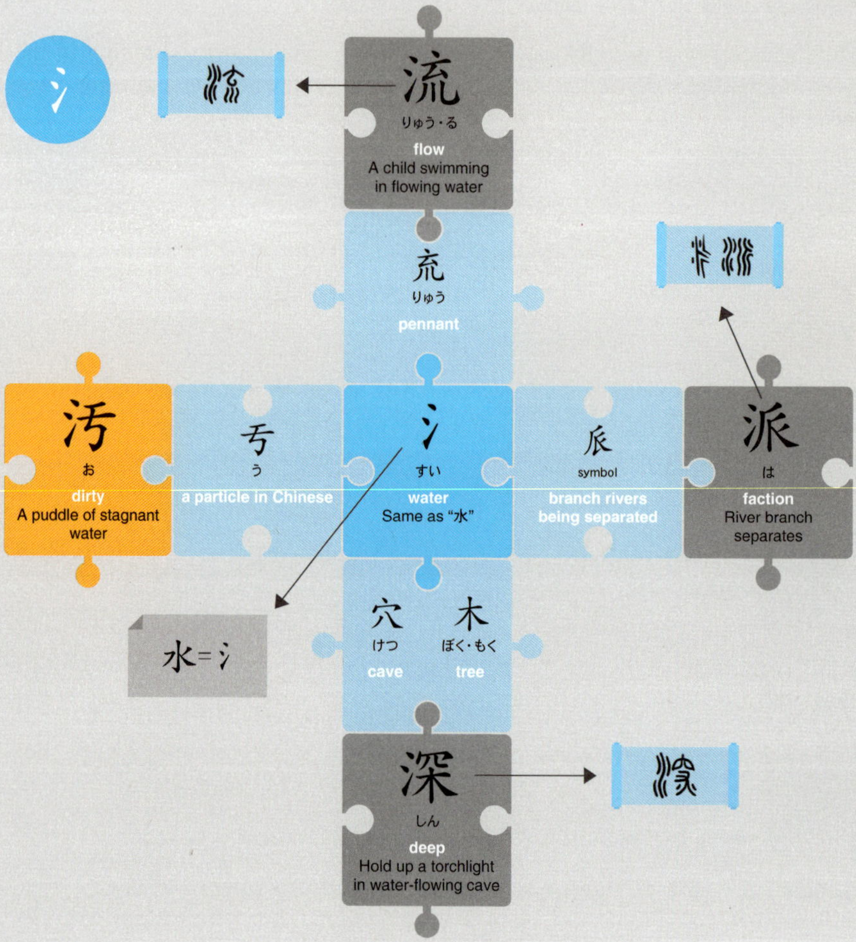

157 氵

スイ

water

A different form of "water 水[156]" which is used only in combination with other characters.

157a 流

リュウ・ル ながれる・ながす

丶 丶 氵 氵 氵 氵 浐 浐 浐 済 流

flow

water 氵 [スイ] + pennant 㐬 [リュウ]

"㐬," which symbolizes a child playing in flowing water is not used by itself. Therefore, water(氵) is added to restore the original meaning of flowing water.

* "㐬" symbolizes a child(𠫓 151c*) swimming in flowing water(川 156e).

流れる[ながれる] flow; run; pass (time)
流す[ながす] let flow; spill; drain
海流[かいりゅう] ocean current -79c 157a
交流[こうりゅう] interchange; alternating current 1a -157a

157b 派

ハ

丶 丶 氵 氵 氵 氵 沂 沂 派

faction; dispatch

water 氵 [スイ] + branch rivers being separated 𠂢 [symbol]

Symbolizes small branch rivers separating(𠂢) from the main stream(氵), which came to mean factions or the act of dispatching someone to another place.

左派[さは] left wing; left faction -155c 157b
派手[はで] showy; loud; flashy; gaudy -157b 28
立派[りっぱ] splendid; fine; handsome; elegant -64 157b

157c 深

シン ふかい・ふかまる・ふかめる

丶 丶 氵 氵 氵 氵 氵 泙 泙 深 深

deep

water 氵 [スイ] + cave 穴→穴 113a [ケツ] + tree 木 164 [ボク・モク]

Symbolizes a man holding(又 30) torch fire(火 124) inside a deep, dark cave (穴) with water(氵) flowing on the floor.

* "木" is a changed form of person holding(又) a fire(火).

深い[ふかい] deep; profound; intense
深まる[ふかまる] deepen; become deeper
深める[ふかめる] deepen; heighten; intensify
深夜[しんや] dead of night; midnight -157c 172c

157d 汚

オ きたない・よごす・よごれる

丶 丶 氵 氵 汚 汚

dirty

water 氵 [スイ] + a particle in Chinese 亏 [ウ]

Water(氵) that can't flow if the draining route is twisted(亏) or blocked becomes 'dirty.'

* "亏" represents sound that comes through the vocal cords.

汚い[きたない] dirty; foul
汚す[よごす] make dirty; defile
汚れる[よごれる] become dirty; become defiled

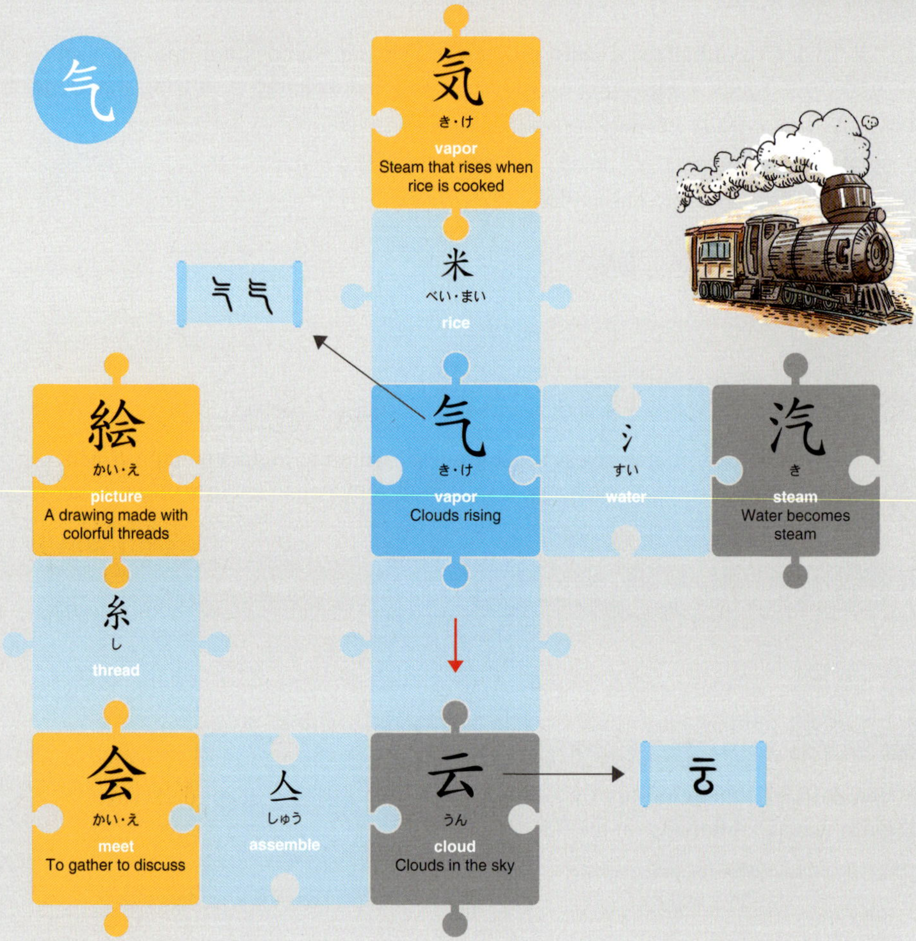

158 气

キ・ケ

vapor; air; energy

Symbolizes clouds or water vapor rising up in the air – derived to mean air or gas in general, or a term for energy.

* A radical that isn't used alone.

158a

気

キ・ケ

ノ 𠂉 𠂉 气 気 気

vapor; air; energy

vapor 气 [キ・ケ] + rice× →米 110 [ベイ・マイ]

Steam(气) that rises when rice(米) is cooking represents 'vapor, air or energy.'

元気[げんき] energy; vitality; vigor -58a 158a
天気[てんき] weather -60b 158a
電気[でんき] electricity -159c 158a
病気[びょうき] disease; illness; sickness -65a 158a

158b

汽

キ

丶 丶 氵 氵 汇 汽 汽

steam

water 氵 157 [スイ] + vapor 气 [キ・ケ]

Water(氵) becomes a form of air(气) – steam – and rises upward.

汽車[きしゃ] train; steam train (original meaning) -158b 97
汽船[きせん] steamship -158b 98a

158c

云

ウン いう

一 二 云 云

cloud; say

Signifies clouds floating in the sky. A floating cloud can also predict rain, which also came to mean 'to say'.

云う[いう] say; such

158d

会

カイ・エ あう

ノ 人 𠆢 亼 会 会

meet

assemble 亼 54 [シュウ] + say/cloud 云 [ウン]

To discuss(云) an issue, people must gather(亼) or meet. When people gather(亼) and discuss(云), good ideas or solutions are obtained.

会う[あう] meet; see; encounter
会社[かいしゃ] company -158d 99e
宴会[えんかい] party; banquet -78b 158d
社会[しゃかい] society; community -99e 158d

158e

絵

カイ・エ

乡 乡 幺 糸 糸 糸 糸 紒 紒 絵 絵 絵

picture

thread 糸 104 [シ] + meet 会 [カイ・エ]

Colorful threads(糸) were put together(会) into fabric or clothes to create patterns, so this character came to mean 'drawing.'

絵画[かいが] picture; painting -158e 122d
絵本[えほん] picture book -158e 165

雨

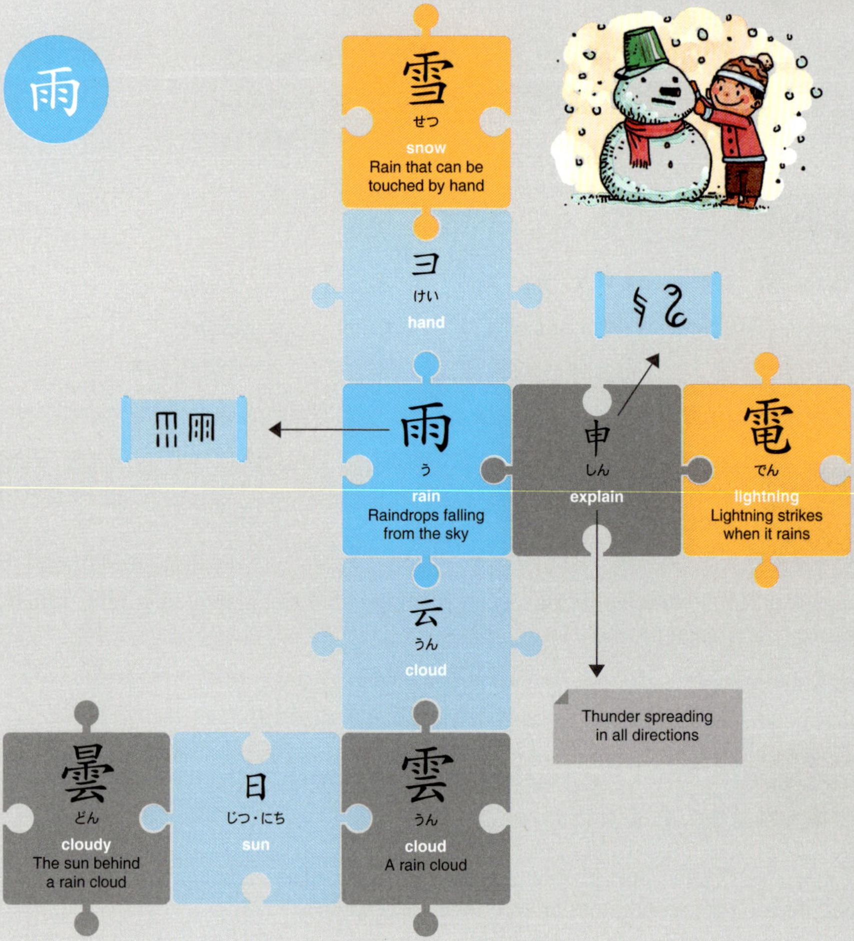

159 雨

ウ あめ・あま

rain

一 丆 亐 币 币 雨 雨 雨

Combination of raindrops(丶) falling(巾) from the sky(一) – meaning rain.

雨戸[あまど] rain shutter door; shutters -159 115d'
大雨[おおあめ] heavy rain, torrential rain, downpour -60 159
梅雨[つゆ・ばいう] rainy season; (summer) monsoon -79b 159

159a 雪

セツ ゆき

一 ｢ 〒 币 币 雨 雨 雨 雪 雪 雪

snow

rain 雨 [ウ] + hand ヨ[32] [ケイ]

A somewhat poetic expression; snow is a form of rain(雨) that can be touched by hand(ヨ).

吹雪[ふぶき] snowstorm; blizzard - 19d 159a

159b 申

シン もうす

丨 冂 日 日 申

explain

Symbolizes thunder that spreads out to all directions. Came to mean explain, as in explaining your opinion or will to all directions.

申す[もうす] speak humbly

159c 電

デン

一 ｢ 〒 币 币 雨 雨 雨 霄 霄 霄 霄 電

lightning

rain 雨 [ウ] + explain 电→申 [シン]

Lightning(申) strikes when the rain(雨) comes. This character is now used as the term for electricity, as thunder is an electrical discharge in the atmosphere.

電気[でんき] electricity - 159c 158a
電話[でんわ] telephone - 159c 20b
電報[でんぽう] telegram - 159c 30b
電車[でんしゃ] electric train, tram - 159c 97
電池[でんち] battery - 159c 68b
電力[でんりょく] electricity; (electric) power - 159c 125

159d 雲

ウン くも

一 ｢ 〒 币 币 雨 雨 雨 雫 雲 雲 雲

cloud

rain 雨 [ウ] + cloud 云[158c] [ウン]

When “云” came to mean ‘to speak,’ a character for cloud was created by adding a cloud(云) above rain(雨).

159e 曇

ドン くもる

丨 冂 日 日 旦 旦 昌 昌 昌 昌 曇 曇 曇 曇 曇 曇

cloudy

sun 日[170] [ジツ・ニチ] + cloud 雲 [ウン]

When the sun(日) goes behind a cloud(雲), the weather becomes cloudy.

曇る[くもる] become cloudy; become dim, be gloomy

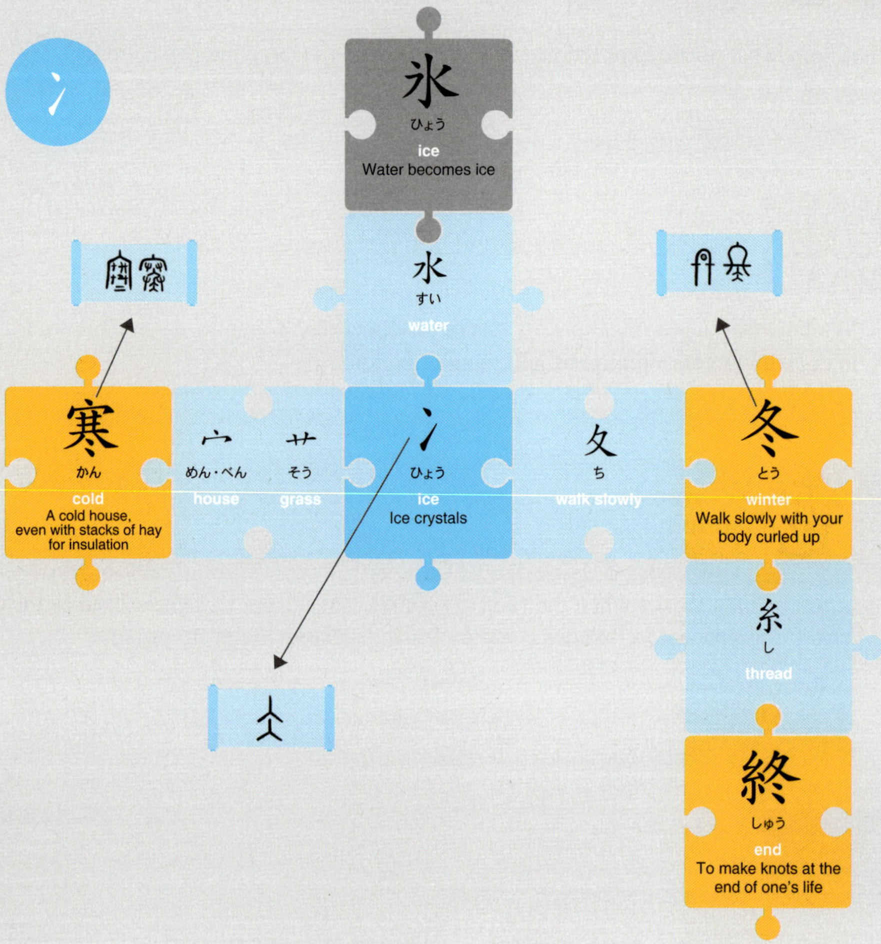

160 冫

ヒョウ

ice

丶 冫

The ancient character used to describe ice by putting together two shapes of ice crystals. Modern reform simplified the crystal into a simple dot(丶) and is used only in combination with other characters to add the meaning of coldness or freezing.

160a **氷**

ヒョウ こおり

亅 才 水 水 氷

ice

ice 丶→冫[ヒョウ] + water 水[156] [スイ]

As the temperature drops below zero, water(水) becomes ice(冫).

* The Chinese use "冰."

160b **冬**

トウ ふゆ

ノ ク 夂 冬 冬

winter

walk slowly 夂[46] [チ] + ice 冫[ヒョウ]

In the bitter cold(冫) of winter, people tend to curl up and walk slow(夂).

* Its ancient character has an image of knots made at both ends of a thread. It describes 'winter' because everything ends its growth in the season of winter.

160c **終**

シュウ おえる・おわる

ㄥ 幺 幺 糸 糸 糸 糸 約 終 終 終

end

thread 糸[104] [シ] + winter 冬 [トウ]

The character "冬" used to mean 'to end or to finish' by making knots at the ends of the thread, but its meaning was transformed into its original meaning 'winter' by the addition of a thread(糸).

終(わ)る[おわる] end; finish; die
終える[おえる] end; finish; complete
終始[しゅうし] from beginning to end; continuously -160c 76c

160d **寒**

カン さむい

丶 丶 宀 宀 宀 宇 宙 寉 実 実 寒 寒

cold

house 宀[113] [メン・ベン] + grass 艸→艹[161] [ソウ] + ice 冫[ヒョウ]

Symbolizes how ice(冫) cold wind still blows into a house(宀), even when the inside is insulated by stacks of hay(共→茻).

* The ancient character shows a person(人[51]) shivering in the cold(冫) wind, in the midst of the hay(茻) put inside of the house(宀).

寒い[さむい] cold; chilly
寒け/寒気[さむけ] cold; chill -160d / 160d 158a

Diagram for 艹

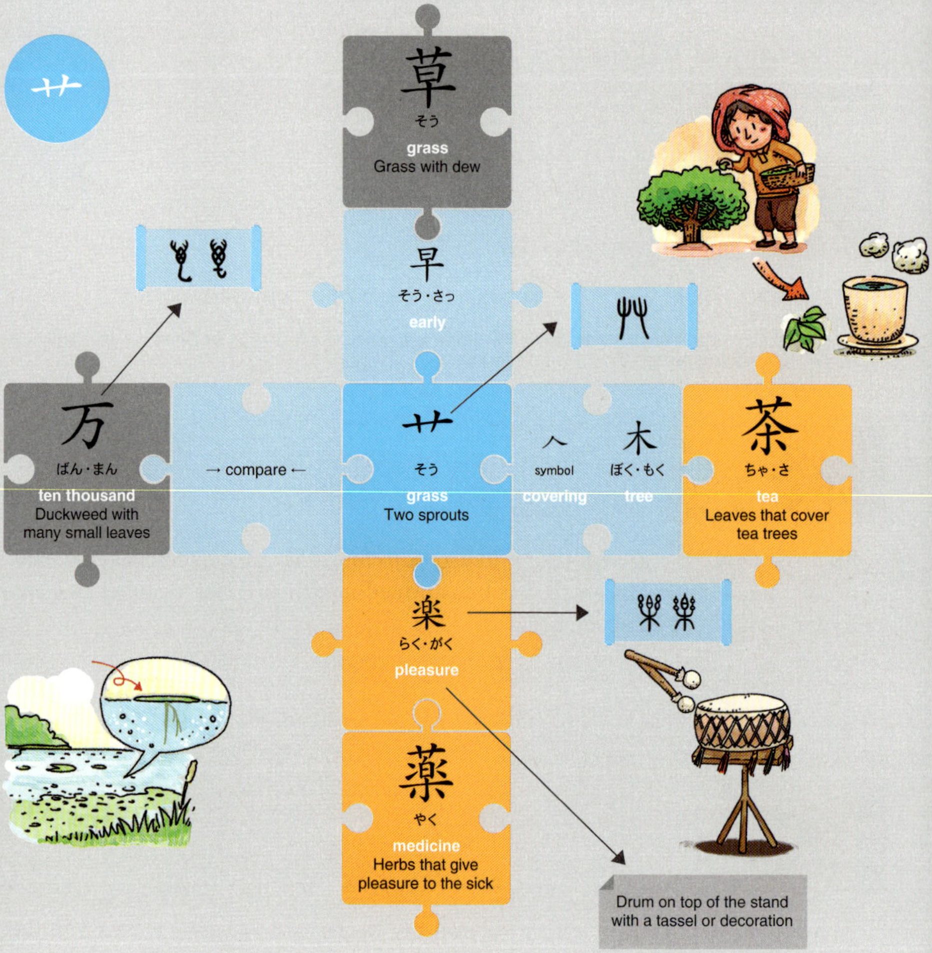

161	艹	ソウ **grass**	一 十 艹

Simplified form of sprouts or grass(艸) formed by combining two sprouts(屮). Used only in combination with other characters and usually placed on top of a character.

161a	草	ソウ　くさ **grass** grass 艹 [ソウ] + early 早 170c [ソウ・サッ]	一 十 艹 艹 艹 苩 苩 荁 草

Grass(艹) on the field shining with the morning sun(早).

* "早" shows the sun(日 170) rising above the horizon(十)in the morning.

161b **茶** チャ・サ 一 十 艹 艾 艾 苁 苶 茶 茶

tea

grass 艹 [ソウ] + covering 𠆢 [symbol] + tree 木 164 [ボク・モク]

Symbolizes the making of tea by processing leaves(艹) that cover(𠆢) the tea trees(木).

* Tea originates from the Szechuan(四川) region of China, and spread to all other regions.

お茶[おちゃ] green tea; tea ceremony	喫茶店[きっさてん] teahouse, tea room -163d 161b 100b
紅茶[こうちゃ] black tea -155b 161b	茶色[ちゃいろ] light brown; brown -161b 75d

161c **楽** ラク・ガク たのしい・たのしむ ′ 亻 自 自 白 伯 泊 泊′ 泊く 泊幺 楽 楽 楽

pleasure; music

white 白 106 [ハク・ビャク] + tassel 𢆶 → 𢆶 [symbol] + tree 木 164 [ボク・モク]

Music is symbolized by a drum(白) with a decoration(𢆶) standing on a drumstand(木). Also derived to mean joy or pleasure in playing with a decorated(𢆶) drum(白) on a drumstand(木).

* The traditional character(樂) shows "幺," which are twisted threads abbreviated into two dots(丶).

楽しい[たのしい] enjoyable; pleasant	楽しむ[たのしむ] enjoy (oneself); take pleasure in
音楽[おんがく] music -18 161c	楽器[がっき] musical instrument -161c 135a

161d **薬** ヤク くすり 一 十 艹 艹 艹 芇 苩 苩 苩 蒩 蒩 蒩 菡 薬 薬 薬

medicine

grass 艹 [ソウ] + pleasure 楽 [ラク・ガク]

A herb(艹) that puts the sick at ease and gives them pleasure(楽) is medicine.

* Chinese medicine does use animal products like a bear's gall bladder and deer antlers, but most ingredients are herbs(艹).

薬局[やっきょく] pharmacy -161d 74c

161e **万** バン・マン 一 丂 万

ten thousand

Symbolizes duckweed which lives on water and has countless number of small leaves. It then became to mean ten thousand.

* Traditional character(萬) represents a scorpion, with two claws(艹) and a long tail(禺) that strikes its prey with poison. Since arthropods like scorpions are known to have many feet, it later became to mean ten thousand. Adding "insect 虫 143 [チュウ]" back into this character(萬) restores the meaning of "scorpion 蠆 [タイ]."

万年筆[まんねんひつ] fountain pen -161e 96e 33d

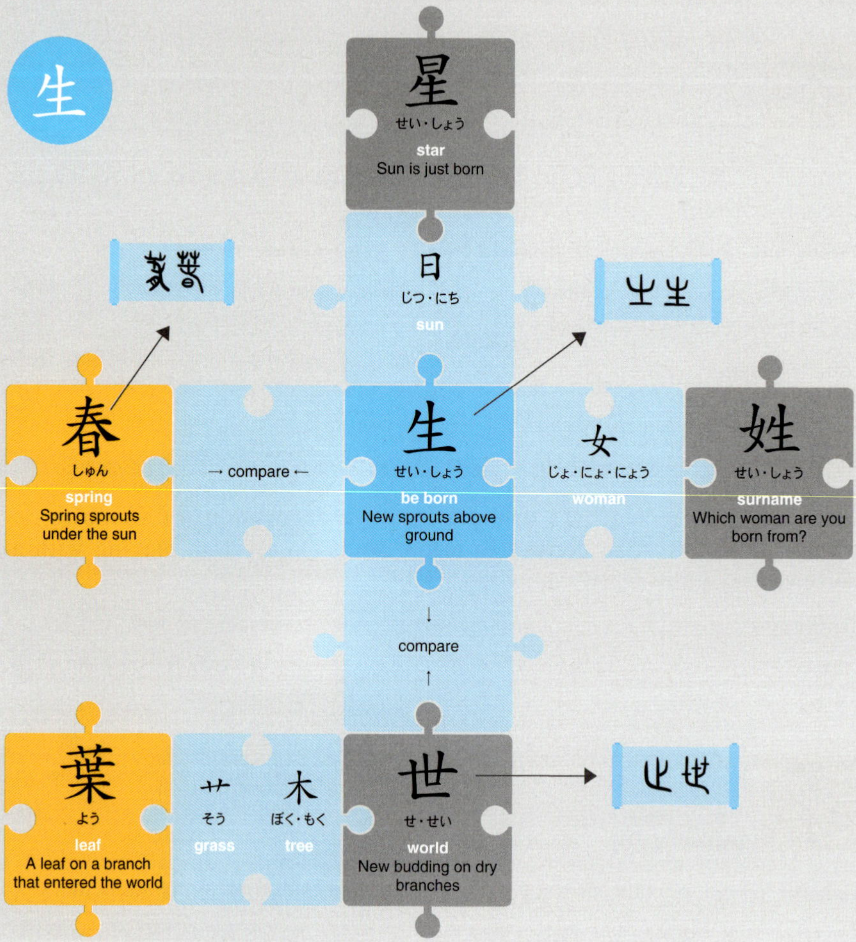

162 生

セイ ショウ いかす・いきる・いける・うまれる・うむ・はえる・なま

ノ 𠂉 𠂉 牛 生

be born; life

New sprouts(屮 161) start growing above ground(土 120) – representing birth and life.

生(ま)れる[うまれる] be born	生かす[いかす] let live; keep alive
生きる[いきる] live; exist	生ける[いける] keep alive; arrange (flowers)
生む[うむ] give birth; produce	生える[はえる] grow; sprout
生[なま] raw; uncooked	学生[がくせい] student -77b 162
先生[せんせい] teacher; doctor; sir (honorific) -58d 162	
生徒[せいと] pupil; student -162 44e	誕生日[たんじょうび] birthday -50e 162 170
留学生[りゅうがくせい] international student; student studying abroad -70d 77b 162	

162a 星

セイ・ショウ ほし

丶 口 日 日 旦 早 星 星 星

star

sun 日[170] [ジツ・ニチ] + be born 生 [セイ・ショウ]

Stars are represented as a baby sun(日) which was just born(生).

晨星[しんせい] morning star; Venus - 168a 162a

162b 姓

セイ・ショウ

ㄑ 女 女 女 女 女 姓 姓

surname

woman 女[78] [ジョ・ニョ・ニョウ] + be born 生 [セイ・ショウ]

Back in the ancient maternal society, a person was given a surname that identified which woman(女) he or she was born(生) from.

姓名[せいめい] full name - 162b 172d

162c 世

セ・セイ よ

一 十 廾 廿 世

world

Symbolizes new sprouts(屮[161]) budding out on a dry branch in the spring, signifying the beginning of life in a new world.

世紀[せいき] century; era - 162c 66c
世界[せかい] the world - 162c 51b

162d 葉

ヨウ は

一 十 艹 芒 芒 芒 苹 萓 萓 葉 葉 葉

leaf

grass 艹[161] [ソウ] + world 世 [セイ・セ] + tree 木[164] [ボク・モク]

New shoots(世) appear on a dry tree branch(木) and the leaves(艹) grow abundantly.

葉書[はがき] postcard - 162d 33e
紅葉[こうよう] autumn colors (leaves) - 155b 162d
言葉[ことば] speech; language; word; phrase - 17 162d

162e 春

シュン はる

一 二 三 声 夫 夫 春 春 春

spring

sprouts 𡗗 [symbol] + sun 日[170] [ニチ・ジツ]

Symbolizes sprouts(𡗗) budding out as spring comes with stronger sunlight(日).

* The ancient character shows "𡗗" as a group of sprouts(屮[161]).

青春[せいしゅん] youth - 107 162e

Diagram for 丰

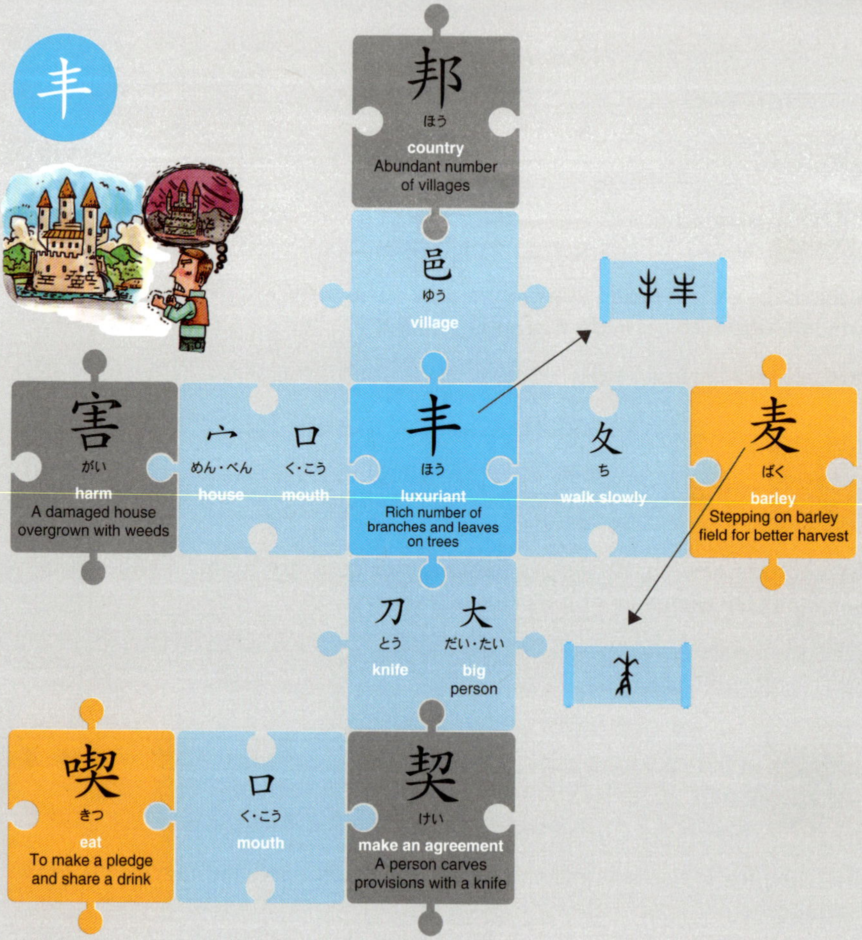

163 丰 ホウ

luxuriant

一 二 三 丰

Signifies how leaves and branches are abundant in trees.

163a 邦

ホウ

一 ＝ 三 丰 邦 邦

country

luxuriant 丰 [ホウ] + village 阝→邑 75c [ユウ]

Signifies that there are an abundant(丰) number of villages(邑) which create a nation or state.

* When "hill 阝 116 [フ]" is placed on the right side of a character, it means the same as "邑."

連邦[れんぽう] federation; union - 97e 163a

163b 麦

バク

一 ＝ 丰 主 夫 麦 麦

barley

luxuriant 丰 [ホウ] + walk slowly 夂 46 [チ]

When growing barley, the field must be stepped (treaded) in order to prevent young barley sprouts from freezing to death. This is symbolized by slowly walking(夂) on the barley field for an abundant(丰) harvest later in the year.

蕎麦[そば] buckwheat; Soba (an abbreviation for 'そばきり') - 3c 163b

163c 契

ケイ ちぎる

一 十 丰 丰 刧 刧 契 契 契

make an agreement

luxuriant 丰 [ホウ] + knife 刀 95 [トウ] + person/big 大 60 [ダイ・タイ]

People(大) gather to make an agreement and use a knife(刀) to carve the various(丰) details.

契る[ちぎる] promise; pledge 契約[けいやく] contract; agreement - 163c 104a

163d 喫

キツ

丨 口 口 口 吋 吋 吽 喆 喆 喫 喫 喫

eat; drink

mouth 口 12 [ク・コウ] + make an agreement 契 [ケイ]

According to tradition, when a treaty or a deal(契) was made, food and drink was shared(口), so this character came to mean 'eat or drink.'

喫茶店[きっさてん] teahouse, tea room - 163d 161b 100b

163e 害

ガイ

丶 丶 宀 宀 宇 宝 宝 害 害 害

harm

house 宀 113 [メン・ベン] + luxuriant 丰 [ホウ] + mouth 口 12 [ク・コウ]

This letter has the image of cursing with one's mouth(口) wishing that the house(宀) of one's enemy would be overgrown(丰) with weeds. Although the enemy's house is located far away and beyond the reach of one's hands, its overgrown weeds may indicate that the enemy may have already been damaged.

公害[こうがい] pollution; public nuisance - 76e 163e 被害[ひがい] damage; harm - 149b 163e

Diagram for 木

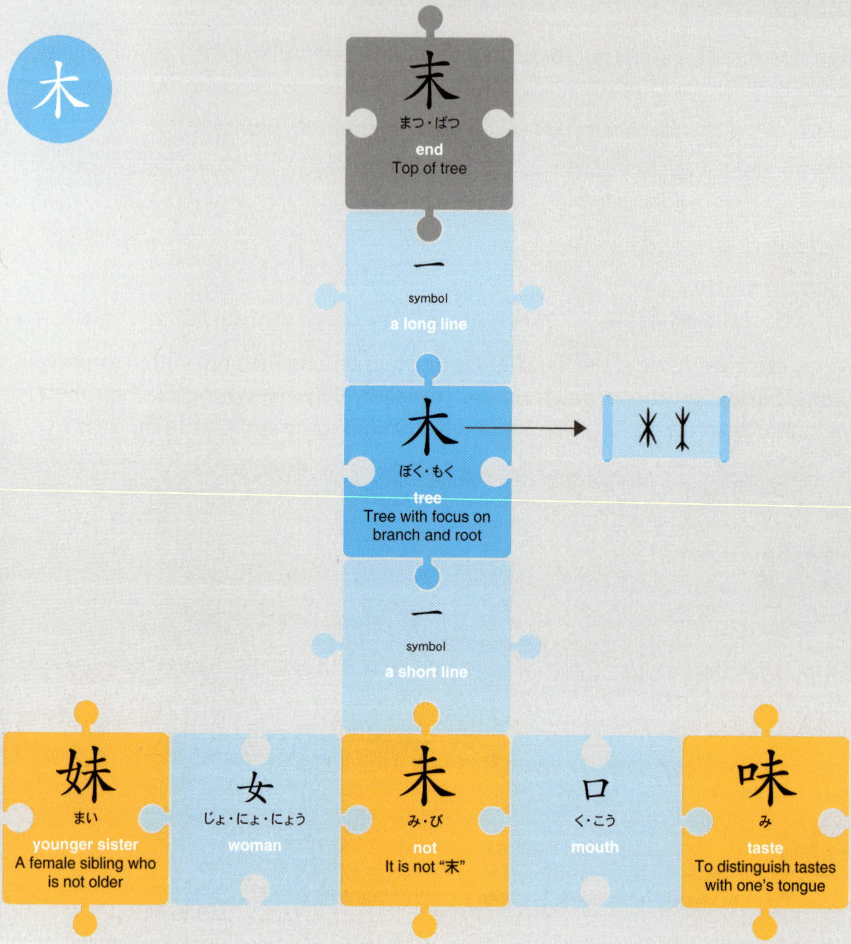

164 **木** ボク・モク き

一 十 才 木

tree; wood

Symbolizes a tree by combining branches(一), root(八), and the stem(丨).

木曜日[もくようび] Thursday -164 141c 170
植木[うえき] garden shrubs; potted plant -8a 164

164a 末

マツ・バツ すえ

一 二 キ 才 末

end

a long line 一 [symbol] + tree 木 [ボク・モク]

A horizontal line(一) is added to the top of "木" to emphasize that the location is the end.

年末[ねんまつ] end of year -96e 164a
週末[しゅうまつ] weekend -122b 164a

164b 未

ミ・ビ いまだ

一 二 キ 才 未

not; un-

a short line 一 [symbol] + tree 木 [ボク・モク]

A shorter horizontal line(一) is added to the top of "木" to emphasize that the growth is not yet finished. The tree is, therefore, not great in size, but rather small trees that are still growing.

未だ[まだ] yet; as yet, up to now
未だ[いまだ] not yet; still, more
未来[みらい] future -164b 110e

164c 味

ミ あじ・あじわう

丨 ㄇ 口 口一 口二 吽 味 味

taste

mouth 口[12] [ク・コウ] + not 未 [ミ・ビ]

A sapling(未) that is still growing is thin and faint. This character means to use one's tongue(口) to distinguish very faint(未) differences in taste.

味わう[あじわう] taste; savor
美味しい[おいしい] delicious; tasty -134c 164c
不味い[まずい] unappetizing; unskillful -173c 164c
意味[いみ] meaning; sense; intention -18b 164c

164d 妹

マイ いもうと

く 女 女 女一 女二 妹 妹 妹

younger sister

woman 女[78] [ジョ・ニョ・ニョウ] + not 未 [ミ・ビ]

Signifies a younger sister who is not(未) above any of the siblings(女).

姉妹[しまい] sisters -103b 164d

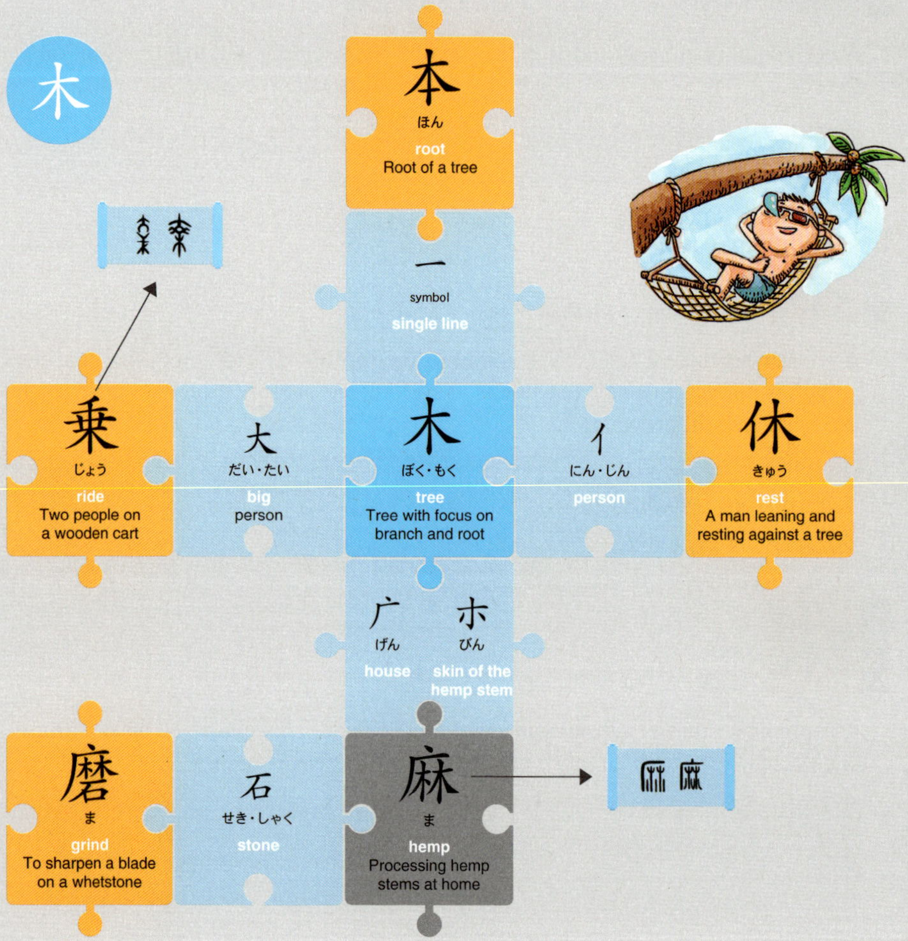

165 本

ホン もと 一 十 才 木 本

root; book; counter for long cylindrical things

tree 木[164] [ボク・モク] + single line 一 [symbol]

A horizontal line(一) is added to the bottom of "木" to emphasize its root. Also signifies book in a sense that a book is the root of knowledge. It's used as a 'counter when counting long and thin objects' such as pencils.

一本[いっぽん] one (long cylindrical things); one book -173 165
何本[なんぼん] how many long cylindrical things -13c 165
絵本[えほん] picture book -158e 165
基本[きほん] foundation; basis -39b 165
本屋[ほんや] bookstore; bookseller -165 74a

165a 休

キュウ やすまる・やすむ・やすめる ノ イ 仁 什 付 休

rest

person イ 52 [ニン・ジン] + tree 木 164 [ボク・モク]

A person(イ) leaning against a tree(木) to rest.

休み[やすみ] rest; relaxation
休む[やすむ] rest; relax; take a rest
休まる[やすまる] feel rested; feel at ease
休める[やすめる] give a rest; suspend
休憩[きゅうけい] rest; recess; interval -165a 20a
休暇[きゅうか] holiday -165a 38e
連休[れんきゅう] consecutive holidays -97e 165a

165b 麻

マ あさ ` 亠 广 广 庁 庁 庄 床 府 麻 麻

hemp

house 广 114 [ゲン] + skin of hemp stem 木→ホ [ビン]

Symbolizes women processing the bark(ホ) of the hemp stems to produce strings in a house(广). Hemp leaves and flowers also contain anesthetic substance, which led to the meaning of numbness.

* Ancient character shows "林"(木) as a shape of the hemp bark(ホ) being taken off.

麻酔[ますい] anesthesia -165b 133b

165c 磨

マ みがく ` 亠 广 广 庁 庁 庄 床 府 麻 麻 麻 磨 磨 磨 磨

grind; polish

hemp 麻 [マ] + stone 石 153a [セキ・シャク]

The meaning of 'grind' came from the image of creating friction(麻) on a whetstone(石) with a dull tool. A hemp(麻) has numbing properties which gives the rubbed area a burning sensation(麻).

磨く[みがく] polish; grind; brush
歯磨(き)[はみがき] brushing one's teeth; tooth powder; toothpaste -21 165c

165d 乗

ジョウ のる・のせる ノ 二 三 乒 乒 乕 乗 乗 乗

ride

tree 禾→木 164 [ボク・モク] + person/big 大 60 [ダイ・タイ]

A person(大) riding on a wooden(木) cart.

* Ancient characters show that "禾 111" is a variation of "木."

乗る[のる] get on (transportation); be loaded
乗せる[のせる] give (someone) a ride; load (up)
乗(り)換え[のりかえ] transfer (trains, buses, etc.); connection -165d 57d
乗客[じょうきゃく] passenger -165d 12c

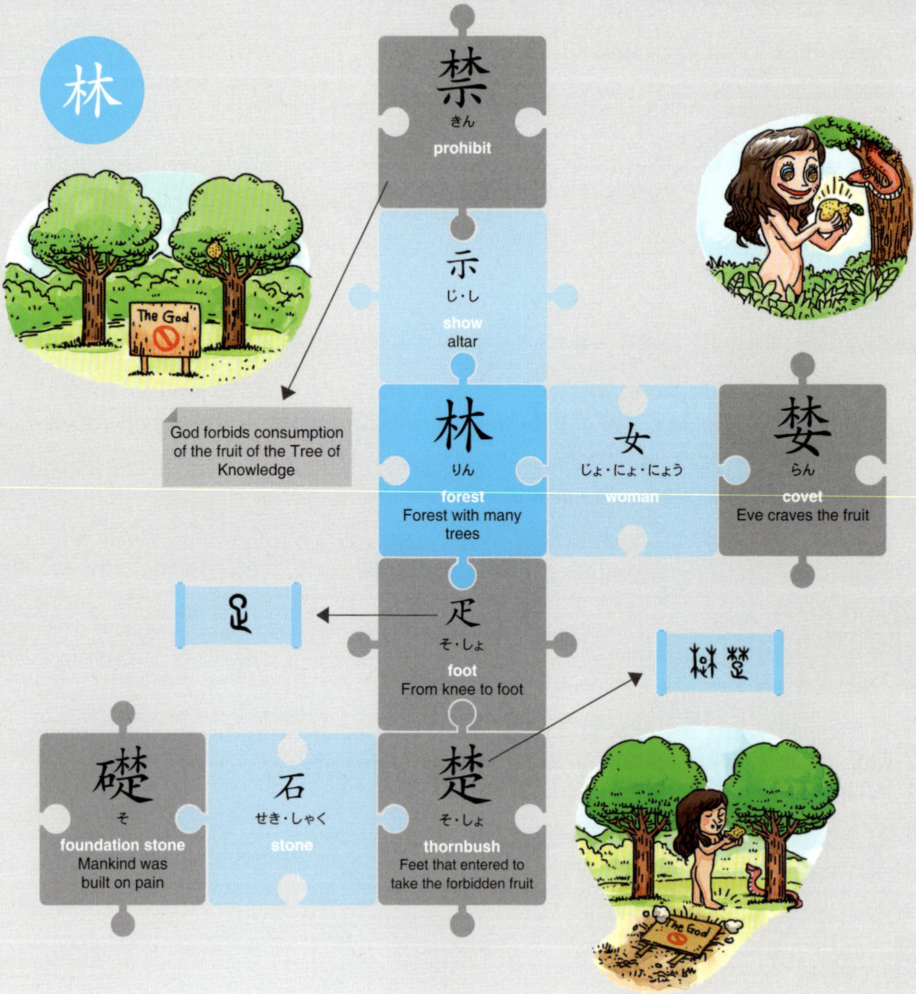

166 林

リン はやし

forest

tree 木[164] [ボク・モク] + tree 木[164] [ボク・モク]

一 十 才 木 木一 村 材 林

Two trees(木) are combined to symbolize forest.

山林[さんりん]forest; forest woods - 153 166

166a 禁

キン

prohibit

tree 木[164] [ボク・モク] + tree 木[164] [ボク・モク] + altar/show 示[99] [ジ・シ]

God(示) forbid Adam and Eve from eating the fruit from the Tree(木) of Knowledge and the Tree(木) of Life.

禁止[きんし] prohibition -166a 44
禁酒[きんしゅ] abstaining (prohibition) from alcohol -166a 133a

166b 婪

ラン

covet

tree 木[164] [ボク・モク] + tree 木[164] [ボク・モク] + woman 女[78] [ジョ・ニョ・ニョウ]

Eve(女) covets the fruit from the Tree(木) of Knowledge and the Tree(木) of Life that God forbade her from touching.

貪婪[たんらん] covetousness; greed

166c 疋

ソ・ショ

foot

It describes the knee to the end of the 'foot.'

* Compare "止[44]" and "足[45]" that also describes feet.

166d 楚

ソ・ショ

thornbush; cane (whip)

tree 木[164] [ボク・モク] + tree 木[164] [ボク・モク] + foot 疋 [ソ・ショ]

The shape of Eve's feet(疋) as she walked between two trees(林) to get to the tree of the knowledge of good and bad(木) from the tree of life(木), something God had clearly ordered her not to touch. Eating the fruit did not improve man's life as the snake said it would. Genesis 3:18 says the ground is full of 'thorns and thistles,' which means it inflicts pain.

苦楚[くそ] suffering; hardship

166e 礎

ソ

foundation stone

stone 石[153a] [セキ・シャク] + thornbush 楚 [ソ・ショ]

The foundation(石) of mankind began with pain(楚) due to someone making the wrong choice.

基礎[きそ] foundation; basis -39b 166e

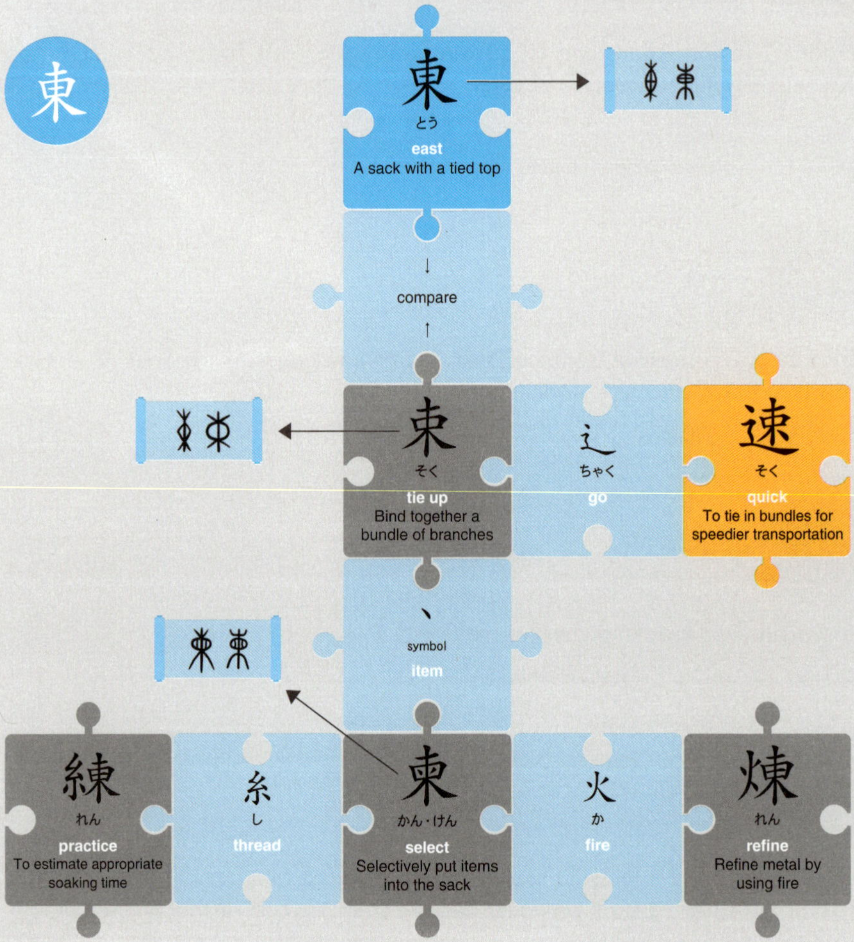

167 東

トウ ひがし

一 ｢ 𠮛 㠯 曰 申 東 東

east

Symbolizes a sack(曰) with its mouth tied(木) up. East, an abstract concept of direction, was something difficult to represent by symbols, and so this character was taken due to its identical pronunciation.

* In China, used together with "west 西[132a] [セイ・サイ]," which was a very common type of pottery that can be seen in any directions, meant "things 東西" in general.

東南アジア[とうなんアジア] Southeast Asia -167 178a
東洋[とうよう] the East; the Orient -167 134d

167a 束

ソク たば

tie up; bundle

tree 木[164] [ボク・モク] + bundle ロ [symbol]

Symbolizes how tree(木) branches are tied and bound(ロ) together for easier transportation.

約束[やくそく] promise; appointment; convention; rule -104a 167a

167b 速

ソク はやい・すみやか

quick

tie up 束 [ソク] + go 辶[49] [チャク]

Scattered objects can be transported(辶) faster and easier when they are tied up(束).

速い[はやい] fast; quick
速やか[すみやか] quick; swift; prompt
速達[そくたつ] express mail; special delivery -167b 49d
速度[そくど] speed; velocity -167b 114b

167c 柬

カン・ケン

select

tie up 束 [ソク] + item 丶 [symbol]

Only necessary items(丶) are selected when packing(束) things into a sack.

167d 煉

レン

refine

fire 火[124] [カ] + select 柬→東 [カン・ケン]

Impurities can be selectively(柬) removed by melting a metal with fire(火) – the process of refining metal.

煉瓦[れんが] brick -167d 64e

167e 練

レン ねる

practice

thread 糸[104] [シ] + select 柬→東 [カン・ケン]

To make silk, the thread(糸) has to be extracted from the silkworm's cocoon, and this is done by soaking them in boiling water. The time has to be estimated(柬) correctly and that requires much practice.

* This character can also be interpreted to mean 'to make the thread soft and whiter.'

練る[ねる] refine; gloss (silk); knead; exercise
練習[れんしゅう] practice; exercise -167e 141a

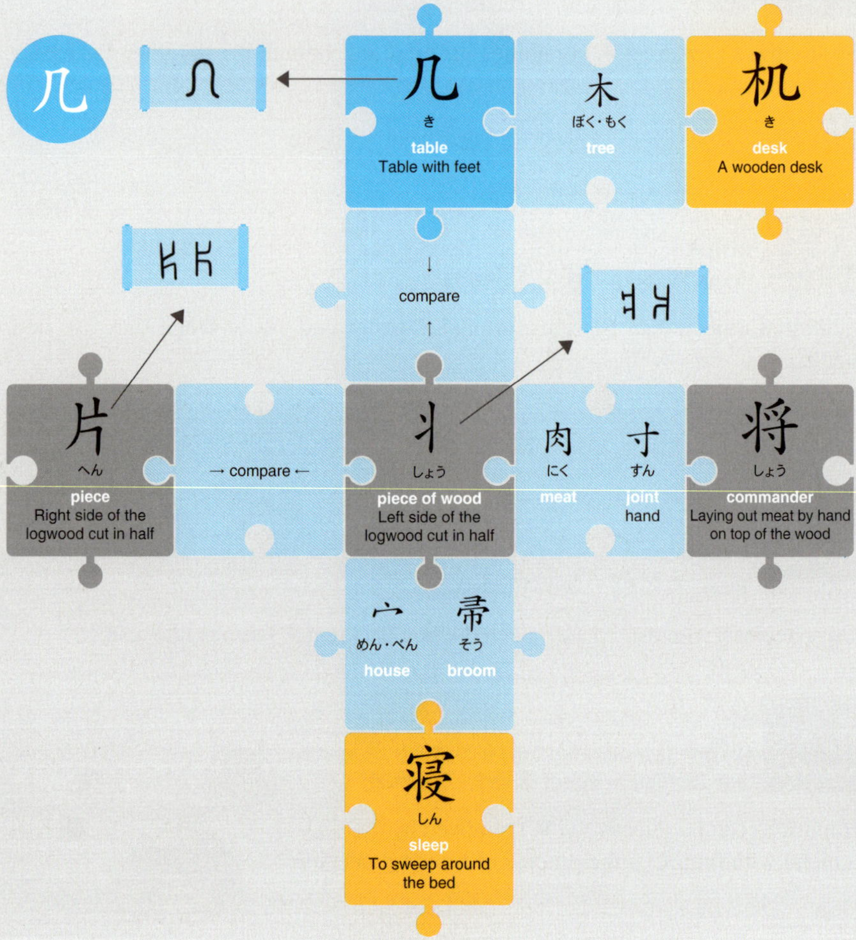

168 几

キ

table

Symbolizes a small table with its feet stretched out.

* Discussed here since the meaning is related with wood.

168a **机**

キ つくえ　一 十 才 木 杉 机

desk

tree 木[164] [ボク・モク] + table 几 [キ]

A desk(几) made with wood(木) is for you to sit at and read or write on.

168b **丬**

ショウ　丶 冫 丬

piece of wood

Symbolizes a flat side of the logwood cut in half, which came to simply mean a piece of wood.

168c **将**

ショウ まさに　丨 丬 丬 丬' 丬ク 丬夕 丬夕 丬夕 将 将

commander; future

piece of wood 丬 [ショウ] + meat ⺼→夕→月→肉[151] [ニク] + hand/joint 寸[35] [スン]

Symbolizes a general laying out of pieces of sacrificial meat(肉) onto a piece of wood(丬) by hand(寸). The sacrificial ceremony was for the blessing of victory in the future – wishing that victory will happen.

* Traditional character(將) shows "夕[172a]" is in fact a simplified form of moon(月[172]), which is a different form of meat.

将に[まさに] just (about to); on the verge
将来[しょうらい] future -168c 110e

168d **寝**

シン ねる　丶 丶 宀 宀 宀 宀 宀 宀 宀 宀 寝 寝 寝

sleep

house 宀[113] [メン・ベン] + piece of wood 丬 [ショウ] + broom 㑒 →帚[103d] [ソウ]

Cleaning the area around your bed(丬) in the house(宀) with a broom(帚) means you are preparing to sleep.

寝る[ねる] sleep; go to bed
寝台[しんだい] bed; berth -168d 76b
昼寝[ひるね] nap (afternoon); siesta -170b 168d

168e **片**

ヘン かた　丿 丿' 片 片

piece

Opposite of "丬," this symbolizes the right side of a log, meaning a thin piece.

片付く[かたづく] be put in order; be solved; be finished -168e 36
片付ける[かたづける] tidy up; put in order; straighten up -168e 36
片道[かたみち] one way -168e 4e

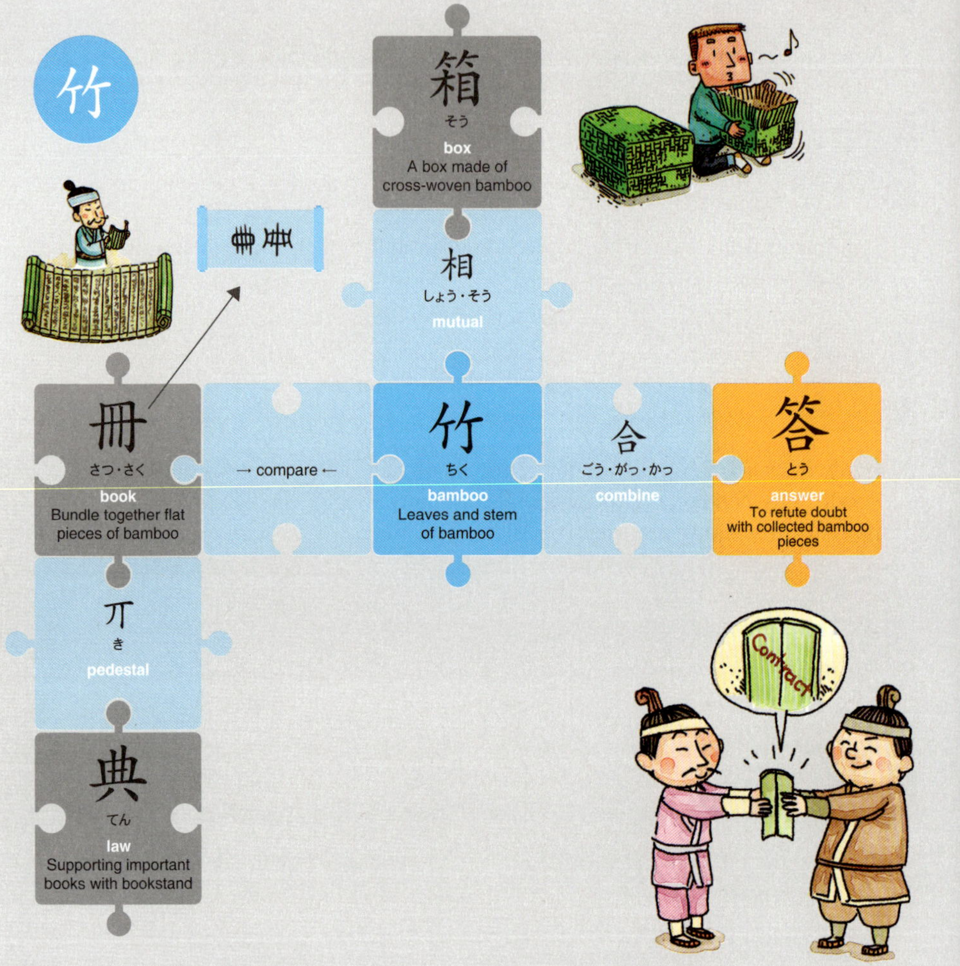

169 竹

チク たけ

bamboo

ノ ⺈ 𠂉 ⺮ 竹 竹

Symbolizes a simplified form of bamboo. Bamboo is used in China as a symbol of longevity due to its long life and evergreen nature, as well as having the same pronunciation as wish "祝[59a] [シュク]."

169a 箱

ソウ はこ ノ ⺈ ⺮ ... 箱

box

bamboo 竹 [チク] + mutual 相[7c] [ショウ・ソウ]

Bamboo is light and easy to bend, but it is not easily breakable. This character portrays a box which is made by processing and cross-weaving(相) the bamboo(竹).

箱船[はこぶね] ark; (i.e. Noah´s ark) -169a 98a

169b 答

トウ こたえ・こたえる ノ ⺈ ⺮ ... 答

answer

bamboo 竹 [チク] + combine 合[54a] [ゴウ・ガッ・カッ]

Before paper was invented, when making a deal, the Chinese wrote on a piece of bamboo(竹) and broke it in half. Later, when they needed to verify facts, they joined the pieces together(合). When there was doubt about the conditions, the bamboo(竹) pieces were joined(合) to get the answer.

答える[こたえる] answer; reply
答(え) [こたえ] answer; solution
問答[もんどう] question and answer -115a 169b

169c 冊

サツ・サク 丨 冂 ⺆ 冊 冊

book

Symbolizes bamboo books(冊), created by bundling together thinly cut plates of bamboo(竹).

* Before paper was invented, bamboo plates(冊) were used to write on.

169d 典

テン 丶 ... 典

law; ceremony

book 曲→冊 [サツ・サク] + pedestal 丌[39] [キ]

Symbolizes placing important books(冊) about national ceremonies or law on bookstands(丌). The meaning of dictionary is also derived from the fact that dictionaries contain all such important writings in one place.

* “丌” symbolizes a supporting stand.

辞典[じてん] dictionary -83d 169d

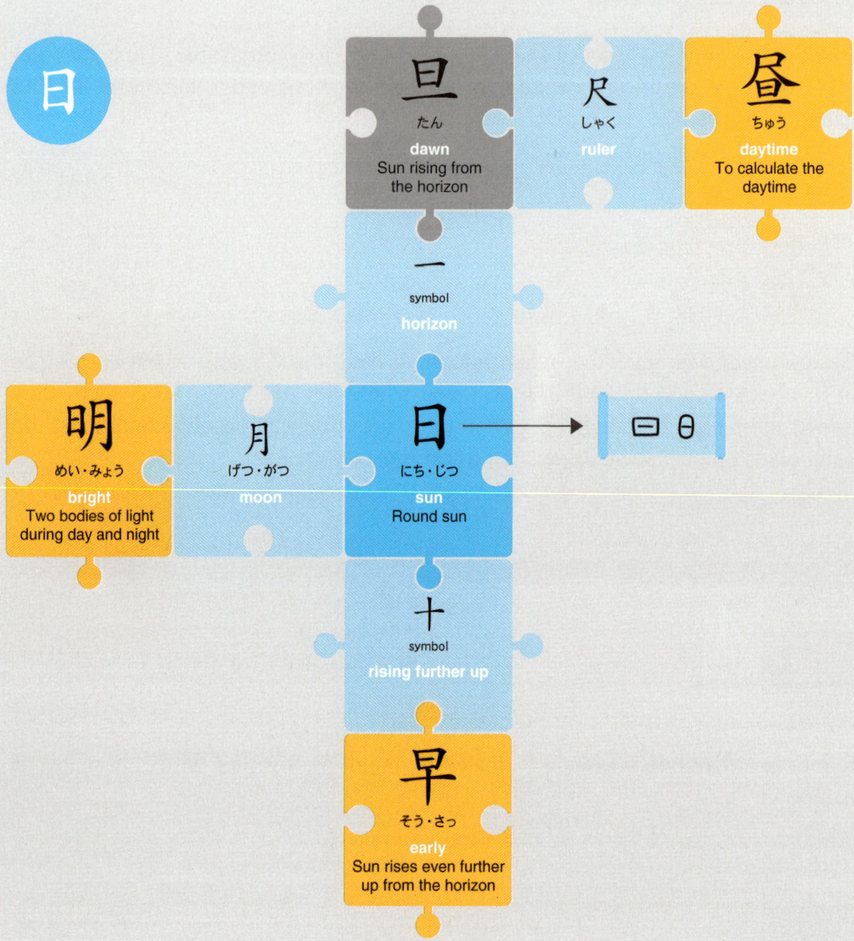

170 日

ニチ・ジツ か ひ

sun; day

丨 冂 月 日

Symbolizes the round sun, also signifying day – a cycle of the sun.

明後日[あさって] day after tomorrow -170d 48c 170
一昨日[おととい] day before yesterday -173 180b 170
今日[きょう] today; this day -54b 170
誕生日[たんじょうび] birthday -50e 162 170
毎日[まいにち] everyday; daily -79a 170
火曜日[かようび] Tuesday -124 141c 170
木曜日[もくようび] Thursday -164 141c 170
土曜日[どようび] Saturday -120 141c 170
明日[あした] tomorrow -170d 170
昨日[きのう] yesterday -180b 170
今日は[こんにちは] good afternoon -54b 170
何日[なんにち] what date; how many days -13c 170
月曜日[げつようび] Monday -172 141c 170
水曜日[すいようび] Wednesday -156 141c 170
金曜日[きんようび] Friday -154 141c 170
日曜日[にちようび] Sunday -170 141c 170

170a 旦

タン

丶 ㄇ 日 日 旦

dawn

sun 日 [ニチ・ジツ] + horizon 一 [symbol]

Dawn arrives as the sun(日) rises just above the horizon(一).

一旦[いったん] once; for a while - 173 170a
元旦[がんたん] New Year's Day - 58a 170a

170b 昼

チュウ ひる

フ コ 尸 尺 尺 尽 吊 昼 昼

daytime; noon

ruler 尺 74b [シャク] + dawn 旦 [タン]

During the day, which is after the sun rises at dawn(旦), time was measured(尺) based on the length of the shadow on the sundial. This character also means 'noon,' the middle of daytime.

* The traditional character(晝) shows someone writing with a brush(聿 33) during the day, after the sun rises at dawn(旦).

昼御飯[ひるごはん] lunch; midday meal - 170b 69c 117b
昼寝[ひるね] nap (afternoon); siesta - 170b 168d

170c 早

ソウ・サッ はやい・はやめる

丶 ㄇ 日 日 旦 早

early

sun 日 [ニチ・ジツ] + rising further up 十 [symbol]

The sun(日) rises further up(十) from dawn "旦," to indicate the start of morning. The day begins every morning, so this character also means 'early.'

早い[はやい] early; fast
早める[はやめる] hasten; quicken
早速[さっそく] at once; immediately - 170c 167b

170d 明

メイ・ミョウ あかす・あかり・あきらか・あかるい・あく・あくる・あける

丨 ㄇ 月 日 日) 明 明 明

bright; next

sun 日 [ニチ・ジツ] + moon 月 172 [ゲツ・ガツ]

Sun(日), light of the day, and the moon(月), light of the night, are combined to signify brightness. Also signifies wishing for a bright future to come next.

明るい[あかるい] bright; light (color)
明く/開く[あく] one's eyes open - 170d / 38d
明(か)す[あかす] disclose; reveal
明(か)り[あかり] light; illumination
明らか[あきらか] clear; obvious
明くる[あくる] next; following
明ける[あける] dawn; become light
明後日[あさって] day after tomorrow - 170d 48c 170
明日[あした] tomorrow - 170d 170

Diagram for 日

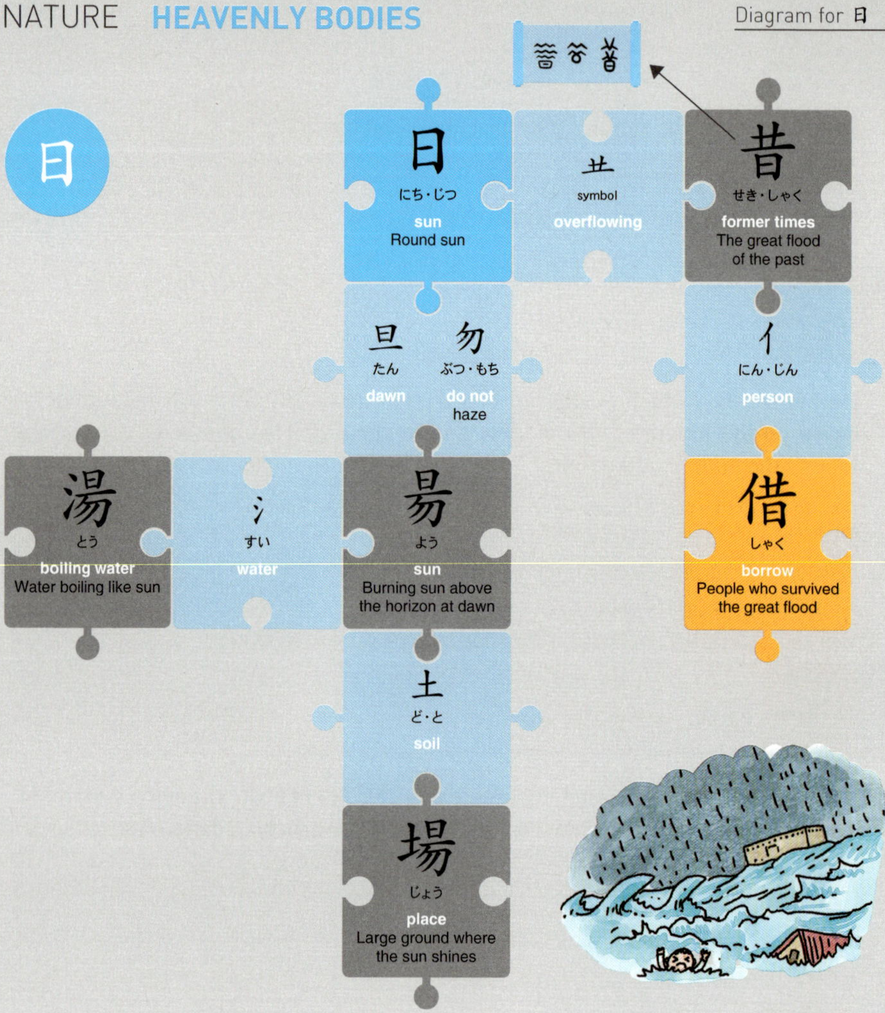

171	昔	セキ・シャク むかし **former times** overflowing 龷 [symbol] + day/sun 日 170 [ジツ・ニチ]	一 十 廾 龷 艹 昔 昔 昔

The largest disaster humans remember in history is the great flood, in which everyone on earth was wiped out except the 8 family members of Noah. It is believed that the character symbolizes the past, or the former days(日) of the flood(龷).

* Ancient inscriptions actually show an overflowing water(龷) and sun(日), representing the particular day.

171a 借

シャク かりる

ノ イ 亻 仁 什 件 供 借 借 借

borrow

person 亻[52] [ニン・ジン] + former times 昔 [セキ・シャク]

The family of Noah, people(亻) who survived the great flood in the past(昔), would not have lived if they had not followed God's words. Their lives are basically borrowed from God.

借りる[かりる] borrow; get a loan
借金[しゃっきん] debt; loan -171a 154

171b 昜

ヨウ

丨 冂 日 日 旦 旦 号 昜 昜

sun

dawn 旦 [タン] + haze/do not 勿[41] [ブツ・モチ]

At dawn(旦), the edge of the just-risen sun burns in a haze(勿).

* When "勿" is used in relation to a non-living thing, it can symbolize haze.

171c 場

ジョウ ば

一 十 土 土 圹 圹 坦 坦 垾 場 場 場

place

soil 土[120] [ド・ト] + sun 昜 [ヨウ]

A large ground(土) with sunlight shining upon it(昜) provides a suitable place for people to gather and hold events.

工場[こうじょう・こうば] factory -155 171c
場合[ばあい] case; situation -54a 171c
場所[ばしょ] place; location -171c 115e
飛行場[ひこうじょう] airfield; airport -128d 48a 171c

171d 湯

トウ ゆ

丶 丶 氵 氵 氾 沪 浔 浔 浔 湯 湯 湯

boiling water

water 氵[157] [スイ] + sun 昜 [ヨウ]

Symbolizes water(氵) boiling like a fierce sun(昜). Also refers to soup in general.

湯気[ゆげ] steam; vapor -171d 158a

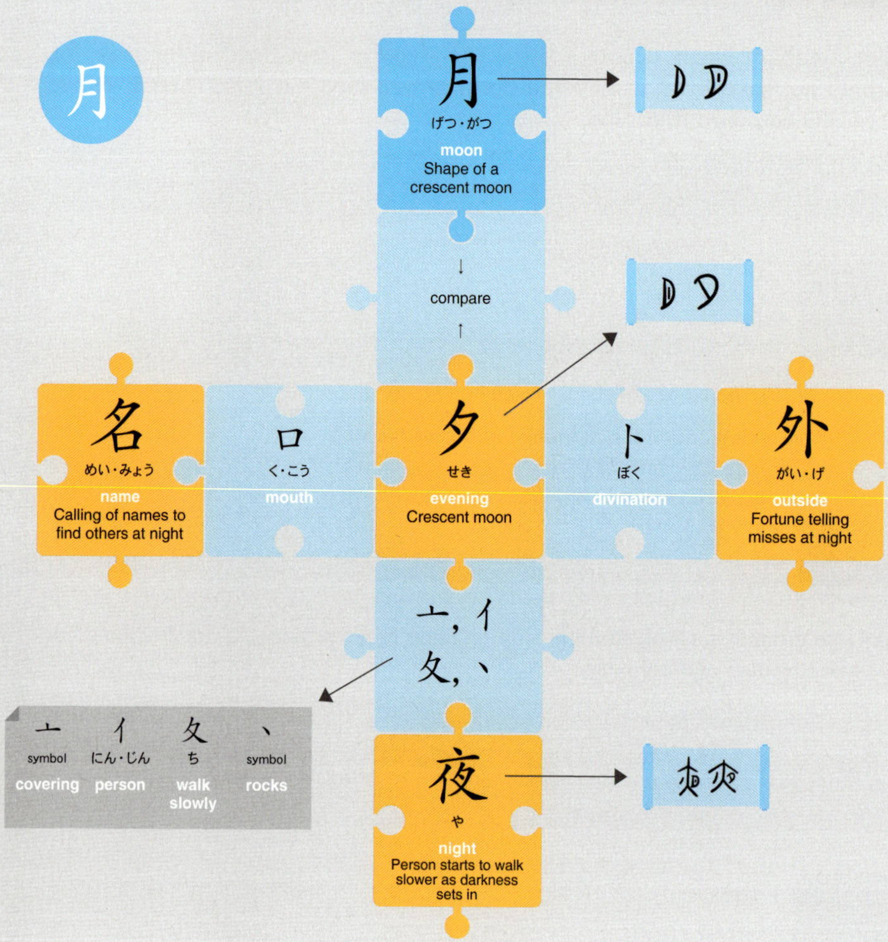

172 月

ゲツ・ガツ つき

moon; month

Symbolizes the shape of the crescent or half moon. When used as part of another more complicated character, this shape can mean 'moon', but also meat(肉 151) or ship(舟 98).

一月[いちがつ] January (Jan.) -173 172	今月[こんげつ] this month -54b 172
月曜日[げつようび] Monday -172 141c 170	先月[せんげつ] last month -58d 172
何月[なんがつ] what month -13c 172	毎月[まいげつ] every month -79a 172
来月[らいげつ] the next month -110e 172	正月[しょうがつ] New Year('s Day); January -45 172

172a 夕

セキ ゆう

丿 ク 夕

evening

Symbolizes the shape of a crescent moon, signifying evening.

夕べ[ゆうべ] evening
夕飯[ゆうはん] evening meal -172a 117b
夕方[ゆうがた] sunset; dusk; evening (time) -172a 126

172b 外

ガイ・ゲ そと・はずす・ほか・はずれる

丿 ク 夕 夕 外

outside

evening 夕 [セキ] + divination 卜 100 [ボク]

Fortune-telling(卜) at night(夕) causes both the teller and the spirits to be exhausted and miss (as in outside of truth) their telling.

外/他[ほか] other (esp. places and things); outside -172b / 68d
外す[はずす] take off; remove; detach
外れる[はずれる] come off; get out of place; slip out
外国人[がいこくじん] foreigner; alien -172b 86a 51
屋外[おくがい] outdoor; open air -74a 172b
例外[れいがい] exception -25c 172b

172c 夜

ヤ よ・よる

丶 亠 广 疒 疒 夜 夜 夜

night

covering 亠 [symbol] + person 亻 52 [ニン・ジン] + walk slowly 夂 46 [チ] + rocks 丶 [symbol]

A person(亻) is walking(夂) slowly in the dark night(亠) to avoid rocks(丶) in the road.

* In the ancient script called 'the bronze inscription,' it is also described as a moon(夕) inside an armpit (丶) of a person(大 60), which is the most dark place in a human body.

今夜[こんや] this evening; tonight -54b 172c
深夜[しんや] dead of night; midnight -157c 172c
夜間[やかん] at night(time) -172c 115b

172d 名

メイ・ミョウ な

丿 ク 夕 夕 名 名

name

evening 夕 [セキ] + mouth 口 12 [ク・コウ]

In the middle of a dark night(夕), one must call(口) out names of others to find or recognize them.

名前[なまえ] name -172d 98b
氏名[しめい] full name; identity -80 172d
姓名[せいめい] full name -162b 172d
有名[ゆうめい] famous; well-known -34b 172d

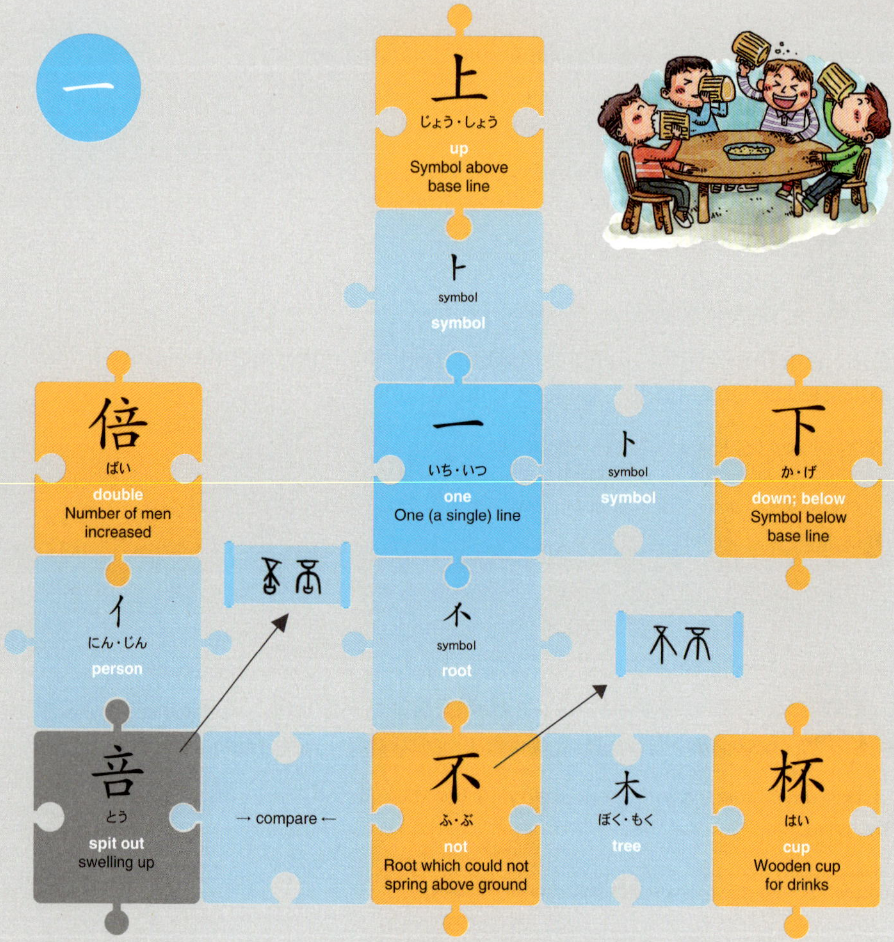

173 一

イチ・イツ　ひと・ひとつ

one; 1

One line is stroked to represent number one.

一つ[ひとつ] one; 1; the same; just
一日[ついたち] first day; a day -173 170
一昨日[おととい] day before yesterday -173 180b 170
一昨年[おととし] year before last -173 180b 96e
一寸[ちょっと] some; a little; a few -173 35

173a 上

ジョウ・ショウ　あがる・あげる・うえ・うわ・かみ　　丨 ⺊ 上

up; above

symbol ⺊ [symbol] + base line 一 [symbol]

A symbol(⺊) above a line serving as a base(一). It can be used differently as a verb.

上がる[あがる] go up; rise; climb
上げる[あげる] raise; increase
上着[うわぎ] coat; outerwear -173a 7b
上手[じょうず] excellent skill, skillful; expert -173a 28

173b **下**

カ・ゲ おりる・くださる・くだる・さがる・さげる・した・しも

一 丅 下

down; below

base line 一 [symbol] + symbol ⺊ [symbol]

A symbol(⺊) below a line serving as a base(一). Opposite of "上, " and can be used differently as verb.

下りる[おりる] go down; come down
下さる[くださる] (honorific) give, confer
下る[くだる] go down; descend
下がる[さがる] come down; hang down
下げる[さげる] lower; bring down
貴方/貴下[あなた] (honorific) you -145c 126 / 145c 173b
靴下[くつした] socks 149d 173b
地下鉄[ちかてつ] subway -68b 173b 154d
下手[へた] unskillful; poor (at); clumsy -173b 28

173c **不**

フ・ブ

一 フ 不 不

not

earth 一 [symbol] + root 朩 [symbol]

Root(朩) of plants will not spring above the ground(一). Used as negation.

* "不" is shown here since "一" is the radical for this character.

不味い[まずい] unappetizing; unskillful -173c 164c
不吉[ふきつ] bad luck; ominous -173c 84a
不断[ふだん] constancy; ceaselessness; continuity -173c 94d
不便[ふべん] inconvenience; inexpediency -173c 31d

173d **杯**

ハイ さかずき

一 十 オ 木 木 杉 杯 杯

cup

tree 木[164] [ボク・モク] + not 不 [フ・ブ]

The meaning of drinking cup (for alcohol) is derived from wooden(木) cups used by people with "不" added as a pronunciation guide.

* Remember how Chinese made toasts: when they toast(干[96] 杯), they empty(不) the glass and show the bottom of the glass(木).

一杯[いっぱい] amount necessary to fill a container; a drink; full -173 173d
何杯[なんばい] how many cups -13c 173d

173e **倍**

バイ

ノ イ イ 仁 仁 什 位 倍 倍 倍

double; times

person 亻[52] [ニン・ジン] + swelling up/spit out 咅 [トウ]

This character means 'double or times' because it signifies that the number of people (亻) have increased(咅).

* Unlike "不," "咅" shows bumps(口) of raised soil because of shoots sprouting up(立). Refer to "部[116d]."

一倍[いちばい] one share; double -173 173e
何倍[なんばい] how many times; several times -13c 173e
二倍[にばい] double; twice -176 173e

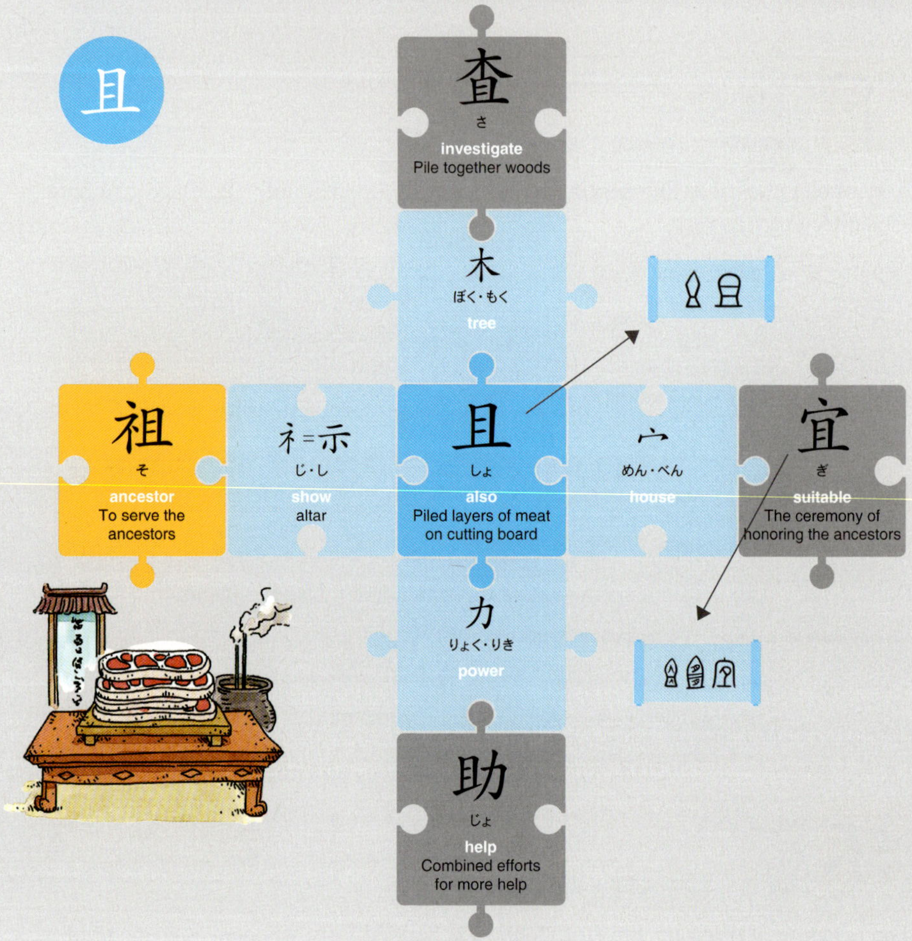

174 且

ショ かつ

丨 冂 月 月 且

also

Meat is piled in layers on a cutting board(一) for the honoring of the ancestors. Since the layers of meat are laid one after the other, meaning of ‘and’ is derived from here.

* “且” is shown here since “一” is the radical for this character.

且つ[かつ] also; at the same time; moreover

174a 査

一 十 才 木 木 杏 杏 杳 査

サ

investigate

tree 木[164] [ボク・モク] + cutting board/also 且 [ショ]

One needs to investigate whether pieces of wood(木) are straight enough to be piled or stacked together – as in the meat on the cutting board(且) – to make a raft of timber.

* The ancient script of "査" has its original meaning of 'timber (or log) raft.'

審査[しんさ] judging; inspection; examination -142c 174a
検査[けんさ] inspection; examination -55a 174a
調査[ちょうさ] investigation; examination -122c 174a

174b 宜

丶 丶 宀 宀 宀 宜 宜 宜

ギ よろしい

suitable

house 宀[113] [メン・ベン] + cutting board/also 且 [ショ]

Signifies an act of honoring the ancestors in a home(宀), which is considered appropriate and suitable, with the meat piled on a cutting board(且).

宜しい[よろしい] all right; well; good
便宜[べんぎ] convenience -31d 174b

174c 助

丨 冂 月 月 且 町 助

ジョ たすかる・たすける

help

cutting board/also 且 [ショ] + power 力[125] [リョク・リキ]

Meaning of to help is derived, as people pile together their efforts(力), like the meat on the cutting board(且).

助かる[たすかる] be helped; be saved; be rescued
助ける[たすける] help; save; rescue
助言[じょげん] advice -174c 17
助手[じょしゅ] assistant -174c 28

174d 祖

丶 ラ 才 ネ 礻 初 初 祖 祖

ソ

ancestor

altar/show ネ=示[99] [ジ・シ] + cutting board/also 且 [ショ]

To place a cutting board(且) full of meat on the altar(ネ) as an offering to one's ancestors.

お祖父さん[おじいさん] (honorific or a friendly) grandfather -174d 30a
お祖母さん[おばあさん] (honorific or a friendly) grandmother -174d 79
祖父[そふ] grandfather -174d 30a
祖母[そぼ] grandmother -174d 79

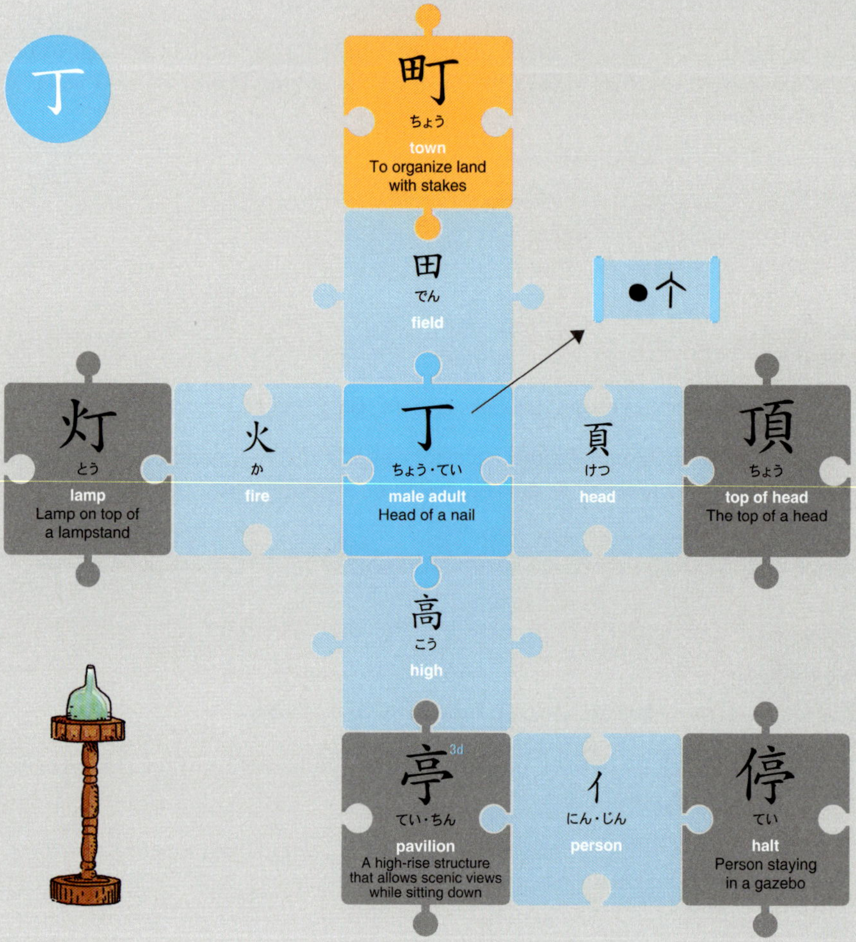

175 丁

チョウ・テイ

male adult

一 丁

Emphasizes the head(一) of a nail(亅). It came to mean an adult 'male.' Just as a nail with a large head is able to use more power, an adult male is able to use all his strength(亅) due to his fully grown head(一).

* "丁" is shown here since "一" is the radical for this character.

175a 町

チョウ　まち

town; block; street

field 田 [122] [デン] + nail/male adult 丁 [チョウ・テイ]

Farmland(田) was separated into individual plots with ridges between them. In an area, town, or block, stakes(丁) were used as markings.

下町[したまち] downtown; business quarters - 173b 175a

175b 頂

チョウ　いただき・いただく

top of head

nail/male adult 丁 [チョウ・テイ] + head 頁 [4] [ケツ]

The crown is the topmost part of one's head(頁) and is indicated by adding 'the head of a nail(丁)' to the character.

頂く[いただく] put on the head; (honorific) receive
絶頂[ぜっちょう] summit; peak; climax - 75a 175b
頂点[ちょうてん] peak; summit; the top - 175b 100c
頂上[ちょうじょう] top; summit - 175b 173a

175c 停

テイ

halt

person 亻[ニン・ジン] + pavilion 亭 [3d] [テイ・チン]

A traveler(亻) stops at a gazebo(亭) to take a rest and admire the view.

* The pronunciation comes from "亭." It depicts a pillar(丁) which has been built with a tall and elevated(高 [3]) posts in a spot of good view.

停車[ていしゃ] stopping (of a vehicle) - 175c 97
停電[ていでん] power failure - 175c 159c
バス停[バスてい] bus stop

175d 灯

トウ

lamp

fire 火 [124] [カ] + lamp stand/male adult 丁 [チョウ・テイ]

Signifies a lamp fire(火) burning on top of a lampstand(丁).

* Traditional character(燈) shows fire(火) raised up high(登112e) – thus "丁" can be said to represent a lampstand.

灯台[とうだい] lighthouse; oil-lamp stand - 175d 76b
電灯[でんとう] electric light; lamp - 159c 175d

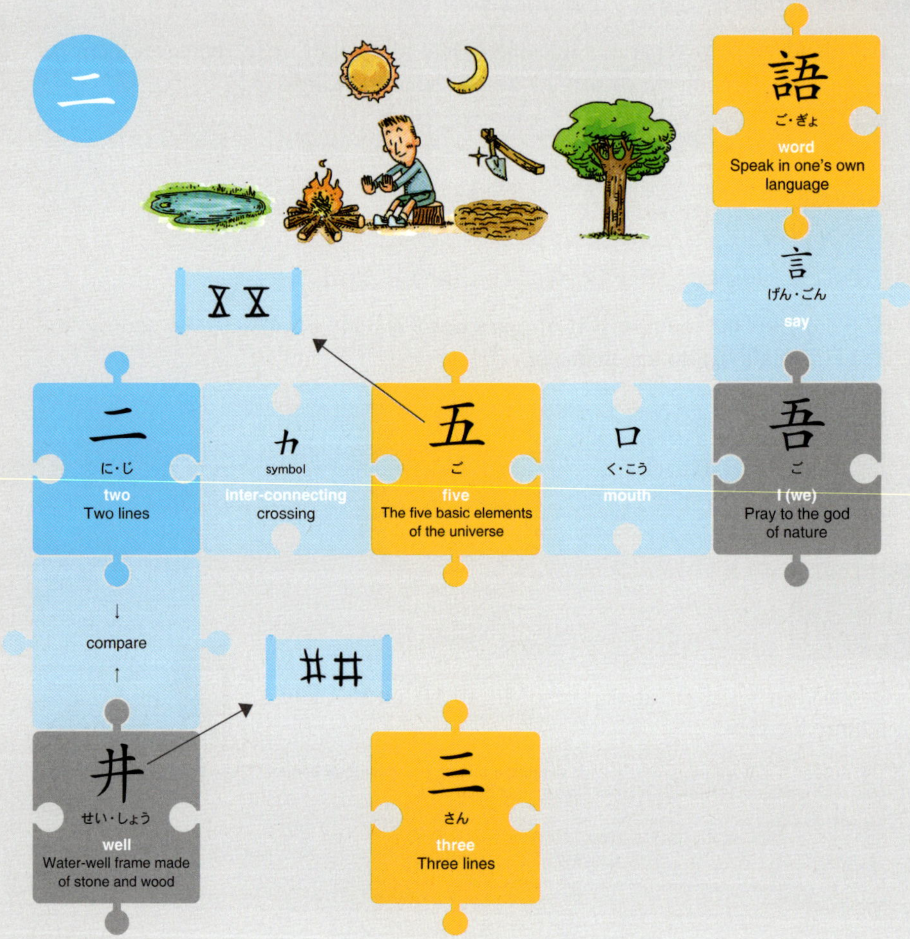

176 **二**

ニ・ジ ふたり

two; 2

Two lines are stroked horizontally to signify number two.

二つ[ふたつ] two; 2
二十歳[はたち] 20 years old; twenty -176 178 44b
二十日[はつか] 20th day; twenty days -176 178 170

176a 五

ゴ いつつ

一 丅 五 五

five; 5

heaven and earth 二 [symbol] + crossing/inter-connecting ㄌ [symbol]

The two horizontal lines(二) signifying heaven and earth is inter-connected(ㄌ) to represent the universe. It was believed that the universe contained five basic elements.

* In the cosmic dual forces and the five elements of the Chinese cosmology, there are five basic natural elements that maintain the natural world: water(水), fire(火), wood(木), metal(金), and earth(土).

五つ[いつつ] five; 5

176b 吾

ゴ われ

一 丅 五 五 吾 吾 吾

I; we

five 五 [ゴ] + mouth ロ 12 [ク・コウ]

Signifies an act of wishing(ロ) for the well-being of myself (I) or ourselves (we) to the god of nature who governs the five(五) basic elements of nature.

吾が/我が[わが] my; our - 176b / 91a

176c 語

ゴ・ギョ かたる

丶 亠 亠 言 言 言 言 言 訂 訂 語 語 語 語

word; language

say 言 17 [ゲン・ゴン] + I (me) 吾 [ゴ]

Signifies an act of prayer(言) to a deity in one's own(吾) language.

語る[かたる] tell; talk
英語[えいご] English - 61c 176c
敬語[けいご] honorific; honorific language - 40d 176c

176d 井

セイ・ショウ

一 二 ナ 井

well

Signifies the frame of a waterwell, created by weaving together stone or wood materials and digging downward.

* "井" is shown here since "二" is the radical for this character.

天井[てんじょう] ceiling - 60b 176d

176e 三

サン みっつ

一 二 三

three; 3

Three strokes of lines are used to represent number three.

三つ[みっつ] three; 3

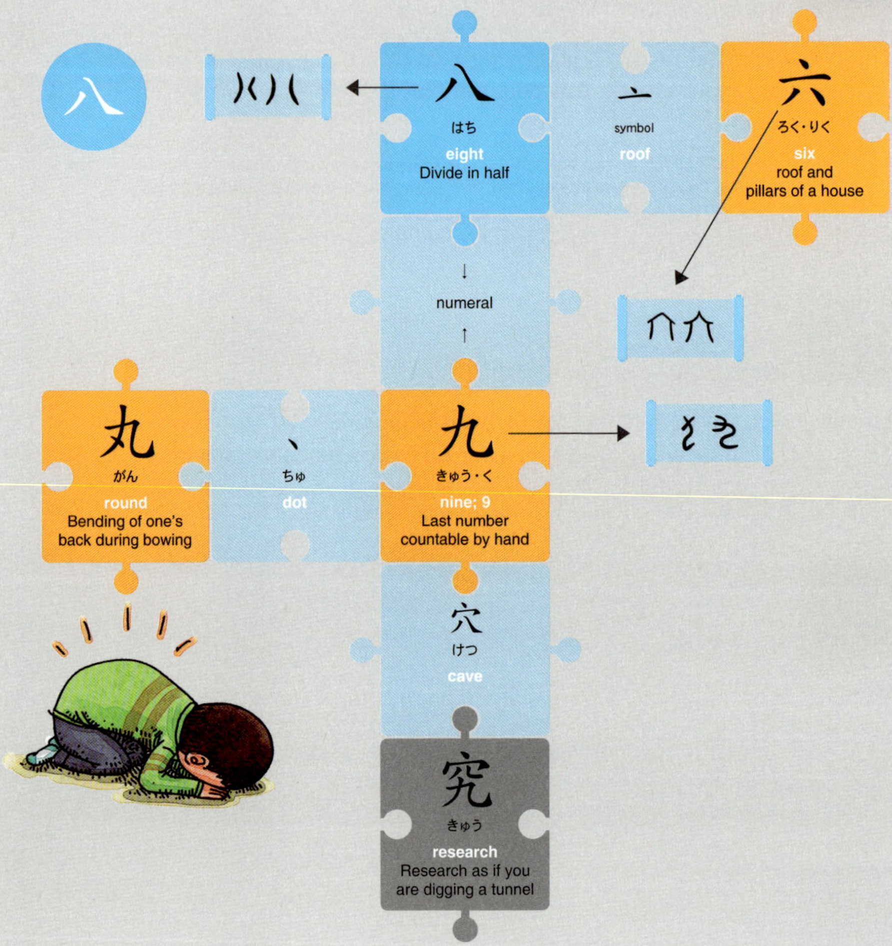

177 **八** ハチ やっつ ノ 八

eight; 8

Shaped as two matching lines in opposite directions, means 'to divide.' Currently means number eight, derived from a number that can be continuously divided(八).

* When written upside down(ソ), it signifies 'heavenly blessing.'

八つ[やっつ] eight; 8
八百屋[やおや] vegetable shop; greengrocer -177 106a 74a

177a **六**

ロク・リク　むっつ

丶 亠 六 六

six; 6

Originally meant a shape of a house with a roof(亠) and pillars(八), but later became to mean the number six.

* The ancient form shows that the picture of the roof(宀[113]) changed to the head(亠).

六つ[むっつ] six; 6

177b **九**

キュウ・ク　ここのつ

丿 九

nine; 9

Signifies number nine by representing the edge of the hand(ナ[34]) in bent(乚) form, meaning the last(乚) decimal number countable by hand.

九つ[ここのつ] nine; 9

177c **究**

キュウ

丶 丶 宀 宀 穴 究 究

research

cave 穴[113a] [ケツ] + nine 九 [キュウ・ク]

Signifies research or investigation, as in digging a deep(九) hole(穴).

* Nine "九" being the last digit in the decimal system reinforces the meaning of depth.

研究[けんきゅう] study; research - 153b 177c

177d **丸**

ガン　まる・まるい・まるめる

丿 九 丸

round

When bowing, a person's back takes a round shape like 'an egg or a pellet.'

* Has no relation to the character "九," meaning number nine.

丸い[まるい] round; spherical
丸める[まるめる] make round; roll up

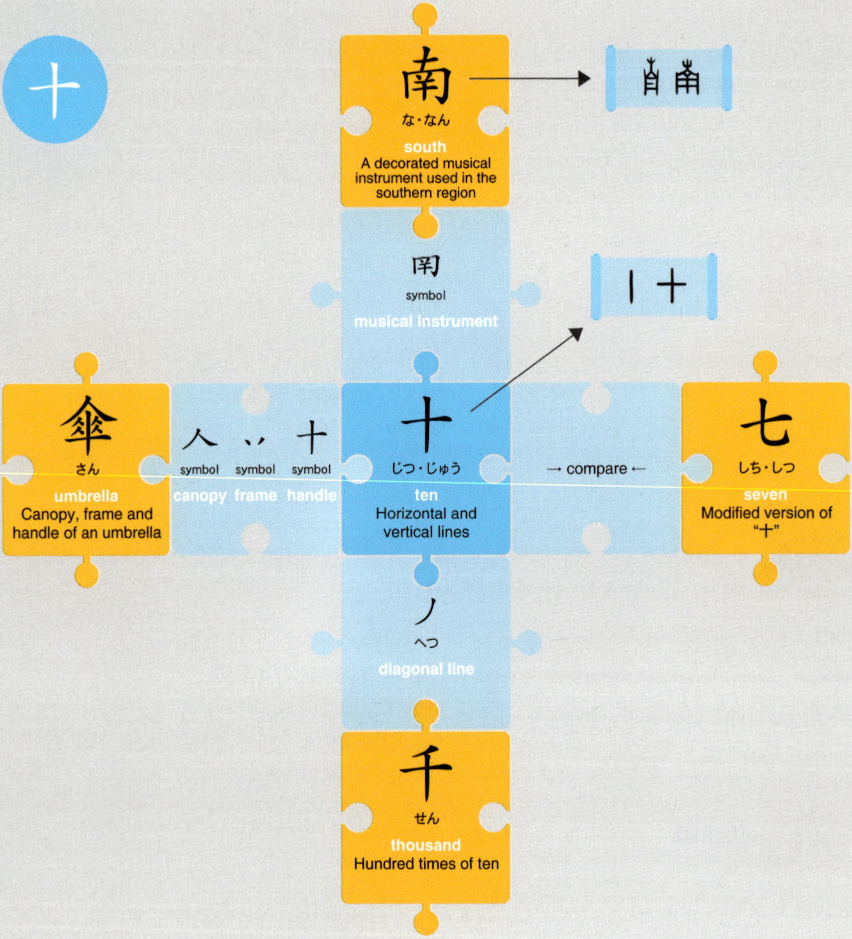

178 **十**

ジツ・ジュウ　とお

一 十

ten; 10

The number ten was originally written as a single vertical line(|) but later added a horizontal line(一) to reduce confusion.

十分[じゅうぶん] plenty; enough -178 95a

178a **南**

ナ・ナン みなみ 一 十 𠂇 冂 冂 冇 冇 南 南

south

hanger decorations 十 [symbol] + musical instrument 用 [symbol]

A clear-sounding percussion instrument(用) with hanging decorations(十) used in southern China, which eventually became to mean south.

* Certain tribes in southern China still have a traditional instrument called "南任."

南米[なんべい] South America -178a 110
南北[なんぼく] south and north -178a 73
東南アジア[とうなんアジア] Southeast Asia -167 178a

178b **七**

シチ・シツ なな・ななつ 一 七

seven; 7

Lower part of "ten 十" is bent to represent number seven, a little less than ten.

七つ[ななつ] seven; 7

178c **千**

セン ち 丿 二 千

thousand

diagonal line 丿 179e [ヘツ] + ten 十 [ジツ・ジュウ]

Number ten "十" is given an additional line(丿) to signify a hundred times of itself – one thousand.

* "丿" does not have a specific definition and can be adapted to many different definitions.

178d **傘**

サン かさ 丿 𠆢 人 仒 仒 仒 仒 仒 仒 伞 傘 傘

umbrella

canopy 𠆢 [symbol] + frame 仌仌[symbol] + handle 十 [symbol]

This character reflects the image of an unfolded umbrella which consists of a canopy(𠆢), frame(仌仌) and a handle(十).

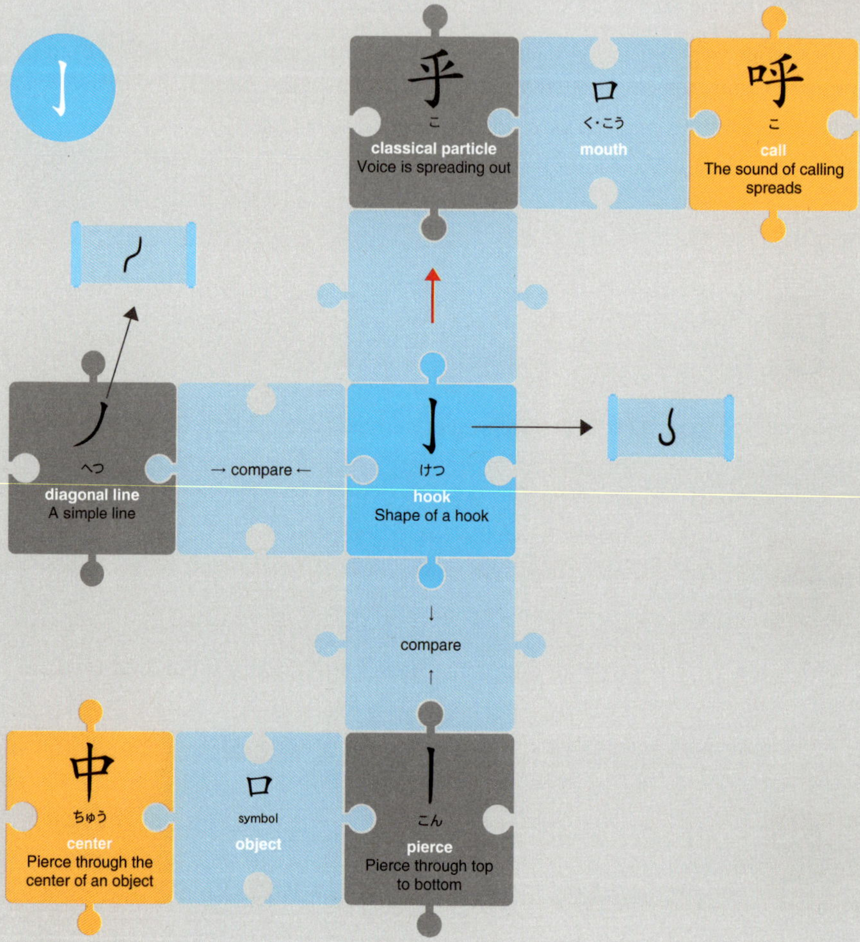

179 亅

ケツ

hook

It is called a hook due to its bent shape at the end. It can only be used when it's combined with other characters.

179a 乎

コ

classical particle

This character depicts the image of calling somebody, when a voice starts to originate out of the throat and spreads out. It is used at the end of a sentence to express 'interrogative or exclamatory particle.'

* Compare with the notes for "汚157d."

179b 呼

コ よぶ

call

mouth 口12 [ク・コウ] + suffix 乎 [コ]

"乎" is a suffix indicating the sound of calling someone loudly, so the character for mouth(口) was added to accentuate its original meaning.

呼ぶ[よぶ] call out
呼吸[こきゅう] breathing; breath -179b 56b

179c 丨

コン

pierce

Signifies action of striking/piercing vertically from top to bottom.

179d 中

チュウ なか

center

object 口 [symbol] + pierce 丨 [コン]

This character describes an object(口) which is pierced(丨) in the middle or the center. It also means that China is the center of the world.

御中[おなか] abdomen; belly; stomach -69c 179d
集中[しゅうちゅう] concentration -140a 179d
中古[ちゅうこ] used article; secondhand article -179d 15

179e 丿

ヘツ

diagonal line

A shape of a simple line stroked from the upper right to the lower left. Can be interpreted in many different ways without a solid definition.

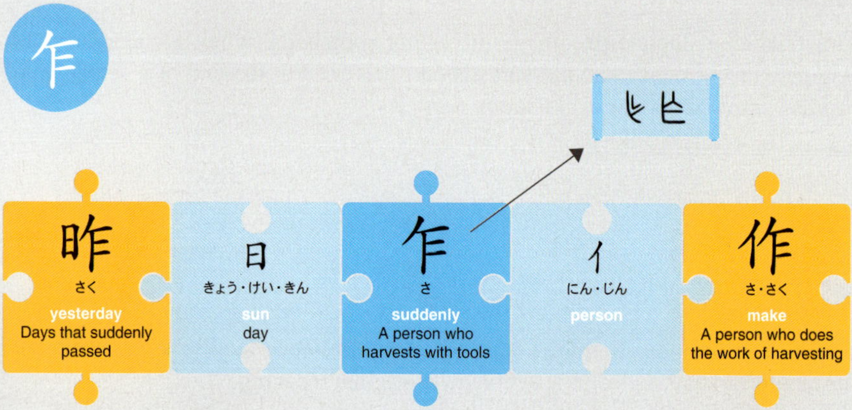

180 乍

サ ながら

ノ 𠂉 𠂉 乍 乍

suddenly

Signifies a person(𠂉→人[51]) harvesting the crops using tools(乍). Crops are harvested suddenly, after waiting a year to grow.

* The reason for introducing "乍" here is due to the fact "丿[179e]" is a radical in this case.

乍ら[ながら] while

180a 作

サ・サク つくる

ノ 亻 亻 作 作 作 作

make

person 亻[52] [ニン・ジン] + suddenly 乍 [サ]

The character "乍," which signifies a person harvesting with tools, is used to mean 'sudden'; by adding the subject person(亻), it reinforces the meaning of to do.

作る[つくる] make; produce
作文[さくぶん] writing; composition -180a 105
作す/為す[なす] do; perform -180a / 136d

180b 昨

サク

丨 ㄇ 日 日 日' 昨 昨 昨 昨

yesterday

day/sun 日[170] [ジツ・ニチ] + suddenly 乍 [サ]

As the old saying goes, time flies – and it really does feel fast. Meaning of yesterday is formed from the day(日) that passed all of a sudden(乍).

一昨年[おととし] year before last -173 180b 96e
一昨日[おととい] day before yesterday -173 180b 170
昨日[きのう] yesterday -180b 170

Diagram for 丶

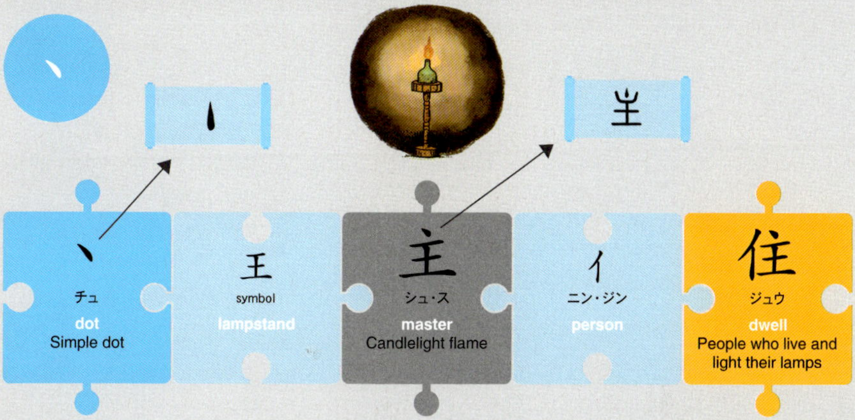

181 丶

チュ

dot

丶

A simple dot. Used often as a symbol of a specific character in the simplification process of traditional characters into simplified versions.

181a 主

シュ・ス　おも・ぬし

丶 亠 亍 干 主

master

flame 丶 [symbol] + lampstand 王 [symbol]

Signifies a flame(丶) that burns on top of the lampstand(王), derived to mean the master, as the flame is the center of all objects and beings in darkness.

* The character may look identical to the character "king 王[86] [オウ]," but it has no relation to any meaning of king or royalty.

主に[おもに] mostly; mainly	君主[くんしゅ] ruler; monarch; sovereign - 32e 181a
主義[しゅぎ] principle; belief - 181a 91b	亭主[ていしゅ] house owner; husband - 3d 181a

181b 住

ジュウ　すむ

丿 亻 亻 仁 什 住 住

dwell

person 亻[52] [ニン・ジン] + lamp/master 主 [シュ・ス]

Meaning of to reside/to live is formed by the people(亻) or residents who light their lamps(主) at night.

住む[すむ] dwell; live; inhabit	住居[じゅうきょ] dwelling; residence; living - 181b 15e

Diagram for 小

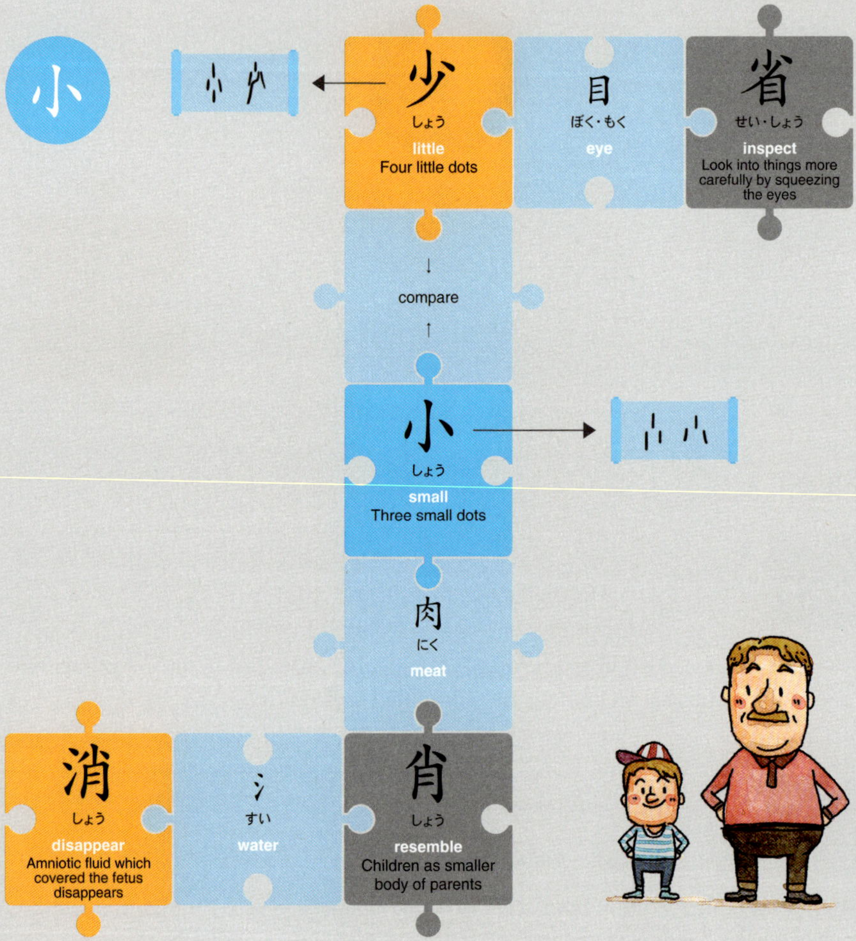

182 **小**

シヨウ お・こ・ちいさい

亅 小 小

small

Signifies a group of three small dots(丶).

小さい[ちいさい] small; little
小さな[ちいさな] small; little
小母さん[おばさん] (honorific) old lady, madam -182 79
小父さん[おじさん] (honorific) uncle, old man, mister -182 30a
小包[こづつみ] package; parcel -182 75a

182a 少

シヨウ すくない・すこし 丨 小 小 少

little

Signifies a group of four little dots(丶).

少ない[すくない] little; few; young
少し[すこし] a little; a few; a bit
少女[しょうじょ]] girl; young lady -182a 78
少年[しょうねん] boy; youth -182a 96e
多少[たしょう] more or less; somewhat; a little -151b 182a

182b 省

セイ・ショウ かえりみる・はぶく 丨 小 小 少 少 省 省 省 省

inspect; economize

little 少 [ショウ] + eye 目[7] [ボク・モク]

This signifies the act of bringing objects into focus – in order to have a better, more careful look – by squeezing(少) the eyes(目). One can then economize by looking into things more carefully.

* In fact, when you squeeze(少) your eyes(目) to focus on something distant, the eyebrows will force the iris to close down, increasing the field of depth and helping you to see better.

省みる[かえりみる] look back (at the past); reflect on the past
省く[はぶく] omit; leave out
反省[はんせい] self-reflection, self-examination -117a 182b

182c 肖

ショウ 丨 丨丶 丨丶 肖 肖 肖 肖

resemble

small ⺌→小 [ショウ] + meat 月→肉[151] [ニク]

A child is described as a small(小) body(肉) – signifying the resemblance with his/her parents.

肖る[にる]resemble; look like

182d 消

ショウ けす・きえる 丶 丶 氵 氵 氵 氵 氵 消 消 消

disappear

water 氵[157] [スイ] + resemble 肖 [ショウ]

A child who takes after his/her parents(肖) is born when the amniotic fluid (氵) bursts and disappears. It also contains the dual meaning of the continuously changing 'news,' as the fetal fluid is continuosly formed and then disappears in a life cycle of a human child.

消す[けす] extinguish, blow out, switch off
消える[きえる] be extinguished; disappear
消化[しょうか] digestion -182d 52a
消息[しょうそく] news -182d 6b

A concluding remark

The fact that you are reading this probably means that you have an interest in kanji and a knowledge that almost rivals that of a scholar. Now is the time to reveal how kanji was made and share the purpose of this book. Doing so will help you approach the thousands of new kanji you will come across with an objective but inquisitive mind.

How the Chinese characters were made.

Pictograms: The origin of Chinese characters are the pictograms of items the ancient Chinese used to communicate with. A tree's branches(一), roots(八), and trunk(丨) became the character "tree 木 [ボク・モク]." Once you know their origins, the 300 odd Chinese pictograms shouldn't be so hard to memorize.

Codes: Codes were used to convey meanings that were difficult to do so with shapes. For example, a long horizontal stroke(一) on top of a tree(木) to emphasize the end of something came to mean "end 末 [マツ・バツ]." There are about 130 such characters. If you remember they are made based on pictograms, these also should be easy to remember.

Ideograms: As time passed, pictograms and codes were combined to make new characters. For example, a person(亻) leaning against a tree(木) means "rest 休 [キュウ]." There are about 1,000 such ideograms. Once you know the pictograms and codes these characters are based on, they shouldn't be such a threat.

Combined characters: The meanings of ideograms can be memorized based on the characters they are composed of, but remembering the pronunciation is a whole new matter. Therefore, the ancient Chinese made new characters by borrowing the meaning of one and the pronunciation of another and combining them. For example, they combined "clothes 衤 [イ・エ]" and "end 末 [マツ・バツ]" to make "socks 袜 [バツ・マチ]." About 97% of all Chinese characters were made this way.

In addition to the above-mentioned characters, there are 'derivative cognates (reciprocal meaning)' and 'rebus (or phonetic loan or borrowed characters).' They have, however, slight variations in meaning or pronunciation, and therefore shouldn't need much effort to remember.

Basic characters as the backbone

We can tell that all ideograms, combined characters, 'derivative cognates (reciprocal meaning)' and 'rebus (or phonetic loan or borrowed character)' were made with pictograms and codes. So if we know all the characters that are pictograms and codes, then we can easily deduce the meaning, which is a unique quality of Chinese characters.

Xu Shen(许慎, 30 AD~124), a Han Dynasty scholar and the author of the first Chinese language dictionary Shuowen Jiezi(说文解字), selected 540 basic characters. Scholars from countries that still use Chinese characters, namely China, Korea, and Japan, selected 200~214 of them and called them 'radicals.' However, there are some basic characters that are not radicals, so including those, there are about 250 basic characters in the Chinese language.

That's it. All languages have a basic form, and Chinese is, of course, no exception. English has the 26-letter alphabet while Korean has 24 vowels and consonants and Japanese has 50 letters. Remember those basics and you can learn the language. 250 basic Chinese characters sounds daunting, but it shouldn't be. English, Korean, and Japanese are phonetic languages, so just because you can read and write doesn't mean you understand. But Chinese characters are ideograms with meaning, and with memorizing comes understanding.

Most Chinese characters are combined

Most Chinese characters are combined characters which are relatively easy to understand because the basic characters that form the whole convey both meaning and pronunciation.

Wang Anshi(王安石, 1021 AD~1086), one of the Eight Giants of the Tang (唐) and Song(宋) Dynasties' literary world suggested that within a combined character, the part that gave its meaning also gave its pronunciation. This is only natural because when making a combined character, the scholar would first look for a character with a similar pronunciation. Let's take a previous example, the character "socks 袜 [バツ・マチ]." The Chinese combined "clothes 衤 [イ・エ]"

for the meaning and "end 末 [マツ・バツ]" for the pronunciation to describe socks(袜), which is clothing(衤) for a part at the end(末) of one's body. Isn't that fascinating! Of course, not all combined characters are like that. Some combined characters have parts that are included only for the pronunciation. For example, to make "狼[ロウ]," the character for 'wolf,' the Chinese combined "dog 犭 [ケン]" and borrowed the pronunciation from "good 良 [リョウ]." Searching for the seemingly invisible or nonsensical connection might help you memorize these kinds of characters. "狼[ロウ]" means a wolf(犭) has a good(良) head. In other words, this character means a wolf is smart. The Native Americans acknowledged this and believed wolves to be sacred animals. This book is a compilation of such stories and explanations that are sure to help you remember Chinese characters.

How to enjoy the hidden meanings of Chinese characters

Now that you know how Chinese characters were formed and why this book was written, we should consider how to apply the characters you have learned so far.

In most cases, this book provides only one English word as the meaning to one given Chinese character. But as is the case with any language, most characters have multiple meanings. Especially so for pictograms, because their meanings change depending on the situation and the reason they are used in a combination. For example, the explanation of "対[タイ・ツイ]" says 'before talking to someone, you would raise the hand(寸) holding the candlestick to check the tattoo(文) to see if the person was friend or foe.' Based on that situation, "対" can mean 'towards, to face, to answer, opposite, compare, equal, even or versus.' It will be much easier to remember the origin of a character and use that to learn the other derivative meanings.

Each time you come across a new, more complicated Chinese character, you'll notice you're breaking them down into smaller components. In most cases, one component will give you the pronunciation and the others will help you deduce the meaning. Keep that fact in mind when studying any Chinese character. Think about the why such components were put together to make a new character and the size of your vocabulary will have no bounds.

On-Kun pronunciation index

Kanji can be read in one of two ways, 'on' or 'kun.' 'on' is when the character sounds like its Chinese or Korean counterpart. The Japanese would consider this pronunciation foreign, so it's marked in katakana. Depending on when a certain character entered the Japanese language, 'kun' can be grouped into Baekje, Han or Tang pronunciations, but this book focuses on the basic *kun* used in JLPT N5~N1 vocabulary and are marked in hiragana.

	On-yomi	Kanji	No.
ア	ア	覀	132
	アイ	愛	29e
	アイ	哀	102a
	アイ	鞋	121c
	アク	悪	26c
	アン	暗	18a
	アン	安	78a
イ	イ	椅	14d
	イ	囗	16
	イ	意	18b
	イ	易	41b
	イ	位	64a
	イ	已	66a
	イ	夷	87d
	イ	医	89a
	イ	衣	101
	イ	為	136d
	イク	育	151c
	イチ	一	173
	イツ	乙	67
	イツ	一	173
	イン	飲	19a
	イン	尹	32d
	イン	廴	50
	イン	院	58c
	イン	因	60d
	イン	乚	67c
	イン	印	69d
	イン	引	87c
	イン	員	147d
ウ	ウ	右	34a
	ウ	有	34b
	ウ	烏	139e
	ウ	羽	141
	ウ	雨	159
	ウン	云	158c
	ウン	雲	159d
エ	エ	回	16c
	エ	衣	101
	エ	画	122d
	エ	会	158d
	エ	絵	158e
	エイ	影	2c
	エイ	英	61c
	エイ	映	61d
	エイ	永	156a
	エイ	泳	156b
	エキ	易	41b
	エキ	駅	74d
	エツ	戉	92b
	エツ	越	92c
	エン	爰	29a
	エン	延	50d
	エン	宴	78b
	エン	塩	85d
	エン	袁	102b
	エン	遠	102c
	エン	園	102d
	エン	円	147e
	エン	鉛	154a
オ	オ	和	12d
	オ	悪	26c
	オ	汚	157d
	オウ	押	28e
	オウ	往	48b
	オウ	央	61b
	オウ	尢	63
	オウ	王	86
	オウ	黄	108
	オウ	横	108a
	オウ	奥	142e
	オク	屋	74a
	オチ	越	92c
	オツ	乙	67
	オン	音	18
	オン	飲	19a
	オン	乚	67c
	オン	遠	102c
	オン	温	132e
カ	カ	和	12d
	カ	可	13
	カ	哥	13a
	カ	歌	13b
	カ	何	13c
	カ	河	13d
	カ	個	15c
	カ	箇	15d
	カ	叚	30d
	カ	暇	30e
	カ	夏	46c
	カ	化	52a
	カ	花	52b
	カ	戈	91
	カ	禾	111
	カ	華	120e
	カ	果	123c
	カ	課	123d
	カ	火	124
	カ	加	125b
	カ	科	128a
	カ	家	136a
	カ	靴	149d
	カ	下	173b
	ガ	牙	21c
	ガ	臥	85a
	ガ	我	91a
	ガ	餓	109a
	ガ	画	122d
	ガ	駕	125c
	ガ	賀	125d
	が	瓦	64e
	カイ	回	16c
	カイ	快	27b
	カイ	開	38d
	カイ	介	51a
	カイ	界	51b
	カイ	夬	62
	カイ	皆	72c
	カイ	階	72d
	カイ	海	79c
	カイ	悔	79d
	カイ	怪	120c
	カイ	挂	121a
	カイ	掛	121b
	カイ	鞋	121c
	カイ	街	121d
	カイ	灰	124a
	カイ	解	150a
	カイ	会	158d
	カイ	絵	158e
	ガイ	街	121d
	ガイ	害	163e
	ガイ	外	172b
	カク	覚	9b
	カク	各	12b
	カク	客	12c
	カク	較	97a
	カク	画	122d
	カク	革	149c
	カク	角	150

On-yomi	Kanji	No.
ガク	学	77b
ガク	楽	161c
カッ	合	54a
カツ	活	20c
カツ	滑	24a
ガッ	合	54a
ガツ	歹	25
ガツ	月	172
カン	看	7a
カン	甘	12a
カン	甲	28d
カン	鹸	55d
カン	奐	57c
カン	換	57d
カン	完	58b
カン	关	62b
カン	監	85b
カン	干	96
カン	漢	108c
カン	間	115b
カン	厂	117
カン	缶	130d
カン	凵	131b
カン	貫	145d
カン	慣	145e
カン	官	152c
カン	館	152d
カン	寒	160d
カン	柬	167c
ガン	顔	5d
ガン	眼	10c
ガン	含	54c
ガン	元	58a
ガン	玩	86c
ガン	㫃	127
ガン	丸	177d
キ		
キ	規	9d
キ	奇	14
キ	騎	14a
キ	寄	14b
キ	綺	14c
キ	其	39
キ	箕	39a
キ	基	39b
キ	期	39c
キ	旗	39d
キ	起	44d
キ	己	66
キ	記	66b
キ	紀	66c
キ	危	69b
キ	季	77d
キ	幾	91d
キ	機	91e
キ	帰	103e
キ	喜	112a
キ	器	135a
キ	貴	145c
キ	气	158
キ	気	158a
キ	汽	158b
キ	几	168
キ	机	168a
ギ	技	42a
ギ	義	91b
ギ	宜	174b
キチ	吉	84a
キツ	吉	84a
キツ	喫	163d
キャク	客	12c
ギャク	玉	86b
キュウ	及	56a
キュウ	吸	56b
キュウ	久	56c
キュウ	急	56d
キュウ	弓	87
キュウ	皀	109c
キュウ	休	165a
キュウ	九	177b
キュウ	究	177c
ギュウ	牛	137
キョ	居	15e
キョ	去	63c
キョ	許	90d
ギョ	御	69c
ギョ	魚	144
ギョ	漁	144b
ギョ	語	176c
キョウ	交	1a
キョウ	校	1b
キョウ	京	2
キョウ	喬	3a
キョウ	橋	3b
キョウ	蕎	3c
キョウ	竟	18d
キョウ	鏡	18e
キョウ	廾	38
キョウ	共	38a
キョウ	供	38b
キョウ	興	38c
キョウ	敬	40d
キョウ	教	43a
キョウ	夾	51c
キョウ	狭	51d
キョウ	兄	59
キョウ	況	59b
キョウ	卬	70
キョウ	経	97d
キョウ	驕	138b
キョウ	強	143a
きょう	警	40e
ギョウ	行	48a
キョク	局	74c
キョク	曲	129d
キン	京	2
キン	今	54b
キン	斤	94
キン	近	94a
キン	巾	103
キン	菫	108b
キン	金	154
キン	禁	166a
ギン	銀	10b
ク		
ク	口	12
ク	供	38b
ク	句	40c
ク	久	56c
ク	公	76e
ク	庫	114e
ク	狗	135c
ク	工	155
ク	功	155a
ク	紅	155b
ク	九	177b
クウ	空	113b
クン	君	32e
ケ		
ケ	化	52a
ケ	花	52b
ケ	悔	79d
ケ	怪	120c
ケ	華	120e
ケ	家	136a
ケ	气	158
ケ	気	158a
ゲ	牙	21c
ゲ	夏	46c
ゲ	華	120e
ゲ	解	150a
ゲ	外	172b
ゲ	下	173b
ケイ	京	2
ケイ	景	2b
ケイ	計	17a
ケイ	憩	20a
ケイ	彐	32
ケイ	敬	40d
ケイ	兄	59
ケイ	巠	97b
ケイ	軽	97c
ケイ	経	97d
ケイ	冂	118
ケイ	圭	121
ケイ	挂	121a
ケイ	匸	131d
ケイ	奚	139a
ケイ	鶏	139b
ケイ	契	163c
ケイ	警	40e
ゲイ	鯨	2a
ゲイ	迎	70a
ケチ	夬	62
ケチ	結	84b
ケツ	頁	4
ケツ	欠	19
ケツ	齧	21a
ケツ	夬	62
ケツ	決	62a
ケツ	結	84b
ケツ	穴	113a
ケツ	亅	179
ゲツ	齧	21a
ゲツ	月	172
ケン	見	9
ケン	建	33b
ケン	鍵	33c
ケン	検	55a
ケン	験	55b
ケン	鹸	55d

	On-yomi	Kanji	No.
	ケン	倹	55e
	ケン	兼	111b
	ケン	嫌	111c
	ケン	間	115b
	ケン	険	116c
	ケン	犬	135
	ケン	犭	135b
	ケン	件	137b
	ケン	研	153b
	ケン	柬	167c
	ゲン	彦	5c
	ゲン	顔	5d
	ゲン	見	9
	ゲン	現	9a
	ゲン	眼	10c
	ゲン	限	10d
	ゲン	言	17
	ゲン	験	55b
	ゲン	元	58a
	ゲン	原	106d
	ゲン	嫌	111c
	ゲン	广	114
	ゲン	研	153b
コ	コ	古	15
	コ	故	15a
	コ	固	15b
	コ	個	15c
	コ	箇	15d
	コ	鼓	42b
	コ	去	63c
	コ	己	66
	コ	庫	114e
	コ	戸	115d
	コ	乎	179a
	コ	呼	179b
	ゴ	期	39c
	ゴ	後	48c
	ゴ	御	69c
	ゴ	午	96c
	ゴ	牛	137
	ゴ	五	176a
	ゴ	吾	176b
	ゴ	語	176c
	コウ	交	1a
	コウ	校	1b
	コウ	高	3
	コウ	口	12

	On-yomi	Kanji	No.
	コウ	嚙	21b
	コウ	甲	28d
	コウ	更	31c
	コウ	興	38c
	コウ	降	47c
	コウ	行	48a
	コウ	後	48c
	コウ	公	76e
	コウ	好	78c
	コウ	孝	81b
	コウ	考	81c
	コウ	幸	83e
	コウ	較	97a
	コウ	黄	108
	コウ	広	114d
	コウ	向	118b
	コウ	工	155
	コウ	功	155a
	コウ	紅	155b
	ゴウ	号	12e
	ゴウ	嚙	21b
	ゴウ	合	54a
	ゴウ	卬	70
	ゴウ	迎	70a
	ゴウ	強	143a
	コク	口	16
	コク	国	86a
	コク	黒	124c
	コク	谷	153c
	コツ	骨	24
	コツ	乞	67a
	コン	艮	10
	コン	根	10a
	コン	困	16a
	コン	建	33b
	コン	今	54b
	コン	昏	80d
	コン	婚	80e
	コン	近	94a
	コン	金	154
	コン	丨	179c
	ゴン	艮	10
	ゴン	言	17
サ	サ	左	155c
	サ	差	155d
	サ	茶	161b
	サ	査	174a

	On-yomi	Kanji	No.
	サ	乍	180
	サ	作	180a
	ザ	坐	120a
	ザ	座	120b
	サイ	彩	5b
	サイ	最	22d
	サイ	殆	25e
	サイ	采	29c
	サイ	菜	29d
	サイ	歳	44b
	サイ	妻	78e
	サイ	切	95b
	サイ	祭	99a
	サイ	細	104c
	サイ	済	105d
	サイ	西	132a
	サイ	隹	140
	サイ	財	145a
	ザイ	財	145a
	サク	錯	154b
	サク	冊	169c
	サク	作	180a
	サク	昨	180b
	サッ	早	170c
	サツ	撮	22e
	サツ	察	99b
	サツ	冊	169c
	ザツ	雑	140b
	サン	彡	5
	サン	参	5a
	サン	算	38e
	サン	散	43b
	サン	産	117e
	サン	山	153
	サン	三	176e
	サン	傘	178d
シ	シ	自	6
	シ	四	16b
	シ	次	19b
	シ	歯	21
	シ	死	25a
	シ	思	26a
	シ	志	26d
	シ	誌	26e
	シ	史	31
	シ	使	31b
	シ	時	37a

	On-yomi	Kanji	No.
	シ	支	42
	シ	止	44
	シ	是	45d
	シ	之	67b
	シ	弛	68c
	シ	此	72a
	シ	旨	73b
	シ	指	73c
	シ	尸	74
	シ	巳	75
	シ	厶	76
	シ	私	76a
	シ	始	76c
	シ	子	77
	シ	氏	80
	シ	紙	80a
	シ	士	84
	シ	仕	84e
	シ	試	88b
	シ	矢	89
	シ	至	90
	シ	示	99
	シ	市	103a
	シ	姉	103b
	シ	糸	104
	シ	豕	136
	シ	師	152b
	ジ	自	6
	ジ	次	19b
	ジ	耳	22
	ジ	事	32c
	ジ	寺	37
	ジ	時	37a
	ジ	持	37b
	ジ	地	68b
	ジ	治	76d
	ジ	字	77a
	ジ	辞	83d
	ジ	仕	84e
	ジ	示	99
	ジ	除	116b
	ジ	二	176
	シキ	色	75d
	シキ	式	88a
	ジキ	直	8
	ジキ	食	109
	シチ	七	178b

	On-yomi	Kanji	No.
	シツ	疾	65b
	シツ	室	90a
	シツ	失	154c
	シツ	七	178b
	ジツ	日	170
	ジツ	十	178
	シャ	射	23a
	シャ	謝	23c
	シャ	者	82
	シャ	煮	82a
	シャ	車	97
	シャ	社	99e
	シャ	写	131a
	ジャ	邪	116e
	シャク	勺	40a
	シャク	尺	74b
	シャク	赤	124b
	シャク	石	153a
	シャク	昔	171
	シャク	借	171a
	ジャク	着	7b
	ジャク	弱	141b
	シュ	首	4d
	シュ	取	22b
	シュ	趣	22c
	シュ	手	28
	シュ	戍	91c
	シュ	殳	93
	シュ	輸	98d
	シュ	種	119d
	シュ	酒	133a
	シュ	主	181a
	ジュ	入	53
	ジュ	就	63b
	ジュ	戍	91c
	シュウ	臭	6d
	シュウ	拾	28b
	シュウ	亼	54
	シュウ	祝	59a
	シュウ	就	63b
	シュウ	舟	98
	シュウ	秋	111a
	シュウ	周	122a
	シュウ	週	122b
	シュウ	集	140a
	シュウ	習	141a
	シュウ	終	160c
	ジュウ	重	119a
	ジュウ	十	178
	ジュウ	住	181b
	シュク	祝	59a
	シュク	宿	106b
	シュツ	出	131c
	シュン	春	162e
	ジュン	準	140c
	ショ	書	33e
	ショ	処	46d
	ショ	暑	82c
	ショ	初	102
	ショ	所	115e
	ショ	疋	166c
	ショ	楚	166d
	ショ	且	174
	ジョ	女	78
	ジョ	如	78d
	ジョ	除	116b
	ジョ	助	174c
	ショウ	相	7c
	ショウ	章	18c
	ショウ	性	27a
	ショウ	正	45
	ショウ	政	45b
	ショウ	笑	61a
	ショウ	咲	62c
	ショウ	妾	83a
	ショウ	商	83c
	ショウ	召	95c
	ショウ	紹	95d
	ショウ	青	107
	ショウ	清	107a
	ショウ	精	107b
	ショウ	請	107c
	ショウ	声	112b
	ショウ	床	114a
	ショウ	尚	118c
	ショウ	升	128c
	ショウ	象	136b
	ショウ	像	136c
	ショウ	生	162
	ショウ	星	162a
	ショウ	姓	162b
	ショウ	丬	168b
	ショウ	将	168c
	ショウ	上	173a
	ショウ	井	176d
	ショウ	小	182
	ショウ	少	182a
	ショウ	省	182b
	ショウ	肖	182c
	ショウ	消	182d
	ジョウ	娘	11a
	ジョウ	情	27e
	ジョウ	静	32b
	ジョウ	丈	34d
	ジョウ	定	45c
	ジョウ	成	92a
	ジョウ	乗	165d
	ジョウ	場	171c
	ジョウ	上	173a
	ショク	植	8a
	ショク	殖	25d
	ショク	色	75d
	ショク	食	109
	ショク	続	146d
	シン	真	8d
	シン	親	9c
	シン	身	23
	シン	心	26
	シン	忄	27
	シン	進	49e
	シン	辛	83
	シン	臣	85
	シン	新	94b
	シン	神	99c
	シン	請	107c
	シン	審	142c
	シン	辰	148
	シン	振	148a
	シン	震	148b
	シン	賑	148c
	シン	深	157c
	シン	申	159b
	シン	寝	168d
	ジン	人	51
	ジン	亻	52
	ジン	⺈	56
	ジン	儿	58
	ジン	臣	85
	ジン	神	99c
	ジン	塵	150d
ス	ス	子	77
	ス	数	110b
	ス	蘇	144c
	ス	主	181a
	ズ	図	16d
	ズ	事	32c
	ズ	豆	112
	ズ	頭	112c
	スイ	誰	17d
	スイ	吹	19d
	スイ	推	28c
	スイ	垂	120d
	スイ	出	131c
	スイ	酔	133b
	スイ	隹	140
	スイ	水	156
	スイ	氺	156c
	スイ	氵	157
	スウ	数	110b
	スン	寸	35
セ	セ	世	162c
	ゼ	是	45d
	セイ	性	27a
	セイ	情	27e
	セイ	静	32b
	セイ	歳	44b
	セイ	正	45
	セイ	政	45b
	セイ	成	92a
	セイ	斉	105c
	セイ	済	105d
	セイ	青	107
	セイ	清	107a
	セイ	精	107b
	セイ	請	107c
	セイ	晴	107d
	セイ	声	112b
	セイ	西	133a
	セイ	生	162
	セイ	星	162a
	セイ	姓	162b
	セイ	世	162c
	セイ	井	176d
	セイ	省	182b
	ゼイ	説	59d
	セキ	射	23a
	セキ	赤	124b
	セキ	隻	140d

	On-yomi	Kanji	No.
	セキ	石	153a
	セキ	昔	171
	セキ	夕	172a
	セチ	節	109e
	セツ	説	59d
	セツ	阝尼	69
	セツ	接	83b
	セツ	折	94c
	セツ	切	95b
	セツ	節	109e
	セツ	雪	159a
	せつ	折	94c
	ゼツ	舌	20
	ゼツ	絶	75e
	セン	穿	21d
	セン	舛	47
	セン	㑒	55
	セン	鹸	55d
	セン	先	58d
	セン	洗	58e
	セン	戔	92d
	セン	浅	92e
	セン	船	98a
	セン	占	100a
	セン	泉	106c
	セン	鮮	144a
	セン	山	153
	セン	川	156e
	セン	千	178c
	ゼン	全	53a
	ゼン	前	98b
	ゼン	然	124d
	ゼン	善	134b
ソ	ソ	組	104b
	ソ	蘇	144c
	ソ	錯	154b
	ソ	疋	166c
	ソ	楚	166d
	ソ	礎	166e
	ソ	祖	174d
	ソウ	相	7c
	ソウ	爪	29
	ソウ	争	32a
	ソウ	走	44c
	ソウ	送	62d
	ソウ	帚	103d
	ソウ	窓	113d
	ソウ	騒	138a
	ソウ	艹	161
	ソウ	草	161a
	ソウ	箱	169a
	ソウ	早	170c
	ゾウ	象	136b
	ゾウ	像	136c
	ゾウ	雑	140b
	ソク	足	45a
	ソク	即	109d
	ソク	則	147a
	ソク	側	147b
	ソク	束	167a
	ソク	速	167b
	ゾク	族	127a
	ゾク	続	146d
	ゾク	俗	153d
	ソク.	息	6b
	ソツ	卒	101d
	ソン	村	35a
	ソン	孫	77c
タ	タ	太	60c
	タ	他	68d
	タ	多	151b
	ダ	打	28a
	ダ	兑	59c
	タイ	体	24b
	タイ	殆	25e
	タイ	待	48d
	タイ	兑	59c
	タイ	大	60
	タイ	太	60c
	タイ	台	76b
	タイ	代	88d
	タイ	貸	88e
	タイ	対	105b
	ダイ	題	45e
	ダイ	内	53b
	ダイ	大	60
	ダイ	台	76b
	ダイ	弟	87a
	ダイ	第	87b
	ダイ	代	88d
	タク	沢	74e
	タク	度	114b
	ダチ	達	49d
	タツ	羍	49c
	タツ	達	49d
	ダツ	脱	59e
	タン	誕	50e
	タン	短	89c
	タン	段	93a
	タン	反	117a
	タン	旦	170a
	ダン	談	17c
	ダン	暖	29b
	ダン	段	93a
	ダン	断	94d
	ダン	男	125a
チ	チ	値	8b
	チ	置	8c
	チ	夂	46
	チ	遅	49b
	チ	池	68a
	チ	地	68b
	チ	弛	68c
	チ	治	76d
	チ	知	89b
	チ	致	90d
	チク	竹	169
	チャ	茶	161b
	チャク	着	7b
	チャク	辶	49
	チュ	丶	181
	チュウ	虫	143
	チュウ	昼	170b
	チュウ	中	179d
	チョ	猪	82b
	チョウ	挺	50c
	チョウ	長	81d
	チョウ	張	81e
	チョウ	超	95e
	チョウ	朝	98e
	チョウ	兆	100d
	チョウ	重	119a
	チョウ	調	122c
	チョウ	鳥	139
	チョウ	丁	175
	チョウ	町	175a
	チョウ	頂	175b
	チョク	直	8
	チン	亭	3d
ツ	ツ	都	82d
	ツ	通	129b
	ツイ	対	105b
	ツイ	口	152
	ツイ	追	152a
	ツウ	痛	65c
	ツウ	通	129b
テ	デ	弟	87a
	テイ	亭	3d
	テイ	体	24b
	テイ	定	45c
	テイ	廷	50a
	テイ	庭	50b
	テイ	挺	50c
	テイ	低	80b
	テイ	帝	84c
	テイ	締	84d
	テイ	弟	87a
	テイ	第	87b
	テイ	鼎	147
	テイ	丁	175
	テイ	停	175c
	テキ	的	40b
	テキ	彳	48
	テツ	鉄	154d
	テン	天	60b
	テン	店	100b
	テン	点	100c
	テン	展	101c
	テン	典	169d
	デン	田	122
	デン	電	159c
ト	ト	図	16d
	ト	徒	44e
	ト	都	82d
	ト	頭	112c
	ト	登	112e
	ト	度	114b
	ト	渡	114c
	ト	土	120
	ト	斗	128
	ド	度	114b
	ド	土	120
	トウ	亠	1
	トウ	道	4e
	トウ	盗	19c
	トウ	討	35d
	トウ	等	37d
	トウ	到	90b

	On-yomi	Kanji	No.
	トウ	倒	90c
	トウ	投	93b
	トウ	刀	95
	トウ	逃	100e
	トウ	唐	110c
	トウ	糖	110d
	トウ	豆	112
	トウ	頭	112c
	トウ	登	112e
	トウ	当	118e
	トウ	萄	130e
	トウ	島	139d
	トウ	読	146c
	トウ	冬	160b
	トウ	東	167
	トウ	答	169b
	トウ	湯	171d
	トウ	灯	175d
	ドウ	道	4e
	ドウ	同	118a
	ドウ	堂	118d
	ドウ	動	119b
	ドウ	働	119c
	ドウ	萄	130e
	トク	得	35b
	トク	特	37c
	トク	読	146c
	ドク	独	143d
	ドク	読	146c
	トツ	突	113c
	ドン	曇	159e
ナ	ナ	南	178a
	ナイ	内	53b
	ナン	難	108d
	ナン	男	125a
	ナン	南	178a
ニ	ニ	二	170
	ニク	肉	151
	ニチ	日	170
	ニャク	疒	65
	ニャク	弱	141b
	ニュウ	入	53
	ニュウ	乳	67d
	ニョ	女	78
	ニョ	如	78d
	ニョウ	女	78
	ニン	人	51
	ニン	亻	52
	ニン	𠆢	56
	ニン	儿	58
ネ	ネン	念	54d
	ネン	年	96e
	ネン	然	124d
ノ	ノウ	能	73d
	ノウ	農	148d
	ノウ	脳	151d
ハ	ハ	巴	75b
	ハ	播	142b
	ハ	派	157b
	バ	馬	138
	ハイ	配	66d
	ハイ	背	73a
	ハイ	貝	145
	ハイ	敗	147c
	ハイ	杯	173d
	バイ	梅	79b
	バイ	貝	145
	バイ	買	146a
	バイ	売	146b
	バイ	倍	173e
	ハク	白	106
	ハク	薄	130b
	バク	麦	163b
	ハチ	八	177
	ハツ	法	63d
	ハツ	癶	112d
	バツ	末	164a
	ハン	煩	4c
	ハン	班	86d
	ハン	般	93c
	ハン	搬	93d
	ハン	反	117a
	ハン	飯	117b
	ハン	板	117c
	ハン	犯	135d
	ハン	半	137a
	ハン	釆	142
	ハン	凡	143b
	バン	曼	27c
	バン	晩	57b
	バン	板	117c
	バン	番	142a
	バン	播	142b
	バン	万	161e
ヒ	ヒ	疲	65d
	ヒ	匕	72
	ヒ	比	72b
	ヒ	飛	128d
	ヒ	非	141d
	ヒ	皮	149
	ヒ	彼	149a
	ヒ	被	149b
	ビ	鼻	6c
	ビ	美	134c
	ビ	未	164b
	ヒツ	必	26b
	ヒツ	筆	33d
	ヒツ	匹	131e
	ヒャク	百	106a
	ビャク	白	106
	ヒョウ	并	64d
	ヒョウ	平	96a
	ヒョウ	苹	96b
	ヒョウ	表	101a
	ヒョウ	冫	160
	ヒョウ	氷	160a
	ビョウ	病	65a
	ビョウ	平	96a
	ビョウ	苗	123
	ビョウ	猫	123a
	ビン	便	31d
	ビン	瓶	64f
フ	フ	父	30a
	フ	付	36
	フ	附	36a
	フ	符	36b
	フ	府	36c
	フ	腐	36d
	フ	歩	44a
	フ	夫	60a
	フ	普	64c
	フ	布	103c
	フ	阝	116
	フ	甫	129c
	フ	傅	130a
	フ	富	133e
	フ	風	143c
	フ	負	145b
	フ	不	173c
	ブ	歩	44a
	ブ	無	47a
	ブ	舞	47b
	ブ	武	88c
	ブ	分	95a
	ブ	部	116d
	ブ	葡	130c
	ブ	豊	148e
	ブ	不	173c
	フウ	封	35c
	フウ	夫	60a
	フウ	富	133e
	フウ	風	143c
	フク	服	30c
	フク	复	46a
	フク	腹	46b
	フク	畐	133c
	フク	福	133d
	ブツ	勿	41
	ブツ	物	41a
	フン	分	95a
	ブン	聞	22a
	ブン	分	95a
	ブン	文	105
ヘ	ヘイ	並	64b
	ヘイ	并	64d
	ヘイ	病	65a
	ヘイ	平	96a
	ヘイ	苹	96b
	ヘイ	閉	115c
	ベイ	米	110
	ベイ	皿	132d
	ベキ	冖	131
	ヘツ	丿	179e
	ヘン	変	43d
	ヘン	辺	49a
	ヘン	返	117d
	ヘン	片	168e
	ベン	便	31d
	ベン	勉	57a
	ベン	宀	113
	ベン	釆	142
ホ	ホ	歩	44a
	ホ	布	103c
	ホ	捕	130
	ホ	葡	130c
	ボ	母	79
	ボ	戊	92
	ホ	甫	129c

	On-yomi	Kanji	No.
	ホウ	報	30b
	ホウ	封	35c
	ホウ	勹	40
	ホウ	法	63d
	ホウ	包	75a
	ホウ	芉	96b
	ホウ	飽	109b
	ホウ	方	126
	ホウ	訪	126a
	ホウ	放	126d
	ホウ	豊	148e
	ホウ	鞄	149e
	ホウ	朋	151a
	ホウ	丰	163
	ホウ	邦	163a
	ボウ	亡	1c
	ボウ	忘	1d
	ボウ	忙	1e
	ボウ	冒	7d
	ボウ	帽	7e
	ボウ	卯	70b
	ボウ	戊	92
	ボウ	旁	126b
	ボウ	傍	126c
	ボウ	网	146
	ホク	北	73
	ボク	目	7
	ボク	攵	43
	ボク	卜	100
	ボク	木	164
	ホッ	法	63d
	ホン	反	117a
	ホン	翻	142d
	ホン	本	165
	ボン	煩	4c
	ボン	犯	135d
	ボン	凡	143b
マ	マ	麻	165b
	マ	磨	165c
	マイ	枚	43c
	マイ	毎	79a
	マイ	米	110
	マイ	売	146b
	マイ	妹	164d
	マツ	末	164a
	マン	曼	27c

	On-yomi	Kanji	No.
	マン	慢	27d
	マン	万	161e
ミ	ミ	美	134c
	ミ	未	164b
	ミ	味	164c
	ミョウ	命	71a
	ミョウ	苗	123
	ミョウ	明	170d
	ミョウ	名	172d
	ミン	民	80c
ム	ム	無	47a
	ム	武	88c
メ	メ	馬	138
	メイ	命	71a
	メイ	鳴	139c
	メイ	明	170d
	メイ	名	172d
	メン	面	6a
	メン	免	57
	メン	宀	113
モ	モ	母	79
	モウ	亡	1c
	モウ	毛	5e
	モウ	网	146
	モク	目	7
	モク	木	164
	モチ	勿	41
	モツ	物	41a
	モン	聞	22a
	モン	文	105
	モン	紋	105a
	モン	門	115
	モン	問	115a
ヤ	ヤ	也	68
	ヤ	野	119e
	ヤ	夜	172c
	ヤク	厄	69a
	ヤク	約	104a
	ヤク	薬	161d
ユ	ユ	俞	98c
	ユ	輸	98d
	ユ	由	123e
	ユ	遊	127d
	ユイ	由	123e
	ユウ	又	30
	ユウ	ナ	34

	On-yomi	Kanji	No.
	ユウ	右	34a
	ユウ	有	34b
	ユウ	友	34c
	ユウ	尤	63a
	ユウ	熊	73e
	ユウ	邑	75c
	ユウ	由	123e
	ユウ	斿	127b
	ユウ	游	127c
	ユウ	遊	127d
	ユウ	酉	133
ヨ	ヨ	予	4a
	ヨ	預	4b
	ヨ	余	116a
	ヨ	斿	127b
	ヨウ	夭	61
	ヨウ	斿	127b
	ヨウ	用	129
	ヨウ	甬	129a
	ヨウ	要	132b
	ヨウ	腰	132c
	ヨウ	羊	134
	ヨウ	様	134a
	ヨウ	洋	134d
	ヨウ	曜	141c
	ヨウ	葉	162d
	ヨウ	昜	171b
	ヨク	弋	88
	ヨク	浴	153e
ラ	ライ	礼	99d
	ライ	来	110e
	ラク	楽	161c
	ラン	乱	20d
	ラン	卵	70c
	ラン	覧	85c
	ラン	婪	166b
リ	リ	吏	31a
	リ	理	86e
	リ	裏	101b
	リ	利	111d
	リ	里	119
	リキ	力	125
	リク	六	177a
	リツ	聿	33
	リツ	律	33a
	リツ	立	64

	On-yomi	Kanji	No.
	リュウ	立	64
	リュウ	留	70d
	リュウ	流	157a
	リョ	旅	127e
	リョウ	涼	2d
	リョウ	良	11
	リョウ	令	71
	リョウ	領	71d
	リョウ	料	128b
	リョウ	漁	144b
	リョク	緑	104d
	リョク	力	125
	リン	粦	47d
	リン	隣	47e
	リン	林	166
ル	ル	留	70d
	ル	娄	110a
	ル	流	157a
	ルイ	累	123b
レ	レイ	例	25c
	レイ	令	71
	レイ	冷	71b
	レイ	零	71c
	レイ	領	71d
	レイ	礼	99d
	レイ	麗	150c
	レツ	列	25b
	レン	連	97e
	レン	煉	167d
	レン	練	167e
ロ	ロ	鹵	55c
	ロウ	狼	11b
	ロウ	浪	11c
	ロウ	郎	11d
	ロウ	廊	11e
	ロウ	耂	81
	ロウ	老	81a
	ロウ	娄	110a
	ロク	緑	104d
	ロク	鹿	150b
	ロク	録	156d
	ロク	六	177a
	ロン	論	17b
	ロン	乱	20d
ワ	ワ	和	12d
	ワ	話	20b

Kun-yomi | あ~う

	Kun-yomi	Kanji	No.
あ	あい	相	7c
	あいだ	間	115b
	あう	合	54a
	あう	会	158d
	あお	青	107
	あおい	青	107
	あか	赤	124b
	あかい	赤	124b
	あかす	明	170d
	あかり	明	170d
	あがる	上	173a
	あかるい	明	170d
	あき	秋	111a
	あきらか	明	170d
	あきる	飽	109b
	あく	開	38d
	あく	空	113b
	あく	明	170d
	あくる	明	170d
	あける	開	38d
	あける	空	113b
	あげる	上	173a
	あける	明	170d
	あさ	朝	98e
	あさ	麻	165b
	あさい	浅	92e
	あざやか	鮮	144a
	あし	足	45a
	あじ	味	164c
	あじわう	味	164c
	あずかる	預	4b
	あずける	預	4b
	あそぶ	遊	127d
	あたい	値	8b
	あたたかい	暖	29b
	あたたまる	暖	29b
	あたためる	暖	29b
	あたま	頭	112c
	あたらしい	新	94b
	あたり	辺	49a
	あたる	当	118e
	あつい	暑	82c
	あつまる	集	140a
	あつめる	集	140a
	あてる	当	118e
	あと	後	48c
	あな	穴	113a

	Kun-yomi	Kanji	No.
	あに	兄	59
	あね	姉	103b
	あびる	浴	153e
	あぶない	危	69b
	あま	雨	159
	あまい	甘	12a
	あまえる	甘	12a
	あまやかす	甘	12a
	あまる	余	116a
	あめ	雨	159
	あやうい	危	69b
	あやしい	怪	120c
	あやまる	謝	23c
	あゆむ	歩	44a
	あらう	洗	58e
	あらかじめ	予	4a
	あらそう	争	32a
	あらた	新	94b
	あらわす	現	9a
	あらわす	表	101a
	あらわれる	現	9a
	ある	有	34b
	あるく	歩	44a
	あわす	合	54a
	あわせる	合	54a
	あわれ	哀	102a
い	いう	言	17
	いう	云	158c
	いえ	家	136a
	いかす	生	162
	いき	息	6b
	いきる	生	162
	いく	行	48a
	いく	幾	91d
	いけ	池	68a
	いける	生	162
	いし	石	153a
	いそがしい	忙	1e
	いそぐ	急	56d
	いた	板	117c
	いたい	痛	65c
	いたす	致	90d
	いただき	頂	175b
	いただく	頂	175b
	いたむ	痛	65c
	いためる	痛	65c
	いたる	至	90

	Kun-yomi	Kanji	No.
	いたる	到	90b
	いち	市	103a
	いつつ	五	176a
	いと	糸	104
	いぬ	犬	135
	いぬ	狗	135c
	いのち	命	71a
	いま	今	54b
	いまだ	未	164b
	いもうと	妹	164d
	いや	嫌	111c
	いる	居	15e
	いる	射	23a
	いる	要	132b
	いれる	入	53
	いろ	色	75d
	いわう	祝	59a
う	うえ	上	173a
	うえる	植	8a
	うえる	餓	109a
	うお	魚	144
	うごかす	動	119b
	うごく	動	119b
	うし	牛	137
	うしなう	失	154c
	うしろ	後	48c
	うすい	薄	130b
	うすめる	薄	130b
	うた	歌	13b
	うたう	歌	13b
	うち	内	53b
	うつ	打	28a
	うつ	討	35d
	うつくしい	美	134c
	うつす	映	61d
	うつす	写	131a
	うつる	映	61d
	うつる	写	131a
	うつわ	器	135a
	うま	馬	138
	うまい	旨	73b
	うまれる	生	162
	うみ	海	79c
	うむ	生	162
	うめ	梅	79b
	うやまう	敬	40d
	うら	裏	101b

	Kun-yomi	Kanji	No.
	うらなう	占	100a
	うらなう	卜	100
	うる	得	35b
	うる	売	146b
	うれる	売	146b
	うわ	上	173a
え	え	重	119a
	えがく	画	122d
	える	得	35b
お	お	小	182
	お	御	69c
	おいる	老	81a
	おう	負	145b
	おう	追	152a
	おえる	終	160c
	おお	大	60
	おおい	多	151b
	おおいに	大	60
	おおかみ	狼	11b
	おおきい	大	60
	おおやけ	公	76e
	おかす	犯	135d
	おきる	起	44d
	おく	置	8c
	おく	奥	142e
	おくる	送	62d
	おくれる	遅	49b
	おこす	起	44d
	おこなう	行	48a
	おこる	起	44d
	おさえる	押	28e
	おさまる	治	76d
	おさめる	治	76d
	おしえる	教	43a
	おす	押	28e
	おそい	遅	49b
	おそわる	教	43a
	おっと	夫	60a
	おと	音	18
	おとうと	弟	87a
	おとこ	男	125a
	おとずれる	訪	126a
	おなじ	同	118a
	おのおの	各	12b
	おのずから	自	6
	おぼえる	覚	9b
	おも	主	181a
	おも	面	6a
	おもい	重	119a
	おもう	思	26a
	おもて	表	101a
	おもむき	趣	22c
	おもんずる	重	119a
	おや	親	9c
	およぐ	游	127c
	およぐ	泳	156b
	およそ	凡	143b
	および	及	56a
	およぶ	及	56a
	およぼす	及	56a
	おり	折	94c
	おりる	降	47c
	おりる	下	173b
	おる	折	94c
	おる	居	15e
	おれる	折	94c
	おろす	降	47c
	おわる	終	160c
	おんな	女	78
か	か	日	170
	かう	買	146a
	かえす	返	117d
	かえりみる	省	182b
	かえる	変	43d
	かえる	換	57d
	かえる	代	88d
	かえる	帰	103e
	かえる	返	117d
	かお	顔	5d
	かがみ	鏡	18e
	かかる	掛	121b
	かぎ	鍵	33c
	かぎる	限	10d
	かく	欠	19
	かく	書	33e
	かげ	影	2c
	かける	欠	19
	かける	掛	121b
	かさ	傘	178d
	かさなる	重	119a
	かさねる	重	119a
	かじる	齧	21a
	かず	数	110b
	かす	貸	88e
	かぜ	風	143c
	かぞえる	数	110b
	かた	方	126
	かた	片	168e
	かたな	刀	95
	かたまる	固	15b
	かためる	固	15b
	かたる	語	176c
	かたわら	傍	126c
	かつ	且	174
	かど	角	150
	かならず	必	26b
	かね	金	154
	かねて	予	4a
	かねる	兼	111b
	かの	彼	149a
	かばん	鞄	149e
	かぶる	被	149b
	かみ	紙	80a
	かみ	神	99c
	かみ	上	173a
	かむ	噛	21b
	かよう	通	129b
	から	空	113b
	からい	辛	83
	からだ	体	24b
	かりる	借	171a
	かるい	軽	97c
	かれ	彼	149a
	かわ	河	13d
	かわ	側	147b
	かわ	皮	149
	かわ	革	149c
	かわ	川	156e
	かわす	交	1a
	かわら	瓦	64e
	かわる	代	88d
	かわる	変	43d
	かんがえる	考	81c
き	き	黄	108
	き	木	164
	きえる	消	182d
	きく	聞	22a
	きこえる	聞	22a
	きざし	兆	100d
	きた	北	73
	きたす	来	110e

	Kun-yomi	Kanji	No.
	きたない	汚	157d
	きたる	来	110e
	きのえ	甲	28d
	きまる	決	62a
	きみ	君	32e
	きめる	決	62a
	きよい	清	107a
	きらう	嫌	111c
	きる	切	95b
	きる	着	7b
	きれる	切	95b
く	くう	食	109
	くさ	草	161a
	くさい	臭	6d
	くさる	腐	36d
	くじら	鯨	2a
	くすり	薬	161d
	くださる	下	173b
	くだる	下	173b
	くち	口	12
	くつ	靴	149d
	くに	国	86a
	くばる	配	66d
	くび	首	4d
	くみ	組	104b
	くむ	組	104b
	くも	雲	159d
	くもる	曇	159e
	くやしい	悔	79d
	くやむ	悔	79d
	くら	庫	114e
	くらい	暗	18a
	くらい	位	64a
	くらべる	比	72b
	くらべる	較	97a
	くる	来	110e
	くるま	車	97
	くろ	黒	124c
	くろい	黒	124c
	くわえる	加	125b
	くわわる	加	125b
け	け	毛	5e
	けす	消	182d
	けわしい	険	116c
こ	こ	小	182
	こ	子	77
	こえ	声	112b
	こえる	越	92c
	こおり	氷	160a
	ここのつ	九	177b

	Kun-yomi	Kanji	No.
	こころ	心	26
	こころざし	志	26d
	こころざす	志	26d
	こころみる	試	88b
	こころよい	快	27b
	こし	腰	132c
	こしかけ	椅	14d
	こす	越	92c
	こたえ	答	169b
	こたえる	答	169b
	こと	言	17
	こと	事	32c
	ことば	辞	83d
	ことわる	断	94d
	この	此	72a
	このむ	好	78c
	こぼれる	零	71c
	こまかい	細	104c
	こまる	困	16a
	ごみ	塵	150d
	こめ	米	110
	これ	之	67b
	これ	此	72a
さ	さいわい	幸	83e
	さが	性	27a
	さかい	界	51b
	さかずき	杯	173d
	さかな	魚	144
	さがる	下	173b
	さき	先	58d
	さく	咲	62c
	さけ	酒	133a
	さけぶ	号	12e
	さげる	下	173b
	ささえる	支	42
	さす	指	73c
	さす	差	155d
	さだまる	定	45c
	さだめる	定	45c
	さと	里	119
	さま	様	134a
	さます	覚	9b
	さます	冷	71b
	さむい	寒	160d
	さめる	冷	71b
	さめる	覚	9b
	さら	皿	132d
	さる	去	63c
	さわ	沢	74e
	さわぐ	騒	138a

	Kun-yomi	Kanji	No.
し	しあわせ	幸	83e
	しいる	強	143a
	しお	塩	85d
	しか	鹿	150b
	しかし	然	124d
	しかり	然	124d
	しずか	静	32b
	しずまる	静	32b
	した	下	173b
	した	舌	20
	したしい	親	9c
	しぬ	死	25a
	しま	島	139d
	しめす	示	99
	しめる	閉	115c
	しめる	締	84d
	しめる	占	100a
	しも	下	173b
	しらべる	調	122c
	しる	知	89b
	しるし	印	69d
	しるす	記	66b
	しろ	白	106
	しろい	白	106
	しろがね	銀	10b
す	すう	吸	56b
	すえ	末	164a
	すく	好	78c
	すく	空	113b
	すくない	少	182a
	すこし	少	182a
	すずしい	涼	2d
	すすむ	進	49e
	すずむ	涼	2d
	すすめる	進	49e
	すでに	已	66a
	すなわち	即	109d
	すべる	滑	24a
	すます	済	105d
	すみ	角	150
	すみやか	速	167b
	すむ	済	105d
	すむ	住	181b
	する	為	136d
	すわる	座	120b
せ	せ	背	73a
	せい	背	73a
そ	そだつ	育	151c
	そだてる	育	151c
	そと	外	172b

	Kun-yomi	Kanji	No.
	その	其	39
	その	園	102d
	そば	傍	126c
	そば	側	147b
	そば	蕎	3c
	そむく	背	73a
	そむける	背	73a
	そら	空	113b
	そらす	反	117a
	そる	反	117a
	それ	其	39
た	た	田	122
	たいら	平	96a
	たえる	絶	75e
	たおす	倒	90c
	たおれる	倒	90c
	たかい	高	3
	たかまる	高	3
	たかめる	高	3
	たけ	丈	34d
	たけ	竹	169
	たす	足	45a
	だす	出	131c
	たすかる	助	174c
	たすける	助	174c
	たずねる	訪	126a
	ただしい	正	45
	ただちに	直	8
	たち	達	49d
	たつ	立	64
	たつ	断	94d
	たつ	経	97d
	たつ	建	33b
	たてる	建	33b
	たてる	立	64
	たとえる	例	25c
	たに	谷	153c
	たね	種	119d
	たのしい	楽	161c
	たのしむ	楽	161c
	たば	束	167a
	たび	度	114b
	たび	旅	127e
	たべる	食	109
	たま	玉	86b
	たまご	卵	70c
	ため	為	136d
	ためす	試	88b
	たより	便	31d
	たりる	足	45a

	Kun-yomi	Kanji	No.
	だれ	誰	17d
	たれる	垂	120d
ち	ち	千	178c
	ちいさい	小	182
	ちかい	近	94a
	ちから	力	125
	ちぎる	契	163c
	ちち	父	30a
	ちち	乳	67d
	ちらかす	散	43b
	ちらかる	散	43b
	ちらす	散	43b
	ちり	塵	150d
	ちる	散	43b
つ	つかう	使	31b
	つかえる	仕	84e
	つかれる	疲	65d
	つぎ	次	19b
	つき	月	172
	つく	着	7b
	つく	付	36
	つく	附	36a
	つく	就	63b
	つく	突	113c
	つぐ	次	19b
	つぐ	接	83b
	つくえ	机	168a
	つくる	作	180a
	つける	付	36
	つける	附	36a
	つける	就	63b
	つける	点	100c
	つち	土	120
	つづく	続	146d
	つつく	突	113c
	つづける	続	146d
	つつむ	包	75a
	つの	角	150
	つま	妻	78e
	つめ	爪	29
	つめたい	冷	71b
	つよい	強	143a
	つよまる	強	143a
	つよめる	強	143a
	つらい	辛	83
	つらなる	連	97e
	つらぬく	貫	145d
	つらねる	連	97e
	つれる	連	97e
て	て	手	28

	Kun-yomi	Kanji	No.
	てら	寺	37
	でる	出	131c
と	と	戸	115d
	とい	問	115a
	とう	問	115a
	とお	十	178
	とおい	遠	102c
	とおす	通	129b
	とおる	通	129b
	とき	時	37a
	とく	解	150a
	とく	説	59d
	とぐ	研	153b
	とける	解	150a
	ところ	処	46d
	ところ	所	115e
	とし	歳	44b
	とし	年	96e
	とじる	閉	115c
	とどまる	止	44
	とどめる	止	44
	となり	隣	47e
	とばす	飛	128d
	とぶ	飛	128d
	とまる	止	44
	とまる	留	70d
	とみ	富	133e
	とむ	富	133e
	とめる	止	44
	とめる	留	70d
	とも	友	34c
	とも	共	38a
	とも	供	38b
	とり	鳥	139
	とる	取	22b
	とる	撮	22e
	とる	采	29c
な	な	名	172d
	ない	無	47a
	なおす	直	8
	なおる	直	8
	なか	中	179d
	ながい	長	81d
	ながい	永	156a
	ながす	流	157a
	なかば	半	137a
	ながら	乍	180
	ながれる	流	157a
	なく	鳴	139c
	なげる	投	93b

	Kun-yomi	Kanji	No.
	なごやか	和	12d
	なさけ	情	27e
	なす	為	136d
	なつ	夏	46c
	など	等	37d
	なな	七	178b
	ななつ	七	178b
	なに	何	13c
	なま	生	162
	なまり	鉛	154a
	なみ	浪	11c
	なみ	並	64b
	なめらか	滑	24a
	ならう	習	141a
	ならす	鳴	139c
	ならびに	並	64b
	ならぶ	並	64b
	ならべる	並	64b
	なる	成	92a
	なる	鳴	139c
	なん	何	13c
に	にえる	煮	82a
	にがす	逃	100e
	にぎやか	賑	148c
	にぎわう	賑	148c
	にげる	逃	100e
	にし	西	132a
	にる	煮	82a
	にわ	庭	50b
	にわとり	鶏	139b
ぬ	ぬぐ	脱	59e
	ぬし	主	181a
	ぬすむ	盗	19c
	ぬの	布	103c
	ぬるい	温	132e
ね	ね	値	8b
	ね	音	18
	ね	根	10a
	ねこ	猫	123a
	ねる	練	167e
	ねる	寝	168d
の	のがす	逃	100e
	のがれる	逃	100e
	のせる	乗	165d
	のぞく	除	116b
	のち	後	48c
	のばす	延	50d
	のびる	延	50d
	のぼる	登	112e
	のむ	飲	19a

	Kun-yomi	Kanji	No.
	のる	乗	165d
は	は	歯	21
	は	葉	162d
	ば	場	171c
	はい	灰	124a
	はいる	入	53
	はえる	生	162
	はかる	計	17a
	はかる	図	16d
	はく	穿	21d
	ばける	化	52a
	はこ	箱	169a
	はし	橋	3b
	はじまる	始	76c
	はじめ	初	102
	はじめて	初	102
	はじめる	始	76c
	はしる	走	44c
	はずす	外	172b
	はずれる	外	172b
	はた	旗	39d
	はたす	果	123c
	はたらく	働	119c
	はつ	初	102
	はて	果	123c
	はてる	果	123c
	はな	鼻	6c
	はな	花	52b
	はな	華	120e
	はなし	話	20b
	はなす	放	126d
	はなす	話	20b
	はなれる	放	126d
	はね	羽	141
	はは	母	79
	はぶく	省	182b
	はやい	速	167b
	はやい	早	170c
	はやし	林	166
	はやめる	早	170c
	はら	原	106d
	はる	張	81e
	はる	春	162e
	はれる	晴	107d
ひ	ひ	火	124
	ひ	日	170
	ひえる	冷	71b
	ひがし	東	167
	ひき	匹	131e
	ひく	引	87c

	Kun-yomi	Kanji	No.
	ひくい	低	80b
	ひさしい	久	56c
	ひだり	左	155c
	ひと	一	173
	ひと	人	51
	ひとしい	等	37d
	ひとつ	一	173
	ひとり	独	143d
	ひま	暇	30e
	ひやかす	冷	71b
	ひやす	冷	71b
	ひらく	開	38d
	ひる	昼	170b
	ひろい	広	114d
	ひろう	拾	28b
	ひろがる	広	114d
	ひろげる	広	114d
	ひろめる	広	114d
ふ	ふえる	殖	25d
	ふかい	深	157c
	ふかまる	深	157c
	ふかめる	深	157c
	ふく	吹	19d
	ふくむ	含	54c
	ふくめる	含	54c
	ふける	老	81a
	ふける	更	31c
	ふし	節	109e
	ふたつ	二	176
	ふで	筆	33d
	ふとい	太	60c
	ふとる	太	60c
	ふね	舟	98
	ふね	船	98a
	ふやす	殖	25d
	ふゆ	冬	160b
	ふる	降	47c
	ふる	振	148a
	ふるい	古	15
	ふるえる	震	148b
へ	べ	辺	49a
	べ	部	116d
	へる	経	97d
ほ	ほうき	帚	103d
	ほうる	放	126d
	ほか	外	172b
	ほか	他	68d
	ほし	星	162a
	ほす	干	96
	ほそい	細	104c

	Kun-yomi	Kanji	No.
	ほどく	解	150a
	ほとり	辺	49a
	ほとんど	殆	25e
	ほね	骨	24
ま	ま	真	8d
	まい	舞	47b
	まいる	参	5a
	まう	舞	47b
	まえ	前	98b
	まかす	負	145b
	まがる	曲	129d
	まく	播	142b
	まげる	曲	129d
	まける	負	145b
	まご	孫	77c
	まさに	将	168c
	まじえる	交	1a
	まじわる	交	1a
	また	又	30
	まち	街	121d
	まち	町	175a
	まつ	待	48d
	まったく	全	53a
	まつり	祭	99a
	まつる	祭	99a
	まと	的	40b
	まど	窓	113d
	まなぶ	学	77b
	まぬかれる	免	57
	まめ	豆	112
	まる	丸	177d
	まるい	丸	177d
	まるい	円	147e
	まるめる	丸	177d
	まわす	回	16c
	まわり	周	122a
	まわる	回	16c
み	み	身	23
	み	箕	39a
	みえる	見	9
	みがく	磨	165c
	みぎ	右	34a
	みじかい	短	89c
	みず	水	156
	みずから	自	6
	みせ	店	100b
	みせる	見	9
	みだす	乱	20d
	みだれる	乱	20d
	みち	道	4e
	みっつ	三	176e
	みどり	緑	104d
	みな	皆	72c
	みなみ	南	178a
	みみ	耳	22
	みやこ	都	82d
	みる	見	9
む	むかう	向	118b
	むかえる	迎	70a
	むかし	昔	171
	むく	向	118b
	むける	向	118b
	むこう	向	118b
	むし	虫	143
	むずかしい	難	108d
	むすぶ	結	84b
	むすめ	娘	11a
	むっつ	六	177a
	むら	村	35a
め	め	目	7
	め	眼	10c
	めし	飯	117b
	めす	召	95c
も	もうす	申	159b
	もちいる	用	129
	もつ	持	37b
	もっとも	最	22d
	もっとも	尤	63a
	もと	基	39b
	もと	元	58a
	もと	原	106d
	もと	本	165
	もの	物	41a
	もの	者	82
や	や	屋	74a
	や	矢	89
	やさしい	易	41b
	やすい	安	78a
	やすまる	休	165a
	やすむ	休	165a
	やすめる	休	165a
	やっつ	八	177
	やど	宿	106b
	やぶれる	敗	147c
	やま	山	153
	やむ	止	44
	やむ	病	65a
	やめる	止	44
	やめる	辞	83d
	やわらげる	和	12d
ゆ	ゆ	湯	171d
	ゆう	夕	172a
	ゆえ	故	15a
	ゆか	床	114a
	ゆき	雪	159a
	ゆく	行	48a
	ゆたか	豊	148e
	ゆび	指	73c
	ゆみ	弓	87
	ゆるす	許	96d
	ゆるむ	弛	68c
よ	よ	夜	172c
	よ	世	162c
	よい	酔	133b
	よい	良	11
	よい	善	134b
	よう	酔	133b
	よこ	横	108a
	よごす	汚	157d
	よごれる	汚	157d
	よせる	寄	14b
	よっつ	四	16b
	よぶ	呼	179b
	よみがえる	蘇	144c
	よむ	読	146c
	よる	寄	14b
	よる	因	60d
	よる	夜	172c
	よろこぶ	喜	112a
	よろしい	宜	174b
	よわい	弱	141b
	よわまる	弱	141b
	よわめる	弱	141b
	よわる	弱	141b
	よん	四	16b
わ	わ	我	91a
	わかる	分	95a
	わかれる	分	95a
	わける	分	95a
	わざ	技	42a
	わすれる	忘	1d
	わたくし	私	76a
	わたし	私	76a
	わたす	渡	114c
	わたる	渡	114c
	わらう	笑	61a
	わるい	悪	26c
	われ	我	91a
	われ	吾	176b

Meaning index

Strictly speaking, to the Japanese, kanji is a foreign language. To the reader, Japanese is also a foreign language. The hardest part of learning a foreign language is learning how the words conjugate. Sometimes you will find a word that corresponds directly to one in your native language, but in most cases there won't be a direct correlation. Take the character "語[ゴ・ギョ]" for example. It can be translated into 'word, language, speech, tell, talk, say'. It is very difficult to allocate just one meaning to each kanji. For that reason, we suggest you avoid using this index, if possible. Although you will be tempted to look up a word from your native language.

	Meaning	Kanji	Ref.
a	abdomen	腹	46b
	ability	能	73d
	above	上	173a
	accomplish	就	63b
	accomplished	達	49d
	accomplished man	彦	5c
	accustomed	慣	145e
	achieve	成	92a
	achievement	功	155a
	add	加	125b
	advance	進	49e
	advantage	利	111d
	affair	件	137b
	affair	事	32c
	after	後	48c
	again	又	30
	age	歳	44b
	ahead	先	58d
	air	气	158
	air	気	158a
	air	空	113b
	alcohol	酒	133a
	alert	警	40e
	all	⼈	55
	all	皆	72c
	almost	殆	25e
	alone	独	143d
	already	已	66a
	also	且	174
	ancestor	祖	174d
	angle	角	150
	answer	答	169b
	apologize	謝	23c
	appear	現	9a
	apple	苹	96b
	argue	論	17b
	armor	甲	28d
	arrive	到	90b
	arrive	至	90
	arrogant	慢	27d
	arrow	矢	89
	as	如	78d
	ascend	登	112e
	ascend	升	128c
	ash	灰	124a
	ask	問	115a
	assemble	亼	54
	associate with	交	1a
	attach	付	36
	attach	附	36a
	attack	討	35d
	augment	殖	25d
	autumn	秋	111a
	awake	覚	9b
	ax	斤	94
	ax	戉	92b
b	back	後	48c
	back	背	73a
	back (rear)	裏	101b
	bad	悪	26c
	bad	歹	25
	bag	鞄	149e
	bamboo	竹	169
	barbarian	夷	87d
	barley	麦	163b
	base	基	39b
	bathe	浴	153e
	be born	生	162
	be born (nativity)	誕	50e
	be defeated	敗	147c
	be in trouble	困	16a
	beans	豆	112
	bear	負	145b
	bear	熊	73e
	bear (fruit)	結	84b
	bear debt	負	145b
	beautiful	美	134c
	beautiful	綺	14c
	beautiful	麗	150c
	bed	床	114a
	before	前	98b
	beforehand	予	4a
	beg	乞	67a
	begin	始	76c
	below	下	173b
	bend	曲	129d
	beside	旁	126b
	beside	傍	126c
	betray	背	73a
	between	間	115b
	big	大	60
	bird	鳥	139
	bird	隹	140
	bite	噛	21b
	black	黒	124c
	bless	祝	59a
	blessing	福	133d
	block	町	175a
	bloom	咲	62c

blow	吹	19d
blue	青	107
board	板	117c
boat	舟	98
body	身	23
body	己	66
body	体	24b
boil	煮	82a
boiling water	湯	171d
bone	骨	24
book	本	165
book	冊	169c
bore through	穿	21d
borrow	貸	88e
borrow	借	171a
borrow	段	30d
bottle	瓶	64f
boundary	界	51b
bow (archery)	弓	87
box	箱	169a
brain	脳	151d
branch	支	42
break	折	94c
breath	息	6b
breathe in	吸	56b
bridge	橋	3b
bright	曜	141c
bright	明	170d
bright	奐	57c
bring about	致	90d
broad	広	114d
broom	帚	103d
buckwheat	蕎	3c
Buddhist temple	寺	37
build	建	33b
bull' s-eye	的	40b
bundle	束	167a
bureau	局	74c
busy	忙	1e
buy	買	146a
c		
calculate	算	38e
call	呼	179b
call	召	95c
calm	平	96a
can	可	13
cane (whip)	楚	166d
capital	京	2

capital	都	82d
car	車	97
carapace	甲	28d
cart	車	97
cat	猫	123a
catch	捕	130
cause	因	60d
cave	穴	113a
cease	已	66a
celebrate	祝	59a
center	中	179d
center	央	61b
ceremony	典	169d
ceremony	式	88a
ceremony	礼	99d
chair	椅	14d
change	変	43d
change	化	52a
chapter	章	18c
character	文	105
character	字	77a
chase	追	152a
chicken	鶏	139b
chief	長	81d
child	子	77
China	漢	108c
circle	円	147e
circuit	周	122a
circumference	周	122a
city	市	103a
clamor	騒	138a
class	等	37d
classical copula	也	68
classical particle	乎	179a
clean	清	107a
clear up	晴	107d
cliff	厂	117
climb up	登	112e
close	閉	115c
close	关	62b
closing	封	35c
cloth	布	103c
clothes	衣	101
clothes	服	30c
cloud	云	158c
cloud	雲	159d
cloudy	曇	159e

cold	寒	160d
cold	冷	71b
color	色	75d
coloring	彩	5b
combine	合	54a
come	来	110e
command	令	71
commander	将	168c
commit (a sin)	犯	135d
compare	比	72b
compare	較	97a
complete	完	58b
compute	計	17a
concubine	妾	83a
concurrently	兼	111b
condition	況	59b
confused	錯	154b
congratulate	賀	125d
connect	接	83b
connect	紹	95d
connect	連	97e
consider	考	81c
contact	接	83b
contain	含	54c
container	器	135a
contend	争	32a
continue	続	146d
convenient	便	31d
cooked rice	飯	117b
cool	涼	2d
copy	写	131a
corpse	尸	74
corridor	廊	11e
count	数	110b
count (up)	料	128b
counter for animals	匹	131e
counter for flat thing	枚	43c
counter for items	箇	15d
counter for long cylindrical things	本	165
country	邦	163a
country	国	86a
courtyard	庭	50b
cover	覀	132
cover	冖	131
covet	婪	166b
cow	牛	137

	crest	紋	105a
	crimson	紅	155b
	cross (over)	済	105d
	cross (over)	渡	114c
	crow	烏	139e
	cry	鳴	139c
	cup	杯	173d
	currency	貝	145
	curve	曲	129d
	custom	俗	153d
	cut	切	95b
	cut off	断	94d
d	dance	舞	47b
	danger	険	116c
	dangerous	殆	25e
	dangerous	危	69b
	dark	昏	80d
	darkness	暗	18a
	dawn	旦	170a
	day	日	170
	day of the week	曜	141c
	daytime	昼	170b
	decide	決	62a
	deep	深	157c
	deer	鹿	150b
	degree	度	114b
	deposit	預	4b
	descend	降	47c
	desk	机	168a
	diagonal line	丿	179e
	die	亡	1c
	die	死	25a
	difference	差	155d
	difficult	難	108d
	direction	方	126
	dirty	汚	157d
	disappear	消	182d
	discipline	紀	66c
	discuss	討	35d
	disease	疾	65b
	dish	皿	132d
	dislike	嫌	111c
	disordered	乱	20d
	dispatch	派	157b
	display	展	101c
	distant	遠	102c
	distinguish	釆	142
	distribute	配	66d
	divide	分	95a
	divination	卜	100
	do	為	136d
	do not	勿	41
	doctor	医	89a
	dog	犬	135
	dog	犭	135b
	dog	狗	135c
	dominion	領	71d
	door	門	115
	door	戸	115d
	dot	点	100c
	dot	丶	181
	double	倍	173e
	down	下	173b
	drag	娄	110a
	draw	画	122d
	drawing	図	16d
	drink	喫	163d
	drink	飲	19a
	droop	垂	120d
	drop	零	71c
	drum	鼓	42b
	drunk	酔	133b
	dry	干	96
	dust	塵	150d
	dwell	住	181b
	dynasty	朝	98e
e	each	各	12b
	ear	耳	22
	early	早	170c
	east	東	167
	easy	易	41b
	eat	食	109
	eat	喫	163d
	economize	省	182b
	egg	卵	70c
	eight	八	177
	elder brother	兄	59
	elder brother	哥	13a
	elder sister	姉	103b
	elephant	象	136b
	emperor	帝	84c
	empty	空	113b
	empty box	匚	131d
	enclose	口	16
	end	卒	101d
	end	終	160c
	end	末	164a
	endeavor	勉	57a
	energy	气	158
	energy	気	158a
	enter	入	53
	entire	全	53a
	envoy	使	31b
	equal	斉	105c
	equal	等	37d
	-er (person)	者	82
	error	舛	47
	escape	逃	100e
	esteem	尚	118c
	eternal	永	156a
	even	斉	105c
	even	調	122c
	evening	晩	57b
	evening	夕	172a
	every	各	12b
	every	毎	79a
	evil	悪	26c
	examine	審	142c
	examine	検	55a
	examine	察	99b
	example	例	25c
	excellent	英	61c
	exchange	易	41b
	exchange	換	57d
	exchange	兑	59c
	exciting	興	38c
	exempt	免	57
	exist	有	34b
	explain	申	159b
	explain	説	59d
	extremely	絶	75e
	eye	目	7
	eye	眼	10c
f	face	面	6a
	face	向	118b
	face	顔	5d
	face to face	対	105b
	faction	派	157b
	fall	秋	111a
	family	族	127a
	family name	氏	80

	far	遠	102c
	far	冂	118
	farming	農	148d
	father	父	30a
	feast	宴	78b
	feather	羽	141
	feeling	情	27e
	field	田	122
	field	野	119e
	filial piety	孝	81b
	finally	竟	18d
	finger	指	73c
	finish	卒	101d
	finish	済	105d
	fire	火	124
	first	初	102
	fish	魚	144
	fishing	漁	144b
	five	五	176a
	fix	定	45c
	flag	斿	127b
	flag	旗	39d
	flat	平	96a
	float	游	127c
	floor	床	114a
	flour	面	6a
	flourish	賑	148c
	flow	流	157a
	flower	花	52b
	flowing water	巠	97b
	flutter	㫃	127
	fly	飛	128d
	-fold	重	119a
	food	食	109
	foot	疋	166c
	foot	足	45a
	forest	林	166
	forget	忘	1d
	former times	昔	171
	fortunate	幸	83e
	foundation stone	礎	166e
	fountain	泉	106c
	four	四	16b
	fragrant	皀	109c
	fresh	鮮	144a
	friend	朋	151a
	friend	友	34c
	front	前	98b
	frugal	倹	55e
	fruit	果	123c
	full	畐	133c
	future	将	168c
g	gain	得	35b
	garden	園	102d
	garden	庭	50b
	gate	門	115
	gather	集	140a
	gather	社	99e
	general counter	個	15c
	get	得	35b
	give	予	4a
	give birth	産	117e
	gnaw	齧	21a
	gnaw	嚙	21b
	go	辶	49
	go	行	48a
	go	往	48b
	go	之	67b
	go away	去	63c
	go out	出	131c
	gods	神	99c
	gold	金	154
	good	良	11
	goodness	善	134b
	govern	御	69c
	govern	治	76d
	government	官	152c
	government	府	36c
	grain	皀	109c
	grandchild	孫	77c
	grape	葡	130c
	grape	萄	130e
	grass	艹	161
	grass	草	161a
	great	太	60c
	green	緑	104d
	green	青	107
	greet	迎	70a
	grind	磨	165c
	grind	研	153b
	ground	地	68b
	group	徒	44e
	grow up	育	151c
	guard	戍	91c
	guest	客	12c
h	hair	彡	5
	hair	毛	5e
	half	半	137a
	hall	堂	118d
	halt	停	175c
	hand	手	28
	hand	彐	32
	hand	𠂇	34
	hand over	付	36
	hand-tablet	圭	121
	hang	掛	121b
	hang	挂	121a
	happening	故	15a
	harden	固	15b
	harm	害	163e
	harmonious	和	12d
	hate	嫌	111c
	haughtiness	驕	138b
	have	有	34b
	have	持	37b
	head	亠	1
	head	頁	4
	head	頭	112c
	head	首	4d
	headgear	帽	7e
	hear	聞	22a
	heart	心	26
	heart	忄	27
	heavy	重	119a
	help	助	174c
	hemp	麻	165b
	hide	匸	131d
	hide	乚	67c
	high	高	3
	hill	阝	116
	history	史	31
	hit	打	28a
	hit	当	118e
	hold	持	37b
	hole	穴	113a
	hook	亅	179
	hope	巴	75b
	horizontal	横	108a
	horn	角	150
	horse	馬	138
	hot	暑	82c

	house	宀	113
	house	广	114
	house	家	136a
	house	屋	74a
	hundred	百	106a
	hungry	餓	109a
	husband	夫	60a
i	I	吾	176b
	I	我	91a
	ice	冫	160
	ice	氷	160a
	ignis fatuus	粦	47d
	image	像	136c
	important	要	132b
	in advance	預	4b
	increase	殖	25d
	individual	個	15c
	inform	報	30b
	insect	虫	143
	insert (between)	夾	51c
	inside	裏	101b
	inside	内	53b
	inspect	省	182b
	institution	院	58c
	intention	志	26d
	interior	奥	142e
	interpose	介	51a
	interval	間	115b
	intimate	親	9c
	investigate	調	122c
	investigate	査	174a
	iron	鉄	154d
	island	島	139d
	-ist	者	82
j	jade	玉	86b
	Japan	和	12d
	joint	節	109e
	joint	寸	35
	judge	審	142c
	just	甫	129c
k	key	鍵	33c
	king	王	86
	kitchen garden	甫	129c
	knife	刀	95
	know	知	89b
l	ladle	勺	40a
	lamb	羍	49c
	lame	尢	63
	lamp	灯	175d
	language	語	176c
	late	遅	49b
	late	晩	57b
	laugh	笑	61a
	law	典	169d
	law	律	33a
	law	法	63d
	laziness	慢	27d
	lead	鉛	154a
	leaf	葉	162d
	leather	革	149c
	left	左	155c
	lens	鏡	18e
	letter	字	77a
	lie down	臥	85a
	life	命	71a
	life	生	162
	light	軽	97c
	lightning	電	159c
	like	好	78c
	like	如	78d
	limit	限	10d
	line	列	25b
	little	少	182a
	live	活	20c
	lodging	宿	106b
	lofty	卬	70
	long	長	81d
	long clothing	袁	102b
	long time	久	56c
	long walk	廴	50
	long-drawn-out	曼	27c
	look at	覧	85c
	lose	失	154c
	love	愛	29e
	low	低	80b
	lucky	吉	84a
	luxuriant	丰	163
m	mace	圭	121
	machine	機	91e
	make	作	180a
	make an agreement	契	163c
	male adult	丁	175
	man	男	125a
	many	多	151b
	mark	符	36b
	market	市	103a
	marry	婚	80e
	master	師	152b
	master	主	181a
	materials	料	128b
	meal	飯	117b
	meaning	意	18b
	meat	肉	151
	meat (sacrifice)	口	152
	medicine	薬	161d
	meet	会	158d
	member	員	147d
	merits	功	155a
	metal	金	154
	military	武	88c
	milk	乳	67d
	mirror	鏡	18e
	misfortune	厄	69a
	mix	錯	154b
	mixed	雑	140b
	month	月	172
	moon	月	172
	moral	道	4e
	more	兪	98c
	morning	朝	98e
	most	最	22d
	mother	母	79
	mountain	山	153
	mouth	口	12
	move	動	119b
	move	搬	93d
	music	楽	161c
	mutual	相	7c
n	nail	爪	29
	name	号	12e
	name	名	173d
	narrow	狭	51d
	nature	性	27a
	near	近	94a
	neighbor	隣	47e
	net	网	146
	new	新	94b
	next	来	110e
	next	明	170d
	next	次	19b
	nibble	齧	21a

	night	夜	172c
	nine	九	177b
	node	節	109e
	noon	昼	170b
	noon	午	96c
	north	北	73
	nose	鼻	6c
	not	非	141d
	not	未	164b
	not	不	173c
	nothingness	無	47a
	now	今	54b
	number	数	110b
	number	号	12e
	numberical order	番	142a
o	obey	服	30c
	occupy	占	100a
	ocean	洋	134d
	offer	供	38b
	official	吏	31a
	old	耂	81
	old	古	15
	old	老	81a
	old man	丈	34d
	omen	兆	100d
	one	一	173
	one's back	癶	112d
	oneself	己	66
	open	夬	62
	open	開	38d
	open box	凵	131b
	opposite	対	105b
	opposite	反	117a
	order	命	71a
	order	第	87b
	ordinary	凡	143b
	origin	元	58a
	original	原	106d
	other	他	68d
	outside	外	172b
	outstanding	挺	50c
	outstanding	尤	63a
	oversee	監	85b
p	pain	辛	83
	pain	痛	65c
	pair (mate)	匹	131e
	paper	紙	80a
	parent	親	9c
	park	園	102d
	participate	参	5a
	pass through	通	129b
	pattern	紋	105a
	pavilion	亭	3d
	peaceful	安	78a
	pedestal	台	76b
	people	民	80c
	period	紀	66c
	period	期	39c
	period	代	88d
	permit	許	96d
	person	者	82
	person	人	51
	person	亻	52
	person	⺈	56
	person	儿	58
	person	卩/㔾	69
	personal	厶	76
	phrase	句	40c
	pick	采	29c
	pick up	拾	28b
	picture	画	122d
	picture	絵	158e
	piece	片	168e
	piece of wood	丬	168b
	pierce	丨	179c
	pierce	貫	145d
	pig	豕	136
	pig	猪	82b
	pity	哀	102a
	place	処	46d
	place	所	115e
	place	座	120b
	place	場	171c
	plan	図	16d
	plant	植	8a
	plate	皿	132d
	play	遊	127d
	play	玩	86c
	pleasure	楽	161c
	plentiful	豊	148e
	plum	梅	79b
	point	点	100c
	point to	指	73c
	polish	磨	165c
	politics	政	45b
	pond	池	68a
	pond	沢	74e
	position	位	64a
	pottery	缶	130d
	power	力	125
	practice	習	141a
	practice	練	167e
	precious	貴	145c
	press	押	28e
	print	印	69d
	private	私	76a
	process	課	123d
	produce	産	117e
	profession suffix	士	84
	prohibit	禁	166a
	project	映	61d
	prolong	延	50d
	promise	約	104a
	promptly	即	109d
	property	財	145a
	protect	戍	91c
	public	公	76e
	public building	館	152d
	pull	娄	110a
	pull	引	87c
	pungent	辛	83
	pure	清	107a
	purpose	旨	73b
	purpose	趣	22c
	push	推	28c
	push	押	28e
	put	置	8c
	put together	并	64d
q	quake	震	148b
	queer	怪	120c
	question	問	115a
	quick	速	167b
	quick	快	27b
	quiet	静	32b
r	rain	雨	159
	raise (bring up)	育	151c
	reach	達	49d
	reach	及	56a
	reach	到	90b
	read	読	146c
	reason	由	123e

Meaning	Kanji	Ref.
reason	故	15a
reason	理	86e
record	録	156d
records	誌	26e
red	赤	124b
red clay	堇	108b
refine	煉	167d
refined	精	107b
reflect	映	61d
reform	革	149c
regret	悔	79d
regulation	規	9d
rejoice	喜	112a
relax	憩	20a
release	夬	62
release	放	126d
relieve	賑	148c
remaining	余	116a
remember	記	66b
remove	除	116b
renew	更	31c
repeat	复	46a
repent	悔	79d
request	請	107c
requite	報	30b
research	究	177c
resemble	肖	182c
reside	居	15e
resign	辞	83d
respect	敬	40d
rest	休	165a
rest	憩	20a
rest	息	6b
retainer	臣	85
return	帰	103e
return	返	117d
revive	蘇	144c
reward	謝	23c
rice	米	110
rice paddy	田	122
rice plant	禾	111
ride	駕	125c
ride	乗	165d
ride on horseback	騎	14a
right	当	118e
right	然	124d
right	正	45
right	右	34a
right	是	45d
righteousness	義	91b
rise	起	44d
risk	冒	7d
rite	礼	99d
river	河	13d
river	川	156e
road-way	道	4e
room	室	90a
root	本	165
root	根	10a
rot	腐	36d
round	丸	177d
row	列	25b
royal court	廷	50a
rule	則	147a
rule	尹	32d
ruler	尺	74b
ruler	君	32e
run	走	44c
S sacrifice	祭	99a
sake	酒	133a
salt	鹵	55c
salt	塩	85d
saltiness	鹸	55d
same	同	118a
sated	飽	109b
say	言	17
say	云	158c
scatter	散	43b
scholar	士	84
school	校	1b
script	文	105
sea	海	79c
seal	封	35c
seal	印	69d
season	季	77d
seat	座	120b
section	部	116d
section	段	93a
section	課	123d
section	科	128a
see	見	9
see	看	7a
seed	種	119d
seedling	苗	123
select	柬	167c
self	自	6
sell	売	146b
send	寄	14b
send	送	62d
sequence	番	142a
servant	奚	139a
serve	供	38b
serve (work)	仕	84e
set	掛	121b
set	置	8c
seven	七	178b
sever	絶	75e
several	幾	91d
sex	性	27a
shadow	景	2b
shadow	影	2c
shake	振	148a
Shaku	尺	74b
shallow	浅	92e
shape	様	134a
sharp	利	111d
sheep	羊	134
shellfish	貝	145
shine	華	120e
ship	船	98a
SHO (unit of measure)	升	128c
shoe	鞋	121c
shoes	靴	149d
shoot	射	23a
shop	店	100b
short	短	89c
show	示	99
shut	閉	115c
sick	疒	65
sickness	病	65a
side	側	147b
side by side	並	64b
sideways	横	108a
sign	符	36b
silk	綺	14c
silver	銀	10b
single	隻	140d
Sino-	漢	108c
sit	坐	120a
situation	局	74c
six	六	177a

skill	技	42a
skin	皮	149
sky	空	113b
sky	天	60b
slacken	弛	68c
sleep	寝	168d
slender	細	104c
slippery	滑	24a
slow	遅	49b
small	小	182
small	戔	92d
smell	臭	6d
snap	折	94c
snow	雪	159a
so	然	124d
soil	土	120
song	歌	13b
sorrow	哀	102a
sort	般	93c
sound	音	18
sound	声	112b
source	原	106d
south	南	178a
sow	播	142b
spare time	暇	30e
speak	話	20b
spear	戈	91
spear	殳	93
special	特	37c
splay	癶	112d
spoon	匕	72
spread	布	103c
spread	張	81e
spring	泉	106c
spring	春	162e
squad	班	86d
square	方	126
stair	階	72d
stand	台	76b
stand	立	64
standard	準	140c
star	星	162a
starve	餓	109a
station	駅	74d
statue	像	136c
stay	宿	106b
stay	留	70d

stay	処	46d
steal	盗	19c
steam	汽	158b
step	歩	44a
step	段	93a
stick	着	7b
stone	石	153a
stop	止	44
stopping	艮	10
store	店	100b
storey	階	72d
straight	直	8
strange	奇	14
stream	川	156e
street	街	121d
street	町	175a
stretching	延	50d
strike	攵	43
strike	打	28a
stringed arrow	弋	88
strong	強	143a
study	学	77b
study abroad	留	70d
stuffed	飽	109b
style	式	88a
subject	題	45e
substitute	代	88d
suddenly	乍	180
suddenly	突	113c
suffix	子	77
sugar	糖	110d
suitable	当	118e
suitable	宜	174b
summer	夏	46c
summer heat	暑	82c
sun	日	170
sun	昜	171b
super	超	95e
support	支	42
support	推	28c
surface	表	101a
surname	姓	162b
surpass	越	92c
sweet	甘	12a
swim	游	127c
swim	泳	156b
swing	振	148a

t

table	几	168
take	取	22b
take off	脱	59e
take pictures	撮	22e
talk	談	17c
tall	喬	3a
Tang Dynasty (618-907)	唐	110c
taste	味	164c
tasty	旨	73b
tea	茶	161b
teach	教	43a
team	班	86d
ten	十	178
ten thousand	万	161e
test	験	55b
test	試	88b
that	彼	149a
that	其	39
the	彼	149a
therefore	爰	29a
thin	細	104c
thin	薄	130b
thing	件	137b
thing	物	41a
think	思	26a
this	此	72a
thornbush	楚	166d
thought	念	54d
thousand	千	178c
thread	糸	104
three	三	176e
three-legged caldron	鼎	147
throw	投	93b
thunder	震	148b
tie	結	84b
tie	締	84d
tie up	束	167a
tie up	累	123b
tighten	締	84d
tile	瓦	64e
time	時	37a
times	回	16c
times	倍	173e
tired	疲	65d
title	題	45e
TO	斗	128
together	共	38a

	tone	調	122c
	tongue	舌	20
	tooth	歯	21
	top of head	頂	175b
	topple	倒	90c
	touch	着	7b
	toward	向	118b
	towel	巾	103
	town	町	175a
	town	村	35a
	trade	商	83c
	transcend	超	95e
	transport	輸	98d
	trash	塵	150d
	travel	旅	127e
	tree	木	164
	tribe	族	127a
	trip	旅	127e
	true	真	8d
	tube	甬	129a
	turn over	翻	142d
	turn round	回	16c
	tusk	牙	21c
	tutor	傅	130a
	two	二	176
	two hands	廾	38
u	umbrella	傘	178d
	un-	非	141d
	un-	未	164b
	understanding	解	150a
	unfold	展	101c
	untie	解	150a
	unusual	変	43d
	up	上	173a
	urgent	急	56d
	use	用	129
	use	使	31b
	utensil	器	135a
v	valley	谷	153c
	value	値	8b
	vapor	气	158
	vapor	氣	158a
	vegetable	菜	29d
	vexed	煩	4c
	vicinity	辺	49a
	village	村	35a
	village	里	119
	village	邑	75c
	visit	訪	126a
	voice	声	112b
w	waist	腰	132c
	wait	待	48d
	walk	彳	48
	walk	歩	44a
	walk slowly	夊	46
	warehouse	庫	114e
	warm	温	132e
	warm	暖	29b
	warp threads	経	97d
	wash	洗	58e
	water	氵	157
	water	水	156
	water	氺	156c
	wave	浪	11c
	we	吾	176b
	we	我	91a
	weak	弱	141b
	wealthy	富	133e
	wear	被	149b
	wear	穿	21d
	weave	組	104b
	week	週	122b
	well	井	176d
	west	西	132a
	whale	鯨	2a
	what	奚	139a
	what	何	13c
	white	白	106
	who	誰	17d
	wicked	邪	116e
	wide	広	114d
	widespread	普	64c
	wife	妻	78e
	wind	風	143c
	window	窓	113d
	wine-bottle	酉	133
	winnowing basket	箕	39a
	winter	冬	160b
	without fail	必	26b
	wolf	狼	11b
	woman	女	78
	wood	木	164
	word	語	176c
	word	辞	83d
	work	働	119c
	workman	工	155
	world	世	162c
	worm	虫	143
	wrap	勹	40
	wrap	包	75a
	write	書	33e
	write down	記	66b
	writing	書	33e
	writing brush	聿	33
	writing brush	筆	33d
y	yawn	欠	19
	year	歳	44b
	year	年	96e
	yellow	黄	108
	yen	円	147e
	yesterday	昨	180b
	young	夭	61
	young lady	娘	11a
	young man	郎	11d
	younger brother	弟	87a
	younger sister	妹	164d
z	zero	零	71c
numbers	1	一	173
	2	二	176
	3	三	176e
	4	四	16b
	5	五	176a
	6	六	177a
	7	七	178b
	8	八	177
	9	九	177b
	10	十	178
	100	百	106a
	2rd/10	乙	67
	4th/12	卯	70b
	5th/10	戊	92
	5th/12	辰	148
	6th/12	巳	75

Radical index

When looking for kanji in a dictionary without knowing its pronunciation, one must use the radical-based index to find a specific character. However, this can be a difficult task to perform in the early stages of learning. This index includes the base characters that form part of a composite character that will enable readers to find a correct character based on its base.

1 stroke

乙67	乞67a 之67b 乚67c 乳67d 也68 九177b 究177c 丸177d 七178b
一173	号12e 体24b 吏31a 更31c 夫60a 天60b 病65a 百106a 同118a 興38c 畐133c 万161e 世162c 葉162d 末164a 未164b 本165 冊169c 旦170a 上173a 下173b 不173c 杯173d 三176e 七178b
亅179	争32a 静32b 事32c 行48a 乎179a 呼179b
丨179c	引87c 中179d
丿179e	必26b 爱29a 史31 勿41 廷50a 庭50b 挺50c 延50d 誕50e 夭61 孫77c 戊92 升128c 飛128d 為136d 気158a 万161e 千178c 乎179a 呼179b 乍180
丶181	勺40a 的40b 往48b 太60c 尤63a 就63b 低80b 監85b 覧85c 国86a 玉86b 永156a 氷160a 柬167c 煉167d 練167e 夜172c 主181a 住181b

2 strokes

亠1	交1a 亡1c 京2 変43d 卒101d 市103a 育151c 流157a 夜172c 六177a
又30	取22b 趣22c 最22d 撮22e 曼27c 慢27d 爱29a 暖29b 報30b 服30c 段30d 暇30e 友34c 支42 及56a 吸56b 殳93 祭99a 察99b 度114b 渡114c 反117a 飯117b 板117c 返117d 怪120c 騒138a 隻140d 寝168d
ナ34	右34a 有34b 友34c 丈34d 布103c 灰124a 左155c 差155d
勹40	号12e 勺40a 的40b 句40c 敬40d 警40e 勿41 包75a 葡130c 萄130e
人51	介51a 界51b 夾51c 亼54 僉55 臥85a 卒101d 坐120a 座120b 旅127 茶161b 傘178d
亻52	値8b 何13c 個15c 体24b 例25c 使31b 便31d 付36 供38b 化52a 花52b 倹55e 位64a 他68d 低80b 仕84e 代88d 貸88e 倒90c 宿106b 働119c 傍126c 傅130a 像136c 件137b 側147b 俗153d 休165a 借171a 夜172c 倍173e 停175c 作180a 住181b
入53	全53a 内53b 病65a

⺈56 | 争32a 静32b 及56a 吸56b 久56c 急56d 免57 奂57c 換57d 危69b 色75d 絶75e 負145b
𠂉 | 腹46b 乞67a 毎79a 梅79b 海79c 悔79d 監85b 覧85c 塩85d 年96e 族127a 斿127b 游127c 遊127d 旅127e
儿58 | 四16b 竟18d 免57 奂57c 換57d 元58a 完58b 院58c 先58d 洗58e 兄59 商83c 匹131e 売146b 読146c 続146d
卩/㔾69 | 報30b 服30c 厄69a 危69b 御69c 印69d 卬70 令71 即109d 犯135d
匕72 | 死25a 化52a 花52b 此72a 比72b 皆72c 階72d 北73 背73a 乗165d 旨73b 指73c 能73d 熊73e 老81a 皀109c 即109d 節109e 鹿150b
厶76 | 参5a 殆25e 去63c 法63d 私76a 台76b 始76c 治76d 公76e 窓113d 広114d 強143a 育151c 流157a 云158c
刀95 | 勿41 辺49a 留70d 分95a 切95b 召95c 紹95d 超95e 初102 解150a 契163c 喫163d 鬱21a
刂95 | 列25b 例25c 班86d 到90b 倒90c 前98b 兪98c 輸98d 帰103e 利111d 則147a 側147b
卜100 | 占100a 店100b 点100c 掛121b 外172b
厂117 | 彦5c 顔5d 厄69a 危69b 段93a 原106d 反117a 飯117b 板117c 返117d 産117e
冂118 | 冒7d 帽7e 内53b 奂57c 換57d 央61b 英61c 映61d 病65a 商83c 同118a 興38c 周122a 円147e 冊169c 南178a
力125 | 勉57a 動119b 働119c 男125a 加125b 駕125c 賀125d 功155a 助174c
冖131 | 覚9b 愛29e 学77b 帝84c 締84d 帚103d 帰103e 写131a 売146b 読146c 続146d 寝168d
凵131b | 齒/歯21 出131c 脳151d
匚131d | 医89a 匹131e
冫160 | 冷71b 冬160b 終160c 寒160d
几168 | 処46d 机168a
丁175 | 亭3d 停175c 打28a 町175a 頂175b 灯175d
二176 | 次19b 悪26c 行48a 元58a 云158c 汚157d 五176a 吾176b 語176c 井176d
八/丷177 | 真8d 共38a 供38b 興38c 其39 介51a 界51b 兑59c 説59d 脱59e 关62b 咲62c 送62d 并64d 公76e 殳93 分95a 船98a 鉛154a 兼111b 穴113a 尚118c 堂118d 当118e 半137a 典169d 六177a
十178 | 直8 古15 計17a 章18c 卒101d 酔133b 準140c 早170c 南178a 千178c 傘178d

3 strokes

亡1c | 忘1d 忙1e

彡5	影2c 参5a 彩5b 彦5c 顔5d
口12	各12b 客12c 和12d 号12e 可13 古15 回16c 言17 吹19d 舌20 噛21b 殆25e 拾28b 史31 事32c 君32e 右34a 句40c 敬40d 警40e 合54a 含54c 㑒55 吸56b 免57 兄59 咲62c 命71a 局74c 邑/阝75c 台76b 如78d 商83c 吉84a 結84b 知89b 召95c 紹95d 超95e 船98a 鉛154a 占100a 店100b 点100c 哀102a 袁102b 遠102c 園102d 唐110c 糖110d 喜112a 問115a 部116d 倍173e 同118a 興38c 向118b 尚118c 堂118d 周122a 加125b 駕125c 賀125d 畐133c 器135a 鳴139c 員147d 谷153c 喫163d 害163e 味164c 東167a 名172d 吾176b 呼179b 中179d
囗16	固15b 困16a 四16b 回16c 図16d 因60d 国86a 園102d
忄27	忙1e 性27a 快27b 慢27d 情27e 悔79d 怪120c 慣145e
扌/手28	撮22e 打28a 拾28b 推28c 押28e 持37b 技42a 挺50c 換57d 指73c 接83b 投93b 搬93d 折94c 挂121a 掛121b 捕130 播142b 振148a
才	閉115c 財145a
ヨ32	争32a 静32b 事32c 尹32d 君32e 聿33 興38c 急56d 妻78e 帚103d 帰103e 唐110c 糖110d 兼111b 嫌111c 当118e 録156d 雪159a 寝168d
寸35	射23a 村35a 得35b 封35c 討35d 付36 寺37 対105b 傅130a 薄130b 将168c
廾38	共38a 供38b 開38d 算38e 升128c 飛128d 研153b
夂46	各12b 愛29e 変43d 复46a 腹46b 夏46c 処46d 降47c 後48c 冬160b 麦163b 夜172c
彳48	律33a 得35b 徒44e 行48a 往48b 後48c 待48d 御69c 彼149a
辶(⻌)49	道4e 辺49a 遅49b 達49d 進49e 送62d 迎70a 近94a 連97e 逃100e 遠102c 返117d 週122b 遊127d 通129b 追152a 速167b
廴50	建33b 鍵33c 廷50a 庭50b 挺50c 延50d 誕50e
亼54	論17b 合54a 拾28b 今54b 含54c 念54d 㑒55 令71 俞98c 輸98d 会158d 絵158e
大60	参5a 奇14 快27b 夆49c 夾51c 狭51d 奐57c 換57d 夫60a 規9d 天60b 太60c 因60d 夭61 央61b 英61c 映61d 夬62 決62a 关62b 咲62c 送62d 夷87d 美134c 犬135 奚139a 鶏139b 奥142e 失154c 鉄154d 契163c 喫163d
尤63	尤63a 就63b
己66	起44d 已66a 記66b 紀66c 配66d
也68	池68a 地68b 弛68c 他68d
尸74	居15e 遅49b 屋74a 尺74b 局74c 駅74d 沢74e 展101c
巳75	包75a 巴75b 邑/阝75c 色75d 絶75e
子77	孝81b 教43a 乳67d 字77a 学77b 孫77c 季77d 好78c 斿127b 游127c 遊127d

Radical | 3~4 strokes

女78	娘11a 始76c 安78a 宴78b 好78c 如78d 妻78e 婚80e 妾83a 接83b 姉103b 娄110a 数110b 嫌111c 要132b 腰132c 姓162b 妹164d 婪166b
士84	志26d 喜112a 鼓42b 廷50a 庭50b 挺50c 吉84a 結84b 仕84e 声112b 売146b 読146c 続146d
弓87	弛68c 張81e 弟87a 第87b 引87c 夷87d 弱141b 強143a
弋88	式88a 試88b 武88c 代88d 貸88e 戈91
干96	并64d 御69c 幸83e 平96a 苹96b 午96c 許96d 年96e
巾103	帽7e 帝84c 締84d 市103a 姉103b 布103c 帚103d 帰103e 師152b
宀113	客12c 寄14b 定45c 完58b 院58c 字77a 安78a 宴78b 室90a 察99b 宿106b 穴113a 向118b 尚118c 堂118d 富133e 家136a 審142c 奥142e 官152c 館152d 寒160d 害163e 寝168d 宜174b
广114	廊11e 府36c 腐36d 庭50b 店100b 唐110c 糖110d 床114a 度114b 渡114c 広114d 庫114e 座120b 鹿150b 麻165b 磨165c
阝116	限10d 附36a 降47c 隣47e 院58c 階72d 除116b 険116c
阝(邑)75c	郎11d 廊11e 都82d 部116d 邪116e 邦163a
土120	寺37 基39b 走44c 去63c 法63d 地68b 塩85d 社99e 袁102b 遠102c 園102d 菫108b 堂118d 里119 坐120a 座120b 怪120c 垂120d 華120e 圭121 周122a 赤124b 塵150d 場171c
犭/犬135	狼11b 狭51d 猪82b 猫123a 狗135c 犯135d 独143d
山153	島139d
工155	式88a 試88b 空113b 功155a 紅155b 左155c 差155d
川156e	流157a
氵157	涼2d 浪11c 河13d 活20c 滑24a 洗58e 況59b 決62a 法63d 池68a 沢74e 治76d 海79c 浅92e 済105d 清107a 漢108c 渡114c 游127c 薄130b 温132e 酒133a 洋134d 準140c 漁144b 浴153e 泳156b 流157a 派157b 深157c 汚157d 汽158b 湯171d 消182d
艹161	蕎3c 菜29d 敬40d 警40e 花52b 英61c 苹96b 華120e 苗123 猫123a 薄130b 葡130c 萄130e 蘇144c 寒160d 草161a 茶161b 薬161d 葉162d
丬/爿168b	将168c 寝168d
夕172a	多151b 外172b 名172d
小182	原106d 少182a 省182b 肖182c 消182d

4 strokes

予4a	預4b 野119e
毛5e	表101a
日	最22d 撮22e 曼27c 慢27d 更31c 便31d 書33e 曲129d 農148d 豊148e 典169d
欠19	歌13b 飲19a 次19b 盗19c 吹19d

牙21c	穿21d 邪116e
歹25	死25a 列25b 例25c 殖25d 殆25e
心26	忘1d 息6b 意18b 聴20a 思26a 必26b 悪26c 志26d 誌26e 愛29e 念54d 急56d 窓113d
手/扌28	看7a
爪/爫29	爰29a 暖29b 采29c 菜29d 彩5b 愛29e 乳67d 印69d 為136d 奚139a 鶏139b 将168c
父30a	交1a
勿41	物41a 易41b 昜171b 場171c 湯171d
支42	技42a 鼓42b
攵43	故15a 敬40d 警40e 教43a 散43b 枚43c 政45b 致90d 数110b 放126d 敗147c
止44	齒/歯21 歩44a 歳44b 走44c 正45 御69c 此72a 武88c
夭61	喬3a 橋3b 蕎3c 驕138b 笑61a
卬70	迎70a 卯70b 卵70c
氏80	紙80a 低80b 民80c 昏80d 婚80e
王/玉86	全53a 国 86a 玉86b 玩86c 班86d 理86e 主181a 住181b 往48b
戈91	我91a 義91b 戍91c 幾91d 機91e 戊92 戔92d 浅92e
殳93	段93a 投93b 般93c 搬93d
斤94	近94a 新94b 折94c 断94d 所115e
ネ/示99	礼99d
文105	紋105a 対105b 斉105c 済105d
戸115d	所115e
火124	煩4c 談17c 秋111a 灰124a 赤124b 煉167d 灯175d
灬124	無47a 熊73e 煮82a 点100c 黒124c 然124d 為136d 馬138 鳥139
方126	訪126a 旁126b 傍126c 放126d 㫃127
斗128	科128a 料128b
犬/犭135	臭6d 突113c 然124d 器135a
牛137	特37c 物41a 半137a 件137b 解150a
水156	泉106c 永156a 泳156b 氷160a
气158	気158a 汽158b
云158c	会158d 絵158e 雲159d 曇159e
丰163	邦163a 麦163b 契163c 喫163d 齧21a 害163e
木164	校1b 橋3b 相7c 植8a 親9c 根10a 椅14d 困16a 体24b 采29c 菜29d 彩5b 村35a 枚43c 検55a 梅79b 機91e 新94b 横108a 来110e 禾111 床114a 板117c 果123c 課123d 様134a 集140a 雑140b 深157c 茶161b 楽161c 薬161d 葉162d 末164a 未164b 味164c 妹164d 本165 休165a 乗165d 林166 東167 束167a 机168a 杯173d 査174a
片168e	
日170	景2b 音18 暗18a 暖29b 暇30e 時37a 易41b 是45d 題45e

Radical | 4~5 strokes

	腹46b 晩57b 映61d 普64c 旨73b 指73c 宴78b 昏80d 婚80e
	暑82c 朝98e 晴107d 間115b 温132e 曜141c 曇159e 星162a 春162e
旦170a	早170c 明170d 昔171 東167 昨180b
月172	骨24 服30c 有34b 期39c 散43b 腹46b 脱59e 背73a 前98b
侖98c	輸98d 朝98e 祭99a 察99b 然124d 腰132c 朋151a 育151c
	脳151d 明170d 肖182c 消182d

5 strokes

目7	看7a 着7b 相7c 冒7d 帽7e 真8d 見9 眼10c 殖25d
	算38e 省182b
甘12a	
可13	哥13a 歌13b 何13c 河13d 奇14
古15	故15a 固15b 個15c 箇15d 居15e
史31	吏31a 使31b 更31c 便31d
付36	附36a 符36b 府36c 腐36d
正/⻗45	政45b 定45c 是45d 題45e
兄59	祝59a 況59b 兑59c 説59d 脱59e
立64	彦5c 顔5d 音18 位64a 並64b 普64c 商83c 帝84c 締84d
部116d	倍173e 産117e 旁126b 傍126c
瓦64e	瓶64f
疒65	病65a 疾65b 痛65c 疲65d
令71	命71a 冷71b 零71c 領71d
母/毋79	毎79a 梅79b 海79c 悔79d 貫145d 慣145e
矢89	疾65b 医89a 知89b 短89c 族127a
戊92	歳44b 成92a 戉92b 越92c
圣/巠97b	軽97c 経97d
示/ネ99	祝59a 祭99a 察99b 神99c 社99e 福133d 禁166a 祖174d
衤/衣101	初102 被149b
白106	的40b 皆72c 階72d 百106a 宿106b 泉106c 原106d 皀109c 即109d
節109e	習141a 楽161c 薬161d
禾111	和12d 私76a 季77d 秋111a 嫌111c 利111d 種119d 科128a 蘇144c
癶112d	登112e
穴113a	穿21d 空113b 突113c 窓113d
田122	思26a 甲28d 押28e 界51b 留70d 里119 画122d 苗123 猫123a
累123b	果123c 課123d 由123e 男125a 薄130b 畐133c 番142a 播142b
審142c	翻142d 町175a 申159b
用129	甬129a 通129b 甫129c 捕130 傅130a 葡130c
皿132d	盗19c 監85b 塩85d 温132e
罒/网146	置8c 曼27c 慢27d 買146a
皮149	疲65d 彼149a 被149b

石153a	研153b 磨165c 礎166e
氺156c	録156d
申159b	神99c 電159c
生162	性27a 産117e 星162a 姓162b
疋166c	楚166d
冊169c	論17b
旦170a	得35b 昼170b 昜171b 場171c 場171c 湯171d
且174	組104b 査174a 宜174b 助174c 祖174d
乍180	作180a 昨180b
交1a	校1b 較97a

6 strokes

自6	息6b 鼻6c 臭6d 憩20a
艮10	根10a 銀10b 眼10c 限10d
舌20	憩20a 話20b 活20c 乱20d 辞83d
耳22	聞22a 取22b 趣22c 最22d 撮22e
聿33	律33a 建33b 鍵33c 筆33d 書33e
寺37	時37a 持37b 特37c 等37d 待48d
舛47	無47a 舞47b 降47c 粦47d 隣47e
色75d	
耂81	孝81b 教43a 老81a 考81c
至90	屋74a 室90a 到90b 倒90c 致90d
舟98	般93c
兆100d	逃100e
衣101	表101a 裏101b 展101c 哀102a 袁102b 遠102c 園102d
糸104	綺14c 後48c 紀66c 絶75e 孫77c 紙80a 結84b 締84d 紹95d
経97d	約104a 組104b 細104c 緑104d 紋105a 累123b 奚139a 鶏139b 続146d
紅155b	絵158e 終160c 練167e
米110	粦47d 隣47e 断94d 精107b 娄110a 数110b 糖110d 来110e 料128b
圭121	封35c 挂121a 掛121b 鞋121c 街121d
㫃/方127	旗39d 族127a 斿127b 游127c 遊127d 旅127e
缶130d	萄130e
覀/西132	西132a 要132b 腰132c 酉133
羊134	着7b 遅49b 羍49c 達49d 義91b 様134a 善134b 美134c 洋134d 鮮144a 差155d
羽141	習141a 弱141b 曜141c 翻142d
虫143	騒138a 強143a 風143c 独143d
肉151	腐36d
𠂤152	追152a 師152b 官152c 館152d
竹169	箇15d 筆33d 符36b 等37d 算38e 箕39a 笑61a 第87b 節109e

	箱169a 答169b

7 strokes

見9	現9a 覚9b 親9c 規9d 覧85c
良11	娘11a 狼11b 浪11c 郎11d 廊11e
言17	計17a 論17b 談17c 誰17d 話20b 謝23c 誌26e 討35d 警40e 誕50e 説59d 記66b 試88b 許96d 請107c 調122c 課123d 訪126a 読146c 語176c
身23	射23a 謝23c
走44c	趣22c 起44d 徒44e 越92c 超95e
足45a	
辛83	親9c 報30b 妾83a 接83b 辞83d 幸83e 新94b
臣85	臥85a 監85b 覧85c
車97	較97a 軽97c 連97e 輸98d 庫114e
豆112	喜112a 鼓42b 短89c 頭112c 登112e 豊148e
里119	理86e 裏101b 重119a 動119b 働119c 種119d 野119e 黒124c
酉133	配66d 酒133a 酔133b
豕136	家136a 象136b 像136c
釆142	番142a 播142b 審142c 翻142d 奥142e
貝145	貸88e 賀125d 財145a 負145b 貴145c 貫145d 慣145e 買146a 販148c
貝(鼎)147	則147a 側147b 敗147c 員147d
辰148	振148a 震148b 賑148c 農148d
角150	解150a
谷153c	俗153d 浴153e
麦163b	
束167a	速167b 東167c 煉167d 練167e

8 strokes

京2	鯨2a 景2b 影2c 涼2d 就63b
直8	植8a 値8b 置8c 殖25d
奇14	騎14a 寄14b 綺14c 椅14d
其39	箕39a 基39b 期39c 旗39d
㑒/僉55	検55a 験55b 鹸55d 倹55e 険116c
免57	勉57a 晩57b
長81d	張81e
者82	煮82a 猪82b 暑82c 都82d
青107	情27e 静32b 清107a 精107b 請107c 晴107d
飠/食109	飲19a 餓109a 飽109b 飯117b 館152d
門115	聞22a 開38d 問115a 間115b 閉115c

周122a | 週122b 調122c
隹140 | 誰17d 推28c 進49e 難108d 集140a 雑140b 準140c 隻140d 曜141c
非141d |
金154 | 銀10b 鏡18e 鍵33c 鉛154a 錯154b 鉄154d 録156d
雨159 | 零71c 震148b 雪159a 電159c 雲159d 曇159e
林166 | 麻165b 磨165c 禁166a 婪166b 楚166d 礎166e
昔171 | 錯154b 借171a

9 strokes

頁4 | 預4b 煩4c 顔5d 題45e 夏46c 領71d 頭112c 頂175b
首4d | 道4e
面6a |
音18 | 暗18a 意18b 章18c 竟18d 鏡18e
畐133c | 福133d 富133e
風143c |
革149c | 鞋121c 靴149d 鞄149e
飛128d |

10 strokes

高3 | 喬3a 橋3b 蕎3c 驕138b 亭3d 停175c
骨24 | 滑24a
馬138 | 騎14a 験55b 駅74d 駕125c 騒138a 驕138b

11 strokes

鹵55c | 鹸55d
黄108 | 横108a 菫108b 漢108c 難108d
鳥139 | 鶏139b 鳴139c 島139d 烏139e
魚144 | 鯨2a 鮮144a 144b 蘇144c
鹿150b | 麗150c 塵150d

14 strokes

鼻6c |

15 strokes

齒/歯21 | 齧21a 噛21b

Pattern index

You can use this index to locate a certain kanji with its root character. Dissect the kanji you are looking for and decide which pattern will help you find it quicker. Kanji with multiple root characters or patterns are mentioned multiple times so that you can choose any option. But everything is based on how every character is dissected in this book. For example, to locate "喬," you can look up both "夭" and "高" in its abbreviated form.

2 strokes	亠1	交1a 亡1c 忘1d 京2 高3 亭3d 変43d 立64 衣101 裏101b 卒101d 哀102a 市103a 文105 夜172c 六177a
	ナ34	右34a 有34b 友34c 布103c 左155c
	人51	介51a 亼54 合54a 今54b 含54c 㑒55 令71 命71a 俞98c 食109 余116a 金154 会158d 傘178d
	入53	全53a
	⺈56	欠19 争32a 久56c 急56d 免57 奐57c 危69b 色75d 象136b 魚144 負145b 角150
	𠂉	复46a 無47a 舞47b 乞67a 毎79a 午96c 年96e 缶130d 気158 氛158a
	匕72	旨73b
	厶76	参5a 台76b
	刀95	召95c
	卜100	占100a 点100c 上173a
	冖131	写131a
	二176	云158c
	八/丷177	关62b 並64b 普64c 并64d 公76e 父93 分95a 前98b 兼111b 尚118c 堂118d 当118e 半137a 谷153c
	十178	直8 真8d 古15 南178a
3 strokes	口12	号12e 邑75c 員147d
	ヨ32	帚103d
	夂46	各12b 冬160b
	大60	奇14 奎49c
	士84	志26d 吉84a 喜112a 声112b 売146b
	宀113	客12c 寄14b 定45c 完58b 字77a 安78a 宴78b 室90a 察99b 宿106b 穴113a 向118b 富133e 家136a 審142c 奥142e 官152c 寒160d

		害163e 寝168d 宜174b
	土120	寺37 走44c 去63c 幸83e 袁102b 圭121 赤124b
	艹161	蕎3c 菜29d 花52b 英61c 苹96b 華120e 苗123 薄130b 葡130c 萄130e 蘇144c 草161a 茶161b 薬161d 葉162d
	夕172a	多151b 名172d
	小182	少182a 省182b 肖182c
4 strokes	手28	看7a
	爪/爫29	爰29a 采29c 愛29e 奚139a
	止44	齒/歯21 歩44a 歳44b
	夭61	喬3a
	氏80	昏80d
	戈91	戔92d
	文105	斉105c
	气158	気158a
	丰163	麦163b
	木164	査174a
	日/曰170	景2b 冒7d 最22d 曼27c 易41b 是45d 暑82c 曇159e 星162a 旦170a 早170c 昜171b
5 strokes	目7	見9 貝145
	可13	哥13a
	立64	彦5c 音18 意18b 章18c 竟18d 辛83 妾83a 商83c 帝84c 産117e 旁126b
	白106	泉106c 皀109c
	禾111	季77d
	癶112d	登112e
	穴113a	穿21d 空113b 突113c 窓113d 究177c
	田122	思26a 界51b 累123b 果123c 男125a
	罒/网146	置8c 買146a
6 strokes	自6	息6b 鼻6c 臭6d
	聿33	書33e
	耂81	老81a 孝81b 考81c 者82 煮82a
	米110	粦47d 娄110a
	曲129d	農148d 豊148e 典169d
	覀/西132	要132b
	羊134	着7b 義91b 善134b 美134c 差155d

	羽141	習141a
	竹169	箇15d 筆33d 符36b 等37d 算38e 箕39a 第87b 節109e 箱169a 答169b
7	里119	黒124c
	采142	番142a
8 strokes	其39	基39b
	隹140	集140a 隻140d
	雨159	零71c 震148b 雪159a 電159c 雲159d

2 strokes	又30	曼27c 爰29a 友34c 及56a 殳93 隻140d
	人51	欠19 食55
	儿58	見9 竟18d 免57 元58a 完58b 先58d 兄59 兑59c 売146b
	卩/㔾69	令71 零71c
	匕72	老81a 皀109c
	厶76	去63c 公76e 云158c 会158d 雲159d 曇159e
	刀95	分95a
	卜100	下173b
	力125	男125a
	冫160	冬160b 寒160d
	丁175	亭3d
	八/丌177	頁4 鼻6c 真8d 共38a 興38c 其39 箕39a 黄108 穴113a 典169d 六177a
	十178	章18c 辛83 午96c 卒101d 準140c 草161a 早170c 傘178d
3 strokes	彡5	参5a 彦5c
	口12	各12b 客12c 古15 言17 舌20 君32e 右34a 合54a 含54c 台76b 吉84a 召95c 占100a 喜112a 善134b 石153a 谷153c 害163e 答169b 名172d 吾176b
	ヨ32	雪159a
	寸35	寺37
	廾38	算38e
	夂46	愛29e 変43d 复46a 夏46c 麦163b
	大60	奥57c 天60b 夭61 笑61a 央61b 英61c 关62b 美134c 奚139a

		奥142e 契163c
	子77	字77a 学77b 季77d 孝81b
	女78	安78a 宴78b 妻78e 妾83a 娄110a 要132b 婪166b
	巾103	帝84c 市103a 布103c 帚103d
	土120	基39b 至90 堇108b 里119 圭121
	山153	島139d
	工155	巠97b 空113b 左155c 差155d
	夕172a	多151b
4 strokes	父30a	交1a
	牙21c	穿21d
	心26	忘1d 息6b 意18b 憩20a 思26a 悪26c 志26d 念54d 急56d 窓113d
	止/龰44	走44c 正45 足45a 定45c 是45d
	王/玉86	全53a 主181a
	戈91	戔92d
	灬124	無47a 熊73e 煮82a 点100c 黒124c 然124d 為136d 馬138 鳥139 烏139e
	方126	旁126b
	犬135	臭6d 突113c
	水156	泉106c 永156a 氷160a
	木164	采29c 菜29d 禾111 果123c 集140a 茶161b 楽161c 薬161d 葉162d
	日/曰170	音18 書33e 普64c 旨73b 昏80d 者82 暑82c 春162e 昔171 省182b
	月172	有34b 背73a 育151c 肖182c
5 strokes	目7	看7a 着7b 冒7d
	可13	哥13a 奇14 寄14b
	母/毋79	毎79a
	示99	祭99a 察99b 禁166a
	白106	皆72c 百106a 習141a
	田122	留70d 苗123 畐133c 番142a 審142c
	用129	甬129a 甫129c
	皿132d	盗19c 監85b
	生162	星162a
	疋166c	楚166d
	且174	査174a 宜174b

6 strokes	聿33	筆33d
	舛47	舞47b 粦47d
	至90	室90a
	衣101	表101a 裏101b
	糸104	累123b
	羊134	羍49c
	羽141	弱141b
	𠂤152	官152c
7 strokes	見9	覚9b 覧85c
	言17	警40e
	豆112	登112e 豊148e
	里119	重119a
	豕136	家136a 象136b
	貝145	貸88e 賀125d 負145b 貴145c 貫145d 買146a 員147d
	辰148	震148b 農148d
8	京2	景2b
10	高3	喬3a 蕎3c
	馬138	駕125c
15	齒/歯21	齧21a

2 strokes	亻52	値8b 何13c 個15c 体24b 例25c 便31d 付36 供38b 化52a 倹55e 位64a 他68d 低80b 仕84e 代88d 倒90c 働119c 傍126c 傅130a 像136c 件137b 側147b 俗153d 休165a 借171a 倍173e 停175c 作180a 住181b
	刂95	帰103e
	力125	加125b
	冫160	冷71b
	丁175	頂175b
	二176	次19b
3 strokes	口12	吹19d 噛21b 吸56b 咲62c 鳴139c 喫163d 味164c 呼179b
	忄27	忙1e 性27a 快27b 慢27d 情27e 悔79d 怪120c 慣145e

扌/手28	撮22e 打28a 拾28b 推28c 押28e 持37b 技42a 挺50c 換57d 指73c 接83b 投93b 搬93d 折94c 挂121a 捕130 播142b 振148a
夂46	処46d
彳48	律33a 得35b 徒44e 行48a 往48b 後48c 待48d 御69c 街121d 彼149a
子77	孫77c
女78	娘11a 始76c 好78c 如78d 婚80e 姉103b 嫌111c 姓162b 妹164d
弓87	弛68c 張81e 引87c 強143a
巾103	帽7e
阝116	限10d 附36a 降47c 隣47e 院58c 階72d 除116b 険116c
土120	地68b 塩85d 場171c
犭/犬135b	狼11b 狭51d 猪82b 猫123a 狗135c 犯135d 独143d
工155	功155a
氵157	涼2d 浪11c 河13d 活20c 滑24a 洗58e 況59b 決62a 法63d 池68a 沢74e 治76d 海79c 浅92e 済105d 清107a 漢108c 渡114c 游127c 温132e 酒133a 洋134d 漁144b 浴153e 泳156b 流157a 派157b 深157c 汚157d 汽158b 湯171d 消182d
丬/爿168b	将168c
夕172a	外172b
4 strokes	
予4a	預4b
歹25	死25a 列25b 殖25d 殆25e
止44	此72a
王/玉86	現9a 玩86c 班86d 理86e
文105	対105b
戸115d	所115e
火124	煩4c 煉167d 灯175d
方126	旗39d 放126d 㫃127 族127a 斿127b 旅127e
牛137	特37c 物41a
丰163	邦163a
木164	校1b 橋3b 相7c 植8a 根10a 椅14d 村35a 枚43c 検55a 梅79b 機91e 横108a 板117c 様134a 林166 机168a 杯173d
日170	暗18a 暖29b 暇30e 時37a 晩57b 映61d 晴107d 曜141c 明170d 昨180b
月172	服30c 腹46b 脱59e 腰132c 朋151a 脳151d

Pattern | ◧

5 strokes	目7	眼10c
	古15	故15a
	矢89	知89b 短89c
	示/ネ99	祝59a 神99c 礼99d 社99e 福133d 祖174d
	衤/衣101	初102 被149b
	白106	的40b
	禾111	和12d 私76a 秋111a 利111d 種119d 科128a
	田122	町175a
	石153a	研153b 礎166e
	且174	助174c
6 strokes	舌20	乱20d 辞83d
	耳22	取22b
	至90	到90b 致90d
	舟98	般93c 船98a
	糸104	綺14c 紀66c 絶75e 紙80a 結84b 締84d 紹95d 経97d 約104a
		組104b 細104c 緑104d 紋105a 続146d 紅155b 絵158e 終160c 練167e
	米110	精107b 糖110d 料128b
	自152	師152b
7 strokes	良11	郎11d
	言17	計17a 論17b 談17c 誰17d 話20b 謝23c 誌26e 討35d 誕50e
	説59d	記66b 試88b 許96d 請107c 調122c 課123d 訪126a
	読146c	語176c
	身23	射23a
	走44c	趣22c 起44d 越92c 超95e
	臣85	臥85a
	車97	較97a 軽97c 輸98d
	豆112	頭112c
	里119	野119e
	酉133	配66d 酔133b
	貝145	財145a 則147a 敗147c 販148c
	角150	解150a
8 strokes	京2	就63b
	其39	期39c
	免57	勉57a
	青107	静32b

Strokes	Component	Kanji
	飠/食109	飲19a 餓109a 飽109b 飯117b 館152d
	金154	銀10b 鏡18e 鍵33c 鉛154a 錯154b 鉄154d 録156d
9	革149c	鞋121c 靴149d 鞄149e
10	馬138	騎14a 験55b 駅74d 騒138a 驕138b
11	鹵55c	鹸55d
	魚144	鯨2a 鮮144a

Strokes	Component	Kanji
2 strokes	又30	取22b 趣22c 及56a
	人51	臥85a
	卩/㔾69	御69c 印69d 卬70 卯70b 卵70c 即109d 犯135d
	匕72	死25a 化52a 此72a 比72b 北73 靴149d
	厶76	私76a
	刀/刂95	列25b 例25c 到90b 倒90c 切95b 初102 則147a 側147b
	卜100	掛121b 外172b
	力125	勉57a 動119b 働119c 功155a 助174c
	几168	処46d 机168a
	丁175	打28a 町175a 灯175d
	十178	計17a
3 strokes	彡5	影2c 彩5b
	口12	和12d 如78d 知89b 加125b
	寸35	射23a 謝23c 村35a 封35c 討35d 付36 附36a 対105b
	己66	起44d 記66b 紀66c 配66d
	也68	池68a 地68b 弛68c 他68d
	阝/邑75c	郎11d 都82d 部116d 邪116e 邦163a
	子77	好78c
	士84	仕84e
	弋88	代88d
	土120	社99e
	工155	紅155b
4 strokes	欠19	歌13b 飲19a 次19b 吹19d
	支42	技42a 鼓42b

	攵43	故15a 敬40d 教43a 散43b 枚43c 政45b 致90d 数110b 放126d 敗147c
	氏80	紙80a
	王/玉86	班86d
	戈 91	我91a 戍91c 戊92 成92a 戉92b
	殳93	段93a 投93b 般93c 搬93d
	斤94	新94b 折94c 断94d 所115e
	文105	紋105a
	火124	秋111a
	方126	訪126a
	斗128	科128a 料128b
	牛137	件137b
	气158	汽158b
	木164	休165a 林166
	月172	期39c 朝98e 朋151a 明170d
5 strokes	目7	相7c
	可13	何13c 河13d
	立64	位64a
	瓦64e	瓶64f
	田122	細104c
	皮149	彼149a 被149b
	生162	性27a 姓162b
	且174	組104b 祖174d
6 strokes	交1a	校1b 較97a
	艮10	根10a 銀10b 眼10c 限10d
	舌20	話20b 活20c
	聿33	律33a
	圭121	挂121a 鞋121c
	羊134	洋134d 鮮144a
	羽141	翻142d
	虫143	独143d
7 strokes	見9	現9a 親9c 規9d
	良11	娘11a 狼11b 浪11c
	走44c	徒44e
	辛83	辞83d

	里119	理86e
	酉133	酒133a
	辰148	振148a 賑148c
8 strokes	京2	鯨2a 涼2d
	直8	植8a 値8b
	免57	晩57b
	長81d	張81e
	青107	情27e 清107a 精107b 請107c 晴107d
	隹140	誰17d 推28c 難108d 雑140b
9	頁4	預4b 煩4c 顔5d 題45e 領71d 頭112c 頂175b
	音18	暗18a
10	骨24	滑24a
11 strokes	黄108	横108a
	鳥139	鶏139b 鳴139c
	魚144	漁144b
15	歯/齒21	噛21b

☐

2 strokes	勹40	勺40a 句40c 匆41 包75a
	厂117	厄69a 原106d 反117a 灰124a
	冂118	内53b 同118a 周122a 円147e 网146 肉151 冊169c
	凵131b	画122d 出131c 山153
	匚131d	医89a 匹131e
	几168	凡143b 風143c
3 strokes	囗16	固15b 困16a 四16b 回16c 図16d 因60d 国86a 園102d
	辶(⻌)49	道4e 辺49a 遅49b 達49d 進49e 送62d 迎70a 近94a 連97e 逃100e 遠102c 返117d 週122b 遊127d 通129b 追152a 速167b
	廴50	建33b 廷50a 延50d
	尸74	居15e 屋74a 尺74b 局74c 展101c 昼170b
	广114	廊11e 府36c 腐36d 庭50b 店100b 唐110c 床114a 度114b 広114d 庫114e 座120b 鹿150b 塵150d 麻165b 磨165c
4	气158	気158a

5	疒65	病65a 疾65b 痛65c 疲65d
8	門115	聞22a 開38d 問115a 間115b 閉115c

■

1 strokes	乙/乚67	乱20d 己66 已66a 乞67a 乳67d 巳75 巴75b 毛5e 九177b 丸177d 七178b
	一173	甘12a 丈34d 尢63 尤63a 万161e 世162c 不173c 三176e
	亅179	予4a 争32a 事32c 氷156c 丁175
	丨179c	引87c 川156e 丰163 中179d
	丿179e	必26b 尢63 尤63a 戊92 成92a 毛5e 乗165d 九177b 丸177d 千178c 乎179a 乍180 少182a
	丶181	尤63a 之67b 凡143b 永156a 氷160a 丸177d 主181a
2 strokes	儿58	兆100d
	二176	五176a 井176d
	十178	升128c 千178c
3 strokes	口12	可13 史31 吏31a 哀102a 袁102b 向118b 器135a 中179d
	ヨ32	争32a 事32c 尹32d
	大60	夾51c 夫60a 太60c 夭61 央62 夷87d 失154c
	弓87	弟87a 夷87d 引87c
	弋88	式88a 武88c
	干96	幸83e 平96a 午96c 年96e
	土120	坐120a 垂120d
4 strokes	戈91	我91a 戍91c 幾91d 戊92 成92a 戉92b
	犬135	器135a
	木104	來110e 未104a 末104b 本105 乗105d 東107 束107a 柬107c
	日/曰170	更31c 曲129d
5	田122	甲28d 画122d 由123e 申159b

Others

首4d 面6a 報30b 段30d 能73d 民80c 菫108b 兼111b 飛128d 為136d 非141d 麗150c 片168e